Up to the Challenge?

International Development

Tapping into the Global Network

▶ *International Management*

THIRD EDITION

International Management

Strategic Opportunities and Cultural Challenges

Dean B. McFarlin
UNIVERSITY OF DAYTON

Paul D. Sweeney
UNIVERSITY OF DAYTON

Houghton Mifflin Company
Boston   New York

To Laurie, Andrew, Elizabeth, and Nathaniel . . . no one could ask for a better family!

–DEAN B. MCFARLIN

To Emily, Farrell, and M.L. Hohman.

–PAUL D. SWEENEY

Publisher: Charles Hartford
Editor in Chief: George T. Hoffman
Development Manager: Susan M. Kahn
Associate Editor: Jessica Carlisle
Project Editor: Marilyn Rothenberger
Manufacturing Manager: Karen Banks
Executive Marketing Manager: Steven W. Mikels
Senior Marketing Manager: Todd Berman
Marketing Associate: Lisa E. Boden

Cover images: "People in airport," © Terry Vine/Getty Images; "Blurred binary and money symbols," © Getty Images

Printed in the U.S.A.

Library of Congress Control Number: 2004114516

ISBN: 0-618-51983-1

123456789-DOW-09 08 07 06 05

Brief Contents

Contents

Chapter 3
Doing Things Right: International Ethics and Social Responsibility   80

Chapter 13

Chapter 14

Exploring the Opportunities and Challenges of International Management

The field of international management changes rapidly, which is one of the things that draws us to it. While it is interesting to study, the rapid evolution of the field also makes writing a book on the subject a challenge. Because this area is relatively new and changes quickly, there's no precise set of topics that must be covered in an international management text. This gives authors like us tremendous flexibility in what material we cover and how we cover it. We hope you'll agree with our choices and will conclude that our text offers the most up-to-date and comprehensive coverage of key issues in international management on the market today.

Balancing Strategy and People In a nutshell, our vision is to bring students inside the real world of international management. The field is rapidly evolving, challenging students, professors, and businesspeople alike. Economies around the world are becoming increasingly integrated, presenting both unprecedented opportunities and tremendous exposure to a sweeping array of risks. We believe that tackling international management in such a volatile environment requires a balanced approach. Some texts emphasize a strategic orientation in grappling with international management. Others emphasize a people-oriented approach, focusing primarily on employee behavior. But our view is that neither approach should dominate at the expense of the other. Today, perspectives can be buffeted quickly by tremendous change, and there is a need to adapt fast.

Consequently, our approach is one that blends perspectives and is firm enough to offer guidance. Management needs to think creatively and analytically about potential international opportunities, weighing internal strengths and weaknesses as well as possible competitive threats in the process. Ultimately, that process should culminate in the formation of strategies and methods designed to take advantage of those opportunities. But actually capitalizing on them is another matter entirely. It means executing and implementing. That takes time—and events can overtake a well-laid plan in a heartbeat.

Then there's the human side of the equation. Many plans derail because they fail to anticipate people-related complexities and complications. And when you come down to it, in the international environment those people and culture challenges probably trip up companies just as much as misguided business strategies do—maybe more. So strategy development and cross-cultural management skills are both critically important. Ideally, they should be interrelated. Possible cross-cultural challenges should inform strategy creation. And strategic needs should help shape management approaches and human resource policies around the world. Neither is more important than the other.

We present our balanced perspective in a lively fashion. Generally speaking, we take an applications-oriented approach that is solidly grounded in the latest research. Both instructors and students have told us our approach is fresh and engaging. We hope you enjoy it!

Intended Audience   This book will appeal to a wide audience. Students with limited exposure to international issues will appreciate the basic foundations and concepts that are laid out in each chapter. At the same time, students with some international coursework or work experience will be attracted by the book's depth. From a pedagogical perspective, the book will work well as a primary text in a course on international management. It can also be used in a management-oriented international business course. The strong focus on applications, with a variety of applications-oriented features, appeals to both students and instructors who wish to take a hands-on approach to the study of international management. But before we describe those features in detail, first we'll explain how the book is organized and walk you through our table of contents.

Organizing the Challenge of International Management

The organization of this revised edition of our book continues to reflect our belief that successful international management consists of four basic parts. First, *managers need to understand the broad context of international business*. Specifically, that includes critical trends impacting international management and the legal and political forces driving international business. Managers must also have a solid grounding in the ethical and cultural dilemmas that can pop up in international settings, and must realize what to do about them when borders are crossed. Second, *managers need to master the essential elements of effective interaction in the international arena*. That means learning how culture affects some of the basics that they may take for granted. Understanding how different cultures perceive and process information, developing skills in cross-cultural communication, and figuring out how to negotiate successful cross-border deals are all examples of this. Third, *effective international management means being able to recognize and take advantage of strategic opportunities*. That often means deciding how best to enter foreign markets and then figuring out how to operate successfully once there. Finally, *international managers must motivate and lead people from a variety of cultures and be able to build effective international teams*. It also means taking an international perspective on the hiring, training, and development of employees—if for no other reason than the rules of the game on factors like compensation and labor relations may be very different when borders are crossed. All this reflects our blended approach. For example, compensation practices are often rooted in a culture or country, and understanding these people-related issues is important. Indeed, a firm's strategy may be shaped by this understanding as well.

Chapter Preview   Our chapters are organized around a four-part scheme. We'll present our chapter preview by walking you through each part of the book.

Part I: On a Global Stage: The Context of International Management   This first part includes Chapters 1–4 and covers the essential foundations for successful international management. *Chapter 1* discusses the basics of international competition, trends impacting international management, and developments in countries and regions around the world. In this edition, Chapter 1 was extensively updated. Next, *Chapter 2* focuses on legal and political issues that managers need to take into account in their international operations. We discuss the different legal and political systems that exist around the world and their effects on international business. The chapter also tackles various types of political risk that managers may face in foreign markets and what they can do about them. This revision includes the latest business risk data that was available at the time we were writing. *Chapter 3* examines ethical values and corporate social responsibility in an international environment. Specific ethical issues, such as bribery, human rights abuses, and social upheavals, are considered in detail. And we offer guidance for responding to various ethical dilemmas (e.g., developing and adhering to corporate codes of conduct). *Chapter 4* concludes the first part of the book by examining culture in more detail. Specifically, we discuss the pervasive impact of culture on international management. We present frameworks that help explain basic cultural dimensions and their implications for managing people around the world. We include several new box features that provide examples of how firms reacted to these challenges.

Part II: Interacting Effectively in an International Environment   The second part of the book includes Chapters 5–7. The effect of culture on interpersonal interactions is a strong theme throughout this section. In other words, these chapters are natural extensions of the cultural issues raised in Chapter 4. As you'll see, *Chapter 5* examines how culture can affect employees' perceptions of their work environment, their jobs, and the people around them. The chapter also explains how to manage perception problems—such as stereotyping—in a culturally diverse business environment. *Chapter 6* shows how cultural differences can impede communication and offers advice for improving verbal, nonverbal, and written communication in an international environment. *Chapter 7* wraps up this part of the book by examining how to manage international conflicts and conduct successful cross-border business negotiations. Clearly, effective negotiation requires outstanding preparation and an appreciation of how negotiation strategies vary across cultures.

Part III: Capitalizing on International Opportunities   The third part of the book includes Chapters 8–10 and addresses the broad strategic and operational decisions faced by international managers. *Chapter 8* focuses on defining and developing international business strategy. First, we distinguish among common international strategies and explain when they might be pursued. In doing so, we also present some of the special challenges small firms face in developing an international strategy. Next, we provide detailed coverage of the process involved in developing winning international strategies (e.g., conducting a SWOT analysis). We conclude by discussing how companies need to ensure that their internal systems are aligned to support their international strategy if they want to succeed. *Chapter 9* takes things one step further by considering implementation issues that companies face in executing their international strategies. We present the various options available for entering foreign markets, including the pros and cons of each. In essence, each option can work under the right conditions, whether we're talking about exporting, licensing, or foreign acquisitions, just to name a few possibilities. Consequently, we also make suggestions for weighing and choosing among the options available. *Chapter 10* extends this discussion by examining how managers can make their entry choices work and keep their international operations running smoothly. That includes topics such as developing mechanisms to help coordinate international operations, managing business alliances (e.g., international joint ventures) successfully, and maintaining a technological edge abroad.

Part IV: Managing People in the International Arena   The final part of the book includes Chapters 11–14 and focuses squarely on the people side of the international management equation. And last is by no means least! Mishandling people-related issues can jeopardize even the best strategy, if not the best intentions, of management. *Chapter 11* tackles the challenge of how best to motivate and lead employees across cultures. We argue that cultural values can affect how employees behave and that managers should alter their style accordingly. *Chapter 12* explains how managers can build an effective international workforce. That process starts by taking a strategic approach to international human resource management—one that aligns human resource needs with the firm's international business strategy. Next, we discuss the options firms have for staffing foreign operations (e.g., hire locals or send expatriates?) and developing their international talent. We conclude with a presentation of strategies that firms can use to help expatriates succeed through appropriate selection mechanisms, training practices, and support systems. *Chapter 13* continues this theme by discussing how to ensure the success of an international workforce once it's in place. That means figuring out how to appraise performance and design compensation systems for employees around the world. *Chapter 14* concludes Part IV by examining some of the most vexing "people problems" facing international managers. In particular, we discuss how managers can develop effective international teams, especially in an environment of increasing diversity. We also suggest ways to strategically manage unions and labor relations around the world. These are no small challenges since the scope, purpose, and historical roles of unions vary dramatically across countries.

Cases   Given our strong application orientation, each section contains two substantial cases designed to accompany each of the chapters in Parts I–IV. These cases can be used to highlight issues from particular chapters or to provide a capstone experience that integrates material across chapters. They provide an excellent opportunity for students to analyze real international management problems in depth. All cases are current, of uniformly high quality, and come from the best providers available.

Changes to This Edition

For those professors who have used earlier editions of our book, we thank you. We'd also like to take the opportunity to highlight a number of changes we've made to this edition that we think you'll agree are improvements. For one, all the chapters have been updated with the latest articles from *The Wall Street Journal*, *The Economist*, and the *Financial Times*, among many other sources. Indeed, we believe we've captured some of the most contemporary thinking about issues and opportunities in international management. Likewise, we hope you'll appreciate the many new references to academic journals that include the *Journal of International Business Studies*, *Academy of Management Journal*, and *Strategic Management Journal*, again among many others. We've also made considerable effort to integrate web and Internet-related resources and exercises throughout the book. Some feedback on earlier editions, in fact, called for more such integration. To respond to this feedback, we've included a new end-of-chapter feature that we call *Tapping into the Global Network*. Each chapter now includes up-to-date and substantive assignments that have a strong web component to them (we say more about this below).

Additionally, we've dramatically updated the cases included in the book. Our goal was to choose the most contemporary cases—cases that reflect the latest issues in a dramatically changing field. You will be the judge of whether we met our goal. Likewise, we've streamlined the whole book chapter by chapter. Reviewers have told us that they spend considerable time on exercises, cases, and other material to augment the text in class and that they might be better served by a streamlining process. We hope we have met this need. Moreover, we believe the book has some key features that distinguish us from others in the market.

Key Features That Set Us Apart

We hope you'll find our unique array of features hard to resist. Moreover, we've gone to great lengths to support those features and provide additional information in our *Instructor's Resource Manual* and website.

Up-to-Date and Quality Sources   As highlighted above, our chapters rely on the most recent and most prestigious publications available. They include first-class research journals (e.g., *Academy of Management Journal* and *Journal of International Business Studies*) as well as publications aimed squarely at practicing managers (e.g., *Harvard Business Review* and *The Wall Street Journal*). We believe students must become good consumers of new knowledge and have an appreciation for research about international management. After all, research provides the building blocks for most successful applications in international management.

The Writing: Accessible, Engaging, and Action Oriented   Of course, international management is ultimately about *application* and figuring out what works. Consequently, each chapter is chock full of examples and illustrations from corporations around the world. We've also included concrete guidelines and action recommendations in each chapter. In doing so, we use an accessible and engaging writing style that is also direct, getting quickly to the point. Our job is to pull students in and make them as excited about international management as we are—whether we're describing a piece of research or pitching suggestions for action.

Getting "Real World" with Cases   Each chapter opens with an *International Challenge*, a short case that challenges students with a real problem facing an international manager or company. These problems are directly connected to the content of each chapter. The case concludes by posing questions for students (e.g., Why is this happening and what should be done about it?). As they read through each chapter, students will be exposed to concepts, ideas, and applications that will help them digest the problems and issues raised. A companion case called *Up to the Challenge?* closes each chapter and reveals the steps actually taken to address the problem raised in the chapter-opening case. As they make these connections, students are asked to reflect on the steps taken (e.g., Will they ultimately succeed? Is additional action needed?). Additional follow-up information on the opening and closing case for each chapter is presented in the *Instructor's Resource Manual* and may be used by instructors to supplement what is already covered in the opening and closing features.

As we noted in our chapter preview, more substantive cases are provided at the end of each part. These comprehensive cases allow students to integrate what they have learned across several chapters and apply that knowledge to a practical problem. Supplementary case material for instructors is also provided in the *Instructor's Resource Manual*.

Special Features   Besides cases, we also include boxed text sections in each chapter. These sections, entitled *International Insights*, report on cutting-edge and creative approaches taken by companies or people grappling with unusual international management issues in particular countries. Of course, these detailed and up-to-date examples dovetail with the topics discussed in each chapter. On the student website (with additional support in the *Instructor's Resource Manual*), we also include a feature called *Reality Check*. This feature is designed to provide an "in-the-trenches" snapshot, one that instructors may wish to use as an introduction to each new section or chapter. Using an interview format, this feature asks international managers, trade officials, and others impacted by international business in their jobs for their perspectives on issues related to each chapter. Put simply, we let real people doing real work describe, in their own words, the challenges they face and what's important to them. In doing so, they provide some fascinating insights into the nuts and bolts of international management.

Getting "Hands On" with Exercises and Applications   Students will find two special sections at the end of each chapter. The section labeled *International Development* presents students with an exercise or self-assessment designed to build self-insight and promote skill development in chapter-relevant areas. New to this edition, *Tapping into the Global Network* takes things one step further and gives students reason to use the Internet and related resources to pursue a project involving work that should be completed outside class. Each project is designed to directly apply chapter concepts or assess how international firms are implementing them. If desired, students can present their findings in class.

Other Important Pedagogical Features   To help guide students through the content by pointing out and summarizing key topics, each chapter begins with a set of *Learning Objectives* and concludes with a *Chapter Summary* and *Discussion Questions*. Finally, we've made extensive use of exhibits throughout the book to make it easier to digest information as well as to increase readability and visual appeal. Speaking of visual appeal, we've also included **a full-color insert from the World Bank Atlas** containing maps and charts that help give students a broad snapshot of the world of business.

Supplementary Materials

Accompanying this book is an outstanding set of supplements:

- **An excellent *Instructor's Resource Manual with Test Items*** includes chapter outlines, plenty of supplementary lecture materials such as the previously mentioned *Reality Checks*, comments on special text features, teaching notes for the cases, and recommended videos.

- **PowerPoint slide shows for each chapter,** available on the instructor website, outline chapter material and present key chapter exhibits as well as supplementary materials.

- ***HMTesting*** is a computerized version of the multiple-choice and essay test items found in the *Instructor's Resource Manual*. This easy-to-use program, available on CD, allows instructors to generate and change tests. The program includes an online testing feature by which instructors can administer tests via their local area network or over the web. It also has a gradebook feature that lets users set up classes, record and track grades from tests or assignments, analyze grades, and produce class and individual statistics.

- **A comprehensive video package** includes several segments that illustrate chapter concepts using examples of real-world organizations. Teaching notes and suggested uses for the segments appear in the accompanying Video Guide.

- **Student and Instructor websites** are also available. For students, we offer links to related websites, including the sites for those companies highlighted in the text, and self-test questions that are scored for immediate feedback. For instructors, we offer PowerPoint slides, downloadable files from the *Instructor's Resource Manual* that can be edited or used as is to meet specific course needs, and sample syllabi.

Giving Thanks

Behind every successful book project is a set of professionals who provide the support, guidance, and advice so vital to making everything click. We are extremely grateful for the outstanding reviewers who contributed their time, energy, and academic expertise toward the development of this project: Lawrence A. Beer, Arizona State University; Charles Byles, Virginia Commonwealth University; John E. Call, New Mexico State University; Norma Carr-Ruffino, San Francisco State University; Lauryn McManus, University of Central Florida; Mark Fenton, University of Wisconsin-Stout; Joseph Fontana, George Mason University; Bob Goddard, Appalachian State University; Selim Ilter, St. John Fisher College; Robert Isaak, Pace University; Daniel James, University of Northern Colorado; Dong I. Jung, San Diego State University; Marios Katsioloudes, West Chester University of Pennsylvania; Amy McMillan, Louisiana Tech University; Behnam Nakhai, Millersville University of Pennsylvania; Lynn Neeley, Northern Illinois University; John O'Del, Rhode Island College; Tara Radin, Hofstra University; Roy W. Reeber, Hawaii Pacific University; Daniel James Rowley, University of Northern Colorado; Deepak Sethi, University of Texas at Dallas; Arnold Sherman, University of Montana; John Stanbury, Frostburg State University; Richard Steers, University of Oregon; and Kara Swanson, Boise State University.

Likewise, it goes without saying that we owe an enormous debt of gratitude to our wonderful Houghton Mifflin team. First, we want to thank our editor Jessica Carlisle. Jessica has an uncanny ability to motivate us to get things done. Her ability to recognize small victories along the way helped us a lot. We also are very grateful to Susan Kahn. Susan has so many skills and wears so many hats that were helpful to us on this and previous projects. Thank you, Susan. Finally, we want to thank George Hoffman for believing in this project and sticking with us! And for helping to spread the word both before and after publication, we thank our marketing team of Steve Mikels and Lisa Boden.

We continue to owe an enormous debt of gratitude to our dear friend Amy Anderson. No one could ask for a better author for an *Instructor's Resource Manual*, particularly on international management! Amy's extensive international experience—she's lived and worked in several countries, run an international studies center at a major university, and completed her doctoral thesis on international business education—made her an easy choice. And we'll always be grateful that she signed on with us and has continued through this edition.

▶ *International Management*

PART I

On a Global Stage: The Context of International Management

1

An Overview of Global Trends and Challenges

Learning Objectives

After reading this chapter, you should be able to:

▶ Understand the general competitive environment in international business as well as the major and emerging players in the global economy.

▶ Identify major trends in international business, both positive and negative.

▶ Understand the role of management in responding to evolving international business challenges.

▶ Understand key foundation concepts in international management

INTERNATIONAL CHALLENGE

Balancing Act for New Balance: How Far Can It Run with Production in the United States?

THE ODDS ARE that you own at least one pair of athletic shoes. Indeed, athletic shoes are ubiquitous, as are familiar American brand names Nike and Reebok. What's also interesting is that the industry's biggest players have all of their shoes made in low-wage locations like China, Vietnam, and Indonesia, usually in factories owned and run by foreign subcontractors.

And then there's New Balance Athletic Shoe, Inc. In 1972, owner Jim Davis bought the firm for $100,000. Today, with over $1.3 billion in sales, New Balance is the fourth largest player in the athletic shoe industry worldwide (in the United States, the firm ranks second behind Nike). New Balance also has foreign subcontractors. Stroll down the aisle of a subcontractor's plant in China and you'll see young women repeating the same dull sewing tasks on old equipment to produce New Balance shoes. And the pay is a pittance (20–40 cents an hour). Of course, by reaping such labor savings, so the theory goes, companies can earn much higher profits. Plus, some argue that the U.S. economy is better off when low-skill, low-wage jobs can migrate to countries where labor is cheap and plentiful. That allows U.S. firms to concentrate on areas where more capital and higher skills are needed, which helps America's advanced economy sustain its edge and keeps living standards rising.

But New Balance really is different. Unlike its competitors, New Balance also has 1,200 employees making shoes in five U.S. facilities. Indeed, its American workforce has increased over 50 percent in the past several years. Overall, New Balance makes about 25 percent of its shoes in the United States, a percentage that owner Jim Davis would like to increase. Production employees at New Balance earn about $14 an hour, up to seventy times as much as their Chinese counterparts. But what's interesting is that the enormous gap in labor costs notwithstanding, the difference in *total* costs between the Chinese and American plants isn't that great. In China, the total cost of producing a pair of shoes is about $1.30, compared to $4 in New Balance's American plants. The resulting cost differential of $2.70 only represents 4 percent of the $70 price for the average shoe. And that 4 percent is manageable, especially since U.S. production means New Balance can fill orders and change styles more quickly than its competitors in North American markets.

But how does New Balance narrow the costs of producing in the United States enough to compete effectively? Clearly, New Balance's U.S. plants are extraordinarily efficient. Its American employees produce a shoe from scratch in less than 25 minutes compared to three hours in China. So what accounts for the American plants' productivity and efficiency? How can this feat be accomplished with the low-skill jobs and low-tech products that many companies have exported to low-wage locations? And what's the role of management in all of this?

As you read through this introductory chapter, you'll find that when it comes to international business, change is a constant theme. And adapting to change often means challenging old beliefs and coming up with new paradigms, even if they go against what passes for conventional wisdom. After you've read the chapter and digested our thumbnail sketch of international business, take a look at our closing *Up to the Challenge?* section for an overview of New Balance's approach.[1]

▶ *International Business in the Twenty-first Century*

In 1903, Dayton, Ohio, natives Orville and Wilbur Wright launched their flimsy craft over the sands of Kitty Hawk. The Wright brothers' persistence and engineering brilliance changed the world forever, revolutionizing transportation and business as we know it. Part of their incredible legacy can be seen at the Dayton airport today, where Menlo Worldwide operates its international air freight hub. Dozens of freighters depart daily, shipping machinery, materials, and parts to factories around the world. It's all part of global trends toward increased outsourcing of components, flexible manufacturing, and greater reliance on logistics systems that can deliver parts as needed (i.e., on a "just-in-time" basis). In electronics alone, contract manufacturers increased their production 400 percent between 1996 and 2003.[2] Of course, besides flight, astounding innovations in computers and information technologies have made it possible for transportation companies, as well as firms in many industries, to manage inventories, collect customer information, and track shipments around the world twenty-four hours a day, seven days a week.

And that's just the tip of the iceberg. The combination of cheap, pervasive fiber-optic cables straddling the globe and the increasingly ubiquitous availability of PCs makes for a flexible worldwide information flow that allows workers anywhere, and at any time, to interact.

One result of this is a surge in offshoring of jobs as companies everywhere scour the planet for the best talent at the best price.[3] Overall, the broad, long-term trend is the continued growth of international business, something that will, in addition to technology, increasingly weave national economies together. This ongoing connecting process is known as **globalization**.[4]

Many experts predict that this process ultimately will increase international cooperation and reinforce overall growth. Over time, tariffs will gradually disappear, worldwide accounting practices will emerge, and business practices that encourage more competition will become widespread.[5]

globalization
Process by which national economies are increasingly woven together worldwide

Of course, concerns and doubts remain. For instance, some question the efficiency and effectiveness of the **World Trade Organization** (WTO). This governing body, made up of 147 member countries, establishes worldwide rules for trade and commerce. Members hash out these rules during complex and protracted negotiations, the latest series of which is known as the Doha Round. The WTO also monitors trade regulations and has elaborate mechanisms to enforce its rulings on trade disputes between member nations. A key goal for the WTO is to reduce barriers and stimulate trade around the world. But the WTO is also a battleground for national interests as well as a lightning rod for critics who argue that globalization has drawbacks, including lost jobs, painful workforce migrations, social upheavals, and greater threats to the environment.

Clearly, the mission of the WTO and the worldwide trade issues that it wrestles with are complex. The original principles governing the WTO are outlined in a document that's a mind-numbing 27,000 pages long. A single dispute between the United States and the European Union (EU) over banana **tariffs** levied against American firms took several years to resolve. Likewise, in 2004 the WTO issued a 350-page "interim ruling" that favored Brazil's allegations that U.S. government subsidies paid to American cotton farmers drove down prices and unfairly allowed U.S. farmers to increase their global market share.[6]

Just securing WTO membership in the first place can prove incredibly challenging. For example, China's 2002 entry into the WTO was the culmination of protracted negotiations spanning fifteen years. Indeed, the full effects of China's membership will take years to fully unfold. China must execute the daunting changes it promised to make as a condition of membership (e.g., to revamp banking rules, securities regulations, and import-export restrictions, just to name a few). On top of that, China's WTO membership increased international pressure about issues such as ongoing product piracy and human rights abuses.[7]

Indeed, from the U.S. perspective at least, China has a ways to go when it comes to WTO regulations. Current complaints about China from the American side include intellectual property protection issues (e.g., that China isn't doing enough to combat product and brand piracy), "excessive" tax rebates given to Chinese computer chipmakers (which allegedly make it harder for American firms like Intel to sell chips in China), product dumping (that Chinese electronics and furniture companies allegedly are selling goods in the United States at below-market rates), and Chinese regulations that prohibit the import of certain U.S. farm products. Of course, as Brazil's cotton subsidy case suggests, compliance with WTO regulations is in the eye of the beholder![8]

It's also important to note that the WTO isn't the only body that governs international trade. The growth of regional and bilateral trade agreements in recent years is seen as something of a mixed bag. While these agreements have many pluses and are generally positive, they also can make managing broader economic issues more difficult, especially as new powerhouses like Brazil, China, and India continue flexing their economic muscles.[9]

The bottom line is that downturns and setbacks will occur along the way, the WTO notwithstanding. And setbacks can occur in the blink of an eye. A horrific example is the terrorist attacks that took place in New York City and Washington on September 11, 2001. In addition to the devastating loss of innocent lives, stock markets around the world lost trillions of dollars worth of value within days and growth prospects in many countries dimmed in the short term.[10]

World Trade Organization
Governing body that establishes worldwide rules for trade and commerce

tariff
A government-imposed tax on imports

EXHIBIT 1.1   *The Top Ten Business Threats: What International CEOs See as the Biggest Threats*

Threat Category	Overall Rank	Percent Mentioning
Over-regulation	1st	18%
Increased international competition	2nd	17%
Currency fluctuations	3rd	15%
Price deflation	4th	11%
Loss of critical talent	5th	11%
Global terrorism	6th	10%
Risk to reputation (i.e., anything that might hurt the firm's image or reputation)	7th	10%
Cost of capital	8th	8%
Emerging technologies	9th	6%
Corporate governance issues	10th	5%

Source: Adapted from Champion, M. (2004). CEOs' worst nightmares. *The Wall Street Journal*, January 21, A13. Note that the total percentage exceeds 100 percent since CEOs could mention multiple threats.

Overall, grappling with the sheer speed of change and the increasing complexity of international business makes the role of management—and the stakes—more important than ever.[11] And sometimes management is blindsided, even in the best companies, by sudden economic shifts. Just ask networking giant Cisco Systems about the rapid downturn it experienced in early 2001. In announcing layoffs, Cisco effectively reversed plans it had sketched out just weeks earlier to have 100,000 network professionals in place in India by 2006. Overall, there are a variety of threats and risks facing international business leaders. Take a look at Exhibit 1.1 to see what we mean—it summarizes the threat perceptions of roughly 1,400 international CEOs who participated in a survey conducted by PricewaterhouseCoopers. As you'll see, global terrorism is considered a threat, but it is by no means at the top of the list. As it turns out, international executives have plenty of threats to worry about.[12]

Of course, all businesses face risks and managing them effectively is a key challenge for management. Indeed, there are many good reasons to be fundamentally optimistic about the long-term prospects for international business. Consequently, the goal of this chapter is to give you a sense of the trends and challenges facing international managers in the twenty-first century. Many of these changes are positive and represent huge opportunities. In pursuing these opportunities, management must guard against the accompanying risks and dangers, which often rear up suddenly and unexpectedly. We also want to sketch out how firms approach international competition as well as provide a snapshot of the major players in the global economy. In doing so, we'll be presenting some basic concepts and ideas that will be used throughout the book. But we'll start this chapter by describing the growth of international business and profiling the role countries and regions around the world are playing in that growth.

▶ *Globalization and the Growth of International Business*

Today, the lines between international and domestic operations are gone or continue to blur. Many companies look for ideas, workers, materials, and customers everywhere. Likewise, tough competitors can appear from anywhere. Just ask Motorola about Finland's Nokia! Of course, many industries already operate on a global basis (e.g., computers) or are moving in that direction (e.g., automotive parts). These days, as one European manager put it, "The scope of every manager is the world."

Needless to say, managing that way isn't easy. Among other things, it requires worldwide information networks, a supportive corporate culture, and the ability to take advantage of local needs, strengths, and initiatives when they exist. For instance, Philips, the Dutch electronics giant, deliberately moves unit headquarters to wherever the hottest consumer trends appear for a particular line of business (e.g., Hong Kong for audio products and California for digital set-top boxes). But there's no single answer. For some companies, just letting local managers pursue their own ideas is a step forward. Coca-Cola freed its Turkish unit, for example, to pursue a new pear-flavored drink for the local market.[13]

The Hottest Growth Areas

So where is all the growth in international business occurring? One way to measure things is by the flow of **foreign direct investment** (FDI) into a particular country over several years. More than just capital, FDI also means that managerial knowledge and technical know-how is moving into a country from outside its borders. As such, FDI is a good measure of a country's prospects on the international business stage, either as an established market or an emerging one.

foreign direct investment
Capital and knowledge that flows into a country from outside its borders

The total worldwide flow of FDI hit $1.1 trillion in 2000 and was predicted to exceed $10 trillion in 2005. Exhibit 1.2 lists the top ten projected recipients of FDI through 2005. As you can see, the list is dominated by established players, such as the United States, as well as by high-growth developing markets, such as China. Although it's not captured in the exhibit, another encouraging trend is that the growth of FDI inflows into poor, developing countries should continue to exceed the growth rates experienced by their industrialized counterparts. By 2005, poor countries were expected to receive nearly 30 percent of global FDI inflows.[14]

In fact, much of the growth in international business is occurring *outside* traditional economic powerhouses like the United States, the European Union, and Japan (these three regions are often referred to as the Triad.)[15] For instance, in 2003 China had the largest percentage increase in international trade of any country worldwide. China was both the fastest-growing exporter in the world that year (enjoying a 22 percent annual increase) as well as its fastest-growing importer (a 40 percent increase, with most of that growth accounted for by imports from Japan, Taiwan, and South Korea).[16] Granted, the United States may not be the world's fastest-growing nation, but it's still the biggest economy (at $10.7 trillion, the U.S. economy eclipses China's at $6.3 trillion in equivalent

EXHIBIT 1.2   *Foreign Direct Investment Magnets: The Top Ten*

Country	Projected Yearly FDI Inflow, 2001–2005 (in US$ billions)	Share of Worldwide Inflows (%)
United States	236.2	26.6
United Kingdom	82.5	9.3
Germany	68.9	7.8
China	57.6	6.5
France	41.8	4.7
Netherlands	36.1	4.1
Belgium	30.2	3.4
Canada	29.6	3.3
Hong Kong	20.5	2.3
Brazil	18.8	2.1

Source: Adapted from ———. (2001). The cutting edge. *The Economist*, February 24, 80.

purchasing power).[17] Still, these growth statistics underscore that trade among the United States, Japan, and the European Union is becoming less and less important over time.[18] For instance, in 1993, Japan accounted for almost 15 percent of America's trade. By 2000, Japan's share had fallen to less than 11 percent, with **North American Free Trade Agreement** (NAFTA) partners Mexico and Canada making up the difference. Moreover, developing markets are increasingly becoming important export targets for the Triad. Mexico, for example, buys 75 percent of its imports from the United States, while the Czech Republic and Hungary buy 65 percent of their imports from the European Union.[19]

Clearly, the total value of economic activity in a country, or **gross domestic product** (GDP), is growing at a faster rate in developing nations than in the Triad. Indeed, developing countries are expected to capture 50 percent of *world* GDP in the near future. The bottom line is that consumer demand in developing markets is rising as they become more affluent.[20] Overall, global GDP is expected to hit $48 trillion by 2010, a figure over 80 percent higher than 1994.[21] Take a look at Exhibit 1.3—it lists the 2004 GDP growth rates for twenty-five developing nations as well as GDP per person (a measure of a country's relative wealth). As you can see, China and India are among the fastest-growing countries in the world, but are also among the poorest (by comparison, the 2004 GDP growth rate for the United States was about 5 percent and its 2003 GDP per person was $35,992).[22]

Consequently, many American firms consider developing countries as more than just sources of cheap labor. They're also places to build new markets and tap populations eager for new products and services as their income and wealth rise.[23] That's why Citibank spent years building its credit card business in developing markets like Indonesia and Thailand. And in 2004, Citibank started issuing credit cards in China, the first foreign bank to do so.[24]

But don't forget small companies. They fuel much of the growth in international business. In 1995, firms with fewer than 500 employees accounted for a bigger share of total manufactured exports than large firms for the first time.[25]

North American Free Trade Agreement
Trade agreement linking Canada, Mexico, and the United States

gross domestic product
The total value of economic activity in a country

EXHIBIT 1.3   *Gross Domestic Product Statistics for Selected Developing Nations*

Country	Projected 2004 GDP Growth (percentage change over 2003)	2003 GDP per Person (US$)
Argentina	6.9%	$10,423
Brazil	3.6%	$7,559
Chile	4.7%	$9,965
China	8.9%	$4,654
Colombia	3.9%	$6,039
Egypt	3.2%	$3,879
Hong Kong	6.5%	$26,845
India	7.2%	$2,538
Indonesia	4.6%	$3,041
Israel	2.4%	$19,194
Malaysia	6.1%	$8,591
Mexico	3.4%	$8,812
Peru	3.9%	$4,886
Philippines	4.1%	$4,487
Russia	6.6%	$9,749
Singapore	5.9%	$24,389
South Africa	2.6%	$10,000
South Korea	5.4%	$19,497
Taiwan	5.4%	$17,962
Thailand	7.2%	$6,937
Turkey	4.8%	$7,189
Venezuela	7.8%	$5,342

Source: Adapted from ———. (2004). *The Economist* poll of forecasters. *The Economist*, April 24, 110; **http://www.nationmaster.com**.

And small firms aren't just shipping products abroad. Many are setting up outposts on foreign turf. Yellow Springs Instruments (YSI) is a case in point. This small Ohio firm, with $50 million in sales, makes, among other things, monitoring equipment that measures water flow and pollution levels. In 2001, YSI opened a sales office in the Chinese city of Qingdao and has plans for several more. With 22 percent of the world's people but less than 10 percent of its fresh water, China has a severe shortage of clean water. As YSI's president put it, "We think we can make a difference there."[26]

▸ A Snapshot of Regional Trends

This section offers brief snapshots of important trends in specific countries and regions. We'll pay special attention to established, dominant countries as well as emerging markets expected to grow rapidly in the years ahead.

The Americas: Searching for Trade Ties That Bind

Free Trade Area of the Americas Proposed free trade zone covering 800 million people in thirty-four countries in the Western Hemisphere

A big question mark is whether a proposed continental free trade zone stretching from Alaska to the tip of South America will become reality. Targeted to be in place by 2006, the **Free Trade Area of the Americas** (FTAA) aims to create a free trade zone covering 800 million people in thirty-four countries. But getting the nations involved to agree on FTAA terms has been challenging. For instance, countries like Brazil worry that the United States has more to gain than they do if FTAA is implemented and competition becomes unfettered as tariffs and other restrictions fade. Mexico, in contrast, would lose its exclusive access to American markets. Since NAFTA became a reality in 1994, Mexico's exports have surged threefold, with nearly 90 percent headed for the United States.[27]

As a consequence, the U.S. government has focused on building smaller free trade deals within the region, in the hopes of building support for larger agreements like the FTAA over time (e.g., by showing skeptical nations such as Brazil that the United States isn't the only beneficiary of such arrangements). That seems to be part of the logic behind the Central American Free Trade Agreement (or CAFTA), a deal that was reached in 2003 between the United States and four Central American countries (i.e., El Salvador, Guatemala, Honduras, and Nicaragua; with talks ongoing to bring in Costa Rica and other countries as well). Two-way trade between these countries and the United States hit $30 billion in 2003 (a figure that eclipses the total value of trade that the United States has with both India and Russia put together). Generally speaking, all countries within CAFTA would enjoy duty-free trade with each other's markets for virtually all products as the agreement is phased in.[28]

For a summary of recent two-way trade within and between regions in the Americas, take a look at Exhibit 1.4. Merchandise trade levels in four of the five regions within the hemisphere grew faster than the world average over the past ten years. And that's a trend proponents hope will accelerate if FTAA becomes a reality. We'll take a look at NAFTA partners Canada, Mexico, and the United States before turning our attention to key countries in South America. NAFTA has dramatically increased trade and investment among the three countries by gradually eliminating tariffs, import quotas, and barriers to foreign ownership.[29]

Canada For the most part, the past several years have been good to Canada. The country's growth rates were steady, if unspectacular (e.g., GDP growth was 2.2 percent in 2003), and inflation and interest rates remained under control. Nevertheless, Canada's relationship with its southern neighbor, and the world's largest economy, is fraught with awkward comparisons. Canada and the United States are each other's largest trading partner, with two-way trade between the countries topping $393 billion in 2003. But Canada's smaller economy is much more dependent on foreign trade than America's (foreign trade equals about 80 percent of GDP in Canada, but only about 25 percent in the United States). Canada frets about keeping up with its giant neighbor, at least in certain respects. On living standards, for instance, Canada comes up short, with the average Canadian family's after-tax income running about 30 percent lower than their American counterpart's. Put simply, Canadians are taxed more and paid less than their American neighbors. That said, Canada's situation is enviable, both as a place to live and a place to invest. Traditionally known for its natural resources (e.g., timber, minerals, fish), Canada has received major

EXHIBIT 1.4   *Commerce in the Americas: Levels of Inter- and Intraregional Trade between Nations*

Region	Trade Flows (in US$ billions)*				
	AC	CC	CA	MR	NA
Andean Community (AC) (Bolivia, Colombia, Ecuador, Peru, Venezuela)	($5.4)				
Caribbean Community (CC) (e.g., Guyana, Jamaica, Suriname)	$0.5	($1.1)			
Central America (CA) (Costa Rica, El Salvador, Guatemala, Honduras, Nicaragua)	$1.3	$0.2	($2.5)		
Mercosur (MR) (Argentina, Brazil, Paraguay, Uruguay)	$5.9	$0.3	$0.4	($18.3)	
NAFTA (NA) (Canada, Mexico, U.S.)	$43.4	$8.6	$15.6	$42.7	($702.5)

*Trade *within* a region is in parentheses; all other figures reflect *interregional* trade.
Source: Adapted from ———. (2001). Trade in the Americas: All in the familia. *The Economist,* April 21, 19–22.

investments across a range of industries from foreign companies, often to take advantage of lower costs and a skilled workforce. For example, in the auto industry, the major U.S. (Ford and General Motors) and Japanese (Honda and Toyota) companies all operate factories in Canada, along with scores of suppliers. And the reverse is also true. Canadian corporations have invested heavily abroad, especially in the United States. For instance, Canadian Pacific has almost a third of its railroad tracks in the United States and is one of the biggest owners of luxury hotels in America.[30]

Mexico   Predating NAFTA was the *maquiladora* sector. Established by the government, **maquiladoras** are foreign factories that can import parts and materials into Mexico duty free, as long as they are used to make products for export. Most *maquiladoras* are in Mexico's northern states, adjacent to the primary destination for their exports—the United States. NAFTA's implementation was a huge boost to the *maquiladora* sector. Between 1993 and 2001, *maquiladoras* created some 800,000 new jobs as foreign companies, including American household names such as Ford, came in to set up shop.[31]

    Like Canada, Mexico now seems inextricably tied to its American neighbor. Indeed, Mexico sends 90 percent of its exports to the United States. That said, China and India are challenging Mexico's twin advantages of NAFTA and proximity when it comes to the U.S. market. Cheaper labor and improving infrastructure have caused thousands of *maquiladora* jobs to vanish in recent years as companies pulled out to go to China (or other cheaper locations). Likewise, India has jumped in front of Mexico in terms of service exports, carving out a niche in technological services, thanks to a ready pool of skilled professionals and modern communications systems. But, Mexico's exposure to the

maquiladoras
Foreign factories in Mexico that can import materials duty free and are usually located close to the U.S. border

rest of the world has also grown, thanks to NAFTA and the presence of world-class firms such as Volkswagen and Matsushita. In the process, Mexican firms learned about the practices, standards, and technologies used by foreign firms, with many becoming formidable international competitors in their own right. Consider Grupo Industrial Bimbo SA (GIB), a Mexican food company and McDonald's exclusive bun supplier in Mexico. GIB recently set up a candy factory in a cheap labor country to serve a rich market next door. The factory is in the Czech Republic and the market is western Europe.[32]

Overall, Mexico is now healthier for all of this, experiencing fewer dramatic boom-and-bust swings than in the past (e.g., the 1994 debt crisis that caused the collapse of the peso). Yet it's hard to predict when job and wage growth in Mexico will be strong enough to significantly reduce immigration, particularly of the illegal variety, to the United States. Should that occur, any continuing immigration from Mexico may largely consist of people looking for higher-paying jobs as opposed to just having a job at all. But it seems unlikely that American demand for low-wage Mexican labor will evaporate any time soon. And since Mexico still has major problems (e.g., poverty) and economic development is uneven (i.e., concentrated in certain areas and sectors), many of its citizens will undoubtedly continue to look for opportunities elsewhere.[33]

In any case, Mexico is the United States' second largest trading partner, with two-way trade between the countries pushing $236 billion in 2003. Since NAFTA was implemented, foreign direct investment in Mexico has averaged $12 billion annually. Of course, being connected at the hip to the United States could mean being dragged down when the economy up north goes south. That point was underscored in 2001 when DaimlerChrysler said it would shut down three factories in Mexico, a move costing 2,600 jobs. And auto-related exports make up 20 percent of Mexico's total. But for the long haul, both foreign and Mexican-owned suppliers are cautiously optimistic.[34]

The United States Although the United States experienced a recession in 2001, by 2004 prospects for faster near-term growth were looking good. And despite the woes of 2001–2003 (e.g., dot.com debacles, terrorist attacks, war in Iraq, wild stock market swings, weak economic growth, and accounting scandals at Enron and elsewhere), productivity growth continues to be strong. Moreover, as we've said, the United States is still the world's biggest economy and the biggest magnet for foreign investment. Many foreign companies find the United States an attractive place to set up operations or acquire firms (witness all the plants that BMW, Mercedes, and Nissan have built in the past few years). The United States also leads in knowledge creation, financial services, and information technology, positions that will be important in the years ahead. For example, the United States has the most creative economic environment in the world, one where it's easy to start new businesses and access sophisticated technologies.[35]

Today, American multinationals operate around the world, with many enjoying dominant positions in their respective industries. Colgate-Palmolive, for instance, operates in over 150 countries, with foreign sales accounting for 75 percent of its revenues. In fact, 185 of the 500 largest multinationals in the world are American (take a look at Exhibit 1.5 for a list of the world's ten largest companies).

However, the United States still runs large trade deficits. In 2003, both imports and exports were up over the previous year (8.3 percent and 4.6 percent, respectively). Overall, imports of goods and services soared to almost $1.5

EXHIBIT 1.5   *World's Largest Companies by Revenue: The Top Ten in 2003*

Rank/Company	2002 Revenues (US$ billions)	Headquarters	Industry
1. Wal-Mart	240,525	United States	Retail
2. General Motors	186,763	United States	Automotive
3. ExxonMobil	182,466	United States	Energy
4. Royal Dutch/Shell	179,431	Netherlands/Britain	Energy
5. British Petroleum	178,721	Britain	Energy
6. Ford Motor	163,871	United States	Automotive
7. DaimlerChrysler	141,421	Germany	Automotive
8. Toyota Motor	131,754	Japan	Automotive
9. General Electric	131,698	United States	Diversified
10. Mitsubishi	109,386	Japan	Trading/diversified

Source: Adapted from ———. (2003). Global 500: The world's largest corporations. *Fortune,* July 21, 106.

EXHIBIT 1.6   *America's Trade Imbalances: The Top Five Goods Deficits and Surpluses*

Top Five Deficits	2003 Deficit (US$ billions)	Top Five Surpluses	2003 Surplus (US$ billons)
1. China	-123,960	1. Netherlands	+9,731
2. Japan	-65,965	2. Australia	+6,689
3. Canada	-54,685	3. Belgium	+5,077
4. Mexico	-40,615	4. Hong Kong	+4,691
5. Germany	-39,199	5. United Arab Emirates	+2,381

Source: Adapted from **http://www.census.gov/foreign-trade/top/dst/2003/12**.

trillion, while exports from the United States hit $1 trillion. The resulting $490 billion deficit was an all-time record, with China alone accounting for $124 billion of the total. Of course, the United States does have trade surpluses with a variety of countries. Exhibit 1.6 lists the countries producing the top five deficits and top five surpluses with the United States in 2003.[36]

Trends in South America In the 1980s, South American countries were awash in debt, hyperinflation, and fear. They watched as East Asia leapfrogged South America onto the world economic stage. In the 1990s, many South American governments acted to transform the region's 500 million people into a competitive regional trading bloc. In particular, they privatized state-owned industries, reduced tariffs, made it easier for foreigners to invest, and set up free trade agreements with neighbors and the United States.[37] That said, in 2004 there was considerable skepticism across the region about the value of such reforms and freer trade in general, particularly as it related to the poor and job creation. Indeed, leaders of countries such as Brazil and Argentina called on the United States to do more to open its own markets and to cut subsidies for American farmers.[38]

Nevertheless, many foreign companies are convinced that economic reforms will continue and eventually succeed in South America. Looking back, however, the results of reforms show that while progress has been made, there's still a considerable way to go. GDP growth in the region averaged 3 percent in the 1990s, a figure that lagged behind that of many Asian economies. Still, things were looking up in 2004, with GDP growth expected to average 4 percent across Latin America. Likewise, foreign direct investment more than doubled from 2002 to 2004. Generally speaking, countries enacting the most significant reforms, such as Chile, did better than countries that made fewer changes, such as Ecuador. The region has also been prone to instability because of its dependence on foreign capital. In short, capital can move in or out of the region quickly, depending on the whims of foreign investors and external events. Speaking of instability, political upheavals and guerrilla movements have dogged Colombia, Ecuador, and Peru in recent years, putting a crimp on business. And poverty, slow job growth, stifling regulations, and weak business infrastructures remain region-wide concerns.[39]

The region's three economic powerhouses are Argentina, Chile, and Brazil. Chile has the most successful track record in recent years, both in terms of reform and its economic performance as an exporter. On the other hand, Argentina suffered through a stubborn recession from 1999 to 2001. At the end of 2001, Argentina experienced a financial collapse precipitated by an inability to pay back foreign loans that was then followed by a GDP drop of over 10 percent in 2002. Among the reasons cited for Argentina's problems during this period were high foreign debt, an overvalued currency, burdensome regulations, and onerous taxes on investment and production. But Argentina devalued its currency and unpegged it from the U.S. dollar, renegotiated foreign loan terms, and kept a lid on government spending. These steps and overseas demand for Argentine products helped GDP growth jump up almost 9 percent in 2003 and an expected 7 percent in 2004. Whether Argentina's recovery is sustainable remains to be seen. But Argentina's experience underscores the challenge of creating stable, open economies in emerging markets—be they in South America or anywhere else.[40]

Brazil is by far the biggest economy in South America. Brazil's currency sank in 2000–2001, bringing with it renewed fears about inflation and interest rate hikes. Moreover, the spillover from problems in neighboring Argentina helped slow Brazil's economic growth and caused many foreign companies to cut back production in the short term. But going forward, the picture seems a bit more positive, thanks to a combination of government fiscal policies and greater demand for Brazilian exports. GDP growth for 2004 was expected to hit 3.6 percent. Brazil's attractiveness is perhaps best illustrated by the moves car companies have made in recent years. American, European, and Japanese car firms all have world-class manufacturing facilities in Brazil. Simply put, Brazil and the region have a pent up demand for cars.[41]

Mercosur
A trading block consisting of Argentina, Brazil, Paraguay, and Uruguay

So there's reason to be cautiously optimistic about the long-term future for South America. Many South American countries are looking beyond the region for trading partners. For instance, among **Mercosur** members (a trading block consisting of Argentina, Brazil, Paraguay, and Uruguay), exports to other South

EXHIBIT 1.7 *A Profile of Selected Asian Nations*

Nation	Rank: Corporate Governance Quality	Rank: Transparency	Top Fifteen Family Control (percent)	Rank: Global Resilience to Shocks
China	8	10	Unavailable	4
Hong Kong	2	2	84	3
Indonesia	9	7	22	8
Japan	3	3	2	not ranked
Malaysia	6	4	76	6
Philippines	4	5	47	9
Singapore	1	1	48	1
South Korea	10	9	13	2
Taiwan	5	6	17	5
Thailand	7	7	39	7

*For ranked items, 1 = best (i.e., best corporate governance, most transparency, most resilience). The numbers under Family Control refer to the percentage of a country's GDP accounted for by the corporate assets under the control of that country's top fifteen families.

Sources: Adapted from ———. (2001). Singapore: Death by a thousand cuts. *The Economist*, September 15, 38; ———. (2001). In praise of rules: A survey of Asian business. *The Economist*, April 7, 1–18; ———. (2001). Emerging market indicators. *The Economist*, January 26, 98; ———. (2001). A global game of dominos. *The Economist*, August 25, 22–24; Balfour, F., & Clifford, M.L. (2001). Hong Kong: A city under siege. *Business Week*, July 23, 48–49; Bremner, B., Balfour, F., Shari, M., Ihlwan, M., & Engardio, P. (2001). Asia: The big chill. *Business Week*, April 2, 48–50; Pura, R., & Borsuk, R. (2001). Politics-as-usual hinders Southeast Asia. *The Wall Street Journal*, July 30, A15, A16.

American nations account for less than 30 percent of the total. Over 40 percent of Mercosur exports go to the European Union and the United States. And South America is a fast-growing market for imports from the United States.[42]

The Asia-Pacific Mix: Growth, Stagnation, and Economic Dips

The Asia-Pacific region may become the most dominant economic area in the world in the next few years. But along the way there have been plenty of hiccups. Moreover, the countries of Asia have some similarities, but also many differences. Countries that have structural problems (e.g., high government debt, weak corporate governance, poor legal protections) and are highly dependent on key overseas markets tend to be most vulnerable to economic shocks. An interesting aspect of business in Asia is that many of the region's most successful companies are part of family-owned empires. These Asian empires are often formidable competitors that pursue opportunities at home as well as abroad. But the degree of family control varies across the region. In some Asian countries (e.g., Malaysia), a handful of powerful families control 50 percent of all local companies. On the other hand, family control of companies is minuscule in Japan, with the level of family control about the same as it is in Europe (less than 10 percent of all companies). Take a look at Exhibit 1.7 for a profile of some corporate governance and related issues in selected Asian countries.[43]

In any case, many of the current concerns about Asia revolve around the growing clout of China, its ongoing problems, and the spillover effects that might occur around the world should those problems not be contained. This prevailing mood highlights the fact that companies need to balance China's potential, as well as the region's prospects, against underlying issues that continue to hold back some Asian countries.[44] These issues include:

- **Infrastructure problems** (e.g., inadequate power and transportation networks, pollution issues, etc.)

- **Rising costs** (e.g., for labor, housing, capital, and materials, especially in certain countries)

- **Excessive manufacturing capacity in certain industries** (e.g., semiconductors)

- **Insufficient innovation** (worker training is weak in some Asian countries)

- **Weak banking systems** (e.g., unchecked lending practices that result in billions of unprofitable loans)[45]

Next, we'll take a closer look at recent trends in emerging markets in the Asia-Pacific region (e.g., China, India) as well as the more established economic powerhouses (e.g., Japan).

China Over the past quarter-century, China's ascendance has been astounding, with GDP growth averaging about 9 percent annually and foreign trade growth averaging about 15 percent. Moreover, foreign direct investment has been pouring in at around $1 billion per week in recent years, as companies worldwide salivate at the prospect of serving 1.3 billion potential (and increasingly affluent) consumers or tapping a seemingly endless supply of cheap labor. No wonder China is now tightly woven into the world's economy and, as of 2004, had a total GDP worth $1.4 trillion, good for sixth place globally.[46]

guanxi
Relationships or connections that can facilitate business in China

Nevertheless, China presents some formidable problems to foreign businesses, including a weak legal system and opaque government policies. It's a place where business is often guided by **guanxi** (relationships or connections) rather than by rules and laws. Other challenges for foreign companies include China's incredible ethnic, cultural, and linguistic diversity. Regional differences are huge, and much of the population (70 percent) lives in rural areas and is quite poor. Put simply, China is *not* a single, homogenous market. Indeed, the percentage of Chinese with disposable incomes sufficient to buy cell phones, much less cars, is still relatively small. That's why Motorola and Nokia enjoyed a quick spike in sales initially, only to see it level off in the last few years. Although only about 20 percent of Chinese have cell phones, slowing growth suggests that most of the population that can afford to buy a cell phone have done so. On top of that, foreign multinationals like Nokia and Motorola have seen 40 local competitors pop up in recent years, causing cell phone prices in China to drop.[47]

competitive intensity
The extent to which a fast-paced and highly competitive business environment exists in a country

Overall, Motorola's and Nokia's experience underscores China's **competitive intensity**. Competitors are legion and the pace of business activity is frenetic. Nearly 150,000 foreign companies operate in China, including 40 percent of the world's largest 500 firms, a figure that's steadily rising. No other country has experienced this kind of corporate influx in such a short period. Plus, 6 million privately owned firms offer plenty of formidable competition in China.

When we visited China, a manager at a U.S. consumer products firm said that in addition to competing against other world-class multinationals such as Unilever, the company faced thousands of local competitors (mostly small, family-run enterprises) just in Shanghai alone! Indeed, the foreign companies that have been most consistently profitable in China, at least so far, have not focused on selling into the domestic Chinese market. Instead, the most profitable firms are those using China as a cheap platform for manufacturing and exporting goods (the average Chinese factory worker pulls in $80 a month—a figure that an American paid the minimum wage earns in less than two days).[48]

Clearly, foreign companies often underestimate the difficulties of doing business in China. But even firms that grasp those difficulties are willing to put up with them for the simple reason that China is still the world's largest emerging market, one with tremendous potential for ongoing growth. China is also run by a government that, despite its many failings, is eager to build the country's economic prowess.[49]

The road ahead includes a variety of challenges for China. As of 2004, rapid business expansion and the continuing influx of foreign direct investment ($53.5 billion in 2003) were causing GDP growth to advance strongly. But power rationing was necessary in some of the booming coastal cities as demand exceeded supply. Speaking of supplies, China's hungry factories are prompting worries about inflation and higher commodity prices worldwide as the country consumes an increasingly big chunk of production-related raw materials. For instance, in 2004, China devoured 7 percent of the world's crude oil, 30 percent of its iron ore, and 27 percent of its steel. Likewise, fully half of the worldwide increase in demand for cement in 2004 was due to China. Indeed, these trends should continue as both foreign multinationals and their local counterparts, such as telecom-equipment supplier Huawei Technologies Company, continue to build manufacturing capacity in China at a rapid rate. Coupled with an inefficient banking system, such fast-paced growth fuels a speculative lending environment, one that the central government may have to rein in strongly at some point. Doing so, however, could help slow China's economy, possibly unhinging neighboring Asian economies (e.g., Japan, Taiwan) that are increasingly connected to China.[50]

In the meantime, the Chinese government continues to weigh the pace of reforms demanded by the country's 2002 entry into the World Trade Organization. For example, the Chinese government has pledged to:

- Spend billions to modernize its infrastructure (e.g., new roads, power plants).

- Dismantle state-owned firms in most industries (which still account for a big slice of the economy) and encourage those that stay in business to improve their competitiveness (e.g., by setting up joint ventures with foreign companies).

- Eliminate most import barriers and reduce tariffs.

Many foreign companies look forward to the day when they can import products, distribute goods, invest, and own businesses in China without significant restrictions. Kodak, for instance, has sunk over $1.2 billion into factories in China in the past few years, buying them from uncompetitive Chinese manufacturers. The firm also opened over 6,000 Kodak outlets there and expects China to knock the United States off as the top market for its film by 2010. As Kodak's Asia president put it, "China is the potential opportunity of a lifetime."

For its part, China wants the ability to export goods ranging from computers to shoes without quota restrictions by 2005. If that happens, China may capture 50 percent of the world's export market for certain goods in the apparel, machinery, and electronics sectors within a few years (an increase over 100 percent in some cases). Such prospects worry many of China's low-wage competitors in places like India, Indonesia, and Mexico.[51]

India Speaking of India, the country's population is 1.05 billion. But by 2045 or so, India will eclipse China, creating the biggest potential market in the world. And while India is getting ready, it's starting from behind compared to China, with slower economic growth, much less foreign direct investment, a lower literacy rate, and a larger percentage of its population in poverty. Overall, many view India as a less successful and less formidable competitor than China. And a recent survey of international executives found that nearly 60 percent were more likely to invest in China than India, with only 14 percent saying the reverse. But the gap with China is closing, especially in India's southern states. Indeed, more than 50 percent of the population in these states, where much of India's booming technology industry is based, should achieve middle-class status by around 2025. And India's 8.1 percent GDP growth rate in 2003 actually surpassed China's (India's growth rate is expected to average 6–7 percent in the years ahead). Experts urge the Indian government to speed reform along by taking a number of steps:

- Accelerating the sell-off of state-owned enterprises.
- Reforming India's complex and restrictive labor laws.
- Deregulating various industries (e.g., textiles) and continuing to reduce tariffs.
- Encouraging private banking and relaxing currency restrictions.
- Continuing to improve the business infrastructure, including a shaky power grid.[52]

Many of India's biggest foreign investors have been automobile companies, with several forming partnerships with local firms in recent years. Consumer products giants like Coca-Cola and Unilever have also moved into the Indian market. But India's biggest impact on the global economic scene is probably in information technology (IT). In 1991, India's IT industry was valued at a scant $50 million. In 1999, the figure was $4 billion. And by 2008, India's high-tech industry may hit $77 billion, providing 2 million jobs (compared to about 800,000 in 2004), and about 30 percent of the country's total exports, in the process. India is a source of cheap, well-educated, English-speaking high-tech labor for U.S. firms and their software code-writing needs. For instance, General Electric, IBM, Microsoft, and Intel are among the American companies with R&D facilities in India. In fact, nearly 40 percent of the world's biggest 500 multinationals outsource some of their IT needs to Indian firms. Moreover, leading Indian IT firms like Infosys and Wipro Technologies are becoming world-class competitors in their own right, aggressively developing new software and offering their consulting services globally in high-margin areas like strategic planning and IT system implementation.[53]

Japan As the world's second largest economy, Japan had a 2.7 percent GDP growth rate in 2003—after spending much of the previous decade in the economic doldrums. Ironically, part of the reason for Japan's resurgence is that China is now a major consumer in its own right, driving up demand for the kind of complex goods that many Japanese firms can now make efficiently at home (e.g., Japan's Hitachi Construction has seen soaring Chinese demand for its power shovels). Indeed, Japanese exports to China hit $60 billion in 2003, and, for the immediate future, prospects for continued GDP growth look reasonably good.[54]

Still, risks and challenges remain for Japan. In 2001, for instance, government debt was running about 120 percent of GDP. However, by 2004, government debt had increased to 144 percent of GDP, more than twice the U.S. rate. In part, problems with Japan's debt and its financial system reflect the government's efforts to simultaneously protect weak domestic industries (e.g., chemicals, financial services, retailing) and maintain a thriving export machine. In a nutshell, weak industries hurt the economy, driving up both the cost of living and the cost of doing business in Japan. Consequently, Japanese companies have been voting with their feet for years, leaving the country to pursue lower costs and better markets (e.g., elsewhere in Asia, the Americas, etc.).[55]

That said, Japan has taken steps to clean up banks riddled with bad debts, encourage foreign investment, reduce import barriers, and increase domestic demand (including the $1.1 trillion in recent years that the government has spent on various domestic projects). But continuing reforms are needed to improve the banking system, eliminate stifling regulations, and reduce the cost of doing business.[56]

Moreover, many Japanese manufacturers set up operations in cheaper locations without eliminating capacity at home or trimming bloated workforces. While admirable in some respects and consistent with corporate tradition in Japan, these actions have resulted in lower profits for Japanese firms, if not weakened their competitive position worldwide. For example, Japanese car companies' domestic demand has fallen around 25 percent in the past decade. Over the same period, their excess capacity rose to around 25 percent and their collective labor forces have dropped less than 5 percent. But times may be changing, with Nissan, Mazda, and Mitsubishi all announcing domestic layoffs and plant closings in recent years.

Even Japanese **keiretsu**, huge groups of companies with interlocking ownership ties and business interests, are slowly unraveling. The cozy groups of owner relationships behind names such as Sumitomo and Mitsubishi (corporate "families" with dozens of firms, including banks, manufacturers, and trading companies), are becoming too expensive to maintain. The percentage of equities on the Tokyo stock exchange held in these stable relationships has dropped considerably in the past few years, while the percentage of foreign ownership has risen.[57]

keiretsu
Large groups of Japanese firms with interlocking ownership ties and business interests

Regardless of its problems, Japan is a formidable international competitor. The country has some impressive assets, including a highly educated workforce, many world-class firms, and excellent capabilities in technology. Japanese firms continue to have enormous success in foreign markets in everything from video games to robotics to automobiles (e.g., Sony, Nintendo, Toyota, etc.).[58]

Southeast Asia's Other Developed and Emerging Countries Hong Kong, Singapore, South Korea, and Taiwan represent the other developed economies in the region. Of course, Hong Kong has been reunited with China since 1997. The uncertainty about Hong Kong's long-term prospects as a capitalist bastion with low taxes and little government interference revolve around its liabilities (e.g., it's the sixth most expensive city in the world) and autonomy. China has promised Hong Kong autonomy for fifty years. The worry is that if Hong Kong's freedoms and rule of law erode too much, its status as a great place for multinationals to do business could be jeopardized. On the other hand, much lower costs in other mainland cities like Shanghai for everything from office space to apartments to taxis may do more to lure business away than anything else.[59]

Taiwan also has a tricky relationship with China, especially about its perceived autonomy and its defense connections with the United States. But the growing trade and business linkages between China and its "renegade province" (the label China often applies to Taiwan) paint a more optimistic long-term picture. Taiwan's ongoing efforts to liberalize trade restrictions with China should also help smooth out relations. Already, some 40,000 Taiwanese companies operating on the mainland account for over 10 percent of China's exports. For many of Taiwan's increasingly sophisticated firms, China is a welcome source of inexpensive labor. China, in return, gains from the influx of capital ($40 billion in the past several years), jobs, and technological savvy that Taiwanese firms like computer-maker Acer bring.[60]

Moving on to Singapore, the city-state has the highest standard of living in the region, with a per-person GDP over $24,000. Well known for its efficient government, openness to foreign investment, and well-trained workforce, Singapore has proved to be stable and resilient in the face of the region's ups and downs. Although Malaysia's prosperity falls short of Singapore's, it has also been stable, with relatively inexpensive labor and good business infrastructure. In any case, both Malaysia and Singapore need to do more to cut costs and encourage entrepreneurship if they are to remain competitive, especially since their counterparts in the region all have lower labor costs (e.g., China, India, Indonesia, and Vietnam).[61]

Finally, South Korea is a key player in the region, with a $950 billion economy, a highly skilled workforce, an improved banking system, and a burgeoning information technology industry. Clearly, South Korea has come a long way in recent years, with per-person GDP pushing $20,000 and 68 percent of households having broadband Internet access (only 15 percent of American and 8 percent of European households can say the same). But South Korea's challenges include an education system that is still too rigid, a relatively inflexible labor market, and a need to continue reforming the **chaebol** (huge diversified conglomerates such as Samsung that still account for a big slice of the economy). Accountability remains a problem for many such firms. For example, regulators charged managers from the SK Group with exaggerating profits by $1.2 billion. And Ssangyong Cement Industrial Co. racked up billions in debt by plowing resources into questionable ventures that had nothing to do with its core business. But instead of letting the firm go under, the government bailed it out and spent billions on public works projects to generate contracts for Ssangyong and other chaebol.[62]

Some officials feel that South Korea can't afford to let firms in strategic sectors (e.g., electronics, automobiles) die, especially since they provide jobs and help support thousands of vendors and suppliers. Others counter that South Korea would be better off in the long run if the chaebol sold off or shut down losing businesses. In fact, many chaebol have disappeared over the past five years, crushed by their mountains of debt. A good example is Daewoo, which made everything from fertilizers to cars around the world. After running up $80

chaebol
Huge diversified conglomerates in South Korea

billion in debt, it was split into twelve separate companies. But such corporate collapses seems to stimulate entrepreneurial activity. South Koreans are less enamored with the chaebol and are willing to embrace greater risk than ever before. Today, the percentage of South Korean adults working in firms less than four years old is far higher than in other industrialized countries (and twice the rate in the United States). On top of that, South Koreans are becoming more consumer-oriented, something that may contribute to an increasingly diverse South Korean economy.[63]

Next, let's turn to the region's emerging nations. Indonesia, the Philippines, Thailand, and Vietnam all offer inexpensive labor, large populations, and a variety of assets and resources. Except for Vietnam, these countries all have experienced serious political and social instability in recent years. For example, cries about corruption and heavy-handedness in government have been heard frequently in the Philippines and Thailand. And flare-ups of scandals and political instability tend to have a chilling effect on foreign direct investment, as these countries have found out. Take Indonesia. The country has suffered from high government debt and low investor confidence due, at least in part, to political uncertainty and a string of government corruption scandals. Ethnic frustrations and local rebellions erupted in 2001, causing security headaches for foreign companies. For instance, ExxonMobil shut down its Indonesia facilities after secessionist guerrillas shot at airplanes carrying its employees.[64]

The issue in Vietnam is how changes in the communist leadership over time may impact business. And despite its low labor costs, Vietnam needs to catch up with its more competitive Asian brethren. Although Vietnam's GDP has doubled in the past decade thanks in large measure to fewer restrictions on entrepreneurship and foreign investment, the pace of growth needs to quicken so that the 1.4 million people who enter the workforce each year can find jobs. Plus, the private sector in Vietnam is still overshadowed by protected and unprofitable state firms, propped up in many cases by a state-run banking system. Vietnam also has some serious corruption problems and large gaps in living standards between the big cities and the poor countryside, where 75 percent of the population lives.[65]

Europe: East Meets West

Over the past fifteen years, staggering political and economic changes have occurred in Europe, especially in Russia and its former satellites. The 600 million people of the region have arguably seen more change in a shorter period than anywhere else in the world. Europe continues to evolve toward greater economic integration. The European Union and its currency, the euro, are established facts of life. And on May 1, 2004, the fifteen nations of the European Union became the EU 25 as Cyprus, Malta, and eight Eastern European countries became new members. More expansion may be coming in the years ahead, with Romania and Bulgaria hoping for membership in 2007 and Turkey and Balkan countries (e.g., Croatia) waiting in the wings after that.

That said, many challenges and obstacles still lie in the path of greater economic integration. For instance, the rate of progress varies considerably across countries. Some, like Poland, have done well by embracing free markets and transforming their management talent to match; while others, such as Albania and Ukraine, still have a long way to go. And the Balkans is still Europe's most unstable and unpredictable region, a potential flashpoint that has chilled business investment in the area. We'll take a quick look at the European Union before turning our attention to Russia and the developing nations of central and eastern Europe.[66]

Maastricht Treaty
Agreement that provided the basis for the formation of the European Union

The European Union: Growing and Evolving   The European Union was created in 1993 by the signing of the **Maastricht Treaty**. The EU model is unique and clearly reflects European cultures, history, and languages. But like the United States, the European Union aims to operate as a single, integrated economic market that uses one currency and is guided by a central bank. The European Union aims to have a unified customs system, no trade barriers, and an umbrella economic strategy for dealing with the rest of the world across member countries. And therein lies both the opportunity and the challenge for international companies. On one hand, manufacturing in the European Union allows firms to move their products to any member country without duties or currency hassles, a highly attractive prospect to say the least. Of course, that's prompted billions in foreign investment in recent years. However, a unified market doesn't mean that Europe's diverse cultures—and the needs and desires that go with them—have disappeared. So companies doing business in Europe often need to be highly responsive to local product preferences if they want to do well, the European Union notwithstanding.[67]

Euro-zone
European Union countries using the euro in cross-border trade

But the European Union is a formidable economic force, with a collective economy larger than that of the United States or Japan. That said, achieving the European Union's ultimate integration goals won't be easy. Take the euro. On January 1, 2002, the euro began circulating, replacing national currencies in the twelve EU countries comprising the **Euro-zone** (i.e., members using the euro in cross-border trade since 1999). But three EU members, Denmark, the United Kingdom, and Sweden, have decided, at least for now, to keep their own currencies. Plus, the European Union's ten newest members are several years away from currency integration with the euro. Another challenge is how to wrestle with power differences and other disputes (e.g., about movement of labor, corporate tax rates, farm reform, etc.) in the EU's complex governance structure. And then there's the issue of integrating the EU's newest members as well as wrestling with future expansion possibilities (countries must meet certain debt, inflation, and interest rate targets to join). Take a look at Exhibit 1.8 for a snapshot of the European Union's ten newest members from central and eastern Europe as well as the fifteen nations comprising the European Union prior to May 1, 2004. As you can see from the exhibit, the new member countries are poorer than the EU 15 (in terms of per capita GDP), but faster-growing. Moreover, the new members generally have cheaper skilled labor and faster-growing productivity than their EU 15 counterparts, thanks to swelling foreign direct investment (though overall productivity is still lower). These factors, when combined with lower corporate tax rates (about 20 percent for the EU 10 versus over 30 percent on average for the EU 15), suggest that the EU 10 will continue to be an attractive target for foreign direct investment, and, as a consequence, put pressure on the more established economies of the EU 15 (e.g., Germany, France) to reform their more costly tax, welfare, and labor systems.[68]

Indeed, the EU markets are, generally speaking, less efficient and less flexible than the American market for reasons including onerous taxes, red tape, and rigid labor laws. Such factors could limit the European Union's GDP growth, at least until additional reforms occur. In fact, high labor costs and rigid employment rules are among the reasons that German giant Siemens has been

EXHIBIT 1.8 *The European Union: 15 Plus 10 Equals 25 Countries and Counting*

EU 15	2003 GDP growth (percent change over 2002)	Population (millions)	2003 GDP per capita (US$)	As of 2004 using the Euro?	EU 10 (newest members as of May 1, 2004)	2003 GDP growth (percent change over 2002)	Population (millions)	2003 GDP per capita (US$)	Year expected to begin using Euro
Luxembourg	1.2%	<1	$48,309	yes	Malta	4.1%	<1	$10,000	2007
Ireland	1.8%	3.7	$28,975	yes	Cyprus	3.4%	<1	$17,564	2007
Finland	1.9%	5.2	$25,766	yes	Estonia	4.8%	1.4	$6,815	2007
Denmark	0.4%	5.3	$28,843	no	Slovenia	3.2%	2.0	$16,100	2008
Austria	0.7%	8.1	$27,808	yes	Latvia	3.9%	2.4	$4,421	2008
Sweden	1.6%	8.9	$25,985	no	Lithuania	3.8%	3.7	$5,942	2007
Portugal	-0.8%	10.0	$19,323	yes	Slovakia	4.0%	5.4	$6,985	2009–2010
Belgium	1.1%	10.2	$29,128	yes	Poland	3.8%	38.6	$5943	2009–2010
Greece	4.7%	10.5	$19,061	yes	Hungary	4.0%	10.0	$9721	2008–2009
Netherlands	-0.5%	15.8	$27,108	yes	Czech Republic	3.7%	10.3	$9,336	2010
Spain	2.4%	39.4	$21,153	yes					
Italy	0.3%	57.6	$25,087	yes					
France	0.1%	59.0	$25,889	yes					
United Kingdom	2.2%	59.2	$25,427	no					
Germany	-0.1%	82.0	$26,214	yes					
Regional Data									
EU 15	0.7%	381	$28,389						
New EU 10	3.1%	74	$13,343						
EU 25	0.7%	455	$25,384						

Sources: Adapted from ———. (2003). When east meets west: A survey of EU enlargement. *The Economist,* November 22, 1–16; ———. (2003). A big payoff from a bigger EU. *Business Week,* November 10, 36; Karmin, C. (2004). As EU grows, no big bang in Europe's stocks. *The Wall Street Journal,* March, 29, C1, C16; Rhoads, C., & Champion, M. (2004). As Europe expands, new union faces problems of scale. *The Wall Street Journal,* April 29, A1, A8; **http://www.nationmaster.com**

shifting jobs and production capacity from Germany (where a single union employee may earn $60,000 a year) to lower-cost locations such as Hungary, Brazil, and China. In the last decade, Siemens has eliminated 51,000 positions in Germany while its worldwide workforce grew by 39,000.[69]

This underscores the fact that EU 15 firms have been looking outward for places to invest for some time. For instance, while firms in the EU 15 have invested heavily in the EU 10, they have also poured hundreds of billions into the United States in recent years, in effect connecting the European Union more tightly to the ups and downs of the American economy. German companies alone have some 800,000 American employees. Overall, the European Union may be more economically resilient in the near term than either the United States or Japan. For instance, trade in the Euro-zone is pretty diversified. Of the Euro-zone's top ten trading partners, none has even a 20 percent share (the United States' second-ranked share is about 17 percent). Other positives for Euro-zone countries at this point include lower household and corporate debt relative to the United States.[70]

Spain is a good example of a country that has gained enormously from EU membership. Thanks to the European Union and the euro, combined with government tax cuts, deregulation, and privatization, Spain's economic growth has soared in the past several years, allowing the country to shed its earlier image as the poor sister of western Europe. Now Spanish firms raise capital throughout the European Union for expansion and foreign acquisitions. Spain's Repsol did just that to buy Argentina's YPF for $15.4 billion and become the seventh largest oil firm in the world. In Latin America alone, Spanish companies have spent some $60 billion in recent years. And at home, richer Spaniards are facing some of the problems that accompany success. For example, illegal immigration has soared as people from places like Morocco and Ecuador have sought jobs that Spaniards no longer want.[71]

Central and Eastern Europe: Leaders and Laggards Of course, many countries in central and eastern Europe would love to be in Spain's shoes. Among the ten new members of the European Union from central and eastern Europe, monthly wages are 85 percent less and per-person GDP less than half, on average, of those in EU 15 nations. Images of booming capitals like Prague aside, much of central and eastern Europe is rural and poor. And in potential future EU members such as Belarus, Bulgaria, and Ukraine, things are even worse, with monthly wages averaging less than $100 a month.[72]

Actually, East Germany's experience offers insights about the challenges of catching up. Since Germany was reunited more than a decade ago, the German government has spent over $1.3 trillion to help the eastern half of the country erase the impact of sixty years of communism. And the job's not over yet, with the German government paying about 4 percent of the country's GDP annually to support the east. And unemployment in the east remains stubbornly high (around 20 percent), more than double the rate in the western half of Germany. Granted, the east now has excellent roads, superior telecommunications, and many gleaming new factories. But productivity, wages, and GDP growth still lag behind the western half of the country.[73]

If we want to mark progress in central and eastern Europe, it's clear that new EU members Poland, Hungary, and the Czech Republic are the economic leaders. All three nations moved farther and faster than their European counterparts to open up their economies and privatize state-owned industries. They also had the advantage of offering inexpensive, high-quality labor right next door to western Europe. Tens of billions have flowed into the three nations in the past decade, with American, Asian, and western European firms all taking part. Sony, for instance, built a consumer electronics plant in Hungary. Of course, foreign investment means more jobs and rising incomes for local citizens. And that fuels additional investment from companies eager to serve new consumers. That's why GE Capital moved into Poland and bought part of a Hungarian bank—to offer central Europeans credit cards and loans. It's also why Poland, the Czech Republic, and Hungary are expected to attract the lion's share of foreign direct investment in eastern and central Europe over the next several years.[74]

That said, Poland is probably the key player to watch among the ten new EU members. Poland alone accounts for over 40 percent of the GDP and over 50 percent of the population of the EU 10. And with $12 billion in new foreign direct investment (Whirlpool and Gillette are among the American multinationals making major investments), along with an expected 6 percent GDP growth rate in 2004, Poland's future appears relatively bright. That is, if Poland's notorious red tape, inefficient agriculture sector, and swelling government deficits can be brought to heel. But EU membership should open European markets and boost Polish exports.[75]

Russia Of course, an even bigger player lies east of Poland. On the GDP front, Russia's economic output actually shrank during much of the 1990s. However, early into the twenty-first century, the country got back on a growth track, with GDP growth increasing over 6 percent annually in the past few years. One measure of how far Russia has come recently is that some experts predict that the country will join the World Trade Organization in 2006. Granted, higher energy prices and a large devaluation of the ruble in 1998 helped the GDP picture improve. But the Russian government deserves credit for moving to privatize and restructure state-owned firms, many of which now make money. Likewise, the government continues to push regulatory, tax, legal, land ownership, and banking reforms. Some changes, like a new, simplified flat-rate income tax system, have already been put into effect. Other changes have yet to be implemented or need more time before we can judge their success. But the economic environment has stabilized, at least for now. The flight of Russian capital has slowed as business leaders keep more money at home instead of shifting it offshore. And foreign investment has been slowly rising.[76]

Yet another hopeful sign is Russia's growing, affluent middle class. Many are either entrepreneurs or managers in big multinational or local firms. Today, as many as 30 million Russians (some 20 percent of the population) enjoy middle-class status. To many companies this means a larger pool of potential customers with disposable income. That's why Sweden's IKEA, a home furnishings chain, took the plunge in 2000 and opened its first Russian store in a Moscow suburb. On opening day, 40,000 Russians sat in a two-mile traffic jam just to reach the store.[77]

That said, Russia faces significant problems and challenges. Inflation is still relatively high. Foreign investment remains minuscule compared to smaller emerging markets like Poland. Indeed, over the past fifteen years, foreign direct investment in Russia has averaged a mere $50 per person on an annual basis, compared with $1,000 in Poland. Government involvement in the economy is still too high. Forty million Russians remain mired in poverty, and unemployment

International Insights

Russia: Taming the Wild, Wild East

MANY THINK OF Russia as a place where the rule of law is weak. Throw in widespread violence, crime, and corruption aimed at businesses and you have a risky scenario indeed. One western banker said he would "rather eat nuclear waste" than sink money into Russia. Of course, that's overly harsh. But as Russia slowly dismantled its state-run economy, scam artists, gangsters, and corrupt officials emerged to fill the void. Doing business in Russia has been compared to frontier life in nineteenth-century America. In the old West, American firms often had to rely on themselves for protection against criminals or business shenanigans since there was no strong legal system or law enforcement presence to fall back on.

And today, although many changes and improvements have taken place, similar challenges still occur in Russia. For example, many Russian laws are hazy or poorly enforced, creating opportunities for scams and rip-offs. Big Russian firms are routinely accused of hiding assets and cash from stockholders and investors. For instance, questions were raised about why energy giant Gazprom, Russia's largest company (the government owns 38 percent of Gazprom), did $1 billion in business annually with an obscure firm whose majority owners were relatives of Gazprom's senior executives. During a recent crackdown, government officials and several of Russia's well-known business tycoons (e.g., Mikhail Khordokovsky, CEO of the huge Russian oil firm Yukos) were accused of tax evasion, embezzlement, and money laundering, among other things. But the end result of such investigations, according to critics, often depends on whether the individuals charged have friends in high places or were victims of political motivations in the first place. For instance, CEO Khordokovsky's allies alleged that his real "crime" was supporting political rivals of Russian President Vladimir Putin. In any

case, crony capitalism still plays an enormous role in Russia, with connections at the highest levels of government enhancing business prospects and, perhaps, the ability to skirt the law.

And consider this. According to some estimates, 40 percent of the Russian economy and 50 percent of Russian banks are controlled by organized criminal groups. Contract killings over disputed business turf still occur. Moreover, payoffs and bribes are relatively common. For instance, many businesses willingly pay 10–20 percent of their monthly profits to criminal elements for *krisha* (the Russian word for "roof"). Having *krisha* means your business will be "protected" against vandals, pesky government officials, and other "large and unpredictable costs." Likewise, if a company wants to build a factory, it may have to pay one official to get it started and another to keep it going. And Swiss food giant Nestlé says that it even competes against organized crime at the retail level in Russia. The can of coffee you buy off a Russian shelf may have been put there by criminal gangs that have "arranged" for products to be imported without paying duties.

Perhaps what's most disturbing about all of this is that the criminal figures involved are often part of local firms or even, in many cases, the government itself. But experts say that this kind of lawlessness is nothing new in Russia. The old communist regime, and the czars before that, basically took what they wanted. Consequently, while some semblance of stability existed, there was also plenty of underlying crime and corruption. The good news is that the Russian government is more serious about reining in corruption than ever. But until corruption is under control, the question remains—why do business in such a difficult environment? Because while the risks are great, so are the potential rewards in Russia's large market of 145 million.[78]

rates need to come down. And then there's Russia's crumbling infrastructure. It may cost $100 billion to put things right. The list of problems is numbing: bad roads, rampant industrial accidents, toxic waste dumps, decrepit railroads, intermittent electric power, and leaking gas pipelines. The government has plans to sell off utility monopolies to raise money. But finding the money, much less actually repairing and modernizing the infrastructure, will take years. Finally, corruption and organized crime continue to plague Russia and its foreign investors. Take a look at the accompanying International Insights box to see what we mean.[79]

The Middle East and Africa: Uncertain Territory and Untapped Potential

Speaking of regions that come with plenty of risk, uncertainty, and unrealized potential, we turn our attention in this section to the Middle East and Africa.

The Shadow on the Middle East Despite having some impressive assets, most notably oil, the ongoing Arab-Israeli conflict, terrorism threats from Islamic militants, and turmoil in Iraq cast a shadow on economic growth in the Middle East. For instance, as violence increased in 2001, Palestinian incomes plunged along with Israel's GDP growth and trade with its neighbors. Of course, spikes in oil prices can spur export revenues in the region's oil-producing states (e.g., Saudi Arabia, United Arab Emirates), helping to partially offset weakness in other areas, such as textiles.

Tourism is also a potentially huge draw in the Middle East, thanks to its numerous historical and religious sites. However, tourism is stagnant, undeveloped, or held hostage to the vagaries of the area's peace prospects. In recent years, Saudi Arabia, Jordan, and Egypt spent billions to attract foreign tourists (e.g., on hotel construction). Even Libya has gotten into the act, building luxury hotels on its shorelines in the hopes of attracting more than the paltry 40,000 tourists that visited in 2003. Likewise, the Syrian government wants to attract more non-Arab visitors (nearly 80 percent of its tourists are from neighboring Arab states) as well as increase the total number of annual visitors. To do that, it hopes to increase the number of hotel beds available by 500 percent over the next decade or two. But without stability, it's unlikely those beds will be filled.

Overall, long-term prospects for regional GDP growth are uncertain. The Middle East faces major hurdles to becoming an integrated economic power. Israel is the only country in the region to resemble a dynamic, modern economy—with a true middle class and some globally competitive companies. This comes despite the fact that Israel has lived with terrorism, wars, and heavy government involvement in its economy for decades. Of course, Saudi Arabia has also seen a spike in economic activity in recent years (e.g., GDP growth was 6.4 percent in 2003), despite internal terrorist threats and conflict in next-door Iraq. There are also some successes (e.g., greater foreign direct investments, more government encouragement of entrepreneurship) in places as diverse as Dubai, Egypt, and Jordan. That said, countries such as Saudi Arabia and Israel arguably need to spur more foreign investment and create more jobs. In the case of Saudi Arabia, that might involve greater efforts to privatize state-owned firms, lower government spending, increase government transparency, eliminate barriers to foreign business ownership, and reduce social welfare benefits. Saudi Arabia also hopes to diversify its economy in the years ahead (oil and gas currently account for over 30 percent of Saudi GDP).[80]

Africa Untapped Untapped potential is the phrase that comes to mind about Africa. Sub-Saharan Africa is the poorest region in the world. Of the region's 600 million people, nearly half live on less than $1 a day. On top of that, some African countries are beset with heavy government intervention in their economies, official corruption, tribal conflicts, and weak business infrastructures. AIDS also threatens sub-Saharan Africa's workforce. The region has over 70 percent of the world's HIV/AIDS cases, the vast majority of which involve heterosexual transmission and include up to 30 percent of the population in some countries. All of these factors contribute to the perception that Africa is risky for international companies.[81]

But developed countries have played a role in holding Africa back. Trade barriers and farm subsidies in the United States, the European Union, and Japan cost sub-Saharan nations billions annually in lost exports. In addition, foreign direct investment in sub-Saharan Africa has been low (e.g., less than $4 billion in 2002), despite the fact that the region provides the highest returns on FDI in the world. On the one hand, this suggests that the perceived risks are such that only quick, high-profit projects have a chance of attracting foreign capital. On the other hand, the high returns also imply that the risks of doing business in the region are overstated. Indeed, most of the continent is at peace and, over the past decade, most African countries enacted more pro-business regulations. Of course, there still are horror stories, such as Zimbabwe, which can no longer feed itself, especially given its shrinking economy and extreme inflation rate (the world's highest in 2003 at 385 percent). That said, Africa also has some of the world's fastest-growing economies (e.g., Chad and Equatorial Guinea had the top two spots in 2004, largely thanks to rising oil output).[82]

Speaking with one economic voice would help Africa obtain more foreign direct investment and better access to EU and American markets, especially for its quality textile and agricultural products. More than ten different economic blocs are present in Africa (e.g., the Southern African Customs Union, consisting of Botswana, Namibia, Lesotho, South Africa, and Swaziland). So far, progress on regional, much less continental, integration has been slow. Today, Africa accounts for only about 2 percent of global trade.[83]

To improve regional cooperation and self-reliance, the presidents of several sub-Saharan countries developed plans to create "sustainable economic development" across the continent. These plans focused on improving African infrastructure (roads, telecommunications, and air service), sharing resources, eliminating internal trade restrictions, and lobbying for easier access to developed markets. Time will tell how effective these efforts will be.[84]

Nevertheless, there are signs of progress throughout the African continent, especially in the sub-Saharan region. Indeed, over the next several years, regional GDP growth is predicted to increase, mainly because of changes in a variety of government and economic policies. That said, the overall growth rate in Africa may still lag behind that of other emerging nations. And big differences will be present among African countries, both in terms of their near- and long-term prospects. As a result, we'll take a closer look at South Africa, a country that continues to show promise and, with nearly 50 percent of the GDP in sub-Saharan Africa, is widely viewed as the economic anchor of the region.[85]

South Africa South Africa's peaceful transformation from a racist, white minority government to an elected majority-rule democracy led by Nelson Mandela inspired the world. Today, South Africa is both a rich and a poor country, one with extreme income gaps paralleled only by Brazil. But the gap is shrinking slowly, thanks to a growing black middle class.[86]

Still, economic growth needs to quicken if a significant dent is to be made in South Africa's official unemployment rate of 25 percent (some say the figure is really 40 percent). Specifically, GDP growth needs to be at least 5–6 percent, something that South Africa has not yet achieved (GDP growth from 1994 to 2003 averaged around 3 percent). Of course, foreign investment can help move things along. And South Africa does have a lot to offer, including excellent roads, ports, and telecommunications facilities. It also has abundant natural resources, a growing high-tech industry, open government, a good legal system, and ongoing privatization efforts. In fact, foreign investment has been rising in South Africa since 1994. The world's car companies are a good example of that investment. BMW, Fiat, Ford, GM, Toyota, and Volkswagen all operate in South Africa, employing some 280,000 South Africans and continuing to ramp up production. Indeed, automobile production in South Africa increased 500 percent between 1998 and 2003. Mercedes, for instance, makes all of its C-class cars with right-hand drive in South Africa.[87]

Realizing South Africa's potential will not be easy, however. The country has to deal with the legacy of forty years of apartheid, a system that made the black South African majority second-class citizens in everything from housing to education to health care. And that means spending money to electrify houses and bring clean water to poor areas. Plus, international companies have many emerging markets to choose from for their investments, including places without South Africa's AIDS epidemic, active unions, and tough labor laws.[88]

▶ *Key Challenges Facing International Business*

Our discussion of regional trends underscores the fact that growth and prosperity in the world are not guaranteed. Optimistic projections could be derailed by a variety of factors, including political uncertainty, corruption, disputes over trade issues, tough new competitors, and fiscal mismanagement, just to name a few. Plus, major threats can pop up quickly anytime, anywhere. Indeed, these may be among the most challenging times for global economic development.[89]

Technological Sophistication and International Volatility

There's little doubt that foreign markets have become increasingly important for American, Asian, and European multinationals over the years. Of course, innovations in transportation, communications, information technology, and manufacturing have created new foreign markets and helped firms conduct international business. For example, the growth of computer use and Internet activity in a country may increase international trade flows, a pattern that's most robust in poorer countries. But to obtain a major boost from Internet technology, poor countries must catch up and put the necessary infrastructure in place (e.g., a reliable power supply, high-speed digital connections). Fortunately, the costs of installing a digital infrastructure are falling (e.g., computers, fiber-optic cable, etc.). That said, to realize the benefits of technology, countries need an educated population as well as affordable access. As you might expect, that's a tall order in some cases. Nevertheless, computer use in countries like China, India, Russia, and Brazil has jumped over 500 percent in recent years.[90]

Nevertheless, technological advances per se do little to eliminate international business problems driven by cultural differences, political upheavals, corruption, and mismanagement. And technology can create new challenges by accelerating how quickly crises hit. As the importance of international business grows, the fallout from those crises becomes more serious.[91]

Currency Volatility and Implications for Management In 1994, Mexico faced a financial crisis triggered by its inability to pay off foreign bondholders. Alarmed bondholders fled Mexico in droves, sending the Mexican peso plunging and causing ripple effects worldwide as investors pulled money out of emerging markets. But in early 2001, the reverse happened when some $10 billion in foreign capital flowed into Mexico in a few months, attracted by a rising peso. Likewise, the euro plunged in value against the U.S. dollar from its introduction in 1999 to mid-2001, only to reverse course, rising 50 percent against the dollar through early 2004.[92]

These volatile currency fluctuations underscore the impact of rapidly shifting business conditions as well as the use of technology by sophisticated investors. Virtually anywhere, anytime, an investor can electronically move in or out of international currency markets. Billions of dollars can flow in and out of a country in *minutes*, whether sparked by a real crisis or just a herd mentality. Plus, the sheer size of the currency markets (over $1 trillion is traded *daily*) makes stabilizing currencies difficult.[93]

Sudden currency updrafts can make a firm's exports more expensive overnight, increasing the pressure to reduce costs (e.g., by shopping globally for supplies, moving production to cheaper locations). Such was the case for Volkswagen. Thanks to the rising euro, its European-produced cars became more expensive to export to the United States, something that Volkswagen said helped account for a $1.25 billion drop in its 2003 profits. On the other side of the coin, however, sharp currency downdrafts can make a company's exports cheaper. Some suggest that a weak dollar helps U.S. companies succeed overseas more than any corporate action to improve competitiveness. Indeed, while Volkswagen suffered because of the rising euro, American companies exporting to Europe were gleeful. Farm equipment giant Deere & Company was a good example—its exports and profits surged in 2003 thanks, at least in part, to the weaker dollar.[94]

That said, currency volatility clearly increases the risks inherent in international business. Not paying close attention to currency issues can be disastrous. Take Xerox. Analysts alleged that poor management oversight cost the firm $1 billion in foreign currency losses in 1999 (much of it in volatile Brazil).[95] But even with good financial management, currency shocks can impact firms dramatically, especially if companies are earning a big chunk of their revenues overseas and are exposed in dozens of foreign markets. Personal-care product giant Colgate-Palmolive is a good case in point. In 2002, the company enjoyed almost $9.3 billion in sales and was operating in some 170 countries. But thanks to currency fluctuations and the associated costs, the company estimated that its global sales took a $465 million hit (about 5 percent of total revenues).[96]

So what can international firms do to combat wild currency fluctuations? **Currency hedging** is an option. Companies can buy currency options that fix exchange rates for a period of time. That's how Coca-Cola managed to sidestep the euro's drop in 2000 and any damage to its European earnings. And from 2002 to 2004, many big European firms did the same, buying hedges to protect

currency hedging
Buying currency options that fix exchange rates for a period of time to guard against currency fluctuations

dollar-based revenues earned in the United States from the falling U.S. dollar. Indeed, Porsche decided to buy hedges to protect its dollar-based revenues through 2007. But hedging is basically pricey, complex guesswork. Coke would have lost out had the euro soared, and Porsche will lose if the dollar does the same. Then there's the expense. Let's take a simple example. Say a company wants to protect $500 million in earnings from a drop in the dollar against the euro. If the dollar's value slipped 10 percent, then that $500 million would be worth only $450 million. But the cost of that protection could run a steep $26 million. Another way to minimize risks associated with exchange rate swings is to use local suppliers and make more products in the places where you sell them. This is referred to as **natural hedging**. Honda, for instance, manufactures three out of every four cars it sells in the United States in American factories, isolating U.S. sales from a rising yen. Likewise, DaimlerChrysler makes its M-class Mercedes at a plant in Alabama, allowing it to sidestep the impact of the rising euro on American sales in 2003–2004 (and make a hefty profit at the same time by shipping U.S.-made M-class cars to Europe). And some companies use both options. Dow Chemical, for example, uses financial hedges and scatters its production facilities around the world.[97]

> **natural hedging**
> Using local suppliers and plants to help minimize exchange rate swings

Actually, some large firms view their facilities as modular. Put simply, when currency gyrations make life difficult in one place, you quickly shift locations. For instance, in 1999 some two dozen major companies operating in Argentina suddenly left to set up shop in neighboring Brazil. Why? A 35 percent plunge in the Brazilian *real* had a lot to do with it. Overnight, it became cheaper to manufacture in Brazil. It also made Argentinean products a lot less attractive to Brazilian consumers. In the process, thousands of jobs were lost in Argentina.[98]

Of course, currency volatility often hits small firms hardest. While currency fluctuations may slice a sizeable chunk off a multinational corporation's earnings, it's often just a nibble in the overall scheme of things. And such firms typically have more experience with currency problems and more options for dealing with them than their smaller brethren. Consequently, more small firms, like Iowa-based Vermeer Manufacturing, are copying bigger firms by shopping for materials from cheaper locations, opening overseas operations in major markets, looking for foreign partners, and dabbling in currency hedging. Nevertheless, many of these steps are beyond the reach of small firms that want to sell abroad.[99]

Overall, while technology helps stitch national economies together, it also makes international business a volatile proposition. As we've seen, one way that firms try to minimize that volatility is by scattering facilities and suppliers across many countries. But those moves lead to another set of challenges, including managing people from diverse cultures. We'll consider some of those workforce challenges next.

International Workforce Challenges

What's also driving the increasing complexity of international management is that companies need innovative and productive employees to compete. And not just in manufacturing. Clearly, America's manufacturing prowess remains formidable. In fact, output has generally risen over the past twenty-five years despite occasional downturns. Of course, one of the reasons why manufacturing's share of U.S. GDP has been fairly constant over the past two decades is the tremendous growth in the service economy and the jobs that go with it. But whether it's manufacturing or services, companies are increasingly scouring the globe to find the most talented employees at the most reasonable overall cost.[100]

offshoring
The process of exporting jobs abroad, often to lower wage locations

Offshoring and Global Job Dispersion   This process, sometimes referred to as **offshoring**, isn't something limited to big multinationals. Small firms are also a large part of the offshoring trend. Indeed, according to some American venture capital firms, up to 75 percent of the small companies they invest in disperse jobs abroad. Consider American software developers Jboss and Model N—both of these small firms (neither had more than 100 employees in 2004) offshored jobs like customer support and software testing to places as diverse as Greece, India, and the Ukraine.[101]

Of course, along with finding the most talented employees, companies often offshore with the expectation of realizing huge labor cost savings (on the order of 25–75 percent). But offshoring requires good management. Without laying out expectations clearly, providing needed support to offshore employees, and effectively dealing with cultural differences, any anticipated savings can vanish. That's what happened to California-based security software firm ValiCert when it first started offshoring software development work to India. The firm's Indian software engineers really didn't understand how ValiCert's software was used (because they weren't told) and, as a consequence, left out features American customers wanted in new products. When customers balked, trying to solve the problem quickly across more than a dozen time zones turned into an expensive nightmare that hurt relationships on both sides. Eventually, ValiCert was able to learn its lessons and turn things around with Indian employees. But sometimes firms just give up, as Dell Computer did when it brought certain help desk and call-center operations back to the United States from India in the face of mounting customer complaints. Indeed, offshoring requires careful thought about what jobs should be sent abroad as well as the due diligence needed to find outstanding foreign employees. Generally speaking, jobs that do not require superior English or an in-depth understanding of American laws, markets, and culture are the safest offshoring bets.[102]

Besides these management challenges, offshoring has also become something of a political hot potato in recent years, particularly in the United States. On one side are politicians who respond to (and tap into) rising public concerns about job losses (and increasingly skilled and high-paying jobs at that), to lower-wage countries. On the other side are executives who view offshoring as a worldwide competition for jobs. As Hewlett-Packard CEO Carly Fiorina put it, "There is no job that is America's God-given right anymore." Of course, the realities associated with the offshoring trend are complex. For instance, some argue that thanks to foreign companies who set up shop in the United States, the number of "imported" jobs (which tend to be high-paying, skilled jobs) exceed the number of "exported" jobs (which are more likely to be low-paying, unskilled jobs) by 200–300 percent. Critics also argue that offshoring helps American companies to save money, thereby allowing more high-skilled hiring at home as well as cheaper goods and services for customers. Moreover, they point out that offshoring numbers pale in comparison to the jobs that are always being destroyed and created inside the United States (more than 2 million jobs monthly).

That said, these arguments are likely to be cold comfort to American employees stuck in repetitive, routine work (i.e., jobs most likely to be offshored) or in certain highly skilled professions that have been hit hard by offshoring. For instance, software application developers and database engineers have seen job opportunities as well as salaries drop in recent years. As one American executive put it, these Americans ". . . are competing with everyone else in the world who has a PC." And who will work for 80 percent less pay.[103]

But neither political controversy nor management setbacks seem to be slowing the offshoring trend. In fact, in certain parts of the world, offshoring is booming. For instance, the call center business in the Philippines has been growing fast, thanks, in major part, to foreign multinationals such as U.S.-based Convergys Corp. The attractions? Filipinos' good English skills, an excellent communications infrastructure, and low wage costs. In the past several years, 30,000 call-center jobs have been created in the Philippines, a number expected to hit 100,000 in 2005. Likewise, American companies as diverse as GE Capital Services, Intel, J. P. Morgan Chase, and Microsoft have flocked to places like India and the Philippines to take advantage of their relatively inexpensive but highly skilled English-speaking labor forces. Indeed, estimates are that 3.3 million customer service and related call-center jobs (along with wages worth $136 billion), will move from the United States to China, India, the Philippines, and Russia in the next few years. And companies outside the United States are making similar moves. Spanish phone company Telefonica, for instance, has over 2,000 Morocco-based employees handling service calls for French and Spanish customers.[104]

Granted, many of these offshored jobs are lower level, providing basic customer and service support functions. But not all. For instance, dozens of American firms such as IBM and Motorola also do much of their software development in India to take advantage of skilled local programmers and lower wages. In fact, General Electric has over 17,000 employees in India, many of them scientists and professionals. Skilled professional and service jobs, such as scientific research and pharmaceutical development, are increasingly moving to "centers of excellence" worldwide. And maintaining these jobs offshore is often much less expensive than it would be in the United States or Europe, especially when foreign governments offer help. For example, India's southern state of Tamil Nadu opened an $85 million high-tech complex aimed at attracting skilled work from around the world. On top of that, the state pumps $10 million a year into local schools for computer equipment and computer literacy training. As a result, one Indian official noted that "by 2008, all the citizens in Tamil Nadu will be computer literate." And studies suggest that poor nations, like India, reap double benefits by boosting education and investing in their technological infrastructures. Not only do they increase their ability to use new technologies, they enjoy stronger income growth to boot. Over the long haul, that may reduce the income gap between rich and poor countries.[105]

In the meantime, workforces will continue to become globally dispersed. According to one estimate, by 2015 up to 90 percent of the clerical and white-collar jobs that existed in the United States at the dawn of the third millennium will be offshored to some degree. American skills need to be upgraded to keep up.[106] For instance, despite rising demand, just 13 percent of American college graduates earn degrees in the sciences or engineering annually. And at the moment jobs requiring those degrees are being filled overseas, either as American firms move high-tech positions abroad or bring in foreigners (via immigration or temporary visas) to fill jobs in the United States.[107]

Workforce Quality The bottom line is that international firms need employees who can handle increasingly complex work. Consequently, the number of American manufacturers that train workers in new skills has doubled in the past decade or so. And the best workforce usually wins and keeps their jobs in the process. For instance, Siemens, the German industrial and communications giant, has doubled the skilled jobs in its workforce in recent years while cutting the number of semiskilled positions in half.[108]

All of this raises a question. What makes for a highly qualified workforce? The answer is complex, but education, on-the-job training, motivation, and computer literacy all matter. Plus, there's little doubt that workforce quality is an important factor for determining how competitive a country is—or at least how competitive a country's companies are in a particular industry. India's increasingly competitive IT service companies are a case in point. Indian IT

EXHIBIT 1.9   *Which Countries Are Most Competitive? The Top 25*

2004 Rank (2003 Rank)	Country
1 (1)	United States
2 (4)	Singapore
3 (6)	Canada
4 (7)	Australia
5 (8)	Iceland
6 (10)	Hong Kong
7 (5)	Denmark
8 (3)	Finland
9 (2)	Luxembourg
10 (11)	Ireland
11 (12)	Sweden
12 (17)	Taiwan
13 (14)	Austria
14 (9)	Switzerland
15 (13)	Netherlands
16 (21)	Malaysia
17 (15)	Norway
18 (16)	New Zealand
19 (20)	Germany
20 (19)	United Kingdom
21 (25)	Japan
22 (29)	China (Mainland)
23 (18)	Belgium
24 (26)	Chile
25 (22)	Estonia

Source: Adapted from The International Institute for Management Development's (IMD) *2004 World Competitiveness Scoreboard* (http://www02.imd.ch/wcy/ranking).

firms like Infosys, Wipro, and Tata offer cheaper prices than their Western counterparts; they are increasingly a force to be reckoned with in the $600 billion technology services industry. Part of their success is a testimonial to India's well-educated, high-skilled, and experienced workforce of IT professionals. Indeed, American IT service competitors like IBM are lowering prices and cutting costs as a result of this Indian competition. And one of the ways IBM is cutting costs is by offshoring more skilled IT jobs to a variety of lower wage locations, including, you guessed it, India.

Take a look at Exhibit 1.9. It ranks the world's twenty-five most competitive countries. You'll notice that India is not on the list. While there's little doubt that India's IT workforce is superb in many respects, the country as a whole still faces enormous challenges with respect to raising the incomes and educating a large swath of its population. Indeed, although they have many differences, a common thread among the top countries in Exhibit 1.9 is the *overall* quality of their workforces. But harbor no illusions about what can be done *anywhere* given good worker training and the right infrastructure. After touring several award-winning Mexican plants, one American union official put it this way: "The workers at those plants make a fraction of what American workers make, but there's no drop in quality. Most Third World countries are turning out world-class products."[109]

Increasing Workforce Diversity Globalization is also bringing people from diverse cultures and backgrounds together. Many American and European companies aggressively recruit foreign immigrants, especially for jobs requiring specific technical skills.[110] Demographic shifts within nations are having a similar impact. In the United States, for example, people of Hispanic descent will represent almost 25 percent of the population by 2050, up from 10 percent in 1995. At the same time, the share for non-Hispanic whites will drop to around 50 percent from over 70 percent in 1995.[111] And a diverse workforce can help firms better serve an increasingly diverse customer base. In the United States, African Americans, Asians, and Hispanics collectively represent a huge chunk of purchasing power (Hispanics alone have over $650 billion in disposable income to spend). Targeting these and other groups in recruiting brings in employees who can help connect firms with important segments of their customer base. For example, Procter & Gamble had greater success penetrating the Hispanic population in the United States after it set up a bilingual team of sixty-five employees to do so. Today, according to one P&G executive, "Hispanics are a cornerstone of our growth in North America."[112]

So if diversity can make the difference between success and failure, companies can't afford to let antiquated attitudes permeate the workforce. For instance, key corporate decisions are increasingly made in cross-functional groups. Such groups automatically bring together people from diverse backgrounds, making their effective interaction critical. In fact, experts recommend introducing cultural diversity into decision-making groups and teams, putting a premium on managers' abilities to overcome the difficulties of making it all work.[113]

But relatively few companies have created an atmosphere where diversity is taken seriously. In one survey, less than 10 percent of firms felt they did a very good job of supporting diversity. Not surprisingly, failure can be costly. Higher turnover rates mean higher recruiting and training expenses. And for some occupations, those costs can exceed $100,000 per job.[114]

EXHIBIT 1.10   *Try These Questions on for Size: Challenges Facing International Management*

Most Critical and Important	Also Very Important
Who are our international competitors and how should we deal with them?	How important is a firm's reputation in global versus domestic competition?
What global leadership approaches will allow us to perform better as a firm?	What can we do to break the inertia of a domestic orientation?
How do managers in our company become more global?	What factors cause a shift to a more global corporate identity?
What are the requirements of a global firm?	How can management design a global human resource strategy?
How do we integrate competing values in our firm (e.g., across functions and across borders)?	How does a firm's brand image or reputation cross borders?
How do we best acquire and distribute knowledge throughout the firm?	

Source: Adapted from Zahra, S. A., & O'Neill, H. M. (1998). Charting the landscape of global competition: Reflections on emerging organizational challenges and their implications for senior executives. *Academy of Management Executive, 12*, 13–21.

Managing in a Volatile and Challenging International Environment

All of this raises a larger question about the impact of today's volatile and challenging international environment on management. Clearly, the goal of international management is to achieve the firm's international objectives by effectively procuring, distributing, and using company resources (e.g., people, capital, know-how, physical assets) across countries.[115]

So what happens if management decides that China (or wherever) is a place to develop, manufacture, or sell a product? What then? How should managers *manage* in the environment they find themselves in? As you will see, this is a tough question to answer. Just imagine all the contextual challenges facing managers in firms that operate in dozens of countries. How do they develop business strategies that take such diversity into account? Or find and effectively manage the best talent worldwide? After all, business practices, laws, languages, cultural values, and market structures may all vary across countries, globalization notwithstanding. These factors can affect every aspect of management, including communication, motivation, compensation, employee development, business strategy, and ethics.[116]

To get a sense of the challenges that international managers are concerned about right now, take a look at Exhibit 1.10. These days, executives are feeling the pressure, especially those charged with running complex global empires. For instance, two decades ago, P&G was big, with $7 billion in sales, 50,000 employees, and facilities in twenty-three countries. Today, the firm is downright gargantuan, with over $43 billion in revenues, almost 100,000 employees, and facilities in several dozen nations. As one executive put it, P&G today is "a much more diverse, much more culturally different, much more global company." Senior leaders worry about how to manage their vast operations when information and capital fly around the world in a heartbeat, economies bounce around rapidly, and customer preferences are fickle. Many want to improve communications and somehow knit together company outposts to be more responsive to, if not anticipate, changes in international business.[117]

Overall, this book will provide some guidelines, if not answers, for responding to these challenges. For now, we'll sketch out some principles for international managers who want to succeed in the twenty-first century. Today, successful international firms will be led by managers who

- Value ethnic diversity and have multicultural experience.

- Embrace teamwork and information sharing.

- Act globally where possible (e.g., selling similar products worldwide) while fine-tuning things for local markets where necessary.

- Look to local managers abroad for ideas and give them a great deal of control.

- Offer employees around the world an implicit contract in which high-quality work will be rewarded with decent wages, continuous learning, and recognition.[118]

But embracing these ideas may require new assumptions about how to run a business. For example, many managers still see their roles in command and control terms, with corporate headquarters making decisions for foreign subsidiaries. Unfortunately, this orientation doesn't take full advantage of local expertise, nor does it permit a quick response to rapidly changing local conditions. In fact, international corporations with a rigid hierarchy and a control mentality are slowly fading from the scene. Wholly owned subsidiaries are giving way to networks of alliances between organizations. Growing a company this way, however, requires flexible managers who are willing to accept the ambiguity inherent in relationships not based on control.[119]

Basic Conceptual Foundations

Many of the points we've made in this chapter rest on a variety of management concepts. Although we'll cover these concepts in detail later, introducing a few of them now will help you approach the rest of the book.

Defining Culture   There's no doubt that culture plays a big role in determining success or failure in international management. Culture can affect how managers lead, hire, and compete in various countries. But what exactly is **culture**? We agree with Hofstede, who defined culture as "the collective programming of the mind which distinguishes one group or category of people from another." This "programming" can't be observed directly. Rather, it can only be *inferred* from behavior. Likewise, people are often unaware of the pervasive impact of culture on their own attitudes, beliefs, and behaviors.[120] Culture is a concept that's only useful if it can accurately predict behavior. And although cultural values can change dramatically when borders are crossed, this isn't always the case. Furthermore, many distinct cultural groups can coexist within individual countries. Despite these complexities, it's important to understand country-specific differences in cultural values that exist and how they impact international management.

culture
Collective mental programming that distinguishes one group of people from another

International Corporations and Their Evolution Firms tackle international business in many different ways. Some export products from a home base while others have sales facilities in foreign countries to handle their exported products. Other firms build or buy facilities abroad to manufacture products or deliver services. We'll cover the various approaches to international business in later chapters. For now, a basic understanding of how firms approach the international business arena might be very helpful.

multinational enterprises
Large, well-developed international companies operating in a variety of overseas locations

In particular, you've already been reading about **multinational enterprises** (referred to as *multinationals* throughout the rest of the book). Multinationals are large, well-developed international firms that operate facilities to produce products or deliver services in a variety of overseas locations and have considerable resources invested abroad. And if you're wondering how much influence multinationals have today, consider this. The number of multinationals around the globe has soared over 800 percent in the last three decades (as of 2000, there were 63,000 multinationals competing around the world). Over 50 of the 100 biggest "economies" on the planet are actually multinationals. Gigantic multinationals like Wal-Mart and General Motors have annual sales that surpass the total GDP of about 90 percent of the countries in the world. Moreover, the world's 1,000 biggest multinationals are responsible for about 80 percent of industrial production worldwide. Overall, multinationals pay 90 million employees worldwide some $1.5 trillion in salaries and wages. And among the 500 biggest multinationals today, just over a third are based in the United States—down from about 60 percent in 1962.[121]

Managers in multinationals often make decisions based on their assessment of business opportunities and threats around the world. This doesn't mean, however, that multinationals all compete in some identical "global" fashion. As you'll see later, some multinationals (like those in the semiconductor industry) compete in global industries where few if any location-specific preferences exist. Other multinationals, however, operate in industries where a high degree of local tailoring has to be done.

Even within industries, multinationals may operate quite differently. This variation results from many factors, including firm values and the moves of competitors. Some multinationals, for instance, have facilities in many countries but try to use the same basic structure, technologies, and human resource practices everywhere. In these multinationals, the "home country" is where the headquarters resides and where decisions about firm culture, policies, and practices are made.

For other multinationals, however, local operations have more freedom to make their own decisions. Such multinationals tend to be more diverse internally in terms of both culture and structure. Business practices, technologies, and cultural values may all vary depending on the needs of particular locations where the firm operates. In short, headquarters may offer suggestions and guidance, but it's up to local managers to make operational choices. This emphasis is often reflected in multinationals that rely on local managers to run foreign operations (as opposed to sending an expatriate from the home country to run things).

Some multinationals, however, take diversity one step further. Their firm cultures have evolved to the point where organizational diversity is a core value. This value, along with a few other core beliefs, is the glue that both holds the firm together and allows enormous flexibility. Such multinationals tend to be run by teams of managers from several countries. In fact, other than a few

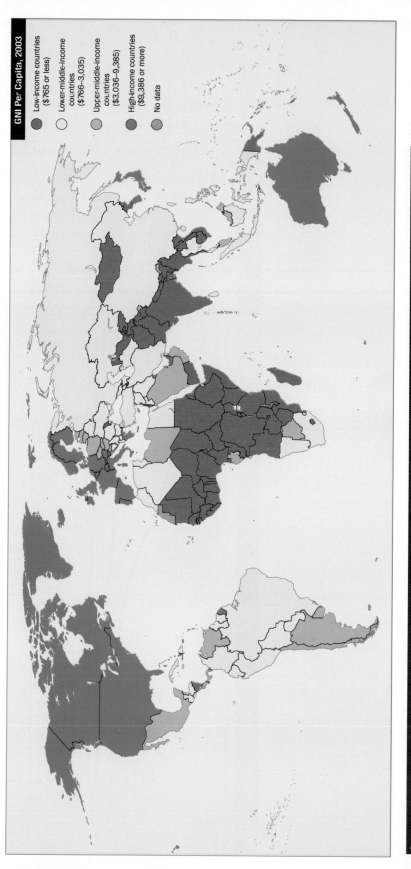

GNI Per Capita, 2003

- ● Low-income countries ($765 or less)
- ○ Lower-middle-income countries ($766–3,035)
- ● Upper-middle-income countries ($3,036–9,385)
- ● High-income countries ($9,386 or more)
- ● No data

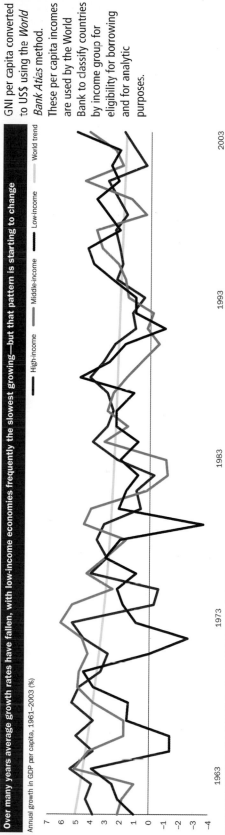

Over many years average growth rates have fallen, with low-income economies frequently the slowest growing—but that pattern is starting to change

Annual growth in GDP per capita, 1961–2003 (%)

— High-income — Middle-income — Low-income — World trend

1963   1973   1983   1993   2003

GNI per capita converted to US$ using the *World Bank Atlas* method.

These per capita incomes are used by the World Bank to classify countries by income group for eligibility for borrowing and for analytic purposes.

Map from 2004 WORLD BANK ATLAS, p. 7, GNI per Capita, 2003. © 2004 International Bank for Reconstruction and Development/The World Bank. Used with permission.

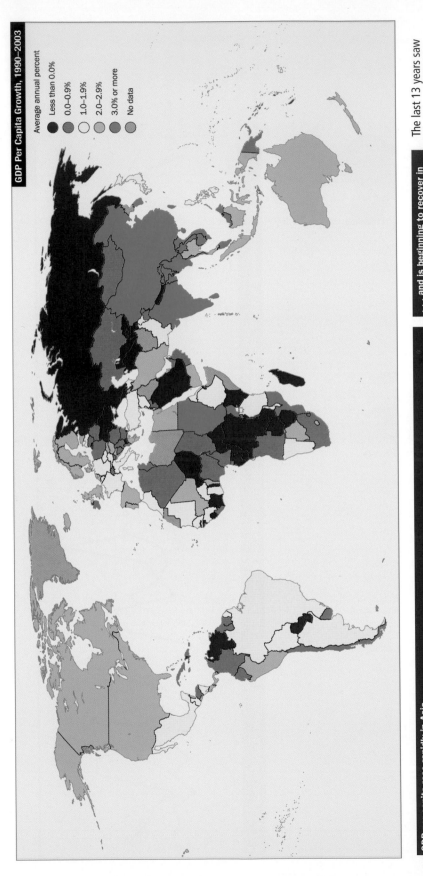

GDP Per Capita Growth, 1990–2003

Average annual percent

- ● Less than 0.0%
- ● 0.0–0.9%
- ○ 1.0–1.9%
- ● 2.0–2.9%
- ● 3.0% or more
- ● No data

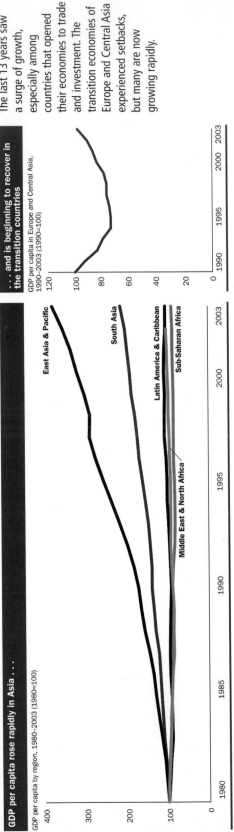

GDP per capita rose rapidly in Asia . . .

GDP per capita by region, 1980–2003 (1980=100)

East Asia & Pacific

South Asia

Latin America & Caribbean

Middle East & North Africa

Sub-Saharan Africa

. . . and is beginning to recover in the transition countries

GDP per capita in Europe and Central Asia, 1990–2003 (1990=100)

The last 13 years saw a surge of growth, especially among countries that opened their economies to trade and investment. The transition economies of Europe and Central Asia experienced setbacks, but many are now growing rapidly.

Map from 2004 WORLD BANK ATLAS, p. 35. GDP per Capita Growth, 1990–2003. © 2004 International Bank for Reconstruction and Development/The World Bank. Used with permission.

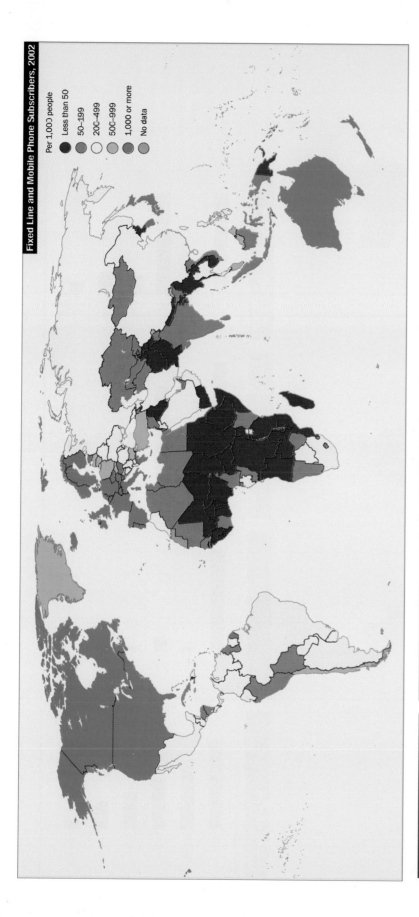

Fixed Line and Mobile Phone Subscribers, 2002

Per 1,000 people

- Less than 50
- 50–199
- 200–499
- 500–999
- 1,000 or more
- No data

Water, sanitation, and electricity are good for health and education

- In Bangladesh, installing facilities with clean water and sanitation for girls increased their school attendance by 15 percent.
- Access to sewerage in some urban Nicaraguan communities reduced child mortality by 50 percent.
- In households with electricity, children read and study more, improving educational performance.

Electrification rates range from near complete coverage to less than 10%

Households with access to electricity, 2000–02 (%)

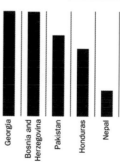

Georgia
Bosnia and Herzegovina
Pakistan
Honduras
Nepal
Cambodia
Mali

0 20 40 60 80 100

Transport is important for school attendance and health care

- In Morocco, girls' attendance in primary school more than tripled after a paved road was built.
- In Africa, 11 percent of people surveyed say that the high cost of transport—or poor access—is the major barrier to health care.
- In Andhra Pradesh, India, the female literacy rate is 60 percent higher in villages with all-season road access than in villages with sporadic access.

Rural roads are key to travelling to health clinics, schools, and jobs

Share of rural population with access to an all-season road, most recent year available (%)

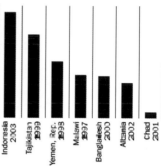

Indonesia 2003
Tajikistan 1999
Yemen, Rep. 1998
Malawi 1997
Bangladesh 2000
Albania 2002
Chad 2001

0 20 40 60 80 100

The combined mobile and fixed telephone lines per 1,000 people is a measure of access to information and communications technology. In 2002 more than 120 countries had more mobile than fixed line subscribers, including Austria, the Czech Republic, Malaysia, Uganda, and Venezuela.

Map from 2004 WORLD BANK ATLAS, p. 45, Fixed Line and Mobile Phone Subscribers, 2002. © 2004 International Bank for Reconstruction and Development/The World Bank. Used with permission.

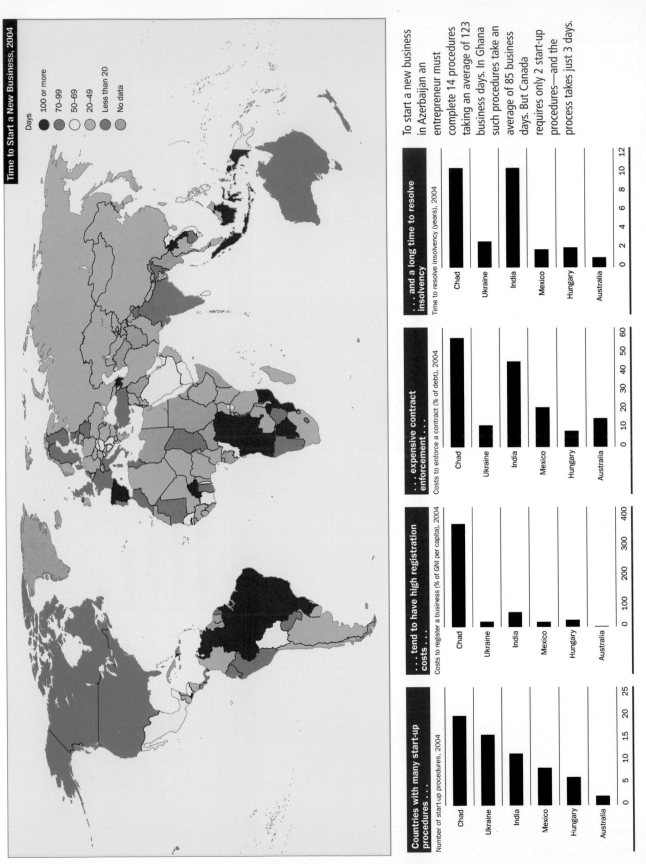

Time to Start a New Business, 2004

Days
- 100 or more
- 70–99
- 50–69
- 20–49
- Less than 20
- No data

To start a new business in Azerbaijan an entrepreneur must complete 14 procedures taking an average of 123 business days. In Ghana such procedures take an average of 85 business days. But Canada requires only 2 start-up procedures—and the process takes just 3 days.

Countries with many start-up procedures . . .
Number of start-up procedures, 2004

Chad, Ukraine, India, Mexico, Hungary, Australia
0   5   10   15   20   25

. . . tend to have high registration costs . . .
Costs to register a business (% of GNI per capita), 2004

Chad, Ukraine, India, Mexico, Hungary, Australia
0   100   200   300   400

. . . expensive contract enforcement . . .
Costs to enforce a contract (% of debt), 2004

Chad, Ukraine, India, Mexico, Hungary, Australia
0   10   20   30   40   50   60

. . . and a long time to resolve insolvency
Time to resolve insolvency (years), 2004

Chad, Ukraine, India, Mexico, Hungary, Australia
0   2   4   6   8   10   12

Map from 2004 WORLD BANK ATLAS, p. 41, Time to Start a New Business, 2004. © 2004 International Bank for Reconstruction and Development/The World Bank. Used with permission.

practices that are not subject to negotiation, such as indoctrinating employees in the firm's core values, these multinationals operate on a diverse basis. Relatively few multinationals have reached this status.[122]

We'll conclude with an evolutionary snapshot of how multinationals have changed in the last 100 years. As you can see in Exhibit 1.11, multinationals have gradually changed both their geographic scope and their orientation toward foreign subsidiaries. But not all multinationals develop in the same way or at the same rate. Nevertheless, multinationals are generally expected to continue moving toward the more liberal model in the years ahead.

EXHIBIT 1.11   *The Evolution of Multinationals and Their Approach to Innovation: Three Eras*

Era	Time Frame	Description of Multinational Operations
Paternalism	1900–1960s	Firms innovate in the home country, moving products out to the rest of the world from there. As foreign subsidiaries evolved, however, it became clear that the home office did not have a monopoly on good ideas. IBM and Procter & Gamble are prominent examples during this period.
Expansionism	1970s–1980s	Some firms set up R&D or other units abroad in an effort to capture ideas in key markets. But these outposts had difficulty integrating ideas across the company and holding headquarters' attention. Plus, establishing these outposts signaled to other foreign facilities that their ideas weren't needed (e.g., because they weren't in a big enough market or important enough to warrant an R&D operation).
Liberalism	1990s–today	The emerging approach takes a more democratic twist to the pursuit of new ideas. It assumes that great ideas can come from anywhere, especially in parts of the firm that are directly connected to customers or other outside constituencies. It also assumes that the farther a foreign outpost is from the home office, the less constrained it is by corporate traditions and beliefs. So foreign subsidiaries are better viewed as peninsulas than as islands. With that in mind, firms can expect some of their most creative and innovative ideas to come from the edges of the organization instead of the center. How to tap and leverage those ideas are key challenges for management.

Source: Adapted from Birkinshaw, J., & Hood, N. (2001). Unleash innovation in foreign subsidiaries. *Harvard Business Review* (March), 79, 131–138.

Chapter Summary

The purpose of this chapter was to describe the basic landscape of international business and the competitive environment that it represents. We began by describing *globalization* and prospects for increasing international business growth worldwide. Also discussed was the *World Trade Organization*, the body that governs worldwide rules for trade. In any case, the strongest growth will most likely be in emerging markets, although long-term prospects in many developed markets are also good. And as we noted, an important way to assess those prospects is by examining the flows of *foreign direct investment*. Next, we examined trends in specific regions of the world.

In the *Americas*, prospects for greater economic integration are being debated. The *Free Trade Area of the Americas* (FTAA), for instance, holds out the prospect of a continental free trade zone stretching from Alaska to the tip of South America. Clearly, the United States is the region's dominant player, though Canada and Mexico have generally done well in many respects since the *North American Free Trade Agreement* (NAFTA) was implemented. In South America, long-term growth prospects look good. In the short run, however, countries in the region continue to experience significant problems.

The *Asia-Pacific* region may become the world's most dominant economic area in the years ahead. But important differences exist across countries in the region in terms of their current performance, future prospects, and existing problems. Although there may be some setbacks—and major challenges exist in some Asian countries (such as rising costs, political instability, high debt, and weak infrastructures)—growth should continue over the long haul. Clearly, China has a large economy and the strongest growth in the region, though it may eventually be eclipsed by India. China is also a challenging place to do business for a variety of reasons, including its *competitive intensity* (i.e., many competitors operate and the pace of business activity is frenetic).

The transformation of *Europe* is continuing. On May 1, 2004, the European Union expanded its membership to twenty-five, adding ten new countries from central and eastern Europe. Countries nearest to western Europe (Poland, Hungary, and the Czech Republic) have performed the best so far. Russia has recently steadied itself economically and resumed a growth track while continuing to combat ongoing problems with regulation, laws, infrastructure, and organized crime. Overall, the prospect of an expanding, integrated European market with a common currency is a tantalizing one that continues to fuel foreign investment.

In the *Middle East and Africa*, major problems, such as political conflicts, war, poverty, corruption, and weak business infrastructure, still exist. Nevertheless, headway is being made. For example, Saudi Arabia has embarked on reforms to open its economy. Likewise, if South Africa can build on its accomplishments, it will be an important barometer for the rest of sub-Saharan Africa.

From there we moved to a discussion of some key challenges in international business. These included sweeping technological changes and the increasing volatility of international business. We examined how rapid currency fluctuations can impact business and what management can do in response (e.g., *currency hedging* and *natural hedging*). Small firms are particularly vulnerable to such fluctuations, especially since their resources (and consequently, their ability to cope) are often more limited than those of larger firms. Another set of challenges involves *offshoring* and the increasing internationalization of workforces around the world. Companies are willing to look anywhere in the world to find employees with the right skills at the right price for just about any job. So jobs are dispersing throughout the world as never before. And countries are more formidable competitors when they can offer firms a hardworking and skilled pool of employees.

For international executives, maintaining workforce quality and managing diversity are important challenges. And in big global empires, the management challenges are even greater. To meet these challenges, international managers must, among other things, value ethnic diversity, have multicultural experience, embrace teamwork, and be open to ideas from anywhere. Finally, we concluded by discussing the role of *culture* (the collective mental "programming" that sets groups of people apart) in international management and how *multinational enterprises* (large, well-developed international firms) have grown and evolved over the last 100 years.

Discussion Questions

1. What are the most important trends in international business? Which are the biggest management challenges for international firms? Why? What can firms do in response?

2. Which markets represent the biggest opportunities for international firms? Which markets represent the biggest risks? Why?

3. What is culture? Why is it important for international management?

4. In your view, what are the pros and cons about the scope, influence, and reach of multinationals on the global economic scene?

5. How have multinationals evolved over the years? What are the implications of this for management?

Up to the Challenge?

How New Balance Makes "Made in the U.S.A." Work, at Least for Now

AT THE START of this chapter we said that New Balance was unique among major athletic shoe companies in that it manufactures 25 percent of its shoes in the United States. In doing so, New Balance has minimized the cost gap with Asian subcontractors to the point where it can remain competitive. Put simply, owner Jim Davis felt obligated to manufacture in the United States. The son of successful immigrants, Davis said, "It's part of the company's culture to design and manufacture here." Plus, being close to customers in a major market offers speed advantages in terms of fulfilling orders and changing styles.

But making this philosophy work essentially meant shifting from low tech to high tech, both in terms of equipment and employee skills. Borrowing a page from manufacturing methods in higher-tech industries, New Balance had employees take classes on computerized manufacturing techniques and sophisticated teamwork. On the factory floor, employees operate in small, flexible teams. Employees must master a variety of skills, switch jobs continuously, help each other out, and take responsibility for production activities. And employee training is constant and ongoing.

New Balance also took a creative approach in adapting high-tech equipment from other industries to its needs. For instance, the company bought seventy computerized sewing machines that came with templates designed for other products. New Balance factories ripped out the templates and set up facilities to make their own (about thirty templates are needed for the average shoe). Once the right templates were in place, the computerized machines could guide twenty sewing heads at once. The result was a technology-intensive manufacturing operation for athletic shoes. And with a highly skilled workforce to run the equipment, New Balance factories in the United States need only one employee for every six that plants using ordinary sewing machines require.

The New Balance story raises some interesting questions. On the one hand, it suggests that American firms can avoid shifting production abroad by upgrading the skill levels of work at home. Indeed, the reality is that while the manufacturing workforce in the U.S. has been shrinking, productivity has been rising, with the result that American manufacturing output has soared 100 percent over the past decade. But what are the limits to this? Moreover, what are the costs and risks associated with New Balance's approach? What might happen if demand spikes up sharply or drops precipitously? Is New Balance at a disadvantage because it owns and operates some factories, whereas Nike and Reebok don't? Only time will tell if New Balance's approach represents a long-term competitive advantage for the company.[123]

International Development

International Management: Should It Be Life at 35,000 Feet?

Purpose

To offer a snapshot of what life is like as an international manager, to discuss the implications of that life, and to present some of the execution challenges companies face in running their international operations.

Instructions

Read the following short case (either before or in class). Then have a class discussion around the questions raised at the end of the case. Alternatively, your instructor will divide the class into groups of three to six and ask each group to consider the discussion questions and develop a list of their three most important reactions or ideas (20 minutes). If time allows, your group could then make brief presentations about its findings to the class (20 minutes). You may conclude with a general discussion about the rigors of life as an international manager and the implications of those rigors for corporations (15 minutes).

Case: Have Manager, Should Travel?

Accounting powerhouse PricewaterhouseCoopers (PWC) is a bona fide global empire, with almost $15 billion in revenues and over 120,000 employees serving clients all over the world. And Ellen Knapp's job is to help keep that empire running well. As PWC's chief knowledge officer and chief information officer, Knapp spends much of her time traveling overseas.

And Knapp's situation isn't unique. Knapp once survived three international red-eye flights crammed into less than a week. In the process, she ran into a colleague in London who was about to endure two such flights in two days. On another occasion, she ran into an acquaintance from consulting giant McKinsey at the Philadelphia airport. He was bound for New Delhi while Knapp was in transit to London and Frankfurt.

These days, international travel isn't confined to CEOs who hop on corporate jets for two-week business trips spanning a dozen time zones. Increasingly, the growth of international business means that managers like Knapp slog through airports as they crisscross the globe on their firm's behalf. But at least Knapp gets to fly business class. Employees who are a notch or two below Knapp on the corporate ladder must endure international travel wedged into economy seats.

Nevertheless, how does Knapp survive? A constellation of skills and abilities clearly help Knapp endure. These include being extremely organized, dedicated, optimistic, and, by a lucky twist, amazingly immune to jet lag. On the home front, Knapp has few complications since her two children are grown. Her two administrative assistants also keep Knapp plugged in at the home office. PWC tries to help by holding meetings near big airports and giving traveling managers like Knapp a phone and a desk when they arrive at a company outpost.

If you're wondering why Knapp has to travel overseas so much, the answer can be summed up in one word: bonding. Most of Knapp's travels are aimed at building relationships and trust between PWC people scattered around the world. The idea, at least in theory, is that over time better relationships will encourage cross-border information sharing and greater collaboration. That said, some question whether direct, face-to-face contact is the best, if not only, way to encourage international sharing and collaboration. Clearly, many believe that relationship building requires plenty of informal face time (e.g., over lunch). Whether Knapp's traveling really pays off or not is debatable, but one thing is certain: Knapp makes airlines happy.

Discussion Questions

1. How does Knapp's work life sound to you? Attractive? Tiring? Why or why not?

2. How would Knapp manage if she had younger children at home? What if she had younger children and a spouse with a demanding career on top of it?

3. Is all this flitting around the world really necessary? How might technology be used to eliminate some of this travel? What are the potential costs and benefits? To whom? The limitations? Can technology really substitute for relationship building, especially in far-flung corporate empires?

Adapted from: ———. (1999). On a wing and a hotel room. *The Economist*, January 9, 64.

 Tapping into the Global Network

Hitting Home: Understanding Your Local "China Syndrome"

Purpose

Much has been written in recent years about China's booming exports as well as the pressures (and benefits) that this has brought to manufacturing firms in places like America, Europe, and Japan. For instance, Chinese firms import a variety of goods to the United States, including office equipment, toys, computer components, and sporting goods, just to name a few. Consequently, what about your local companies? What role do they play in Chinese imports (e.g., have they decided to import products from China rather than make them locally)? Conversely, what role do your local companies play in exporting to China? Are any local firms realizing a good portion of their revenue by exporting products to China? Overall, the purpose of this exercise is to conduct an analysis of companies that import from and export to China in your local environment. The local environment will be defined by your instructor but could be a state, a province, a county, or a city.

Instructions

1. Outside class, break into small groups (ideally 3–6) to do research to answer these basic questions: Which companies are major importers from and exporters to China in the local environment (city, state, etc.)? What industries do they represent? What efforts, if any, are being made to encourage or help local companies to export to China (or to discourage imports)? For some general background information about challenges facing American manufacturers because of imports, the growth of China's economy, and formidable Chinese exporters, you may want to read the following:

   Ansberry, C., & Aeppel, T. (2004). Surviving the onslaught. *The Wall Street Journal*, October 6, B1, B6 (subscribers see **www.wsj.com**).

   Lieberthal, K., & Lieberthal, G. (2003). The great transition. *Harvard Business Review*, October, 70–81 (subscribers see **www.hbr.org**).

   Zeng, M., & Williamson, P. J. (2003). The hidden dragons. *Harvard Business Review*, October, 92–103 (subscribers see **www.hbr.org**).

   For more information about exporting to China, visit the U.S. Commercial Service's website for helpful information and a variety of links (**http://www.buyusa.gov/china/en/**). Part of the U.S. Department of Commerce, the Commerical Service is a government agency that helps American firms do business in China and other countries. The U.S. Commercial Service has been in existence for over two decades and has almost 2,000 trade experts in more than 100 American cities and 150 government offices outside the United States (e.g., in American trade centers and embassies).

2. If the class is small enough, your instructor may have your groups make brief presentations (ten minutes) about your findings to the class. This may be followed by a discussion about the level of involvement with China by local firms. Alternatively, your instructor may make this an individual assignment and have you write a report and ask you to take part in a general class discussion on the issues raised.

2

Legal and Political Foundations of International Management

INTERNATIONAL CHALLENGE

Crouching Dragon, Hidden Knockoffs: Piracy in the Middle Kingdom

Learning Objectives

After reading this chapter, you should be able to:

▸ Identify at least three major legal systems in place around the globe today.

▸ Pinpoint important effects that these legal systems have on commerce that is conducted within their jurisdictions.

▸ Define political risk and understand some of the specific effects it has on international business.

▸ Understand some of the ways that risk can be managed, reduced, or avoided altogether.

SIMON LICHTENBERG IS A 41-year-old Danish businessman with a stubborn streak. But stubbornness can be a virtue, especially when you need a whole lot of persistence to protect your product and copyright material in China. Mr. Lichtenberg came to Shanghai in 1993 and by 1995 opened a Bo Concepts franchise with his $30,000 dollars and Chinese language skills. Bo Concepts is a high-end furniture company that sells contemporary products through department stores and furniture malls. Business was good. The modern Danish designs appealed to the growing young urban professionals who were proliferating in the dynamically growing city of Shanghai. In 1995, the first year of business, sales were $3.6 million and then jumped to $6 million the very next year. By the end of 1997, Lichtenberg had fourteen franchise outlets in Shanghai, Guangzhou, and Beijing. And he was making money. But this is when the trouble started.

To take advantage of the expanding home improvement trend fueled by the growing professional set, Bo Concepts was joined in business by some 3,000 furniture companies selling all sorts of interesting products. While Lichtenberg did not mind competition, even of this magnitude, this wasn't the real problem. The real issue was that over twelve companies in the Shanghai area alone started to pump out furniture that "bore an uncanny likeness to Bo Concepts' designs."[1]

That was a nice way of saying that Lichtenberg and Bo Concepts were getting ripped off by pirates. Not only was the furniture a drop-dead look alike, some of the stores actually used the Bo Concepts logo as their own in their showrooms. The resemblance was uncanny. Other copycats had the Bo Concept catalog and models in their stores so that customers could peruse the products. Still others went a step further by printing their own catalogs with pictures and marketing concepts taken directly from the Bo Concepts catalog. Consider the comments of salesman Zheng Yong at the Xujiahui Furniture Company, part of a large department store in a shopping district of Shanghai, the kind of place that an up and coming family would go to get a nice couch, a bed, or their first computer armoire. "I can make furniture just like Bo Concepts'," bragged Mr. Yong. "We can change the length and the width to your specifications. We can stain it whatever tint you want. You don't want to bargain. This is our lowest price," he said, talking right below the Bo Concept's company logo on the wall behind him. And Mr. Yong was probably right; the $600 teak bed sold by Bo Concepts was only $96 at his store.

So that was the situation. As is the case in other industries, Chinese companies can create uncanny knockoffs and take a big bite out of a firm's profits. By 1998 to 2000, the knockoffs in combination with the Asian financial crisis were taking their toll. Bo Concept's revenue declined by 10 percent and the outlook was even worse. And as Mr. Lichtenberg put it, "When the company president visits China once a year, he almost has a heart attack when he sees the copies." This is extra pressure that Lichtenberg doesn't need. As you read this chapter, think of options, both legal and political, that Bo Concepts could use to stem the rising tide of counterfeiting and piracy. Then take a look at our *Up to the Challenge?* at the end of the chapter for an update on Bo Concepts' plan of attack.[2]

▶ *Legal Issues in International Management*

In this chapter we discuss two related issues—the political and legal sytems used in various countries where multinationals do business. Laws are the written codes of conduct that constrain and guide the actions of companies. You may be aware there are many different legal systems used around the globe—even among those nations that share a common heritage. This is the subject of the first part of this chapter. At the same time, however, a law may be constrained, altered, or ignored altogether because of political concerns. Worse yet, if political power changes hands, the legal framework may be changed again. Therefore, in addition to the formal, written legal code, multinationals should closely watch the political activity occurring at home and in the foreign countries where they operate. International companies may also wish to engage in political activity to gain an advantage. So although there is a close relation between a country's legal framework and its typical political activity, each should and must be carefully monitored. We will discuss both of these areas in turn.

Types of Legal Systems

Several systems have been devised for categorizing the types of legal systems within countries. Although no approach covers every legal system in operation, one approach that helps familiarize us with cultural variations among laws is presented in Exhibit 2.1.[3] As you'll note, the number and types of laws are varied and complex. Across all countries, however, the most frequently used systems are civil and common law.

Civil Law **Civil law**, found in over seventy countries, is the most frequently used system in the world.[4] Also referred to as *code law*, civil law approach is based on an elaborate and detailed set of rules. A major goal of a civil law system is to design as complete a set of regulations about what is right and wrong as is

civil or code law
Relies on pre-existing codes and is the most frequently used legal system in the world

EXHIBIT 2.1   *International Legal Systems*

Type of Legal System	Characteristics of the System
Civil law	• Codified • Based on abstract principles • Predictable because of elaborate code
Common law	• Based on precedent • Emphasis on procedures • Flexible
Islamic law	• Religious/faith-based code • Codified and predictable • Applicable to daily life
Communist/socialist law	• Based on ideology • Based on bureaucracy • Minimal private rights
Sub-Saharan African law	• Community oriented • Based on custom • Group-based outcomes
Asian law	• Social order/harmony stressed • Low use of legal mechanisms • Bureaucratized

Source: Adapted from Richards, F. L. (1994). *Law for global business.* Boston, MA: Irwin.

possible. In Western culture the system was formed in Roman times. Major developments have subsequently included the Napoleonic code and its spread throughout French colonial possessions during the last century as well as the impact of German civil code on that country's colonial possessions. In addition to France and Germany, the Czech Republic, Greece, Indonesia, Japan, Turkey, and many South American and African countries use the civil law system. Because of the existing code of legal regulations, there is great consistency among countries in the conduct of legal proceedings, especially in contrast to the common law system.

common law
Relies on the balance of previous cases or precedent to resolve legal disputes

Common Law Common law is practiced in about thirty countries, including the United Kingdom and most of its former colonies, the United States, Canada, Australia, and Ireland.[5]

Instead of relying on preexisting codes, common law uses the balance of previous cases (common use) or precedent to resolve legal disputes. Because of the focus on the case at hand and its similarity to previous cases—instead of an application of general principles/codes—there is great emphasis on procedural issues in common law. In fact, a judge in a common law system is relatively passive, typically functioning as a neutral referee. The lawyers for the plaintiff and defendant are expected to present evidence and develop the legal case in order

EXHIBIT 2.2   *Number of Lawyers and Tort Costs in Various Countries*

Country	Number of Lawyers per 100,000 People	Country	Tort Costs (as % of GDP)
Pakistan	508.4	United States	2.40
Singapore	396.0	Switzerland	.70
United States	312.0	France	.55
Belgium	214.0	Canada	.55
Germany	190.1	Austria	.53
Canada	168.5	Belgium	.50
Australia	145.7	Germany	.45
United Kingdom	133.8	United Kingdom	.45
Japan	101.6	Italy	.45
Italy	81.2	Spain	.35
Brazil	69.1	Japan	.35
France	49.1	Denmark	.35
India	34.4	Australia	.30
South Korea	7.7		
China	4.2		

Source: ———. (1994). *The Economist*, March 5, 36; ———. (1992). *The Economist*. July 18, 13. Reprinted by permission.

to resolve the dispute. In the civil law system, however, a judge takes a much greater part in the proceedings, including the decisions about what evidence will be presented to the court. To those unfamiliar with the common law system, rulings seem widely discrepant, often changing from year to year and even case to case. To an extent, this is true, and easily traced to reliance on precedent. In other words, the effect of previous rulings, court interpretations, and legal modifications lends itself to some inconsistency—especially compared to civil law.

Some have said that the common law emphasis on the active role of litigants promotes high numbers of attorneys and lawsuits.[6] Exhibit 2.2 presents some data that support this claim. The left side of this exhibit shows the percentage of lawyers in a variety of different countries—some with civil and some with common law systems. In general, there is a tendency for civil law countries (e.g., South Korea, Japan, and France) to have relatively few lawyers, whereas common law countries (e.g., the United States, Canada, Pakistan) have a relatively high number. In fact, the United States alone has nearly 40 percent of the world's lawyers, whereas Japan seems to have only a small fraction of this percentage (see the International Insights on the role of litigation outside the United States). Exhibit 2.2 also provides data on this point; it shows the tort costs as a percentage of GDP in a number of different countries. Roughly, this figure refers to the costs (legal, repayment, and damage awards) associated with lawsuits involving products (e.g., automobiles, cigarettes) and services (e.g., malpractice) and other civil actions. The United States (at 2.4 percent) has about four times the amount of costs as the next closest country (Switzerland, at .7 percent). We should note, however, that tort costs are not completely the result of the form of legal system—while the U.S. legal system has not changed over

🌐 International Insights

Courting Trouble: American Lawyers and Litigation in Japan

FOREIGN LAW FIRMS in Japan must abide by a number of rules that don't apply to their domestic counterparts. For instance, foreign firms must first list the name of their resident partner in Japan, followed by a Japanese phrase meaning "foreign business lawyer," and only then display their trademark firm name by which they're known to the rest of the world. So on their office doors, business cards, stationery, and even in the directory of the American Chamber of Commerce, the Tokyo office of the well-known U.S. firm of Coudert Brothers is called "Stevens *gaikokuho-jimu-bengoshi* Coudert Brothers." The firm of Milbank, Tweed, Hadley & McCloy (already a mouthful) becomes "Dickson, Green, Benson, *gaikokuho-jimu-bengoshi*, Tweed, Hadley & McCloy."

Foreign lawyers, or *gai-ben*, as they are known, say these rules on names are really only a minor irritation compared to other restrictions. For example, foreign lawyers cannot advise on Japanese law, nor can they employ Japanese lawyers who are permitted to give such advice. In fact, foreigners aren't permitted to join with national firms to get around the restriction.

Perhaps most important, *gai-ben* are barred from arbitration proceedings. This is no small matter since arbitration is common and litigation is rare. Partly this results from the Japanese tendency to avoid conflict, but the slowness of courts is also a factor. Cases can take ten years or more to go to trial.

The Japanese bar opposed the opening of the nation's legal market, and they support the current set of restrictions. They still fear foreign competition—even though fewer than fifty *gai-ben* (mostly Americans) have registered there, in comparison to 124,000 registered Japanese legal professionals. Despite fears of opening the market, "the hordes of lawyers the Japanese worried about didn't materialize," says Charles Stevens, the Coudert Brothers *gai-ben*. Those who have come would like to see more freedom to work. This is important, they say, because Japanese lawyers sometimes don't represent foreign clients well; they are seen as overly concerned with preserving social harmony and the existing business relations they have with their fellow Japanese. In one case, a big Japanese brokerage house was tipped off about a company's bankruptcy; thanks to this

---

the past twenty years, the relative growth of tort costs has risen dramatically. In fact, from 1970 to 1990, tort costs (relative to GDP) in the United States tripled.[7]

Further, managers should be aware of important differences even among similar systems. The United States and the United Kingdom, for example, both use a common law system, yet each has unique practices. For example, the discovery process in the United States is extensive and open. A defendant's counsel is well aware of the witnesses that will be called by the prosecution, and they may also depose those witnesses to find out exactly what they will testify. In the United Kingdom, however, no extensive discovery process exists; often a defendant will simply be provided a list of potential witnesses and a brief summary of why they were called. Likewise, contingency fee arrangements (whereby an attorney might take 30 to 40 percent of the trial judgment), while common in the United States, are considered unethical in the United Kingdom where clients pay hourly rates. Indeed, it is common in the United Kingdom for the losing party to pay trial costs and the attorney fees of their opposition.[8]

islamic law
Relies upon religious stipulations in the Quran—also known as **sharia** (or God's rules)

Islamic Law   Islamic law relies upon religious stipulations in the Quran—the holy book of Islam. **Islamic law** is also known as **sharia** (or God's rules) and is basically a moral code. While the Quran is not, strictly speaking, a code of law, it

information they obtained assets that were claimed by a consortium of foreign banks. The Japanese lawyers representing the banks never told the bank executives for fear that it would offend the brokerage house.

Despite the problems with the Japanese system, a major benefit is that these very *gai-ben*—particularly the aggressive American type—are limited in their practice. Consider some of the American behavior that Japanese would find offensive. Within twenty-four hours after a major accident at a Union Carbide plant in India, American lawyers were on the ground soliciting clients, and within four days they were back home and had already filed many lawsuits. The Japanese react very differently to these situations. For example, after a JAL flight crashed near Tokyo not long ago, the airline's president, Yasumoto Takagi, humbly bowed to families of the victims and apologized "from the bottom of our hearts." He vowed to resign once the investigation was complete. Next of kin received condolence payments and negotiated settlements with the airline. Similarly, when another JAL flight crashed into Tokyo Bay, the president also visited families and offered gifts while kneeling before funeral altars. The airline quickly paid families $2,000 each for condolence payments, then reached settlements ranging up to $450,000. Only one lawsuit was filed. Contrast this behavior with a crash of a Delta Airlines plane at Dallas. After this tragedy, lawyers rushed to set up shop at the airport Marriott. The well-known attorney

Melvin Belli said, "I'm not an ambulance chaser—I get there before the ambulance." And one of his associates bragged, "We always file the first suit." Belli told the media that they wanted "to get to the bottom of this and to make ourselves available." Within three days, the first of many lawsuits had been filed against Delta.

The Japanese legal system, as well as many European ones, does not promote this type of activity. For one thing, since there are relatively few attorneys, they don't descend in droves on an accident because they are too busy. In Japan, only 500 lawyers are admitted to the bar each year, and there are fewer judges per capita now than there were in 1890. Moreover, contingent fee arrangements (where the winning attorney gets one third of the judgment) are not common in Japan; they are illegal and even considered immoral in parts of Europe. European systems require additionally that the losing party pay the winner's legal fees—a strong deterrent to the wanton litigation seen in the United States. Finally, the legal system itself may not allow for litigation on certain topics, such as product liability. Japan has never had any laws directly aimed at protecting the public from defective goods. As a result, there have only been about 100 such cases brought to Japanese courts from 1945 through 1991.[9] It remains to be seen what will happen in Japan if the legal market opens even wider. For now, however, things are likely to stay much the same.[10]

---

includes covenants of relevance to business, including admonitions to honor agreements and to observe good faith in business transactions. The Islamic system considers that God's law was given to the prophet Mohammed. Some experts claim that by the end of the tenth century religious scholars had determined that divine law had been translated and clarified sufficiently and that no more substantial interpretation (*ijtihad*) was necessary.[11]

As with the other legal systems, while there are differences across the thirty or so countries that embrace Islamic law, the fact that much of the code was developed centuries ago and endures today with relatively few changes can create problems for multinationals. Consider the basic principle in many Western countries of interest earned on an investment. Islamic law requires obedience to the principle of *riba*, which prohibits the collection of interest on loans in deference and respect to the poor. And many Islamic courts have acted consistent with such principles. A federal court in Pakistan, for example, ruled that interest earned on an investment was non-Islamic and illegal. The Pakistani Supreme Court subsequently sided with that court, and went further by ruling that over twenty laws dealing with financial and banking issues were in violation of Islamic law.[12] A government commission formed in response to the court's dictates recommended that a banking system without interest be instituted. As you might imagine, several banks have challenged the rulings and recommendations. And the finance minister, Mr. Sardar Asif Ahmed Ali, stated that the ruling would negatively affect foreign investment and the treatment of Pakistan by international agencies such as the World Bank.[13]

To overcome some of the problems this observance presents in international commerce, Muslim businesses have devised some unique approaches. In Iran, for example, banks have charged upfront fees for a loan in lieu of interest payments or have devised leasing arrangements that comply with Islamic law. Likewise, some U.S. banks have developed creative financing arrangements to overcome the Quran's prescription that interest cannot be paid or received. For example, when Dr. Ala-ud-Din, a dentist in San Jose, California, wanted to buy a house in this most expensive of U.S. real estate markets, he faced problems. Fortunately, a small Islamic financing company actually bought the house for Dr. Din and leased it to him over a fifteen-year period that eventually made him the owner.[14] Banks in some countries, eager to be seen as respectful of sharia principles but also eager to do business, try to uphold the spirit of the law by doing the same thing. Many times they will engage in *ijara*—they'll acquire a capital item for a firm and then lease it to them. Aggressive banks will also issue interest-free bonds at a discount to par.[15] Even a few U.S. mutual funds have emerged that follow Islamic law. Companies with a presence in Islamic countries have been advised to be aware of issues involved in topics ranging from hiring practices to business entertainment (especially alcohol-related events) to investment policies. Some Western firms, including banks such as Citibank, J. P. Morgan, and Deutsche Bank, have operations in Islamic countries and have benefited from this understanding.[16]

Other Legal Systems   There are other legal systems in operation today, including socialist/communist or bureaucratic law and sub-Saharan African law, among others.[17] In China, for example, the legal system is a complex combination of several systems. Like many aspects of Chinese culture, the operation of the legal system is hard for Westerners to understand. Take traffic laws as an example. Many firms do not permit their expatriate employees to drive; instead, they provide even low-level managers with cars and drivers. Mostly, this is because in the event of a collision with a cyclist or pedestrian, Chinese law may hold the vehicle operator partially responsible. There is a well-known story of a stationary car (parked by a foreigner) that was hit by a bicyclist. The car's owner was assessed 10 percent of the blame because "if you had not come to China, this would not have happened."[18] Chinese laws now represent an interesting case, one that should be watched closely by Western and other firms eager to enter and capture that market. In late 2004, at the national Communist Party meeting, Hu Jintao is expected to introduce a far-reaching plan to overhaul laws dealing with China's burgeoning market economy. Some say that this will represent the biggest economic change since Deng Xiaoping's introduction of the "socialist market economy." Many in China feel this reform will yield internal benefits, such as greater barriers to bureaucratic corruption. For example, experts such as Professor Li Shuguang at the China University of Science and Law voice this needed change: "China has been operating under a market economy for 20 years, but it doesn't even have such basic laws as a bankruptcy law or a monopoly law to ensure fair competition."[19] With China's recent WTO membership, there are external reasons for this dramatic updating.

China aside, many feel that systems around the world share more and more in common as decades pass. It remains to be seen if this is actually the case. For now, however, we do note that these legal perspectives can result in varying degrees of protection against discrimination across countries.[20] In the United States, for example, the Civil Rights Act of 1964 (and the 1990/91 amendment) forbids U.S. firms from discriminating against employees at home and in foreign countries. Foreign multinationals are also subject to the Civil Rights Act while operating in the United States. Gender discrimination is prohibited in Belgium. In the United States, age discrimination is also outlawed, whereas it is permitted in France. Interestingly, Greece has a wide degree of protections against discrimination (e.g., gender, race, religion), but no laws dealing with age or national origin. Pakistan also has many forms of legal protection, but an employer could legally use gender as a job qualification variable. Finally, some countries have no specific antidiscrimination laws whatsoever (e.g., Venezuela). Therefore, it is important to be aware of the legal system that operates where a multinational has a presence.[21] One way that firms can do this is to join forces, as with the merger between the UK firm Freshfields and Germany's Bruckhaus Westrick Heller Loeber creating a legal powerhouse of nearly 2,000 attorneys.[22] Even beyond this, as economies and financial markets outgrow national borders, countries are compelled to blend regulations.[23] For example, when a Saudi broker buys shares of a British company on the NASDAQ exchange, there will be some need to reconcile differences. Interestingly, in many cases there is a tendency toward common law rules and standards (e.g., the system used in the United States and the United Kingdom), but this trend is far from universal and there is resistance among countries that use different methods.

As with many things, however, the devil may be in the details rather than the system or label. Exhibit 2.3 illustrates what we mean. This figure presents data collected from over 10,000 business executives from around the globe on their views about whether justice is administered fairly in forty-nine different countries. As you'll see, many more developing or emerging economies fall at the bottom of these rankings (we show the top and bottom ten countries in this exhibit). While not shown in this exhibit, the United States ranks at

EXHIBIT 2.3   *Ratings of the Fairness with Which Justice Is Administered in Various Countries: The Top Ten and Bottom Ten*

1	Denmark	9.14	40	Mexico	3.09
2	Finland	8.91	41	Slovak Rep	2.96
3	Canada	8.56	42	Philippines	2.89
4	Norway	8.56	43	Portugal	2.83
5	Austria	8.54	44	Poland	2.57
6	Iceland	8.51	45	Colombia	2.51
7	Singapore	8.50	46	Russia	2.42
8	Sweden	8.36	47	Indonesia	1.74
9	New Zealand	8.32	48	Venezuela	1.68
10	Switzerland	8.32	49	Argentina	0.83

Source: Adapted from The World Competitiveness Yearbook, 2002, Lausanne, Switzerland: IMD.

number 16 (a rating of 7.73, with higher ratings equating to better justice) and China is ranked number 28 (a rating of 5.15). All this suggests that one additional source of regulation that multinationals need to pay attention to is international law.

International Law

While no single body of law or code applies across borders, some sets of rules or guidelines do exist. Moreover, some important agreements have been reached over the years that can serve as relatively clear guidelines for international law. These agreements have resulted in a number of standing organizations that seek to promote international commerce law.

General Agreement on Trade and Tariffs
An agreement that affects commerce on an international level

GATT/WTO The **General Agreement on Trade and Tariffs** (GATT) is one such agreement that affects commerce on an international level. GATT resulted from a conference in 1948 of fifty-three nations that were concerned with the effect of protectionism and high tariffs on the world economy and political stability. The purpose of the GATT was to extend fair and similar trading and tariff policies to all members. These members are supposed to be extended the benefits of a most-favored-nation status (a set of preferential tariff fees). Currently, over 140 nations are members of the World Trade Organization (WTO) (the successor to GATT, established in 1995), many others are not members but receive special trade considerations, and still others are seeking membership. The membership process can prove long and contentious. For example, China's 1986 application for entry into the WTO was initially delayed by a public fight between the United States and the European Union over insurance. One complicating factor was whether AIG, the largest insurance company in the United States, should continue to receive preferential treatment by China at the expense of its EU competitors.[24]

Once it becomes a member, however, a nation is required to make its tariff and other business laws consistent ("harmonize") with guidelines, or it is liable to face rebukes and sanctions from the WTO. (This most-favored-nation status is not automatically extended to nations who are not full members.) China, which finally became a WTO member in January 2002, will be required to remove a large number of barriers to trade. For example, it must slash import tariffs from 21 percent to 8 percent. Likewise, importers currently consult the voluminous (over 100 pages) *Harmonized Tariff Schedule of the U.S.* if they wish to import to the United States. WTO agreements are reworked every several years during scheduled negotiation periods (or "rounds"). Ostensibly, this multicountry negotiation process is supposed to replace a large number of bilateral trade agreements, although clearly the latter still occur. While the WTO has resulted in several positive outcomes (such as a set of international legal guidelines regarding tariffs), it has also been criticized. For one, the organization is often seen as too slow moving—perhaps because over 140 countries must be heard during the negotiation process, and because it occurs only every few years.[25] Additionally, there are some escape clauses in the WTO structure that allow countries to have disparity, not harmony, in their tariffs on a selected few products (as the United States has done in the past for textiles, steel, and motorcycles). Despite its reputation as a bit of a bully, the WTO has also been criticized by the *Wall Street Journal* as being indecisive and not powerful enough.[26] In addition, there is a recent trend for countries to act on their own to strike deals with a few others, especially as the international tensions caused by the war in Iraq continue to reverberate.[27]

Many other agreements provide legal regulation of international commerce, including the European Union, NAFTA, and others. Similarly, the United Nations and its many allied organizations (e.g., International Labor Organization, World Bank, International Monetary Fund) provide the legal and regulatory context in which global business operates. The World Bank, for example, was founded in 1944 in large part to deal with war-torn Europe. It is owned by 181 member nations but is dominated by the United States.[28] The World Bank has a loan portfolio of nearly $120 billion, with a focus now on Asia, Africa, eastern Europe, and Latin America. While the bank does not run the projects it finances—that is left to the governments that borrow the money—it does exercise control through a complex set of requirements and regulations.

Resolving International Disputes   Of course, the mere presence of an agreement to oversee trade doesn't mean that there won't be conflict between countries. There is considerable trade and legal disagreement among countries. Resolving any disputes across borders can be very complex. Partly this is because the trade conflict may be viewed or treated differently by international and domestic laws. The United States, for example, has been castigated by some other countries for trying to restrict U.S. and foreign exports to nations with which it is in conflict, such as Cuba or Iraq. They claim the U.S. action violates WTO stipulations, whereas U.S. officials point to domestic laws and constraints that force their hand. An important question in situations like this is: Where should the issue be resolved? Which court or country has or should have jurisdiction in situations like this?

Source of Jurisdiction   One of the most important examples in this regard happened in 1984, when one of the deadliest industrial accidents in history occurred near Bhopal, India. Union Carbide India, Limited (UCIL), an Indian corporation, operated a chemical plant near Bhopal. An accident, allegedly resulting from negligence of the operators, was catastrophic. Winds blew a lethal gas into the densely populated city and the death toll was staggering. Over 2,100 people lost their lives and nearly 200,000 other people suffered injuries—some of which were debilitating. It is important to note that UCIL was incorporated under Indian laws and its stock was traded publicly on the Bombay Exchange. A majority of its stock (50.9 percent) was owned by Union Carbide Corporation (UCC), a U.S. company; 22 percent of the stock was owned by the Indian government, and the remaining 27 percent by private Indian investors.

Immediately after the accident, American lawyers traveled to India and signed up many Indian clients (all those affected, including all the plant employees, were Indian). Within four days of the accident, the first of over 100 legal actions was filed in U.S. District Court. To justify the filing of these suits in U.S. courts, the argument was made that the American parent corporation (UCC) controlled the subsidiary (UCIL). Union Carbide countered by claiming that they no longer had operational control over this or the other seven UCIL plants in India. UCC's participation via employees and plant operation was terminated at least a year before the accident. They claimed, therefore, that Indian courts were the correct forum to hear the case. All parties (UCC, the U.S. lawyers, and the victims' families) were, of course, aware that any damage awards would be substantially higher in U.S. courts than in India. In addition, the fact that the lawyers would get one-third of the awards as their fees likely prompted the action in U.S. courts. As it turned out, the U.S. Circuit Court of Appeals ruled in 1987 that India was in fact the appropriate forum to hear the case, provided that UCC submit to the jurisdiction of Indian courts and agree to satisfy any judgment reached against them in those courts. Eventually, Union Carbide (U.S.) reached an agreement with the Indian Supreme Court to pay $480 million to the victims, a relatively small amount by U.S. standards.

A much more complex issue currently looms for international law—that of the Internet and digitized products. As in other business domains, countries are very reluctant to cede away sovereignty in the Internet realm. A case involving a Russian programmer at Moscow-based Elcomsoft Co. illustrates this point. Dmitry Sklyarov was arrested in Las Vegas in 2001 and accused of overriding an Adobe Systems security feature that protects electronic books. However, his program is legal in Russia; in fact, it's sold and marketed there. Eventually, a U.S. district court acquitted Elcomsoft and Mr. Sklyarov, to the chagrin of Adobe and other U.S firms. In a more far-reaching case, an Australian court ruled in early 2003 that an Australian businessman, Joseph Gutnick, could sue (New York–based) Dow Jones & Co. (owners of the *Wall Street Journal Online*). Mr. Gutnick claims that an article published in the United States and distributed via the Internet defamed his reputation. The *Wall Street Journal Online* will now have to defend itself in this distant venue if another court does not intervene. Many companies are watching this case closely as it raises complex and troubling issues. For example, what if an Englishman sues an American publisher for defamation and the American firm must defend itself under British legal code? Libel laws in the United States place the burden on the plaintiff to show intent to defame, whereas the burden falls on the defendant in British courts. Or, what might happen to an American firm that made a movie with nude scenes? Could it be prosecuted in countries that ban such scenes? While many companies are watching these cases closely, some others have already acted. Intuit, the database software maker, has pulled its products from countries such as France as a protective reaction to avoid libel, product-liability, and other legal actions.[29]

These cases raise issues about whether foreign companies are responsible for the effects of their products and alliances in foreign markets and illustrate that it is difficult to decide which country's courts and laws apply in Internet and other situations. Often, this confusion may be the result of political issues surrounding the legal one. We now turn our attention to these political concerns.

▶ *Political Issues and Risks in International Management*

We have already shown that it is important to be aware of the prevailing legal system and methods that operate in any one country. Legal systems, however, affect and are affected by the prevailing political situation in the country; this in turn can shape the ability of a multinational to run its business. Many multinationals are experienced at evaluating the political environment of their home country. They are less experienced and comfortable, however, with making judgments about other countries. Nevertheless, such predictions can be important for the firm. Obviously, it is difficult for a multinational to run smoothly in times of great political strife, let alone during revolution or war. Less obvious, however, is the fact that there are many other less conspicuous sources of risk for international managers to consider. In this part of the chapter, we will first define political risk, give examples of various forms of risk to a business, discuss predictors of risk that a multinational may wish to use to evaluate a particular subsidiary, and then talk about ways to manage or reduce risk.

What Is Political Risk?

Political Risks are the actions by groups of people or governments that have the potential to affect the immediate and/or long-term viability of a firm. This definition encompasses a large number of events—all the way from a revolution that results in confiscation of a firm's operations down to small changes in the tax code. Some of what we will discuss directly involves legal issues (e.g., a law that does not permit exports to a certain country). We discuss them in this part of the chapter rather than earlier because, although they may be based on legal code, their enforcement or existence itself represents a form of political risk for a multinational.

political risk
The extent to which actions by people or governments in a country may affect the viability of a firm

Many of the factors involved in determining political risk are difficult to predict or anticipate, even for an expert in international politics. For example, many of those experts believed that Iraq would not invade Kuwait in 1990 and therefore did not consider the potential negative effects on business operations in that country. Although the Middle East is generally viewed as risky, there are forms of risk inherent in most areas and countries of the world. For example, the European Union severely restricts Japanese auto imports, whereas the United States has a history of tight control over foreign investment in the banking and airline industries—and there appear to be internal political reasons for such restrictions.

Since even experts have difficulty with political predictions, it may be even harder for business leaders to anticipate all the political risks affecting their many international operations. All the same, because of the potentially catastrophic effects of political events, management needs to do at least two things: (1) investigate political risk before entering a new market, and (2) continually monitor political events that may affect ongoing operations. Some firms, for example, maintain and consult timely descriptions of the political environment in an effort to predict the effects on their operations. In general, the extent of concern with political risk is often negatively related to the amount of investment in that country.

Types of Political Risk

What is the nature of the many political risks involved in international operations? Some feel that there are too many to account for, and this may be true. Even so, there have been some efforts to help companies respond by classifying political risks into manageable categories. One system divides types of threats or risks into three main categories. These include risks resulting from (1) the *political/economic environment*, (2) prevailing *domestic economic* conditions, and (3) *external economic* relations.[30]

Exhibit 2.4 presents examples of each of these three main categories, and we will talk about each of these in turn. Before we do, however, please note in Exhibit 2.4 that numbers are assigned to each risk variable. This effort to quantify many different threats to doing business in a particular country has two

EXHIBIT 2.4   *A Method for Rating Political Risk Across Countries*

Type of Risk	Examples	Minimum Score	Maximum Score
Political/economic environment	1. Stability of political system	3	14
	2. Possibility of internal conflicts	0	14
	3. External threats to stability	0	12
	4. Degree of economic control	5	9
	5. Dependability as trading partner	4	12
	6. Provision for constitutional guarantees	2	12
	7. Effectiveness of public administration	3	12
	8. Quality of labor relations/ social peace	3	15
Domestic economic conditions	9. Size of population	4	8
	10. Per capita income to foreigners	2	10
	11. Economic growth, last 5 years	2	7
	12. Potential growth, next 3 years	3	10
	13. Inflation, last 2 years	2	10
	14. Openness of cap market to foreigners	3	7
	15. Availability of high-quality labor force	2	8
	16. Ability to hire foreign nationals	2	8
	17. Availability of energy resources	2	14
	18. Regulations on environment/ pollution	4	8
	19. Degree of infrastructure development	2	14
External economic relations	20. Import restrictions	2	10
	21. Export restrictions	2	10
	22. Foreign investment restrictions	3	9
	23. Ability to enter into partnerships	3	9
	24. Protection for brands, trademarks	3	9
	25. Restrictions on money transfers	2	8
	26. Currency revaluation previous 5 years	2	7
	27. Balance of payments condition	2	9
	28. Amount of oil/energy imports	3	14
	29. International financial standing	3	8
	30. Currency exchange restrictions	2	8

Source: Adapted from Dichtl, E., & Koeglmayr, H. G. (1986). Country Risk Ratings. *Management International Review, 26,* 4–11.

main purposes. First, if you sum up the total scores for each country, you can get a relatively accurate way to compare the risks of doing business internationally. Second, by quantifying specific types of risk, a company can target and work on specific threats. For example, if there are severe restrictions on money transfers from a country that your firm otherwise finds attractive, this category system can focus your entry efforts on dealing with that threat. Perhaps you can strike a deal with the government that would reduce such restrictions for a reasonable period of time. Let's look more closely at all three types of risk that a company may face.

Political/Economic Environment Risk First, there are many types of political/economic variables that could increase risk. For example, the stability of a country's government and political system are important sources of uncertainty. In recent years, we have seen the effects of dramatic and sometimes violent changes in political systems, and these changes have had major negative effects on the multinationals operating in those countries.

Perhaps the most important risk faced by firms in such situations is **nationalization**. This occurs when a government forces the transfer of ownership from private to state control. The height of this activity occurred from the 1960s through the 1970s, during which time over 1,500 firms were nationalized by about seventy different countries. Industries that were capital intensive and based on indigenous resources such as crude oil production, mining, and steel were most susceptible to nationalization. The reasons for government takeover of an industry are many. For one, a new government may wish to show that it is tough—tough enough to stand up to foreign powers and businesses. A government may also nationalize a company or industry because of its value to state defense or because of the power that industry may wield globally. The crude oil industry is an excellent example of this reason. At the beginning of the century most crude oil operations were foreign owned. Through the decades, especially the 1970s, oil operations were nationalized—so much so that most oil production facilities are now domestically owned.[31]

If a government nationalizes an industry or company and then compensates the multinational that is affected, that action is called **expropriation**. Many countries (including the United States) recognize the right of a country to expropriate assets via a principle called **sovereign immunity**. Basically this principle holds that no nation has the right to judge or challenge the internal actions of another state, provided that state has proceeded justly.[32] Although the concept of just action is complex and open to interpretation, it appears as though a government cannot expropriate property or other assets unless three requirements are met:

1. The expropriation must be for a public purpose.
2. The action must be performed in a nondiscriminatory way—foreign investors must be treated the same way as domestic investors.
3. Investors must be provided prompt, adequate, and effective compensation for their equity holdings.

Courts have typically ruled that if a sovereign government acts consistently toward domestic and foreign firms, then full compensation may not even be necessary.[33] The mass nationalization of the crude oil industries by many countries in the Middle East and North Africa in the 1970s is an example of expropriation since foreign and domestic firms were typically offered compensation for their

nationalization
Occurs when a government forces the transfer of ownership from private to state control

expropriation
Occurs when a government compensates a company after nationalizing its assets

sovereign immunity
Principle that no nation has the right to challenge the internal actions of another state, if that state has proceeded justly

🌐 International Insights

In Harm's Way: The Danger in Doing Business Abroad

IF YOU'RE GOING OVERSEAS TO do business, you'd better leave your Rolex watch and your Armani suits at home! And you're better off renting a midsize Ford rather than a Mercedes. Why? Well, because in addition to the many opportunities offered by the global economy, there also come some very great hazards. One very dangerous possibility is the threat of kidnapping or violence to the employees of global companies with deep pockets.

In fact, U.S. businesspeople are victims of nearly 100 violent attacks a year while doing business in foreign countries. According to the State Department, there were more attacks on businesspeople than on all U.S. diplomatic or military personnel in all worldwide embassies (Iraq now aside). In fact, *Business Week* reports that the frequency of kidnapping, robberies, and other crimes rose throughout the 1990s. Given the overthrow of the Taliban in Afghanistan and the

second Gulf War, one can only expect this rate, as well as other types of crime, to accelerate. Beyond their political presence in the world, another reason for this increased crime on Americans is much simpler and more old-fashioned: they are seen as easy targets.[34] Only recently have U.S. multinationals systematically provided security for their executives traveling abroad. And, the elimination of security staff is one of the first things to go when a firm is in a downsizing mode.

Even if you're not an executive, you should have reason to worry about your safety. We know that terrorists often target high-profile executives before they even set foot in a country. Increasingly, the lower- and midlevel employee is also feeling the negative effects of crime; this is the group that is least likely to be protected by a security service. How can this group—or anyone, for that matter—travel and do business more safely? One way is to follow the advice of Chuck.

---

confiscation
When nationalization of foreign firms occurs with little or no compensation offered

losses. Although there may be long-term negative effects for a country that expropriates property (such as future reluctance to invest by foreigners), usually an agreement is reached that both parties find at least acceptable.

When nationalization discriminates against foreign firms by offering little or no compensation for loss of property, however, this action is called **confiscation**. In these circumstances, courts have typically ruled that property owners are entitled to full compensation. Regardless of a court ruling in its favor, a multinational can be devastated by confiscation and there are many recent examples to point to. For instance, in the years following World War II, governments in China and eastern Europe confiscated a great deal of private property with little or no compensation to foreign investors. The same practice was observed in Cuba following the communist takeover in 1959, and more recent examples include Chile, Peru, and Zimbabwe.

Although expropriation and confiscation were rare in the 1990s and early 2000s, multinationals should be aware of the risks of these events, especially because when they do occur, their effect is substantial. As shown in Exhibit 2.4, however, many political/economic events can take place. With the recent wave of nationalism occurring all over the world, civil war represents a greater risk to doing business for a multinational than it has for some time. The recent events in the former Yugoslavia have shown this, and there are many other conflicts that could have the same effects in coming years. Clearly, civil war can result in disruption of production and productivity as well as more important things like threats of injury and possibly even death to employees or their families.

Vance, a former Secret Service agent who worked for three presidents and now has clients in over 1,500 companies in more than fifty countries (**www.vancesecurity.com**). One of Vance's best pieces of advice is "Learn how to blend in with the scenery." You may become a target simply because you look very foreign and rich. So don't wear an expensive watch or other jewelry. And fly commercial, not the corporate jet. Criminals monitor the airports and use this as a marker for a good target. Fly nonstop; take-offs and landings are the most dangerous times. Also, rent a car common in the country you are visiting; don't take a big limo or some other luxury car. If you are one of Vance's famous clients and are willing to spend the money—like Henry Kissinger, General Schwarzkopf, or Salman Rushdie—he will make sure there is no trouble ahead of time. Vance International Security Services agents will travel to the country in advance of your visit to scout the airport, your proposed routes, and your hotel. If you can't afford these services, Vance recommends that you do your own homework. You can call any or all of these three groups: (1) the regional security officer at the U.S.

embassy in the country you're visiting, (2) the State Department's Overseas Security Advisory Council for free tips (**http://travel.state.gov/index.html** or call 202-663-0533), or (3) the U.S. Department of Commerce for more country-specific advice (**http://home.doc.gov/; 800-USA-TRAD**).

One last piece of advice from Vance: "Think like the terrorist. If I were going to knock me on the head, where would I do it? When would I strike?" This means that once you've landed, stay alert and vary your daily routine. Don't eat every night at the same bistro at 8 p.m. or go jogging every morning at 7 a.m. Swap cars with other employees unpredictably and take cabs at other times. Don't share any personal information, including your hotel, cell number, or the like; give out your work address and phone at most. Of course, not every business trip overseas is terribly dangerous, but you have put yourself in harm's way. Countries that make Vance's danger list include Colombia as well as Kenya, Nigeria, Peru, the Philippines, Russia, South Africa, and increasingly China. History shows that wherever international business goes, bandits are sure to follow![35]

Similarly, we well know that radical political activity such as terrorism and other forms of violence can and have created great hardship and problems in many different countries, including the United States.[36] One specific risk that a multinational takes is the threat of kidnapping. The news is full of these crimes, including several kidnappings of foreign executives in Iraq, Colombia, and Mexico, among other countries. Latin American countries in general have some of the highest kidnapping rates in the world, but in Colombia where about 3,000 kidnappings occur every year, this is a burgeoning business.[37] It's estimated that millions of dollars and up to one-third of executives' time is spent on security issues and coordination while in Colombia.[38] More detail on this topic and what firms can do about it is provided in the accompanying International Insights.

Exhibit 2.4 presents other forms of political risk. These other forms, although less sensational in their effects, are probably more common. For example, the climate surrounding a country's labor relations is something to consider in every region where a multinational might do business. As we'll discuss later in Chapter 14, labor regulations vary dramatically, and some are not favorable to business. It is important to review those relations periodically in the countries where the company already has a presence. Regardless, like the other specific examples of political threats or risks, each can be evaluated and scored by the concerned company.

Domestic Economic Conditions as Risk Factors Exhibit 2.4 presents a number of domestic economic criteria that could make a foreign investment more or less risky. As you can see there, domestic conditions such as per capita income and economic growth rate and the presence of roads, airports, and communication systems can add to or reduce the amount of risk a company may face. Ordinarily, good infrastructure support reduces risk and thereby facilitates entry and expansion of business. At the same time, however, risk can present opportunity. Take, for example, the telephone infrastructure in Hungary, where in the early 1990s there were only ninety-six phone lines per 1,000 people (the U.S. rate is 545 per 1,000), and the installation of a new line required a five-year wait. A U.S. firm, Qwest, viewed this as an opportunity and entered the Hungarian market with their cellular division. Business boomed; they immediately received over 10,000 requests for service.[39] While Hungary is widely viewed as one of the most stable and risk-free economies around, our point highlights the fact that risk evaluation systems should not be applied thoughtlessly or without creativity. [40] Other domestic risk factors include the passage of legal regulations on environmental pollution. The enforcement of such laws could restrict how a multinational may operate in a foreign country. These restrictions almost always increase operation costs to the company. For example, in Germany, companies must abide by rigid packaging laws when selling and shipping their products. This "green dot" law requires businesses to do two things: (1) accept back from consumers all excess packing materials, and (2) encourage recycling of the materials by alerting customers about this option with a green dot on the material and with prominent recycling facilities at the point of purchase.

In Germany, as in the United States, there are also many restrictive environmental laws that affect the production and disposal of industrial wastes. In some countries, however, environmental laws are almost nonexistent. In part this absence of regulation occurs because developing countries are struggling to improve economic conditions and often wish to do as little as possible to discourage foreign investment. As a result, these countries may become places for

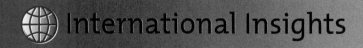 International Insights

The Greening of the River Huai: Environmental Issues in Newly Industrialized China

IT APPEARS THAT MANY NEWLY industrialized countries are facing many of the same environmental problems the United States faced after its rapid period of industrial growth—one of which is environmental pollution. This list of countries would certainly have to include Mexico and the not so newly industrialized, but newly politicized Russia. Topping this list, however, is the People's Republic of China.

Huainan, China, a big city on the Huai River in Anhui Province about 200 miles from Shanghai, has lots of problems. Workers at the Xicheng paper factory arrived one day to find a warning posted on the gates: "Factory closed by order of the Environmental Protection Bureau." Like many formal edicts in

China, this one was ignored and workers went in and began their daily shift. Later that afternoon, however, the presses jerked to a halt and all the lights went out. Apparently, this time it was for real, and shortly after that a delegation of officials showed up and told them that this time there was no way out.

Paper mills like this one on the river are responsible for generating much of the toxic sludge that has turned the once beautiful Huai River to the color of coal. When environmentalists won an order to shut down nearly 1,000 plants in China, they had a rare "green" moment. It is rare because so many environmental hazards pile up every day in China. One-fifth of China's river water can no longer be used

waste-producing countries to dump this material. To deal with this problem, over fifty countries became signatories to the Basel Convention, an agreement on the international transport of hazardous wastes. A key element of the agreement is that informed consent about the movement of the toxic waste must be given and permission received from all countries through which it passes. The exporting country cannot move the waste until it receives written permission, obtains insurance coverage against damage, and enacts domestic laws making it a crime to violate the agreement.

The accompanying International Insights reviews the environmental issues that are present in China, a country that is undergoing dramatic industrial growth. As this material illustrates, many countries are increasingly concerned with the effect of industry on their environment. In addition to the direct costs to firms doing business, there are also indirect effects of concern for the environment. Because of several major environmental disasters, such as the one mentioned earlier at Bhopal, India, awareness of these important issues has intensified. Some countries such as Germany even have major political parties organized around environmental issues. Thus, there are direct and indirect forms of risk associated with this factor. Clearly, these affect the business decisions of multinationals. A consumer products company may build its plant in Mexico rather than in the United States (their intended market) because U.S. pollution control regulations require expensive equipment and monitoring. Similarly, a chemical company may manufacture in Indonesia rather than in Germany because of the extensive industry restrictions. These examples raise ethical and other issues, such as whether a multinational should capitalize on weaker restrictions in another country, a topic discussed in the next chapter. For now, we note that the relative presence or absence of legal restrictions in any one country is often considered in an overall risk rating system like that presented in Exhibit 2.4.

---

to irrigate land. Almost everyone in urban settings buys and drinks bottled water. Hotels catering to foreigners—even the five-star variety, like the Shangri-La resort hotels in Guangzhou and Shanghai—caution visitors not to use the water or even to brush their teeth with it. In fact, 82 percent of Chinese rivers are polluted, and 20 percent are not even usable for irrigation. Most coal is burned without emission controls, and the Chinese urban population breathes polluted air that exceeds World Health Organization safety levels by anywhere from four to ten times. Vaclav Smil, a China specialist at the University of Manitoba in Canada, estimates that the problems resulting from environmental pollution (from lost farmland to higher cancer rates) cost China as much as 15 percent of its GNP. This proportion is much larger than in older industrialized economies.

As far as the Huai River is concerned, Chinese environmentalists have made it a priority in order to symbolize their concerns about the country as a whole. For years, many paper mills, printing and dye plants, and other factories sprang up along the river. Their growth was largely unchecked and their toxic discharge flowed untreated into the Huai. Many of the firms were small, but they generated jobs in addition to pollution. So they were tolerated if not encouraged. To Liang Congjie, an environmentalist in Beijing, it is a sign of progress that some of those factories have now been closed—in some cases, with doors chained and windows boarded. Still, Mr. Liang notes that it took years to make this progress, and he fears operations may just move to another location or province. Nevertheless, he says, "I consider it the beginning of a turning point. China needs decades before it outgrows the first stage of wealth creation, like the United States one hundred years ago."

The reactions to the closures are mixed. One young farmer said his elder brother lost his job at the mill because of the closures, but he also understands the government's actions. "You can't even take a bath in this water now without smelling bad. It wasn't that way when I was a kid."[41]

External Economic Relations as Risk Factors As shown in Exhibit 2.4, a large number of factors influence how a country relates economically to another country. These may be especially important to study. Whereas some of the earlier factors we considered were rare (e.g., civil war), virtually every country restricts its external economic relations in several ways. For example, many countries have restrictions on imports, usually in the form of **tariffs**. A tariff is a fee paid by an exporter to the country of import. A tariff, therefore, would increase the price of a foreign product or service relative to the domestic counterpart. Through the use of import taxes like these, a country can partially restrict imports and provide protection for domestic industry. This type of restriction presents a risk for the foreign multinational.

Tariffs are not the only way imports can be restricted. One country may wish to limit imports in order to force another country to expand its markets to accept more of its goods. The European Union, for example, limits the import of Japanese autos to a percentage of the total autos sold in the European Union. Likewise, the United States had restricted the number of automobiles that Japan may import in order to pressure Japan into purchasing more American-made components. Japan had restricted the latter via subtle, informal measures. Regardless of their cause, these limits may also act to increase the price of the product. Finally, a country may restrict imports when they are perceived as a threat to the health or safety of its citizens. In 1996 and again in 2001, British (and other European) cattle were affected by "mad cow disease"—an affliction that produces many nervous system symptoms and eventually death. Although the British argued that the disease did not affect the harvesting of the beef, many countries (including EU countries) temporarily banned the import of beef raised in Britain. British farmers incurred great losses as a result of this ban and eventually destroyed nearly half of the cows in Britain. In the United States, foreign producers of food must receive FDA approval regarding their hygiene standards prior to importing their products.

Export controls or restrictions are important concerns for international managers. There are many types of export restrictions. For example, *sanctions*, *embargoes*, and *boycotts* are all examples of restrictions that can affect an international business. Each could also extend to import restrictions, and many times these terms are used interchangeably. All three refer to actions by a country that constrain free trade for political rather than economic reasons, but they differ in their intended magnitude. **Sanctions**, or sets of specific restraints involving trade, can take many different forms. For example, a country may cancel its preferential tariff fees for another country (most-favored-nation status), restrict access to computers or other high technology, or prohibit the export of certain weapons. Some of these sanctions were used by the United States against China after that government's violence against the pro-democracy movement in 1989, and again in Haiti in 1994 in an effort to restore a democratically elected government; they were in place against Iraq until after the second Gulf War, and are still levied against countries such as Syria as of 2004.

An **embargo** is an all-out prohibition of trade with another country—not just commerce in several specific or critical goods and services. Usually embargoes are imposed in order to protect national security or to promote a certain foreign policy, and they have been used by the United States since the Revolutionary War. Often embargoes are instituted during times of war, but they are erected during peacetime as well. The president of the United States has considerable discretion to enact an embargo. The president can direct the

tariffs
Fees paid by an exporter to the country of import

export controls
Restrictions imposed by governments on what can be exported from a country

sanctions
Sets of specific restraints imposed by governments on international trade

embargo
Government-imposed unilateral prohibition of trade with another country

Department of Commerce's Bureau of Export Administration to add a country to an embargo list based on the following criteria:

- The extent to which the country's actions affect U.S. national security
- The country's current/future relations with the United States or its allies or enemies
- Whether the country is or is not communist
- The country's nuclear, chemical, and biological weapon policy and degree of compliance with world agreements on these weapons[42]

Based on these criteria, the United States currently has designated Cuba, Iran, Libya, North Korea, Sudan, and Syria as countries for which this broad set of controls applies.[43] The embargo against Cuba, for example, has been in place since 1961, when the attempted invasion of U.S.-backed forces was crushed by Cuban forces. An extremely strong anti-Castro lobby in the United States has kept this embargo in place despite some efforts to remove it.

Critics have pointed out that the use of embargoes (and sanctions) is not that effective. For example, an analysis of the nearly fifty different uses of sanctions and embargoes to achieve political goals from 1970 to 1983 showed that few were successful.[44] Partly this lack of success resulted from the diffuse focus of the sanctions, some dealing with improvement of human rights and others as protests against terrorism. But mainly the restrictions were ineffective because other countries filled the void left by the sanctioning country. This is one of the major complaints from the business community about such restrictions. American businesspeople sometimes object by saying, "Why should we be penalized by our government from doing business in China because their human rights record is not up to our standards?" Some maintain that U.S. multinationals are unfairly punished because American sanctions are often not observed by other countries. Thus, South Korea or Japan, while expressing genuine outrage over China's policies, continued to do business and even take advantage of opportunities created by American sanctions.

The relevant U.S. government agencies (such as the Departments of Commerce, Defense, and State) that are responsible for developing and implementing sanctions and embargoes are familiar with and probably sympathetic to these complaints about controls. The Commerce Department (via its Bureau of Export Administration) is in fact charged with issuing licenses for exports, some of which may override existing sanctions. A business must file an application for an export license, the first step of which is to properly classify for the government the commodity that is proposed for export. This is a complex process that involves classifying the type of product, where the product is going, and the nature of the restrictions that are in place. An application for the export of scuba gear and outboard engines to Iran, for example, might not be permitted because of fears of attacks on oil tankers in the Gulf.[45] After receiving an application, the Department of Commerce then has ninety days to issue or deny a license to export the product(s), although approval recently has averaged only about five days.

The application for license, like a tax return, is a self-report of one's behavior. As with a tax return, there are some applicants who don't tell the truth. One example is those who mislead about the nature of their product or where it is going. An infamous example of this occurred in 1986, when the U.S. Navy determined that Soviet submarines were somehow able to move without any detectable noise. Over the next several months, it was revealed that the Soviets had acquired advanced equipment from Toshiba in violation of Japanese and U.S. export laws. It was discovered that Toshiba received permission to export because they had deceived the Japanese government by changing the description of the exported equipment. Because of this threat to its security, the United States reacted strongly. Government contracts totaling over $200 million with Toshiba were canceled, and Congress banned the company from doing business with the government for three years. The Japanese government reacted lightly to the infractions, suspending the sentences given to Toshiba executives and imposing only a $16,000 fine. Cases such as this are enforced by the U.S. Treasury's Office of Foreign Assets Control, and most investigations result in civil actions against companies. In 2001, for example, the agency made nearly 1,600 referrals to the Justice Department, and they typically result in large fines paid by the offending company. It is rare that criminal action is taken, although more aggressive action is being taken since 9/11. Currently, for example, a Luxembourg shipping firm called Stolt-Nielsen with offices in Connecticut is under a criminal probe for its dealings with Iran and has already paid fines for illegal dealings with Sudan. Records show Stolt-Nielsen filed phony cargo documents, ordered its ship captains to use code words on the radio to refer to embargoed ports they visited (e.g., Cuba was "Port Charlie"), and removed Iranian names from shipments and documents.[46]

diversion

Using an export license to provide materials to a third party not included on the license

More common but much less known, however, is the problem of **diversion**. This term refers to the use of an export license to provide materials to a third party not included on the license. For example, a U.S. oil company may seek a license to export oilfield equipment to one country, which would in turn send the equipment to Tripoli—in violation of the U.S. export embargo on Libya. This situation is more common than we would like to think, and has led courts to rule that the burden is on the exporter. That is, it is the exporter's responsibility to screen and proceed diligently with foreign buyers regarding intended uses of the product. There are very extensive civil and criminal penalties in place for those found in violation of export laws.

Even if a company proceeded with good faith, filed a legitimate application for license, and then went to great lengths to investigate a customer, it still may be denied a license. Most likely this will be because of the national importance of the export controls that have been implemented (such as weapons technology). Nevertheless, companies still have an avenue of appeal. A firm could request that the Secretary of Commerce determine the foreign availability of your product. If there is a non-U.S. source of the product that is comparable in quality, a firm may be granted a license to export despite the controls that are in place. Almost certainly, however, an application and appeal will be denied if the business involves exporting controlled weaponry (such as missile technology or nuclear equipment and materials). Supercomputers are also highly controlled because of their strategic significance. There are many global agreements on the trade in these items, and several organizations were devoted to the control of such exports. COCOM (Coordinating Committee for Multilateral Export Control), in particular, was formed in 1949 to prevent the Soviets from acquiring technology that could lead to a military advantage. The organization grew to seventeen members and many affiliates, but after the breakup of the Soviet Union the perceived need for the group faded and the organization has since been disbanded.

⊕ International Insights

Baxter International and the Arab Boycott of Israel

BAXTER INTERNATIONAL IS A Chicago-based manufacturer of hospital supplies. They do business in many different countries, including Israel. For years, however, they wished to expand their business to the lucrative Middle East market; by all estimates this market seemed destined to produce sales in the billions of dollars in the upcoming years. Over the years, Baxter tried a number of strategies to enter this market, including the acquisition of firms that already had a presence there. For example, Baxter spent $53 million in 1982 to acquire Medcom, Inc., a New York–based manufacturer of hospital supplies that had close relations with Saudi Arabia. Their hope was to exploit MedCom's connections with the Saudis to kick-start their Middle East business. After losing money for over a year, Baxter executives were told by Saudi government officials to "stop wasting their time in the Middle East," according to a company document obtained by the *Wall Street Journal*. After several more years in the red, Baxter sold MedCom in 1986 for just $4 million—or just 7 percent of what it had paid for the company. What was the problem here?

The problem, as it turned out, was Baxter's Israeli business. As a result of this business, Baxter was on the Arab League boycott list and the Saudis wanted nothing to do with Baxter. Being shut out of the Middle East, however, bothered Baxter executives. The recently gained riches from oil sales in the 1970s and 1980s promised rich rewards for the company that gained an early footing there. Baxter executives repeatedly discussed entry strategies with a number of Arab countries, like Syria. They also spoke with prominent Syrian lawyers and specialists on the boycott, some even at their Illinois headquarters. These talks did not result in any concrete agreements. In 1988, Baxter suddenly sold their intravenous fluids plant in Israel, although they claim they had been seeking a buyer for some time. And they almost simultaneously announced plans to build a similar plant in Syria in a joint venture operation with the Syrian army. Within the year, Baxter was dropped from the Arab blacklist.

Although these events were noted by prominent observers, they may have just been seen as a very unusual coincidence by skeptics had it not been for some of Baxter's former executives who criticized Baxter's actions. Based on their testimony and other evidence, the Department of Justice filed criminal charges against Baxter. The U.S. grand jury heard evidence about Baxter's sale of discounted hospital supplies to Syria, allegedly as a bribe for being removed from the list. Later, the Department of Commerce also filed civil suits against the company, and shareholders followed with further legal action. In 1993, Baxter pleaded guilty to the criminal charges, paid a large fine ($6.6 million), and suffered other penalties for their violation of the antiboycott law. For example, the government slapped a two-year ban on exports to Syria and Saudi Arabia. Under intense criticism, the Baxter CEO was even forced to resign his position on the board of trustees at Yale University.[47]

As we have said, export controls—such as sanctions, embargoes, and control lists—can often be ineffective because the products can be provided by other countries who are not so constrained. If the issue is important enough, a set of countries may wish to go one step further to restrict trade by enacting a **boycott**. If sanctions and embargoes represent a unilateral unwillingness to engage in trade (such as the United States embargo against Cuba), a boycott is a multilateral or collaborative effort to do the same thing. Examples of the collaboration of many countries to try to restrict trade include: (1) the COCOM group just mentioned, and (2) the international coalition formed to confront Iraq's invasion of Kuwait in 1990. That coalition survived until the invasion of

boycott
Collaborative effort among countries to prohibit international trade with another nation

Iraq over ten years later. Boycotts have the same purpose as sanctions, embargoes, and other controls; they are simply more extreme in their scope. Because of the collaborative nature of boycotts, they tend to be more effective than export controls established by only one country. This also means that boycotts are very much more difficult to organize and implement, as illustrated by the incredible effort of getting traditional enemies—Israel and Jordan or Saudi Arabia—on the same side against Iraq.

One other problem with boycotts is that unless the organizing is very complete, it can polarize sides against one another. An example of this situation is the boycott instituted against Israel in December 1954 by the League of Arab States. The League (currently composed of twenty-one nations) agreed that companies that traded with Israel could be blacklisted and not permitted to do business with League members. Because of its close political ties with Israel, the United States enacted *antiboycott* laws that prohibit American firms from complying with or otherwise supporting the boycott by refusing to do business with Israel or a blacklisted firm. Courts have ruled that merely by returning an Arab League questionnaire that sought information about business relations with Israel, Briggs and Stratton Corporation was in violation of the law.[48] Given the volatile situation in the Middle East, it remains to be seen what will happen regarding business risk for firms vis-à-vis the boycott. After the Gulf War, some Arab countries (like Kuwait) resumed doing business with Israel, but events that occurred since the beginning of the Palestinian Intifada in 2000 have crushed any hopes that the nearly fifty-year boycott may be coming to an end. Clearly, this presents a risk to U.S. business that some other countries do not face, and the accompanying International Insights on U.S-based Baxter International shows that the penalties for violating this law include large fines.

But businesses in other countries can face even bigger hurdles. Consider the plight of Nassar Investment Company, a Palestinian firm that exports stone and tile products around the world. They face pressures, not only from the Israeli military, but also from their Arab neighbors. Last year, during Operation Defensive Shield (Israel's response to a wave of terrorist attacks), troops took over Nassar's stone-cutting facility and used it as a camp to interrogate suspected militants. The plant was shut down for nearly two months. In 2001 terrorists had taken refuge along the periphery of the plant, leading to a shelling by Israeli tanks that resulted in a million-dollar loss of cranes, forklifts, and more. Not only that, but Nassar simultaneously faces a boycott of all Palestinian products by Lebanon and Syria and suspicion by other countries of anything that comes from the West Bank and Gaza for fear it has some Israeli content. Nassar's solution to these big problems is ingenious. To protect against holdups at Israeli checkpoints, it has built up a three-year supply reserve; to get around restrictions on Palestinian vehicles entering Israel, it has set up a separate company in Jerusalem using Israeli trucks driven by Israeli workers; and finally, it has set up factories in Arab countries to avoid the boycott. While nearly 20 percent of Palestinian exporters have gone out of business since the intifada began and the rest have laid off nearly 40 percent of their workforces, Nassar's steps have kept them in business and successful.[49]

To summarize, it is important to consider the extent of export controls as risk factors in international business. Exports are significant parts of the economy of every country; they provide a much-needed foreign exchange and are the source of many jobs. But they are only one (important) example of external economic risk factors. In Exhibit 2.4, we presented many other types of risk, including restrictions on foreign investment. For example, one risk factor is the presence of restrictions on the extent of foreign investment in a particular country. Most EU countries, for example, restrict the ownership of television and radio stations to nationals. Germany gives preference to companies that are majority-owned by its nationals when awarding licenses to broadcast. The United States requires foreign ownership of radio and TV stations to be limited to 25 percent, whereas Greece and Portugal restrict such ownership to 25 and 15 percent, respectively. Typically, restrictions like these are imposed to prevent foreign control of critical industries (e.g., finance, communications, etc.). Clearly, these restrictions increase the risk of doing business since they prevent the foreign multinational from having sole control of the operation of a firm. Interestingly, they have not stopped Australian, British, and Japanese firms from investing in such restricted U.S. industries, although these firms probably weighed the risks against potential rewards.

One of the biggest external risks that companies face is the lack of legal protection for their products and trademarks in a foreign country. The most common legal protections are the use of patents, trademarks, and copyrights. A number of international agreements are in place to provide protection. The Paris Convention, for example, is a set of international guidelines recognized by nearly eighty countries. Ultimately, however, a multinational must rely on the enforcement of laws within a country to protect its products and intellectual property rights. To comply with WTO requirements, in the year 2005 India will again begin to honor international pharmaceutical patents—something it has not done since the early 1970s. Since that time, the market share of foreign drug firms has dropped considerably, but with regulations on the horizon foreign direct investment is again pouring into India.[50] Nevertheless, if the reward is great enough, a firm may wish to take the risk of operating without legal protection altogether or run the risk in a country where the enforcement is lax at best. Such is the case in Spain, where unlicensed generics create a major headache for U.S. drug firms. Spain has a complex court system, one with no special courts or judges with expertise in patent law or the complex pharmaceutical industry. So, when U.S.-based Merck sued the Spanish generic maker Chemo-Iberica for violating its patent on Zocor (the anticholesterol drug), the case was mired in Spanish courts for years. At one point, Chemo even claimed it had developed a new fungus fermentation process (aspergillus obscurus) to produce Zocor, thereby bypassing Merck's patent (the generic price was about $11 vs. Zocor's price of $24). This procedure was "obscurus" all right—in fact, mycology experts finally convinced the court this procedure just didn't exist! Finally, Spanish courts ruled for Merck; but they awarded no damages and the patent expired two days later anyway.[51]

Take another example, the Chinese market. Firms that enter China are often required by the government to reveal the critical design features or recipes of their products.[52] Professor Kenneth DeWoskin, a China expert at the University of Michigan School of Business, says, "Chinese research and design institutes look for the best technology in the country and spread it around. They also examine plans and specifications of new ventures, so there's bound to be some leakage."[53] Clearly, there is a good deal of "leakage," and the losses extend beyond the entertainment and computer industry. For example, after DuPont introduced its Londax herbicide in China, it decided to build a $25-million plant in Shanghai to produce the chemical. By then, however, a state-owned company jumped into the market with a much cheaper knockoff of Londax. Likewise, shortly after Pilkington opened a plant in China to make glass, a state glass factory sent an order for production equipment to Germany—complete with detailed and obviously pirated plans that were emblazoned with Pilkington's name! And in plain sight of police on main streets in Guangzhou and Shanghai, Chinese music fans can pick up the latest popular music CDs or Microsoft Office for about $1.50. The U.S. Trade Representative's office says, "Anyone can walk into a store in Beijing and buy a pirated copy of Microsoft software. The store simply copies it onto a few blank diskettes while you wait." Toy makers such as Mattel and Hasbro are especially concerned, as it is common for their new toys on display at the international Hong Kong Toy Fair to be displayed by a Chinese competitor. Since China makes about 70 percent of world's toys, including those of American companies, the design can easily be copied. After Mattel decided to prototype their new designs in-house and then bring them to the Hong Kong fair, their staff had to chase away would-be copiers who were using spy cameras, copiers, and Palm Pilot sketch pads to copy designs. Mattel no longer attends the fair.[54]

It's not just products, either—protecting a brand name in the China market is difficult at best. A bogus Chinese breakfast cereal product called Kongalu Cornstrips has a trademark and packaging identical to that of Kellogg's Cornflakes. A small Chinese computer manufacturer, called Mr. Sun, has used Sun Microsystem's trademark for all its machines.[55] And Shanghai consumers can now enjoy coffee at a series of Xing Ba Ke stores. The loose translation of this is "Shanghai Starbucks," although you don't have to read closely as their logo looks identical to that of Starbucks. The general manager of Xing Ba Ke says "we have a totally different operation" and cites waiters and higher prices as examples of this "new" business model. Starbucks is hardly convinced and had gone to the mat before to protect its brand/logo by suing companies called "Mr. Charbucks" and "Sambucks" among others.[56]

Despite this danger of product piracy once a product's critical features are revealed, many companies move into the Chinese market anyway. Coca-Cola is one firm, however, that steadfastly refuses such revelations and thus has been careful in China. And because of a similar restriction in India, at one point the firm left that country altogether. Coca-Cola quit India after the government demanded that they reveal their secret recipe and transfer other technical information to local management.[57] Likewise, two years of negotiating for an important minivan venture between Chrysler and the Chinese government fell apart at the last minute when China demanded that Chrysler reveal its manufacturing techniques. Many companies, such as Pilkington, are now wary of seeing their partners become their rivals. New Balance is aggressive in this regard. At a shoe factory in Southern China, a man named George Arnold closely inspected the stitching and workmanship of a run of nearly 7,000 New Balance shoes. Mr. Arnold pronounced the lot as real and promised Horace Chang, the plant owner, that he'd wire the $120,000 payment soon. But, in fact, this was a sting orchestrated by New Balance using private detectives. They and others such as Rolex, Reebok, Gucci, and Cartier are making these interdiction efforts to stem the tide of counterfeiting. Interestingly, Mr. Chang was a licensed supplier and manufacturer for New Balance, one whom they had worked with since 1995. But after a disagreement with him in regard to shoe quality and brand name, and armed with evidence that his factory was producing "on the side," New Balance began its crackdown. It was galling for them to see their $60 shoe being sold for around $20, with the latter emerging from Mr. Chang's factory. This case is still

EXHIBIT 2.5   *Business Software Piracy Rates in Various Countries*

Country	Piracy Rate
China	96%
France	47%
Germany	30%
Japan	38%
Russia	89%
Thailand	79%
United States	24%
Vietnam	97%

Source: Adapted from ____ (2003). Business Software Alliance (BSA) Website, **www.bsa.org**.

being worked out as of 2004, but New Balance has severed its relation with Mr. Chang and is worried about his near half-million-shoe inventory. This reflects an increasing trend for *real* products—not knockoffs—to be in competition in the marketplace. Procter & Gamble recently fired a supplier that sold their empty shampoo bottles to a counterfeiter who filled them with different product, and Unilever recently found its partner was producing extra soap and selling it directly to stores.[58]

Stopping this illegal activity is difficult, especially at the company level. In general, however, research shows that the presence of laws protecting intellectual property rights has a positive impact on foreign direct investment and that this is especially the case among developing countries.[59] Piracy, the software variety in particular, seems to happen in many places, not just China or other developing nations. For example, the *Wall Street Journal* reported on a raid by the Spanish police at a Madrid monastery where Jesuit priests trained their students in computers—relying mostly on pirated software.[60] Exhibit 2.5 shows that while piracy is a big problem in China, there are other problem markets. In fact, while the U.S. piracy rate is among the lowest in the world, the total cost is among the highest (because of the number of computer users in the U.S. relative to other countries). Likewise, many of these knockoffs and originals alike are targeted to the U.S. market. Exhibit 2.6 shows the top source country of fake products seized by U.S. Customs as well as the most common products that are faked. Of course, many items get through. We recently saw knockoffs of $250 Oakley sunglasses going for $15 near the Pike Street Market in Seattle. And, students here at the University of Dayton were themselves a source of some leakage. On a summer exchange program in Thailand, they brought home DVD copies of the hit movie *Finding Nemo*, even before it had been released to video stores in the United States. The price on Bangkok streets was $1.[61] Given the importance that knowledge plays in the economy, some analysts have targeted intellectual property as America's main competitive advantage in the 21st century.[62] Thus, the ability to preserve those property rights may become an even more important risk factor for the U.S. economy in the near future. By 2006, all WTO members are to have implemented basic rules for protection and enforcement of counterfeiting and intellectual property protection.

EXHIBIT 2.6   *Frequency and Brand of Counterfeit Goods Confiscated*

Country of Origin for All Illegal Goods Seized by U.S. Customs		Brand of Illegal Good Seized (Listed by # of shipments seized)	
China	47%	Nintendo	350
Taiwan	26%	Nike	250
Pakistan	7%	Adidas	200
South Korea	6%	Nokia	150
Indonesia	4%	Louis Vuitton	49
Thailand	3%		

Source: Adapted from ____ (2003). Imitating property is theft. *The Economist*, May 17. 51–54.

EXHIBIT 2.7   *The Ten Least and Most Risky Countries in Which to Do Business*

Countries with the Most Business Risk	Countries with the Least Business Risk
1. Ecuador	1. Luxembourg
2. Iraq	2. Norway
3. Cuba	3. Singapore
4. Russia	4. Finland
5. Myanmar	5. Switzerland
6. Sudan	6. Netherlands
7. Vietnam	7. Ireland
8. Cameroon	8. Denmark
9. Pakistan	9. Brunei
10. Nigeria	10. Canada

Source: "The Ten Least and Most Risky Countries in Which to Do Business" from **www.prsgroup.com/commonhtml/toorank.html**. Copyright ©PRS Group. Used with permission.

Summary of Risk Factors As we have demonstrated, there are a large number of legal and political risk factors associated with doing business in a foreign country. One of the pluses of using a category system like the one we presented in Exhibit 2.4 is that factors can be itemized and evaluated. A firm considering a big investment in a foreign country may wish to systematically weight all these factors themselves or use information provided by companies specializing in risk assessment. Exhibit 2.7 presents the top ten most and least risky countries in which to do business (out of nearly 130 countries). China, for example, had an overall risk ranking of 32 relative to the other 130 countries. Despite this rating and the large number of risks it represents, many countries are rushing to invest in China. These facts show that a firm must still make a judgment about the overall risk of doing business. If the overall score is indeed too high, a multinational might drop that country from consideration unless the risk can be managed or reduced in some way.

EXHIBIT 2.8   *A Classification of Approaches to Managing Risk*

	Direct	Indirect
Defensive/Reactive	• Take legal action • Make operations dependent on parent company • Control makeup of management	• Risk insurance • Contingency planning method • Home country government pressure
Linking/Merging	• Long-term agreements (e.g., NAFTA) • Joint ventures • Promoting host goals	• Lobbying of foreign governments • Becoming good corporate citizen to host country

Managing Political Risk

One advantage of quantifying risk is the ability to make better decisions about entering or avoiding a country or whether to scale back existing operations in a particularly risky country. Leaving or scaling back are not, however, your only options. Another advantage of using a rating scheme such as the one discussed earlier is that serious sources of risk can be isolated. It may then be possible for a firm to influence or manage some of the factors that cause the risk. Take, for example, a situation where labor relations are shaky at best. If this is a critical risk factor, then the multinational must recognize the fact that risk is not static. Good management might be able to deal with poor labor relations by making some concessions.

Categorizing Risk Reduction   There are a large number of ways a multinational could potentially stave off risk. In fact, there are probably as many methods to reduce risk as there are sources of risk. For our purposes, however, we can classify all these techniques into a more manageable set of categories. For example, there are *defensive/reactive strategies* that a multinational could use to deal with risk.[63] These types of methods try to keep company operations or other assets out of the reach of the risk factor—such as a hostile government. There are also *linking/merging strategies*. These usually entail methods by which a firm tries to get closer to the risky country, perhaps even making itself indispensable to the local economy. Each of these types of strategies can be direct, in that it tries to take on the problem in a head-on way, such as by legal action. The strategy could also be indirect, approaching the risk in a roundabout way, with hopes that in the long run risk will be reduced. Exhibit 2.8 presents some examples of each of the four types of risk management.

Examples of Risk Reduction   Let's look at a few examples of each of these strategies. A type of *direct/defensive* risk reduction is to make operations in the target country dependent on your operations in one or more other countries that are less risky. This dependency allows your firm to preserve control over key supplies, components, and critical technology that are necessary to run the subsidiary, and it can have a number of positive effects on the firm's exposure to risk. For example, operation dependency would make your subsidiary less attractive for expropriation by host government X. This is because the plant could not operate without supplies you provide via a plant in country Y. This strategy would also leave your firm less open to risks of trademark or copyright theft if critical technology was deployed in another country. Thus, a multinational can reap multiple benefits from one action, a characteristic typical of many of the risk management strategies listed in Exhibit 2.8.

A firm can also use several different risk management techniques simultaneously and may also wish to use some *direct/linking strategies*. For example, a multinational may wish to enter into long-term agreements with a foreign country that *specify* treatment of its subsidiary, and the home country may do the same. The North American Free Trade Agreement that we discussed earlier is one recent example of this method. The option to enter into joint ventures (discussed in Chapters 8 and 9) may be available; in this case, the subsidiary is already jointly owned by either the host government or a firm headquartered in the host country. In situations like this, a multinational has less equity at risk and other national firms share a good deal of the risk, but there are significant barriers to overcome in order to have successful links.[64]

Concurrently, a multinational may also wish to use a set of indirect methods. It may purchase political risk insurance as an *indirect/defensive* strategy. Political risk insurance is an indirect strategy because it does nothing to deal with or alter the risk; it simply tries to protect the firm if and when the risk materializes. Several private firms provide insurance to cover some risks that may be realized in doing international business. In the United States, a federal agency, the Overseas Private Investment Corporation (OPIC), also provides similar coverage. Started in 1971 in order to promote private American business investment in developing countries, OPIC is self-sustaining, has recorded a positive net income every year of operation, and thus runs at no net cost to U.S. taxpayers. Currently, the insurance programs are available for new and expanding business in over 140 countries.

Risk insurance covers some, but certainly not all of the risks we discussed earlier. A company can purchase protection against expropriation and confiscation of its foreign enterprise or coverage for property and income losses caused by political violence. For example, the effects of declared or undeclared wars, civil war, revolutions, and many types of civil strife (terrorism and sabotage) are covered; OPIC compensates the investor's share of income losses resulting from political violence and other risk factors. A multinational can even purchase an offsite rider to the policy that compensates for losses resulting from damage outside its facility that affect its business (e.g., damage to railways, power stations, and suppliers). Finally, OPIC also protects the multinational against currency inconvertibility. This is not insurance against currency devaluation; the company has to assume this risk itself. Instead, investors are compensated if they suffer new currency restrictions that prevent the conversion and transfer of profits from their foreign investment. In general, this insurance is very comprehensive and can help many firms overcome their reluctance to deal with risk factors in a foreign operation or investment.[65] You will learn a lot more about OPIC by completing the exercise at the end of this chapter.

Other examples of indirect/defensive strategies are presented in Exhibit 2.8. For example, although many firms clearly recognize that the risk of doing business in a certain country is high, they are willing to take on the risk if a set of contingency plans provides a viable way to manage it. This "scenario planning" approach, proven in military applications, is becoming an increasingly popular method for balancing risk in business.[66] Or a firm could gradually increase its investment in a foreign operation while appealing to its government to pressure the other host government. This is now a common practice in Japan, where American automakers (among other industries) perceive that the risks of closed markets and opportunities can be altered by pressuring the U.S. administration to get concessions from the Japanese.

Finally, a multinational can use *indirect/linking* strategies to remove or reduce some forms of risk. One way it can do this is by making itself a "good corporate citizen." For example, the multinational could contribute to local charities, support public projects, or otherwise promote its good deeds. Clearly, this strategy involves merging with the local community as opposed to pulling away, and it is indirect because it is hoped that the goodwill generated by the donations will eventually spread to the company itself. Starbucks' approach is a good example of marketing locally while thinking or doing business globally. While we discussed their effort to protect their trademark in China, they also have made efforts to position their stores as members of the local community. Their twenty-nine stores in Beijing, for example, support local groups, and they have developed inexpensive moon cakes for the traditional Autumn moon festival. When the mistaken U.S. bombing of the Chinese embassy in Belgrade occurred in 1999, protestors cut through Starbucks, buying coffee on their way to (violent) protests at the U.S. embassy. Sales actually rose at Starbucks that day, whereas other prominent American businesses suffered some damage.[67]

Indirect and linking strategies are very common for many multinationals. Japanese efforts to increase their U.S. philanthropic activity in the late 1980s and early 1990s are an example. Finally, lobbying is another method of this type of risk reduction. In the United States, special interest groups in the areas of steel, automobiles, textiles, and computer chips have been adept at gaining import restrictions that reduce the risk in their businesses.[68] Conversely, foreign firms long ago recognized the important role that lobbying plays in the operation of the U.S. federal government. Indeed, the number of registered lobbyists to the federal government grew from about 7,000 in 1991 to over 15,000 in 1999. As an alternative strategy of this type, a government itself could invest in a venture in another country, as Thailand has done with its plans to open over 1,000 Thai restaurants in the United States.[69]

Investing in Risky Countries   These are just a few of the many methods that firms use to reduce their risks in doing international business. Apparently, these methods are enough to convince firms to make what would otherwise be considered unwise investments. As mentioned, the situation in China now is a good example. China is rated by several groups as a relatively risky place to invest, yet foreign capital is rushing into the country. Many of these foreign enterprises have tried to temper their risk by entering into joint ventures and by lobbying their own and the Chinese government.

This situation is equally true in eastern Europe, where companies feel that they face a variety of problems and risks. A survey of eighty-seven companies that have invested in eastern Europe suggests that most of the challenges of doing business in these formerly communist countries involve political, economic, and legal uncertainties or risks.[70] Just as with China, however, these risks have apparently failed to deter Western investors. More than half report that they have increased their stakes in eastern Europe. And even though they report that the former Soviet Union is fraught with risks, 52 percent say they are still considering this area for investment. This trend suggests that for some firms quantitative analysis (as in risk assessment) is helpful, but it does not always and directly lead to a decision. There is not always a clear link between the results of the analysis and the decision to be made. This is even truer when the decision concerns ethical or social responsibility issues. These issues are the subject of our next chapter.

Chapter Summary

We reviewed several of the most important legal systems in operation around the world today, including the *civil law, common law*, and *Islamic law* systems. Each system has different implications for commerce that takes place under its jurisdiction. In common law systems, for example, businesses can experience a good deal of litigation because continual interpretation of statutes is typical in such systems. The other systems have their own characteristics and constraints.

Laws operate (or sometimes fail to operate) within a particular political system, and a new political regime can dramatically change the legal system. So we highlighted the importance of these issues above and beyond the rule of law. We also showed that the amount of *political risk* incurred by a multinational can have major negative effects. Political risk can result from a large number of events or actions taken by governments or groups of people. Examples of political/economic risk faced by a multinational include *nationalization* and *expropriation* of its assets by a foreign government, each of which can have disastrous consequences for a firm. A variety of domestic economic conditions can also affect a multinational's business, including a lack of infrastructure and the enactment of strict environmental laws. Finally, a third set of risk factors include those external economic relations one country has with another. These include *tariffs* and a variety of export controls (e.g., *sanctions, embargoes*, and others). We provided an example of the U.S. export control

system and its complexities to illustrate our point. We also discussed other important risks that businesses face and how their impact can be calibrated.

We finished the chapter with a discussion of one of the most important points of all—what a multinational can and should do after it acknowledges the risks it faces. The options include strategies of *direct risk reduction* (e.g., negotiating with the foreign government) and/or *indirect* efforts to stave off potentially catastrophic effects if the risk materializes (e.g., purchasing U.S. government–backed risk insurance). Finally, we recognize that while some multinational actions might be both legally consistent and politically astute or expedient, the action might still be inconsistent with company or society values.

Discussion Questions

1. What are the major differences among the three main legal systems that exist? How might each affect commerce that is conducted within its purview?

2. How might a Japanese and American lawyer react in each other's country? What behaviors might you see, and which ones could you tie to their respective legal systems?

3. What are some of the forms of political risk? Why might Nigeria, Peru, or Indonesia be considered relatively risky places to do business?

4. What steps would you recommend to deal with forms of risk in the above countries?

Up to the Challenge?

Bo Concepts: How Do You Knock Out the Knockoffs?

IN THE OPENING box we presented a tough situation for Bo Concepts. Their thriving business in China was being dramatically threatened by Chinese copycats; revenues were dropping

dramatically and the number of copycat competitors was growing exponentially. Worse yet, copying is common in China because it's easy to get away with. Laws are sketchy and ambiguous and enforcement is suspect, to say the least. Keeping all this in mind—as well as the issues raised in the chapter—what are Bo Concepts and its franchise owner Simon Lichtenberg to do?

In his home country and some others, Lichtenberg would begin by asking a judge to order a preliminary injunction to stop the firms from copying. But China does not have a set of detailed procedures for such injunctions, and as a result their judges rarely invoke them. Undeterred, Lichtenberg hired private investigators from Pinkerton to collect evidence and present it to the Chinese agency responsible for such transgressions (the State Administration for Industry and Commerce, SAIC). This was also a dead end; nothing resulted from the investigation.

With sales continuing to drop, Lichtenberg didn't let the matter sit for long. Six months later, he was back at the SAIC's doorstep. But who was he to talk with about this? Though he could speak Mandarin, who would he speak it with? The agency has literally hundreds of departments, and only one officer in each with the authority to take action. "The system is not made for foreign investors to find these guys," said Lichtenberg. So instead of the rule of law, he used good old-fashioned connections—called *guanxi* in China. A friend of Lichtenberg's knew the head of Shanghai's SAIC and informed him of the situation. This person in turn called a district director, who assembled a committee of twenty-five experts to review the matter. Lichtenberg was keen to convince the committee that using the company's name and catalog was unfair. Unbelievably, these items are not specifically covered in Chinese law, and thus officials are loath to rule on them for fear it would upset a superior who more properly should decide.

It was even worse among some Chinese officials. "Their attitude was, if your furniture sells well, why wouldn't others copy it?" Lichtenberg reported. It took nearly four months to do the convincing, but once done, the board moved quickly. By early 1999, a set of committee-ordered raids resulted in confiscations and some changes. These and related efforts reduced the pirating of Bo Concepts' product and catalog. Part of the stoppage came from the intimidation of facing the SAIC board. But not all were so persuaded. No arrests were made, nor were any fines handed out.

And the committee did not perceive jurisdiction over design infringement, only the brand issue and some unfair competition. To deal with the infringement issue, the persistent Lichtenberg turned to the Chinese patent bureau, which he found was located on the third floor of an old building in a seedy part of Shanghai. The toilets were backed up and stank and the place was in very poor shape, but the old men who sat at their desks drinking green tea got to work looking at the problem.

This group was also helpful to Bo Concepts. The bureau began a series of meetings with an intimidated group of copycatters. Some claimed they weren't copying and others said they didn't know it was illegal; regardless, the board was convincing and required the firms to cease and desist or to combine forces with Bo Concepts in a joint venture. On a final front, Bo Concepts brought suit against one of the larger firms it thought was responsible for a majority of the copying, asking for $180,000. The case is currently stuck in the Intermediate Court, and it's not clear that Bo Concepts will win this one. The defendant claims that Bo Concepts did not apply for patents in China during the six-month period after it filed the original patents in Denmark, a Chinese requirement and a mistake often made by foreigners. The Counterfeiting Coalition actually recommends to foreign businesses that they automatically apply for such patents, even if they don't plan to do business in China in the foreseeable future, to protect themselves.

Whatever happens with this case, Bo Concepts feels it has made significant progress. Even though some new and smaller copycats pop up now and then, they no longer represent that much of a threat to the company. And many of the high-end outlets that sell Bo Concepts products are also refusing to stock the knockoffs because of the legal action and the effect on their image. For Lichtenberg, persistence paid off. While it required considerable time and money to protect their product, along with some significant help from the Danish embassy, it does seem possible to stem the knockoff tide in China. You may wish to look closer at this particular company (**www.boconcept.com**) to follow up on Bo Concepts' efforts at protecting its products, and to match this with current views about business risk in China (**www.prsgroup. com**).[71]

International Development

Culture Knowledge Quiz

Purpose

Few, if any, traditions and values are universally held. Many business dealings have succeeded or failed because of a manager's awareness or lack of understanding of the traditions and values of his or her foreign counterparts. With the world business community so closely intertwined and interdependent, it is critical that managers today become increasingly aware of the differences that exist. Toward that end, the purpose of this exercise is the following:

- To stimulate awareness of cultural differences
- To promote consideration of the impact of cultural differences in a global economy
- To stimulate dialogue between domestic and international students
- To explore issues raised by culturally diverse workforces

Instructions

Working alone or with a small group, complete the sentences. If you are taking the quiz with students from countries other than your own, explore what the answer might be in your country and theirs. Your instructor will lead a discussion of the correct answers in class.

1. In Japan, loudly slurping your soup is considered to be
   a. rude and obnoxious.
   b. a sign that you like the soup.
   c. okay at home but not in public.
   d. something only foreigners do.

2. In Korea, business leaders tend to
   a. encourage strong commitment to teamwork and cooperation.
   b. encourage competition among subordinates.
   c. discourage subordinates from reporting directly, preferring information to come through well-defined channels.
   d. encourage close relationships with their subordinates.

3. In Japan, virtually every kind of drink is sold in public vending machines except for
   a. beer.
   b. diet drinks with saccharin.
   c. already sweetened coffee.
   d. soft drinks from U.S. companies.

4. In Latin America, managers
   a. are most likely to hire members of their own families.
   b. consider hiring members of their own families to be inappropriate.
   c. stress the importance of hiring members of minority groups.
   d. usually hire more people than are actually needed to do a job.

5. In Ethiopia, when a woman opens the front door of her home, it means
   a. she is ready to receive guests for a meal.
   b. only family members may enter.
   c. religious spirits may move freely in and out of the home.
   d. she has agreed to have sex with any man who enters.

6. In Latin America, businesspeople
   a. consider it impolite to make eye contact while talking to one another.
   b. always wait until the other person is finished speaking before starting to speak.
   c. touch each other more than North Americans do under similar circumstances.
   d. avoid touching one another as it is considered an invasion of privacy.

7. The principal religion in Malaysia is
   a. Buddhism.
   b. Judaism.
   c. Christianity.
   d. Islam.

8. In Thailand
   a. it is common to see men walking along holding hands.
   b. it is common to see a man and a woman holding hands in public.
   c. it is rude for men and women to walk together.
   d. men and women traditionally kiss each other on meeting in the street.

9. When eating in India, it is appropriate to
   a. take food with your right hand and eat with your left.
   b. take food with your left hand and eat with your right.
   c. take food and eat it with your left hand.
   d. take food and eat it with your right hand.

10. Pointing your toes at someone in Thailand is
    a. a symbol of respect, much like the Japanese bow.
    b. considered rude even if it is done by accident.
    c. an invitation to dance.
    d. the standard public greeting.

11. American managers tend to base the performance appraisals of their subordinates on performance, while in Iran, managers are more likely to base their performance appraisals on
    a. religion.
    b. seniority.
    c. friendship.
    d. ability.

12. In China, the status of every business negotiation is
    a. reported daily in the press.
    b. private, and details are not discussed publicly.
    c. subjected to scrutiny by a public tribunal on a regular basis.
    d. directed by the elders of every commune.

13. When rewarding an Hispanic worker for a job well done, it is best not to
    a. praise him or her publicly.
    b. say "thank you."
    c. offer a raise.
    d. offer a promotion.

14. In some South American countries, it is considered normal and acceptable to show up for a social appointment
    a. ten to fifteen minutes early.
    b. ten to fifteen minutes late.
    c. fifteen minutes to an hour late.
    d. one to two hours late.

15. In France, when friends talk to one another
    a. they generally stand about three feet apart.
    b. it is typical to shout.
    c. they stand closer to one another than Americans do.
    d. it is always with a third party present.

16. When giving flowers as gifts in western Europe, be careful not to give
    a. tulips and jonquils.
    b. daisies and lilacs.
    c. chrysanthemums and calla lilies.
    d. lilacs and apple blossoms.

17. The appropriate gift-giving protocol for a male executive doing business in Saudi Arabia is to
    a. give a man a gift from you to his wife.
    b. present gifts to the wife or wives in person.
    c. give gifts only to the eldest wife.
    d. not give a gift to the wife at all.

18. If you want to give a necktie or a scarf to a Latin American, it is best to avoid the color
    a. red.
    b. purple.
    c. green.
    d. black.

19. The doors in German offices and homes are generally kept
    a. wide open to symbolize an acceptance and welcome of friends and strangers.
    b. slightly ajar to suggest that people should knock before entering.
    c. half-opened suggesting that some people are welcome and others are not.
    d. tightly shut to preserve privacy and personal space.

20. In the area that was formerly West Germany, leaders who display charisma are
    a. not among the most desired.
    b. the ones most respected and sought after.
    c. invited frequently to serve on boards of cultural organizations.
    d. pushed to get involved in political activities.

21. American managers running businesses in Mexico have found that by increasing the salaries of Mexican workers, they
    a. increased the numbers of hours the workers were willing to work.
    b. enticed more workers to work night shifts.
    c. decreased the number of hours workers would agree to work.
    d. decreased production rates.

22. Chinese culture teaches people
    a. to seek psychiatric help for personal problems.
    b. to avoid conflict and internalize personal problems.
    c. to deal with conflict with immediate confrontation.
    d. to seek help from authorities whenever conflict arises.

23. One wedding gift that should not be given to a Chinese couple would be
    a. a jade bowl.
    b. a clock.
    c. a basket of oranges.
    d. shirts embroidered with dragon patterns.

24. In Venezuela, New Year's Eve is generally spent
    a. in quiet family gatherings.
    b. at wild neighborhood street parties.
    c. in restaurants with horns, hats, and live music and dancing.
    d. at pig roasts on the beach.

25. If you order "bubble and squeak" in a London pub, you will get
    a. two goldfish fried in olive oil.
    b. a very cold beer in a chilled glass, rather than the usual warm beer.
    c. Alka Seltzer® and a glass of water.
    d. chopped cabbage and mashed potatoes fried together.

26. When a stranger in India wants to know what you do for a living and how much you earn, he will
    a. ask your guide.
    b. invite you to his home and, after getting to know you, will ask.
    c. come over and ask you directly, without introduction.
    d. respect your privacy above all.

27. When you feel you are being taken advantage of in a business exchange in Vietnam, it is important to
    a. let the anger show in your face but not in your words.
    b. say that you are angry, but keep your facial expression neutral.
    c. not show any anger in any way.
    d. end the business dealings immediately and walk away.

28. When a taxi driver in India shakes his head from side to side, it probably means
    a. he thinks your price is too high.
    b. he isn't going in your direction.
    c. he will take you where you want to go.
    d. he doesn't understand what you're asking.

29. In England, holding your index and middle fingers up in a vee with the back of your hand facing another person is seen as
    a. a gesture of peace.
    b. a gesture of victory.
    c. a signal that you want two of something.
    d. a vulgar gesture.

Tapping into the Global Network

Calibrating International Business Risk

Purpose

To provide some hands-on understanding of risk in an international environment and to apply that to one or more specific countries.

Instructions

In this chapter we talked a good bit about managing risk. The Overseas Private Investment Corporation (OPIC) is a U.S. federal agency whose purpose is to provide services, including insurance, to companies that invest overseas. One of the services they offer is political risk insurance to protect firms against the risks of expropriation, war, revolution, and some negative economic events (e.g., inconvertibility of local currency). The OPIC is particularly well organized and service oriented. Their website is excellent and they also have an automated information line that allows customers to request many documents explaining OPIC programs. For this exercise, we want you to choose one or two countries in conjunction with your instructor. Once you target your countries, either check out the OPIC webpage (**www.opic.gov**) or call their information line (202-336-8651) to request information.

This website is easy to use. It is chock full of information. Click on the Program Handbook icon as well as the help/site information tab for important information. After you locate the documents, look through them and see what information you would find useful for investigating the countries you have chosen. Call or visit the OPIC webpage again and obtain any additional documents.

Using all of your sources of information, prepare a brief (one page or less) report on your country/countries. Some of the questions you may wish to address in this report are:

- In general, what is the OPIC and what is its purpose?
- Are your countries eligible for OPIC support?
- In particular, what kind of support is available?
- How would you or an interested company request support?
- What exactly is insured by your participation in the program?
- What is the approximate cost to your company of such insurance?

To complete this report, you may wish to provide the political risk rating of your chosen countries. To get this number and an interpretation, you will need to refer to one of three sources: (1) Euromoney's Annual Survey of Country Risk, (2) a more widely available source, such as the annual risk ratings that appear in the *Wall Street Journal*, or (3) the *Planning Review*'s annual issue on political and economic risk for 101 countries. If the countries you choose are not on this list, select others that you think are similar in political risk and briefly mention in your report why you think the risk is similar. Finally, you may wish to contact the Department of Commerce Trade Information Center (**http://www.trade.gov/td/tic/** or 1-800-USA-TRADE) and/or the Export-Import Bank Export Financing Hotline (**http://www.exim.gov/** or 1-800-424-5201) for further information about the countries you have chosen for your report.

3

Doing Things Right: International Ethics and Social Responsibility

Learning Objectives

After reading this chapter, you should be able to:

▸ Distinguish between the two major approaches to ethics in international management: universalism and relativism.

▸ Identify cross-national differences in ethical views and practices.

▸ Recognize how multinationals deal with unethical practices by foreign governments.

▸ Understand the Foreign Corrupt Practices Act and its implications for U.S. multinationals.

▸ Pinpoint the social costs that accompany the ongoing economic transition occurring in many countries and how multinationals may contribute to them.

INTERNATIONAL CHALLENGE

Competitive Intelligence: Dumpster Diving for That Extra Edge

❝I DON'T EVER want to be in a fair fight. I want an edge everyplace I go."—Herbert M. Baum, CEO of Quaker State Corp.

Mr. Baum's comment gives you a sense of the high stakes in the competitive fight facing many multinationals. The "edge" that he refers to, however, could be *competitive intelligence* (CI). While it isn't supposed to involve blatantly illegal acts like stealing another firm's proprietary documents, CI is often a fuzzy business that skates close to (and sometimes over) the line when it comes to ethics and legality. In some ways, therefore, CI is a gentle term for what we know to be spying! When Oracle went dumpster diving in Microsoft's trashcans for documents and hints of that company's moves, the whole notion of CI received much attention. But most companies have more panache than Oracle. Indeed, that trash operation "was the sort of thing that gives legitimate business intelligence a bad name," say Alden Taylor of Kroll Associates, a large CI firm in New York.

But what exactly is CI? Part strategic planning, CI is designed to anticipate competitors' moves and includes a range of data collection techniques. CI often involves sifting through vast amounts of information for emerging trends and what competitors might be doing about them. Who does CI? Analysts range from librarians to ex-spies, from in-house experts to outside consulting firms. They prowl web pages and trade shows, tramp through the patent office, and keep their eyes and ears open in airports. Companies like Real World Intelligence, for instance, offer customized versions of software created for the CIA. The software scans through voluminous Internet data, such as new product information on firms' web pages. European and Asian multinationals also engage in CI (and industrial espionage, too); they've actually been in the CI business longer than their American counterparts.

How well does CI work? Pretty well, according to insiders. Former bosses of Monsanto's CI unit estimated returns to the tune of $50 million annually. Motorola's former chair, Robert Galvin, hired former intelligence officers to set up a CI unit for the firm back in the 1970s. Since then, Motorola has never been blindsided in the way Xerox was in the 1980s, when Japanese firms cut into the firm's copier market share. Indeed, their unit is now directed by its third ex-CIA operative in a row!

The real issue for business ethicists isn't whether CI helps the bottom line, but whether it is morally defensible. Consider this sequence of events carried out by a food company that wanted to win market share from a competitor with a surprise price cut. First, CI agents interviewed ex-employees of the competitor. The idea was to find out when the competitor's sales reps had to get approval from senior management before giving retailers a discount (e.g., after a rival had cut prices). Next, the *neighbors* of the competitor's senior executives were telephoned under various pretexts in an effort to learn about their schedules. That's when it was discovered that the competitor's executives were on a European plant tour. An unwitting but cooperative travel agent even handed over their entire itinerary! As a result, the food company's price cuts were launched immediately. Because their approval was needed and they were several time zones away, the competitor's executives couldn't respond quickly. The competitor lost business as a result.

CI and its related activity are on the rise. The number of countries spying on U.S. industry has actually increased—not declined—since the end of the Cold War. A study recently published by PricewaterhouseCoopers claims that economic espionage is on the rise and that it's currently responsible for about $45 billion in annual losses among the Fortune 1000 (U.S.) companies. Some of it is relatively blatant, as when several years ago then Russian President Boris Yeltsin chided domestic business leaders for not effectively using stolen technological secrets! Being an ally is no assurance you'll be free from CI. The former head of French intelligence publicly admitted that he organized a unit to spy on U.S. firms. He also revealed that Air France flight attendants eavesdropped and taped conversations of American businesspeople flying on that airline. Likewise, several prominent cases of theft of industrial secrets from U.S. firms involving Chinese citizens have raised the profile of CI. Mr. Yan Ming Shan, an employee of PetroChina, a state-owned oil company in China, was recently charged with stealing the source code for one of the world's most powerful programs for locating oil and gas deposits. Mr. Shan was training on the software at 3DGeo Development corporation in San Francisco. Employees of 3D noticed something had gone awry with this seismic imaging software and traced the problem to Mr. Shan, who they said transferred this code from their network to his computer. A week after 3D officials confronted him, Mr. Shan was arrested at the San Francisco airport as he was about to board a flight to Shanghai. Officials found the source code on his laptop as well as several programs used to break passwords and gain illegal access (one was called "Crack"). The indictment shows that several weeks prior to Shan's arrest, officials from his company (PetroChina) had visited him and brought him a drive that was capable of storing large amounts of data. Company officials have not yet been charged. 3DGeo's CEO acknowledges "it could have killed the company," but all the same he hopes to continue working with PetroChina—which told the CEO it had no knowledge of Mr. Shan's theft.[1]

So here's your challenge. It's easy to see unethical qualities when someone is arrested and charged with a felony. But, what about more subtle CI activity? Is that unethical? For example, think about whether the following information-gathering activities are unethical:

- Digging through a company's trash on public property.

- Deliberately eavesdropping on private company conversations.

- Sending phony job seekers in response to a competitor's want ads.

- Hiring a competitor's former employees.

- Sending phony visitors to tour a competitor's facilities.
- Attending trade shows where a competitor's wares are displayed.

Take a look at the *Up to the Challenge?* box at end of this chapter for some surprising answers to these questions. Before that, however, try to think of some recommendations you might have for multinationals interested in protecting their secrets from competitors' snooping.[2]

▶ *Ethics and Social Responsibility in International Management*

In this chapter we discuss international issues related to ethics and corporate social responsibility. This topic goes beyond the discussion of politics and laws presented in the previous chapter. Although certain business activities may not violate any legal codes or political norms, they can be seen as simply the wrong thing to do. Of course, many firms have already dealt with ethical issues in the domestic arena. However, with falling trade barriers and rising international commerce, it seems likely that many companies will have to confront ethical issues on a global level in the years ahead.

As we showed, international managers must understand the legal and political framework of the countries in which they do business. However, the fact that some business steps are legal or politically expedient doesn't mean that action should be taken. There are many cases where an action might raise a larger personal, organizational, or societal concern.[3] As a result, firms might be better served in the long run by acting within a broad set of value-based guidelines. Although guidelines are difficult to develop and implement, following such rules may increase customer good will, help avoid future litigation, and even benefit society in various ways.[4] All these concerns bring us into the realm of ethics and the effects that they have (or should have) on the way business is done.

ethical values
Individuals' moral judgments about what is right or wrong

We'll start by discussing **ethical values**, with the focus on individuals' moral judgments about what is right or wrong. Then we will move beyond personal guidelines and consider how companies can serve the communities and nations in which they do business. Many experts have called on multinationals to build such corporate social responsibility explicitly into their international business strategies.[5] In fact, several frameworks exist to help multinationals move in this direction by distinguishing between various types of ethical and socially responsible corporate behavior.[6] In general, however, the topic of ethics traditionally focuses on more narrow personal issues, while corporate social responsibility is more general since it is driven by the ethical posture of the firm as a whole.

Even with the great strides made in international business over the last twenty-five years, many still feel that the concept of business ethics is murky at best and, at worst, impossible to really use. Part of the problem is that ethics, already a complicated issue, ends up being an even more intricate and tangled issue when we move from country to country. The political and economic systems we discussed in Chapter 2 have direct and indirect effects on the moral values held by people doing international business. In turn, such philosophies affect what people in different cultures think is ethical behavior.[7] Finally, these perceptions can drive behavior, such as questionable payments, human rights at work, and standards for treating employees. We will talk about each of these in this chapter.

Philosophies and Perspectives on Ethics

How should we act and how should others behave? These are major and enduring philosophical questions that have been debated for centuries. This ongoing debate has made it clear that there are many answers to these questions, strong feelings associated with each, and many different justifications on which the answers could be based. Since these philosophies are not our direct concern here, we'll boil them all down to two main positions, universalism and relativism. These two perspectives suggest sharply different behavior for international managers.[8]

Universalism, as the label implies, holds that there are widespread and objective sets of guidelines that cut across countries and cultures. Advocates of this position agree that there are moral rules that everyone should follow. These universalists point to the fact that there are behaviors that almost every culture considers wrong (e.g., harming others or their property).

universalism
Perspective that widespread and objective sets of ethical guidelines exist across countries

Advocates point out that there is wide acceptance of some basic principles for doing business. For example, virtually every country in the world has some sort of law that prohibits bribery, lying, and stealing in a business context.[9] Of course, as we'll show later, not every country enforces such laws, and many choose to "look the other way." Nevertheless, our point is that many people believe that there are widely applicable "rules" for doing business that everyone should obey. Universalists typically are not content to sit back passively and hope that people will discover these basic principles and then act accordingly. Instead, a common strategy has been to actively develop a set of behaviors that constitute universal guidelines. Transnational or global codes of ethics that managers should follow have been developed.[10] For example, universalists have developed a set of minimal rights for international workers. Among other things, these include the right to physical security, free speech, subsistence, and nondiscriminatory treatment.[11]

Exhibit 3.1 lists a few of the better-known global guidelines.[12] These codes deal with topics as diverse as basic human rights, product safety, environmental concerns, and illegal payments. To give you a more in-depth look, we present

EXHIBIT 3.1   *Sets of Ethical Obligations for Firms Conducting International Business*

1. UN Universal Declaration of Human Rights
2. Organization for Economic Cooperation and Development Guidelines for Multinational Enterprises
3. European Convention on Human Rights
4. Helsinki Final Act
5. International Labor Organization's Declaration of Principles Concerning Multinational Enterprises and Social Policy
6. International Covenant on Economic, Social, and Cultural Rights
7. International Covenant on Civil and Political Rights
8. UN Code of Conduct on Transnational Corporations
9. European Economic Community Code of Conduct for Companies with Interests in South Africa
10. Sullivan Principles: A set of seven rules, set forth by Rev. Leon Sullivan of the United States, for companies doing business in South Africa during the apartheid-era regimes (pre-1994). They include issues of equal treatment for all races in terms of pay, advancement, and other employment practices.

EXHIBIT 3.2   *DeGeorge's (1993) Seven Basic Ethical Principles for Multinationals*

1. Multinationals should do no intentional direct harm.
2. Multinationals should produce more good than harm for the host country.
3. Multinationals should contribute by their activity to the host country's development.
4. Multinationals should respect the human rights of their employees.
5. To the extent that local culture does not violate ethical norms, multinationals should respect the local culture and work with and not against it.
6. Multinationals should pay their fair share of taxes.
7. Multinationals should cooperate with the local government in developing and enforcing just-background institutions.

one such code in detail in Exhibit 3.2. This code consists of seven ethical principles that multinationals should follow. Of course, these principles aren't intended to exhaust a firm's ethical responsibilities but rather exemplify the things multinationals should take into account to operate with integrity.

In practice, however, at least two problems emerge with the implementation of universal principles such as these. First, because the codes try to be broad and universal, there is plenty of ambiguity about how they should be interpreted. This has led to inconsistency in the way that different multinationals view and use principles such as "favorable working conditions" and "cooperation with local government."

A second issue is that many countries and companies have not officially adopted all (or even some) of these ethical obligations. For example, although the United States is often seen as being highly concerned with ethical issues, it has not signed on to several sets of these global principles.[13] Partly this is because the United States disagrees with certain aspects of the guidelines, and in part it's also due to internal political pressures. On the other hand, sometimes the United States has endorsed various international agreements dealing with ethical issues but has had trouble getting other countries to cooperate. Even when many countries have signed on in principle, things don't always go the way the United States wants them to. In the last chapter, for example, we discussed the battles that the United States has been losing—and may continue to lose—in the World Trade Organization. In 1996, for example, the United States lost the first case it brought before the WTO court in Geneva. American representatives wanted to make foreign oil suppliers follow pollution standards in the U.S. Clean Air Act in the operation of their (foreign) refineries and plants. Unfortunately, from the American perspective, the WTO ruled that U.S. law discriminated against foreign suppliers in this case. These and other defeats have made the United States distance itself from the WTO. In another case, the United States backed away from slapping Japan with sanctions about some of their trade practices out of fear of losing at the WTO.[14]

cultural relativism
Perspective that ethical behavior in a country is determined by its own unique culture, laws, and business practices

Relativism For these reasons and more, **cultural relativism** has become a popular alternative to universalism.[15] Proponents of relativism believe that ethical behavior in any one country is determined by its own unique culture, laws, and business practices. Therefore, if it is common to provide a public official with a nominal payment to process paperwork for your imports, this may be the thing to do—even though it may be illegal in your own country. This perspective of "when in Rome, do as the Romans do" is often justified on several counts. Perhaps the most important argument is that to do otherwise is to disrespect the culture into which you come as a guest. The obvious implication of this argument is that international managers should follow the practices of the country in which they are doing business.

An example of this situation occurred some time ago when American actress Michelle Pfeiffer was in Moscow filming the movie *The Russia House*. She left the set after a few weeks of filming to protest the fact that Russian extras were not allowed to eat the lavishly catered food provided to foreign actors. She was embarrassed by this since the movie was being made at a time and in a place where it was often difficult or very expensive to get quality food, soap, and other necessities. There was a law, however, forbidding Western film companies from feeding the Russian extras they employed. Local officials were called in to beg Ms. Pfeiffer to return to the set; they explained that this was just the way things were done in Russia. Pfeiffer was eventually convinced, stating, "I didn't sleep that night. Then I realized, this is so typically American of you. Whether I was right or wrong wasn't the issue. The issue was, do I have the right as an outsider to come in and force my sensibilities on this culture?"[16] Ms. Pfeiffer's reaction here is a good example of cultural relativism in practice.

Becoming a relativist—if only temporarily—doesn't give the manager a "get out of ethics jail free" card; unfamiliar and perhaps distasteful customs aren't immune from managerial analysis or judgment. For example, most people would not agree that suppressing political freedom, using slave or prison labor, and other violations of human rights are morally acceptable because it happens in Rangoon rather than Lagos, Jakarta, or New York.[17] Most people are in fact universalists as far as these extreme behaviors are concerned.

This particular attitude, however, does not always translate into action. There are a variety of possible responses and justifications for continuing a firm's business activity in countries where indisputably immoral actions are taking place. In apartheid-era South Africa, for example, many multinationals argued that if they divested their interests in South Africa, greater harm would result to those whom sanctions were intended to help, at least temporarily. In particular, they thought that divestiture would cause many black employees to lose their jobs. Some multinationals also argued that they would be better able to push for government reforms by remaining a player in the South African economy.[18] Similar arguments continue to be made by the many U.S. multinationals that currently do a good deal of international business.[19]

PepsiCo used the same justification to continue its business in Burma (also known as Myanmar), a country run by a repressive military regime.[20] However, under increasing pressure from the U.S. government and human rights organizations, PepsiCo decided in 1997 to end its presence in Myanmar.[21] This is the same year that international economic sanctions were imposed on the country. Unfortunately for Myanmar, although many companies such as PepsiCo have pulled out of the country, the military regime has stepped into the breech. To maintain its grip on power, the military is exploiting one of Myanmar's most precious resources—their vast acreage in old-growth forests. Many experts point out that the revenue derived from the teak trade might be the most significant factor in maintaining the junta's grip on power.[22] In fact, Burmese timber was responsible for 11 percent of the country's legal foreign exchange earnings in 2003. Other data, however, suggest that the actual amount of exports might be double this figure. One reason is that the military—some 350,000 strong—

uses this money to supplement its budget. The military has also cut deals with companies inside the country to solidify their power, and they provide cut-rate prices to China in exchange for that country's support of the illegal government in Myanmar.

Corporations who seek to act as relativists aren't always given a free pass, as suggested by the governmental pressure on PepsiCo. The first line of pressure, however, is often the organized protest by special-interest groups. Protestors, for example, showed up at Unocal gas stations in the United States and claimed the firm helped support the authoritarian regime in Myanmar via a partnership to develop a gas field. Other companies such as Heineken and Carlsberg terminated their investments in Myanmar after similar protests. Still other firms have worked with governments, environmentalists, and other organized groups up front before such protests occur. Chevron has given money to protect forests in New Guinea, Royal Dutch/Shell now meets with Amnesty International, and other firms donate up to 1 percent of annual revenues to be spent on education and health care of local populations.[23] Kraft Foods, which buys about 10 percent of the world's coffee beans, recently reached an agreement with Rainforest Alliance, an environmental group, to purchase beans grown using sustainable methods, something Chiquita Brands and others before them have done.[24] Finally, GM—the world's largest car maker—has tried to blunt criticism from environmental groups of its gas-guzzling 2.8 ton Hummer H2 vehicle by touting its work on hydrogen-powered cars. GM prominently points out that over one-quarter of all its research spending goes into these vehicles whose only emission is water.[25] It appears as if continuing pressure is beginning to change the mind, if not the hearts, of many multinationals.

Cross-National Differences in Ethical Perspectives

The universalism–relativism debate raises the question of whether countries diverge in how they view and act on ethical principles in business. The many studies on this topic generally confirm that there are widely different ways to approach ethical issues across countries. One study, for instance, found that American managers were more likely to view human relations issues (such as employee theft and misuse of company information) in ethical terms than were their counterparts from Austria and Germany. On the other hand, Austrian and German managers were more likely to view involvement in local politics in ethical terms. These differences may reflect cultural values. Americans tend to be highly individualistic and, as a result, may feel that the individual is the main source of ethical values. Germans and Austrians, however, tend to be more community oriented. In fact, business ethics in these countries has been described in terms of the relationship between businesses and their local environments.[26]

Another interesting study compared the reactions of managers in the United States, France, and Germany to several important ethical topics, including illegal payments, coercion, conflict of interest, and environmental concerns. These issues were presented to the managers in the form of short stories that provided background. Here is an example of one of the stories that managers read:

> Rollfast Bicycle Company has been barred from entering the market in a large
> Asian country by collusive efforts of the local bicycle manufacturers. Rollfast could
> expect to net $5 million per year from sales if it could penetrate the market. Last

🌐 International Insights

In the International Bribery Game, U.S. Multinationals Lag Behind

A RECENT U.S. government report revealed how far American multinationals lag behind their French, German, and Japanese competitors in the use of bribery to secure international business deals. In addition to outright payoffs, some of America's competitors offer inducements to their international customers or attach "conditions" to foreign aid (like signing business deals). Consider these alleged improprieties:

- France offered aid to Vietnam in exchange for 20 percent of the Vietnamese telecom market. Likewise, France said it would pull loan guarantees to an African nation unless a French firm won a $20-million telecom contract there.

- A European aerospace firm said it would lobby against European Union membership for Turkey unless the country bought its airplanes.

- A German high-tech firm used bribes to help win eleven contracts over a ten-year period.

- Japan offered to cancel $30 million of Brazil's debt to Tokyo if it purchased a supercomputer from a Japanese multinational. The computer's price tag was $30 million.

- Several high-ranking Indian government officials, including an ousted prime minister, were indicted on corruption and extortion charges—some of which involved U.S. firms such as the now infamous Enron Corporation.

So what do such "greased palm" approaches cost U.S. multinationals? According to one estimate in the mid-1990s, foreign multinationals used bribery in efforts to secure 100 business deals worth $45 billion. Although it wasn't clear that corrupt practices were responsible, 80 percent of those deals were actually won by foreign multinationals. Plus, with nearly $1 trillion in foreign infrastructure projects available through 2006, there is a lot at stake for U.S. multinationals.

Foreign officials have long complained about a U.S. double standard on these issues. They point out that diplomats in America's 162 foreign embassies often help U.S. multinationals land contracts and push products. In fact, U.S. multinationals have been caught in their own bribery tangles. In 1995 a former executive at Lockheed Martin was sentenced to prison for using bribery to secure a cargo plane deal from an Egyptian government official, a clear violation of the U.S. law that forbids American firms from using bribery to get business. Other U.S. multinationals, however, have tried more unique methods to nail down international deals, including flying foreign officials to the United States where they can be wined and dined and given "spending money" for shopping.

Nevertheless, U.S. multinationals are clearly also-rans when it comes to bribery and other forms of corruption. In fact, bribery is culturally and legally permissible in many countries. In France, paying off foreigners can be written off as a tax deduction. Germany's tax laws contain similar allowances. Many U.S. business and government leaders say the answer lies in a more aggressive effort to push foreign multinationals to play the international business game by American ethical rules. In all likelihood, however, such an effort will be a tough uphill battle.[27]

week a businessman from the country contacted the management of Rollfast and stated that he could smooth the way for the company to sell in his country for a price of $500,000.

The managers were then asked whether they would pay the bribe. In most cases, U.S. managers were less likely to pay the bribe than either of the European managers, who did not really differ all that much from one another. Managers were also asked about the *reasons* for their behavioral reactions. Not surprisingly, the reasons varied across countries. For example, nearly 50 percent of the U.S. managers said they would not pay a bribe because they thought it was unethical, illegal, or against company policy. Only 15 percent of the French and 9 percent of the Germans mentioned these reasons. Instead, the Europeans were much more likely to say that it was competition that forced them to act that way ("It is the price to be paid to do business in that country" or "Competition forces us to take the offer"). Overall, the U.S. managers were more concerned about ethical issues, while the Europeans were more concerned about maintaining a competitive business presence.[28]

Other researchers using different research methods in other countries have reached similar conclusions.[29] Interestingly, studies have also shown that even when attitudes about ethical issues are similar across countries, they may be the result of *different* moral reasoning processes.[30] These different perspectives may result from the legal frameworks of each country, their economic environments, or their unique cultural values. As a result, cross-national differences in ethics may also be fairly resistant to change in the short term, even if the political, social, and economic conditions in a country are shifting dramatically. For instance, despite the incredible changes that have occurred in South Africa over the past few years, attitudes towards ethical business practices in the country have remained remarkably stable.[31]

Codes of Ethics Another example of the different emphasis nations place on ethics can be found by looking at the presence (or absence) of corporate codes of conduct across countries.[32] One important study looked at this issue by comparing 600 European firms (British, French, and German) with a similar sample of American companies. The results? First, U.S. firms were more likely to have ethical codes in the first place. Only about 30 percent of French firms had codes of ethics in place, and in German and British firms the corresponding percentages were 51 percent and 41 percent. These numbers don't even come close to the 75 percent of American companies that said they had a written code of ethics in place.[33]

Also, most European firms that did have codes of conduct had instituted them after 1984. The Zeiss company of Germany introduced a code for its employees as early as 1896, but this is the exception rather than the rule. What is more, European firms with corporate codes are much more likely to have a strong U.S. connection than those without codes. For example, 25 percent of the European firms with codes are actually subsidiaries of U.S. multinationals, whereas only 2 percent without such codes are U.S. subsidiaries.[34]

In addition to looking at whether a company had a code in place, research has also looked at differences in the *content* of the codes.[35] Although there are some differences among European companies, when considered as a whole they differ sharply from the codes of U.S. firms. For example, 100 percent of European firms mentioned employee conduct somewhere in their corporate codes; only 55 percent of U.S. firms dealt with this issue. In keeping with the traditional American focus on marketing, however, U.S. firms (80 percent) were more likely to mention customers than European companies (67 percent). Likewise, U.S. firms (86 percent) referred to government relations much more frequently than their European counterparts (20 percent).

What the codes say about political issues also reveals important things about their outlook. Many U.S. firms state their commitment to abiding by the law but appear to mistrust the role of government in business. The corporate code of Dow Chemical, for example, states, "We pay our taxes *gladly*, yes, but we do not pay them *blindly*. We have the right to question the wisdom of regulatory zeal" (Dow's emphasis, not ours). In contrast, the few times when European firms mention political issues, they do so in general, positive ways. For example, Bertelsmann (Germany) states that it "supports a free, democratic and socially responsible society" and Wella Corp. (Germany) says that it "welcomes political, social, and cultural activities of employees."

Ethical Behavior and Human Rights

As we said earlier, almost everyone agrees certain behavior is wrong. The question that many multinationals face, however, is how should they react when they are doing business in countries run by governments that commit these wrong acts against their citizens. The reactions of firms run the gamut of possibilities. A few (such as Levi Strauss), have steadfastly refused to do business in such circumstances; whereas others (such as Mobil and Ford) continue to do business, arguing that more good can be accomplished by staying in a country.

Human Rights Issues in South Africa   A well-known example of this range of reactions was seen in apartheid-era South Africa. Practiced by the white South African government for several decades, **apartheid** prohibited blacks from voting and from living in white areas, permitted job and pay discrimination against blacks, and required blacks get special permission to enter certain areas. For many years, it was clear that most of the world found these practices reprehensible and morally wrong. Nevertheless, South Africa remained an economic power in Africa during apartheid, accounting for 25 percent of the GNP of the whole continent. In fact, much of the world continued to do business with South Africa while apartheid was in force.

apartheid
A system formerly applied by the white minority government in South Africa that discriminated against blacks in housing, jobs, and political participation

In the 1970s and 1980s, however, the issue of apartheid became more acute for multinationals doing business in South Africa. Multinationals began to feel pressure from civil rights activists and stockholders to curtail their business with South Africa. In 1977, Rev. Leon Sullivan, a Baptist minister and member of the board of directors of General Motors, developed guidelines for firms doing business in South Africa. The essence of his seven principles was that U.S. multinationals should not obey apartheid laws. To their credit, many U.S. multinationals did not—with General Motors taking the lead.[36] Ten years later, Rev. Sullivan concluded that the principles failed to result in any government changes. As a result, he changed his position and advocated a divestment strategy as well as a trade embargo rather than "constructive engagement."

Many shareholders of U.S. corporations, including large pension funds, eventually adopted the same perspective. Likewise, about 25 percent of the U.S. multinationals doing business with South Africa pulled out of the country. Nelson Mandela's support for divestment in his 1990 tour of the United States, in addition to his criticism of U.S. and European firms, pushed this further. By 1991, there were only about 110 U.S. multinationals operating in South Africa compared to 267 in 1986. However, these figures do not include joint ventures or forms of indirect investment (e.g., Ford sold parts to a South African firm, even though it no longer made cars there).[37] In any case, it wasn't exactly clear how important the corporate boycotts were in leading to the 1994 election of President Nelson Mandela.

Ironically, U.S. multinationals like Honeywell found that the route back into South Africa was as difficult as their original decision to leave.[38] While a main concern was the potential for making money, multinationals returning to

South Africa also were urged to help redress the inequities that still remained from the apartheid era.[39] For example, some multinationals contributed money to build homes and schools in the squalid townships where many of the black majority still lived.[40] Overall, the trends showed a steady return of U.S. multinationals to South Africa. By the time President Mandela was elected in 1994, some 150 U.S. multinationals were operating in South Africa, a 40 percent increase over the previous three years. This activity leveled off at the end of the 1990s. In any case, multinationals' behavior in South Africa illustrates that even when most of the international community finds a nation's behavior morally reprehensible, a clear and consistent reaction from corporations does not necessarily follow.[41]

Human Rights Issues in China   This last statement can also apply to China. This country has seen an enormous influx of foreign investment in recent years and, as we have documented in earlier chapters, is booming in many ways. The trouble, however, is that by many accounts China is responsible for a wide variety of human rights violations. According to groups like Amnesty International and Human Rights Watch, the Chinese government is responsible for suppressing individual freedoms that many countries take as a given and for other serious abuses.

These groups have accused China of operating nearly 1,000 prison labor camps (where the majority of prisoners are political criminals), capricious arrests, the use of child labor, and unsafe working conditions (outside prison camps). A recent U.S. State Department report on human rights in China provided some support to such allegations by referencing a variety of human rights abuses that included arbitrary detention and forced confessions.[42] The following International Insights documents what happened to one Chinese man who was employed by Chrysler at its joint venture operation in China.

Nevertheless, most U.S. multinationals—as well as the U.S. government—continue to press a familiar argument. They say that a business presence in China must be maintained in order to influence the human rights situation there, the same argument used decades earlier in South Africa. It may be the right one. In fact, experts say that by improving working conditions in China, multinationals can help change attitudes towards human rights in general and workers in particular. This can operate in tandem with the effects of setting a positive example by providing good pay and a safe working environment. For instance, multinationals can give local employees opportunities for personal growth and development, including training designed to increase respect for individuals and tolerance of differences. For instance, firms can provide training that could increase upward mobility within the multinational and create additional opportunities for employment. Over time, these steps may help contribute to the development of a more sophisticated and enlightened workforce in China.[43]

Others, however, feel that doing business with countries like China only condones a poor human rights record. In fact, this is the position of the Laogai Research Foundation, headed by Harry Wu of Stanford University. The institute claims that despite the increasing presence of foreign multinationals, conditions are not getting better. Mr. Wu himself spent nineteen years in Chinese prison labor camps for his public criticism of Chinese support for the 1956 Soviet invasion of Hungary. Since then he has been a thorn in China's side by revealing evidence of many human rights violations. A few years ago, Mr. Wu entered China

International Insights

Human Rights Issues for U.S. Multinationals in China: The Case of Gao Feng

GAO FENG was an employee at Beijing Jeep, a joint venture between Chrysler Corporation and the Chinese government. We say "was an employee" because he was suspended and told to either resign or be fired by the company. His offense? A serious level of absenteeism by the standards of almost any company—he was a no-show for over a month! However, there is much more to the story than this.

When he returned to the factory after his month-long absence, Gao told his boss that he had been arrested by the police. During a Christian memorial service that commemorated the victims of the government crackdown and violence in 1989, police raided the location and arrested the participants, among them Gao, and held them for over four weeks. Because the police failed to provide proof of his whereabouts during this period of time, Beijing Jeep suspended Gao and gave him the resign-or-else ultimatum.

This may have just been another of many sad cases had the Associated Press not picked up the story. A few months later, the media also linked Chrysler's Chinese partner with a sweatshop that used forced prison labor for production. Chrysler has denied the reports, reiterating its pledge not to use components that are produced by prison labor. All this had occurred in the context of a failed negotiation with the Chinese government to produce minivans and reports that Chinese factories were manufacturing low-cost, knockoff versions of the Chrysler Jeep. Therefore,

even if the prison labor claims were not true, they were bad publicity for Chrysler. That publicity—in combination with the acknowledged troubles that Chrysler was having—made doing business in China all the more difficult. So Gao's case was something of an embarrassment.

Gao told reporters that he refused to quit. Eventually he was reinstated by Beijing Jeep. He attributes his success to a sense of moral obligation from the company, to public pressure from the media, and to Human Rights Watch (the organization that championed his case). Chrysler's side of the story was that Gao was never suspended or dismissed. He simply overreacted when he returned to see his job posted and jumped to the wrong conclusions. Chrysler said jobs were routinely posted after two weeks of absence. Plus, no one told Beijing Jeep of Gao's whereabouts, and the police denied holding him more than one day. Chrysler also said that it could not check into the incident further because doing so would be inconsistent with the way business is done in China. In effect, Chrysler worried that it would be unable to push Chinese authorities to the extent that it would in the United States. The concern was that if Chrysler criticized the actions of the police, it might offend Chinese authorities to the point where they would tell the firm to leave. By maintaining a low-key approach, Chrysler felt it was helping China become a better place for all employees at Beijing Jeep.

---

illegally (he is a U.S. citizen) and videotaped several prison labor camps, such as the Hangzhou Hardware & Tool Works, where nearly 1,600 political prisoners march to work every day. Tools from the factory are exported all over the world, including to the United States. The institute estimates that nearly 10 million people are being held in such camps, most of whom were sent there for speaking out against the government. These people are forced to work against their will in dangerous conditions for many hours a day; they are often beaten, tortured, and poorly fed.[44]

Despite these revelations—that few outside China deny—almost no multinationals have taken stands similar to those that were seen in South Africa. There are a few prominent exceptions. Reebok International, while continuing their presence in China, has at the same time made their position clear to the government. The company sent an unambiguous notice to the Chinese government after the Tiananmen Square massacre in 1989 by creating a human rights award. The award was given to the four main leaders of the Chinese democracy movement. To further ensure that its Chinese partners don't use prison labor, Reebok asks them to sign affidavits. So far, the response has been good. Reebok, along with rock star Peter Gabriel and the Lawyers Committee for Human Rights, also provides financial support for the group Witness. This group provides video cameras and fax machines to local human rights groups all over the world, including those in China.

Other firms, like the Timberland Company, a shoe and apparel manufacturer, pulled out of China in 1993 because the government did not support the firm's beliefs about the value of employees. Levi Strauss, the San Francisco–based firm that is among the world's largest apparel makers, also pulled out of China. Levi Strauss is internationally known for their products. What is not so well known is the clear and strong stand the firm takes on ethical guidelines for conducting international business. The company is one of the few American multinationals that has gone against the grain with their business practices around the globe in general, and in China in particular.

Levi Strauss's interests in China were not large, amounting to about $50 million per year. But in May 1993 the firm announced that it would phase out operations in China. The decision to leave China was based on an application of a clear set of corporate values that had been developed a few years earlier. In fact, since the mid-1980s, the firm has embraced a management style that emphasizes values and ethical practices.[45] During that time, a company task force worked for three years on developing a set of guidelines for doing business overseas. The result was a two-part set of guidelines (see Exhibit 3.3) that Levi Strauss uses with foreign contractors and business partners. The first part, called *Business Partner Terms of Engagement*, deals with issues that its business partners can control. As you can see, these include issues such as workplace health and safety, employment practices, and general ethics. For example, Levi Strauss clearly states that it will not do business with partners who use prison or child labor.

According to Levi Strauss, most of its foreign partners want to treat their employees well, and even those partners not in compliance are often interested in working toward adherence to company principles. Nevertheless, Levi Strauss did find that a portion (about 5 percent) was not meeting the guidelines and there was no indication that those partners ever would. As a result, Levi Strauss terminated those business relationships. This was true in China, where Levi Strauss had great concern about worker safety, prison labor, and China's one-child policy. Arriving at this decision was difficult and took weeks of meetings and debates among Levi Strauss's China policy group.[46]

Eventually, the firm chose to drop China. Levi Strauss continues to review such decisions via their terms of engagement (Exhibit 3.3) and other country selection criteria. As far as China is concerned, however, critics of Levi Strauss have suggested that leaving was nothing more than a public relations move. They noted that the company had little direct investment in China and would have no trouble finding contractors to operate in other low-cost countries. Levi Strauss admitted that its decision could be an image boost but still claimed that it sacrificed great economic potential by leaving China.[47] In 1998, the company lifted its self-imposed restrictions on doing business in China after one of its

EXHIBIT 3.3 *Levi Strauss Co.'s Business Partner Terms of Engagement*

1. **Ethical Standards:**

   We will seek to identify and utilize business partners who aspire as individuals and in the conduct of all their businesses to a set of ethical standards not incompatible with our own.

2. **Legal Requirements:**

   We expect our business partners to be law abiding as individuals and to comply with legal requirements relevant to the conduct of all their businesses.

3. **Environmental Requirements:**

   We will only do business with partners who share our commitment to the environment and who conduct their business in a way that is consistent with Levi Strauss & Co.'s Environmental Philosophy and Guiding Principles.

4. **Community Involvement:**

   We will favor business partners who share our commitment to improving community conditions

5. **Employment Standards:**

   We will only do business with partners who adhere to the following guidelines:

   - **Child Labor:** Use of child labor is not permissible. Workers can be no less than 15 years of age and not younger than the compulsory age to be in school. We will not utilize partners who use child labor in any of their facilities. We support the development of legitimate workplace apprenticeship programs for the educational benefit of younger people.
   - **Prison Labor/Forced Labor:** We will not utilize prison or forced labor in contracting relationships in the manufacture and finishing of our products. We will not utilize or purchase materials from a business partner utilizing prison or forced labor.
   - **Disciplinary Practices:** We will not utilize business partners who use corporal punishment or other forms of mental or physical coercion.
   - **Working Hours:** While permitting flexibility in scheduling, we will identify prevailing local work hours and seek business partners who do not exceed them except for appropriately compensated overtime. While we favor partners who utilize less than 60-hour workweeks, we will not use contractors who, on a regularly scheduled basis, require in excess of a 60-hour week. Employees should be allowed at least one day off in seven.
   - **Wages and Benefits:** We will only do business with partners who provide wages and benefits that comply with any applicable law and match the prevailing local manufacturing or finishing industry practices.
   - **Freedom of Association:** We respect workers' rights to form and join organizations of their choice and to bargain collectively. We expect our suppliers to respect the right to free association and the right to organize and bargain collectively without unlawful interference. Business partners should ensure that workers who make such decisions or participate in such organizations are not the objects of discrimination or punitive disciplinary actions and that the representatives of such organizations have access to their members under conditions established either by local laws or mutual agreement between the employer and the worker organizations.
   - **Discrimination:** While we recognize and respect cultural differences, we believe that workers should be employed on the basis of their ability to do the job, rather than on the basis of personal characteristics or beliefs. We will favor business partners who share this value.
   - **Health & Safety:** We will only utilize business partners who provide workers with a safe and healthy work environment. Business partners who provide residential facilities for their workers must provide safe and healthy facilities.

periodic reviews. With a changing competitive landscape, and more experience in working with contractors to assure they work within the terms of engagement, Levi Strauss felt the change of policy was warranted.

Overall, however, Levi Strauss clearly considers many ethical issues to be universal in nature and believes that these principles should guide corporate behavior. To ensure this, Levi Strauss believes the best answer is to develop and enforce a specific set of conduct codes that foreign business partners must follow. At the same time, however, the firm became aware a few years ago that two of its contractors in Bangladesh were employing children under fourteen years of age. Although acceptable under Bangladesh law, it violated international labor standards and Levi's code. After studying the situation further, however, the company discovered that the underage children were often the sole source of support for their families. Levi Strauss asked the contractor to have the children quit work and go back to school at the company's expense (including books, tuition, uniforms) until they came of age.[48]

Enforcement Issues with Codes of Conduct In fact, the use of such conduct codes has been increasing lately, at least among U.S. multinationals. Unlike Levi Strauss, however, many multinationals take a more relativistic view in their codes for foreign business partners. For instance, Nike's policy at one point suggested it would be sufficient if its foreign contractors adhered to local labor laws. Nike toughened its code after critics said that requiring contractors to comply with local laws did little to protect workers in places like China and Indonesia because the laws were so weak to begin with.[49]

But tougher codes aren't always enough. The real issue may be enforcement. For instance, Levi Strauss conducts periodic audits of all its partners to see if they are in compliance with its conduct code. In 1992, an audit of over 700 partners in more than fifty countries showed relatively high compliance rates, with nearly 70 percent found to be observing company standards.[50]

Despite its industry-leading systematic enforcement efforts, Levi Strauss has admitted that it doesn't catch everything. Part of the reason is that code inspectors may refrain from probing too deeply so as not to cause offense to their partners/contractors. Other companies, however, rely on contractors to police themselves. For instance, J.C. Penney Co. has foreign suppliers sign a conduct code that prohibits violations of local labor laws. But Penney's own Guatemalan contractors say that the company is only concerned with product quality and that it doesn't check on working conditions in their operations. In fact, these contractors sometimes use child labor, pay less than the legal minimum wage, and require unpaid overtime when producing apparel for Penney's. The response of Penney's, and other U.S. retailers such as Target, is that enforcing conduct codes is virtually impossible because suppliers are spread across thousands of factories in dozens of countries. But even limited enforcement may help. Wal-Mart, for example, conducts occasional inspections at its Guatemalan plants, and this practice resulted in fewer labor violations than did comparable factories doing work for Penney's.

Overall, critics charge that without enforcement, conduct codes are nothing more than public relations efforts designed to assuage customers about poor working conditions in developing countries.[51] Evidence certainly supports the presence of poor conditions. So poor are they in some countries that workers are even willing to pay to take jobs in foreign countries. Some have called this practice debt bondage, and Western firms are indirect participants. A specific example illustrates an uncomfortably common occurrence. Consider Mary, a Filipina worker desperate for work, who took a job in Taiwan for a Motorola subcontractor. She borrowed $2,400 to pay a labor broker in the Philippines for that job lead, but borrowed the money from a local lender at a 10 percent interest rate—per month! The $460 a month she earns in Taiwan gets eaten up to pay interest, Taiwanese income tax, room and board, and more. In fact, she and many other such workers often go further into debt.[52] Even among countries with legal protections, however, there can be similar problems. Indeed, a cover story in a recent *Business Week*, titled "Workers in Bondage," documented these same effects in many European countries.[53] Western Europeans have long prided themselves on the high standards they impose on employers. And workers have many more legal protections than in the United States. Yet despite this, the hundreds of thousands of economic refugees who are pouring into Europe from China, India, the old Soviet bloc, and elsewhere sometimes face horrific conditions in countries such as England, France, Italy, and Spain.

A positive trend of late holds promise to improve the enforcement of codes. The criticism of codes is that they represent more public relations than social responsibility in action. Supporting this view is the practice by Western companies of conducting audits of foreign operations, but not releasing the results of that audit. Recently, however, a few firms—including Nike, Reebok, and Van Heusen among others—have gone public with those audits. In 2003 for the first time, these audits are available on the Internet (**www.fairlabor.org**) for public scrutiny. This may put pressure on Wal-Mart, Disney, the Gap, and other firms to do the same.[54]

Ethics Associated with Questionable Payments and Bribery

Concerns about whether multinationals are responsible for protecting workers— even when they work for foreign contractors—are big ethical questions, to be sure. However, there are many other issues around which the universalism versus relativism debate swirls. In Saudi Arabia, for example, it is illegal to hire female managers for many jobs.[55] For an American, however, there is legal protection for gender discrimination in employment. So is it unethical to do business in Saudi Arabia? Likewise, is it unethical to avoid strict environmental laws by locating facilities offshore? Finally, is it right for a U.S. multinational to market a drug in Malaysia that failed to receive U.S. government approval because there are questions about a possible link to cancer?

U.S. multinationals in many of these cases have cogently argued that their ethically questionable actions are justified and even morally correct. Indeed, as we mentioned earlier, the relativist position enjoys a great deal of credence and is apparently attractive to some multinationals, even though some prominent observers have rejected it.

One common practice in international business that intersects with ethical relativism is the use of **questionable payments**. This refers to practices like bribery, extortion, and "grease" payments to bureaucrats and business leaders, both foreign and domestic. Bribery and related activity have a long and venerable history in international business.[56] In addition to direct monetary payments, this activity also includes things such as giving expensive gifts (jewelry, art, and other collectibles), providing lavish entertainment, and offering free trips to foreign or domestic dignitaries.

questionable payments Refers to ethics of bribery, extortion, and "grease" payments to bureaucrats and business leaders

EXHIBIT 3.4   *Words That May Connote Bribery in Different Countries*

Country	Word	Country	Word
Brazil	*jeitinho*	Japan	*wairo*
Egypt	*baksheesh*	Malaysia	*makan siap*
France	*pot au vin*	Mexico	*mordida*
Germany	*trink gelt/schmiergeld*	Nigeria	*dash*
Greece	*baksissi*	Pakistan	*roshvat*
Honduras	*pajada*	Peru	*coima*
Hong Kong	*hatchien*	Philippines	*lagay*
India	*speed money/baksheesh*	Russia	*vzyatha*
Indonesia	*uong sogok*	Thailand	*sin bone*
Iran	*roshveh*	United States	*grease money/payola*
Italy	*bustarella*	Zaire	*tarif de verre*

Source: Adapted from Jacoby, N. H., Nehemkis, P., & Eells, R. (1977). *Bribery and extortion in world business: A study of corporate political payments abroad.* New York: Macmillan.

In fact, the use of illegal or questionable payments has been common practice in many societies throughout recorded history—whether it is Africa, Asia, the Middle East, Europe, or the Americas.[57] Records of many early civilizations show that bribery was common. Indeed, bribery is so much a part of nearly every culture that most languages have a word for it.[58] While we're certainly not suggesting you use these words in business dealings, Exhibit 3.4 does show examples of words from around the world that may reflect such questionable payments.

For example, the payment of *baksheesh* in some Arab and Turkish-speaking countries reflects the questionable or illegal payoffs to which we are referring. The presence and frequency of political payments in such countries may reflect centuries of rule by an all-powerful state (like the Ottoman Empire). Here, *baksheesh* could provide the protection for businesses that an imperfect and abusive legal system could not. Likewise, in Mexico the term *la mordida* (literally, "the bite") might reflect a similar history and sense of powerlessness with the government bureaucracy.[59] The terms in other languages—like the Italian *bustarella* ("little envelope") and the French *pot au vin* ("jug of wine")—carry vivid and evocative images. In Nigeria, the foreign firm that doesn't "dash" local bureaucrats may not be able to function in that country.

Interestingly, almost every country in the world explicitly outlaws bribery of its own officials.[60] So, if an illegal payment is made to a foreign official, that person or corporation risks prosecution. Despite this near universal view of bribery, countries vary dramatically in terms of how much they tolerate and

EXHIBIT 3.5   *Rankings of the Ten Most Corrupt and Ten Least Corrupt Nations*

Rank/Nation	CPI Rating	Rank/Nation	CPI Rating
1. Bangladesh	1.3	124. Switzerland	8.8
2. Nigeria	1.4	125. Norway	8.8
3. Haiti	1.5	126. Australia	8.8
4. Paraguay	1.6	127. The Netherlands	8.9
5. Burma	1.6	128. Sweden	9.3
6. Tajikistan	1.8	129. Singapore	9.4
7. Georgia	1.8	130. New Zealand	9.5
8. Cameroon	1.8	131. Denmark	9.5
9. Azerbaijan	1.8	132. Iceland	9.6
10. Angola	1.9	133. Finland	9.7

Source: Adapted from Transparency International (2003; **www.transparency.de**). The higher the rank and the CPI score, the lower the corruption; 133 total countries rated.

practice corruption. In some countries there is actually little or no risk involved since bribery is commonplace if not expected. Consider the results of a recent survey of a large number of Indonesian businesspeople, government officials, and general citizenry. Among other results, over 65 percent of households said they'd been asked for "unofficial" payments from public officials. Likewise, over 50 percent also said it was common practice for teachers to ask for payments to ensure a child's continued enrollment in school. Even public officials themselves acknowledged their role—nearly 50 percent admitted they received "under the table" payments. In other cases, however, the magnitude of the bribery and other forms of corruption (like embezzlement of company or government funds) may be just too great to ignore, even if bribery is an accepted and common practice. In fact, nearly two-thirds of the Indonesian businesspeople said they would willingly pay up to 5 percent of their revenue in additional taxes if it would be used to battle corruption.[61]

When this occurs, the corrupt official or business leader may be hauled into court and prosecuted. In Exhibit 3.5, we present the results of a survey conducted annually by Transparency International, a nonprofit organization that tracks corruption worldwide. The survey ranked 133 nations based on the overall level of corruption as perceived by various international institutions and businesspeople. **Corruption** was defined as the amount of bribery, embezzlement, and behind-the-scenes activity typically involved in doing business. In the exhibit we present a set of the ten most corrupt and the ten least corrupt nations. The U.S. ranking of 118 (out of 133) in the survey compared well to the highest-rated (least corrupt) country, Finland.[62]

corruption
The extent to which bribery, embezzlement, and other illegal behind-the-scenes activity occurs in business or government

Bribery across countries   France presents an interesting case of a crackdown on corruption, led by French magistrates who are fed up with an elitist system of cozy relationships between business and government. The magistrates have zeroed in on the widespread corruption (bribery, kickbacks, and embezzlement) that is a side effect of this system (known in France as *dirigisme*). Part of their motivation is a concern that pervasive corruption has contributed to France's anemic economy, high unemployment rate, and inward-looking, uncompetitive companies. What's stunning about the French crackdown is its scope. Since 1995, *dozens* of top executives and politicians have been targeted for investigation, if not already convicted and jailed, and these include leaders of some of France's most well-known companies.[63] France, and some other European countries, have immunity laws that protect those with high government roles from prosecution. This law recently helped Jacques Chirac, the French president, avoid facing charges of financial impropriety that allegedly occurred while he was mayor of Paris. During Mr. Chirac's recent re-election campaign, opponents carried pictures of him that read "Vote for me or I go to jail."[64]

France is hardly the only country where concern about bribery and other corrupt practices have prompted concern and crackdowns.[65] Consider this roster of incidents that have either resulted in criminal convictions or that have prompted various investigations:

- A $350-billion bad loan scandal in Japan exposed the close cooperation that often exists between Ministry of Finance bureaucrats, political leaders, bankers, and organized criminal gangs (collectively known as the *yakuza*). Questionable loans were allegedly made to yakuza front companies even as yakuza members were attending fundraisers for Japanese politicians.[66]

- Mr. Chey Tae-won, Chairman of South Korea's SK Corp., was released from prison after serving only three months for a multibillion-dollar tax fraud. Koreans reacted with outcry and suspicion. Mr. Chey, the son-in-law of a former South Korean president, was convicted of wide-ranging corruption. Nevertheless, Mr. Chey kept his position as chairman of SK—the country's third largest conglomerate—and expected to return to management. After a brief rest, he was to take over from another executive who ran the firm in Mr. Chey's absence—and who himself was convicted for his part in the fraud but received a suspended sentence![67]

- Corruption in China is a major issue for the government with more than 43,000 cases of graft and corruption investigated in 2001. Government officials estimated that between 1995 and 2000, annual economic losses due to corruption amounted to anywhere from 13 to 17 percent of GDP. And a lot of this involved government officials themselves! Convictions in the last few years included: A sixteen-year sentence for the Beijing mayor and Communist Party secretary, a suspended death sentence for the mayor of Shenyang for corruption and ties to gangsters, another suspended death sentence for the vice-minister of public security, and a completed death sentence for the vice chairman of the Chinese Parliament.[68]

- Opposition party leaders in Moscow threatened investigations and legislative changes to curb emerging Russian conglomerates that seem to have "uncles" (*dyadyas*) within the government to watch out for them. They provide the conglomerates with breaks on taxes, import duties, and legislation involving foreign competitors, allegedly in return for payoffs. Some thirty-two of these Russian industrial giants run 500 factories and seventy-two banks that have 2.5 million employees.[69]

Of course, the United States is hardly the perfect bastion of proper business practices. The history of American business is replete with examples of such corruption. In fact, some experts feel that certain U.S. industries, such as food, retail, and construction, are still fertile areas for corruption. What is worse, people from other nations often think Americans fail to acknowledge their own ethical foibles. As a result, the United States is sometimes seen as being pious or hypocritical—especially considering that Americans have had their share of scandals and ethical problems, even before the recent wave of scandals involving Enron, WorldCom, Tyco, and others. Europeans, for instance, think the United States needs to "lighten up a little" and be less naive about separating business and personal ethics.[70]

All of the examples that we've been talking about so far involve investigations of internal forms of possible bribery and corruption, where a country's political or business leaders may somehow be "on the take." Very few countries, however, outlaw bribes by their citizens to public officials of a *foreign* country. Most countries take the "when in Rome" perspective, maintaining that common practice should be followed by its citizens in that foreign nation. In fact, some countries like Switzerland go further than that by allowing their businesses to take tax write-offs for bribes paid to foreign governments.[71] This is at minimum a tacit endorsement of such practices.

Until a few decades ago, payoffs by U.S. firms to foreign representatives were also common. In the mid-1970s, however, several high-level cases of corporate corruption became widely publicized. At the time, the United States was very sensitive to corruption because of the Watergate scandal that eventually caused President Richard Nixon to resign. For instance, Carl Kotchian, president of Lockheed, made payments to Japanese government officials and agents in order to secure a large contract from Nippon Air to buy Lockheed airliners. Mr. Kotchian was contacted by Japanese officials and told that if Lockheed wanted the contract, they would have to make some payments to close the sale. He was approached several additional times for further payments, which ended up totaling $12.5 million.[72] When the press uncovered the Lockheed payments, the firm was charged with many tax code violations as well as with falsifying records. Interestingly, experts point out that although such illicit payments were supposed to be a common business practice in Japan, the public disclosure of the Lockheed payments created quite a furor in that country as well.[73] Government officials involved in this incident were criminally charged and one even committed suicide.[74]

In any case, the Lockheed incident received wide attention and explanation, including an article detailing the events by Mr. Kotchian himself.[75] More detailed analysis shows that this represented only one facet of Lockheed's foreign bribery payments.[76] Lockheed, however, was hardly alone. Apparently, nearly 450 U.S. corporations made inappropriate payments to foreign officials or companies during the period of 1974 to 1976 when the Lockheed situation occurred. The reaction of the already outraged American public pushed Congress to pass the **Foreign Corrupt Practices Act (FCPA)**, which became law in 1977 and was later amended to clarify some ambiguous provisions.

Foreign Corrupt Practices Act
Set of U.S. laws making it illegal to pay or offer to pay officials of foreign governments to gain or increase business

The Foreign Corrupt Practices Act   The FCPA made it illegal to pay or offer to pay officials of foreign governments to gain or increase business. Penalties for violators include fines up to $1 million for companies, as well as fines and up to five years' imprisonment for the individuals involved. Interestingly, the current version of the FCPA *does not* prohibit all "questionable" payments to foreign officials or governments. Actually, a distinction is made between bribes and

grease payments
Payments made to officials to facilitate the performance of functions that they ordinarily do as part of their jobs

facilitating payments. The latter are often called **grease payments** because they are made to "grease the wheels" of business. It is not illegal to make payments to low- and middle-level officials so that they will perform functions that they are ordinarily obliged to do as part of their jobs.

For example, in many countries, it is absolutely necessary to provide small payments to customs officials in order to get them to do what they legally should do, such as inspect and pass the imports of a U.S. multinational. Sometimes foreign customs officials will impede or backlog a shipment until they receive the grease payments. Other examples of grease payments that are not illegal under the FCPA include: (1) providing "gifts" that help overcome bureaucratic technicalities that impede business; (2) "gifts" given to supplement an environment of low wages, with the gifts acting as gratuities for services performed; and (3) the facilitation of permits and equipment that are allotted via the extra payments. Essentially, the difference between a bribe and a grease payment usually is that grease payments are relatively small and they are not offered to get anything more than a business is entitled to anyway (such as an import license). To some ethicists, however, this is a distinction without a difference.

Effects of the FCPA Although the FCPA was signed by then President Jimmy Carter with some fanfare, a number of U.S. multinationals complained about it. The complaints largely centered around the effect of the law on the competitiveness of American business. Several prominent business leaders pointed out that they had lost contracts with foreign governments in the past because they refused to pay requested bribes. In fact, they noted that companies with inferior products and services—who in a fair environment would not receive the contract—often ended up getting the business.

These business leaders argued that the FCPA would dramatically exaggerate this effect. In order to compete effectively, U.S. businesses must also be allowed to use methods of competition—including bribery—that foreign multinationals are able to use.[77] Furthermore, as we pointed out earlier, some executives noted that other governments not only do not outlaw bribes, they sometimes sanction them by allowing bribes to be tax deductible (e.g., Germany and Switzerland). This situation changed in 1999 with the passage of European antibribery statutes, laws that have many elements similar to the U.S. FCPA. Nevertheless, executives then and now ask: How can U.S. business compete in world markets with such restrictions?[78]

Actually, research has been done to answer the question of whether or not the FCPA had a negative effect on the competitiveness of U.S. business. One study looked at the market share of U.S. business since the passage of the FCPA in two different types of countries. This involved surveying U.S. embassy and Department of Commerce officials about business practices in over fifty different countries. The goal of this part of the study was to identify countries where the prevalence of improper payments was very high and countries where this practice was rare. Having done this, the study then examined whether the passage of the FCPA was more likely to be an export disincentive in countries where illegal payments are common. It also looked at change in market share before the passage of the FCPA (1971–1976) and after passage (1977–1980). Interestingly, the FCPA did not decrease the overall competitiveness of American multinationals overseas. In fact, there were no differences in market shares between the two types of countries either before or after the passage of the FCPA.[79]

However, this study does have some limitations. For one, the researchers studied the effects over a relatively short time interval, after passage of the FCPA. Competitiveness could decline slowly over time as a result of the act. Second, the market share data themselves are quite variable. For example, in the airline industry it was common to observe market share changes of nearly 100 percent over a year. Although this was not consistently associated with countries where bribery is common, it does show that the data can jump around dramatically. Boeing, for example, may sign a contract with Saudi Arabia one year and be shut out entirely next year when Airbus Industrie gets the next Saudi contract.[80]

Nevertheless, although the data are far from perfect, an initial conclusion would be that the FCPA does not significantly affect American international competitiveness overall. This doesn't mean, however, that U.S. multinationals don't lose out on specific business ventures because they won't provide a cut to a foreign partner. For example, American telecom firms complained about being shut out of contracts awarded by Ecuador as it privatized the state-run phone company. Some 90 percent of the nearly 200 contracts awarded went to non-U.S. firms, allegedly because American firms wouldn't pay 10 percent of a contract's value to government officials.[81] Likewise, Ford Motor Co. felt it lost out on a car venture in Indonesia because rival Hyundai cut a sweetheart deal with one of President Suharto's sons. In fact, some multinationals at the time felt that without an ally in the Suharto family, business deals simply didn't get done in Indonesia. Plus, having one of President Suharto's six children as a joint venture partner wasn't illegal per se under American law.[82] However, such a situation serves to illustrate once again the many ethical gray areas that exist in international business.

Summing Up Questionable Payments At this point, we can only speculate about the level of corrupt activities currently being carried out by American multinationals. Certainly, some questionable behavior is occurring. With few exceptions, however, American multinationals have done quite a bit to eliminate corruption in their international dealings. For example, it is rare to see cases such as the one in 1988 that implicated one of the largest ad agencies in the world, Young & Rubicam (Y&R)—and three of its executives. The U.S. Justice Department claimed that the firm had violated the act by using one of its Jamaican agents to indirectly bribe the Jamaican minister of tourism in an illegal effort to obtain business. Y&R agreed to pay a $500,000 fine to settle the case brought under the FCPA.[83]

One response of many U.S. firms—like Y&R—is to develop clear corporate guidelines about illegal payments and to communicate them directly to their managers. In fact, it is estimated that almost 80 percent of U.S. multinationals have incorporated such guidelines into their operations. As we pointed out earlier, the percentage for U.S. multinationals with such guidelines is much larger than for multinationals of several other nations. Some of these codes, like Caterpillar's, provide detailed guidelines about what payments are and are not permitted. In fact, some corporate codes, like IBM's (and now Y&R's), take a very strong ethical position. IBM, for instance, does not allow its managers to even use grease payments that are legally permitted under the FCPA. In general, however, these codes are not very precise, and they usually tell managers what they shouldn't do as opposed to what they should.[84]

🌐 International Insights

Making Friends and Influencing People: How U.S. Firms Compete Where Bribes Flourish

U.S. MULTINATIONALS are often constrained by their own corporate codes of conduct as well as by the Foreign Corrupt Practices Act (FCPA). The bottom line is that U.S. firms can't engage in many of the practices that some other countries permit their firms to do. So how do U.S. firms compete in this environment? Well, consider Percy Chubb III. He's spent a million dollars trying to make friends and presumably influence people. Mr. Chubb, while serving as vice chairman of Chubb Insurance, wanted a license from Chinese officials in order to tap that country's potentially large insurance market. So the company set up a $1 million program to teach insurance at Shanghai University. It has also named as board members some of the officials who eventually will decide if Chubb gets its license. "You try to show them this is a two-way street," explains Mr. Chubb, who says his company has spent "millions" on similar projects to improve its prospects overseas.

Such behavior exemplifies the strategy used by many U.S. firms, an approach that contrasts with the blatant bribery that is still common in much of the world. Aggressive foreign companies commonly use payoffs to gain access to big, fast-developing markets. There is little doubt that some U.S. firms are doing the same thing. Unlike their European and Asian counterparts, however, they are subject to the big teeth of the FCPA if they get caught. For instance, Lockheed-Martin Corp. was convicted in 1995 of paying $1.5 million to an Egyptian official who helped the firm get an aircraft contract. The company paid $24 million in fines, which was more than twice the profits from the contract itself. Likewise, GE paid a $69-million fine after one of their employees bribed an Israeli general.

Prosecutions under the FCPA, however, are relatively rare; less than 50 cases have been filed as of 2003. Partly this is because cases often require cooperation from the countries where the violation occurred, and this is difficult. This is the very mechanism by which U.S. officials were tipped off about a scandal involving ExxonMobil. In what is the largest

As a result, some experts actually recommend that multinationals set up ethics hotlines that employees can call anonymously.[85] Although there are many hurdles to overcome, including how to deal with false allegations, at least some firms are starting such hotlines. Another proactive step that some U.S. multinationals are taking is to make efforts to convince foreign multinationals and their governments—mostly through U.S. government channels—to implement stronger laws against bribery and other corrupt practices.[86] In general, however, such efforts have not been very successful. The accompanying International Insights provides more details on these and other obstructions that U.S. managers face in conducting international business.

▶ Ethical Issues Emerging from Countries Converting to Capitalism

In this final section, we examine the social problems that multinationals may help create in countries moving toward more competitive market economies. For instance, privatization is a trend sweeping the globe. This is especially true in China, Latin America, the former Soviet Union, and eastern Europe. Africa is

investigation of possible bribery since the passage of the FCPA, the Department of Justice has opened an inquiry into Mobil's involvement into oil deals in Kazakhstan (home of the world's largest oil discovery in the last thirty years) and the routing of $78 million in payments through the Swiss accounts of Kazakh officials (including their president). With help of Swiss authorities, records have resulted in indictments of a now-retired Mobil executive. For its part, Mobil has denied knowledge of such payments or awareness of such activity among its employees. Other firms are similarly involved, including some European firms. But those officials are not likely to be charged since the illegal activity occurred before passage of the European equivalent of the FCPA in 1999.[87]

Bribery aside, a much more common strategy for U.S. firms is to influence by making friends. The Chubb approach of using donations and other "philanthropic" activity to exert influence is perfectly acceptable under the FCPA. When IBM chairman Louis Gerstner visited Beijing in 1995, for instance, the company donated $25 million in hardware and software to twenty Chinese universities. Another common example of this strategy is to offer foreign officials trips to the United States. "Those trips provide an excellent opportunity to build relations with customers," said William Warwick, chairman of the China operations for AT&T Corp. For instance, when Union Texas Petroleum formed a joint venture with Pakistan's government, the company said it would spend more than $200,000 a year training those government officials in the United States and Europe. Once in the United States, foreign officials often spend at least part of their time visiting factories and the like. But side trips to places such as Disney World, Las Vegas, and Atlantic City appear to be very common. For example, Dow Jones & Co. arranged an Atlantic City trip for one delegation from China.

None of these payments is illegal under the FCPA. "But is it corruption?" an executive asks. "I mean, if someone came up to me and offered me something worth eighteen months' salary, it would certainly get my attention." Even the U.S. government lends a hand. A U.S. diplomat in eastern Europe says that sometimes the government will pay for a ministry head to visit America before a U.S. company bids on a big contract. The U.S. Department of Commerce employs this strategy with many countries around the world. According to Transparency International, an international corruption oversight organization, Russian, Chinese, and South Korean companies are "paying bribes in developing countries on an exceptional and intolerable scale" (with the U.S. having problems of its own in this area).[88] As a result, we can only predict that these creative strategies among U.S. firms are likely to continue.[89]

likely to follow in a big way.[90] Multinationals often view this trend as an opportunity to buy up state-owned firms, thereby providing a foothold in what are becoming important emerging markets. Likewise, low wage rates in developing nations have become an irresistible lure for many multinationals.

However, multinationals also need to be aware of the social problems that they may contribute to as a result of increased economic activity. For instance, because of weak regulations in many emerging countries, as their economic growth rates have shot up, so has the pollution of their water and air. In fact, the deteriorating environment in these countries threatens to be an expensive social headache and major source of conflict. Just creating the infrastructure to provide an adequate water supply for developing Asian nations cost an estimated $100 billion in 2002. Another $50 billion or more will be needed to combat serious air pollution problems in many Asian cities. Recently, officials in India's Delhi state say court-ordered shutdowns of small polluting industrial units will eliminate the jobs of two million people.[91] India has also turned its attention to foreign firms and problems to which they may contribute. Environmental groups in India recently charged that soft drinks sold there by PepsiCo and Coca-Cola contain traces of pesticides.[92] While this remains to be proven, many feel this is also an indirect shot over the bow of the Indian government and their weak attention to massive pollution and water problems in the country.[93] Attacks on multinationals such as these strike a chord with Indians, and activists hope this will transfer to feelings about Indian inaction. Either way, foreign firms must deal with these issues.

Another social problem that multinationals are faced with or are being forced to deal with is the AIDS malady. AIDS epidemics around the world have, in some cases, had sufficient impact to damage and/or bring down an economy. Nowhere has this been truer than in Botswana. This country in southern Africa had seen dramatic economic growth in the thirty years before the huge growth of AIDS began in the mid-1990s. Per capita income jumped from just $300 to nearly $3,500, school enrollment went from 50 percent to 97 percent, and infant mortality dropped sharply. As might be expected, AIDS is a much greater problem among countries that suffer from poverty. Now, however, things seemingly couldn't be much worse: AIDS is responsible for eating up 30 percent of the economic growth, employers can only count on an average of five years of productive labor from employees, and more than 20 percent of children are likely to be orphans. Many employers simply cannot find healthy workers; it's common to find hospitals where 75 percent of the beds are filled with AIDS patients. The government estimates that it will cost $500 million over the next five years to provide its people with treatment and drugs—many of which are developed and sold by highly developed countries. Increasingly, these companies, including many U.S. drug firms, are feeling the pressure exerted on them to reduce the price of drugs—particularly to the poorest of countries.[94] South Africa has been particularly aggressive, especially with its sanctioning of "parallel importing." This law permits importers to buy drugs from the cheapest source, whether or not those sources have patents or approval from patent holders.[95] Fights over anticancer and AIDS drugs were partially responsible for the general failure of the recent WTO conference in Cancun.[96] The need for these drugs is high since overall nearly 36 percent of adults in Botswana are inflicted with HIV/AIDS. While this is the highest on the continent, other countries such as Swaziland (25 percent), Zimbabwe (25 percent), and South Africa (20 percent) report enormously high rates as well. Beyond the massive toll in human suffering, these economies are no longer market outlets but instead present a huge problem and drain on global resources.

And, ironically, the movement to a market economy can also contribute to poverty. A recent UN report suggests that the economic growth of many countries that are transitioning to market-based systems masks the fact that millions of people are becoming impoverished along the way.[97] For example, millions of workers lost their jobs in state-owned firms in eastern Europe in recent years. In places such as the Czech Republic, Hungary, and Poland, multinationals have purchased many former state enterprises and promptly proceeded to slash workforces. Granted, many communist-era state businesses were overstaffed, backward, and inefficient. Nevertheless, wholesale terminations have raised unemployment rates, hurt worker morale, and caused resentment.[98] In some places, the numbers are staggering. The unemployment rate in eastern Germany is about 17 percent, roughly twice the rate in the western half of the country. Almost 200,000 jobs in this former communist country were lost in 1996 alone.[99]

A similar trend exists in many Latin American countries like Argentina. There, privatizations are resulting in massive layoffs that are driving up unemployment and poverty.[100] Likewise, many African countries have bloated and inefficient state-owned businesses, but privatizing them will mean job losses

EXHIBIT 3.6   *Estimated Percentages of Children Who Work in Specific Countries*

Country	Estimated Percentage of Children Who Work	Country	Estimated Percentage of Children Who Work
Kenya	42	Thailand	16
Malaysia	37	India	14
Bangladesh	30	China	11
Haiti	25	Egypt	11
Turkey	24	Indonesia	10
Pakistan	17	Vietnam	9
Brazil	16	Philippines	8
Guatemala	16	Mexico	7

Source: Adapted from Zachary. ———. (1994). Levi's tries to make sure contract plants in Asia treat workers well. *Wall Street Journal*, July 28, A1, A6.

and increased social costs. Africa also faces some unique difficulties because of its already high level of poverty. For instance, in Kenya, Del Monte grows pineapples on former state farms. As a result, Kenya earns critical foreign exchange through exports of the fruit. However, the huge plots of land controlled by Del Monte means that less land is available for subsistence farming, making the Kenyans in the area among the poorest people in the country.[101]

In China, tens of millions of workers are idled as state-owned enterprises crumble before the onslaught of foreign multinationals or strive to be "leaner and meaner" in partnership with Western firms. According to some experts, if this trend continues, it could lead to a variety of devastating social problems, if not outright rebellion. Why? Little or no social safety net exists for Chinese workers—there is no significant equivalent to unemployment compensation or social security.[102] Plus, because most of the available jobs are in cities and coastal areas, millions of Chinese are flocking in from the provinces looking for work, some as young as 10 or 11. In the process, families are being split up and crime in the cities is on the rise.[103]

This desperation can also result in what some would call the exploitation of workers, often by multinationals or their foreign partners. Because of low wages and high levels of poverty in many developing countries, adults are often unemployed or underemployed. In Africa alone poverty is pervasive—nearly nine of ten people in twenty-four African countries live on less than $2 a day, and two-thirds live on less than $1.[104] The result there and elsewhere? Children are going to work to help feed the family. In 1999, a staggering 250 million children under 15 were estimated to be working in developing nations. Many of these children end up working for foreign contractors that supply multinationals. Exhibit 3.6 lists the percentage of children under 15 who work in certain developing countries. For another look at what might be considered exploitation, read about what Hong Xiaohui went through in landing a job for U.S.-based toymaker Mattel in the following International Insights.

As you might suspect, there are no easy answers here. Clearly, multinationals offer many benefits to emerging economies. However, they can also contribute to the social problems that accompany the transition to market-based

🌐 International Insights

A Job Seeker's Odyssey

ONE OF THE greatest migrations in history is under way now. Some estimate that as many as 100 million Chinese are on the move. Millions of peasants are fleeing their villages for the lure of economic prosperity in big cities such as Shanghai and Guangzhou. One of these stories is about Hong Xiaohui, who traveled 1,200 miles from her remote village in China to Mattel's Barbie doll plant in Guangdong province. This 18-year-old's journey says a lot about what it's like to be in the middle of the economic upheaval reshaping China. Unfortunately, it isn't a very pretty story. In fact, it's one that raises a variety of ethical concerns about the responsibilities that multinationals have in recruiting their Chinese workforces. But one thing is clear. Hong Xiaohui's odyssey is one that 100 million Chinese from the interior provinces are making in the quest for work.

To reach the Mattel factory, Ms. Hong spent several days (and sleepless nights) on a bouncing, rickety bus. There was no food or water provided except what Ms. Hong brought herself or was willing to pay for. After a while, the bus reeked from sweat, vomit, and rotting food. Bathroom breaks often meant finding a spot on the side of the road or waiting in line with the 100 other women traveling on the bus to use a country outhouse. Believe it or not, the women on the bus had

to *pay* 415 yuan (about $50) for this trip. But they did so willingly. When local labor officials showed up at their villages to recruit workers for Mattel, many leapt at the chance to escape China's grim rural poverty.

However, when Ms. Hong reached the Mattel plant, there were some unpleasant surprises. Mattel offered a pay level of 200 yuan per month (about $25), despite the fact that the labor officials recruiting for Mattel had promised her 350 yuan. The factory is also run strictly, with three absences resulting in termination. Off the job, Ms. Hong is housed (crammed, actually) in a small room with eleven other employees. The amenities? A concrete floor, a single light bulb, and a tiny bathroom with no hot water.

Nevertheless, Ms. Hong signed a contract to work at Mattel for three years. Doing what? Putting the hair on Barbie doll heads—a sometimes painful job that requires punching holes in the heads and weaving in the hair. When asked about working conditions and the other things that Hong Xiaohui had to suffer through, Mattel refused to comment. In spite of everything, though, Ms. Hong says she'd make the same choice again. To do otherwise would leave her "like a flower in a greenhouse. It can't feel the wind blow and it can't grow stronger."[105]

---

economies. So what should multinationals do as a result? At a minimum, we suggest that multinationals learn to be sensitive to the fact that some of their actions may have negative effects on local populations, unintended or not. There also seems to be an assumption among some multinationals that any suffering (from layoffs, pollution, etc.) is a "necessary" or "inevitable" part of a "temporary" transition process. While it is too soon to tell, in many cases multinationals may be underestimating how long it will take to halt the "temporary" suffering.

All of this argues for a greater emphasis on ethical behavior and social responsibility by multinationals. Experts suggest, for example, that multinationals adopt strict codes of conduct for their own behavior on environmental issues. In fact, multinationals have also been encouraged to raise environmental awareness in the nations where they do business and to make investments in local efforts to clean up and protect the environment.[106]

Similarly, investments in the community (in schools, hospitals, retraining programs, land grants to farmers, etc.) may help lessen the social impact of economic change. Multinationals may also want to help governments in emerging nations develop and implement policies similar to those that already exist in many Western industrialized countries (such as programs designed to provide unemployment benefits, assist budding entrepreneurs, and provide loans to existing local businesses). One such program is being established by Hewlett-Packard.[107] Even with HP stock in the doldrums, CEO Carly Fiorina is thinking long term. She recently unveiled an impressive program to sell products to the poor of the world. The program is called World e-Inclusion and is on the leading edge of a trend some call B2-4B, or "business to four billion." In the next few years, HP will sell, lease, or donate $1 billion of its products to governments and agencies in countries such as Bangladesh and Senegal. Fiorina feels this will eventually position HP to be in on the ground floor of a huge market and to tackle some issues immediately. To support this giveaway, HP will also set up funds for potential entrepreneurs, low-power devices for the equipment, and more. There are critics to be sure, but Fiorina is no wide-eyed philanthropist. "There's a big difference between creating a sustainable business model around products and services that raise the standard of living and . . . just pouring in money on an ongoing basis." Time will tell. Nevertheless, such steps might smooth out some of the bumps in the road that emerging nations must endure on the way to becoming market-based economies.

Chapter Summary

In this chapter we dealt with *ethical values* and *corporate social responsibility*. We reviewed two major perspectives on ethics. On one hand, *universalism* argues that there are sets of ethical values that should apply everywhere, and many international and corporate codes of conduct have been developed based on this perspective. On the other hand, *relativism* is a perspective that embraces the idea that countries often have different sets of ethical values that are shaped by their own unique laws and practices. The implication for business in this case is "When in Rome, do as the Romans do."

Next, we considered cross-national differences in ethical perspectives. Most research suggests that Americans tend to be more concerned with ethical issues than their counterparts in Europe, Asia, and other parts of the world. U.S. multinationals are also more likely to have written codes of conduct in place that spell out what is considered unethical behavior than are European multinationals.

We then moved on to consider specific unethical practices by foreign governments and what firms are willing to do about them. With respect to human rights, we noted that there is general agreement that certain types of behavior are unacceptable. What is less clear, however, is what multinationals should do as a result. In apartheid-era South Africa, for instance, some multinationals believed that they could have more influence by remaining engaged in that country's economy, whereas others decided to withdraw to protest racist policies. Despite well-documented human rights abuses now in China, few multinationals have pulled out; one exception was Levi Strauss.

Likewise, multinationals need to confront the issue of *bribery* in international business. In many countries, such payoffs are common if not expected. Most nations, however, have laws that prohibit the bribery of officials. Few, however, actually outlaw bribes that their citizens may pay to foreigners. Many nations, in fact, view bribery as just part of the cost of doing international business. Bribing foreigners to get business was sometimes practiced among U.S. multinationals, although the high-profile cases that came to light in the 1970s eventually led to the passage of the *Foreign Corrupt Practices Act* (FCPA). While this law made it illegal to pay foreigners bribes in an effort to win business, the FCPA does allow for *facilitating payments* that will ensure foreign officials do what they are supposed to do (e.g., clear a shipment through customs). Research done on the FCPA's impact suggests that there is no systematic disadvantage suffered by U.S. multinationals because of the act's prohibitions.

We concluded this chapter by discussing some of the social costs that are associated with many nations' ongoing transition to more competitive, market-based economies. In doing so, we looked at how multinationals may sometimes contribute to the suffering of the people living through such transitions (such as by exploiting local workers or increasing pollution, unemployment, and poverty) as well as how multinationals might be able to improve the situation.

Discussion Questions

1. What role do universalism and relativism play for international management?

2. How should multinationals deal with human rights abuses by foreign governments?

Bribery attempts? Other questionable practices? Should they involve themselves in the issues at all? Why or why not?

3. What is your assessment of the Foreign Corrupt Practices Act? Is it likely to be a major hindrance for U.S. multinationals? What position should the U.S. government take regarding the tactics used by foreign multinationals in international competition?

4. What are some of the social costs associated with emerging nations' ongoing transition to market-based economies? How do multinationals contribute to these problems? What should they do about them, if anything? Why?

Up to the Challenge?

Competitive Intelligence: Lots of Gray Areas, No Easy Answers

WE CHALLENGED YOU AT THE beginning of this chapter to make some judgments about the ethics and legality of some specific behaviors associated with the increasingly popular practice of competitive intelligence gathering. The following exhibit summarizes the behavioral incidents we mentioned and whether, according to experts, they are legal, illegal, or in an ethically gray area. In essence, deliberate theft of company materials or secrets from company property is illegal, at least in the United States. However, several of the examples of competitive intelligence we've cited would be considered unethical by many Americans.

Many of these situations have involved U.S. companies. For example, a crayon company employee posed as a potential customer and easily gained access to the firm's production processes. While this is unethical, what about standing outside a plant to count employees who leave various shifts? What about the Japanese firm that sent employees to measure the thickness of rust on train tracks leaving a U.S. plant and then used that data to estimate plant output?[108] Of course, U.S. firms aren't immune to this activity. Just last year Raytheon Co., the defense contractor, agreed to pay a multimillion settlement to resolve charges

that it hired private detectives to eavesdrop in a failed attempt to outrun Ages Group's bid for a U.S. Air Force service contract. Even universities are getting into the act. At the University of Missouri classes are taught in how to do "pipeline" analysis in the drug industry. This involves using public sources to ferret out what products are in the competition's research pipeline.[109]

The early 2000s experienced a down market, but some companies still found the funds to engage in CI. Whereas in the late 1990s, Mr. Michael Mace—the chief competitive officer at Palm—didn't have a second thought about commissioning a $70,000 "scouting report" on the Japanese PDA market, now he will have to be more careful. But his CI work has actually increased in frequency—he's just gotten cleverer about methods. John Nolan, a former defense intelligence officer who now runs a training business on legal (and inexpensive) CI, said it best: "Nothing changes table manners faster than a smaller pie." Indeed, data shows that among firms without an organized CI capability, 45 percent said they planned to start one the following year. [110]

If CI is on the rise and itself getting more competitive, what should a firm do? In our opening box we asked about recommendations that you might give multinationals interested in protecting their secrets from competitors' prying. Here are some tips:

- Have all joint venture partners and consultants the multinational works with sign nondisclosure agreements.
- Make sure the multinational tightly controls access to all facilities and electronic mail systems.

- Use written policies to make all employees more aware of the risks of security lapses.
- Test areas within the firm itself that might be vulnerable to information leaks.
- Establish a centralized electronic reporting system that will allow employees to report any suspicious incidents.

Behavioral Example	U.S. Legal/Ethical Status
1. Calling neighbors under false pretenses to assess managers' whereabouts	Ethically gray area
2. Securing a copy of a competitor's travel itinerary from a travel agent	Ethically gray area
3. Digging through a company's trash on public property	Legal
4. Deliberately eavesdropping on private company conversations	Illegal
5. Sending phony job seekers in response to a competitor's want ads	Ethically gray area
6. Hiring a competitor's former employees	Legal
7. Sending phony visitors to tour a competitor's facilities	Ethically gray area
8. Attending trade shows where a competitor's wares are displayed	Legal

International Development

Bribery in International Business

Purpose

The goal is to discuss ethical issues associated with bribery and corrupt practices that may be encountered in international business dealings. To accomplish this, twelve short minicases are presented that are designed to get you thinking about ethical issues associated with bribery. Your instructor may review the Foreign Corrupt Practices Act and Kohlberg's stages of moral reasoning as background before getting started. These brief minicases deal with issues including bribes versus grease payments, whistle-blowing, the black market, and governmental interaction.

Instructions

Your instructor will divide the class into groups of four to six members. Depending on the time available and number of groups, your group may be assigned all twelve or some subset (like four or six) of the minicases. Discuss each minicase with your group and decide what course of action should be taken (20–30 minutes, depending on the number of cases your group must tackle).

Your instructor will then lead a discussion about the ethical issues raised by the minicases (20–30 minutes, depending on whether your group will be asked to present its recommended courses of action).

Minicases

1. You are driving to a nearby country from your job as a manager of a foreign subsidiary. In your car are a number of rather expensive gifts for family and friends in the country you are visiting. When you cross the border, the customs official tells you the duty will be equivalent to $200. Then he smiles, hands back your passport, and quietly suggests you put a smaller sum, say $20, in the passport and hand it back to him. What do you do?

2. You have been hired as an independent consultant on a U.S. development grant. Part of your job involves working with the Ministry of Health in a developing country. Your assignment is to help standardize some procedures to test for various diseases in the population.

After two weeks on the job, a higher-level manager complains to you that money donated by the World Health Organization to the ministry for purchasing vaccines has actually been used to buy expensive computers for top-ranking officials. What do you do?

3. You have been trying for several months to privatize what was formerly a state-owned business. The company has been doing well and will likely do better in private hands. Unfortunately, the paperwork is slow and it may take many more months to finish. An official who can help suggests that if you pay expenses for him and his family to visit the parent company in the United States (plus a two-week vacation at Disney World and in New York), the paperwork can be complete within one week. What do you do?

4. One of your top managers in a Middle Eastern country has been kidnapped by a terrorist group that has demanded a ransom of $2 million, plus food assistance for refugees in a specified camp. If the ransom is not paid, they threaten to kill him. What do you do?

5. On a business trip to a developing country, you see a leather briefcase (which you badly need) for a reasonable price in the local currency (the equivalent of $200 at the standard exchange rate). In this country, however, it is difficult for the locals to get U.S. dollars or other hard currency. The shop clerk offers you the briefcase for $100 if you pay in U.S. dollars. What do you do?

6. You are the manager of a foreign subsidiary and have brought your car with you from the United States. Because it is a foreign-purchased car, you must go through a complicated web of lines and bureaucracy (and you must do it yourself—no one can do it for you), which takes anywhere from twenty to forty hours. One official tells you, however, that he can "help" if you "loan" him $100 and buy him some good U.S. bourbon. What do you do?

7. Your company has been trying to get foreign contracts in this developing country for several months. Yesterday, the brother-in-law of the finance minister offered to work as a consultant to help you secure contracts. He charges one and one-half times more than anyone else in a similar situation. What do you do?

8. You have been working as the director of the foreign subsidiary for several months. This week, you learned several valued employees have part-time businesses that they run while on the job. One of them exchanges foreign currency for employees and visitors. Another rents a few cars to visitors. And so on. You are told this has been acceptable behavior for years. What do you do?

9. As manager of a foreign subsidiary, you recently discovered your chief of operations has authorized a very convoluted accounting system, most likely to hide many costs that go into his pocket. Right now, you have no real proof, but rumors are circulating to that effect as well. This chief, however, has close ties to officials in the government who can make or break your company in this country. What do you do?

10. You have been hired to do some management training in a developing country. The costs of the program are almost entirely covered by a U.S. government agency. The people responsible for setting up one of the programs in a large company tells you they want the program to be held in a resort hotel (which is not much more expensive than any other) in a beautiful part of the country. Further, because they are so busy with all the changes in their country, they cannot come to a five-day program, which is what has been funded. Could you please make it a little longer each day and shorten it to three days? You would get paid the same. What do you do?

11. You have been hired by an investment firm funded by U.S. dollars. Your job is to finance companies in several former communist countries. If you do not meet your quota for each of three months, you will lose your job, or at least have your salary severely cut back. One of the countries is still run by communists, though they have changed the name of their political party. They want you to finance three companies that would still be tightly controlled by the state. You know

they would hire their relatives to run those companies. Yet if you don't support them, no other opportunities will exist for you in this country. What do you do?

12. Your new job is to secure contracts with foreign governments in several developing countries. One of your colleagues takes you aside one day to give you "tips" on how to make sure you get the contracts you are after. He tells you what each nationality likes to hear to soothe their egos or other psychological needs. For example, people in one country like to be told they will have a better

image with the U.S. government if they contract with your company (of course, this is not true). If you tell them these things, he says, they will most definitely give you the contracts. If not, someone in another company will tell them similar things and they will get the contracts. What do you do?

Source: From *International Management Cases and Exercises*, 2nd edition by D. Marcic and S. Puffer, pp. 93–96. © 1994. Reprinted with permission of South-Western College Publishing, a division of Thomson Learning. Fax 800-730-2215.

 # Tapping into the Global Network

Analyzing Corporate Codes

Purpose

To understand important elements of corporate codes and the complexities involved in constructing such guidelines for behavior.

Instructions

In this chapter, we talked a good deal about corporate codes of ethics and the ways they are both similar and different. For this exercise, do some research to find codes of conduct for three multinational corporations. Using websites or library information, compare the codes and evaluate them. After getting this information, please do the following:

1. Answer these questions about the codes you've chosen and those of others discussed in class. What topics are covered in the codes? Which topics are not covered? How are these issues communicated in the codes? The instructor may wish to keep a tally of the common themes across the various companies. Compile a list by industry and jot down what you think the reasons are for possible differences across those industries.

2. Put together *your* version of a generic corporate code of ethics. Many international accords exist that provide a good base for your work (and for corporations), and a variety of websites are useful for this purpose and for answering the questions raised above:

- **www.ethics.ubc.ca/resources/business** This site includes a discussion of many business ethics issues as well as links and discussion of corporate codes of ethics.

- **ecampus.bentley.edu/dept/cbe** The site of Bentley College's Center for Business Ethics and the source of a good deal of information on this topic.

- **commerce.depaul.edu/ethics** The site of DePaul University's business ethics center.

- **www.ethics.org/glossary.html** A general and valuable resource for business ethics in general and ethical codes in particular.

- **www.transparency.de** The site on international corruption mentioned earlier in this chapter.

4

Cultural Dimensions: Implications for International Management

Learning Objectives

After reading this chapter, you should be able to:

▸ Understand how countries can be clustered according to their cultural values.

▸ Describe how cultural values can affect employee attitudes about work.

▸ Understand the implications of cultural values and dimensions for international management.

▸ Understand how employees and corporations can go about making better sense of culture.

INTERNATIONAL CHALLENGE

Two Sides of the Japanese-American Cultural Divide

MAKING GENERALIZATIONS about culture is always a risky proposition. But it's safe to say that the culture gap between American and Japanese society is sizable. And to the extent that such a gap filters down to individual employees, it can make working together difficult. Take a look at Exhibit 4.1, which summarizes the value differences that may exist between American and Japanese employees.

Now imagine that you're an American, working in the United States for a Japanese-owned subsidiary, and your immediate supervisor is Japanese. What issues might that present for you in terms of performance appraisals and promotions? Or how about the reverse? What kinds of challenges and difficulties do you think a Japanese supervisor would run into with American subordinates? Think about these issues as you read this chapter. You'll be learning a great deal about cultural values and some of their managerial implications. Then take a look at *Up to the Challenge?* at the end of this chapter for some insights into the difficulties that can come up when Americans and Japanese work together and how to bridge them.[1]

EXHIBIT 4.1   *Summary of Contrasting Japanese and American Values and Behavior*

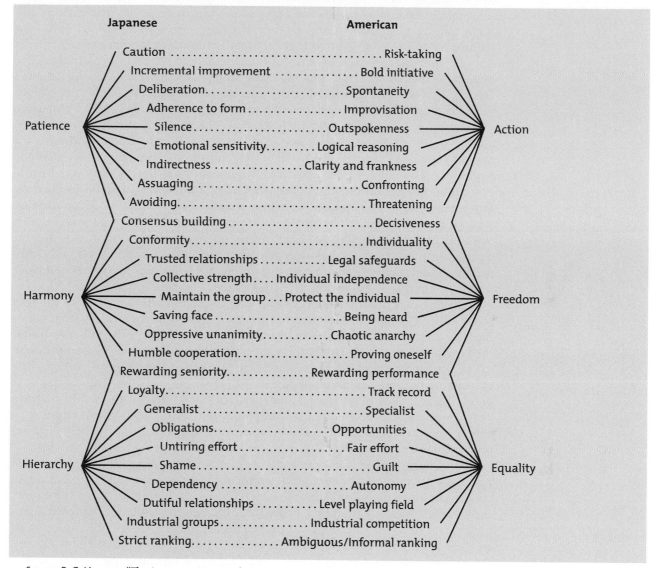

	Japanese	American	
Patience	Caution . . . . Risk-taking		Action
	Incremental improvement . . . . Bold initiative		
	Deliberation. . . . . Spontaneity		
	Adherence to form . . . . Improvisation		
	Silence. . . . . Outspokenness		
	Emotional sensitivity. . . . . Logical reasoning		
	Indirectness . . . . Clarity and frankness		
	Assuaging . . . . Confronting		
	Avoiding. . . . . Threatening		
	Consensus building . . . . Decisiveness		
Harmony	Conformity. . . . . Individuality		Freedom
	Trusted relationships . . . . Legal safeguards		
	Collective strength. . . . Individual independence		
	Maintain the group . . . Protect the individual		
	Saving face . . . . Being heard		
	Oppressive unanimity. . . . . Chaotic anarchy		
	Humble cooperation. . . . . Proving oneself		
	Rewarding seniority. . . . . Rewarding performance		
	Loyalty. . . . . Track record		
	Generalist . . . . Specialist		
Hierarchy	Obligations. Opportunities		Equality
	Untiring effort . . . . Fair effort		
	Shame . . . . Guilt		
	Dependency . . . . Autonomy		
	Dutiful relationships . . . . Level playing field		
	Industrial groups. . . . . Industrial competition		
	Strict ranking. . . . . Ambiguous/Informal ranking		

Source: R. G. Linowes, "The Japanese Manager's Traumatic Entry into the United States: Understanding the American-Japanese Cultural Divide," *Academy of Management Executive,* Vol. 7, p. 24. Copyright © 1993 by the Academy of Management. Reprinted by permission.

▶ *Revisiting Culture*

In Chapter 1 we defined culture as "the collective programming of the mind which distinguishes one group or category of people from another." We also pointed out that people are unlikely to be fully aware of the pervasive impact of culture on their own attitudes, beliefs, and behaviors.[2] But there's plenty of evidence that culture has a major impact on the management of international business, often in some surprising ways. In fact, cultural differences can impact everything from what employees expect from their companies to how expatriates adapt in foreign environments to how firms invest overseas. And the impact itself may cut both ways. In other words, cultural differences have the potential to produce friction and disruption as well as enormous benefits (e.g., better international performance if firms are able to put the best of what various cultures offer to good use).[3] Consequently, the chapters in this book explore how culture plays a role in just about every facet of international business.

Of course, the stakes, at least for management, have never been higher. The ongoing growth of international business brings with it the increasing demands associated with managing culturally diverse workforces. And cultural values (such as a belief in the importance of hard work and thrift) may affect employee motivation in ways that can help explain different economic growth rates among nations.[4] So managers need to know which motivation strategies are applicable across cultures and which are culture specific. But that's just the beginning. Human resource practices, organization structure, strategy formation and implementation, conflict management approaches, negotiation tactics, and leadership styles can also vary dramatically across cultures.[5] Even the reasons entrepreneurs start companies to begin with can be driven, at least in part, by culture. For instance, in East Asian countries (e.g., Indonesia, Korea, Thailand), the level of interest in entrepreneurship may be more strongly connected to social status concerns (e.g., gaining face from success or losing it from failure) than it is in Anglo countries (e.g., Australia, the United States).[6]

In any case, the management challenge is not only to be aware of the role that culture can play, but to turn that awareness into an advantage where possible. For example, research shows that foreign subsidiaries perform better financially (e.g., have a higher return on assets and return on sales) when they use management practices that are consistent with the local culture.[7] Indeed, the ever-changing and rapidly evolving global business environment means that good opportunities may pop up anywhere, often in parts of the world that are poorly understood. Consequently, companies that can quickly grasp and intelligently interpret local cultures and business practices will be in the best position to succeed.[8]

Not surprisingly, however, managing "smart" from a cultural perspective isn't easy. Part of the problem is the complexity of culture itself. The "collective programming of the mind" that characterizes a particular culture can have roots in historical events, geography, shared traditions, economic developments, language, and religion. Moreover, cultural values, while relatively stable in the short run, are constantly evolving. And that means culture is something of a moving target for managers. On top of that, individuals don't always embrace the ostensible values of their cultural group. In other words, you don't have to look very hard to find, for example, Americans who are group oriented as opposed to individualistic and Japanese who are the reverse.[9]

The point is that managers need to be careful not to oversimplify culture and its effects. For example, it's tempting these days to embrace the view that people around the world are increasingly thinking and acting alike, thanks, at least in part, to technological advances (e.g., the Internet) and management development efforts (e.g., training aimed at bringing Western management methods to developing countries). This trend toward **cultural convergence**, some believe, will soon create a "global village" in which it will be possible to manage the same way everywhere. But the reality is that true cultural convergence is a long way off . . . if it comes at all. Indeed, there's evidence that the forces that supposedly are "bringing the world together" have prompted a back-

cultural convergence
The view that people around the world are increasingly thinking and acting alike

lash, reinforcing people's desire to hold on to their own cultural values and traditions. Overall, it would be a mistake to underestimate the continuing power and pull of culture on people's values, attitudes, and behavior.[10]

Another common oversimplification is to view cultural differences as a set of generic labels that can easily be applied to people, nations, and business situations. While this may give managers a basic sketch of what to expect from people in different cultures, it can also create serious new problems. Part of the issue is that research and theory on culture have been unable, at least so far, to both capture all of the cultural complexities that exist and develop specific, tangible advice for managing them.[11] Consequently, the theories and approaches that do exist tend to reduce culture to sets of bipolar adjectives (e.g., individualism–collectivism), which are then used to categorize and classify people and nations. In fact, we will review several prominent perspectives on culture that do just that.

But managers need to be mindful that these perspectives, while useful, can result in a kind of "sophisticated stereotyping" that doesn't fully capture the complexities and nuances of specific cultures. A good way to illustrate the dangers of this approach is by looking at cultural paradoxes. For instance, if Americans are the most individualistic people in the world, then why are Americans so willing to drop everything to help when community emergencies and disasters (e.g., tornados, floods, etc.) strike? Likewise, why do individualistic Americans have the highest rate of charitable gift giving in the world? Here's another example. Many Latin American cultures are well known for the positive regard and warm personal displays shown in interpersonal interactions. Then why do service employees in many Latin American countries express so much indifference to their customers? One survey done in Costa Rica found that many bank customers would rather deal with ATMs (because they were programmed to be polite) than with human tellers.[12]

▶ *The Dimensions of Culture*

In this section, we'll examine the major perspectives on culture that have influenced our thinking about international management. In doing so, we'll acknowledge both the benefits and limitations of these perspectives. We'll conclude this chapter by suggesting ways that both individual managers and international corporations can better understand cultural differences and the dilemmas that may come with them.

Ronen and Shenkar's Country Clusters

Trying to make sense of cross-cultural differences when hundreds of countries and cultures are involved is an extremely difficult task. One way to make things easier is to identify a core set of values that are shared by specific country clusters. Such clusters could help companies modify their management tactics to better reflect the values they expect to encounter in different groups of countries.[13]

In 1985, Ronen and Shenkar created clusters based on their exhaustive and comprehensive review of previous research. This included an assessment of how thousands of employees in nearly fifty countries responded to questions about:

- **The importance of various work goals** (i.e., what employees want from work, such as interesting work, job security, or promotion opportunities)

- **The extent to which work satisfies certain needs** (e.g., for various rewards, personal accomplishment, job satisfaction)

- **Various organizational factors and management issues** (e.g., preferences for autocratic versus democratic leadership)

- **The nature of work roles and interpersonal relationships** (e.g., how well managers relate to subordinates)

In a nutshell, Ronen and Shenkar clustered countries on what they felt were patterns of similarity in employees' attitudes toward work and how well it met their needs.

The clusters Ronen and Shenkar came up with are presented in Exhibit 4.2. Notice that eight country clusters were identified along with four countries that were viewed as separate and independent. Countries within a particular cluster are said to share some basic cultural values. But the exhibit also positions the richer, more developed countries within each cluster closest to the center. For example, the Nordic cluster suggests Sweden is the most highly developed, whereas in the Latin European cluster France is most highly developed.

EXHIBIT 4.2   *Ronen and Shenkar's Synthesized Country Clusters*

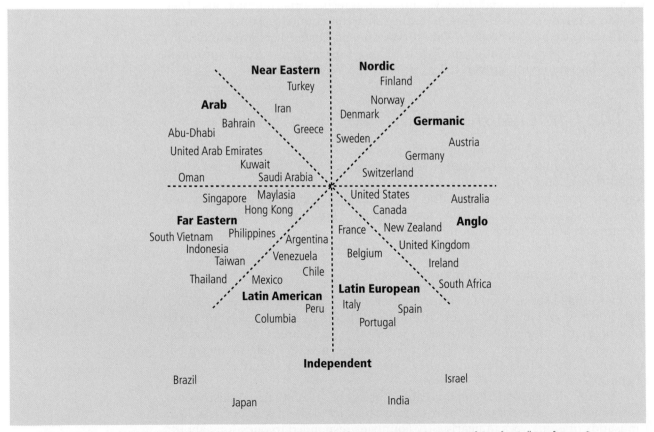

Source: S. Ronen and O. Shenkar, "Clustering Countries on Attitudinal Dimensions: A Review and Synthesis," *Academy of Management Review,* Vol. 10, p. 449. Copyright © 1985 by the Academy of Management. Reprinted by permission.

The level of development and technological progress in a country is one of the factors driving the clustering of countries, according to Ronen and Shenkar. As development proceeds, cultural values may change. You'll also notice that the clusters generally include countries that are close to each other geographically. This reflects the idea that cultural values should develop first in those areas nearest to a particular culture's point of origin. The fact that great geographic distances exist between countries in the Anglo-American cluster may reflect immigration patterns from the British Isles that took Anglo cultural values to many different parts of the globe.

Another similarity within clusters is language. For example, the Latin American cluster contains Spanish-speaking countries and the Anglo cluster English-speaking countries. While the countries in the Latin European cluster have different languages, they are all considered Romance, or Latin-derived, languages. Many work values, goals, and attitudes are shaped by linguistic meanings and interpretations.

Work values and goals may also reflect religious attitudes and beliefs. Catholicism is the major religion in both of the Latin clusters; Buddhist and Confucian values tie the countries together in the Far Eastern cluster. These values emphasize the obligations people have to their families and the shame that is associated with failing to live up to those obligations. Finally, the countries labeled as independent (Brazil, Japan, India, and Israel) have unique religions, languages, and histories. In the case of Japan, this also includes a level of geographic isolation that further contributed to a unique culture.[14]

Overall, Ronen and Shenkar's clusters provide a useful snapshot for international managers interested in knowing where broad similarities and differences may exist between countries in terms of values and attitudes. This is important since such similarities and differences are often reflected in the business practices and approaches used in various countries. Consequently, international managers armed with such knowledge are more likely to operate effectively in foreign environments, everything else being equal. Efforts are underway to refine the concept of country clusters, including the methods used to measure the differences in values between them. As you might suspect, the issues involved are quite complex. For instance, cultures are constantly changing, presenting researchers and managers alike with moving targets. Likewise, the impact of specific cultural differences can vary dramatically, with some differences having very little impact on the performance of international firms and others mattering a great deal. We need to better understand which differences matter most and why.[15]

Limitations of Ronen and Shenkar's Approach   Of course, these complexities also underscore some of the inherent limitations associated with Ronen and Shenkar's approach. For instance, their clusters are missing many countries (e.g., none of the countries in the former Soviet Union are included). In particular, few developing countries (e.g., China) are represented. Where would these countries fit today? Obviously, we don't know for sure, but the answer might be more complex than you would expect. For example, it's easy to imagine a new Asian cluster consisting of Japan, China, and South Korea. All three countries are well known for emphasizing harmony in interpersonal relations, an emphasis traceable to some common Confucian values. However, "harmony" takes on a different meaning in each country. In Japan, harmony is often defined in terms

EXHIBIT 4.3   *Defining "Harmony" Differently in Japan, China, and Korea*

Relevant Harmony Term	Japan *Wa*	China *Guanxi*	Korea *Inhwa*
Definition	Stress on group harmony, mutual cooperation to reach group goals	Stress on friendly relationships that are based on the exchange of favors	Stress on harmony between equals; workers are loyal, bosses are obligated
Employees' commitment	To company	To boss, family	To boss, family
Role of the individual	Be an effective group member	Maintain favorable exchange relations	Be loyal to boss
Decision-making	Participative, consensus-based, illusion of agreement key	Based on personal loyalties and favors owed	Based on family ties, hierarchy
Performance feedback	Indirect, often done via third parties to preserve group harmony	Indirect, often done via third parties to maintain equity in relationships	Indirect, often done via third parties to preserve harmony among unequals
Management style	Group facilitation	Benevolent paternalism	Clan management

Source: Adapted from Alston, J. P. (1989). Wa, guanxi, and inhwa: Managerial principles in Japan, China, and Korea. *Business Horizons*, March–April, 26–31.

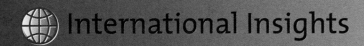

International Insights

Looking for Rugged Individualists . . . in Japan?

JAPAN SPENT MUCH of the 1990s in a protracted domestic slump. Now into the third millennium, angst continues in the wake of failed banks, takeovers, and layoffs, all shocking inconsistencies relative to Japan's traditional "contract" with employees. That social contract between companies and employees traded job security and generous benefits for an emphasis on tranquility, consensus, and the greater good.

The result? Doubts about the viability of the old social contract are leading many Japanese to conclude that building their lives around a relationship with one company is a huge mistake. Consequently, some Japanese are embracing individualism and personal responsibility as never before. One Japanese manager, who saw his forty-year career at a securities firm come to a screeching halt, put it this way: "I have to stand firmly on my own and think for myself. I wish I had realized this earlier in life." And if you don't, according to the same manager, "In this age of cut-throat competition, you'll just end up drowning." Some Japanese corporations also are picking up on this theme, pushing personal responsibility as a way to grow the economy.

of group activities and membership, whereas in China and Korea harmony is often defined in terms of relationships between individuals (Exhibit 4.3 presents a summary of these differences).

As a consequence, Japanese may value *wa* (i.e., group cohesion and group loyalty) above individual needs. Japanese often work for the group's benefit and identify strongly with their company. Since harmonious group relations are so important, interpersonal conflict tends to be minimized. For example, achieving consensus in decision making is critical, even if it requires maintaining an illusion of agreement among everyone during the decision-making process. Open disagreements tend to be avoided. While American managers often disagree in frank terms, some Japanese managers avoid conflicting views at all costs. For Americans, the word *sincerity* means telling the truth. The closest Japanese equivalent, *makoto*, means promoting harmony and showing support for colleagues.[16]

Of course, as we mentioned earlier, cultural values are always evolving. Although that process may be slow and incremental, it's often observable. That may indeed be the case with Japan, a society that's faced tough economic times in recent years. Take a look at the accompanying International Insights to see what we mean.

In China, however, harmony is expressed by *guanxi*, the special relationship that two Chinese have when they are mutually obligated to each other. This obligation includes the fair exchange of favors and can take precedence over laws, firm procedures, and company goals. A failure to return favors results in a loss of face and may lead to the end of the relationship. Employees tend to be loyal to their individual *guanxi* relationships, rather than to the company. *Guanxi* can exist between two people of unequal status, like a manager and a subordinate. In this case, the subordinate will be loyal in exchange for being

Of course, there's always the possibility that the luster of individualism in Japan is merely a passing fad. When the United States experienced economic doldrums in the 1980s, for instance, some Americans faddishly embraced the Japanese emphasis on harmony and consensus. Nevertheless, meaningful signs of real change are also present in Japan. Consider:

- The number of personal injury lawsuits is rising.

- Whistleblowing activity is increasing.

- Entrepreneurship is becoming more attractive as an alternative to corporate careers (e.g., parents can enroll their 4-year-olds in "Sun Kids," a privately run course designed to teach basic entrepreneurial principles and counteract Japan's traditional educational focus on rote learning and group consensus).

- More Japanese companies, like trading giant Itochu, are using merit-based pay and promotion systems.

- Death from overwork (*karoshi*) and workplace bullying by managers (*ijime*) are now important social issues.

But don't equate Japan and America just yet, especially when it comes to individualism and entrepreneurship. World-class entrepreneurs from Japan are still relatively infrequent. And while the feelings of intense gratitude and obligation toward employers have weakened, they still persist. Eliminating these aspects of Japanese culture will take a lot more time. And perhaps a lot more layoffs.[17]

taken care of by the manager. This unequal exchange honors the more powerful member of the relationship and is linked to Confucian expectations that powerful family members help weaker members.

The result in China is a benevolent paternalism where managers may act as kindly father figures who provide for their "children" (subordinates). These complex but informal relationships affect how business gets done; laws, procedures, and regulations are routinely circumvented because of *guanxi*. In fact, developing *guanxi*-based "connections" can help foreign companies succeed in China.[18]

Like China, the South Korean version of harmony (*inhwa*) is defined by relationships between individuals. In South Korea, however, the relationship is explicitly between people of unequal status and power. The guiding principle is the Confucian norm that individuals be loyal to parents and authority figures. So harmony is a function of observing hierarchical rankings. At work, managers often expect the same loyalty and obedience a person would give to a parent. In fact, in many large Korean firms *real* parent-child relationships exist in executive ranks. Traditionally, a company's founder brings members of his family or clan into top positions. Nevertheless, all parties are expected to be emotionally supportive of each other, regardless of their rank or family status. One consequence is a strong reluctance to engage in direct criticism or provide negative performance feedback.[19]

Overall, these differences among Japan, China, and Korea illustrate the limitations of clustering countries that appear to have very similar cultural values. In fact, significant differences also exist among countries within the other clusters identified by Ronen and Shenkar. For example, in the Anglo cluster, British managers tend to be more formal, more class conscious, and more autocratic than their American counterparts.[20] Likewise, research shows that while countries in the Latin American cluster are similar in some respects, they also diverge on some important values (e.g., personal ambition). These differences have implications for how employees need to be managed, business negotiations conducted, and key decisions made across countries in Latin America. In a nutshell, it would be a mistake to assume a high degree of cultural homogeneity in the region.[21]

Moreover, *within-country* differences cannot be ignored. For instance, in the United States new immigrant populations have put managers in the position of having to motivate employees from diverse cultural backgrounds. Doing a better job of managing this diversity can enhance the competitiveness of American companies.[22] Another example of a country with big *internal* differences is South Africa. Approximately 10 percent of South Africa's 45 million people are white descendants of Dutch and British settlers. South Africa's black citizens come from several ethnic groups (e.g., Zulus, Xhosas).[23] Given this diversity, it isn't surprising that cultural differences affect work in South Africa in complex ways.[24]

In summary, Ronen and Shenkar's approach to clustering countries has important limitations. Indeed, these limitations are shared by *all* cluster frameworks to an extent. Hofstede's effort to cluster countries is no exception.

Hofstede: Clustering Countries on Work-Related Value Dimensions

Geert Hofstede's work represents the largest and most influential effort to cluster countries by cultural values. And the impact of his work continues to rise.[25] Hofstede's conclusions are based on a survey that asked over 116,000 employees in more than seventy countries about their values and beliefs. From these data, Hofstede extracted four basic cultural dimensions: individualism–collectivism, masculinity–femininity, power distance, and uncertainty avoidance. To help integrate his results, Hofstede also created cultural "maps" that position each country in terms of pairs of culture dimensions. Since countries also tend to cluster, similarities and differences between groups of countries can be assessed. Overall, Hofstede's work has important implications for managing employees around the world. We'll begin our discussion by defining Hofstede's four basic cultural dimensions.[26]

Individualism–Collectivism This dimension describes whether people in a culture tend to view themselves primarily as individuals or as members of a group. In individualistic cultures, people are expected to take care of themselves, and a high value is placed on autonomy, individual achievement, and privacy. In collectivist cultures, however, people are more likely to view themselves as part of a group that protects and takes care of them in exchange for loyalty and devotion. The group may be the family, a clan or tribe, or an organization.

individualism–collectivism Cultural dimension describing whether people tend to view themselves primarily as individuals or as members of a group

Individualism–collectivism is the most widely studied of Hofstede's cultural dimensions, and it also may be among the most complex. Recent research suggests that collectivism and individualism are actually multifaceted values that people view in terms of a variety of components. For instance, individualism may include both economic (e.g., "I achieve things by competing") and expressive (e.g., "I want to be seen as a unique person") elements. Likewise, collectivism may also contain economic (e.g., "members of the group should share resources") as well as expressive (e.g., "group members should be emotionally involved with each other") components. On top of that, cultures may vary considerably when it comes to how they view a particular component of individualism or collectivism. For example, while cultures that share Confucian and Latin roots tend toward collectivism, at least compared to the United States, they may view expressiveness quite differently. In many Latin American countries, open displays of emotion and warmth are expected and encouraged. On the other hand, such displays are much less likely to be found in Japan. In short, what constitutes "collectivism" (or "individualism," for that matter) may vary from place to place.[27]

Masculinity–Femininity The **masculinity–feminity** dimension describes whether success and the assertive acquisition of money and power (at the expense of others, if necessary) is highly valued, or whether people, the quality of life, and good relationships with co-workers should take precedence. Hofstede noted that in most cultures men were more likely to endorse the assertive (or "masculine") view of things. Masculine cultures are strongly achievement oriented, tend to view the ambitious pursuit of high performance as the ideal, and feel that men are better suited for positions of power. School systems in such cultures tend to identify and develop "high performers." Likewise, an important social value is having a "successful career." Workplaces tend to be competitive, stressful, and prone to conflict.

masculinity–femininity Cultural dimension describing whether success and assertive acquisition or people and relationships are more highly valued

Feminine cultures, on the other hand, emphasize the equality of men and women, place a high value on taking care of the disadvantaged, and desire harmony in the workplace. Consequently, there is a stronger emphasis on job security and creating stress-free work environments. Career pressures also tend to be lower and labor-management discord less likely.

power distance
Cultural dimension describing the extent to which people can accept large differences in power between individuals or groups

Power Distance The **power distance** dimension reflects the extent to which people in a culture can accept large differences in power between individuals or groups in an organization. Put simply, how acceptable is it to have power distributed in an unequal manner? In high power distance cultures, people are more likely to accept their station in life and follow whatever commands those with greater authority are likely to issue. The view is that some people are destined to be in command and others are not. So a company hierarchy that spreads powers unequally is acceptable because managers and subordinates are seen as different types of people. As you might suspect, managerial authority tends to be more concentrated in high power distance cultures.

People in low power distance cultures, in contrast, are more likely to fear concentration of authority. Consequently, power is more likely to be used in a

EXHIBIT 4.4 *Abbreviations for Countries and Regions Used in Hofstede's Culture Maps*

ARA	Arab countries (Egypt, Lebanon, Libya, Kuwait, Iraq, Saudi Arabia, UAE)	JAM	Jamaica
		JPN	Japan
		KOR	South Korea
ARG	Argentina	MAL	Malaysia
AUL	Australia	MEX	Mexico
AUT	Austria	NET	Netherlands
BEL	Belgium	NOR	Norway
BRA	Brazil	NZL	New Zealand
CAN	Canada	PAK	Pakistan
CHL	Chile	PAN	Panama
COL	Colombia	PER	Peru
COS	Costa Rica	PHI	Philippines
DEN	Denmark	POR	Portugal
EAF	East Africa (Kenya, Ethiopia, Zambia)	SAF	South Africa
		SAL	El Salvador
EQA	Ecuador	SIN	Singapore
FIN	Finland	SPA	Spain
FRA	France	SWE	Sweden
GBR	Great Britain	SWI	Switzerland
GER	Germany	TAI	Taiwan
GRE	Greece	THA	Thailand
GUA	Guatemala	TUR	Turkey
HOK	Hong Kong	URU	Uruguay
IDO	Indonesia	USA	United States
IND	India	VEN	Venezuela
IRA	Iran	WAF	West Africa (Nigeria, Ghana, Sierra Leone)
IRE	Ireland		
ISR	Israel	YUG	Former Yugoslavia
ITA	Italy		

decentralized way, with companies having fewer layers of management. In such cultures, managers tend to develop close, trusting relationships with their subordinates and use their power with care. The use of power in such cultures is often subject to a variety of laws, procedures, and standards, which, if violated, can create a backlash as well as other problems for managers.

Uncertainty Avoidance   How people react to uncertain or ambiguous events defines Hofstede's **uncertainty avoidance** dimension. People in cultures that are weak in uncertainty avoidance embrace the idea that life is unpredictable by definition. As a result, there is less concern with or adherence to rules, procedures, or organizational hierarchies. Risk taking, especially in the pursuit of individual achievement, is desirable. Competition and conflict are both viewed as inevitable parts of life in an organization.

> **uncertainty avoidance**
> Cultural dimension describing the extent to which people tolerate uncertain or ambiguous events

People in cultures where uncertainty avoidance is strong, however, tend to feel threatened by ambiguity and will go to great lengths to create stable and predictable work environments. In such cultures, there is an emphasis on absolute truths, and unusual behavior or ideas tend to be rejected. As a result, rules and procedures designed to keep uncertainty at bay proliferate. Likewise, there tends to be less risk taking and personal initiative (e.g., in decision making or your own career moves) in strong uncertainty avoidance cultures.

Hofstede's Cultural Maps   Hofstede created three cultural maps by crossing pairs of cultural dimensions and plotting the corresponding scores for each country. Each map is divided into quadrants representing different combinations of the dimensions plotted. Countries whose pairs of scores tend to cluster together are also identified. The basic idea is that countries may possess certain combinations of cultural values that have unique managerial implications. We'll address these implications in more detail later. For now, we'll focus on understanding Hofstede's culture maps. Exhibit 4.4 shows the abbreviations for the countries used in Hofstede's research.

We'll start with the positions of countries on the individualism–collectivism and power-distance dimensions. As Exhibit 4.5 shows, only Costa Rica combines collectivism and small power distance. Instead, large power distance and collectivism go together, with most countries in this quadrant being either Asian or Latin American. Similarly, small power distance and individualism go together, with northern European and Anglo countries such as Sweden and Great Britain dominating this quadrant.

Exhibit 4.6 displays the map crossing the uncertainty avoidance and masculinity–femininity dimensions. Hofstede suggested that cultures with weak uncertainty avoidance and masculine values will be *achievement oriented*. These tend to be Anglo countries or their former colonies (such as India, Hong Kong, and the Philippines). The second quadrant, combining strong uncertainty avoidance and masculinity, produces *security motivation*. For countries in this quadrant, both performance and job security are valued. In contrast, the combination of feminine values and strong uncertainty avoidance produces *social motivation*. Here job security, positive relationships, and a good quality of life are prized. Scandinavian countries dominate the fourth quadrant, which combines feminine values and weak uncertainty avoidance. In these countries, risk and performance are acceptable, but social relationships and a high *quality of work life* are valued more than individual achievement.

EXHIBIT 4.5   *Culture Map for Power Distance and Individualism*

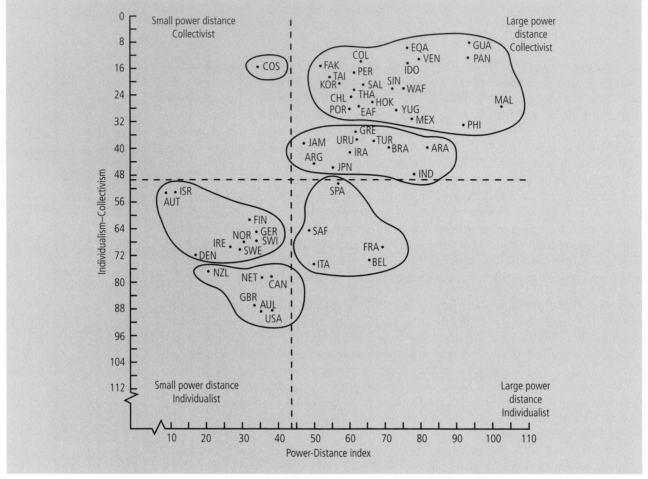

Source: Hofstede, G. (1991). *Cultures and organizations: Software of the mind.* London: McGraw-Hill U.K., 54. Used with permission.

Exhibit 4.7 displays the final map crossing uncertainty avoidance and power distance. Asian countries dominate the *family quadrant* (large power distance and weak uncertainty avoidance). In these countries, there's often less concern about laws and procedures than on being loyal to strong, paternalistic leaders. In contrast, the *pyramid of people quadrant* (large power distance and strong uncertainty avoidance) produces cultures accepting of powerful leaders, but in a context that is fairly hierarchical and rule bound. This diverse quadrant contains Mediterranean, Latin, and some Asian countries.

Germanic countries dominate the *well-oiled machine quadrant* (small power distance and strong uncertainty avoidance). In this environment, leaders are less important than having clear rules and procedures that promote efficiency. Finally, the *village market quadrant* contains Anglo and Scandinavian countries. Here the combination of small power distance and weak uncertainty avoidance allows for a great deal of experimentation and risk taking that's not automatically limited by powerful leaders. In such cultures, good negotiation and conflict management skills may be critical for getting things done since elaborate procedures or dominant leaders are often absent.

EXHIBIT 4.6   *Culture Map for Uncertainty Avoidance and Masculinity–Femininity*

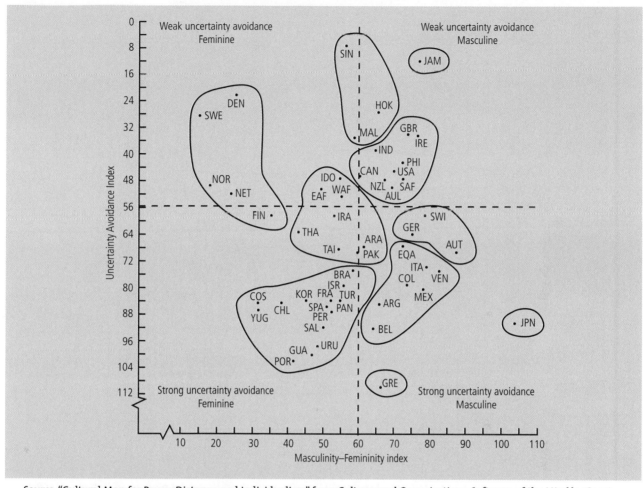

Source: "Cultural Map for Power Distance and Individualism" from *Cultures and Organizations: Software of the Mind* by Geert Hofstede. Copyright © 1991 Geert Hofstede. Reprinted by permission.

Long- Versus Short-Term Orientation: A Recent Addition to Hofstede's Cultural Dimensions More recently, Hofstede proposed a fifth cultural dimension, **long-versus short-term orientation**, which evolved from his work on Asian cultures with colleague Michael Harris Bond. This dimension helps distinguish between cultures that have a forward-looking perspective on life and those that are more concerned with the past and present. Specifically, cultures that are long-term oriented feel that values focusing on the future (e.g., frugality, hard work, adaptability, persistence) are most important. Indeed, many Asian societies are long-term oriented, something that may help explain the recent economic success enjoyed by some Asian countries (e.g., South Korea). On the other hand, cultures that are short-term oriented feel that values focusing on the past and present, (e.g., respect for tradition, stability, fulfillment of social obligations) are most important (e.g., Pakistan).

Take a look at Exhibit 4.8 for a list of twenty-three countries that, according to Hofstede, can be compared in terms of their tendency to embrace a long-term or short-term orientation. You'll notice that while Asian countries in this group tend to have the strongest long-term orientation, the short-term distinction

EXHIBIT 4.7   *Culture Map for Power Distance and Uncertainty Avoidance*

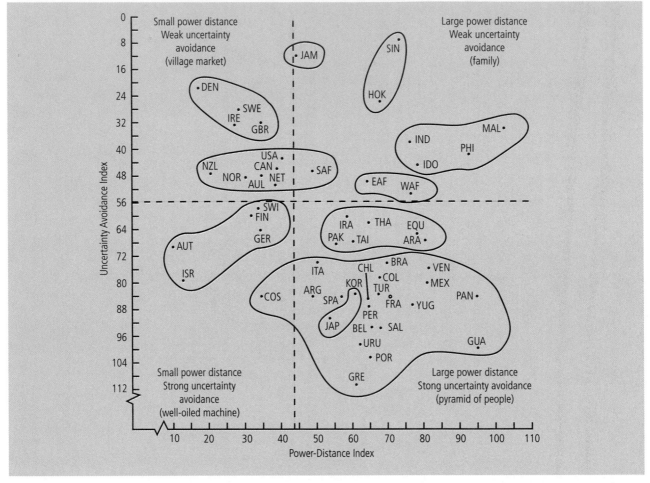

Source: "Cultural Map for Uncertainty Avoidance and Masculinity-Femininity" from *Cultures and Organizations: Software of the Mind* by Geert Hofstede. Copyright © 1991 Geert Hofstede. Reprinted by permission.

is not cleanly divided between "Eastern" and "Western" countries. If you're wondering about how long- versus short-term orientation relates to Hofstede's other four dimensions, the answer is fairly complex. That said, there is some evidence that wealthier countries that strongly embrace a long-term orientation also tend to be high on power distance and low on individualism (South Korea being a good example).[28]

Limitations of Hofstede's Cultural Dimensions Like Ronen and Shenkar, Hofstede misses some key countries in his clustering effort. For example, countries in eastern Europe are basically missing, as are developing Asian nations like Vietnam. To help rectify this, Hofstede's more recent work includes cultural value estimates for emerging economic powers like China and Russia. For instance, he views China as a country that is long-term oriented, high on power distance, low on individualism, and moderate on uncertainty avoidance and masculinity. Russia, on the other hand, is seen as short-term oriented, high on power distance, strong on uncertainty avoidance, moderate on individualism, and low on masculinity. Nevertheless, certain regions of the world remain underrepresented even in the most recent efforts to cluster countries by culture.[29]

EXHIBIT 4.8   *Long- Versus Short-Term Orientation: Where Do Twenty-three Countries Stack Up?*

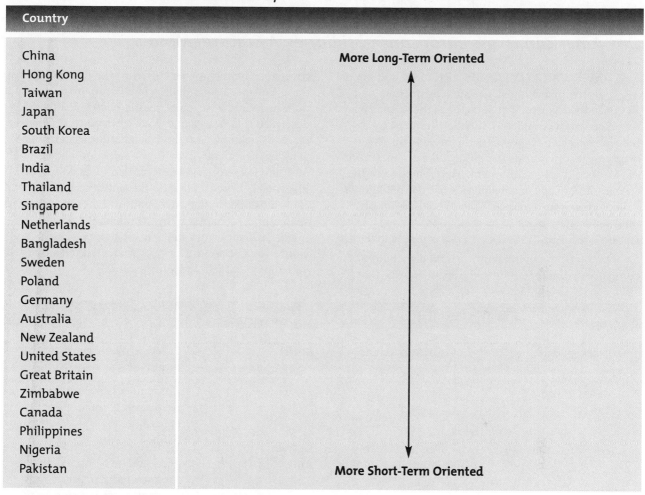

Country
China
Hong Kong
Taiwan
Japan
South Korea
Brazil
India
Thailand
Singapore
Netherlands
Bangladesh
Sweden
Poland
Germany
Australia
New Zealand
United States
Great Britain
Zimbabwe
Canada
Philippines
Nigeria
Pakistan

Source: "Cultural Map for Power Distance and Uncertainty Orientation" from *Cultures and Organizations: Software of the Mind* by Geert Hofstede. Copyright © 1991 Geert Hofstede. Reprinted by permission.

Another limitation of Hofstede's work is that it ignores differences that exist between countries within a specific cluster or quadrant. Research suggests, for example, that cultural differences exist between the United States and Australia despite their similar scores on Hofstede's cultural dimensions. Specifically, Americans tend to be more interested in intrinsic rewards like responsibility and recognition, while Australians tend to be more interested in having job security and a good income.[30] Hofstede's framework has a hard time explaining these results.

Despite its limitations, however, Hofstede's work continues to have a tremendous impact on the field of international management and remains a valuable guide for interpreting the effects of culture. Indeed, recent research has reinforced both the value and applicability of Hofstede's cultural dimensions.[31] One study, for instance, found that business leaders were seen as prioritizing their goals in ways that reflected their national cultures. Specifically, business leaders in countries with high power distance are perceived to value personal honor, family interests, and power more than business leaders in countries with

International Insights

One American Firm's European Subsidiaries: A Cultural Mosaic

AMERICAN COMPANIES ARE often well known for emphasizing values such as freedom and individualism. But sometimes those American values may not completely survive a move abroad. Indeed, when an American company sets up shop overseas, its operations there may take on hues from the local cultural environment. That seems to be the case in the European subsidiaries of one well-known icon of corporate America. This particular company sells about 25 percent of its annual production abroad, with Europe being a major overseas market.

On top of its regional offices and distributors, the company operates five subsidiaries in Europe that cover specific territories. Recently, the firm profiled these European subsidiaries in a company publication, including how employees in each subsidiary described themselves and their work culture. The result is a glimpse into how local cultures can shape work environments, even in the midst of what is one of America's strongest corporate cultures and most identifiable brands. How do the self-descriptions of each subsidiary relate to the cultural dimensions presented in this chapter? Then think about what it might be like to work in each subsidiary. Which would you choose to work in? And what does that tell you about yourself and your values?[32]

Subsidiary Location	Territory Covered	Employees	Self-Description
1. Brackley England,	UK and Ireland	British	Creative, inventive, reserved, multicultural, resourceful
2. Paris, France	France	French	Generally dislike authority; we always complain but we enjoy life (good food, wine)
3. Frankfurt, Germany	Austria, Czech Republic, Hungary, Poland, Slovenia	German, American, French	Hard-working, punctual, accurate, tidy-minded, thirst for knowledge, open to new technology, enjoy food/wine
4. Milan, Italy	Italy	Italian	Chic, passionate, and stylish
5. Amsterdam, Netherlands	Benelux countries	Dutch, Belgian	Dutch are direct and tolerant; Belgians are more modest and always friendly.

low power distance.[33] Take a look at the accompanying International Insights and think about how you might apply Hofstede's cultural dimensions if you were managing this American firm's foreign subsidiaries.

Trompenaars's Alternative: Another Look at Cultural Dimensions

Fons Trompenaars's recent work represents perhaps the most ambitious attempt to identify cultural dimensions besides Hofstede's. Focusing on values and rela-

EXHIBIT 4.9   *Trompenaars's Key Cultural Dimensions and Representative Countries*

Universalism	Neutral	Specific	Achievement	Individualism
↑ United States	↑ Japan	↑ Austria	↑ Austria	↑ United States
Austria	United Kingdom	United Kingdom	United States	Czech Republic
Germany	Singapore	United States	Switzerland	Argentina
Switzerland	Austria	Switzerland	United Kingdom	former Soviet Union
Sweden	Indonesia	France	Sweden	Mexico
Hong Kong	Brazil	Singapore	Singapore	France
China	China	Hong Kong	former Soviet Union	Indonesia
Indonesia	Switzerland	Spain	China	Japan
former Soviet Union	Netherlands	China	Indonesia	Thailand
↓ Venezuela	↓ Mexico	↓ Venezuela	↓ Venezuela	↓ Singapore
Particularism	**Emotional**	**Diffuse**	**Ascription**	**Communitarianism**

Sources: Adapted from Trompenaars, F. (1993). *Riding the waves of culture.* London: Brealey; Trompenaars, F., & Hampden-Turner, C. (1998). *Riding the waves of culture: Understanding cultural diversity in global business* (2nd Ed.). New York: McGraw-Hill.

tionships, Trompenaars surveyed more than 15,000 managers over a ten-year span. These managers represented twenty-eight countries, and Trompenaars was able to identify a variety of bipolar cultural dimensions as a result.[34]

For example, people may differ in terms of how they view their environment. **Outer-directed** employees tend to accommodate their behavior to their situation in life. Why? Because they feel that life's outcomes aren't under their control. Such employees may desire stability as well as have a strong need for harmonious relationships. In contrast, **inner-directed** employees tend to believe they control their own destinies. Consequently, they're likely to be more willing to change their environment and pursue their own goals. According to Trompenaars, Americans tend to be inner-directed, while at the other extreme Chinese tend to be outer-directed.

Along the same lines, research comparing managers from the United States and four Arab countries found that inner-directed values were endorsed most by the Americans, while outer-directed values were more dominant on the Arab side. Because of outer-directed concerns, business in Arab countries often functions on a more relationship-oriented basis than it does in Western nations.[35]

Speaking of relationships, several of the most important cultural dimensions identified by Trompenaars are explicitly relationship-oriented. Exhibit 4.9 presents five of these dimensions along with rankings for countries most representative of each polar extreme. We'll turn our attention to these dimensions next.

Universalism–Particularism This distinction refers to the extent to which people usually believe that one set of rules and practices should apply to everyone (universalism) or whether the rules should be adjusted depending on the person or situation (particularism). Many countries stress good relations with family and friends (particularism) rather than focusing just on the performance-based considerations (universalism) that dominate in countries like the United States. However, countries as diverse as Venezuela, Indonesia, and China tend toward

outer-directed
People who feel that life's outcomes aren't under their control

inner-directed
People who tend to believe they control their own destinies

particularism. Overall, managers from cultures that embrace particularism are more likely to take an employee's personal family troubles and job demands into account when deciding on rewards than are managers from cultures that embrace universalism.

Neutral–Emotional Cultures in which emotions are suppressed and stoicism is important are said to be on the neutral end of this dimension. For example, the Japanese are well known for their reserve and composure. The flip side, of course, is an emotional culture, where feelings are expressed with gusto. Mexico is a good example of an emotional culture. You can imagine some of the challenges that might occur if employees from neutral cultures find themselves in an emotional culture or vice versa. In either case, adapting to the rules of the game that you're in is probably the best bet (e.g., by being more expressive in an emotional culture or more reserved in a neutral culture).

Specific–Diffuse In specific cultures such as the United States, life tends to be compartmentalized. Work and family roles, for instance, are kept relatively separate. Consequently, the behavior you see, the titles used, and the level of formality displayed will all vary depending on what role people happen to be in (e.g., boss, personal friend, co-worker, family member). And that means that having a relationship with someone carries little risk, at least initially. Why? Because the relationship can be limited to a specific role (e.g., you can be very friendly with people on the job but never see them outside of the workplace). But in diffuse cultures like China, the lines between roles are fuzzy. For instance, a person's job title might affect the way that person is treated and viewed in many other spheres of life. Consequently, people in such cultures tend to be somewhat cautious in dealing with others for the first time, especially since access to one area of life may mean access to all.

Achievement–Ascription In achievement cultures, your status depends on how you've performed and the goals you've been able to reach. That might mean obtaining a degree from a top university or landing a prestigious promotion. "Being the best" at whatever it is that you do carries a great deal of weight. In ascription cultures, in contrast, status depends on things like age, connections, class, or gender. For instance, connections are likely to have a larger impact on hiring and other business decisions in ascription cultures like China, Indonesia, or Venezuela than in achievement cultures like the United States.

Individualism–Communitarianism This dimension is similar to the distinction Hofstede draws between individualism and collectivism. Basically, individualism means that you think of yourself as an individual first, while communitarianism means that you think of yourself as part of a group first. A comparison of the two frameworks, however, reveals some differences. For instance, Argentina and Mexico are described as relatively group-oriented by Hofstede but as individualistic by Trompenaars. Why this is the case isn't completely clear. One possibility is that each researcher has defined his terms somewhat differently. Another possibility is that Trompenaars's newer data may be revealing shifts in cultural values that have occurred over the years. As we said earlier, cultures are constantly evolving and changing. Trompenaars's work may help underscore that point.

▶ *The Implications of Culture for International Management*

Up to now, we've provided some brief commentary about the implications of culture for management. We've also noted that culture can potentially impact just about everything, from how international business strategy is formed to specific human resource management practices. In fact, we'll explore some of these issues in later chapters. For now, however, we'll examine how culture may affect what people want from their jobs and how they view leadership. We'll conclude the chapter by offering some specific, practical suggestions for moving beyond the kind of "sophisticated stereotyping" that comes with the limitations of current culture frameworks.

Culture and What People Want from Work

How central is work in the lives of employees? Do employees work primarily for relationships, money, or for the job itself? The answers have important implications for how managers should approach employees in various cultures. Research suggests that what we want from work may, to an extent, depend on our culture. For instance, a survey of 14,000 employees in eight countries (Belgium, Britain, Germany, Israel, Japan, the Netherlands, the United States, and the former Yugoslavia) found that **work centrality** (how important work is in the lives of employees) varied across countries. Americans fell in the middle of the pack, while the British had the lowest work centrality scores and the Japanese the highest. In fact, the Japanese not only had the highest centrality score, they were also significantly ahead of the other seven countries as a group.[36]

work centrality
How important work is in the lives of employees

Of course, it's likely that work centrality in Japan has eroded in recent years (see our earlier International Insights box). That said, the tendency to view work as a critical part of life will undoubtedly persist at some level in Japanese culture. Why? One reason is that it's hard to imagine long-standing Japanese traditions being completely undercut in just a decade or two. For centuries Japan was a society made up of small, isolated farming communities. Such isolation required hard work and cooperation to ensure community survival. This agrarian system began changing significantly only within the last 100 years. The legacy of this system in modern industrial Japan is the value placed on hard work and group solidarity.[37]

This belief in work, combined with a still-strong emphasis on the group, may help explain the high degree of commitment many Japanese still feel toward their firms. It may also explain the Japanese willingness to put up with things that workers elsewhere find tough to swallow. How many Americans, for example, would trade places with the average Japanese white-collar worker, someone who routinely puts in 60 plus hour work weeks, endures two-hour commutes, rarely takes vacations, and feels obligated to spend several nights a week socializing with co-workers?[38] On the other hand, over the past ten years, the total amount of time Americans work annually has risen by nearly sixty hours while the Japanese total has fallen by almost 200 hours.[39]

Part of this workload pullback in Japan may be a response to rising Japanese concern about onerous working conditions. According to a recent survey of employees in industrialized countries, Japanese respondents came in last in terms of morale. Only 44 percent of the Japanese workers surveyed said they were satisfied with their employers. In contrast, 65 percent of the Americans surveyed were satisfied. The percentages were even higher for German (66 percent), Canadian (73 percent), and Swiss (82 percent) workers. In addition, less than 40 percent of the Japanese surveyed thought they were fairly paid. Finally, only 33 percent of Japanese said their firms were well managed, compared to 45 percent in an earlier survey. These numbers appear to reflect a growing feeling among Japanese that big employers are less likely to provide benefits, such as lifetime employment, that made enduring difficult working conditions tolerable.[40]

But what about other aspects of work? Exhibit 4.10 summarizes the importance of eleven different work goals across eight countries. You'll notice that employees in most countries ranked interesting work first or second in importance. Good pay also was an important goal for most employees, although Dutch and Japanese employees both ranked it lower. Substantial differences across countries were found for most of the remaining work goals. For example, job security was very important to Germans, but not very important to Israelis. The Japanese felt that achieving a good match between their job demands and their talents was the most important work goal, while most countries rated it

EXHIBIT 4.10 *Rankings of the Importance of Work Goals by Country*

Work Goal	Belgium	Germany	Israel	Japan	Netherlands	U.S.	Former Yugoslavia	U.K.
Interesting work	1	3	1	2	2	1	2	1
Good pay	2	1	3	5	5	2	3	2
Good interpersonal relations	5	4	2	6	3	7	1	4
Good job security	3	2	10	4	7	3	9	3
Good match between you and your job	8	5	6	1	6	4	5	6
A lot of autonomy	4	8	4	3	1	8	8	10
Opportunity to learn	7	9	5	7	9	5	4	8
Work variety	6	6	11	9	4	6	7	7
Convenient hours	9	6	7	8	8	9	10	5
Good physical working conditions	11	11	9	10	10	11	6	9
Good opportunity for promotion	10	10	8	11	11	10	11	11

Note: 1 = most important, 11 = least important
Source: Adapted from MOW International Research Team. (1987). *The meaning of working.* London: Academic Press, 123.

fifth or lower. Finally, while having autonomy was the most important work goal for Dutch employees, British employees rated it near the bottom.[41]

Nevertheless, these results suggest that providing interesting work will have a positive effect on workers in all eight countries. If these findings generalize to other nations and cultures, managers could view "interesting work" as something that employees universally want from their jobs. The results also suggest that managers need to adjust their approach to match the values of specific cultures. Of course, this adjustment must be made cautiously. After all, cultures change. Moreover, individual values, needs, and goals may diverge from existing cultural norms in any case.

Other studies have produced similar findings and implications. One survey, for example, found that both American and Asian executives valued hard work. But Americans tended to value personal achievement much more than the Asians, while the reverse was true for respect for learning. Also interesting was the fact that there was considerable divergence in values among Asian managers. Executives from Japan, for instance, were more concerned with harmony than their counterparts from Singapore and Hong Kong.[42]

Culture and Views about Leadership

Speaking of executives, the culture we're imbedded in inevitably colors our views about leadership.[43] As a result, the definition of leadership can vary because of cultural factors like history and shared experience. Americans, for instance, tend to see leadership as an influence process in which the leader shapes the attitudes and behaviors of employees in ways that allow company goals to be achieved.[44] In short, the leader's job is to motivate others to produce. To many Americans, leaders are "heroes" who make the organization work. In contrast, the engineer, not the manager, is held in high esteem in Germany. The German tradition of craftsmanship and emphasis on apprenticeships, which dates back to the Middle Ages, means that for many Germans the purpose of management is to attack technical problems and to distribute tasks, not to "motivate" employees.[45]

Research on management philosophies in Europe, Asia, and the United States supports the idea that culture impacts how the role of leadership is perceived. In one survey, less than 20 percent of American, Dutch, and Swedish managers thought it was important to have exact answers ready in response to questions that subordinates might have. In these countries, managers felt that they should help subordinates to find their own answers and solve their own problems. On the other hand, almost half the German managers (46 percent) and more than half of French (53 percent), Italian (66 percent), Indonesian (73 percent), and Japanese (78 percent) managers wanted to have precise answers ready for subordinates. In these countries, projecting an image of expertise that provides comfort and stability to subordinates is often viewed as an important part of a leader's job.[46]

Where leaders come from can also vary across countries because of culture. Japan, for instance, is a classless country in which merit largely determines who ends up in positions of leadership. "Merit" is defined here in terms of successful performance in highly selective schools designed to funnel students into specific roles. Anyone who demonstrates the necessary capabilities can succeed in this context, regardless of his or her particular background. In other countries, however, business leaders tend to come from certain classes of society. For instance, Turkish leaders usually come from the upper classes. Likewise, in certain Arab countries, prominent leaders usually emerge from powerful tribal families.[47]

Culture may also affect assumptions about the characteristics that business leaders need to be effective. For example, Americans tend to think that a leader's success depends on personal traits such as intelligence, self-confidence, and decisiveness. Most of these traits have been associated with cultures that value individual performance. But should we expect countries with different cultural values to use the same criteria to judge managerial effectiveness? In many cases, the answer is clearly "no." That said, there's also evidence that attitudes about what makes for effective leadership have been changing.[48]

In one study, senior managers working in eight different countries for large multinationals were given a list of leader characteristics and asked to select the five that were most important. A few characteristics (e.g., the ability to articulate a vision) were ranked in the top five by managers in most countries. This suggests that senior executives everywhere share certain challenges, especially in large international firms. However, there were no countries that had identical sets of rankings. And for certain pairs of countries, there was little or no overlap between the characteristics ranked in the top five. Cultural values may explain these differences. For instance, only Japanese executives ranked empowering others in the top three. The focus on group-oriented work in Japanese culture lends itself toward seeing effective leaders as people who share power and encourage a harmonious work environment. Likewise, the American, Australian, and British emphasis on "getting results" is consistent with the value Anglo cultures place on individual performance.[49]

Finally, there's been considerable interest in discovering whether cultural perspectives on leadership are converging. One clever investigation compared the relationship between personal characteristics and evaluations of managerial effectiveness in Canada, Hong Kong, and China. The characteristics examined tend to be valued in Anglo countries (e.g., achievement motivation, interest in realizing your highest potential, intellectual ability). The idea was that if cultural values affect the importance of managerial characteristics, then executives in Canada, Hong Kong, and China should differ in terms of how they rate the effectiveness of the managers that work for them. Chinese executives, for instance, might not see a relationship between "Western" criteria and managerial effectiveness. On the other hand, if attitudes toward leadership are converging as industrialization proceeds worldwide and countries like China become more "modern," then the criteria for effective management should be similar in all three countries.[50]

The results painted a mixed picture. Canadian executives felt that interest in realizing your highest potential was most important for managerial effectiveness. However, Chinese executives felt that a manager's intellectual ability was most important. These results support the idea that culture continues to affect which characteristics are seen as critical for effective management. That said, although the rankings were different, most characteristics were viewed as indicators of effectiveness by all executives. This supports the convergence idea since only "Western" characteristics were included. In fact, the Chinese executives in the study all worked for large, modern firms in urban areas and had been exposed to North American management techniques. So the results may reflect the ongoing evolution of Chinese leadership, with "traditional" values being slowly eroded by Western philosophies. Indeed, a similar evolution has been observed in many former communist countries such as Poland and eastern Germany.[51] Nevertheless, it would be a mistake to assume that local values will be completely supplanted by "Western" values in China (or elsewhere) anytime soon—if ever. Indeed, research continues to suggest that convergence forces are typically slowed or offset by aspects of the local cultural environment.[52]

How Individuals and Corporations Can Make Better Sense of Culture

This discussion underscores the complexities associated with culture, a point we've been making throughout the chapter. So far we've presented a series of cultural frameworks and dimensions. We've also discussed their limitations, including the broad-brush portraits they often paint of cultures around the world. And even if we view these "sophisticated stereotypes" as helpful and useful, they may, at least to some extent, already be outdated. After all, cultures may be stable most of the time, but they're certainly not static.

Of course, sometimes managers carry around cultural stereotypes about different parts of the world that can derail effective decision making. Fortunately, Flextronics CEO Michael Marks avoided this problem when he considered whether to build a manufacturing plant in Mexico. Some of the people around him advised against building the plant, suggesting that the cost savings of manufacturing in Mexico would be eaten up by local employees and their "siesta culture." Mr. Marks ignored this stereotype-driven advice and built the plant anyway, a facility that ended up producing over $1 billion in revenues inside of five years. Indeed, Mr. Marks felt that experience highlighted the "corrosive effect of stereotypes" on the ability to make good international business decisions. Of course, cultural stereotyping is typically more subtle than the Flextronics example. As Mr. Marks put it:

> "Managers often pick up the impression that the Chinese are good at this, the Germans are good at that, and so on. But I have learned that in every place that we operate, in every country, the people want to do a good job... This isn't to say that we approach every region with a cookie-cutter uniformity. We may need to train workers differently in different parts of the world."[53]

Of course, to effectively train workers in various parts of the world, managers must understand employees—including the ways in which their culture and context impact how they learn as well as what they need to learn. So how can managers working in a new country—or international corporations, for that matter—do a better job of accurately figuring out the cultures they have to operate in? Let's start with some suggestions for international managers:

- **Approach other cultures with the idea of testing your "sophisticated stereotypes."** In other words, be aware of any cultural stereotypes that you might possess and treat them not as "truths," but as hypotheses to be tested. The most effective international managers change their stereotypes about people from other cultures and countries during the course of interacting with them.

- **Find cultural informants and mentors to help.** Look for someone who: (1) can really make sense of a culture's nuances, paradoxes, and internal logic; and (2) is willing to share his or her insights and information. After all, the more you understand a culture, the more tolerant and effective you'll become.

- **Carefully assess information that seems inconsistent with cultural stereotypes.** Sometimes managers can "plateau" in their learning about another culture without realizing it. This may occur when managers have done pretty well, at least initially, in other cultures and, as a result, become less open to deeper learning. In doing so, managers may be more likely to make bad decisions based on faulty assumptions or a superficial understanding of the culture. This trap can be avoided if managers seek deeper meaning by looking for and analyzing behavior that seems paradoxical to a culture's basic values (e.g., why are many U.S. executives autocratic if Americans pride themselves on equality and egalitarianism?).

- **Learn mental maps that will increase effectiveness in different cultures.** This doesn't mean trying to uncover all the rules of a different culture. What it does mean is that understanding the core values behind the mental maps used in a culture will help you behave more appropriately in that context. And doing so will increase both your effectiveness and self-confidence.

Finally, what about suggestions at a broader level? Here are some ideas for international corporations to consider if they want to make better sense of culture:

- **Put people who have cognitive complexity in international positions.** In short, the last thing companies should want is black-and-white thinkers in international positions. Instead, select people based on their ability to handle alternative viewpoints as well as plenty of ambiguity. Employees with such skills are best equipped to make sense of the complexities and paradoxes inherent in all cultures.

- **Emphasize in-country training for people going overseas.** Too often, cultural training (1) takes place in a classroom environment back home and (2) emphasizes concepts and facts instead of hands-on experience. So, if at all possible, put people on the ground in the culture where they're going to work and challenge them to figure out answers to actual cultural problems. That's likely to produce more motivation to figure out what's going on.

- **Assess the level of cultural expertise among expatriates or other personnel posted in a particular country.** The idea here is that not everyone will be on the same page from a cultural learning perspective. There will be different levels of understanding. Part of this variation may reflect individual differences in skills as well as the amount of time spent in the country. In fact, a good reason to assess cultural expertise is to help the firm figure out how long personnel should stay in a country to achieve the cultural understanding needed to function well.

- **Become a learning organization when it comes to cultural understanding.** In short, put mechanisms into place that will help share and disseminate knowledge about different cultures. For example, have expatriates report their insights and understanding about a culture once they return home. This type of sharing can both increase the firm's collective know-how about different cultures and help expatriates make sense of their cross-cultural experiences.[54]

Chapter Summary

We began this chapter by saying that culture has a pervasive impact on the management of international business. Human resource practices, organization structure, strategy formation and implementation, conflict management approaches, negotiation tactics, and leadership styles can vary dramatically across cultures. And the importance of understanding culture, at least for management, has never been higher because of the ongoing growth of international business.

But *culture* is a complex concept. The "collective programming of the mind" that characterizes a particular culture can have roots in historical events, geography, shared traditions, economic developments, language, and religion, among other things. Plus, cultures are constantly evolving, presenting something of a moving target for managers. So managers need to be careful not to oversimplify culture.

We reviewed prominent efforts to cluster countries by shared cultural values. For instance, Ronen and Shenkar found eight major *country clusters* based on shared cultural values. Geography, language, and religion are all factors that contribute to shared cultural values across specific groups of countries. However, one limitation of Ronen and Shenkar's effort is that many developing countries were not included. In addition, clustering countries together runs the risk of ignoring real cultural differences that exist between countries as well as the cultural diversity that may exist within a single country.

These limitations are also shared by Hofstede's effort to cluster countries on work-related cultural dimensions. Nevertheless, Hofstede's work continues to be a valuable guide for international managers. Hofstede argued that all cultures could be described in terms of four basic dimensions. *Individualism–collectivism* reflects the extent to which people in a particular culture see themselves as individuals or as members of a group. *Masculinity–femininity* describes whether people in a culture place a higher priority on the acquisition of money and power or on things like good relationships with co-workers. *Power distance* reflects the extent to which people in a culture can accept large power differences across ranks in an organization. Finally, *uncertainty avoidance* reflects the level of tolerance people in a particular culture have for ambiguity and uncertainty.

By crossing pairs of these dimensions, Hofstede produced some valuable *cultural maps* that allow international managers to identify countries in terms of various combinations of cultural dimensions and how they cluster together. Hofstede's findings have implications for motivating employees in different countries. For example, countries with weak uncertainty avoidance and masculine values tend to be achievement oriented. The combination of strong uncertainty avoidance and masculine values tends to produce security motivation. Social motivation may result from the combination of femininity and strong uncertainty avoidance.

More recently, Hofstede has introduced a fifth cultural dimension, long-term versus short-term orientation. In a nutshell, cultures that are long-term oriented feel that values focusing on the future (e.g., hard work) are most important. Cultures that are short-term oriented, however, feel that values focusing on the past and present, (e.g., respect for tradition) are most important. Other recent efforts to cluster countries by shared cultural values have tended to support Hofstede's views and have added to our knowledge about developing countries.

In particular, Trompenaars identified several cultural dimensions based on his research. For example, employees in *outer-directed cultures* feel that life's outcomes aren't within their control, whereas employees in *inner-directed cultures* believe they control their own destinies. *Universalism–particularism* refers to the extent to which people usually believe that one set of rules and practices should apply to everyone (universalism) or whether the rules should be adjusted depending on the subordinate or situation (particularism). Cultures in which emotions are suppressed and stoicism is important are said to be *neutral*. The flip side is an *emotional culture*, in which feelings are openly expressed. In *specific* cultures, life tends to be compartmentalized. But in *diffuse* cultures, the lines between roles are fuzzy. In *achievement cultures*, your status depends on how you've performed and the goals you've been able to reach. That might mean obtaining a degree from a top university or landing a prestigious promotion; "being the best" at whatever it is that you do carries a great deal of weight. On the other hand, in *ascription cultures*, status depends on things like age, connections, class, or gender. Finally, *individualism* means that you think of yourself as an individual first, while *communitarianism* means that you think of yourself as part of a group first.

Next, we explored how culture may affect what people want from their jobs as well as their perspectives about leadership. Even the origins of leaders can be driven by culture, at least in part. We concluded with practical suggestions for moving beyond the kind of "sophisticated stereotyping" that comes with the limitations of current culture frameworks. Specifically, for managers and employees, that involved (1) approaching other cultures with the idea of testing your "sophisticated stereotypes," (2) finding cultural informants and mentors to help, (3) carefully assessing information that seems inconsistent with cultural stereotypes, and (4) learning mental maps that will allow you to be more effective in different cultures. For corporations, suggestions included: (1) putting people who have "cognitive complexity" in international positions, (2) emphasizing in-country training for people going overseas, (3) assessing the level of cultural expertise among expatriates or other personnel posted in a particular country, and (4) becoming a learning organization when it comes to cultural understanding.

Discussion Questions

1. Describe the basic cultural dimensions proposed by Hofstede and Trompenaars. What are their similarities, differences, and limitations? How do these dimensions relate to Ronen and Shenkar's country clusters?

2. How might international managers use information about cultural dimensions? Why is understanding culture such an important part of success in international business?

3. Are there any work-related goals that appear to be universal? Which work-related goals vary significantly across countries? How might cultural values impact these work-related goals?

4. How can companies and international managers go beyond the "sophisticated stereotyping" that a superficial understanding of cultures might produce? What are some of the challenges or difficulties associated with doing so?

Up to the Challenge?

Working Together in the U.S.: Implications for Managing the Japanese-American Cultural Divide

A T THE BEGINNING OF THE chapter, we asked you to think about what it might be like for Americans and Japanese to work together. We were especially interested in how potential gaps in cultural values might complicate life for American subordinates and Japanese managers. Here are a few examples of the problems those gaps can create.

Performance Appraisal

Most Americans expect positive reinforcement for their efforts and see performance feedback as providing motivation for higher achievement. Criticism is fine, too, as long as it's constructive and delivered in private. Many Japanese managers, however, find touting personal achievements unacceptable and expect great modesty from sub-

ordinates. Japanese managers may criticize subordinates in front of other co-workers. To Japanese subordinates, this can mean that their boss sees them as having potential. Plus, on-the-job criticisms are usually offset by the "stroking" that Japanese managers informally give subordinates during after-hours socializing. In fact, much criticism is only symbolic since in many Japanese firms the human resources department, rather than the manager, controls personnel decisions. Japanese managers are often surprised when their American subordinates expect them to regularly provide detailed performance appraisals.

As a result, Americans may be puzzled when their Japanese managers provide less performance feedback and career guidance than they expect. When Japanese managers do give formal feedback, it's often delivered in a vague, impersonal fashion (e.g., a brief letter thanking employees for their service). Since Americans are less likely to participate in the Japanese tendency to socialize regularly after work, they may miss opportunities to receive more informal and positive feedback. Americans often see such socializing as cutting into their leisure and family time, while Japanese often see it as an essential part of maintaining work group harmony.

Promotions

Many Americans working for Japanese companies complain about slow promotions and their inability to penetrate upper management ranks, a phenomenon referred to as the *Gaijin ceiling* (*Gaijin* is Japanese for "foreigner"). Many Americans see themselves as individualists out to fulfill their career goals. In contrast, many Japanese think such self-focused behavior creates too much conflict. Americans sometimes fail to appreciate the strong collective orientation of many Japanese managers and the fact that seniority may still count for a great deal when it comes to promotions in Japanese firms.

Small wonder, then, that Japanese managers sometimes have trouble "reaching" their American employees. For example, one Japanese manager gave a speech to motivate his American subordinates. It had the opposite effect. The Japanese manager said the company was doing poorly and urged the Americans to work harder to turn things around. Many Japanese subordinates would accept blame for this situation and redouble their efforts to rectify it. Instead, the Americans polished their résumés and mailed them out in droves. Soon most of the Japanese manager's best American employees had left for jobs elsewhere.

Japanese executives are sometimes reluctant to put Americans in top management jobs because of the language barrier. Few Americans speak Japanese well, forcing Japanese managers to use English. This can create problems if Japanese managers are embarrassed by putting their English language weaknesses on display for American subordinates. On the other hand, even Americans who speak Japanese can commit linguistic gaffes that threaten their careers in Japanese firms. In Japan, the context is very important for interpreting meaning. It took one American manager at Matsushita five years before she finally understood that when told by her Japanese superiors that a proposal "needs more study," several interpretations were possible. In some contexts, it meant "the proposal needs some fine-tuning," while in others it meant "the proposal is dead."

Bridging the Cultural Gap

Resolving these cultural differences takes time and effort. Americans must learn to respect the idea that many Japanese place a higher value on things such as group harmony. Likewise, Japanese must learn to appreciate the fact that many Americans are quite comfortable being assertive and individualistic. Both sides must learn to be more accommodating while retaining their own unique cultural values. That said, how can this be done? How can greater understanding and a "meeting of the minds" translate into different management practices?[55] As you ponder this question, you may want to do some additional research on doing business in Japan and Japanese business culture. One good place to start is the Japan External Trade Organization (**www.jetro.go.jp**). A government-supported organization, JETRO's mission includes helping foreign businesses enter and succeed in the Japanese market. If you can't find what you're looking for about Japan on JETRO's website, chances are you'll find a link that will direct you to an appropriate source. Another good source of information, especially about Japanese business culture and customs, is Executive Planet (see **www.execu tiveplanet.com/business-etiquette/ Japan.html**).

International Development

Understanding Your Orientation toward Individualism–Collectivism

Purpose

To develop a greater understanding of your own attitudes toward individualism and collectivism.

Instructions

Assume that you are in the United States or Canada and want to have a good career in an American or

Canadian corporation. Please answer the following questions about your behavior in the workplace. Using the accompanying scale, please place the appropriate number in the blank before each question.

5	4	3	2	1
strongly agree	agree	not sure	disagree	strongly disagree

1. _____ I would offer my seat in a bus to my supervisor.

2. _____ I prefer to be direct and forthright when dealing with people.

3. _____ I enjoy developing long-term relationships among the people with whom I work.

4. _____ I am very modest when talking about my own accomplishments.

5. _____ When I give gifts to people whose cooperation I need in my work, I feel I am indulging in questionable behavior.

6. _____ If I want my subordinate to perform a task, I tell the person that my superiors want me to get that task done.

7. _____ I prefer to give opinions that will help people save face rather than give a statement of the truth.

8. _____ I say "No" directly when I have to.

9. _____ To increase sales, I would announce that the individual salesperson with the highest sales would be given the "Distinguished Salesperson" award.

10. _____ I enjoy being emotionally close to the people with whom I work.

11. _____ It is important to develop a network of people in my community who can help me when I have tasks to accomplish.

12. _____ I enjoy feeling that I am looked upon as equal in worth to my superiors.

13. _____ I have respect for the authority figures with whom I interact.

14. _____ If I want a person to perform a certain task, I try to show how the task will benefit others in the person's group.

Now, imagine yourself working in one of the following countries. Choose the country about which you have the most knowledge because of actual overseas experience, reading, having friends from that country, classes that you have taken, and so forth.

Japan	Mexico	Brazil
Philippines	Hong Kong	Thailand
Taiwan	Peru	Venezuela
India	Argentina	Greece

If you do not have enough knowledge about any of these countries, imagine yourself working on a class project with three foreign students from any of these countries.

The next part of the exercise is to answer the same fourteen questions, but to do so while imagining that you are working in one of the countries listed above or working on a class project with three students from that country. Imagine that you will be living in that country for a long period of time and want to have a good career in a corporation there. Use the same scale and numbers.

1. _____	8. _____
2. _____	9. _____
3. _____	10. _____
4. _____	11. _____
5. _____	12. _____
6. _____	13. _____
7. _____	14. _____

Scoring

The scoring of this exercise is different from most in that it involves comparison of the two sets of numbers (i.e., your set of numbers for imagining a career in the United States or Canada and your set for imagining a career in one of the other listed countries).

Let's call the first time you answered the questions the "first pass" and the other time the "second pass." In scoring, give yourself 1 point according to the following guidelines.

Question 1: Give yourself a point if your number in the second pass is higher than in the first pass.

Question 2: Give yourself a point if your number in the first pass is higher than in the second pass.

Question 3: A point if number is higher in the second pass.

Question 4: A point if number is higher in the second pass.

Question 5: A point if number is higher in the first pass.

Question 6: A point if number is higher in the second pass.

Question 7: A point if number is higher in the second pass.

Question 8: A point if number is higher in the first pass.

Question 9:   A point if number is higher in the first pass.

Question 10: A point if number is higher in the second pass.

Question 11: A point if number is higher in the first pass.

Question 12: A point if number is higher in the first pass.

Question 13: A point if number is higher in the second pass.

Question 14: A point if number is higher in the second pass.

If you scored 6 or more points, it means that you are sensitive to the cultural differences summarized by the concepts of individualism and collectivism. You are sensitive to the fact that different behaviors are likely to lead to the accomplishment of goals and to success in one's career depending on the emphasis on individualism or collectivism in the culture.

Source: "Understanding your Orientation Toward Individualism-Collectivism" from R. W. Brislin and T. Yoshida (eds.), *Improving Intercultural Interactions; Modules for Cross-Cultural Training Programs.* Copyright © 1994 Sage Publications. Reprinted by permission of Sage Publications, Inc.

 Tapping into the Global Network

The Cultural Minefield of International Gift Giving

Purpose

The objective here is to explore cultural differences in the gift-giving process. In doing so, you have the opportunity to learn something about the complex historical, religious, and linguistic factors that have shaped gift giving in particular countries.

Instructions

Read the background material below outside class (unless your instructor tells you otherwise).

Your instructor will assign you to small groups of three to six and give each group a specific country to research outside class. A variety of websites are available that offer additional detail and resources about international gift-giving issues. For instance, you may want to consult Expat Exchange, an online forum that is full of advice about work-ing and living abroad. And of course,

that includes gift giving (see **www.expatexchange.com/lib.cfm?networkID=159&articleID=191**)!

Your group should be prepared to present your findings in a subsequent class (10–15 minutes per group) and/or prepare a group report. Alternatively, your instructor may make this an individual assignment and have you write a report. Be prepared to take part in a general class discussion on the specific countries assigned. In any case, you should focus on answering these gift-giving questions for the country assigned:

- What gifts might be appropriate for the country in a business context or business relationship?

- When should gifts be given, generally speaking? What about gift giving if you're visiting the country in question on business?

- How should gifts be wrapped? What colors are appropriate or inappropriate? What presentation issues come into play (e.g., when should a gift be presented during a visit)? What other delivery issues might come into play?
- What gifts should be avoided?

Some Background on Gift Giving in an International Context

Differences in cultural values around the world can make managing an international business a tricky proposition. Even behavior that has the best of intentions—like gift giving—can be complex and have great potential to give offense. In many countries, it is appropriate to give foreign clients, contacts, customers, and employees a gift as a sign of appreciation. However, what constitutes an acceptable gift can vary widely. The failure to understand local rules can create hard feelings or even lead to the loss of overseas business.

This begs the question of what you should give as gifts in other countries. Many experts recommend giving something that is unique to your own country or that would otherwise be difficult for the recipient to obtain. For an American, this might mean giving Native American handicrafts or books about the United States. But in other cases, it might be best to research the cultural, religious, and holiday traditions of a particular country to figure out what might make an appropriate gift. Better yet, get to know your foreign contacts well enough so that you begin to understand their individual hobbies, tastes, and so on.

Giving gifts overseas, however, means more than just finding an appropriate item. In many countries, there are fairly elaborate rules regarding how gifts should be wrapped and presented. For instance, yellow and red have positive connotations in India. Likewise, white is a bad choice for many Asian countries (it's associated with death) while gold or red would be better selections. Then there is the presentation of the gift itself. In many Asian countries, using both hands to give and receive gifts is a sign of courtesy. However, if you find yourself in an Islamic country you would want to present a gift with just the right hand since the left hand is viewed as unsanitary.

Timing gift giving is also important. The Christmas season is generally pretty safe because most countries celebrate a major holiday around this time period. Usually, giving gifts in private is the best bet. However, Japanese typically engage in gift giving after business is concluded, while the Chinese usually present gifts at the beginning of a visit. In any case, don't necessarily expect Asians to praise aspects of the gifts you give; it is considered impolite to open gifts in front of the giver. Finally, it should be obvious that we're just scratching the surface here on gift giving overseas. If you have a foreign trip coming up and you're looking for specific gift-giving advice, do your homework and call the embassy of the country that you'll be traveling to.

For a brief snapshot of what we've been talking about, take a look at some recommendations of what to give, when to give, and what to avoid giving for the four countries listed here.[56]

Country	Good Gifts	When to Give Gifts	Gifts to Avoid (with explanation)
China	Ties, pens, modest items	Chinese New Year (January or February)	Clocks (the Mandarin word for clock is similar to "final resting place")
India	Sweets, nuts, fruit	Hindu Diwali Festival (October or November)	Leather goods (cows are sacred to Hindus)
Japan	Americana, liquor	Oseibo (January 1)	Four of anything (associated with death)
Saudi Arabia	Compasses, cashmere	Id al-Fitr (December or January)	Liquor (Islam prohibits alcohol consumption)

CASE 1

Third-World Families at Work: Child Labor or Child Care?

Jonathan Stein, the new vice president of international contracts for Timothy & Thomas North America, shifted restlessly in his plane seat. During his two-month swing through Asia, he'd been on more planes than he could remember, many of them far more uncomfortable than this flight back to Boston. But he couldn't forget the Pakistani girls who had looked no older than ten years old, sweeping the floor between the rows of sewing machines the women worked on.

In that plant in Lahore, the women and girls had been hard at work assembling T&T shorts—currently the hottest item in Timothy & Thomas's 40-year-old line of casual clothes. Like the rest of the company's products, the shorts had that wholesome American "feel good look good" image.

But that image didn't fit the image of those girls at work, and the contradiction left Stein with a quandary. In keeping with Timothy & Thomas's reputation for social responsibility, the company's new Global Guidelines for Business Partners prohibited the use of child labor—with "child" defined as anyone under 14 or the compulsory school age. Until his trip to Asia, Stein had felt good about working for a company that valued employee empowerment and diversity. Yet when it came to Pakistan and other developing countries, he'd found the company's policies no help at all.

In Lahore, Stein had enjoyed the city itself, which was a thriving textile and market center. Its colorful bazaar, wedged between the opulently wealthy and extremely poor districts of the city, was full of silks and the hand-embroidered clothing Lahore was famous for. He had liked the desert landscape and bright white walls, all backed by a cold blue sky. When Stein first met Timothy & Thomas's Pakistani sourcing manager, on a taxi ride to one of the local plants, he was still distracted by so many new sights.

"I should warn you," said Yusuf Ahmed, the sourcing manager, just minutes after shaking Stein's hand. "There's some confusion about the guidelines."

Stein stopped admiring the scenery. "What do you mean?"

"All the good contractors use kids. The little girls come to the plant with their mothers, and I know there are others on the machines who are younger than 14. That's just how it's done here."

"Haven't you told them they have to do it differently?" Stein's hands tensed on his knees. The taxi jounced through the narrow streets, no longer surrounded by the picturesque overflow from the bazaar.

"I'm not a cop," Ahmed said. "Besides, I'm not sure you'd really want me to do that. The situation is more complicated than you think."

"What's complicated? You say contractors aren't in compliance, so we threaten to cut off the contracts until they are."

Ahmed leaned forward impatiently. "Do you realize how committed we are? We've got the Lahore contractors alone assembling half a million T&T products a year—at competitive prices, I can assure you."

"I know the numbers," Stein said. "But that doesn't change the guidelines. We can't have kids in the plants, right?"

"Third-World Families at Work: Child Labor or Child Care?" by Martha Nichols et al., *Harvard Business Review*, Jan/Feb 1993, Vol. 71, Issue 1. Copyright © 1993 by the Harvard Business School Publishing Corporation. Reprinted by permission of Harvard Business School Publishing. All rights reserved.

Ahmed wiped his brow. He looked more than hot under his neatly pressed collar and dark tie. Although he had gone to the University of Pennsylvania and worked in the United States, Yusuf Ahmed had been back in Pakistan as Timothy & Thomas's sourcing manager for the past two years.

"We're lucky to have these guys, if you want the truth," Ahmed said. "Our contractors produce on time and with good quality, which is no small feat. They could set up somewhere else, but in their heart of hearts, many of these guys want to stay in Pakistan, to improve the quality of life a little bit, if they can, by bringing in jobs. Then here we come, the big company from the United States, saying we won't buy what they produce unless it comes incredibly cheap, but of course they have to follow our company guidelines, even if it means that their costs go up—"

"Hold on," Stein broke in. "We have contractors in other countries who are complying with the guidelines, and they seem to be producing just fine."

Now the sourcing manager looked more tired than angry. "Sure. If we ask them to, the contractors here will fire any kids who are under 14. But that will affect at least 60 families, all of them very poor in the first place, do you realize that? And the contractors will still want assurances from us. These guys will want to know that we'll pay our share, even if the price goes up and we have to renegotiate the contracts."

"How much are we talking about?" Stein asked.

"The young kids who come with their mothers do more than you think. They are paid nothing, of course," Ahmed said. "Even the older ones on the machines get paid subminimum wages as trainees, so labor will go up by at least a third to pay adults minimum wage—or more for skilled work. Or if our contractors stick with the kids, they'll have to document that they're really 14. In Pakistan, you can't count on birth registrations, and I'm sure you've seen enough in Asia to know that most kids look younger than their real age."

"So how could you tell they were too young?"

"You can tell." Ahmed shrugged. "With some it's hard, and maybe the only way to be certain is to have a doctor examine them. The children them-selves will lie. They'll say they're 14, because they need the work. What are their alternatives, really? They can hire themselves out as maids for almost nothing, or spend hours on embroidery at home, work that is not regulated at all. Or they can go to a carpet factory, would you like that any better?"

Stein shook his head. "I don't feel good about any of this."

The sourcing manager turned away. "I can't help you there. I don't agree with the guidelines, you know, but since I work for the company, I'll do what I'm told." Ahmed lit a cigarette and stared out the taxi's dirty window. "Forgive me for being blunt, but sometimes I don't know what you managers in Boston are thinking about, I really don't. As far as I'm concerned, imposing American values on the Third World just creates more problems. You have no idea what it's like to live in Pakistan, do you?"

"That's why I'm here."

"For one week. Fine. Then let me tell you about the reality. You don't know what those kids want." Ahmed unrolled the window. He raised his voice above the raucous street sounds outside. "We're not just talking about Pakistan. You can go to Bangladesh, Sri Lanka, Brazil, Mexico, the Azores—you're a Timothy & Thomas man, so you know what I mean. You can go all over the world and find street kids hustling and trying to make some money. Don't you think any of them would rather be working for one of our contractors? I'd say we're doing everyone here a favor."

Stein didn't answer, since by then the taxi had screeched to a halt. However, at the first plant they visited, he still felt uneasy. All of the workers on the floor were girls or women, because working side by side with men was considered improper. Ahmed had explained that this plant owner provided separate buses to bring the women to work. Farhan Hanafi, who led them on a tour of the plant, also made clear to Stein that he provided meals for his workers and wages of 5,000 rupees a month, or about $200, for the skilled women—much more than the minimum wage of 1,200 rupees, Hanafi insisted.

The plant floor wasn't dirty or overcrowded, but there was no heat. The women wore layers of long blouses over thin flowing pants, and many of their heads were covered with brightly woven shawls.

Their bare hands, reddened in the cold room, still moved deftly around the mechanical needles, pushing the pre-cut pieces of cloth forward. He saw small girls winding thread on sewing machine spools for their mothers. Some older girls squatted near piles of patterns and cast-off cloth, stacking and sorting, talking as they worked. They only became silent when Stein and the other men moved closer.

Yusuf Ahmed asked one of the girls some questions in Punjabi. The girl kept her head bowed down and answered in a low voice, shrugging her thin shoulders as she spoke. The girl was about the same height as Stein's eight-year-old daughter, and he had always considered Jessica small for her age.

"She says she likes to work here." Ahmed glanced at the plant owner. "Mr. Hanafi is very kind to them and pays them very well. They have a roof over their heads, and they can keep their hands clean. She's old enough, she claims, because all her friends are here, and they are all the same age. They are all very good workers, she wants Mr. Hanafi to know this."

"But why aren't they in school?" Stein asked.

"The families need them to work," Ahmed said. "I think at least half of the kids in Pakistan don't make it to primary school, and it's more important for boys to get an education, if the families can afford it."

Ahmed's answer depressed Stein even more. Based on the rest of his Asian trip, he knew conditions in this particular Pakistani plant weren't bad. He told himself that the workers were probably grateful for walls that kept out the grit and dry wind outside, for decent lighting and a clean concrete floor. Lahore wasn't Calcutta, of course, but Stein remembered the crowds of people in the poor district outside the plant, many sleeping or begging in the dirt. They had rolled to the side just in time when their taxi honked through. The women were probably glad to have their young daughters inside with them, where the girls could also be useful.

But Stein imagined *60 Minutes* sinking its teeth into this story—a real exposé of how those popular T&T shorts, brought to you by lovable, reliable Timothy & Thomas, were stitched together by poor Pakistani kids. It wouldn't play well in Poughkeepsie.

Now, on the plane back to Boston and company headquarters, Stein twisted around in his seat, trying to get comfortable. If he didn't renew the Lahore contracts, the girls and their families would lose a major source of income. Or was that just a convenient rationale for looking the other way? After all, adhering to the company guidelines would send production costs for the T&T line, at least temporarily, through the roof. Timothy & Thomas's clothing empire was now scrambling to keep its edge in the North American and European markets. There were U.S. warehouses and stores depending on shipments of T&T products, Stein thought. A high volume of shorts and blouses that, to date, had been produced quickly and cheaply by the contractors in Lahore.

The Pakistani girls posed the first test of the Global Guidelines for Business Partners. Yet being on the cutting edge of company policy just made his decision more difficult. Jonathan Stein realized that he was now responsible for the outcome. Unfortunately, all the talk of values and social responsibility in the world didn't erase the bottom line.

Assignment Questions

1. What are some of Stein's options for dealing with the Lahore contractors?

2. How can Stein balance the company's guidelines on child labor with the company's need to make a profit and still not turn a blind eye to the poverty facing employees' families in Pakistan?

3. Ultimately, what would you advise Stein to do? Why? What are the benefits, risks, and costs?

4. Overall, what are a multinational's responsibilities, if any, when it comes to addressing poverty, working conditions, and child labor issues in the places it does business?

CASE 2

Chiba International, Inc.

Ken Morikawa, the general manager for administration of a Japanese manufacturing plant under construction in rural Georgia, was troubled. This morning his American personnel manager, John Sinclair, had walked eagerly across the temporary open-plan office and announced: "I've found a professor of Japanese at Georgia State University who is willing to help translate our corporate philosophy. I would like to hire him for the job."

Ken felt pressured. He thought that John Sinclair, like many Americans, was expecting too much of Japanese companies. The company philosophy that he, Ken, had learned to live by in Tokyo would continue to guide him, but he did not feel that Americans would welcome or even understand a Japanese company philosophy.

Ken had a very large task to do in supervising the building of a plant that might ultimately provide jobs for up to 2,000 employees in an area where very few workers had had any industrial experience. He wished to show that his was a company that cared about the welfare of its workers and their job security, and could be trusted to treat them fairly and not to lay them off. He believed that such a philosophy, if it could be properly explained to workers and carefully implemented, would help to build a high morale among the employees and consequently improve productivity.

Ken also wanted to ensure that high morale be maintained as the workforce expanded to full capacity. Indeed, aside from issues of ease of transportation and distribution, the characteristics of the local workforce, their "Japanese" work ethic, had been one of the primary reasons for establishing the plant here. He believed that the training costs involved in transforming very "green" workers were well worth it, to avoid people who had picked up "bad habits" or had had their morale lowered in prior industrial jobs. In Japan, teaching company philosophy is an important part of the company's introductory training program. But will it work here?

Ken wondered if his new administrative duties were lowering his concern for personnel matters. Ever since he had to read Alfred Sloan's *My Years with General Motors* during the company training program and had written a review that focused on human resource issues, he had held positions related to his field. Even though he had majored in mathematical economics in college, his first assignment had been in the personnel "design center," which controlled training and salary administration for white-collar employees. After two years he was sent to a district office as a salesman. He returned after thirteen months to the employee welfare section of the personnel department at the head office, administering such programs as house loans and recreational activities. Eight years with the company had passed by the time he was sent to an American college to study personnel-related subjects and improve his English.

After receiving his MBA he returned to the head office. His most recent assignment before coming to Georgia was in personnel development research, planning new wages systems. It was expected that in his new job in Georgia he would eventually hand the reins over to an American general manager and remain only in an advisory capacity. However, he felt that it was at this vital stage that the corporation depended on his human

This case was written by Nina Hatvany and Vladimir Pucik for class discussion only. None of this material is to be quoted or reproduced without the permission of the authors.

relations expertise to set the scene for future success. Was he neglecting an area in which he had been trained to be sensitive?

He brought the subject up at lunch with John Sinclair. "Let me tell you something, John. I have a hunch why the Japanese are more successful in achieving high quality and productivity than Americans have been recently. It has to do with application, rather than ideas. Many great ideas have come from the United States, but the Japanese concentrate on applying them very carefully. Americans emphasize creating something new and then moving on. The Japanese meticulously analyze a problem from all angles and see how a solution might be implemented.

"As they say, Rome wasn't built in a day. I'm not sure our American workers will understand what it really means to have a company philosophy. Let's take it slowly and see what kind of people we hire and then see what best meets their needs."

John, who had worked at a rather traditional U.S. company for eleven years and had become increasingly interested in how Japanese companies managed their U.S. employees, had been eager to join a Japanese company. He wanted to see in action such "Japanese" strategies as long-term employment, the expression of a company philosophy, and careful attention to integrating the employees into the company. He answered comfortingly, "Ken, I know you hate conflict. But I also know that you think it important to gather information. One of our purchasing agents, Billy, told me about a Japanese company that he recently visited, Chiba International. Apparently, they already have a fully developed company philosophy and I understand that they're doing very well with it. Why don't we go out to California and talk with their management and try and understand how and why they concentrated on communicating their philosophy?"

"And soak up some sun, too," beamed Ken. "You're on!"

The Company

Chiba International Inc. in San Jose, California, makes high-precision, sophisticated electronics parts used in the final assembly of customized and semi-customized integrated circuits—particularly the expensive memory chips used in computers and military hardware. In such products, reliability is everything, price a lesser consideration. The similar but cheaper parts that manufacturers use once a product reaches a high volume are left for others to make.

Chiba International is a subsidiary of Chiba Electronics Company. *Nihon Keizai Shimbun*, Japan's preeminent business paper, recently ranked Chiba Electronics as one of the foremost companies in Japan on the basis of its management earnings stability and performance, ahead of such better-known giants as Sony, Matsushita Electric, and Toyota Motor. Chiba Electronics Co. has 70 percent of the world market for its products. Chiba International likewise has a 70 percent share of the U.S. market.

Chiba International started in the United States twelve years ago, with a small sales office. A manufacturing plant that had been losing $100,000 to $200,000 a month was acquired from an American competitor. The American management was terminated, and a team of Japanese, headed by a Canadian-born Japanese-reared executive, succeeded in turning it around within two years.

Today fourteen out of the twenty-four top executives and sixty-five out of seventy salesmen at Chiba are Americans. All the employees in other categories are also American.

Chiba's Philosophy

"As the sun rises brilliantly in the sky,
Revealing the size of the mountain, the market,
Oh this is our goal.
With the highest degree of mission in our heart
we serve our industry,
Meeting the strictest degree of customer
requirement.
We are the leader in this industry and our
future path
Is ever so bright and satisfying."

"That's a translation of our company song," said a high-ranking Japanese executive, one of the group of Japanese and American managers who had agreed to meet with Ken and John. "But we haven't introduced it to our employees yet. That's typical of the way we brought the company philosophy to our employees—slowly and carefully. Every line worker gets a leaflet explaining our company philosophy when he or she starts work. We don't have a specific training session on it and we don't force them to swallow it. It's up to them to digest and understand it."

"What about when you acquire a company as you have done over the past few years?" asked John.

"The same thing. It's very gradual. If we force it, it causes nothing but indigestion. Here it has been easy, the work is very labor intensive, repetitive, tedious assembly. In other places the soil is different. At one, for example, almost all the employees are exempts. They understand the philosophy but won't necessarily go by it. Engineers and technical people also seem to be less receptive than people in sales, personnel, and administration. In other sites, though, where the technology is more similar to this, we have had no problem at all."

One of the other managers present in the group, this one American, interrupted to show Ken and John a copy of the leaflet. It was quite rhetorical in tone, but a few paragraphs struck them as particularly interesting.

Management Philosophy
Our goal is to strive toward both the material and spiritual fulfillment of all employees in the Company, and through this successful fulfillment, serve mankind in its progress and prosperity.

Management Policy
(...) Our purpose is to fully satisfy the needs of our customers and in return gain a just profit for ourselves. We are a family united in common bonds and singular goals. One of these bonds is the respect and support we feel for our fellow family co-workers.

Also, the following exhortation:

When there is a need, we all rally to meet it and consider no task too menial or demeaning; all that matters is that it should be done! We are all ready to sweep floors, sort parts, take inventory, clean machines, inspect parts, load trucks, carry boxes, wash windows, file papers, run furnaces, and do just about anything that has to be done.

Meetings

"Daily meetings at the beginning of each shift are held in the courtyard," explained the group. "All the workers stand in lines (indicated by metal dots in the asphalt). Each day, a different member of management speaks for about five minutes. On Mondays executives speak, on Tuesday, personnel and administration are represented, Wednesdays are about safety concerns, and on Thursdays and Fridays, members of production and sales speak. They are all free to say whatever they like. The shift workers tend to develop favorites, especially among the more extroverted sales managers.

"Then a personnel coordinator delivers news about sports events and so on, and perhaps a motivational message, and goes on to lead the group in exercises for one minute. These calisthenics are voluntary, but most of the employees join in. After that, the large group breaks up for brief departmental meetings.

"Again, in the departmental meetings, a speaker is chosen for the day and speaks for about five minutes. Even people at the lowest exempt level find themselves speaking. Then the department manager discusses yesterday's performance, today's schedule and any other messages, such as that housekeeping is inadequate or that certain raw materials are in short supply.

"Once a month, there is an announcement of total company performance versus plans. This is important, as all company employees share at the same rate in the annual company bonus, which is based on profitability and usually equals about one month's salary or wages."

Another Japanese manager continued, "Years ago, there were complaints about having so many meetings, but I haven't heard any for a long time now. The employees like to hear important announcements and even less important ones, such as who is selling theater tickets, bowling league reports, and tennis match dates."

The American personnel manager chimed in: "I was the one who came up with the idea of exercises. I saw it on my visit to Japan. They are just a part of the rituals and symbols that you need in order to get better mutual understanding. The atmosphere was right and the timing was good. Even so, because they weren't mandatory, it took about one-and-a-half years until everyone joined in.

Now most people understand the meaning behind it. If we were to stop it now, we'd get complaints.

"Besides the morning meeting, we have several other meetings. On Mondays, we have a very large liaison meeting for information sharing. All the executives attend: sales managers and staff managers, the plant manager and the assistant plant manager. On Tuesdays, we have a production meeting attended by the production managers and any staff involved with their problems. On Monday at four o'clock every second week we have a supervisors' meeting, mainly for one-way communication to them. On the alternating weeks we have a training meeting. The whole personnel department also meets every week.

"Less formally, we have many sales meetings about, for example, new products. We have combination sales and production meetings, which are called on an as-needed basis. Team meetings on the production line are also called whenever needed.

"All these formal meetings are supplemented by many company-sponsored activities. We have a company bowling league, tennis matches, softball, fishing, and skiing. We often organize discount tickets. We're planning the Christmas party. Each employee can bring a guest, so it costs us about $40,000. Our company picnic costs $29,000."

"It sounds very well worked out for the non-exempts," commented John. "How about for the exempts?"

Sales Force

They started with the largely American sales force.

"They're a very different species. They have tremendous professional pride. Most of the American sales engineers have a very arrogant take-it-or-leave-it attitude. Our attitude is almost the complete opposite. We try to serve our customer's needs, almost like a geisha girl, who makes her customer feel that he is the only one served by her.

"We try to communicate the following motto to them:

S incerity
A bility
L ove
E nergy
S ervice

Sincerity is the basic attitude you need to have, as well as the ability to convince the customer. You must love the products that you sell or you can't convince the customer. You must have energy because at the end of the day it's always the case that you could have done one more thing or made one more sales call. Finally, the mentality of serving the customer is the most important.

"We communicate that to our sales force and they like it, especially when they don't have to tell white lies to customers or put up with harassment from customers. We also want them to be honest with us, even about their mistakes. Quite often we depend on the salesmen's input for our understanding of customers, so an objective daily report by telex or phone is very important to us.

"No one in our company works on a commission basis, not even salesmen. We would lose market share for products that are difficult to promote. Also, the nature of different sales territories would make commissions unfair.

"Although we pay on straight salary only, we don't just have a unilateral sales quota. The salesman discusses his targets with his boss. They are purposely set high, so good performance against goals is grounds for a merit increase the next year.

"We don't really have a marketing department. We feel that it is an expensive luxury, and while we have a Vice President in charge of marketing, his is almost a corporate sales staff function."

U.S. Management

John was curious about how American line managers reacted to working in a Japanese company.

A Japanese manager explained: "When Americans join us, they expect the usual great deal of internal politicking. They scan people in meetings, looking for those with real power, looking, to use our expression, for whose apple he should polish. It takes time for them to realize that it's unnecessary.

"When we interview American executives for a job, we do it collectively so five to ten interviewers are present. This usually puzzles the interviewee. He wonders whom he will report to. We reply that he will be hired by the company, although he may report to one individual. As in Japan, the company will take care of him, so it does not depend on his loyalty to one individual."

"What about your company criteria for hiring managers?" asked John.

"His way of thinking, not necessarily his ability. Although a Harvard MBA is welcomed, it is not essential. In fact, no one here has one. We don't provide an elegant fit to his social elite. There are no private offices. Salary and benefits are up to par for the location (and industry) but not especially high. We work long hours.

"We're looking for devotion and dedication as well as an aggressive attitude. We conduct two or three long interviews for an important position. We ask questions like 'What is your shortcoming?' We're interested not in the answer itself but in the kind of thinking behind it. We do make mistakes sometimes, but our batting average is good.

"Sometimes there's a very deep communication gap between Japanese management and U.S. management because we believe in dedication and devotion to the company. They do, too, but only to a certain point. We often tell them that the joy of working for the company can be identical to personal happiness with the family. I ask my wife for her understanding of that, and I work six days a week, from seven o'clock to ten o'clock. Their wives place demands on them to come home at six o'clock. U.S. executives put personal and family happiness first. I'm not telling you which is right. But it is second nature for me to think about the future of the company. So long as I have challenging assignments and job opportunities, I will put the company before my personal happiness."

"What do American interviewees feel about all this?" asked John.

"One problem is that they ask, 'What's my real future? Can I be considered for President?' There's no real answer because it probably will be a Japanese. However, we don't like to close those doors to a really capable American.

"The issue of communication between Japanese and Americans is still a problem. After the Americans go home, the Japanese get together at seven or eight o'clock and talk in Japanese about problems and make decisions without the Americans present. Naturally this makes the Americans feel very apprehensive. We're trying to rectify it by asking the Japanese managers not to make decisions alone and asking the Americans to stay as late as possible.

"More important, if we could really have our philosophy permeate the American managers, we Japanese could all go back to Japan and not worry about it. Our mission is to expedite that day by education and training.

"So far, however, there is a gap. Americans are more interested in individual accomplishment, remuneration and power. When they are given more responsibility, they don't feel its heavy weight, rather they feel that it extends their sovereign area so that they have more of a whip. That creates power conflicts among U.S. managers."

"Let me tell you, though," summarized the American personnel manager, "I like it. I was recruited by a headhunter. Now, I've been with the company five years and the difference from my former employer is astounding. I don't have to get out there and be two-faced, fudging to keep the union out, hedging for the buck. In general, it's hard to find an American employer that really sincerely cares for the welfare of the low-level employee. This company went almost too far in the opposite direction at first. They wanted to do too much for the employees too quickly, without their earning it. That way, you don't get their respect."

Financial People

"Our financial people throughout the company are proud because of our impressive company performance. Only 20 percent of our financing is through debt, in contrast to many Japanese companies. We also have a rather unique way of treating some of our raw materials internally. We try to expense everything out. It's derived from our founder's very conservative management. We ask the question: 'If we closed down tomorrow, what would our liquid assets be?' In line with that, for example, internally we put our inventory at zero.

"We follow the 'noodle peddler theory.' The noodle peddler is an entrepreneur. He has to borrow his cart, his serving dishes, and his pan to make ramen. He has to be a good marketer to know where to sell. He has to be a good purchasing director and not overbuy noodles, in case it rains. He could buy a fridge but he would need a lot of capital, the taste of noodles would deteriorate, and he would need additional manpower to keep an inventory of the contents of the fridge. The successful noodle peddler puts dollars aside at the end of the day for depreciation and raw materials for tomorrow. Only then does he count profits. That's also why we don't have a marketing department.

The successful peddler doesn't have time to examine opportunities in the next town.

"This is the way a division manager has to operate. In order to maximize output with minimum expenditure, every effort is made to keep track on a daily basis of sales, returns, net shipment costs, and expenses."

Open Communications

"I understand all that you've said so far," mused John, "but how exactly do you take all these abstract philosophical ideas and make them real?"

"Oh, open communications is the key. We have a fairly homogeneous workforce. Most are intelligent, some are even college graduates. Most are also very stable types with dependents or elderly parents they send money to.

"We're lucky, but of course it's not as homogeneous as in Japan where everyone has experienced one culture. So here, the philosophy has to be backed up by a great deal of communication.

"We mentioned the meetings. We also have a suggestion box and we answer all the suggestions in print in the company newspaper. Also, one person from personnel tours the plant all day, for all three shifts, once a week, just chatting and getting in touch with any potential problems as they arise. It's kind of a secondary grievance system. We're not unionized and I guess we'd rather stay that way as it helps us so much with flexibility and job changes among our workforce.

"In the fall, when work is slow, we have many kompas. You may not know about this, John. A kompa is a small gathering off-premises after work. Eight to eighteen people participate and the company pays for their time and for refreshments. They're rarely social, they have an objective. For example, if two departments don't get along and yet they need to work together, they might hold a kompa. A kompa can take place at all levels of the company. Those groups that do it more frequently tend to move on from talking about production problems to more philosophical issues."

Appraisal and Reward Systems

"It all sounds great," sighed Ken, "just as good as Japan. But tell me, how does it tie in with wages and salaries, because people here are used to such different systems?"

"Well, we don't have lifetime employment, but we do have an explicit no-layoff commitment. We are responsible for our employees. This means that employees also have to take responsibility and have broad job categories so we don't have to redo paperwork all the time. We have tried to reduce the number of job classifications to the raw minimum, so we have two pay grades covering 700 workers. At the higher levels, we have three pay grades for craftsmen and two for technicians."

John ventured, "I guess an example of your job flexibility in action is the mechanic you mentioned when we toured the plant."

"Yes, the person you spoke with was a dry press mechanic. He's doing menial labor this week, but his pay hasn't been cut and he knows he wouldn't be taken off his job if it weren't important."

"We don't hire outside, if we can avoid it," added the personnel manager. "Only if the skill is not available in-house. The bulk of our training is on-the-job. We don't utilize job postings. We promote when a person's skills are ripe or when there is a need.

"The job of a 'lead' or team leader is the stepping-stone to supervisor. It's not a separate job status within our system, but the lead is given a few cents an hour extra and wears a pink, not a yellow, smock. The lead is carefully groomed for his or her position, and although a lead might be demoted because a specific need for them no longer existed, a lead would rarely be demoted for lack of skills or leadership ability.

"Rewards are for service and performance. Plant workers, unskilled and semiskilled, are reviewed every six months. The lead completes the evaluation form (see Exhibit 1). This is checked or confirmed by the supervisor and the overall point score translates into cents per hour. There are two copies, one for the supervisor and one for the employee. Depending on the supervisor, some employees get a copy, some don't.

"The office clerical staff are all reviewed on April 1st and October 1st. A similar review form for managers is used to determine overall letter scores. All the scores are posted on a spreadsheet and compared across departments, through numerous meetings of managers and personnel people, until the scores are consistent with one

EXHIBIT 1.

Employee's Name		Clock No.	Dept.	Shift	Over Last 6 Month Period			
					Days Absent	Number Tardies	Number Early Exit	Work Days Leave of Absences
Employee's Job Title		Anniversary						

Rate on Factors Below:		Numerical Score			
		L	S	M	F
1. LOYALTY/DEDICATION	Faithful to the company cause, ideals, philosophy, & customers; a devoting or setting aside for company purposes.				
2. SPIRIT/ZEAL	Amount of interest & enthusiasm shown in work; full of energy, animation, & courage; eagerness & ardent interest in the pursuit of company goals.				
3. COOPERATION	A willingness & ability to work with leaders & fellow employees toward company goals.				
4. QUANTITY OF WORK	Volume of work regularly produced; speed & consistency of output.				
5. QUALITY OF WORK	Extent to which work produced meets quality requirements of accuracy, thoroughness, & effectiveness.				
6. JOB KNOWLEDGE	The fact or condition of knowing the job with familiarity gained through experience, association, & training.				
7. SAFETY ATTITUDE	The willingness & ability to perform work safely.				
8. CREATIVENESS	The ability to produce through imaginative skill.				
9. ATTENDANCE	Includes all types of absence (excused or unexcused), tardies, early exits, L.O.A.'s from scheduled work.				
10. LEADERSHIP	The ability to provide direction, guidance, & training to others.				
OVERALL EVALUATION OF EMPLOYEE PERFORMANCE:					
Supervisor's Approval			Personnel Dept. Approval		
Do Not Write Below This Line — For Human Resource Department Use Only					
Present Base Rate	New Base Rate		Effective Date of Increase	Refer to instructions on the back side of this paper.	

another. Then the scores are tied to dollars. Some managers give feed back, some don't.

"Exempt staff are reviewed on April 1st, and as a separate process, the spreadsheet procedure just outlined is carried out. At least two managers review any exempt employee, but feedback is usually minimal. The reason is that we encourage feedback all year. If there are no surprises for your subordinate at review time, then you've managed well.

"Agreements on reviews for exempt personnel take place in many meetings at various levels. The process is very thorough and exceptionally fair, and contributes to the levels of performance we get."

Quality and Service

A question from John as to how Chiba International was doing as a result of all this elicited much pride.

"Turnover is two and a half percent a month, which is very satisfactory for our kind of labor given a transient society. We rarely have to advertise for new employees now. The community knows about us. But we do select carefully. The personnel department does the initial screening, and then the production managers and supervisors get together and interview people.

"The lack of available technically trained people used to be a big problem, but over the years we've developed the expertise internally. Our productivity is now almost as high as in Japan."

Ken and John asked what other aspects of the company they had not yet discussed. They were told that quality and, hence, customer service, was another central part of the philosophy.

"Our founder, Mr. Amano, firmly believes in zero defect theory. Doctor Deming taught us the concept of quality control. Unfortunately, many American companies did not emphasize this. During World War II, the concept of acceptable quality level was developed in the United States. The idea was that with mass production there will be some defects. Rather than paying for more inspectors on the production line, real problems, for example, with cars, could be identified by the consumer in the field and repaired in the field.

"We don't allow that. We have 100 percent visual inspection of all our tiny parts. They only cost $50 per 1,000 units. We inspect every finished package under a microscope so we have 130 inspectors, which is about one sixth of our production staff.

"The company's founder, Amano, has said to us, 'We try to develop every item our customers want. Being latecomers, we never say no, we never say we can't.' Older ceramic manufacturers would evaluate a proposal on a cost basis and say no. Yet we have been profitable from the start."

As the interview drew to a close, one Japanese manager reflected that Mr. Suzuki has a saying:

Ability $\times$ philosophy $\times$ zeal = performance.

If the philosophy is negative, performance is negative because it's a multiplicative relationship.

"But in our company, which now numbers 2,000, we must also start to have different kinds of thinking. The Japanese sword is strong because it is made of all different kinds of steel wrapped around one another. The Chinese sword is also very strong, but because it's all one material, it's vulnerable to a certain kind of shock. We must bear that in mind so that we have differences within a shared philosophy.

"We're thinking of writing a book on our philosophy, addressing such issues as what loyalty is, by piecing together events and stories from our company history. This would be a book that would assist us in training."

Ken and John walked out into the parking lot. "Whew!" sighed John. "It's more complicated than I had thought."

"Oh, yes! You need a great deal of patience," responded Ken paternally.

"So we'd better get started quickly," enthused John. "Where shall we begin? Perhaps I should call the translator."

Assignment Questions

1. Can Japanese management practices work in the United States without adaptation? Why or why not? What cultural values are relevant?

2. How should Ken and John adapt Chiba's California practices to their situation? What problems will they run into (cultural and otherwise)?

3. What aspects of the Japanese approach used by Chiba are the most interesting or unusual to you? Why?

PART II

Interacting Effectively in an International Environment

5

Perception, Interpretations, and Attitudes across Cultures

INTERNATIONAL CHALLENGE

Doing Business in Vietnam

Learning Objectives

After reading this chapter, you should be able to:

▸ Better understand the influence of culture on our perceptions, interpretations, and resulting attitudes.

▸ Diagnose some of the important ways that perceptual effects can impact our interactions with people from different cultures.

▸ Be able to classify and distinguish cultures along several perceptual dimensions.

▸ Appreciate the importance of some of the verbal and nonverbal ways that people from other cultures will see you, evaluate you, and act toward you.

DIPLOMATIC TIES BETWEEN THE United States and Vietnam have been restored between these former enemies.[1] Past experience has shown that business opportunity often trumps bad feelings for Americans. Accordingly, we predict that you will continue to see U.S. firms moving in to take advantage of a burgeoning business environment in Vietnam. Some experts seem to predict that Vietnam eventually will become Asia's newest tiger because of its many assets. For one, its people are young—80 percent of the population (73 million) is under 40 years old. Additionally, the Vietnamese are well educated and the literacy rate is nearly 90 percent. The Vietnamese people are also said to have a natural sense of entrepreneurship, despite several decades of a communist government. Add all this to the low cost of labor, and it is easy to see why capital should flow into the country.[2]

Just as in China, however, the going will not be easy. There are many potential impediments to economic growth, including an underdeveloped infrastructure, a large bureaucratic government, and corruption. Likewise, as we saw in Chapter 2, a rudimentary legal system permits widespread piracy of intellectual property. Nevertheless, perhaps the biggest challenge for U.S. businesspeople might be a very familiar one—recognizing and understanding cultural differences. In this chapter we discuss the ways that perceptions of others are formed and maintained and the problems that occur in this process. Likewise, we also discuss attitudes toward one's own and other groups. As you read this chapter, please try to think of some of the ways that perception, interpretation, and attitudes might differ in the United States and Vietnam. At the end of the chapter, we'll review some of the actual differences that have been observed between these two countries.[3]

▶ *Perceptions*

perception
The selective mental processes that enable us to interpret and understand our surroundings

The subtlest way that culture can affect us is through our perceptions. **Perception** involves the selective mental processes that enable us to interpret and understand our surroundings. These include attending to or selecting the events in the first place, processing the information that is selected, and finally interpreting the meaning of what was attended to and processed. The key word in this definition is *selective*. We do not perceive all that is going on around us at any one instant. Take right now as an example. You are reading (perceiving) the words on this page, but many other things are also occurring around you. Your stereo may be on, someone may be walking and talking in the hall, noises can be heard outside, and so on. But we do not attend to all these random events. Instead, we selectively attend to stimuli that are important to us or help us make decisions. We certainly do not perceive things at random, but instead we impose order on all the environmental stimuli we are exposed to. (In fact, the defining symptom of schizophrenia is the inability to organize and selectively process one's perceptions!).

If we are imposing order on an inherently disorganized environment, how does this happen, and what role does culture play? It appears that members of a culture teach each other what is important to perceive in our interactions with others. Experts say that what people in one culture need to perceive may be different from what is needed in other cultures. In other words, culture may subtly sensitize people to the information and behavior that is important.[4]

Differences in Perceptions of People and Events across Cultures

Does research support this conjecture about perceptual differences across cultures? And even if differences in perception exist, are there also some similarities in what people look for when they form impressions of others?

Perceptions of People   One group of researchers provided a partial answer to our question about culture and perception.[5] They asked groups of Chinese and Australians to read various descriptions of fictitious people. The descriptions of the people were very detailed, including how conscientious, outgoing, and sensitive they were. Care was taken to see that the Chinese and English versions of the descriptions were similar and thus could not muddy any conclusions. The participants were then asked to predict how these people might behave. The goal was to find out which specific pieces of information would be selected and emphasized by the two groups.

The two cultural groups were chosen deliberately—the Chinese because their culture is oriented to the group and the Australians because their culture is oriented to the individual. For this reason, it was expected that the Chinese would selectively pick out traits that involve consideration of others, whereas the Australians might emphasize more person-oriented traits when forming impressions. The researchers found exactly that—the Chinese were more influenced by a person's conscientiousness toward others in forming their impressions, whereas the Australians focused on outgoingness (a person-focused characteristic) in forming their impressions. Of all the information presented, the Chinese and Australians selected culturally sensitive traits to form their impressions. One lesson to learn here is that it would benefit us to understand how other cultures form opinions of people with whom they negotiate, communicate, and otherwise do business.[6]

In other studies these same researchers provided more evidence for cultural effects on perception.[7] They argued that some cultures are more naturally conscious and respectful of power differences among people, whereas other cultures give less weight to authority. Again, participants were chosen from cultures in which the importance of status varied dramatically. Americans were chosen because they accord relatively little importance to status, whereas Chinese were chosen because they value status highly. The researchers predicted that the Chinese would give more leeway to higher-status persons in their treatment of others than would the Americans—so much so that a high-status Chinese could go as far as to insult another person at a business meeting with little recrimination.

Since it is difficult to observe a personal insult firsthand, researchers instead had people read a story about a business meeting during which a manager publicly insulted an employee. But there were two different versions of the story: In one version the "insulter" was a high-status manager; in the other he was low-status. Participants were asked to read one version of the story and then to offer their perceptions of the insulter. Interestingly, Americans made no distinctions between high- and low-status managers who insulted others; their perceptions of this person were generally negative. The Chinese, however, were less critical of the insulter when he was a high-status manager. These results tell us that culture allows or directs one to be more or less critical of a person depending on that person's status. The results also suggest that different leadership styles (a topic considered in Chapter 11) may be more or less effective in different cultures.

Perception of Events   A follow-up study looked at cultural differences in the perception of everyday events, not people.[8] This study also used Chinese and Australian subjects because of their contrasting group and individual orientations. Everyone read a list of common everyday social events (arriving late to class, going out with friends) and then rated the events on nearly thirty different scales (e.g., boring–interesting, pleasant–unpleasant, etc).

A complicated statistical technique was then used to reduce all these responses to a few underlying dimensions. Interestingly, different dimensions were found for the two groups. The Chinese organized their perceptions of these events mainly along an individual versus group dimension. In other words, the Chinese seemed sensitive to events involving other people; they were more attentive to these events and thought they were more important than events that included few or no other persons. The Australians, however, rated the same everyday events as more enjoyable than the Chinese. Apparently, group events imply more fun to Australians whereas to the Chinese such events conjure up perceptions of social obligation.

Implications of Research on Perceptions of People and Events   All in all, these studies show that culture affects perceptions about life events and the people involved in those events. The insidious thing about perceptions is that most of the time they are "automatic." But automatic does not necessarily mean neutral or unbiased. In fact, these studies actually show that we use filters and organizing tools (i.e., how group-oriented is another person?) that reflect an important part of our culture.

We may rarely question the source of our perceptions because of their automatic nature. As a result, we may rapidly form impressions of business partners that are based on our own cultural filters, and we may equally not appreciate *their* filters. Westerners, for example, prefer abstract and universal principles, whereas East Asians are more likely to seek rules that are specific to the situation at hand. This kind of perception can create problems. For example, one study asked respondents what they would do in regard to a subordinate whose work had been below average for about a year, after they had provided fifteen years of above-average service. The results showed that about 75 percent of Canadians and Americans said they would let the employee go, whereas this figure was only 20 percent for those from Korea and Singapore. In practice, most of these reactions are "automatic" or are done with little thought. This doesn't mean they are hard-wired though: Research has shown that Asians who live in the West (and vice versa) find they adopt these subtle patterns.[9] Another area where there seems to be little conscious decision making about perceptions is in the area of nonverbal behavior.

Perception of Nonverbal Behavior

The studies just cited show that people in different cultures look for and see different things when observing the same behavior. But we must recognize that people use all kinds of cues and information to figure out what others are like, some of which are very subtle and indirect. Some writers, for example, claim that the nonverbal behavior of others offers clues about what they are really like.[10] **Nonverbal behavior** includes features such as people's appearance, facial expressions, and body movements, which can send important signals that affect our perceptions.[11] In fact, sometimes even the way we present our business card becomes an important nonverbal behavior (see the following International Insights).

nonverbal behavior
The subtle cues used to communicate within and across cultures, including facial expressions, appearance, and body movements

personal space
The distance we have between ourselves and others when we talk and interact; different spaces are preferred by different cultures

One example of this effect comes from research on personal space conducted by Edward Hall and his colleagues. They referred to **personal space** as the distance we have between ourselves and others when we talk and interact. This seems like an odd thing for us to consider, but in fact, personal space varies dramatically depending on what you are doing and with whom you are interacting. We regularly make very subtle decisions about how much space to have between ourselves and another person.[12] To illustrate, look at pairs and groups of people talking to one another just after a class break. How did they "decide" to have a foot or two between them and the person with whom they are talking? And please note differences among people if you can. Hall finds that American men like to keep two to four feet between themselves and another man when conversing. Women talking together, however, prefer a smaller amount of space. Hall notes several other interesting facts about personal space, but the most germane here has to do with cross-cultural differences. It seems that Americans and northern Europeans prefer about two feet of personal space when conducting business, whereas Asians prefer about three feet and Arabs typically prefer speaking very close to each other. You can imagine the effect of these differences in a cross-national business interaction. If an American likes about two feet and an Arab businessperson likes about a foot, what is likely to occur? The Arab might perceive the American as stuffy and standoffish, whereas the American businessperson might see the Arab as pushy. Hall believes that knowledge of

🌐 International Insights

Getting "Carded" in Japan: Perception and the Business Card Ritual

BUSINESS CARDS IN the U.S. show little variation. Most are ordered and constructed by assistants or printers; and most people pay little thought to the card style or to the actual exchange of cards with colleagues or clients. The routine is well known to all—you introduce yourself, talk a little bit, and then give the other person your card. You may even toss it across a table as you take the other person's card and shove it in your pocket.

This is so familiar that you're probably wondering why we even bother describing it here. The reason we do so is because other cultures exchange business cards differently. In fact, if you're unaware of their rituals and the resulting perceptions, you may be committing a terrible faux pas. In Japan, the *meishi* (business card) carries much greater importance than in the United States. This importance starts with the construction of the card itself, typically printed on the finest paper. The layout subtly accentuates the importance of the company rather than that of the less important individual. An American card will list your name first, with a title underneath in smaller print, and the firm's name and address below or in a corner. The Japanese *meishi* always presents the company name first and most prominently, then the employee's rank, and next, his or her name—reflecting this decreasing order of importance![13] But there's more. The *meishi* is usually bilingual, with English on one side and Japanese on the other. If you can read the Japanese side, you may pick up additional information. The firm name is often more detailed (and sometimes even different) than on the English side, and the logo usually appears only on this side. Likewise, if the card is printed vertically rather than horizontally, this can mean the firm is more conservative and traditional.

And we haven't even talked about the actual mechanics of exchanging cards yet. This ritual is an elaborate and meaningful act in Japan. Here's how it appears to operate. First, have plenty of cards with you. Not having a card is equivalent to refusing a handshake. The cards should be presented, not passed, with both hands. You should be sure to have your name facing the receiver. And you must bow.

The angle of bowing when presenting a card is a fine art. While Westerners are usually not expected to know the fine points of bowing, a quick, small bow will do the trick. Japanese employees must practice the "house style" during the training they'll get right after joining the firm. Finally, you must be able to receive the card properly as well. Again, you should take it with both hands and spend some time studying it. Examine the Japanese side even if you don't know the language and you'll be given credits by your host or partner. Don't shove the card in your pocket and don't write on the card for the same reason—the *meishi* represents the other person's identity and it's considered rude to treat this symbol disrespectfully. If you're about to have a meeting, place the card (or several cards) down in front of your business partner during the meeting and leave it there until the meeting is over. At that time, pick up the cards. But put them in a special place; they are never to be taken and placed in your pocket casually. Instead it is *de rigueur* to carry a relatively elaborate card holder. Take the holder out of a coat pocket, place the new card in the holder, and then place the holder back in your pocket—as though you really value the card. And, they apparently do value the cards.

The authors recently made a trip to Japan and read in advance about these and other rituals. So, we thought we were prepared for the card exchange. While we were relieved that we had practiced, we made a mistake in a later trip, not realizing how far this ritual extended as a sign of respect. After a long plane flight and several delays (about twenty-five hours total), we arrived exhausted at our hotel outside Tokyo, ready to check in and get some needed sleep. Instinctively, McFarlin took out his credit card to pay the room deposit and he tossed it out on the counter (as we all may have done in the United States). Unfortunately, this act offended the clerk who apparently perceived it as a sign of disrespect. We should have presented the card as we would have a business card. The clerk glared at us thereafter when we strolled through the hotel lobby.[14]

meishi
The business card in Japan, and the important ritual that accompanies its exchange

cultural space preferences can avert a negative perception that could otherwise interfere with a business transaction.

The Perception and Effect of Context

While a person's nonverbal behavior can provide "background" for understanding them, an even more subtle form of influence on our perceptions is the effect of **context**. Our perceptions of the world all occur within some kind of context. For instance, an identical statement could mean dramatically different things, depending, of course, on the context. Many of us know this intuitively, but others have had firsthand experience with this phenomenon (e.g., those who have been quoted "out of context" in the news media). So you could say that the need for context is relatively universal. Nevertheless, Edward Hall and his associates again claim that some cultures are more or less reliant on context in their perceptions of and interactions with others.

Exhibit 5.1 shows how some countries might line up in terms of their general reliance on context. In *low-context* cultures, like the United States or Germany, the interpretation of people and behavior often depends on what is actually said or written. That is, the message is often explicit, with the words themselves carrying most of the real message. In such cultures the meaning of a business interaction would have to be explicitly stated, discussed, and probably mutually agreed upon and written down before any deal could go forward.

However, people in a *high-context* culture might approach a business event very differently. In high-context cultures, the context itself often provides information that can be used to interpret what might otherwise be an ambiguous event. Put simply, people may not require or expect much detailed, explicit information about an event. In such cultures, verbal or written information may take a back seat to what is generally understood via the context. Consequently, high-context cultures tend to be concerned with long-term relationships, a person's word or reputation, and establishing trust over time. In contrast, people from low-context cultures tend to be concerned with getting all the context up front. And this means that they would tend to be concerned about the details of an arrangement and want to be clear about the "rules" for conducting business. Consequently, people from low-context cultures are likely to prefer explicit agendas for meetings and exhaustive legal documents to establish clarity about business deals—as opposed to relying on trust or relationships.

For instance, Japanese tend to be high-context and Americans tend to be low-context in their orientation. This may explain some of the complaints we've heard from Americans about their dealings with the Japanese, and vice versa. Specifically, some Americans claim that it's hard to "get straight answers" from the Japanese, so everything should be explicitly written down. Consider an American who makes a suggestion regarding a possible business deal with a Japanese firm. A Japanese person might reply, "That is interesting and worthy of future study." If the American possessed the high level of context offered by the Japanese culture, he or she would probably understand that this statement may actually mean: "It is unlikely that such an idea is acceptable to us."

The Japanese tend to worry that spelling everything out would be a condescending put-down. Of course, the flip side is that Japanese sometimes say that Americans don't want to spend the time to understand their business environment and are overly oriented to the short term. If the Japanese understood the

---

context
Background information—other than what is said or written—that helps us understand and perceive others; some cultures put great weight on this background information whereas others view it as extraneous

EXHIBIT 5.1   *Comparing High- and Low-Context Cultures*

Culture Example	Context
Chinese Korean Japanese French Arab Greek Spanish Italian English American Scandinavian German Swiss	**HIGH** • What is unsaid but understood carries more weight than written/verbal comments. • Relies on trust for agreement. • Personal relations add to business. **LOW** • Focus on specifics of what was said or written. • Handshake is insufficient. • Trust secured with legal agreement; personal relations detract from business.

Source: Adapted from Hall, E. T. (1976). *Beyond culture.* Garden City, NY: Anchor Press.

low-context culture embraced by many Americans, they would know that Americans' insistence on detailed contracts is a business necessity rather than an indicator of a lack of trust.

Hall argues that differences in context may explain many cross-cultural problems that arise in international business. Accordingly, it's important to know when and how to use context to your advantage. Obviously, you need to keep in mind whom you are dealing with and how much context might be necessary. Consider the following example: A German manager working for a French company was terminated within a year because his performance fell short of company expectations. The German was shocked, especially since "nobody told me what they wanted me to do." A French employee who resigned from a German company had the opposite experience. The French employee became fed up with being constantly told what to do by his German boss. He felt both his pride and intelligence were threatened.

What we have here is different perspectives involving context. The French tend to be high context and typically would expect the German employee to pick up on the message. The low-context German employee, in contrast, would usually expect intervention and direction by the French manager. Unfortunately, that intervention came way too late.[15]

Differences in the Perception of Time

If you're still not convinced that cultural differences in perception are important, you are not alone. Many people feel that perception—like beauty—is in the eye of the beholder. More specifically, some feel that the study of perception is too subjective to be of great value. To answer this criticism, researchers in international management decided to study perceptions of time. They chose to study time because of its objective nature. In fact, we could hardly think of anything more objective than time. Everybody has a watch, waits for a plane according to schedule, plans a travel itinerary, and arranges for a meeting—all on an understood time schedule. Ten minutes is ten minutes, time is time—right?

The answer to this question is no! Even though the whole world is ostensibly on the same time system, there are wide differences in perceptions of this most objective of things—time. At an anecdotal level, this difference can be seen in how some Eastern and Western cultures describe and value time. In Western cultures, time is perceived as a commodity ("time is money," "you're losing/saving time here," "time is running out," etc.). In many Eastern cultures, however, time is seen as more flexible and fluid. Beyond this anecdotal level, however, Robert Levine and his associates have systematically studied this topic.

Research on Time Perception across Cultures   Levine became interested in culture and time when he took a teaching position in Brazil for a year.[16] On the way to his first class meeting he began to worry about his watch since many of the clocks he glanced at (on public buildings, other people's watches) showed a different time. He did, however, arrive at his classroom a few minutes before the start of his class. But no one was there! Instead, many of his students came late, several after a half-hour, a few just about an hour late, and a few others even later than that! Interestingly, no one seemed to be particularly bothered by being late—all wore smiles and gave friendly hellos as they entered class. Since he had taught at California State University for several years, Levine was very surprised by these things; students are definitely expected to arrive on time in the United States. Even more interestingly, however, students in his Brazilian class did not get up and leave when class was over. In California, he was used to being told when class was over (the ubiquitous shifting of books, moving of backpacks, hungry looks, etc.). In Brazil, however, few people left on time. In fact, many lingered to ask questions and interact—many actually staying a half hour or more.

These observations led Levine to conduct a study of American and Brazilian students' perceptions of time in several situations. He found a number of interesting differences in what might be considered "late" for a lunch appointment with a friend. The average American defined "late" as nineteen minutes or more, whereas the Brazilians were more forgiving, defining lateness as about thirty-four minutes or more. Interestingly, he also asked the students about their impressions of people who were late. Brazilians were less likely to blame others for their tardiness than were Americans. The Brazilians typically felt that unforeseen circumstances were important causes of lateness. Americans were more likely to blame the person and to attribute the lateness to a lack of caring. Even more interesting, Brazilians believed that people who were consistently late were more successful than those who were on time. (They are late because they have more friends to talk to, more partners with whom to do business; therefore, lack of punctuality "equals" success!) Although there is some disagreement among Americans in time perceptions, punctuality is relatively critical and lateness is definitely to be avoided.

Levine was not completely satisfied with this study of time. He wanted to show that the effects were not the result of language problems, and he wanted to study several additional countries. The problem clearly facing Levine, however, was exactly how to study time without relying on language and/or self-reports, and he dealt with this problem in a very clever way. He devised several objective indicants of time, ones that did not rely on language or self-report.[17] First, he checked the accuracy of bank clocks by taking a sample of fifteen city banks in various countries and comparing their times with the time provided by the telephone company (Greenwich Mean Time). Banks were of special interest because of their relative formality and because they are tied closely with activity in other countries (e.g., via monetary exchange and interaction). Banking, therefore, is an industry where time is monitored very closely. The researchers reasoned that if cross-cultural differences exist in this critical area, then there are probably lots of other perceptual differences in less important areas of life. Their results showed that bank clocks in Japan were the most accurate— averaging only about thirty seconds off—with U.S. clocks not far behind in accuracy. Clocks in Indonesia were the least accurate, averaging over three minutes late as shown in Exhibit 5.2.

The data presented in Exhibit 5.2 also show some additional findings from Levine's study. Walking speed was another way that time perceptions were measured: Levine clocked how long it took people to walk a 100-foot stretch of downtown that his research team had premeasured. The researchers were careful to randomly choose people who were walking alone in order to avoid those who would talk, socialize, and probably slow down. As you can see from the exhibit, once again the Japanese were at the top of the list—they took about twenty-one seconds to walk the distance (a pretty good clip, if you want to try it!), with the British and Americans tied as very close seconds (about twenty-two seconds each). The Indonesians took about twenty-seven seconds on average to traverse this distance. The difference among countries doesn't seem that long, but if you try counting out six seconds to yourself and consider that the whole "trip" only took about twenty to twenty-five seconds, then you'll probably agree that the difference is significant (six seconds represents a 30 percent difference).

Finally, these researchers measured how long it took a postal clerk in these countries to serve a customer. In each country, including the United States, the researchers presented a clerk with a handwritten note in his or her native language requesting a stamp for a normal letter and gave each clerk an equivalent of a $5 bill. Once again, there was wide variance in the service times, which ranged from a low of twenty-five seconds in Japan to a high of forty-five seconds in Italy.

So what does all this mean? We think it shows that within cultures very subtle processes operate that affect our perceptions of the world, even about one

EXHIBIT 5.2   *Measures of the Pace of Time**

Country	Bank Clock Accuracy	Walking Speed	Post Office Speed
Japan	1	1	1
United States	2	3	2
United Kingdom	4	2	3
Italy	5	4	6
Taiwan	3	5	4
Indonesia	6	6	5

*Numbers are the ranking of each country on the measures of pace of time (1 = top ranking).
Source: Adapted from Levine, R. V., & Bartlett, K. (1984). Pace of life, punctuality, and coronary heart disease in six countries. *Journal of Cross-Cultural Psychology, 15,* 233–255.

of the most objective and indisputable things around—time. In turn, a person who perceives time differently than a business partner from another culture can encounter problems. If we can understand these differences, there is less potential for conflict. One way to better understand these differences is to classify cultures on this time dimension.

Classifying Countries by Their Emphasis on Time   The studies above illustrate how far culture extends into the perceptual domain. The effects are not, however, restricted to topics like accuracy of clocks and walking speed. Some people think that we can actually classify whole groups of countries around this concept of time perception. Edward Hall has weighed in on this topic too. He believes that there are at least two different ways that time is perceived and experienced across cultures: **monochronic time** and **polychronic time**.[18] Roughly, this distinction refers to paying attention to and doing one thing at a time versus doing many things at once. Like most concepts we will discuss in this book, there is considerable variation within cultures and countries in how people view time. Nevertheless, let's focus on cross-national differences.

monochronic vs. polychronic time
Paying attention to one thing at a time versus preferring to do many things at once

In a mostly monochronic culture, time is divided up precisely, with certain slots reserved for certain activities. For monochronic people, a schedule is sacred and to violate it is to face considerable irritation. As mentioned earlier, monochronic people view time as a commodity; they often say that "time is money" or that they are "spending" or "saving" or "borrowing" time. Hall claims that the choice of such economic language to describe time is no accident—it reflects their monochronic view of time. Clearly, monochronic views of time predominate in most business conducted in the United States, and it is probably true of many northern European countries as well. Anyone who has ever traveled on trains throughout Europe knows, however, that there are dramatic differences in how countries view their train schedules. Many a tourist has arrived less than a minute late for a German train only to find it already gone. It is likewise no surprise that the Germans and the Swiss are known for their quality time pieces.

Polychronic cultures, in contrast, take a more flexible view of time. Polychronic cultures seem very foreign and hard for Americans to understand. Hall points out, for example, that some Latins (typically polychronic) would much rather finish an impromptu conversation on the street rather than abruptly (and rudely) terminate it in order to get to an appointment. Polychronic cultures certainly do not have an economic view of time; translations of phrases like "time is money" often don't make a good deal of sense. In Spanish, for example, the closest saying might be the phrase "to pass time."

Time bounces around in a polychronic culture, and "interruptions" are often not seen as such. The word *interruption* implies an unscheduled and unwanted derailing of an activity. To a polychronic person, however, the unscheduled and ad hoc tends to be the expected and so naturally fits in with the way life flows. Two or more activities can be engaged in concurrently or intermittently over a period of time. A U.S. businessperson in Spain, for example, may resent sitting in a waiting room beyond her appointment time while her polychronic contact entertains several other people at once. Since time is so valuable in a monochronic culture, to be kept waiting is a sign of rudeness or irresponsibility. The monochronic American would want an apology. In turn, the polychronic Spaniard may feel that the American has an overly demanding and self-important attitude. Hall contends that this lack of understanding of time perception across cultures has been very costly for business and relates the following example to illustrate:

> A French salesman working for a French company that had recently been bought by Americans found himself with a new American manager who expected instant results and higher profits immediately. Because of the emphasis on personal relationships, it frequently takes years to develop customers in polychronic France, and, in family-owned firms, relationships with customers may span generations. The American manager did not understand this, and ordered the salesman to develop new customers within three months. The salesman knew this was impossible and had to resign, asserting his legal right to take with him all the loyal customers he had developed over the years. Neither side understood what had happened.[19]

Exhibit 5.3 presents some characteristics of people in monochronic and polychronic cultures. Some of these differences have been documented with empirical research. Interestingly, one study found that developing countries (e.g., China, Brazil, Morocco) tend to favor the monochronic interaction style in their business negotiations.[20] Yet their actual behavior is more exemplary of the polychronic style. Regardless, we might interpret extreme monochronic behavior as pushy and overly demanding, and extreme polychronic behavior as a lack of concern or as reflecting a tightly knit group with whom it's difficult to interact. Finally, it is worth noting that Americans' penchant toward monochronic time is well known around the world, and some use our vulnerability to long waits to their advantage. In fact, Hall quotes a Japanese businessperson as saying: "You Americans have one terrible weakness. If we make you wait long enough, you will agree to anything."[21]

Interpretation of Perceptions

Our discussion shows that culture predisposes us to selectively focus on some things (e.g., use of time), and to ignore others (e.g., space differences). We do not mean to imply, however, that all we see is fraught with such perceptual bias. Sometimes—perhaps many times—what we see in others is what is really there. That is, two people or groups may accurately perceive the same behavior occurring in the environment. But even though we may "see" the same thing, we must still *interpret* what we see. In the case of other people, for example, we must make sense of what caused their behavior and what it means. Consider a person

EXHIBIT 5.3   *Differences between Monochronic and Polychronic Time*

Monochronic Time Perspective	Polychronic Time Perspective
• Does one thing at a time	• Does many things at once
• Task oriented	• People oriented
• Comfortable with short-term relations	• Needs longer-term relations
• Sticks to plans	• Often changes plans
• More internally focused	• More externally focused

who completes a project successfully and is presenting the results in a business meeting. It is quite possible that nearly everyone at the meeting perceives that the project is a success. An important issue, however, is our interpretation of *why* the person succeeded. Our answer to this "why" question will have an important effect on our impression of that person and on our future planning. If we see this success as resulting from a lucky break, it will have different implications for the future than if we think the performance came from hard work. The consideration of how we assign causes like these to someone's behavior is the purview of **attribution theory**.

attribution theory
A model of how we come to perceive others' behavior as internally or externally caused

Attribution Theory This theory has been tested extensively in the United States and more recently in many other countries. It predicts that we as humans have a driving need to figure out what makes other people tick. We can never really know the answer to this question since we can't get inside someone's head to read his or her motives or personality. So, our next best method for figuring a person out is to examine his or her behavior. Accordingly, we spend a lot of time scanning and evaluating behavior to figure others out. In other words, because we can't ever really know what other people are like, our best guess is to use their behavior to infer or attribute characteristics they may have. (One point we've made throughout this book is that culture is a big determinant of behavior. So it can often be a mistake to look at a person's behavior and then make a personal attribution when this behavior could be the result of cultural norms!)

self-serving bias
The tendency to take credit (internal attribution) for success but to blame failure on other causes (external attribution)

Self-Attribution Effects One of the most reliable findings in the hundreds of studies done on this topic is known as the **self-serving bias**. This refers to our tendency, when making attributions about our own behavior, to take credit for success (*internal attribution*) and to blame failure on other causes (*external attribution*). This finding may not seem very surprising to you, but it certainly underscores our recognition of the importance of perception in management. The main reason is that the self-serving bias is essentially saying that what happens *after* you performed a behavior affects why you did it in the first place (an internal or external cause). This "back to the future" logic may also stress the extent to which self-serving biases reflect Western cultural norms about work behavior.

A study illustrates what we mean. Researchers interviewed nearly 700 people from five countries—the United States, India, Japan, South Africa, and the former Yugoslavia.[22] These people completed a form that measured their attributions about a variety of life events that could be considered a success or a failure (e.g., performing well at a job). The researchers did a very careful job of translating the questionnaires and of checking the accuracy of the translations. As we might expect from other research, Americans showed the typical self-serving bias. In fact, to an extent the tendency to take more credit for success than failure was observed in all the countries in this study. In comparing results across countries, however, the researchers noted several interesting differences. First, the causal attributions of the Japanese were more internal for failure than were the attributions of people from any of the other countries. In other words, the Japanese were more likely to take responsibility for a failure than anyone else. If these results were accurate, then the stereotype of the American as the take-charge, buck-stops-here manager is not supported by these data.

The Japanese were also the least likely to take credit for success! In fact, this latter effect was dramatic: While the Indians' and Americans' scores were over 8.0 on a 10-point scale and the remaining country scores were over 6, the

Japanese average score was only 3.9. The results of this research were also at least partially supported by another more recent study.[23]

In summary, this study showed two important things. First, the self-serving bias has some cross-national applicability. People from countries as diverse as India, South Africa, and the United States have shown this tendency to take credit for success and to externalize failure. Second, the effect is not universal (probably far from it). In particular, the Japanese showed a strong tendency toward responsibility for failure and modesty regarding success. Clearly, the Japanese are strongly concerned with themselves as members of a group, more so than as individuals per se. Accordingly, **self-effacing behavior** as well as a strong sense of duty toward the work group is common. Therefore, in group-oriented cultures modesty appears to be valued, whereas in individually-oriented cultures (such as that of the United States) a bolder assertion of competence and credit is valued.

self-effacing behavior The tendency among some cultures to be modest in taking credit for success but accepting responsibility for failure

Attributions About Others   A subsequent set of studies looked at the attributions or causes we assign to *others'* behavior.[24] In the first study, Japanese university students read a story about a man who had worked nearly two years for an organization. There were, however, several different versions of the story. Even though most details in the story were the same for everyone, about half were then told that the man was demoted to a lower position after these two years (the "failure" condition). The other half were told that he was promoted to a higher position ("success"). In addition to this factor, the nationality of the man was also varied in the stories. About equal numbers of subjects were told that the man was either (1) a Japanese citizen working in Japan, (2) a U.S. native working in the United States, or (3) a citizen of a developing country who also worked in that country.

After reading the materials, the Japanese students made attributions about the cause of the success (promotion) or failure (demotion) of the other person. It was predicted that the Japanese students would make self-serving attributions for people from all three countries. However, the researchers also predicted an even stronger effect when people were asked to interpret the cause of behavior for someone within—as opposed to outside of—their own group. This in-group bias is similar in form to the self-serving effect. An in-group bias occurs when one is more self-serving for members of one's own cultural group. Interestingly, however, the predictions were not supported—the Japanese students did not show the in-group bias when interpreting the behavior of someone from Japan. In fact, if anything, there appeared to be a pattern that showed a more generous pattern of attributions for people from the other countries (the man who was described as from the United States or a developing country). These findings dovetail with the earlier study that showed that Japanese were less self-serving than those of several other countries. These findings show that Japanese tended to be modest; they were more likely to assign responsibility to themselves for failure and deemphasize credit for success.

Recall that in this study only the Japanese made attributions about others. It would have been nice to include people from those other countries as well and to ask them to read the same description of the promotion and demotion. This is exactly what the researchers did in their second study.[25] Americans and people from a variety of developing countries also read and reacted to the same description of the man just discussed. They found that Americans were more likely to give the man credit for success (internal attribution) than were subjects from developing countries. Since this group included people from many different countries, it is difficult to pinpoint a specific cultural mechanism in operation. Taking both studies into account, however, we can say that Americans are more likely to attribute success to the person—especially compared with the modest Japanese.

In fact, researchers have found similar effects in other group-oriented cultures. This idea was first tested with a group of Chinese.[26] They were asked to rate another person who was either self-effacing in his or her attributions (did not take personal credit for success) or was self-serving (took credit for success). The self-effacing person was much better liked by the Chinese. Finally, this cultural effect is so robust that it apparently even affects our attributions about very bad events. One study found that English-language newspapers were more personal and that Chinese-language newspapers were more situational in their explanations of the same crime.[27] The story, which attracted press attention in both the United States and China, dealt with a Chinese graduate student in the United States who murdered his Ph.D. advisor and several others after losing an award competition. The researchers painstakingly collected all the articles that were written on the topic in the United States and China and then coded the "attributions" about the student's crime into internal (personal) or external (situational) categories. American newspaper reporters were more likely to emphasize internal attributions about the student (quotes included: "very bad temper," "sinister edge to his character well before the shooting," "darkly disturbed man," and "whatever went wrong was internal"). The Chinese reporters, however, were more likely to emphasize situational causes of the murder, including relationships ("did not get along with his advisor," "isolated from the Chinese community"), pressures in Chinese society ("Lu was a victim of the Chinese educational policy"), and aspects of American society ("murder can be traced to the availability of guns").[28]

Implications of Cross-Cultural Attribution These attribution effects emphasize our original point: Perception is not limited to selectively seeing or missing a certain event. Even when many people agree about what they saw, culture can affect the interpretation or assignment of causes as to why something happened. In fact, each study we reviewed made it clear that someone succeeded or failed; there was no ambiguity about these events in this set of studies. Yet perception still had an effect on the interpretation of outcomes that occur to the self and others.

One last example highlights these points.[29] Barbara Walters, of course, is famous for her interviews of notable people, including one several years ago of Muammar Abu Minyar al-Qadhafi, the leader of Libya. Tensions between the United States and Libya were high at the time and the interview centered on this topic. Interestingly, after the interview the media had little to say about the content of what was said. Instead, there was considerable comment about Mr. Qadhafi's behavior. During much of the interview, Mr. Qadhafi shifted his eyes away from Ms. Walters and appeared to be very reluctant to look her in the eyes at all. Ms. Walters herself remarked, "He wouldn't look me in the eye. I found it disconcerting that he kept looking all over the room but rarely at me." The wide and general interpretation of this was that Mr. Qadhafi was shifty and evasive and that the behavior was indicative of someone who was, at best, not telling the whole truth.

Now, whether or not Mr. Qadhafi was telling the truth is not our point here. Our point is instead similar to that made by the attribution researchers. Here we have a case where many people probably saw the same thing (eyes shifting, unwillingness to look someone in the face). But the interpretation of the same event—the attribution—varied dramatically across cultures. To an Arab, Mr. Qadhafi would have been perceived as showing proper respect to another person, especially a woman. To stare at another person—especially a woman—is considered very rude in Arab culture. Thus, instead of the American attribution of the unwillingness to look at Ms. Walters as shifty and untrustworthy, the very same behavior is interpreted as the height of politeness by another culture. This story demonstrates the insidious thing about perception across cultures—it gets you coming (whether you even see the event itself) and it gets you going (even if the outcome is clear, the cause can be attributed differently).

▶ *Attitudes*

Perceptions can start out as isolated events—mostly determined by our environment (loud noise grabs your attention, etc.). Gradually, however, when perceptions occur over and over again, you might form an attitude about them. An **attitude** is a learned tendency to react emotionally toward some object or person. According to social psychologists, we can have attitudes about nearly everything, including ourselves. Attitudes toward the self, toward others/groups, and toward work have all been studied cross-culturally.

attitude
A learned tendency to react emotionally toward some object or person

Attitudes toward the Self

We have attitudes toward many aspects of our lives. Individuals differ in how much control they feel they have over their life, in how much they like themselves, and in their views toward other nationalities. In this section we will focus on attitudes toward the self that are work related or have direct implications for management.

Interdependent and Independent Selves One of the broadest differences in attitudes toward the self deals with the degree of autonomy or uniqueness of the self. The Western view of the self as independent and individualistic is exemplified in cultures that emphasize uniqueness, self-reliance, and individual achievement.[30] American culture is a good example here because it emphasizes independence in so many different ways: Parents encourage their children very early on to be independent, school is by and large structured to foster independent activity, and performance on the job is typically evaluated at the individual level.

interdependent self
The view of oneself as closely linked to others and groups that value paternalism and group cohesion

independent self
The view of oneself as an autonomous or unique individual who values self-reliance and achievement

In contrast, many non-Western views of the self are different. These cultures often make it difficult to separate the self from others and from situations. Great emphasis is put on qualities such as paternalism, interdependence of people, solidarity, and group cohesion. Viewed from this perspective, the self is changeable and deeply affected by others.

Let's take a look at this attitude in some Asian cultures. As we noted earlier, in many of these countries people view themselves as intertwined in complex ways with others. In Japan and China, independence among children is not necessarily emphasized, school activity that joins people with groups is often fostered, and work performance is often defined as group performance. Some U.S. companies use work groups or teams as a defining structure. The rationale

EXHIBIT 5.4   *Two Views of the Self*

Interdependent Self (non-Western)	Independent Self (Western)
• Defines self as part of the group • Focuses on similarity to others • Encourages efforts to sublimate self • Teaches children dependence on/to others • Fears exclusion from others/group • Can "read the mind"/intentions/feelings of others	Defines self apart from group Focuses on uniqueness of self Encourages "finding oneself" Stresses independent children Fears inability to separate from group Believes in importance of "saying what's on your mind"

Sources: Adapted from Markus, H. R., & Kitayama, S. (1998). Culture and the self: Implications for cognition, emotion, and maturation. *Psychological Review, 98,* 224–253; Triandis, H. C. (1989). The self and social behavior in differing cultural contexts. *Psychological Review, 96,* 506–520.

for adopting them is that it is important to let everyone know that "we're all in this thing together" or even to "have people recognize that we're a family here." These statements reflect a non-Western view of the self, one in which individuals are part of—and very much obligated to—the group. It remains to be seen whether these efforts will be successful in the long run. One major obstacle in the way, however, is the lifetime of experience many Westerners have in viewing the self as apart from others, as individuals. In fact, perhaps one reason for the success of such efforts in, say, Japan is that work teams are compatible with cultural norms about the self. A Japanese saying has it that "the nail that sticks out gets hammered down." This proverb refers, in part, to the need for people to fit in well with others.[31] In contrast, a common Western saying is, "The squeaky wheel gets the grease." Exhibit 5.4 provides a summary of these differing attitudes about the self.[32]

Self-Descriptions How do people describe themselves in other cultures? If the preceding distinction is accurate, we should see widely varying self-descriptions between Western and non-Western cultures. This assumption was the starting point of an interesting study.[33] Researchers used a method that was very straightforward—they simply asked U.S. and Japanese students to describe themselves in a very open-ended and unstructured way. They were asked to respond, in any way they wished, to the question "Who am I?" The students were allowed up to twenty responses to this question.

Then the researchers had some hard work to do—they had to take all the responses and place them in categories. Although a number of categories were coded, of special interest to us was how often the students mentioned **abstract** versus **concrete self-descriptions**. Abstract self-descriptions would include general responses like "I am extroverted" or "I am sensitive," whereas concrete descriptions would include statements like "I am happy when I work with my friend" or "In social situations, I tend to hold back." This dimension reflects Western and non-Western views of self. If it is true that Westerners have more independent views of the self, then their self-descriptions should be more abstract and devoid of special or concrete qualifications.[34] Likewise, non-Westerners should describe themselves in ways that are specific and embedded in the concrete as opposed to the abstract. This is exactly what was found:

abstract vs. concrete self-descriptions
General views of the self that are context-free (Western) vs. descriptions of self that are embedded in specific social situations (non-Western)

Americans were more likely to use general trait descriptions of themselves and less likely to use situational descriptions than were the Japanese.[35]

Studies using people from different countries have produced similar results. In one study, people in India and the United States were asked to describe several close friends.[36] These researchers found that 46 percent of the descriptions by Americans were the abstract, context-free variety (e.g., "He is a tightwad"; "She is selfish"). Only 20 percent of Indians, however, made general statements like these. The Indians were much more likely to make situation-specific descriptions ("He is hesitant to give money away to his family"). Other studies found similar results: Americans (40 percent) were more likely than Indians (17 percent) to attribute the behavior of others to abstract dispositions ("He is dishonest") than to situational circumstances ("It is not right, but in this situation, she needed the money").[37] One important way that this differing view about the self is illustrated is via the concept of **face**, the subject of the accompanying International Insights.

face
The need for self-respect, pride, and dignity that varies dramatically across culture

Effects of Having Different Self-Views If some cultures emphasize fitting in rather than standing out, we should also see differences in self-ratings of performance between interdependent and independent cultures. In the United States, self-ratings of job performance are typically higher than corresponding ratings by supervisors or outside raters. This "leniency bias" had led some experts to express misgivings about the use of self-ratings in performance evaluations.[38] Given the nature of the self across cultures, we'd expect that this leniency bias in the United States might not be observed in more interdependent cultures.

This was the premise for a study of nearly 1,000 employees of various organizations in Taiwan.[39] Researchers asked both supervisors and employees to make a variety of ratings of the employees' performance. The ratings for each employee-supervisor pair were then compared. As predicted, the Taiwanese did not show a leniency bias—they were more modest in their self-ratings. Given that there is pressure not to stick out from the group in this interdependent culture, this modesty in self-ratings might be expected. It is important to note that ratings were done anonymously, so the modest tendency probably does reflect an important internalized attitude.

In a subsequent study, workers and supervisors from several Asian (e.g., Korea, Japan) and Western (e.g., the United States, Mexico) countries were compared and similar results were found.[40] This study included nearly 1,000 employees and an elaborate set of controls (e.g, gender, age, religion), yet it still found the effect—a more modest self-rating by Asians. A final study suggested that it is important to consider the nature of the specific culture and not to lump all Asian countries together.[41] It may be a specific set of attitudes in a culture that produces the modesty effect (such as those stressing order and respect for social hierarchy). It is this aspect of culture, not East or West, that drives this effect. As a result, at least some Western countries may also be likely to show modesty effects. If this is correct, we should be examining differences among countries and cultures and specific self-attitudes of interest. The section to follow will discuss some important work attitudes that may directly affect performance on the job.

Protestant work ethic
An attitude that describes differences in the desire to maximize one's material prosperity

Specific Self-Attitudes One self-attitude that falls into this category is the so-called **Protestant work ethic** (PWE). The term refers to the desire to maximize one's material prosperity and is tied closely to strong beliefs in capitalism. The

🌐 International Insights

Face: How to Give It, Get It, and Keep It

PRIDE AND THE respect of others are important in all cultures. Experts, though, say that this need for the regard of others—**face**—may be *the* single most important concept to be aware of in many Asian cultures.[42] One authority claims that "to speak or act in a way that causes an Asian to lose face is tantamount to physical assault in the West." Since many Asian cultures are interdependent, they also try to save face for others. In fact, in a study of 100 Chinese managers, all of them said that face was mutual—that it should be returned when given.[43] For example, if you were to ask an Asian for directions to the post office, he or she may actually take you there, even if it's out of the way. If they don't know where it is, they may still point and say, "That way." To not know is to lose face. Likewise, if you ask Asians to build a product, they will do so even if they know it will fail because of poor design. They would not tell you that your design is flawed up front because doing so may cause *you* to lose face.

Face can explain why some may perceive Asians as indirect.[44] Americans pride themselves on their frankness and honesty and expect similar behavior in others. Asians are also very honest people, but the social demands of face present problems with foreigners. The solution for Americans is complex. They might simply use a more indirect approach than they are used to, such as asking for any suggestions regarding product design that an Asian may be asked to build.

In general, the moral is: Don't mistake smiles as a solid connection with your business contact. In fact, it's possible for an American to create resentment and not even pick up on it. If you did offend, it isn't likely that you will be told, since no one wants you to lose face. Alternatively, you might be told in such a subtle fashion that you would miss the message. For example, you'll find that things will slowly become more difficult, no one will seem very cooperative, and not much will be accomplished.

---

term *Protestant*, however, has been questioned by some since high beliefs in the value of work are observed among non-Protestants, let alone those not adhering to the Christian faith.[45] Nevertheless, to examine the effect of this self-attitude, researchers have developed scales to measure PWE, and a good deal of research has been completed using these scales. For example, one study compared the PWE scores of nearly 2,000 college students from thirteen different countries. The researchers found that PWE is related to a country's emphasis on prestige, wealth, and power. And, they found that countries that had great inequality of wealth and status were more likely to endorse PWE beliefs.[46] Also, in a large study of developing nations, it was found that PWE was also correlated with per capita income.[47] These data suggest that self-attitudes such as PWE may affect economic behavior and growth. For this reason alone, it is very important to study the self-attitude of PWE across cultures.

just world attitude
An attitude that describes differences in the need to believe that people live in a world where people get what they deserve

Another important self-attitude is the belief in a **just world (JW).** This dimension gets at differences among people and countries in the need to believe that we live in a world where people generally get what they deserve. Differences across countries could also be important to those studying international management. Using a well-known scale that measures this attitude, it was found that the higher the gross domestic product of a country, the higher the belief in a just world.[48] This suggests that the belief that the world is just can motivate people to acquire more wealth. Alternatively, the JW belief may simply be a rationalization. In other words, it could indicate that those who are wealthy maintain

There are some general notions to keep in mind about giving, getting, and keeping face that are useful for all concerned:[49]

- Frankness in Asia is almost always rudeness; more subtle, high-context communication is the norm.

- An inviolate rule in Asia is: Compliment but never criticize, even if asked for criticism. You may be tested on small things. Your host may say, "People here are poor workers, aren't they?" If you say yes, you will not pass the test—in fact, you should start packing. One authority goes as far to say that if you can't think of the correct answer to that question—one that saves face for everybody—you shouldn't even be trying to do business in Asia.

- Asians are likely to laugh if you say something that causes loss of face or that demeans their culture or country. Don't mistake the laugh as anything other than defensive—as a way to save face.

- If you ask a question in Asia and don't get an answer, don't push it. It probably has something to do with face. Save it for a later time and setting, preferably a private one.

- Never show anger, even if you feel it. The public display of such a strong emotion will do you no good and you will be labeled a "peasant."

- Do not be in a rush—it is an attack on the face of others. To Asians, your sense of hurry says they are not important enough to spend time with—that you have better places to be.

Some claim that obeying these social rules is akin to capitulating to the demands of the Asian partner. Acknowledging differences, however, does not mean you have to be a pushover. In fact, you could use face to your advantage. Sometimes simply saying, "I would lose face at home if I were to agree to this deal" may carry more weight than a rational, numbers-based argument. Nevertheless, you should be persistently firm, with some flexibility and willingness to explore options. One expert advises business people, "Be firm, but avoid obstinacy and rudeness. A calm and relaxed stubbornness is advised. Be persuasive in a gentle way." That same expert provides this advice above all else: "Go slow, be calm, never loud. Listen more than you talk." This is probably good advice for doing business anywhere—but especially in Asia.

beliefs that they deserve those rewards because the world is just. Regardless of the interpretation, the correlation between JW attitudes and economic behavior is intriguing.

Attitudes about Others and Groups

Attitudes about the self are one thing, but we also hold attitudes toward other groups and cultures. Large numbers of managers are now interacting with their colleagues from different cultural groups and countries. Many even work and reside as expatriates in foreign countries. So it may be more important now than ever to understand other groups.

What are our attitudes toward other countries and people? Most of us have **stereotypes** about people from other countries. Stereotypes are inferences about what other people must be like based on group membership (e.g, racial, religious, cultural groups). A notable percentage of Americans may think the French are romantic, the Germans technical, and the Japanese good at details. Of course, we even have stereotypes about people from other regions, provinces, or states, so cross-national stereotypes are hardly a surprise.

stereotypes
The tendency to infer traits to individuals based on their group membership

Attitudes Toward Americans Some people have clear views about Americans, ones that they most certainly act on. Americans are often said by other cultures to be self-focused. This is part of what is implied by the term *ugly American,*

EXHIBIT 5.5   *Oh, to Know How Others See Us**

Country	Traits Most Often Associated with Americans	Traits Least Often Associated with Americans
Brazil	intelligent inventive energetic industrious greedy	lazy self-Indulgent sexy sophisticated
France	industrious energetic inventive decisive friendly	lazy rude honest sophisticated
Germany	energetic inventive friendly sophisticated intelligent	lazy sexy greedy rude
Japan	nationalistic friendly decisive rude self-indulgent	industrious lazy honest sexy
Mexico	industrious intelligent inventive decisive greedy	lazy honest rude sexy
United Kingdom	friendly self-indulgent energetic industrious nationalistic	lazy sophisticated sexy decisive

*Traits are listed in the order mentioned by respondents from different countries. Respondents were allowed only four responses to the "least often" question.
Source: "How Others See Us" from *Newsweek*, July 11, 1983. © 1983 Newsweek, Inc. All rights reserved. Reprinted by permission.

which refers to an ethnocentric person who believes that the American way is the right and only way. This person is not concerned with other cultures and makes little or no effort to understand the behavior of others. As a result, the ugly American can easily offend a person from a different country or culture.

There may be some larger reasons for why Americans are self-focused and myopic in their attention to other countries (assuming that they are!).[50] For example, the United States is relatively isolated geographically and has a high level of natural resources. Thus, there is little inherent pressure to look abroad. At the same time, however, the United States has always had high levels of foreign investment, and those investments are on the rise. In addition, competition from other countries is fierce. So perhaps more than ever it is necessary to examine our attitudes toward other countries and how these attitudes affect our behavior.

Exhibit 5.5 presents data collected some years ago by *Newsweek* magazine on views that people from six different countries have about Americans. Two questions were asked of the large representative samples in each country. Respondents were asked to go through a large list of trait descriptors (e.g., industrious, honest, etc.) and then choose the traits that were most and least often associated with Americans. As you can see in the exhibit, Americans are stereotypically seen as industrious and energetic by others. In general, people in other countries have fairly positive attitudes about Americans. The Japanese are the only group to use more than two negative characteristics in their description of Americans.[51] If you scan the list of characteristics least often associated with Americans, there is also some agreement. For example, Americans are rarely seen as lazy. On the other hand, Americans apparently aren't seen as either sexy or sophisticated.

More recent data show that pro-American attitudes in Europe have fallen a bit. In a 2002 survey, 75 percent of Britons, 63 percent of French, and 61 percent of Germans had a positive attitude toward the U.S. These numbers and others in Europe have fallen since 2002, but rampant anti-Americanism is exaggerated. Another recent survey, conducted by the German Marshall Fund, asked people to rate countries on a 1 to 100 scale. European countries gave the United States an average rating of 64 (higher than they gave to France), and Americans in turn rated Europeans between 55 (France) and 75 (Britain). Likewise, between two-thirds and three-quarters of Europeans support the U.S.-led war on terror (although about one-half say the United States doesn't take their perspective into account), almost four-fifths called Iraq a serious threat, and everyone expressed admiration for U.S. efforts in science, technology, and pop culture. These attitudes, however, were not expressed among the United States' Muslim allies—it is clear that people from Egypt (6 percent favorable; 69 percent unfavorable), Jordan, Pakistan, and Turkey dislike Americans.[52] But what if you had contact with these other nationalities? Would their stereotypes of Americans fade away and their attitudes improve? To address this question, researchers studied managers from different cultural backgrounds who worked together.[53] Four different groups of managers—British, Japanese, Singaporean, and American—were asked to rate themselves and the other groups on two main dimensions. One dimension measured expectations about typical performance levels (high or low), and the other rating dealt with management style (open vs. closed). Some of the results of the study were interesting. For example, the U.S. and Japanese managers saw themselves as better performers than they are seen by any of the other groups. Another interesting finding was that expatriates rated their host nationals very highly, whereas this was not true if there was no employment relationship. The results on the management style measure were also provocative. The U.S. managers perceived themselves as being much more open (e.g., extroverted, frank, decisive) than the other groups. And this opinion was shared by the other managers, since the U.S. group was actually rated higher in this area by all other groups. The Japanese managers saw themselves as slightly closed (e.g., introverted, cautious, secretive) but were actually regarded as considerably more closed by all the other managerial groups. These results suggest that firms need to be aware of these attitudes and the effect they may have on relations among various managerial groups (e.g., nationals and expatriates). This may be particularly true for American managers, who seem to engender relatively consistent views by other groups.

Formation of Stereotypes How do others get these attitudes or stereotypes about Americans, and conversely, how do Americans form attitudes about others? Given that so few people interact cross-culturally, we have to assume that media portrayals must contribute to stereotypes across countries. For instance, one expert points out that beyond the fact that religious and ideological differences play a role in affecting attitudes toward Arabs, the American media has done more than its share of perpetuating stereotypes.[54] An analysis of TV programs, for example, showed that the Arab was among TV's most popular villain.[55] An analysis of movies made from the 1920s to the present also shows Arabs portrayed as consistently greedy, blood thirsty, and sex-crazed. U.S. newspapers foster this same impression with their portrayals of Arabs. For example, it was not uncommon in the 1980s to see an editorial cartoon that depicted an Arab with loads of money buying up American investments. (Despite this popular belief, Arabs account for less than 3 percent of all foreign investment in the United States.[56]) Likewise, books have a long history of being equally unkind to Arabs. The reaction of an Arab to Jack Kerouac's book about the Beat generation of the 1950s called *On the Road* underscores this point. The reader was bewildered to read passages like the following: "We were like a band of Arabs coming to blow up New York," and "Paul drove into a gas station . . . noticed that the attendant was fast asleep . . . quietly filled the gas tank and rolled off like an Arab."[57]

It is tempting to explain these statements as an attitude of the 1950s since Kerouac wrote during that time. However, a cursory examination of contemporary TV will show the same bias toward other countries. In a *Frasier* episode rerun not long ago, Frasier's brother Miles is lamenting the fact that his wife was spending lots of money ($25,000!) on plastic surgery. In response, Frasier's dad said, "For that, you could get a whole new wife from the Philippines." Of course, this anecdote does not prove the point. What it does show, however, is that we may not be as sophisticated as we might think. In fact, perhaps, it shows that as the media continues to be a powerful influence, the choice of targets has changed from older ones (e.g., Russians, Arabs) to newer ones (e.g., Chinese, French). Interestingly, however, analyses of Arab portrayals in the media since September 11 reveal a relatively evenhanded treatment. Ironically, the wide call to avoid blaming all Arabs or Muslims for the September 11, 2001 murders may have improved the treatment of these groups in the U.S. media. It remains to be

EXHIBIT 5.6   *Attitudes toward Four Countries Held by Americans, 1982 and 1993**

Response Chosen	France 1982	France 1993	United Kingdom 1982	United Kingdom 1993	Israel 1982	Israel 1993	Russia 1983	Russia 1993
Close ally	29	25	57	61	27	26	1	10
Friendly but not a close ally	51	49	34	28	34	43	4	56
Not friendly but not an enemy	13	16	3	3	18	17	30	20
Unfriendly and an enemy	1	3	2	1	5	5	63	7
Not sure	6	7	4	7	16	9	2	7

*Entries in the exhibit are percentages of a national sample who responded to the question "Do you feel that (country) is a close ally of the U.S., is friendly but not an enemy, is not friendly but not an enemy, or is unfriendly and is an enemy of the U.S.?"
Source: Adapted from Hastings, E. H., & Hastings, P. K. (1993). *Index to international public opinion*, 1992–1993. Westport, CT: Greenwood Press.

seen whether more long-term analyses of media and U.S. public opinion will show the same effects, particularly as the United States continues to react to security threats post 9/11.

An analysis of U.S. public opinion about other countries supports these points. Exhibit 5.6 shows how such public opinion/stereotypes can change, given some time and a lot of information.[58] It shows, for example, how attitudes toward Russia as an enemy had atrophied over the 1983–1993 decade, whereas attitudes toward some other countries (e.g., China and Japan) were relatively stable or had declined.[59] One example of such a decline might be observed in contemporary European attitudes toward Americans, a decline that is discussed in the accompanying International Insights.

The In-Group As a Cause of Stereotypes   Besides these media influences, it appears that we simply have a tendency to rate our in-group higher than an out-group. Members of a group tend to emphasize their own positive characteristics and accentuate the negative traits of other groups. This pattern has been noted, for example, in the studies of perceptions between Americans and Russians, Arabs and Israelis, and Catholics and Protestants, among others.[60] In some cases, these stereotypes can manifest themselves in a pattern called **mirror imaging**. This is a case where each group perceives similar positive traits in itself and similar negative traits in the out-group. This pattern is especially likely to occur between groups under conflict (e.g., Arabs and Israelis; Indonesians and Chinese-Indonesians).[61]

Even when mirror imaging is not found, there does appear to be a natural tendency for us to see in-group members as more varied and complex (heterogenous) and out-group members as less varied and more homogenous. Americans, for example, may recognize and perceive wide differences among themselves while perceiving Russians to be relatively similar. Some point out that this contrast is only natural since we have lots of experience with our in-group and are relatively inexperienced with out-groups.

mirror imaging
A stereotypical pattern whereby groups perceive similar positive traits in themselves and similar negative ones in other groups

International Insights

What Sells in Europe? Poking Fun at American Blokes

Critics and supporters alike have long said that advertising reflects real life and that this is why good ads move a product. If this is true, then current European sensibilities about America (and its foreign policies) are reflected in TV and print media ads. While it might be a little too early to say this for sure, early signs are pointing to a strong, resounding, and satirical "yes" as an answer to this question.

Ms. Marie Ridgley, an executive at a British-owned marketing consulting firm has seen a change in the content of ads. "It's not necessarily totally anti-Americanism going on, but it's a reappraisal of the relationship," she said. "We've gone through the stage where we bought into TGI Friday's, McDonald's, and the Nike hook." Apparently, things are changing, perhaps in large part because the Iraq war has inflamed an anti-American sentiment. After the war started, some restaurants in France and other countries took Coca-Cola and Budweiser off their menus because they symbolized the United States. And, while Americans responded to this with some backlash of their own (French fries became "freedom fries"), many in the United States aren't aware of the continuing tit-for-tat (American cheese was called "idiot" cheese by some in France).

But the change in advertising has raised more eyebrows because of its business and mainstream nature. For example, an ad for Heineken (Netherlands) recently showed several Americans in a bar threatening to sue one another over some spilt beer, with the argument eventually reaching the president of the United States. The "conflict" is resolved when one of the men stops his threats and offers to buy more Heineken. The ad campaign is designed to get Brits to buy a higher alcohol beer, one that the rest of Europe already prefers. The campaign's message is that different nationalities like the beer so much that they abandon their stereotypic tendencies. Regarding the United States, therefore, Heineken is so tasty that Americans will even give up their litigious manner.

Another spot that hawks 'I Can't Believe It's Not Butter' makes fun of Americans' exuberance and confidence. The TV spots for the product, made by Unilever (a Dutch-English firm) show Americans dramatically overreacting and incredulous, saying things like "Get out of here!" Finally, a voiceover of a more restrained Brit says "it's not butter." The use of Americans was strategic, according to the British ad agency that created the spot. Even the name of the product is quintessentially American because of its "brash, confident claim." According to the agency, "when Americans get enthusiastic about stuff, they're much more effusive than Brits." Other European ads are much more biting, and again Americans are strategically placed in those ads. Whether these commercials simply reflect light-hearted humor or are deliberately appealing to a seamier side of attitudes is not clear. But there's no denying their success in Europe.[62]

If this is true, then increased contact and interaction with people from different cultures (out-groups) should result in a more articulated view of people in that culture. This prediction was tested with a sample of Americans and Chinese.[63] Researchers assessed the actual amount of contact that each group had with each other. An assessment of both primary contact (actual experience in China/the United States) and secondary contact (number of Chinese/U.S. friends, how often they read about China/the United States, etc.) was made. They also measured the perceived similarity of the other cultural group with questions like "The more I know Chinese, the more similar they are to each other" and "In China, all people tend to behave alike." Results showed that increased contact with the out-group did result in greater heterogeneity. For example, the more contact the Chinese had with Americans, the more likely they were to see variety in Americans' attitudes, behavior, and dress (among other things).

It has also been shown that the familiarity gained through intergroup contact not only resulted in a more varied set of attitudes, it also increased the accuracy of group stereotypes.[64] For instance, perceptions of Japanese and U.S. managers working together for a Japanese-owned commercial bank were compared.[65] These managers were asked to rate themselves and the other group on a variety of trait dimensions. If accuracy is defined as ratings by others that are similar to one's own group rating, then a good deal of accuracy was found. For example, both the Japanese and U.S. managers perceived U.S. employees to be more extroverted, more outspoken, more assertive and less patient than the Japanese. Similar effects were also found among Chinese and U.S. exchange students who had a good deal of interaction with one another.[66]

Although stereotypes often represent biased perceptions of other group members, not all stereotypes are wholly inaccurate. Indeed, research shows that some stereotypes may reflect a partially accurate assessment of some objective group characteristics. In one study, Chinese perceived Americans as more heterogeneous than another group of Chinese, in contrast to the usual in-group/out-group effect noted earlier.[67] The authors claim that this result reflects the greater variety in Americans than in the Chinese and that the ratings were rightfully influenced by this reality. We might expect similar results in Japan where the non-Japanese-born population is only about 2 percent. Such a position reflects the "kernel-of-truth" hypothesis: That stereotypes of another group are at least partially based on some objective characteristics of that group.[68]

The Effects of Attitudes and Stereotypes   One reason to understand these attitude differences across countries is that they may have an impact on whether and how business might be conducted. And, as noted, this impact can change over time. For example, marketers in China claim that macho attitudes among men, which many thought had long since passed, have re-emerged in spades. One study in Shanghai and Chengdu by ad agency Leo Burnett suggested that Chinese men do not relate to guys they often see in TV ads. One participant put it best: "They lack male qualities and it seems that they are just playing the supporting roles to women." So, after decades of government efforts to equalize the role of men and women in society, China again defies prediction. Leo Burnett now recommends to its clients that they emphasize power and "face," rather than brawn or physique, to exemplify Chinese machismo. "Brands should suggest or reinforce a feeling of control." Surveys also show that more and more Chinese men believe their focus should be on their career and that a woman's place is at home. One observer noted this about traditional socialist values of gender equality: "Now those values have really become a joke. If you are making the same money as your wife, you are a loser." Chinese men mentioned Harrison Ford as their prototype male. In the 2002 film *K-19*, Mr. Ford plays "a steady, decisive leader," said one high-income respondent. Procter & Gamble used this strategy in a recent shampoo ad that "turns men's deep seated desire for face into conspicuous consumption."[69]

Another interesting case in point occurred in India, where color TV transmission was first broadcast in 1982.[70] Because there were no Indian color TV manufacturers, the government allowed the domestic firms that already produced black-and-white TVs to import "knocked-down" sets (kits with all the parts, but unassembled) to be assembled and sold in India. Identical kits from German, Japanese, and Korean suppliers were imported and put together with Indian brand names.

country-of-origin stereotype
The belief that the country of origin of various products or services is associated with certain attributes

Interestingly, the German and Japanese TV sets commanded much higher prices than did the Korean sets. In fact, it apparently was common for Indian consumers to bring along a screwdriver to a store in order to open the back of the set to determine the country of origin. Thus, despite identical parts, the Japanese and German companies had an advantage in the marketplace thanks to a **country-of-origin stereotype** among Indians.

Those in marketing have long known about country-of-origin stereotypes and, of course, still make manufacturing decisions based on these stereotypes. For example, the Panasonic line of stereo and related equipment is actually manufactured by Matsushita Electric Company of Japan, although the brand name may not directly bring this country to mind. And even well-known brand names must cultivate and monitor their image in other countries carefully. For example, while McDonald's is the largest fast-food franchise in the world, KFC leads in China because of its careful attention to that market. Likewise, the Carrefour stores of France are a bigger name in China than world-market leader Wal-Mart. Sony is a world leader in electronics and widely seen as a trendsetter in the United States. But, again in China, Sony is seen as a brand for businessmen in their thirties and forties, not the younger, hipper crowd. Instead, Samsung is perceived as fashionable, more fun and sporty, and wilder by the Chinese.[71]

Country-of-origin effects are important in marketing, and they are ones that some advertisers have capitalized on (e.g., the "Made in the U.S.A." television campaign). In fact, a consumer ethnocentrism scale has been developed that measures the tendency to prefer U.S.-made goods.[72] Research has shown that those who score high on this scale accentuate positive aspects of domestic products while overlooking the negative aspects. However, the real trouble may be simply in distinguishing a domestic product from a foreign-made one. Many products have either an ambiguous country of origin or one that belies its source. For example, the Baby Ruth candy bar is made by Nestlé, a Swiss firm, whereas Ghirardelli Chocolate is made in the United States. Grey Poupon and Swiss Miss cocoa are American-owned products. And, while *Bon Appétit* and *Connoisseur* are American-owned magazines, *American Baby* and *Western Sportsman* are not! Likewise, the Honda Accord is made by American workers in Maryville, Ohio, using about 75 percent U.S.-made parts, and the Toyota Camry is made in Kentucky. And, Jaguar, Mazda, Lotus, Saab, and Daewoo are partially or wholly owned by U.S. firms.[73]

Of course, the insidious thing about stereotypes is that some will forget that even at their best stereotypes often reflect only a "kernel of truth" about a specific person. Worse yet, the perceiver may have a brief personal encounter or experience with a member of that group and use this incident as further evidence that all group members are very similar (homogenous). A reasonable perspective on this problem is to recognize that our personal knowledge is very limited, perhaps to a handful or even only one or two persons. Therefore, to categorize a whole group of people (e.g., Arabs, Americans) as having a single trait is a huge and specious leap of inference. Yet, these perceptions and attitudes can have a real impact, regardless of their veracity. For example, some American expatriates report difficulty obtaining a job in a foreign country, even though they are very qualified and successful in the United States. This can occur even in a country and culture similar to the United States, as in Britain where some job-seekers are advised to "temper your American eagerness" and to be "more like the Brits, more reserved."[74]

One objection to all of this that we sometimes hear is that the field of international management itself engages in just this stereotyping. After all, in this chapter we have tried to distinguish Japanese from Americans, Brazilians from Germans, and so on. Although this is generally true, please note that we have usually emphasized relative differences. We certainly are not saying that all Japanese are dissatisfied with their jobs or that all Brazilians don't care about punctuality. We instead refer to observed statistical differences between groups. As you probably know, most statistical tests involve a difference (American vs. Japanese job satisfaction scores, for example) over a pooled variance. The fact that there is variance or differences within groups proves our point. In this book, moreover, we have taken an empirical approach—one based on much data, not just on the opinions of a few people.

Attitudes about Work

People spend a lot of time at work and getting ready to go to work. There are, however, big differences among countries in the number of hours worked. Americans, for example, work about 1,900 hours a year per person. This number is on the high side of the international averages, although the Japanese lead the world by a fair amount. Regardless, we certainly must conclude that work is one of the most important (or at least time-consuming) activities for most Americans and for many other nationalities as well. Accordingly, it should be no surprise that attitudes toward work are one of the most studied issues around.

Job Satisfaction   In fact, the single most studied topic is job satisfaction. Literally thousands of studies have been conducted, mainly with American employees. The prevailing opinion in the popular literature is that Americans rank woefully low in job satisfaction. We are also told that compared to other countries, U.S. workers are particularly dissatisfied with their lot at work. Furthermore, Americans are portrayed as fickle and fidgety as a consequence of this low level of satisfaction. As a result, they are said to have extremely low commitment to their jobs and companies, willing to move or change companies at the drop of a hat.

Have you ever asked yourself, however, why we widely believe this to be the case? On what basis do so many of us have these beliefs about the relatively low level of job satisfaction and commitment of American workers? Many scholars feel that the source of these beliefs are anecdotal stories in the popular media rather than actual study results. Perhaps a reporter or professor briefly visited Japan or Europe for several weeks or months and then wrote an article or book about his or her experience. Although we must and should respect the opinions of others, we also have a responsibility to examine critically the source of the evidence. Who did they speak to? How many people were observed and, more important, how were they selected for observation? Quite often, such observations tend to be nonrepresentative. A foreign observer may be invited to tour or study a factory precisely because it is special or different (nonrepresentative) from the majority. Likewise, we must suspect that companies having great trouble would be unlikely to invite in any observers, let alone foreign ones.

To continue our line of thought here, we ask you to guess what percentage of Japanese workers has what is called "lifetime employment." People in our classes often guess that about 75 percent or more of Japanese workers have lifetime employment. In reality, the figure is closer to 20 percent. Furthermore, this policy is not a long-standing one that emanates from Japanese culture. Rather, it appears to be a post–World War II phenomenon that resulted from deals cut by labor unions with some large companies to end the terrible labor strife that continued into the 1950s. Finally, some companies that have traditionally had lifetime employment policies are now laying off workers (e.g., Matsushita, Nissan, and others). The reason we and most other Americans think that the percentage of Japanese workers covered by lifetime employment policies is higher is not completely clear. Perhaps it is because of the popularized version of Japan we see in well-circulated magazines or in brief TV reports. Regardless, this example suggests that we should examine the source of our international attitudes and then possibly reevaluate them.

Accordingly, we should put more confidence in research studies that systematically examine such issues—especially those conducted on representative samples from two or more countries. Of course, larger-scale and systematic sources of information are in relatively short supply because of their difficulty and expense. Nevertheless, some studies do exist. One such project was conducted by researchers at Indiana University in conjunction with colleagues in Japan.[75] These researchers selected companies randomly so that the sample represented a wide range of industries. This was a first very good step since even some of the better earlier studies only surveyed worker attitudes in the auto or electronics industry. Next, a representative sample of employees from organizations representing these industries was chosen. This second step was all for the better since most earlier research also included nonrepresentative samples of workers. The study ended up surveying over 8,000 employees and included workers from over 100 randomly selected factories in central Japan (fifty-one factories) and in Indiana (fifty-five factories).

The results of this study contradict what many believe about Japanese and American workers and underscore the value of such elaborate and complete studies. For one, it was found that U.S. workers were much *more satisfied* with their jobs than were the Japanese. The researchers went to great lengths to deal with cultural and language differences that might have affected the results. One important potential problem they examined was a tendency for Americans to be typically (and overly) positive and for the Japanese to express even very positive attitudes as neutral, if not bleak. Several patterns in the data, however, eliminate this as a problem. For one, the responses by both groups to different types of job satisfaction questions jumped around. When asked to respond to the question, "All in all, how satisfied would you say you are with your job (1 = not at all, to 5 = very much)?" Americans were much more satisfied than the Japanese. By itself, this result could be explained by the Japanese tendency to be modest. But responses to the question "If a good friend of yours told you that he or she was interested in working at a job like yours at this company, what would you say (0 = advise against it, 1 = would have second thoughts, 2 = would recommend it)?" also showed the same pattern. This question is behavioral and it focuses on others. As a result, it should be less subject to the modesty explanation. Finally, an even stronger pattern of effects was found on another question: Nearly 70 percent of Americans said they would take their job again compared to only about 24 percent of the Japanese.

A closer look at other relevant studies suggests that these findings are accurate. When you look at research that uses different measures and methodologies, nearly every existing study that compares job satisfaction of Japanese and Americans finds the same results.[76] Evidence in support of the position that this is a true difference in job satisfaction between Japanese and Americans comes from yet another study.[77] These researchers asked managers from Canada, France, Japan, and the United Kingdom (around 100 from each country) about their overall level of satisfaction. They also asked, however, about satisfaction with specific components of the job and their work.

Two findings emerged from this study. First, as in previous studies, Japanese were less satisfied than any of the other groups. Second, when the researchers looked at the specific pattern of responses (such as to pay level, working conditions, evaluations of co-workers, etc.), Japanese responses were quite varied. In some cases, they indicated low satisfaction, but in other cases they were among the most satisfied. Thus, the tendency for Japanese to be either systematically bleak or modest in their self-evaluations is less of an issue than was suspected. If bleakness is the driving force, why does it come into play for some aspects of job satisfaction but not for others? Finally, another survey of about 2,500 Japanese workers supported our conclusion. Results similar to those just described were found, but some additional findings are worth mentioning. There was much variation among Japanese workers in their level of satisfaction, which rose strongly with age, seniority, and rank, among other things. These findings tell us that many Japanese are willing to state their level of satisfaction, and some are more willing to do so than others. In fact, older, more senior workers—the very people most likely to hold traditional Japanese values of modesty/self-deprecation—are the ones most likely to say they are happy with their jobs!

We have been focusing on Japanese-American differences in job satisfaction, but obviously there are other countries of interest in the equation.[78] The fact is, however, that most of the research in cross-national job satisfaction focuses on U.S.-Japan differences. Japan was and is one of the major economic powers in the world and a major competitor for the United States, so the high volume of research should be no surprise. And for other work attitudes the same observation could be made. Let us now turn our attention to some of those other important work attitudes.

Organizational commitment Another important and commonly measured work attitude is commitment to one's organization. Just as in our discussion of job satisfaction, the popular belief is that Americans are not as committed to their organizations as workers in other countries. Interestingly, however, few people have actually systematically studied organizational commitment across country and culture. As for job satisfaction, most studies of commitment have been conducted in the United States or in Canada.[79] One exception to this trend is a survey of over 1,600 employees from a wide variety of firms in the United States, Japan, and Korea.[80] Workers in those countries were asked to read and complete a standard and widely used measure of organizational commitment (e.g., "I am willing to work harder than I have to help this company," and "I would turn down another job for more pay in order to stay with this company").

U.S. workers showed significantly higher levels of commitment than either Japanese or Korean employees. The commitment levels of the latter two groups were not different from one another. This finding itself is interesting because, like the findings for job satisfaction, they contradict the popular belief that people from some Asian cultures have higher commitment to their firms. Other studies that employ even more controls have found similar effects.[81] On questions such as "I'm willing to work harder to help the company succeed" and "I'm

organizational commitment Differences among employees in their attachment and allegiance to their organization

proud to work for this company" (among others), U.S. employees scored higher than the Japanese. This was not true of all the commitment questions, however. For example, in response to the question "I would turn down a higher-paying job to stay with this company," there was little difference between U.S. (mean = 2.71) and Japanese (mean = 2.68) employees (on a 5-point scale where 1 = disagree and 5 = agree). In fact, this item showed the least amount of agreement of any of the commitment items; apparently, both Japanese and Americans are willing to entertain higher-paying job offers! Nevertheless, Americans seem to report more commitment to their organizations than do the Japanese. These findings, in combination with the initial belief that Japanese would report higher allegiance to their firms, are an interesting topic that we will return to in later chapters. Earlier research was careful to distinguish *organizational commitment* from *work commitment*. The former refers to the degree to which one identifies and holds allegiance to one's company and is motivated to act on its behalf. Work commitment, on the other hand, refers to the importance of work in one's life— the extent to which it is an important value or motivator relative to other general life activities (e.g., money, family, leisure time, etc.). We've noted that in contrast to what is commonly believed, American workers are as or more committed to their organizations than are Koreans or Japanese. In terms of *work* commitment, however, Japanese appear to be more committed.[82] The Japanese, for example, are more likely to subjugate family issues and problems to those that occur at work. This finding itself is interesting since the Japanese are also popularly thought to place high value on family compared to other cultures.

Before we leave this topic, however, a discussion of one more study may clear up the issue we raised about work (not organizational) commitment across cultures. This study investigated the work involvement of over 5,000 employees of a large multinational firm from twenty different countries from five continents.[83] The results showed that culture (country) had very little predictive value for work commitment or involvement. Instead, a far more important predictor was a person's occupational level. In fact, the author noted that the pattern of work commitment by occupational level was "remarkably similar" across the twenty countries. In particular, as an employee rises in an organization— whether that firm is in Korea, the United States, South Africa, or Israel—so did his or her work commitment.[84] Another way of stating these results is that sometimes situational or personal variables—like occupational level—can be more important predictors than culture or nationality. In this case, there was more commonality among people in the same occupation across national boundaries than among people in different occupations within a country. One lesson we can learn here is that we should try to eliminate situational variables before we leap to the conclusion that country or cultural differences are driving the findings. This will be a special challenge in the remaining chapters, especially as we consider the plight of the expatriate manager.

Chapter Summary

In this chapter, we highlighted the importance of perceptions. While it might be tempting to pass over the study of perceptions as too narrow or idiosyncratic, we showed that not only can they be systematically analyzed but that they can play an important role in cross-cultural interaction. For example, we saw that there are systematic differences in the way that cultures process information about people and events. The perceptions in turn can be modified by differences in nonverbal behavior and in the importance placed in *context* by a given culture. Some cultures are *high context* and provide lots of background information that helps tailor perceptions; other cultures are *low context* and place heavy emphasis on what is explicitly said or written. Interestingly, these perceptual differences even extend to cultural views about time—one of the most objective factors in our lives. We saw that *monochronic cultures* perceive time as an economic commodity that should be carefully monitored and measured, in contrast to *polychronic cultures*, which view time as fluid and flexible.

Perception is one thing, but we also have to make sense of our perceptions. This topic of interpretation—or *attribution*—was discussed next in this chapter. Attribution theorists say that humans are obsessed with asking why something happened. Just because an event catches our attention doesn't mean that we all interpret it the same way. For example, we showed that some cultures make typically more modest attributions about their successes Other cultures, however, seem to encourage a *self-serving attribution*, in which people take credit for success and externalize blame for failures.

If a perception tends to occur over and over again, we may form an attitude about that topic. Accordingly, we next discussed the topic of *attitudes*—both about the self and about others. Again,

there seem to be some cultural determinants of how we view ourselves as well as a tendency to view out-groups (e.g., those from different cultures) in common ways. We concluded the chapter with a discussion of these stereotypic attitudes toward Americans as well as the attitudes of Americans and others toward their jobs and their work.

Discussion Questions

1. Compare the effect of verbal and nonverbal influences on our perceptions. When do nonverbal signs play a bigger role than what is actually said (verbal behavior)? Can you think of an example of such an effect?

2. Think of the ways in which context could affect your perceptions in cross-cultural interactions. For example, what role could it play in communication? What might be the effect in performance evaluations, in meetings, and for a firm's human resource practices as a whole?

3. Reflect on the differences—if any—between the stereotyping process within and across cultures and the process of classifying and distinguishing cultures that we have been engaged in throughout this book. What are your perceptions toward another nation (e.g., France) and why do you have these attitudes?

Up to the Challenge?

Doing Business in Vietnam

WHAT ARE SOME OF THE things you may have picked up throughout this chapter that could be of help in doing business in Vietnam? Maybe the most important thing about this chapter is the point that culture sometimes has a very subtle effect—one that at times is not recognized or appreciated when we interact with others. One of those subtle things is context. Like many Asian countries, Vietnam is a high-context culture. This means that the culture or context itself provides people with a great deal of cues that are used to interpret what might otherwise be an ambiguous event. In such cultures, people do not require or expect much detailed, explicit information about events—the context

often provides this for the Vietnamese. Americans, as you know, are relatively low context—we base our perceptions and interpretations a good deal on what is explicitly said or written.

This basic difference can create some misunderstanding but is easily adjusted to when the difference is recognized. For one, Vietnamese businesspeople will probably want to get to know you personally before getting down to business. Thus, you probably should expect little if anything to be accomplished during initial meetings with Vietnamese—at least from a U.S. cultural perspective, anyway! In fact, what the Vietnamese hope to accomplish is to get some context. During initial meetings, they will want to use that time to understand your background, your temperament, and your interests; all this will help them interpret your verbal and nonverbal behavior. From the U.S. low-context perspective, the amount of time spent discussing "nonproductive" topics could be frustrating. Patience in the form of understanding this basic difference, however, could pay off later.

The question of context brings up a second important issue that was discussed in this chapter—time orientation. As you may also have guessed, the Vietnamese have a more polychronic view of time, viewing it as more flexible and extended than do most monochronic Americans. In part, this orientation results from the agricultural nature of traditional Vietnamese society and its concomitant focus on seasons. At the same time, however, the Confucian virtue of patience emphasizes time flexibility even more. The Vietnamese generally react negatively to a need for urgency in a business deal, whereas the American typically believes that "time is money."

The Vietnamese view of self is *inter*dependent, whereas the American is more likely to have an *in*dependent self. This difference can have many implications for conducting business. For example, because the Vietnamese are more likely to see themselves as interconnected with others, singling out a person (even for praise) is very likely to be embarrassing and may have a backfire effect. These contrasting views of self can be manifested in a number of different attitudes, but perhaps none more diverse than those concerned with the concept of "face." In Vietnam, face is all important. Open criticism in Vietnam is very rare because it can cause irreparable harm to a business relationship. Nevertheless, an American visitor to Ho Chi Minh City will likely view the American War Crimes Museum—if they choose to tour it—as an affront to their face. Our Asia Study Abroad Program students here at the University of Dayton certainly have that reaction every summer during their visit to the city. The name was recently changed to the War Remnants Museum partially because of the many tourists, American and otherwise, who now visit Vietnam. Regardless, all should be cautioned that a loss of temper and overt expression of anger is considered very rude and causes the person who expresses anger to lose face. Criticism and praise are best handled privately when dealing with Vietnamese; the same is probably true, in fact, for criticism for U.S. employees. Finally, other ways to show respect and provide face to a Vietnamese business partner include (1) remaining on the formal side in your interactions, (2) showing great respect for age (the oldest member of a Vietnamese team is usually the most powerful) and (3) giving more interpersonal space to a Vietnamese than you may be used to with U.S. businesspeople. To be effective in doing business with one another, you will need to establish trust. Recognizing and accommodating for differences may provide the foundation for beneficial business relations for Americans and Vietnamese alike.

International Development

Cultural Stereotypes

Purpose
To understand the presence, frequency, and negative effects of various stereotypes.

Instructions
Complete the following questionnaire before class. Your instructor will divide the class into diverse groups of three to six members. Your group will discuss each other's responses to the questionnaire and try to come to a consensus about the stereotypes of the various ethnic groups (20 minutes).

After you have done this, the instructor will lead the whole class in a discussion of the common stereotypes, including similarities and differences between the groups. Finally, you can consider how stereotypes can hinder and block productive business relationships.

Questionnaire
Use one word to describe each of the following groups:
  1. English
  2. French
  3. Norwegians
  4. Latins

5. Japanese
6. Middle Easterners
7. Chinese
8. Africans
9. Italians
10. Americans

Answer the following questions about Canadians (please answer these questions from memory rather than by researching the answers):

1. One word to describe the people.
2. Who is the current prime minister?
3. Name three Canadian historical figures.
4. List four Canadian provinces.
5. What is the main language?
6. What type of government does it have?
7. What is its relationship to England?
8. Name of currency and relationship to U.S. dollar.
9. Main exports to U.S.

Answer the following questions about Mexicans:

1. One word to describe the people.
2. Who is the current president?
3. Name three Mexican historical figures.
4. List three states of Mexico.
5. What is the main language?
6. Type of government.
7. Relationship to Latin America.
8. Name of currency and relationship to U.S. dollar.
9. Main exports to U.S.

Source: Marcic, D., & Puffer, S. (1994). *Management international.* St. Paul, MN: West Publishing. Marcic and Puffer adapted this exercise from Axtell, R. E. (1990). *Do's and taboos around the world.* New York: Wiley and Sons. Reprinted by permission.

 Tapping into the Global Network

Conducting a Cultural Audit of China

Purpose

To familiarize yourself with attitudes toward another culture and to get experience preparing to deal with cultural patterns and attitudes in that country.

Instructions

For this project, you should consider yourself an employee of a smaller firm that has little or no experience in China. Yet, the firm—which manufactures silicon wafers—is seeking to move some of its operations to China in order to be closer to some of its customers and to capitalize on the resulting cost savings.

Your assignment is to produce a "cultural audit" that will better prepare your company for this move. Your goal here is to produce a short manual that will provide an overview of what it's like to do business in China—to provide a "how to" approach that will introduce your representatives and executives to some cultural protocol. You are encouraged to touch on the topics that you've covered thus far in the book (Chapters 1–4) as well as this chapter. If your instructor has asked you to read chapters in a different order, then he or she will advise you on what to eliminate or add in this report. Almost certainly, however, your report will include some treatment of Chinese perceptual tendencies as well as their attitudes toward the United States and ours toward them.

Resources

- **CIA World FactBook (www.cia.gov/cia/ publications/factbook/)**
  This widely referenced document provides a wealth of information about nearly every country in the world. While most of this information deals with basic economic, governmental, and demographic data, it will provide useful information for this exercise.

- **China-Britain Business Council (www.cbbc. org/china-guide)**

  This site offers some very useful background information on understanding basic Chinese business practices. You'll find detailed information on any number of different issues that would arise in doing business in China.

- **The Embassy of the PRC in the United States (www.china-embassy.org/eng/); and The Embassy of the PRC in the United Kingdom (www.chinese-embassy.org. uk/eng/)**

  These sites, the Chinese embassy in the United States and the United Kingdom, offer a lot of background information on the topics that are the subject of this exercise.

- **U.S. State Department Information on China (travel.state.gov/tips_china.html)**

  As the title of this page shows, the U.S. State Department offers information on China that you might find helpful.

6

Communicating Effectively across Cultures

INTERNATIONAL CHALLENGE

Lost in Translation: Bridgestone's Communication Effort Goes Flat

Learning Objectives

After reading this chapter, you should be able to:

▸ Identify and monitor trends in international business communication, both positive and negative.

▸ Be aware that language problems are significant barriers in international business and appreciate that even language proficiency is no guarantee that miscommunication will not occur.

▸ Recognize that there are many different ways that communication can take place and that many cultures place importance on nonverbal communication channels.

IN 2001, JAPAN-BASED Bridgestone Corporation had a major problem. In a nutshell, the company's American subsidiary, Firestone, Inc., was under assault by consumers, lawyers, and even the U.S. government. The reason? Millions of allegedly defective tires that supposedly caused rollover accidents that injured more than 700 people and claimed over 170 lives. Many of the accidents occurred in Ford SUVs, and Firestone alleged that Ford's design was a contributing factor while Ford claimed Firestone's tires were to blame. To make a long story short, Bridgestone eventually recalled millions of tires and provided free replacements.

This series of events was prohibitively expensive for Firestone and disastrous for its brand. Some experts even predicted the Firestone name would eventually disappear as a result. But our purpose here isn't to discuss problems with tires. What we'd like you to focus on are the communication tactics used by Firestone's Japanese parent Bridgestone to manage the situation. These tactics, at least from an American audience's perspective, may have made a bad situation much worse.

First, let's set the stage. Firestone's communication strategy was essentially controlled by Bridgestone executives in Japan. This is common—many Japanese multinationals centralize decision making, with all roads from foreign subsidiaries leading back to Japan. And when faced with problems, many Japanese executives will say nothing in the belief that silence and stoicism communicate that things are being handled calmly and deliberately. Moreover, Japanese executives tend to avoid directly confronting external criticism, preferring instead to stay disengaged.

Even up to Bridgestone's announcement in late 2000 that it would recall millions of Firestone tires, then-President Yoichiro Kaizaki had little to say about the controversy. And despite rising outrage in the United States after the announcement, Bridgestone's Japanese leadership maintained its low profile. Then in September 2000, Firestone CEO Masatoshi Ono went before a U.S. Senate subcommittee to answer questions. Mr. Ono said he took "full and personal responsibility" for some of the accidents involving Firestone's tires. But one senator argued that if Firestone had knowingly put out bad tires, it would be tantamount to "second-degree murder." Mr. Ono's response to this harsh assessment was silence. One American press report described Mr. Ono as "deferential but fumbling" while another said he "came across as tentative and unforthcoming."

Critics argued that Bridgestone's mistake was using Mr. Ono, an executive with weak English skills, to press its case. Indeed, Mr. Ono and many Japanese executives on the Bridgestone crisis management team had trouble following the line of questions. The result, many felt, was that Mr. Ono and Bridgestone were not effectively communicating the message that they wanted the wider American audience to hear.

Days later, President Kaizaki finally stepped into the spotlight during a Tokyo news conference, expressing regret but deflecting blame and strenuously denying a coverup. But he continued to refuse requests for media interviews. Months later, however, Mr. Kaizaki adopted a more open stance and was willing to share important financial information about Firestone's situation. But, it all seemed too late. In early 2001, Mr. Kaizaki stepped down. An American manager who once worked for Bridgestone described the communication tactics that Bridgestone's Japanese executives used this way: "They just don't have a clue how to handle this."

As you read through this chapter, you'll learn a great deal about the myriad communication challenges facing international managers. In doing so, consider these questions. What communication errors did Bridgestone executives make? How would their efforts be interpreted by an American audience? What cultural factors are relevant? And given the damage already done to Firestone's reputation, how should Bridgestone communicate now? Then take a look at the *Up to the Challenge?* box at the end of this chapter for some insights into the communication adjustments that Bridgestone made.[1]

▶ *The Value of Communications Savvy in International Business*

Previously we discussed many important cross-cultural challenges presented by perception issues. Here we pick up right where we left off. That is, once you perceive and interpret the behavior of another person, you need to communicate your feelings or reactions. And that's where your prowess and insight into others' way of thinking is critical, especially in an international environment.

Although it may strike you as obvious that communication comes in many different forms, managers sometimes get themselves into trouble by assuming that communication is the same everywhere. To an American, for instance, a gap in conversation usually is seen as an opportunity to respond. And long gaps tend to create discomfort and a desire to fill in the silence. But in Finland and Japan, longer periods of silence in conversation are normal, even expected. Pauses suggest that someone is carefully contemplating what has been said. In fact, responding too fast can give offense.[2]

So in negotiation situations with the Japanese, unprepared Americans may be very uncomfortable when they encounter silence and may interpret it as dissatisfaction with any offers on the table. Japanese representatives, however, are likely to feel that it is important to consider offers seriously and communicate that by pondering matters in silence. Of course, many astute Japanese negotiators know that Americans are uncomfortable with silence and try to use this cultural trait to their advantage. This underscores the importance of strategically communicating in international business, especially in negotiations.[3] And we'll consider international negotiation in more detail in the next chapter.

EXHIBIT 6.1   *The Ten Most Widely Used Native Languages in the World**

Language	Native Speakers in the World (%)
1. Chinese (Mandarin)	20.0
2. English	6.0
3. Hindustani	4.5
4. Russian	3.5
5. Spanish	3.0
6. Japanese	2.0
7. German	2.0
8. Indonesian	2.0
9. Portuguese	2.0
10. French (tie)	1.5
10. Arabic (tie)	1.5

*These figures reflect only the number of native speakers and do not include those who speak second languages.
Source: Adapted from ———. (1991). *The Economist Atlas*, 116. London: The Economist Books.

But even speaking the "same" language carries pitfalls. Decisions are often a function of culture, background, and experiences, a shared language notwithstanding. Take what often happens when Americans are posted to places such as Australia or the United Kingdom. Not only is the "English" not identical, but the **communication style** is different as well (e.g., the use of irony, sarcasm, understatement). Those differences can cause huge problems if not properly understood. Of course, nonverbal communication matters too. For example, putting your feet up may be acceptable in the United States especially if you want to convey a relaxed and familiar atmosphere, but in most other countries it would be viewed as crude and offensive. The bottom line, as one expert put it, is that "what blows deals is a failure to understand communication styles."[4]

Consequently, this chapter will review various forms of personal communication, both verbal and nonverbal. We'll also look at the ways that multinationals communicate, something that our opening box suggests is important. In addition, we'll review some of the barriers to effective communication across cultures and suggest ways to overcome them.

communication style
A common style of communicating that is tacit and difficult for people in other cultures to appreciate

▶ *Spoken and Written Communication*

The single most important way that we communicate is through language, both spoken and written. Let's look at the role language plays in international communication.

Languages of the World

There are over 2,500 distinct languages currently spoken along with thousands of other offshoots or **dialects**. However, only about 100 of these have more than 1 million speakers. In fact, about ten languages account for most of our communication on the planet (see Exhibit 6.1). A few languages are mostly limited

dialects
The nearly 8,000 different versions of the 2,500 distinct languages that exist in the world

EXHIBIT 6.2   *Americans on Foreign Languages and Foreigners on English*

- Only about 15% of American high school students now study a foreign language, compared to nearly 25% in the 1960s.

- The United States continues to be one of the few places in the world where it is possible to graduate from college without taking even one year of a foreign language.

- While the United States is one of the most ethnically rich nations in the world, the languages accompanying immigrant populations have not spread very widely.

- English is the most popular second language in Europe, the Middle East, Africa, Japan, and China.

- Many foreign companies routinely translate their memos into English.

- The average European knows two languages; many know three or more. Over 40% of the EU speaks English as a second language, and nearly 70% say that "everyone should speak English."

- Chinese children are required to take foreign languages in grade school and to demonstrate mastery prior to college graduation.

Mandarin
The official language of the People's Republic of China, and spoken by over 20 percent of the world's population

to only one nation (e.g., Polish, Japanese, and Greek). Others, however, are spoken across many borders (e.g., English, French). Nevertheless, the dominant language in any one country or region has a great effect on and can even define a particular culture. An interesting case in point is the Chinese government's efforts to promote **Mandarin** as the official national language in a country that arguably has the most linguistic diversity on earth. Used by over 50 percent of China's population, Mandarin is the most common language group in the country. But Mandarin is hard for people from Shanghai and its surrounding provinces to understand. There, various dialects of Wu are common. Some have said that the eight languages of China are as different as Spanish is from French.[5]

Speaking (and Not Speaking) Other Languages

The large number of languages presents several challenges to international managers. First, to be effective you need to communicate in the language of the country in which you are doing business (or be willing to place enormous trust in a translator!). Few Americans, however, speak second or third languages (see Exhibit 6.2). There are many reasons for Americans' general lack of interest in other languages. The most popular explanation is that the United States is relatively isolated geographically and, as a result, has had no great need for additional languages. This explanation, however, doesn't hold up well in the face of the large numbers of immigrants and ethnic minorities in the United States. Plus, technology has made the rapid transmission of information a given, rendering geographic isolation more illusory than real.

Part of the reason for Americans' lack of foreign language proficiency may be ethnocentrism. Perhaps you've heard the story (fictional or not) of the American tourist in Germany who sneezed on a public bus. A German turned and said *"Gesundheit."* As the story goes, the tourist then said to a friend, "How nice—he speaks English." Also, it's possible to graduate from college in the United States without taking a single foreign language course (see Exhibit 6.2). This lack of acknowledgment of other languages reflects the low value that Americans attach to this skill.[6]

One factor that has made it easy for Americans to be complacent about being monolingual is that the rest of the world increasingly uses English in business interactions. For example, English is the language for international air traffic, regardless of city of departure or arrival. And that's not all. Peruse French job ads and you'll find that most management and professional positions require *anglais courant*. English is the official language of oil firm Totalfina, the second biggest company in France—this in a country that ferociously protects its language. In fact, France has created a government ministry of culture to foster the French language and culture. But why is English becoming more pervasive in international business circles, even in France? First, much of the business on the Internet is dominated by American firms. And in the process, the Internet is exposing people everywhere to English more than ever. In support of this conclusion, it's been estimated that about three-quarters of all Internet sites across the globe are in English.[7] Then there's the sheer size of the American economy and the global reach of U.S. multinationals, which effectively makes using English "good business sense," at least in the minds of some. Moreover, English is fairly simple, grammatically speaking, and consequently makes for a relatively easy "common tongue" to use in international business. So when French pharmaceutical firm Rhône-Poulenc merged with German competitor Hoechst a few years ago, English was made the common language of the merged companies.[8]

There are many different languages spoken in EU countries. Yet today more than half the people in the European Union claim to be reasonably conversant in English. In fact, a survey of 16,000 people living in EU countries found that almost 70 percent agreed with the statement "Everyone should speak English." And the Dutch are closest to already being there, with more than 80 percent indicating that they speak English as a second language. English has also been weaving its way into local languages around the world, with Europe no exception. The French term for a self-service restaurant is *le self* and the Russians call denim pants *dzhinsi* (roughly pronounced "jeansy").[9] German has become so littered with English phrases that some now refer to it as *Denglisch*. German executives these days may conduct media interviews in a *Pressebriefingraum* and then go work off their stress at a *Businesssportcenter*. But like the French before them, some German officials worry about the intrusion of English into their culture. One member of the German parliament decried the trend, calling it a "flood of Anglicisms descending on us from the media, advertising, product description and technology."[10]

Nevertheless, this trend seems likely to continue. And if you add all the people who speak English with some competence as a second language to those native English speakers, they become the most numerous in the world (at around 1.3 billion, compared to about 900 million for Mandarin Chinese).[11] Overall, English is the most popular second language in Europe, Africa, Japan, and China, among other places. Consequently, it's probably no exaggeration to consider English as the language of international business. In fact, Exhibit 6.3 provides more detailed evidence to support our statement—apparently much of world business is conducted in English. When people adopt a second language it is often because it is useful in business interactions. In China, for instance, speaking English means better jobs, better pay (often double), and foreign travel opportunities. No wonder teaching English is big business, with up to $3 billion annually being spent on English language training in Asia alone.[12]

EXHIBIT 6.3   *Percentage of World Output Tied to Language Group**

Language	Percentage of World Output by Language Group
1. English	33
2. Mandarin	10
3. Spanish	7
4. German	7
5. French	5
6. Arabic	3
7. Hindi	2
8. All others	33

*World output is defined as the value of goods and services produced by people in each primary language group.
Source: Adapted from Reading, B. (1998). *The Financial Times*, January 17, 21.

That said, other languages really aren't going away, in business or otherwise. For instance, the WTO's costs related to language have soared over 120 percent since it was founded in 1995. Language service to the more than 140 WTO members eats up 22 percent of its budget. It seems that along with global organizations come global-sized bills for translators.[13]

And what does "competence" in English, or any other language that you might speak, really mean? There is no one definition, but there's little doubt that many people overestimate their language skills. And, as noted, perception and decision making may be linked to cultural values regardless of what language is spoken. So communication in international business is likely to have plenty of rough edges to it, even when a "common" language is used. Those rough edges can often create real problems and even great danger, as shown in the following International Insights.

Nevertheless, competence in another language pays dividends in international business. And that's why the American reliance on English represents a distinct disadvantage, one that will continue to cause problems as the ferocity of foreign competition from countries such as China escalates. Many American firms continue to underplay the value of having managers who are fluent in other languages. In one survey, American managers felt that while cross-cultural understanding was valuable, foreign language skills were not as important. The general feeling was that language problems could be overcome by using translators or by hiring foreign nationals.[14] Not surprisingly, studies show that American businesspeople have the lowest foreign language proficiency of any major trading nation in the world.[15] And as you can see in Exhibit 6.4, the United States has received poor grades for knowledge of foreign cultures and languages. In a survey of over 10,000 business people from around the world, the results showed that the United States had the lowest rating of any country.

Communicating in Foreign Languages: Plenty of Room for Error

Clearly, the lack of foreign language skills puts you at a disadvantage in international business. But assuming that you speak Mandarin, French, or Russian, your problems are far from over. Even with great proficiency, many problems

🌐 International Insights

Cross-Cultural Miscommunication in the Air Can Be Dangerous

SECONDS BEFORE KAL flight 2300 landed in a storm in Cheju, South Korea, First Officer Chung Chan Kyu tried to abort the landing by grabbing control of the plane from Captain Barry Woods. The aircraft's black box recorded what happened when the plane was only 30 feet above the ground and about to land. Captain Woods shouts: "Get your hand . . . get off. Get off! Tell me what it is . . .". Seconds later a terrible crunch is heard over the grunts of Mr. Chung and an alarm bell. The plane crashed and burst into flames. Astonishingly, all 157 people aboard escaped with their lives.

Many observers felt that the crash at Cheju reflects a rising occupational hazard—the language obstacle. As fast-growing Asian airlines scoured the world for pilots, cockpit crews have become more culturally and linguistically diverse. The problem in Korea, say foreign pilots, is acute. "It's like an air show up there, and it's hard to tell where everything is because the Koreans are all speaking Korean," said an American who flew for Asiana Airlines for several years before taking a job with a U.S. firm. "There are a lot of opportunities to get hurt."

Under Korean law, foreign pilots must be matched with a Korean first officer so that communication with the control tower is effective. Unfortunately, as was probably the case in the Cheju accident, Korean first officers receive only a rough familiarity with English as they go through flight school. Worse yet, communication may be further hindered by the hierarchical Korean culture that discourages copilots from asking questions or volunteering information. In fact, one foreign pilot who trained many Korean pilots said that in the hundreds of preflight briefings he gave, the trainees did not ask a single question.

These and other factors make flying in Korea more risky than should otherwise be the case. Korea's airlines have higher fatal accident rates than their North American and Latin American counterparts. And investigators acknowledge that miscommunication contributed to the Cheju accident. In fact, as the plane was on its final approach, Captain Woods asked First Officer Chung to turn on the windshield wipers. Because he didn't respond, Mr. Woods repeated the request. A few seconds later, Mr. Chung replied: "yeah . . . wind shears." Apparently, Mr. Woods's order to "get off the controls" also caused confusion. Experts say that a clearer command would have been "Don't touch the controls." Both pilots were charged with criminal neglect.

Clearly, this is a case where culture affected communication. The Confucian tradition in Korea produces a high power distance. This can make it difficult for Korean flight officers to be proactive enough in providing information to superiors. Likewise, asking questions is often regarded as disrespectful. Showing lack of experience or knowledge, even in an airline cockpit, may be considered a loss of face. Fortunately, no lives were lost at Cheju.[16]

---

can arise in verbal communication. First, there can be many dialects within a particular language group. Moreover, major language groups can be found in many countries, as we noted in regard to China. Beyond regional differences in languages, however, there are also accent and usage variations as well as many other subtle differences in language use.

For these reasons, international managers must be sensitive to the possibility that what they intended to communicate was not understood. This is even true with interactions between British and American managers, people who ostensibly share the "same" language. Consider, for instance, how each side interprets the phrase "table the proposal." To Americans, it means that the proposal will be put aside or delayed indefinitely. To the British, however, it means the opposite (i.e., to act immediately on the proposal). There are so many other examples of differences (e.g., flashlight = torch, Band-Aids = plasters,

EXHIBIT 6.4   *The Relative Ranking of Developed and Developing Countries on Knowledge of Foreign Languages and Cultures*

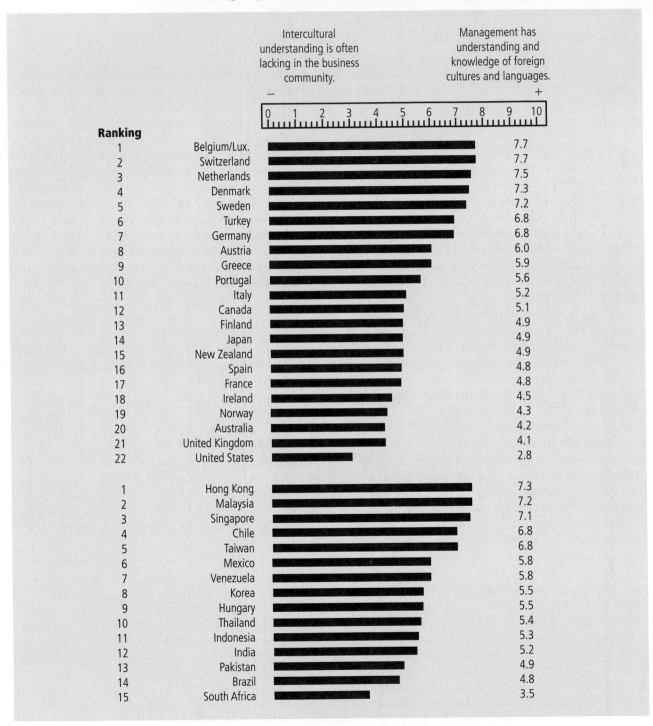

EXHIBIT 6.5   *Communication Blunders Abroad*

Examples of translation errors

- A foreign airline operating in Brazil advertised plush "rendezvous lounges," which in Portuguese implies a room for making love.
- One German translation of the phrase "Come alive with Pepsi" literally meant "Come alive out of the grave with Pepsi."
- A memo from an African subsidiary of Dutch electronics giant Philips referred to "throat-cutting competition" instead of "cut-throat competition."
- A sign on the elevator in a Romanian hotel read: "The lift is being fixed. For the next two days we regret that you will be unbearable."
- A sign in the window of a Paris dress shop said: "Come inside and have a fit."
- A sign in a Japanese hotel read: "You are invited to take advantage of our chambermaid."
- A Bangkok dry cleaner tag line read: "Drop your trousers here for best results."

Examples of failing to appreciate local norms and cultural values when communicating

- One U.S. firm operating in Europe handed out fake coins with "$1 billion" emblazoned on them. Instead of spreading good will, this was largely seen as a reflection of American pomposity and superiority. Europeans wondered why the dollar sign was used instead of local currency.
- In Britain, General Mills used a breakfast cereal package that showed a clean-cut child saying, "See kids, it's great!" Although this was a prototypical American ad, the product received a poor reception. General Mills failed to appreciate that English families are less child-centered when making food purchases than their American counterparts.
- A foreign appliance company used an ad in Middle Eastern markets that showed a refrigerator full of food, including a large ham. The ad was insensitive if not offensive since Muslims are forbidden to eat pork.
- Listerine was introduced in Thailand with an ad that showed a boy and a girl, obviously enthralled with one another. After learning that the public depiction of romantic relationships was objectionable, the ad was adjusted to show two girls discussing bad breath. The revised ad was much more effective.

Source: Adapted from Ricks, D. A. (1983). *Big business blunders: Mistakes in multinational marketing*. Homewood, IL: Dow Jones Irwin.

subway = tube, toilet = loo, etc.) that it is easy to see why Churchill said that the United States and Britain were "a people separated by a common language." Misunderstandings between British and Americans are likely to be cleared up fairly quickly given that the core language is the same. But in transactions involving distinct languages, resolving problems is much more difficult, especially if managers are not fluent in the languages involved and cannot completely check any translations provided.

Even if managers can avoid these problems, they can still make major errors that can harm their international business. For instance, Swedish manufacturer Electrolux once used the phrase "nothing sucks like an Electrolux" to promote their vacuum cleaners. Besides being vaguely obscene, this phrasing could be interpreted as something less than a rousing evaluation of the product! Exhibit 6.5 presents additional communication blunders, committed by companies as they tried to do business internationally. The exhibit shows two main

🌐 International Insights

Habla Usted Español? Microsoft Has to Brush Up

THE LAST THING YOU want to do is offend your customers. And you certainly wouldn't refer to valued clients as vulgar, abrasive, or ridiculous. Apparently, however, this is exactly what Microsoft did to many of its Spanish-speaking customers with one of its products a few years ago. In fact, to some this incident made many of the infamous gaffes of the past look tame.

The problem centered on a Spanish-language version of Microsoft's popular Word program and its thesaurus feature in particular. Unfortunately, the thesaurus function offered a number of offensive synonyms for various ethnic groups, creating a massive public relations headache for the company. The program, for example, suggested that "man-eater," "cannibal" and "barbarian" could be substituted for the Spanish term for black people. The program also likened Indians to man-eating savages and provided the Spanish word for "bastard" as a substitute for people of mixed race. *Lesbian* was equated with "vicious" and "perverse," while *Occidental* was matched with "white," "civilized," and "cultured."

The insulting language was first uncovered in Spain but was later widely discussed in the Mexican press. Microsoft issued a public apology, claimed that the translation errors were "unintentional mistakes," and promised to quickly fix the software. But by then criticism had reverberated in prominent Mexican newspapers and radio stations. In denouncing the program, a local historian told *La Jornada* (a major newspaper in Mexico City) that "those who made this dictionary of synonyms are imbeciles and cretins."

How did a major company like Microsoft get things so wrong? A company representative said that the firm contracted out the thesaurus code to an unnamed American supplier. In turn, Microsoft failed to detect many of the outdated terms and incorrect translations. The representative said, "If you went and bought a printed dictionary in Mexico today, you would find some of these mistakes." Some experts, however, were incredulous and skeptical. "It's unbelievable," said the chair of the Spanish department at the University of California at Berkeley.[17]

types of blunders—errors in translation and errors that violate local norms and culture.[18] If you think such errors are a thing of the distant past, please read the accompanying International Insights about the problems that Microsoft experienced with the translation of its Word program. And consider the fact that even though Microsoft, as well as the companies discussed in Exhibit 6.5, hired professionals to work on and translate their ads or products, they still had problems. So real-time communications in international business are likely to produce as many problems, if not more.

For example, imagine a meeting between American and Japanese managers. Despite accuracy in the literal translation of words, the actual meaning can vary considerably. In Japan, it is generally considered inappropriate to say no in a blunt or direct fashion. The Japanese tend to avoid explicitly saying no to the other party so that both sides retain face. Instead, the Japanese rely on a variety of indirect ways to say no. A person who is not savvy regarding such cultural norms may not understand that "I will consider your proposal" could actually mean no. It is so common for the Japanese to avoid direct negatives that the Japan Export Trade Organization provides a pamphlet to foreigners to help them understand the difference between a yes and a no.[19] Exhibit 6.6 presents some common phrases that actually mean "no" but allow for the bad news to be cushioned. Apparently, even the structure of the language itself seems to be designed in part to preserve this harmony. The verb in Japanese comes at the

EXHIBIT 6.6   *Ten Ways to Avoid Saying No in Japanese*

Phrase That Really Means No	A Common but Incorrect American Interpretation
"That would be very hard to do."	Some adjustments are needed, but the deal is still possible.
"It is very difficult."	The matter is difficult but not impossible.
"I will consider it."	The issue is under consideration for future use.
"I shall give it careful consideration."	Even more attention will be given to the proposal.
"We shall make efforts."	Energy will be put into exploring options.
Silence/delay in response	The other party is thinking about the topic or they are offended by our message; time is being wasted.
A change of subject	The new topic is more important now.
"I'll think about it."	The issue is still alive and under consideration.
"I'll do my best, but I'm in a delicate position."	It will be extremely tricky, but he or she will give it a shot.
"Yes, but . . . ."	Conditional agreement

Source: Adapted from Imai, M. (1975). *Never take yes for an answer*. Tokyo: Simul Press; Ueda, K. (1978). Sixteen ways to avoid saying "no" in Japan. In J. C. Condon & M. Saito (Eds.), *Intercultural encounters with Japan. Communication—contact and conflict*, 185–195. Tokyo, Japan: Simul Press.

end of a sentence. A communicator can present the subject and object first, then alter the verb after gauging the reaction. Further, the speaker can easily add a negative at the end of a sentence that entirely changes the meaning in order to preserve harmony.[20]

Of course, in all cultures it can be difficult to confront someone directly. So it's probably universal to try to cushion bad news to some degree. But Americans in particular are often irritated when they feel they are being "strung along" or not given a "straight answer" when the news is bad.[21] Going back to our Japanese example, the problem is that Americans *should* be hearing a no but they are not. In other words, it's not that the Japanese are insincere, it's just that they are probably working very hard to maintain harmony and show consideration for the feelings of others when communicating a no. A flat-out refusal would certainly be the worst option to take for many Japanese. And conversely, many Japanese perceive the communications of Americans as "blunt," "too insensitive," "overly critical," or just plain "prying." Of course, it would behoove both sides to gain a better understanding of the other.[22]

Embarrassment and Apology as Communication

But what happens once offense is given or a loss of face occurs? Are there cross-cultural differences in how people experience that and respond to it from a communications standpoint? The answer appears to be yes. In one study, Japanese and Americans were asked to describe recent embarrassing situations that they had experienced. The Japanese tended to mention predicaments involving in-group relations (e.g., interactions with family, spouse, friends, and co-workers). American respondents, however, were more likely to mention relations with out-group members (e.g., acquaintances, friends of friends, strangers, and the like). Also interesting were the differences in reactions to these social predicaments. Most of the Americans (65 percent) felt embarrassment, but only a small portion of the Japanese had this reaction (5 percent). On the other hand, the Japanese were much more likely to feel shame (42 percent) in response to the loss of face than were the Americans (4 percent). These findings are supportive of the perspective that Japanese and Americans are generally on opposite ends of the individual–collective dimensions of culture. Our point here is that one major effect of these orientations is a difference in communication styles.[23]

An interesting follow-up issue is how people *resolve* their embarrassments and other interaction predicaments. Of course, one option is to apologize for creating the problem itself, or at least for our part in the social mess. And as it turns out, Japanese and Americans (among others) tend to react differently in situations where one person harms—physically or psychologically—another person. Earlier, we presented the communication problems that occur and contribute to commercial airline accidents. When accidents occur, there's always a major effort made to determine the cause. Some years ago, a Japan Airlines flight crashed into Tokyo Bay at Narita International Airport. Twenty-four people died and many others were hurt. After the accident, the president of JAL publicly apologized, personally visited each family affected by the tragedy, and offered his resignation. It is difficult to imagine the management of an American airline engaging in the same course of action.

Researchers have examined how apologies like these are communicated across cultures. In one study, Japanese and Americans were asked to describe a recent incident in which they had apologized to someone else. The Japanese preferred to apologize directly and extensively (as in the airline example), without offering explanations and reasons for their actions. Interestingly, Americans, while not quite as direct as the Japanese, also generally preferred to apologize directly. However, the American apologies were not as extreme, and they offered many more justifications and attributions to explain their behavior. The Japanese were highly sensitive to lapses in their social obligations and went to great lengths to try to make amends. The American tendency to provide many explanations of "social failure" may reflect the higher value placed on the self in an individualistic culture, which may make the admission of failure or guilt much more difficult. And the concern for the collective or group may make it easier to express such feelings for the Japanese.[24]

In fact, experts suggest that international companies should help their employees understand that the type of apologies and explanations provided by people may be driven by culture-specific values and attitudes. Managers who fail to adjust their communication strategies risk provoking conflict and creating misunderstandings in lots of cross-cultural situations (e.g., negotiations, cross-cultural teams, and performance appraisals, to name just a few).[25] In the accompanying International Insights box we show how a large Japanese firm offered apologies to their customers.

Compliments as Communication

Of course, sometimes we communicate not to deal with interaction problems, but to smooth such interaction in the first place. For example, research shows that Americans praise each other much more frequently than do the Japanese. Americans are also much more likely to commend personal traits and physical appearance than are Japanese. Why these differences? The value placed on the self in U.S. culture—so much so that there is great difficulty in accepting a mistake and apologizing—may lead many Americans to be especially solicitous of compliments that make the self feel better or otherwise stand out.[26]

🌐 International Insights

Japanese Dairy "Pours" on the Apologies

YUMI ITO WAS standing in front of two representatives of Snow Brand, Japan's largest milk company, and they literally "floored" her. Both men were bowing so deeply in apology that their heads touched the floor. In fact, they bowed over and over again to express regret that a batch of their milk had caused Ms. Ito's young daughter to become sick. As their heads literally touched the floor, Ms. Ito said to herself, "This is too painful to watch."

This show of humility was dramatic, even in a country that has made apologies an art form. And Ms. Ito wasn't the only person receiving such attention. In fact, the Snow company asked 2,000 of its employees to personally visit the more than 14,000 people made sick by their milk in order to bow, apologize, and offer cash compensation. Other Japanese firms have asked their employees to pitch in with apologies, but no one has approached the scope of Snow's efforts. To understand this unprecedented campaign, you have to also appreciate what happened and what was at stake for this $12.1-billion food company giant. About two weeks before the apologies such as that received by Ms. Ito, Snow's milk was blamed for causing diarrhea and vomiting in thousands of people. It took several days for the company to isolate a dirty valve at its Osaka plant and then order a recall. Shortly after this event came revelations about contamination in other products, more sick people, and additional recalls. Worse yet, a few days later the government accused Snow of recycling and reselling milk products that had been returned by retail stores. Snow promised a full investigation and closed all twenty-one of its plants temporarily for safety reasons.

In an attempt to regain its reputation, Snow Brand engaged in this mass humility effort. On the weekend after the last allegation, about 700 Snow Brand employees gathered at company headquarters early in the morning for a briefing and instructions on the apology campaign. The basic instructions were to apologize first and then to inquire about the victim's health. Then they were to broach the compensation issue. If there were health-related expenses, the employees were to get a receipt. If none was available or if the victim got mad, employees were instructed to pay them anyway. "How much?" asked one employee. "If the amount is within 30,000 yen [$280], that should be okay," said the supervisor. "And don't talk back, no matter how angry the customer gets." This brings us back to Ms. Ito, who was also presented a white envelope with calligraphy on it that's often used when giving cash to ill people. It included cash and related gift certificates. For Ms. Ito, an apology would have been enough. She refused at first, but the Snow Brand employees implored her to accept the envelope. "We won't be able to go back to our company if you don't take it," they said.[27]

There are wide differences across cultures in terms of how often praise is given, what is praised, and how people respond. For instance, Egyptians tend to have a "complimenting" culture. While they may not compliment as much as Americans, their salutations tend to be longer and have more depth. Here's an example. On one occasion, a host complimented an Egyptian dinner guest on his necktie. The Egyptian promptly took off the tie and gave it to the person who offered the praise. The host politely refused the gift but found it neatly folded on the couch after the party was over.[28]

And consider this. For years American children have been told that "sticks and stones may break my bones, but names will never hurt me." Interestingly, Egyptians have a nearly opposite saying: "A sharp tongue cuts deeper than the sword." Clearly, there are differences in compliments (and insults) across cultures. Some are very stingy with their praise, while others may be willing to give you the ties off their shirts. And this behavior, like other communication, is often linked to underlying cultural norms.[29]

Criticism as Communication

Of course, the opposite of compliments are *criticisms*. Once again, differences across cultures are apparent. One study found that Americans and Japanese tend to use distinctly different styles when criticizing others. The Japanese are more likely to use "passive" forms of criticism, like references to a third party and humorous or ambiguous comments. Americans are much more apt to criticize directly, sometimes with overt anger that might also be accompanied by constructive suggestions. It appears that the need for group harmony in collectivist cultures impacts how people deliver critical comments. Causing someone to lose face through publicly expressed hostility is something to avoid.

And as we implied earlier, this could help explain why it is difficult to say no directly in some cultures. For instance, many foreigners have experienced irritation at the apparent unwillingness of many Chinese to say no directly to an impossible request. Instead, the response is that the request is said to be "complicated" or that "the responsible person is busy at the moment." Likewise, some feel that many Spaniards would sooner take a business loss than openly admit that they made a mistake. These are common observations in more group-oriented cultures.[30]

Monitoring Others as a Communication Tool

If we assume that styles of communication are often taught and learned early in life, then it's probably the case that people in some cultures tend to be more sensitive to other people in the first place. After all, if you're able to communicate in a way that doesn't offend others, then you must have a keen ability to "read" people and related interpersonal clues. In other words, you have to be sensitive enough to know when there is potential for offense (or if you have already given offense) to those around you.

We've all heard about Americans traveling overseas who have no idea how they are coming across to others. Americans are often characterized as blundering loudly through shops and museums, pompously wondering why foreigners don't speak English and why they can't get ice cubes in their drinks. We hope that this thumbnail sketch of the "ugly American," one that says more about the odd tourist than it does about business managers, is fading. Nevertheless, it raises the question of how attuned Americans are, compared to other cultures, to interpreting communication cues from others. Researchers who have studied this **self-monitoring** issue found that Americans and Australians (individualists) are more self-focused than Koreans, Taiwanese, or Japanese (collectivists), who focused more on situational cues (e.g., context, status) than on themselves. This finding suggests that how to act on cues picked up in social situations is something that Koreans, Taiwanese, and Japanese would generally score higher on than Americans and Australians.[31]

self-monitoring
The tendency for differences to occur in people's ability to understand how they are perceived by others in a social setting

Written Communication

One way to avoid all these potential problems is to communicate via letter or e-mail. If you don't speak the language well, you can at least hire someone with writing expertise or carefully craft the message yourself before sending it. But neither option is as simple as it seems on the surface. Hiring writing help is impractical much of the time, given the volume of written communication businesspeople have to deal with.

EXHIBIT 6.7   *An Example of a Japanese Business Letter*

August 21, 2005

Mr. Kaneyuki Taeshiro
International A & M Corp.
Yokohama, Japan

The summer heat is still lingering, but we hope that you are as prosperous as ever and we thank you very much for your constant patronage.

Concerning your request that the inquiry report be sent you by air mail and that two voucher copies be sent you immediately upon publication, we have asked Hitchcock to meet your request as you see in the enclosed copy. We shall be happy if you find it satisfactory.

It has not yet been long since I took over my duties from my predecessor and I may not be up to your expectations in many respects. But I am determined to do my very best, so please give me your further patronage and guidance.

It will be some time before autumn cool. I pray that you take good care of yourself.

Sincerely,
Kazunobu Marusugi

Source: "Japanese Communication Behavior as Reflected in Letter Writing," S. Haneda & H. Shima, *The Journal of Business Communication*, vol. 19, 1982, pp. 19-32.

And according to one estimate, the average corporate e-mail user can expect thirty to forty-five new messages to appear each day. For international managers, the e-mail volume is likely to be much higher. In fact, the growth of international business may account for a good chunk of the rising use of e-mail. Believe it or not, some managers may routinely spend 50 percent of their office time on e-mail. After all, the convenience of e-mail is seductively attractive—a manager in Dayton, Ohio, can quickly fire off a memo to a counterpart in New Delhi without having to think about what time it is on the other side of the world.[32]

How could you construct a letter or e-mail to get your point across, make your supply order clear, or request some key information? If you're an American, you probably would: (1) use English, (2) keep the letter short and to the point, (3) stress the use of the personal tone (personal pronoun) and (4) avoid flowery or exaggerated language.[33] If you were French, however, you would probably be less concise (maybe the letter would spill onto a second page), and your openings and endings would be much more formal and polite. Americans might perceive these parts of the letter to be "old fashioned" or "too formal."[34] Japanese writers often prefer to hint at something, partly because their language itself is ambiguous and partly because, as we've noted, being overly direct could be seen as condescending or an affront to one's face. Exhibit 6.7 shows a sample letter you might receive from a Japanese business partner. Note that it is typical to begin with set phrases about the season or weather and to close with comments that are similar in form. Clearly, the second paragraph is the "real" message and the remaining text (comments about seasons, humble

EXHIBIT 6.8   *An Analysis of Letters Written to and Received from Foreign Countries*

Writing Element	Foreign Letters Received Using a Writing Element (%)	U.S. Letters Sent Using a Writing Element (%)
Use of personal tone (personal pronouns, informal language, etc.)	25	37
Impersonal tone (formal, passive voice)	25	6
Exaggerated courtesy	44	19
Obvious compliments	16	6
Words omitted from sentences	38	6

Source: Adapted from Kilpatrick, R. H. (1984). International business communication practices. *Journal of Business Communication, 21*, 33–44.

attitude) illustrates the cultural norms about communication. Even bad news would be presented very indirectly.[35]

An interesting study of business letter writing involved asking 100 major U.S. corporations for sample letters that they sent to foreign companies as well as letters they received from those foreign firms. Letters were collected from over twenty countries (e.g., Brazil, Mexico, Italy, Thailand, India, Caribbean countries). The results are summarized in Exhibit 6.8. As you can see, Americans sending letters tend to use an informal, casual tone, especially in contrast to the more formal third-person letters they often receive from other countries. Likewise, Americans appear to avoid "exaggerated" courtesy and compliments that other cultures are likely to consider important. Perhaps one lesson to be learned is that if you want to impress someone from another culture, do your best to imitate that person's written communication style.[36]

That said, keep in mind our earlier warnings about the pitfalls inherent in what you might be saying when sending written communications abroad. You may be successful at being more flowery and more subtle than you normally would, but you could still create communication problems in other areas. For example, suppose you send an e-mail to a Japanese business partner about projected profits. Even if you've done everything else right, just the use of the word *profit* may imply something about long-term, collective growth to your Japanese counterpart. To Americans, however, the meaning of the word tends to be multifaceted, with a core theme of personal gain.[37] If your letter had been sent to a Russian, it's possible that the word *profit* (*prybl*) might suggest exploitation.[38] The phenomenon we're describing here is called **bypassing**. It occurs when people define the same words differently. The insidious thing about bypassing is you may not even know it is happening until well after the communication process is over.

In fact, you may wonder if it's possible to come to grips with this and related communication problems on a systematic basis. Ford Motor Company thinks it has, at least when it comes to internal communications across its facilities around the world. The following International Insights describes Ford's approach. As you'll see, it includes both spoken and written communications. It also provides pictures to go with the words. And nonverbal communication is the subject of our next section.

bypassing
When different people use the same words to mean different things

🌐 International Insights

Ford Builds Global Bridges with Communications . . . to a Point

FORD IS VIEWED BY some as a model for internal cross-cultural communications. How to share know-how and information, especially across borders and cultures, is both critical and an enormous challenge in Ford's far-flung global empire. Ford's answer to this challenge is its Best Practices Replication Process.

Employees all over the world are constantly coming up with great ideas in Ford plants. The trick, however, is to somehow share those ideas so that everyone benefits. After all, a great idea that pops up in, say, Mexico, might be able to help the folks in Chicago, too. In the past five years, some 3,000 superior ideas have migrated across all of Ford's manufacturing facilities. Ford estimates the company has saved over $1.25 billion in the process.

Of course, that begs the question of how Ford actually accomplishes this savings. The answer lies in a forty-two-step replication process that involves a clear set of communication strategies and support mechanisms. Basically, it works like this:

- "Community practice" managers look for outstanding new ideas with proven impact wherever they occur worldwide, visiting plants and speaking with local employees to understand how the ideas work.

- Photos are taken of the idea in action (e.g., new manufacturing process, new tools, etc.). Accompanying the photos is a verbal description. Each idea is "translated" into the appropriate jargon used by the manufacturing groups involved and only then converted to other languages for sharing (e.g., an innovation developed in auto painting by French employees would be described in paint-related terminology first, then translated into Spanish so Mexican employees could understand and use it). These words serve as picture captions.

- The pictures and verbiage are then loaded into an existing Internet template and electronically sent to a "community practice administrator" who assesses the idea and, if things look good, forwards it to every plant manager worldwide who might be able to use it.

- Local managers, after receiving an idea, must then officially report a response (adopt, adapt, or reject and provide justification).

But here's an irony to think about. If Ford's so good at communication, why did things with Bridgestone/Firestone get so out of hand (see our chapter opener)? Some say that if information had been shared about the apparent problems associated with pairing Firestone tires and Ford SUVs, the situation would have been brought under control much more quickly. Both companies apparently had information about the mismatch floating around internally.

Part of the issue may be the difference between internal and external communications. Ford's internal information sharing involved like-minded employees with common goals. Firestone, on the other hand, was an external supplier. Neither company had an external communication network that could share the information necessary to discover the tire problems early on. In addition, when information is widely dispersed, mechanisms have to be put into place to support sharing. Managers have to be judged on how well they communicate and processes and procedures have to be in place to support them. Ford's Best Practices Replication Process is a good illustration of that point. But apparently neither Ford nor Bridgestone/Firestone had parallel processes in place to support interfirm communications.[39]

▶ *Nonverbal Communication*

nonverbal communication
The subtle cues used to communicate within and across cultures, including facial expression, appearance, and body movements

Besides the challenges associated with spoken and written communication, nonverbal communication is also important to consider. **Nonverbal communication** is the transmission of messages without the use of words or writing. That is, above and beyond what is being said, often *how* it's being said carries plenty of information value. How you stand and what you wear, for example, can add credibility (or not) to your presentation. Other examples of nonverbal behavior include facial expressions, body posture and alignment, eye contact (or lack of it), movements, and gestures. We'll discuss how nonverbal communication can vary across countries and cultures.

Interpersonal Space

interpersonal space
The distance we have between ourselves and others when we talk and interact; different spaces are preferred by different cultures

One major nonverbal behavior has to do with the amount of **interpersonal space** we prefer to have between us and others in social interaction. As noted in Chapter 5, we actually "choose" to have a certain amount of space between us and another person when we interact with that person. For instance, women tend to have a closer interpersonal space than men do, and friends are physically closer than strangers. And, as we noted in the earlier chapter, a message can be communicated by space differences and violations of norms across cultures.

Touch

haptics
The use touch as a communication tool

Closely related to the concept of space is the use of touch, or **haptics**, with other people. In general, Americans tend not to use touch all that much, except with people with whom they are very familiar or intimate. Touching in some cultures, however, is a natural and expected part of social interaction and communication. One study addressed this issue by observing people as they sat in outdoor cafés in four different countries. During a one-hour timed period, there were 180 touches in San Juan, Puerto Rico; 110 in Paris; one in Gainesville, Florida; and none in London.[40] Likewise, Americans show two to three times greater physical contact with their parents and about two times the amount of contact with friends than do the Japanese.[41]

Arabs tend to use a lot of touching, eye contact, and other nonverbal behavior. The British, however, tend toward the opposite in their nonverbal style, generally avoiding touch and prolonged eye contact. After interacting with each other, many Arabs might feel that the British are aloof and distant, while many British might wonder why Arabs are so interpersonally aggressive and invasive. Actually, this was the starting point for a study that examined the effect of nonverbal training on impressions of people from other cultures. A group of Britons were trained to perform nonverbal behaviors that were appropriate to Arab culture (such as extensive touching, etc.). Next, this group, and a control group that did not receive training, interacted with Arabs. Later, it was found that the Arabs expressed more liking for the Britons who had received the training.[42] This study underscores that nonverbal communications do differ across cultures and can have an impact on relationships. It also tells us that people can be trained in nonverbal communication styles that will have positive effects on international business partners.

Vocal Qualities as Nonverbal Communication

Vocal qualities such as speed and the loudness of your voice can also project an image and add credibility to your explicit message. This topic has been the subject of a considerable amount of cross-cultural research. One study compared the impression conveyed by a message that was delivered either quickly or slowly, even though the message itself was the same. This was done by having Koreans and Americans watch a videotaped speech about the perils of smoking. Although the content of the information presented was always identical, the presentation was varied so that the message was delivered at either a slow, normal, or fast rate while using a technology that retained its natural sound.[43]

After listening to the message, the Koreans and Americans rated the speaker and the speech on a number of characteristics. Americans thought that a relatively fast voice conveyed power and competence. For the Korean subjects, however, a slow delivery was more effective in increasing the credibility of the speaker. One explanation of this difference is that Koreans live in a more collective culture and, as a result, are more concerned with measuring their words carefully so as not to offend.[44] Likewise, Egyptians and many Middle Eastern countries use phrases that reflect a more colorful and emotional stance toward others (e.g., "my most esteemed colleague," or "my honored guest"). These emotional and complimentary communication patterns are reflective of a value placed on creating a sense of warm friendship and personal relations among business partners. In the Muslim faith, reading the Quran aloud in mosques reflects great oratorical skill and is considered a profound occasion. Likewise, the public "cry" for prayer in this faith, not seen in some other faiths, is another example of emotionally charged communication.[45]

Context Revisited

What we've discussed so far should remind us that how something is communicated carries importance above and beyond what is being said. In Chapter 5 we introduced the concept of high- and low-context cultures. Low-context cultures are those that require explicit statement of facts and conclusions in order for a message to be communicated. High-context cultures, in contrast, are those where the setting, surroundings, or cultural mores provide input into the communication process. We concluded that culture may help you interpret an otherwise ambiguous message. So "context" itself may be the ultimate example of nonverbal communication. In fact, your particular context level should provide clues about communication in your culture.

For example, the degree to which you rely on written or verbal communication may be a function of context.[46] In low-context cultures such as Germany and the United States, people tend to rely on written communication because such a medium allows for a permanent and explicit record of a message. In high-context cultures such as Japan, however, people may prefer verbal and face-to-face communications because these modes are more dynamic and allow for greater subtlety than written messages. Indeed, experts warn that international managers need to understand that many Japanese are reluctant to communicate via letters.[47]

But whether we are writing or not, context seems to affect our communication style. One study found that Japanese business communications were indirect and relied on an intuitive style. In contrast, Americans and Canadians

vocal qualities
Characteristics such as speed and loudness of one's voice that project information in communication

EXHIBIT 6.9   *Characteristics of Communication in Low- and High-Context Cultures*

Communication Feature	Low Context	High Context
General approach	direct/explicit	indirect/complex
Degree of precision	literal/exact	approximate/relative
Dependence on words	high	low
Nonverbal dependence	low	high
View of silence	negative; poor/no communication	positive; good communication
Attention to details	high	low
Value placed on intentions	low	high

Source: Adapted from Victor, D. A. (1992). *International business communication*, 153. New York: HarperCollins.

EXHIBIT 6.10   *Improving Your Cross-Cultural Communication Skills: Four Basic Suggestions*

1. Assume that people are different, not similar.

2. Delay judgment; emphasize description of events, not evaluation or interpretation.

3. Practice putting yourself in other people's shoes. If they were visiting the United States, how might you react to them?

4. Treat your interpretations as temporary and subject to further analysis.

Source: Adapted from Adler, N. J. (1997). *International dimensions of organizational behavior* (3rd Ed.). Cincinnati, OH: South-Western.

were much more direct and relied on a rational, fact-based approach to communication.[48] This is consistent with our argument that high or low context can serve as an important nonverbal backdrop to communication.

Along the same lines, other research found that people who were more verbal were perceived as more attractive by Americans (low context), but those who were less verbal were seen as more attractive in Korea (high context).[49] So if you need to communicate in a high-context culture, face-to-face communication is probably a better bet than written communication.[50] In a low-context culture, however, it's usually wise not to "beat around the bush." Communication there will be more effective if concrete, specific, and logical statements are made. Exhibit 6.9 presents some communication characteristics of high- and low-context cultures.

And the following International Insights illustrates how communication can be tailored to cultures that differ in context. In general, however, it might be best to follow the advice presented in Exhibit 6.10 when communication across cultures is required.

International Insights

Is the Grass Greener in German, English, or French? Putting Communication into Context

IN LOW-CONTEXT cultures, communication has pretty much the same meaning regardless of the situation. As a result, messages should be direct and to the point. For this reason people from low-context cultures often seem rude to those from high-context cultures. Letters, meetings, and other forms of communication in high-context cultures must be approached with nuance and subtlety. In turn, this explains the frustration experienced by low-context communicators.

It's rare to see a message that simultaneously communicates well to both types of cultures. One writer, however, told a story about a sign he saw in Switzerland that was translated into three languages—German, English, and French. Equally important, the words were also modified to reflect the different levels of context preferred by these three cultures. In German, the sign read "Walking on the grass is forbidden." This direct, unambiguous message is typical of a low-context culture like Germany. The English portion of the sign read "Please do not walk on the grass." Clearly, the same message was conveyed, but the change reflected the higher level of context among the English. Finally, the French version read "Those who respect their environment will avoid walking on the grass." This is the highest-context message, reflecting that trait among the French. Although the intent of the message is still the same, it is much more indirect and conjures up related issues that may compel the French to comply with it.[51]

Chapter Summary

In this chapter, we discussed the important topic of communication across cultures. Communication comes in many different forms, yet managers sometimes mistakenly assume that communication is the same everywhere.

The single most important way we communicate with others is through the spoken word. Unfortunately, some countries such as the United States are largely monolingual. Indeed, American businesspeople's foreign language skills rank among the weakest in the world. Popular explanations for this situation include geographic isolation and American ethnocentrism. Some U.S. firms feel that Americans' foreign language deficits are not a big problem since English seems to be the de facto language of world business. But native English speakers still run the risk of major communication problems across borders and cultures, many of which were reviewed in this chapter. Part of the reason for these ongoing problems is that communication is filtered through local cultural values and experiences as well as taking place through a variety of different verbal, written, and nonverbal channels.

International managers also need to be aware of the complex ways that cross-cultural differences can manifest themselves in communication. For instance, cultures differ in terms of how they communicate as well as their responses to embarrassment, apology, compliments, and criticism.

Cross-cultural differences are also apparent in written communication styles. Americans, for instance, tend to keep their letters and memos informal, short, and to the point, generally avoiding flowery or exaggerated language in the process. Other cultures, however, have written communication norms that are inconsistent with these customs. But even if you correctly capture the communication style of your international business colleagues, you could still experience the problem called *bypassing*, the miscommunication that occurs when people define the same words differently.

Nonverbal communication is the transmission of messages without the use of words or writing. We discussed cross-cultural differences in *interpersonal space*, touch or *haptics*, *vocal qualities*, and *context interpretation* as well as how these nonverbal channels can create problems for international managers.

Discussion Questions

1. Explain why both spoken and written communication presents many challenges to cross-cultural communications.

2. How might various dimensions of culture (e.g., collectivism, power distance, and uncertainty avoidance) affect various forms of communication across cultures?

3. How would a country's standing on the context dimension affect its communication patterns? Would high-context cultures prefer written or spoken language as a communication medium? What about the preferences of those from low-context cultures?

Up to the Challenge?

Bridgestone Turns the Americans Loose

AT THE BEGINNING of this chapter we described what many American critics saw as a communications debacle in Bridgestone's handling of its "Firestone problem." Allegations that Firestone's tires were defective cost the firm's Japanese parent hundreds of millions of dollars and put its executives' communication skills to the test. And as we suggested, those skills seemed to leave something to be desired, at least from a cross-cultural communication standpoint.

But after succeeding Yoichiro Kaizaki in 2001, Bridgestone's new president, Shigeo Watanabe, took a different tack in the face of a controversy that wasn't going away. Mr. Watanabe adopted a more aggressive communications effort, one in which Americans did the heavy hitting on Firestone's behalf. Mr. Watanabe put the new American CEO of Firestone, John Lampe, in charge of the effort rather than putting Japanese managers in the media limelight. He also gave Mr. Lampe the authority to act without always having to solicit Tokyo's approval first, an unusual step for most Japanese multinationals, especially when such critical decisions are involved.

Given these freedoms, Mr. Lampe went on the offensive. In May 2001, he announced that Firestone would end its century-long status as a Ford supplier. Why? Because the car giant supposedly kept blaming Firestone tires for accidents in Ford Explorers without owning up to alleged safety problems with its SUVs. Bridgestone supported Lampe's decision and his more aggressive approach out of concern that the communication battle was being lost in the United States. Something needed to be done to push back effectively against Ford's public accusations, and the dramatic announcement about cutting ties with Ford was designed, at least in part, to do just that.

And that was just the beginning. CEO Lampe became very active in speaking out publicly on Firestone's behalf. That contrasted sharply with the practice of his predecessor, Masatoshi Ono, perhaps best known for his awkward exchanges with U.S. senators at an earlier public hearing. Speaking of which, Mr. Lampe put a well-known lobbyist in a Washington office to give Firestone a more prominent voice with the U.S. government. Where things will eventually end up with Firestone, its tire problems, and its reputation is still playing out. But from a communications standpoint, the critics seemed to like Bridgestone's new moves. As one auto analyst put it, "It's a credit to the management of Bridgestone in Tokyo that they did replace the linguistically challenged [Mr. Ono] with an American who is prepared to trade punches with [then-Ford CEO] Jacques Nasser."

But what's your assessment of this latest communication effort by Bridgestone? Is it a better match culturally for an American audience? And even if it is, will it be enough to salvage Firestone's damaged brand name in the long run? If not, what other steps would you recommend? Finally, how should Bridgestone have communicated about this problem from the beginning?[52]

International Development

Moshi, Moshi: Overcoming Cultural Barriers to Communication

Purpose

To understand how culture can impact verbal communication in a telephone conversation and to suggest alternative ways to conduct telephone conversations effectively in a given cross-cultural context.

Instructions

Read the following telephone transcript, either inside or outside class. John Smith, an American marketing manager from Weyerhaeuser, is trying to speak with his Japanese counterpart at Rising Sun Company, a Mr. Yamamoto, about a possible business deal.

The conversation:

The phone rings and a woman answers.

Woman: *Moshi, moshi* ["Hello, Hello"].

Smith: Hello, this is John Smith. May I please speak with Mr. Yamamoto?

Woman: Oh, I'm sorry. Who is calling, please?

Smith: This is John Smith calling for Mr. Yamamoto.

Woman: I'm sorry, what is the name of your company?

Smith: I'm calling from Weyerhaeuser.

Woman: I'm sorry, could you spell that please?

Smith: W-E . . .

Woman: I'm sorry, "W-Z"?

Smith: No, W-E-Y-E-R-H-A-E-U-S-E-R. Is Mr. Yamamoto there?

Woman: Oh, Weyerhaeuser. Thank you very much. Your name please?

Smith: John Smith.

Woman: And who do you wish to speak to?

Smith: As I said, Mr. Yamamoto.

Woman: I'm sorry, which department? We have many Yamamotos.

Smith: Uh . . . of course. Mr. Yamamoto in the international marketing department.

Woman: Thank you very much, wait just a minute please. (*Smith is put on hold. Music plays in the background. Meanwhile, a phone rings in a big room where many employees are working at their desks. Someone passing by picks up the phone.*)

Man: *Moshi, moshi.*

Smith: Hello, Mr. Yamamoto?

Man: Oh no, this is Suzuki. Who is calling please?

Smith: This is John Smith calling for Mr. Yamamoto.

Man: I'm sorry, what is the name of your company?

Smith: Weyerhaeuser.

Man: Could you spell that please?

Smith: W-E-Y-E-R-H-A-E-U-S-E-R.

Man: Thank you very much. Just a minute please. (*On hold again. Music plays.*)

Man: I'm very sorry, but Mr. Yamamoto is in a meeting. Could you call again later?

Intensely frustrated, Smith hangs up the phone after "wasting" an international call.

Your instructor will divide the class into small groups of three to six to answer the following questions (15–20 minutes). Your group can present its answers, followed by a general class discussion about international communication and its implications (30 minutes). Alternatively, your instructor may lead a general class discussion about the following questions:

- Why is Smith so frustrated? Would you be in this situation? What cultural factors explain Smith's reaction (and perhaps yours)?

- What mistakes did Smith make, in your opinion? Why? How do Japanese culture and business practices fit in here?
- How would you recommend that Smith approach the call if he had to do it all over again? What specific advice would you offer? Why?

- What if the cultural context was different? For instance, what if Mr. Smith was trying to reach a counterpart in Cairo? How might that shape Mr. Smith's approach to the conversation?

Source: Elashmawi, F., & Harris, P. H. (1993). *Multicultural management: New skills for global success,* 108–111. Houston: Gulf. Reprinted by permission.

Tapping into the Global Network

We Have Ways of Making You Talk: Researching a Foreign Language

Purpose

To examine a few basic elements of a language with which you are not familiar.

Instructions

1. Select a language with which you are not at all familiar. Research some basics about this language and prepare a few statements and greetings from the language to present to class (more detail on this is provided below). Your instructor might want to assign individual students or groups to various languages in order to make sure that several different languages are covered and to make sure that the groups have no familiarity with the language basics. Either way, we recommend looking at the following website that provides briefings on many different languages spoken throughout the world:
   http://123world.com/ languages/index.html
   It is unlikely, for example, that many students (or professors!) are very familiar with languages such as Afrikaans, Arabic, Dutch, Farsi, Hindi, Japanese, Russian, Swahili, Turkish, or many others, and this site will provide many such choices.

2. Once you choose a language, you should begin to gather information that will give you a bit of insight into some basic features of the language and those speaking it. In particular, we recommend you discover the following (with possible supplements provided by your instructor):
   - Where is the language primarily spoken, and how many people speak it? Where

else has it been adopted (if anywhere)?
   - What are the origins of the language and how is it related to other languages and other language families?
   - What is unique or specific to the language (e.g., its grammar, syntax, accent marks, etc.)?
   - Present several basic phrases in that language to the class or in your report. If the report is given verbally, you should try to pronounce those phrases or use some of the sources below to present the phrases to the class (several sites offer .wav files that almost any class computer could read so that the phrase could be heard in a native tongue).
   - What types of challenges might native speakers of this language face when communicating to English speakers? That is, what are some transfer issues they might encounter if they tried to speak in English (e.g, tones, accents, sounds that are wildly different) and if their communication were translated into English by others?
   - Do you have any recommendations for communication training or a possible set of guidelines or advice to give speakers of this language?

3. Once you've chosen a language and considered the above questions, you can begin your research. There are several good sources to begin your work on this assignment (please also see the 123world.com site above):
   - **The Linguist List (http://linguistlist.org/sp/Dict.html)**

This super site, run by Eastern Michigan and Wayne State Universities, presents an amazing number of bilingual and multilingual dictionaries and translation tools. Some of the nearly 200 such dictionaries offer complete translation of phrases that you enter in English.

- **The Linguist List Subpage (http://linguistlist.org/sp/LangAnalysis. html#25)** This page is also part of The Linguist List, but it could be missed in all the wealth of information provided on the site. So, we draw your attention here also. Presented here are a large number of links to language families and many language meta-sites. Some of these will be helpful for the background research required in this assignment.

- **I Love Languages, Guide to Languages on the Web (http://www.ilovelanguages.com/index. php?category=Languages%7CBy+ Language)** This is a wonderful source for common phrases, grammar, and other general features of nearly fifty major languages.

- **Yamada Language Guides (http://babel.uoregon.edu/yamada/ guides.html)** This is another site with a large amount of information about languages and language groups.

7

Conducting Negotiations and Managing Conflicts

Learning Objectives

After reading this chapter, you should be able to:

▸ Appreciate that miscommunication can create conflict among people across cultures.

▸ Diagnose and explain some of the causes of cross-cultural conflict.

▸ Understand some of the ways that cross-cultural conflicts can be managed, and the positive role that negotiations can play.

▸ Explain and apply the four main stages of international negotiations and how cultural values impact the way those stages unfold.

INTERNATIONAL CHALLENGE

Two Sides of a Common Border

YOU'VE PROBABLY READ about negotiations between American companies and their foreign counterparts over various deals. Likewise, the news is full of stories about conflicted negotiations between governments and foreign companies, again over a wide variety of issues. In these cases, much is often made of how the lens of culture shapes each side's views and tactics, often to the point where the parties are looking past each other. You may say to yourself, however, that you don't have to look beyond your own company (or maybe even your family) for examples of conflict and negotiation, and you're probably right. But regardless, we do know that the increasing globalization of business has also internationalized workforces in many companies. And therein lies the potential for increased conflict, even if it doesn't come to a head. As you know or can guess, negotiations are a fact of life within as well as between companies.

So here's the situation we ask you to consider. You're in a room observing negotiations between two departments in the same international company. The issue at hand is who will control the process of buying computers for the firm. On one side of the table are two American managers, who represent the operations area. Operations wants to be able to buy its own equipment and is focused on predictable installation, equipment quality, and outstanding maintenance. On the other side sit two Mexican managers, who represent purchasing. They believe it is their responsibility to do the buying, and their top priority is price, getting the best equipment for the money. Both departments have about the same amount of power, status, and authority within the company. Finally, time is pretty short, especially since major computer needs are on the horizon and actual purchases have to be made.

But as negotiations unfold, it quickly becomes apparent that a clash of cultures that goes beyond any differences of opinion about computers is also occurring. Consider this exchange between one of the Mexican purchasing managers and his American counterpart from operations:

MEXICAN: I think it will better for the total organization, and [smiling] don't forget that we all work for the same company. It will be viewed as better from all points in the corporation if we, the purchasing department, are the ones that take charge of negotiating with the vendor. Although I fully understand that we have to get all the information from you who are going to be using the equipment . . . from a quality of process and strength of position view it really is a better and more natural position to have us talking to them and consulting with you on whether or not the prices seem reasonable. [Is about to continue but the American interrupts . . . a recurring pattern throughout the negotiations.]

AMERICAN: It's unacceptable to us that operations be totally left out of the negotiation process . . . you people have short-term goals regarding price . . . we've got to live with this product month to month . . . so you people zip in there, do your thing, save your 20 percent, look great to the company, and we've got to live with a shoddy product because you've pissed off the vendor, low-balled the price, and then the vendor comes in with a shoddy installation.

MEXICAN: Are you aware that I allowed you to talk? Well, be aware and consider it next time.

AMERICAN: [Ignoring the previous comment] Since the computers are being bought for our department, we've got the bottom line say . . . we understand the technical aspects better than you. Now I want to get this done in a short amount of time so I want to cut to the quick of the matter. I don't want to deal with someone who looks like they are just a messenger.

MEXICAN: I feel, as we say, like the shoemaker to his shoes. We are in the purchasing position, that is precisely our function. When one needs a blender at home, the one who decides what kind to get is the one who will use it. But the one who decides to buy it or not is the one who brings home the money. Excuse me for being so stubborn in this respect, but you could buy a pen, but what do you know about buying a ship? You don't know about ships.

As you read through this chapter, you'll learn how culture can impact international conflict and negotiation. As you'll see, tactics and strategies may to an extent be culturally driven. We'll also discuss ways that international managers can overcome the challenges represented by these issues. In the meantime, what are the specific negotiation tactics, styles, and strategies being used by the Mexican and American in this example? How might they illustrate the cultural values and perspectives of each?

After you've pondered these questions, take a look at the *Up to the Challenge?* box at the end of this chapter for some insights into this exchange.[1]

▶ *A World of Conflict*

As Chapter 6 vividly illustrated, communicating effectively in an international business environment can be quite a challenge. There are many ways that a message can get distorted, confused, or missed altogether across cultures, leaving the door wide open for potential differences and disagreements. In other words, miscommunication can lead to **conflict**. Conflict occurs when disagreements and friction arise in the course of social interaction because of opposing interests, cultural differences in communication styles, and the like. Compounding the communication challenge today is the fact that international managers are more like diplomats than ever, with an increasingly burdensome set of "missions" to carry out—missions that often involve serious disagreements.

conflict
When disagreements and friction arise in the course of interaction because of opposing interests or cultural differences

For example, international managers may have to handle foreign labor strife; negotiate with overseas vendors, clients, partners, and suppliers; lobby governments; soothe relations with outside pressure groups over environmental or other issues; and somehow convince employees with conflicting interests to work together.[2] Additionally, a major reason that firms send expatriates abroad, at least for the short or medium term, is to fix a problem and resolve a conflict.

Not all conflict is bad. In fact, sometimes conflict helps focus people's attention to get things done. In any case, conflict is incredibly common. American managers spend about 20 percent of their time at work dealing with conflict situations.[3] And given all the cross-cultural communication problems we reviewed in the previous chapter, it wouldn't surprise us to learn that conflict occupies an even greater portion of time for managers with international responsibilities.

Consequently, this chapter will review some of the causes of conflict and how to manage it effectively in an international context. And we'll devote a considerable amount of space to the subject of negotiation in international business. As you'll see, how the negotiation process is viewed, as well as the tactics that are used, are the result of many factors. One of the most prominent factors is culture. Failing to understand the role of culture in negotiations will cause conflict and, in the end, undoubtedly cost you business.

Cultural Causes of Conflict in International Management

Given the stakes, international managers need a good understanding of the basic causes of conflict. Some of these causes we've already addressed, at least indirectly. For instance, *language* difficulties represent one such cause. As we pointed out, a misinterpretation because of a poor translation can cause anger on both sides. We also know that differing *cultural norms* may give rise to conflict, especially when each side lacks an appreciation or understanding of the other's cultural frame of reference. More than one American manager has been greatly offended to be kept waiting well beyond a scheduled appointment time in a foreign country, with some even storming out at this "offense."[4] Of course, in this example, the resulting conflict could have been avoided had the American been aware that they were bringing a monochronic perspective about time into a polychronic culture. In addition, had the meeting actually taken place, different norms about the directness of communication (e.g., low vs. high context) might have created conflict and, possibly, a loss of business.

The *decision-making methods* a company uses can also be a potential source of conflict, especially if there's a mismatch with employee values. Some international firms are structured to be highly centralized, with power and decision-making control concentrated in a few people at the top. Other firms, however, operate in a more dispersed fashion, with decision-making control decentralized and pushed down into lower ranks. But employees in high-power-distance cultures may have a preference for centralized and hierarchical decision making. They see it as perfectly acceptable for those higher up in the firm to make important decisions without any of their input. In fact, in such cultures, attempting to decentralize decision making by implementing participative management strategies (e.g., involving employees in setting goals) can backfire, as Exhibit 7.1 suggests. Clearly, conflict in this situation could have been avoided if the American manager had understood the Greek preference for centralization.

EXHIBIT 7.1   *The Road to Conflict Is Paved with Interpretation: A Conversation between a Greek and an American*

Words Spoken	Perception/Interpretation by Each Party
AMERICAN: How long will it take you to finish the report?	AMERICAN: I asked him to participate GREEK: His behavior makes no sense. He is the boss. Why doesn't he tell me?
GREEK: I don't know. How long should it take?	AMERICAN: He has refused to take responsibility. GREEK: I asked him for an order.
AMERICAN: You are in the best position to analyze the time requirements.	AMERICAN: I press him to take responsibility for his actions. GREEK: What nonsense—I'd better give him an answer.
GREEK: Ten days.	AMERICAN: He lacks the ability to estimate his time; this estimate is totally inadequate.
AMERICAN: Take 15. Is it agreed? You will do it in 15 days?	AMERICAN: I offer a contract. GREEK: These are my orders: 15 days.

Source: From *Interpersonal Behavior* by H.C. Triandis. © 1997 Brooks/Cole. Reprinted with permission of Brooks/Cole, an imprint of the Wadsworth Group, a division of Thomson Learning. Fax 800 730-2215

A final cause of conflict that we will mention is the *propensity* for people in a given culture to be involved with conflict in the first place. That is, some cultures go to great lengths to avoid friction between individuals and groups. Indeed, in collective cultures, many different social mechanisms are in place to make conflict less likely to occur. For example, we've mentioned the Japanese tendency to use indirect ways to say no as a way to smooth interpersonal relations. Yet paradoxically this tendency can be extremely frustrating and conflict-provoking when it is used across cultures. Again, the risk of damaging conflict may be highest when a cultural mismatch occurs with another party—say, an American who thinks that conflict should be addressed openly and aggressively. Although a tendency to be open and blunt may be seen as honest and good within American culture, few traits may be more off-putting to a Japanese.

Managing Conflict Effectively

So if conflict is nearly inevitable in international business, how can you manage it effectively to minimize the damage, if not prevent it from happening? To begin with, international managers need to understand that there are different styles for resolving conflict once it occurs.[5] Exhibit 7.2 shows a layout of these styles. Basically, this approach balances concern for your own outcomes against concern for outcomes of others with whom you are interacting. The result is the five relatively distinct styles that are portrayed in the exhibit. There's plenty of research on these styles, although most studies focus on American employees. Of course, even within a culture there are individual differences in style preferences. You can probably think of people who like to confront conflict head-on (**competition**), while others with a similar cultural heritage prefer to try to

competition
A conflict style where one prefers to deal head-on with the issues

EXHIBIT 7.2   *A Typology of Conflict Styles*

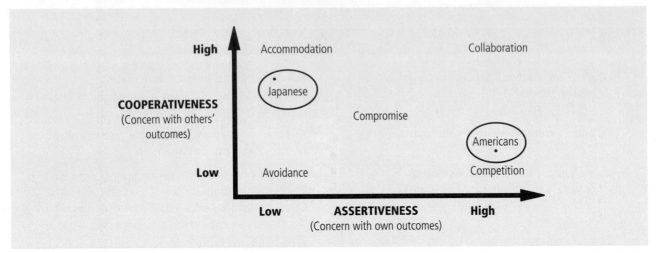

Source: Adapted from Thomas, K. W. (1976). Conflict and conflict management. In M. D. Dunnette (Ed.), *Handbook of Industrial and Organizational Behavior.* Chicago: Rand McNally, 889–935.

avoidance
A conflict style of that entails avoiding as long as possible any disagreements

accommodation
A conflict style that involves high concern with the interests of others, sometimes at the expense of one's own interests

compromise
Conflict style that involves using middle positions whereby both parties give up something to reach an agreement

collaboration
An uncommon conflict-management style that involves skills at inventing new and creative options where both parties "win"

ignore it altogether (**avoidance**). **Accommodation** is another style, one that often involves giving in to the other party. **Compromise** is a familiar term to most, and this term refers to a style where we make trade offs back and forth in order to reach a resolution to conflict. Finally, a relatively rare style called **collaboration** seems to exist. A skilled person might deal with conflict by suggesting new and creative options that are good for both sides, and don't necessarily involve tradeoffs (as in compromise). Once people learn or choose a style, they tend to stick with that approach—it becomes part of their personality. But research does show that some general, culture-based tendencies exist that can distinguish how people tend to handle conflict

For instance, it appears that many Americans like a good argument. One study compared Japanese and Americans on a scale that measured the tendency to either embrace or avoid arguments. The results showed that the Japanese were less inclined to argue in the first place, but once they were involved, their degree of argumentativeness was less than Americans'.[6] Based on this and other studies, some experts have gone so far as to say that Americans feel stimulated by an argument and enjoy the intellectual challenge it provides.[7] The Japanese, on the other hand, are not so fond of open conflict and may even feel mortified that open conflict has occurred and worry that it may disturb group harmony. Based on these findings, it is reasonable to conclude that Americans tend toward the competitive conflict management style while Japanese tend to fall in the avoidance area shown in Exhibit 7.2. That said, we would remind you that these generalizations may not apply to individual Americans or Japanese.

Other studies have compared Americans with people from a variety of other countries on their conflict styles. In general, these studies show that people from collectivist cultures tend to prefer a conflict avoidance style while people from individualistic cultures tend to prefer a direct, competitive style when dealing with conflict. Examples of countries with a collectivist orientation include China, Japan, Korea, and Mexico, while the United States has been the primary individualistic culture studied.[8] So as we suggested earlier, Americans prefer more active, confrontational approaches, while Koreans, Chinese, and Mexicans tend to use more avoidance-type approaches when handling conflict.[9]

Experts also point out that conflict preferences may vary depending on who is party to the conflict. Managers from Turkey and Jordan, for example, tend to use an *overall* conflict-handling style that isn't all that different from their American counterparts. However, when peers are involved, Turkish and Jordanian managers tend to avoid conflict; with subordinates, they take a much more forceful approach when conflict erupts.[10]

Conflict preferences are deeply rooted in culture and extend to a variety of different areas. For instance, people in individualistic cultures often prefer an **equity norm** ("to each according to what they deserve") when dividing up organizational resources.[11] For these individualists, when pay raises for subordinates are determined, individual contributions should be closely related to the eventual raise. In these individualistic cultures (e.g., the United States) this is the "natural" way to figure out who deserves what. In collective cultures, however, people have a tendency to prefer an **equality norm** (every group member gets a more or less equal share of rewards).

Our point here is that these preferences may in part result from inherent cultural differences in dealing with conflict. As we mentioned in a previous chapter, the Japanese say that "the nail that sticks up gets hammered down." Consequently, displaying a direct, out-in-the-open conflict style is a "nail" that sticks out in Japan and other collectivist cultures. In the United States, however, there are many myths and stories that celebrate rugged individualists (the "nails") who oppose and conflict with the majority. Likewise, the tendency to engage in conflict in the first place is also related to the cultural dimension of uncertainty avoidance. Those cultures strong on this value tend to avoid conflict.

Clearly, then, there are cultural prescriptions about how to deal with conflict. There is perhaps no better place to look for those prescriptions than at Disney, an icon of American culture. The U.S. pavilion at Disney's Epcot Center used to display statues that symbolize national virtues. The statues were said to represent the most important American attributes or values. Four of the statues represented "individualism," "self-reliance," "independence," and "freedom." It's unlikely that these four values would stand out in any dramatic way to most Americans. Yet people from other cultures often focus on these attributes because they are so different from their own values. As we've noted, while individualism is a virtue for Americans, it can have negative connotations (e.g., selfishness) in other cultures.[12]

To this point we haven't really explored how people *respond* when conflict rears its head in the form of anger, frustration, or loss of face. What happens in an international business interaction, say, when an American manager gives a Chinese employee a poor performance rating? This feedback could violate social norms in China and result in an enormous loss of face. The result could destroy the employee's commitment and ultimately lead to poorer performance. Likewise, consider a situation where a Mexican host is visibly upset after a visiting American manager says they need to do much more to modernize their "inefficient" plant. In both cases, the reactions to the conflict that's been provoked provide an opening to "repair the damage" to a loss of face or reputation. An astute manager would be sensitive to these messages and might respond with an appropriate **account** (basically an explanation for a negative action that, in part, soothes the pain). Better still, the astute manager might be wise to offer an account even before taking what may be seen as a negative or conflict-provoking step by someone from another culture.

equity norm
A cultural preference for group members to get rewards based on their contributions to the organization

equality norm
A cultural preference for every group member to get a more or less equal share of rewards that functions to keep conflict at a minimum

accounts
Explanations for negative actions that in part are designed to sooth the pain of such actions

EXHIBIT 7.3   *International Conflict Management: Linking Culture and Face to the Account-Giving Process*

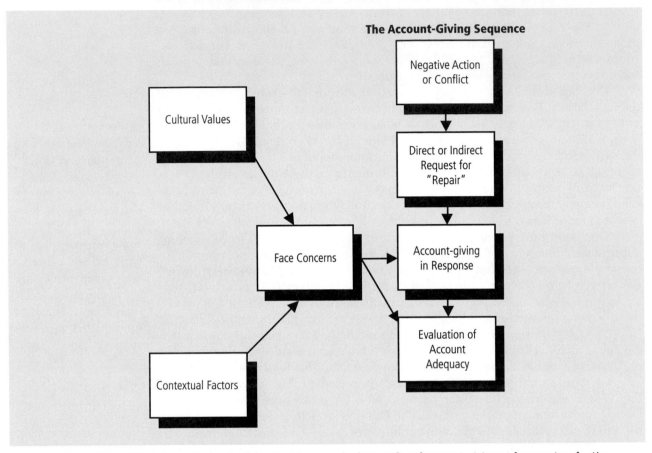

Source: Adapted from Tata, J. (2000). Toward a theoretical framework of intercultural account-giving and account evaluation. *International Journal of Organizational Analysis, 8,* 158.

mitigating accounts
Explanations that are designed to lower tensions caused by the original action or conflict

concession
A type of mitigating account where the person acknowledges the conflict, takes responsibility for it, and offers regrets or perhaps even compensation

The whole issue of managing account-giving across cultures is an emerging area of research in international management. Current thinking is that culture can impact how various actions are perceived and what kinds of accounts might serve to mollify any perceived slights. So managers could benefit from understanding how other people's values might shape both the perceptions of the actions they take in the first place and the accounts they use to explain them later. Take a look at Exhibit 7.3. It provides an overview of the account-giving process we're describing here.

From a conflict management perspective, it's the last two steps in the account sequence that matter most. After all, some negative feedback might be necessary or unavoidable. But a manager's response if offense is taken may go a long way toward determining whether the situation is ultimately salvaged or not.

On one end of the spectrum are **mitigating accounts**, which generally are designed to lower tensions caused by the original action or conflict. For instance, a **concession** is a type of mitigating account where the person acknowledges the conflict, takes responsibility for it, and offers regrets or even some form of compensation (e.g., "It was my poor choice of words that gave offense. For that

I am very sorry."). A **justification** is an account that often provides a less extreme form of mitigation. Here the person admits that the action or conflict has occurred but claims that it wasn't intentional or couldn't be helped under the circumstances (e.g., "I was late for our meeting because an accident on the road caused a major delay."). An **ideological account** may be less satisfying to another party. Here the person owns up to actions taken or the conflict provoked but makes the argument that this was legitimate under the circumstances (e.g., "The poor performance rating I gave you will help make you a better employee in the long run."). Finally, a **refusal** is an account where the person either denies the existence of any negative actions or declines to share the reason for taking them (e.g., "Yes, I'm going to refuse to go along with your request and let's let it go at that—it would take me half the day to explain why."). As you might suspect, this type of account may aggravate rather than reduce tensions.[13]

What would be helpful at this point is a conflict management road map that could explain how specific cultural values are linked to perceived conflicts (e.g., about losing face), the accounts that will be used, and how accounts will be evaluated. It would be very useful to know, for example, which accounts would work best in certain cultural circumstances.

Unfortunately, construction of such a map is very complex. For instance, there's evidence that when Americans or other foreigners make a significant effort to adapt to the interaction rules of collective cultures (e.g., Japanese), it may be viewed quite positively (i.e., as a sign of respect). But let's say we reverse this scenario. If foreigners try to fit in with the interaction and conflict management patterns found in the United States or other individualistic cultures, it may buy them precious little. Why? Because individualists may view such adaptation efforts as failing to present yourself honestly as you really are. In any case, the road map is incomplete at this point and more research needs to be done to flesh out all the issues. And another interesting issue that's starting to receive attention is the nature of work-family conflict. It turns out that cultural factors may impact how work-family overload occurs and the problems it creates. Take a look at the following International Insights to see what we mean.

Nevertheless, we present Exhibit 7.4 as a partial effort to "connect the dots" when it comes to account giving in conflict management. As you can see, it illustrates how combining two of Hofstede's cultural value dimensions (individualism–collectivism and masculinity–femininity) relate to concerns about face and the account-giving and account-receiving process. You might remember from Chapter 4 that masculine cultures tend to stress values like autonomy, achievement, and assertiveness, while feminine cultures tend to place more emphasis on relationships and cooperation.[14]

Knowing how to manage accounts effectively in a cross-cultural negotiation context would be extremely valuable. Negotiations that reach an impasse are also part of the process. Speaking of negotiation, there's been quite a bit of research about how that process unfolds and the factors, including culture, that impact it. We'll turn our attention to negotiation next.

▶ *Understanding International Negotiation*

Negotiation is perhaps one of the best ways to avoid conflict or at least keep it to a minimum. **Negotiation** is the process of communicating back and forth with another person or group with the explicit purpose of making a joint decision or

justification
An account that provides a less extreme form of mitigation; a person admits action occurred, but claims it wasn't intentional or couldn't be helped

ideological accounts
A person owns up to his or her part in the conflict, but argues that it was legitimate under the circumstances

refusals
A form of account whereby one either denies the existence of one's negative actions or where one declines to provide the reason for one's action

negotiation
The process of communicating back and forth with another person or group with the explicit purpose of making a joint decision or reaching agreement about a dispute

🌐 International Insights

Work-Family Conflict: Putting in the Hours . . . for the Family

MANY PEOPLE THINK OF *work-family conflict* as largely a Western phenomenon. But globalization may be changing all that, including in developing nations such as China. That said, attitudes toward work, family, and the relationship between them are inextricably linked to cultural values. So while it's reasonable to expect that employees in the United States and China will both experience work-family conflict, its nature may be quite different in the two countries. In fact, that's a prediction that researchers are starting to explore. And the answers have implications for how a company should

respond to and deal with work-family conflict in their international workforces.

One recent study addressed how time impacted the work-family equation in the United States and China. We're sure most of you can relate to this—time spent on work can make it impossible to spend any "quality time" with family. Likewise, you may start finding it harder to do as much at work if you're cutting out early to engage in family activities. Interestingly, scholars have suggested that individualistic cultures like that in the United States may place a higher value on personal family time than

---

reaching agreement about a particular issue or dispute. Consequently, all negotiations have four key elements:

- Multiple parties (two or more)
- Mixed motives (i.e., areas of disagreement or conflict, but also some interests in common)
- Movement of the parties (e.g., shifting or changing positions over time)
- A goal of reaching an agreement[15]

Basic Approaches to International Negotiation

As we've said, because of the ubiquitous nature of international business negotiation, it has been studied heavily. Indeed, there are two well-established approaches to studying international negotiations.

macrostrategic negotiation
An approach to negotiation that focuses on how the relative bargaining power of the parties impacts outcomes

The **macrostrategic** approach focuses on how negotiation outcomes are affected by the relative bargaining power of the parties. For instance, consider a situation where an American multinational wants to set up operations in a developing country—say, Tanzania. To pursue that, the American firm may end up in a series of negotiations with the Tanzanian government (along with other local constituencies). As the negotiation issues shift from initial entry to site acquisition to ongoing operations, the relative power of the parties may also shift, as illustrated in Exhibit 7.5. Basically, a multinational's leverage tends to decrease once it has made an initial investment, while the local government's power tends to increase. We will address the strategic issues associated with international market entry in the next section of the book (Chapters 8–10).[16] For now, however, we will focus on another approach to international negotiations—the **comparative** perspective.

comparative negotiation
An approach that emphasizes what happens between negotiators during face-to-face interactions and how those shape the results

The primary emphasis of this approach is on what happens between negotiators during face-to-face interactions and how those interactions shape the

do more collectivistic societies, especially in Asia. This hypothesis seems to run counter to our image of Americans as career obsessed and our perception of Chinese as intensely family oriented.

But the basic idea is that when push comes to shove, individualistic Americans will put self-interest (time with family) above collective interest (work). The more collectivistic Chinese may do just the opposite. Another perspective on this issue is that in the United States careers are viewed as vehicles for personal achievement. The stated ethic at least is that "a good family person" won't let personal ambitions harm the family. And having a solid family environment is ostensibly part of the high "American quality of life." In contrast, Chinese employees often seek work as a vehicle for bringing prosperity and honor to their families. So working 120 hours a week and not seeing much of your family would be considered a personal sacrifice you are making for the family rather than a selfish statement about your career objectives that hurts your family in the process.

In short, family demands may cause more work-family conflicts in the United States than in China, while the reverse may be true for work demands. And that's exactly what the study found. Of course, more research needs to be done to tease out the exact role of culture and other factors such as economic development. Nevertheless, managers in China, or anywhere else for that matter, should first try to identify the source of work-family conflict before trying to design "balanced" workplaces that reduce employee strain and stress. Like so many other issues in international management, one size may not fit all when it comes to work-family conflict.[17]

outcomes that result. Consequently, a lot of attention is paid to how cultural factors may affect the way the negotiation process unfolds between individual negotiators.[18]

▶ *Frameworks for Understanding the Process of International Negotiations*

Several frameworks have been developed that can help managers understand the international negotiation process from a comparative perspective. We'll consider two of these frameworks here. The first framework is the broadest. It describes five sets of factors where cultural issues may be relevant in international negotiations, including the frame of reference of the negotiators. This framework is displayed in Exhibit 7.6. However, the exact relationships between the factors listed have yet to be fully researched. Despite this, the framework presents a valuable guide for helping managers grasp the cultural forces that may impact international negotiation outcomes.

The second framework focuses more narrowly on four specific stages that the negotiation process goes through once people begin interacting face to face. Once again, the emphasis is on how cultural differences may impact interactions and outcomes. We'll consider this framework in some depth. First, however, it's best to consider all the planning and preparation that should go into a negotiation prior to beginning the first of the four important steps. So, we'll start by providing advice about this part of the process before we present the four-stage model of negotiations.

Preparing for Negotiations Americans have long been accused of failing to adequately prepare for international negotiations. And concerns about the consequences of inadequate preparation have been around for a long time. Over

EXHIBIT 7.4   *The Use of and Reactions to Accounts in International Conflict: The Impact of Culture and Face*

Cultural Value Combination	Concern with Face	Accounts Most Likely to Be Used	Likelihood of Aggravating Accounts Being Viewed Negatively
Collectivistic-feminine (e.g., Thailand)	High	**Mitigating**	High
Collectivistic-masculine (e.g., Mexico)		(concessions)	
		(justifications)	
Individualistic-feminine (e.g., Sweden)		(ideological)	
Individualistic-masculine (e.g., U.S.)	Low	(refusals/denials)	Low
		Aggravating	

Source: Adapted from Tata, J. (2000). Toward a theoretical framework of intercultural account-giving and account evaluation. *International Journal of Organizational Analysis, 8,* 169.

thirty years ago, one expert cautioned American executives to pay close attention to the Japanese negotiating style. He reasoned that if Americans did a good job of studying Japanese customs and negotiation tactics, the United States would be much better off. In particular, he thought that this kind of homework would help prevent the U.S. trade deficit with Japan from rising to the then "impossible level of $4 billion" (you may recall from Chapter 1 that the U.S. goods deficit with Japan exceeded $65 billion in 2003).[19]

Much of the advice that's been around for decades about how to prepare for international negotiations is still sound. And, since the same advice continues to be echoed today, repetition may indeed be the sincerest form of flattery. Moreover, that advice is often supported by research on international negotiation success and failure.[20] So consider the following general suggestions before undertaking an international negotiation:

- International negotiation is notoriously complex and replete with opportunities to fail; never underestimate it.

- Take whatever steps are necessary to gain an in-depth understanding of the other side—not just on issues of substance, but how their negotiating styles, view of the process, and cultural values may come into play. (Exhibit 7.6 should prove very helpful here in terms of laying out the various issues that need to be considered.) It can be a big mistake to think that everyone is similar to you.[21]

- Seek outside help if the necessary expertise or knowledge is missing inside the company (plenty of consultants and cultural trainers are available for international negotiations).

EXHIBIT 7.5   *Setting Up Shop in Developing Countries: How Negotiating Strength May Shift over Time*

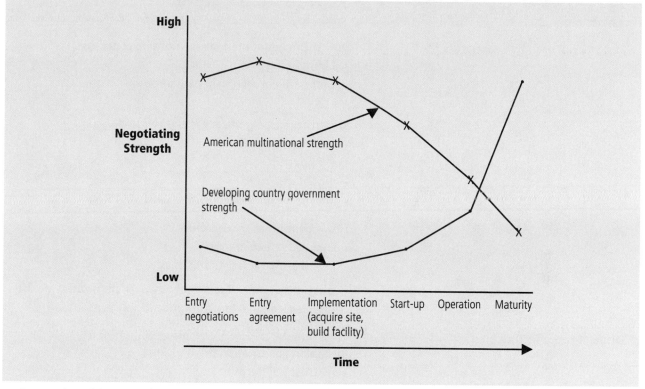

Source: Adapted from Stoever, W. A. (1979). Renegotiations: The cutting edge of relations between MNCs and LDCs. *Columbia Journal of World Business*, Spring, 7.

- If negotiators' language skills are insufficient, use interpreters who are hired by your company (don't rely on interpreters provided by the other side).

- Consider the use of an international negotiating team (more on this later).

- Be prepared to spend significant time and effort on the preparation process. Don't shortchange this process or be impatient in collecting information.

The last point is one that many Americans have trouble with. For example, an American manager leaving the United States for a negotiation in Asia generally should be prepared for a long stay. Many Americans still assume that they can spend a few days on the ground in places such as Japan or China and quickly wrap up a negotiation. In fact, when we were in Shanghai a few years ago, we spoke with an executive from an American automotive company. He groused that he had already "wasted" a week in the country without getting anything done other than "eating and drinking" with officials. And he was angry about having to choose between spending an unknown and indefinite period of time in the country or simply calling the effort a failure and going home. Unfortunately, many people from Asian countries expect a good bit of time to be spent on establishing a rapport, whereas Americans want to "get down to

EXHIBIT 7.6   *Where Culture Comes In: A Framework for Understanding International Negotiations*

General Category	Elements to Consider
Basic model used by negotiators	How the negotiation process might be conceived: • a bargaining effort • joint problem solving or exploration • a debate What the most significant issues might be: • concerns of substance • relationships • procedures/rules • internal or personal goals
Perspectives on individuals	How negotiators are chosen: • knowledge/experience • personal characteristics/status Aspirations of individuals (individual vs. community goals) Group decision making (authoritarian vs. consensual)
Dispositions affecting interactions	Time orientation (monochronic vs. polychronic) Risk-taking orientation (high vs. low) How trust is determined: • intuition • common experiences • reputation • threat of sanctions
Views about the interaction process	Importance of protocol (formal vs. informal) Complexity of communication (low vs. high) Tactics for persuasion: • logic/facts/experience • dogma/tradition • emotion/intuition
Outcomes	Agreement preferences (contractual vs. implicit)

Source: Adapted from Weiss, S. E. (1994). Negotiating with "Romans"—Part I. *Sloan Management Review*, Winter, 53.

business." Worse yet, some foreign negotiators are savvy to Americans' time sensitivities and will end up using this against them.

As we mentioned, using a negotiating team is often advisable in an international context. Once again, however, some Americans believe teams are cumbersome and feel that they're better off going it alone. Sometimes American negotiating teams are small because of the costs associated with larger groups. In other cases, the team is small because of the negotiators' inflated views of their own abilities. Either way, Americans may find themselves outnumbered in international negotiations. And the sheer number of details, let alone the language and cultural issues, often greatly reduce the odds of a good outcome for an understaffed negotiation team.[22]

Even if the team is solid, its members may not be properly prepared or understand how best to work with the team's translator. Experts will often recommend plenty of advance meetings with your interpreter and, ideally, making them a team member from the start. Companies that follow this advice have more success in negotiations. For example, a survey of over one hundred multinationals revealed that nearly 90 percent felt the presence of a bilingual team member improved the quality of their negotiation process with Japanese companies. About the same number of firms thought that such a team member also helped speed up the process. And among those firms without a bilingual team member, most indicated that they would include one in future negotiations. Taking this point a step further, other studies suggest that international negotiating teams should be multicultural. In other words, a company's negotiating team would ideally consist of employees from both the home country as well as the country represented by the other side in the negotiations. This idea goes beyond language issues. A multicultural team could make bargaining perspectives, traditions, and tactics clearer for all sides and help resolve any culturally driven impasses.[23]

But regardless of the size and composition of the negotiating team, we want to repeat the point that familiarity with the prominent features of the host country's culture and customs usually pays big dividends for everyone. When asked about this, Japanese managers said that the most important factor for ensuring success in negotiations with U.S. firms was the willingness of Americans to devote time, effort, and patience to building relationships. Not far behind was "cultural awareness." This included things such as a familiarity with Japanese business norms, customs, and practices. It's likely that these two factors are important in almost all international negotiations, not just those involving the Japanese. Fortunately, these two factors, among the others we discussed, can be worked on and fine-tuned well before the actual negotiation process begins.[24]

That said, we don't want to create the impression that preparation will automatically lead to successful negotiations. The complexities of international negotiation are such that while preparation should improve the odds, there are no guarantees. Even if you are well prepared and display behaviors and tactics that are comfortable for your counterparts, research suggests that your efforts to "adapt" will be viewed more positively in some cultures than in others. In addition, training may not always have the intended effects. Even after they went through identical training in negotiation tactics, Danish and Spanish negotiators in one study still used distinct bargaining styles. The Spaniards tended to connect relationships to the issues at hand and were willing to attack the other side, while the Danes preferred to focus on the issues and avoid direct conflicts. Consequently, Spaniards were likely to view the Danes as being too focused on the business issues and emotionally distant, while the Danes were likely to view the Spaniards as uncooperative and confrontational. All this suggests that training alone is unlikely to completely suppress the styles that people have become comfortable with over the years, whether it results from cultural influences, direct experiences, or both.[25]

Finally, consider this. Whatever its drawbacks and limitations, more training is usually going to be more desirable than less. And that's where big firms have an advantage over small ones. In fact, research shows that larger firms tend to do better in international negotiations than their smaller counterparts. And it's not size per se that counts. Rather, it's the resources that often come with size. Big firms are more likely to have the money for consultants, trainers, and interpreters and perhaps even for role-playing the negotiations.[26] In short, big firms often have the luxury of taking more time to prepare and spending more money in doing so.[27]

International Negotiation: A Four-Stage Process

nontask sounding
The first stage in international negotiations, often the longest in non-Western cultures, whose purpose is to establish rapport or get to know the other party

task-related exchange of information
The second stage of negotiation wherein both parties share their needs and preferences

persuasion
Third stage of negotiation wherein parties make attempts to modify the positions of others

agreement
The fourth and final stage of international negotiations wherein the agreement is reached, but also one in which different modes are used for agreement (e.g., contract, handshake, etc.)

Regardless of the amount (or lack) of preparation, eventually you must begin interaction and negotiation. Experts suggest that the complete negotiation process can be divided up into four main stages.[28] The first stage is called **nontask sounding**. This is often a relatively long stage, especially outside the United States. The basic purpose of this stage is to establish a rapport or to get to know the other party. In other words, interaction in this stage is not directly related to the task of negotiating but instead involves "sounding out" the other party. The next stage involves the **task-related exchange of information**. This process basically involves an exchange of the two parties' needs and preferences as well as an explanation of background issues. After this stage comes the **persuasion** stage of negotiations, in which, as the label implies, there are overt attempts to modify each other's positions. All three of these stages lead to the final **agreement** stage, in which bargains are agreed upon and perhaps contracts signed (see Exhibit 7.7). There is a good deal of research comparing cultures across these four stages, and we'll present some of that work next.

Stage 1: Nontask Sounding   First, let's consider nontask sounding. This is probably a normal stage in most conversations, especially among those meeting for the first time. In fact, the effort to establish rapport or to get to know someone is not only typical across cultures, it is common within cultures. But that doesn't mean that nontask sounding unfolds the same way everywhere. In fact, there often are great differences between Americans and many other cultures about how this stage is approached.

One important variable in the nontask-sounding stage is the amount of time spent on entertaining one's guests in an effort to feel them out and establish personal relationships. You may, for example, encounter people who want to know about you and the company you represent in great detail. In fact, they may even identify themselves when first introduced as belonging to that company. For instance, in many Asian cultures we would introduce ourselves by saying, "We are the University of Dayton's Paul Sweeney and Dean McFarlin." Obviously, in the United States we would almost certainly introduce ourselves by saying, "Hi, I'm Paul Sweeney and this is Dean McFarlin; we're with the University of Dayton." This is a subtle difference, but substantial in its underlying meaning. It reflects what we have already discussed—that people in individualistic cultures like the United States tend to give primary emphasis to the person, while people in collectivistic cultures give primacy to the group (the organization, in this case).

But nontask sounding goes well beyond this. What to an American might seem to be discussions about irrelevant personal details or tangential issues often means a great deal to, say, a Chinese negotiator. In fact, it might be vital from their perspective to have such "irrelevant" discussions early on. Remember that people from low-context cultures often don't want a lot of personal "back-

EXHIBIT 7.7   *Stages in the International Negotiation Process*

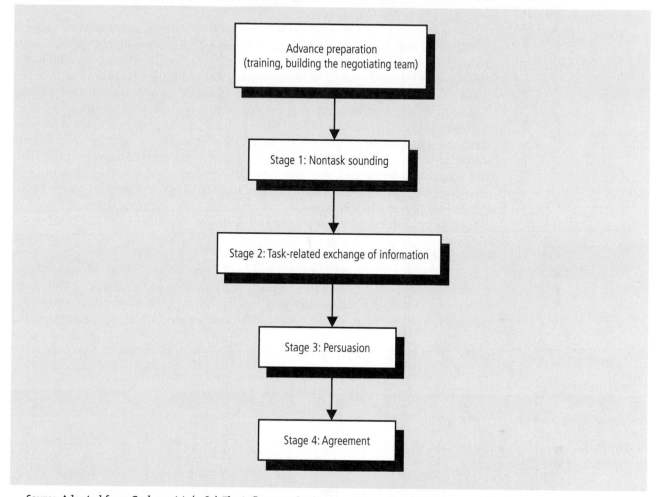

Source: Adapted from Graham, J. L. (1985). The influence of culture on the process of business negotiations: An exploratory study. *Journal of International Business Studies, 16,* 81–96.

ground" before undertaking negotiations. Generally, their perspective is that since a "contextless" contract (one that's explicit and in writing) should be the result of the negotiation process; spending enormous amounts of time to get to know the other party is unimportant and possibly an impediment to reaching one's goal. The perspective of people from high-context cultures such as China, Japan, and Mexico is often precisely the opposite, making it extremely important to spend a significant amount of time on nontask sounding. The personal and organizational information that they seek provides the context that is critical for understanding messages in their culture. Exhibit 7.8 summarizes this and other differences that might be observed between high- and low-context cultures in the nontask sounding stage.

So the amount of time spent on what Americans might consider "meaningless" interaction can vary dramatically across cultures. And in high-context cultures, it really does matter in ways that impact final outcomes. For example, one study showed that for Brazilian and Japanese negotiators, interpersonal comfort was much more likely to lead to outcomes that satisfied the negotiating partner than it was for Americans. This finding underscores the role of nontask sounding in building the personal relationships that are essential for successful negotiations in high-context cultures.[29]

Another sign of a culture's emphasis on the "getting to know you" stage is the importance negotiators place on status. The status of the participants involved in the negotiation, while not directly relevant to the issues being discussed, is relevant in some cultures during the nontask-sounding stage. Once again, the distinction between high- and low-context cultures is useful for making this point. Negotiations among equals are much more common in low-context cultures such as the United States. American negotiators often downplay status in any number of ways (e.g., by using first names, dressing casually, and soliciting input from all team members). But in many high-context cultures, title and status are very important and interactions are more formal.[30] It would be rare, for example, for a high-context negotiator to address the other party by his or her first name. The Chinese, for instance, are very aware of status differences among people on negotiation teams and prefer to negotiate with the head of the foreign company.[31] This is also an apparent preference among Japanese and French negotiators.[32]

Status or position provides background to upcoming negotiations for high-context negotiators, but it is less important in low-context cultures. To illustrate this point, one study had groups of English, French, Germans, and Americans participate in a simulated negotiation. The study found that the French (i.e., the

EXHIBIT 7.8   *Behavior in the Stages of Negotiation: Differences across Low- and High-Context Cultures*

Stage of Negotiation	Low-Context Culture	High-Context Culture
Stage 1: Nontask Sounding	• Briefly exchange social niceties • Will get to the point (i.e., stage 3) quickly • Not especially concerned with status of other group	• Will want to know all about you and your company • Long presentations and meetings in order to get to know you • Give careful attention to age, rank, status of other negotiators
Stage 2: Task-Related Exchange of Information	• Relatively brief stage • Young, ambitious, likely to do well	• Among the longer stages • Advantage given to older, higher-status team member
Stage 3: Persuasion	• Argumentative • The most important stage • "To the point" negotiating style • Cost-benefit approach; face saving not very important	• Declarative • The least important stage • More guarded style • Face saving very important
Stage 4: Concession/ Agreement	• Favor or require detailed written contract • Decision/agreement is impersonal • Profit motive determines agreement	• Less emphasis on long contracts • Deal is sealed on the basis of the contextual variables • Good setting necessary for final agreements

highest context of the four groups) were most interested in and affected by the status of other negotiation team members. Another study involved observations from more than 700 business people from eleven different cultures. The cultures ranged from very low context (e.g., the United States, Germany) to very high context (e.g., Korea, China, Taiwan). This study also found that high status and personal relations mattered more to people from high-context cultures. In Japan, for example, status distinctions can be based on age, gender, and relative position in the firm. So if you're older, male, and higher up in the firm, the odds are it will impress a Japanese bargainer.[33] In the low-context United States, however, Americans often want to establish equality between people, even where it clearly does not exist.[34]

Stage 2: Task-related Exchange of Information This second stage involves the exchange of both parties' needs and preferences. For some cultures this is the most important step in the negotiating process. In high-context cultures such as Japan, long and in-depth explanations of initial bargaining positions are expected. This exchange and the meetings that go along with it will probably be long and drawn out and will involve receiving many questions from the other negotiating party. The long-term approach taken by high-context cultures also means you're likely to see an initial offer that is not very favorable. The belief is that a poor initial offer will leave plenty of room to maneuver in later stages of the negotiation process. For example, one study had groups of businessmen from the United States, Japan, and Brazil participate in simulated negotiations. The Japanese asked for higher profit outcomes in their initial offer than their American and Brazilian counterparts. The American negotiators, however, were more likely to offer a price that was closer to the eventual terms agreed upon by both parties. And the Americans and Brazilians were irritated at the Japanese for their "greedy" initial offers. A second study with the same three cultural groups found that American bargainers could reduce this irritation and improve their outcomes by stretching out this second stage of negotiations. In particular, the more Americans encouraged information exchange from their bargaining partners, the better their financial outcomes in the negotiation.[35]

Stage 3: Persuasion Still, Americans are often skimpy in the attention they pay to task-related information exchange. Sure, Americans may spend some time talking about sports or their families, but dramatically little time compared to other cultures. Instead, a slight glance at the wristwatch is enough to move an American onto the next stage of negotiations. This third stage—persuasion—involves explicit attempts to modify each other's positions. To Americans, this is the most important step in the negotiating process. And it's the stage where they expect to spend most of their time. But how the persuasion stage unfolds in other cultures may end up surprising many Americans.

Consider the amount of time spent at this stage. As we've said, Americans usually spend relatively little time and effort in the earlier two stages in order to spend greater amounts of time here. Other cultures, such as the Japanese, take the time to sound each other out earlier and therefore they spend relatively little time engaging in the kind of overt persuasion many Americans are used to.

Then there are the actual tactics used to persuade. As you might expect, most Americans believe that this stage is where the "real" negotiating takes place. So Americans typically pay very close attention to the interactions that occur in this stage. For example, throughout this part of the process, Americans will often continuously compromise and make modifications to their initial bargaining position. Concessions are common throughout all stages of negotiations for most Americans. However, unlike American bargainers, Japanese negotiators tend to wait until the end of negotiations before making any concessions.[36] Consequently, Americans engaged in international negotiations may go too far and give too much away in an effort to compromise in this persuasion stage.[37] On top of that, the meaning of compromise can differ dramatically across cultures, as shown in the following International Insights.

Another reflection of the American belief that this is where the real negotiation takes place is that they now are ready to "lay their cards on the table." Basically, this means that Americans give, and expect to receive in return, "honest" information during this stage of negotiations. For example, in one study examining the appropriateness of various bargaining methods, Americans were less likely to endorse tactics such as bluffing, feigning threats, or misrepresenting information than were Brazilians.[38]

Fundamentally, Americans believe that the ideal position for both parties should be put on the table, at which time progress can be made—often on an issue-by-issue basis—toward some kind of compromise. But "honesty" issues aside, this style often does not mesh well with the bargaining approaches used in other countries and cultures. The Chinese, for example, often make sudden demands that are presented as nonnegotiable. Such demands often place Westerners at a disadvantage if they're not well prepared.[39] With sufficient patience, however, Americans might find that concessions will appear from the Chinese side at the last minute.[40]

🌐 International Insights

The Devil Is in the Details: The Meaning of Compromise across Cultures

IF YOU'RE WONDERING ABOUT how important language is in international business, consider the language of negotiation. Take the word *compromise*, which generally has very positive connotations for Americans. The United States was founded on compromise and many famous compromises have dotted its history. Americans may be among the world's best compromisers. It follows, of course, that compromise has been an essential part of American business dealings as well. In fact, to many Americans a compromise or concession is a very strong sign of good faith and fair play between negotiators.

Interestingly, however, the word *compromise* has some very different meanings in other cultures. And many of those meanings are far more negative than those conjured up by Americans. In the Middle East, for example, *compromise* carries with it many negative associations, as in the phrase "his virtue was compromised." The Persian word for *mediator* translates to "meddler." In many Latin American cultures, compromise presents an issue of personal honor; here, compromise could connote giving in. Since "giving in" raises many issues of face and personal integrity for Mexicans, it can prove problematic in negotiations. Russians typically see compromise as a sign of weakness. To concede even a minor point can suggest a loss of control or the influence of another's will. As a result, negotiations with Russians can be confrontational.

Likewise, many other terms that relate to the negotiation process are open to different interpretation. The word *aggressive* may be an insult to the British or Japanese, while to Americans such a characterization may indicate a tough, respected bargainer. So it clearly pays to become aware of national sensitivities, especially as far as communication about negotiation goes.[41]

EXHIBIT 7.9   *Ten Elements of the American Negotiating Style (the John Wayne Style)*

American Style	Prescriptions for Use in Other Countries
1. **I can go it alone:** We're often convinced that we can handle complex negotiations by ourselves.	1. **Use team assistance wisely:** Don't hesitate to include extra team members with expertise in technical areas or language.
2. **Just call me John:** Americans downplay status and titles, as well as other formalities like lengthy introductions.	2. **Follow local customs:** Our informality is simply out of place in most other cultures; foreign clients are more comfortable when we follow their customs.
3. **Pardon my French:** We're not much good at speaking other languages—and often we don't make any apologies either!	3. **Speak the (a) language:** Even a rudimentary knowledge of foreign terms can be useful.
4. **Get to the point:** Americans, like no others, want to dispense with the small talk and get down to business.	4. **Getting down to business:** This is defined differently across culture; getting to know the other party is important in many countries.
5. **Lay your cards on the table:** We expect honest information at the bargaining table ("You tell me what you want and I'll tell you what I want").	5. **Hold something back:** Foreign executives seldom lay everything on the table; the negotiating process is expected to take time with concessions made along the way.
6. **Don't just sit there, speak up:** Americans don't deal well with silence—we get into trouble by feeling pressured to fill in silence with possible concessions.	6. **Silence can be a powerful negotiating tool:** Consider its use, but also be aware of its use against you.
7. **Don't take no for an answer:** We are taught to be persistent and not to give up; negotiation is mostly persuasion.	7. **Minds are often changed behind the scenes:** If an impasse is reached, ask more questions; take a recess; try a more subtle approach.
8. **One thing at a time:** Americans approach a negotiating task sequentially ("Let's settle the quantity issue first, and then discuss price").	8. **Postpone concessions:** Until you've had a chance to get all issues on the table; don't measure progress by the number of issues that have been settled.
9. **A deal is a deal:** When we make an agreement, we give our word. We expect to honor the agreement no matter the circumstances.	9. **What we take as a commitment:** Means different things in Tokyo, Rio, or Riyadh; deals, particularly new ones, are more uncertain than we're used to.
10. **I am what I am:** Few Americans take pride in changing their minds, even in difficult circumstances.	10. **Flexibility:** Is very important in cross-national negotiations—we must adapt to changing economic circumstances and interdependence.

Source: Adapted from Graham, J. L., & Herberger, R. A. (1982). Negotiators abroad—don't shoot from the hip. *Harvard Business Review,* July–August, 160–168.

Exhibit 7.9 presents ten elements of what might be considered the American negotiating style. Most of these elements play a role here in the persuasion stage of negotiations. Put simply, some argue that the quintessential American style is that of the frontiersman or cowboy in the old West. This "John

Wayne" style of interaction may work well within the United States, but the characteristics that define American individualism can be received poorly on a foreign stage. After all, negotiation is by definition interdependent. And interdependence, in most shapes or forms, has not been a major emphasis in American culture.[42]

So what can happen when the John Wayne negotiator meets another culture—say, an Asian one? Americans would, in all likelihood, quickly present a complex set of arguments. They may conclude their presentation with an offer that is not too far from what they eventually expect. A Japanese or Chinese businessperson may be surprised by the abruptness of the offer but will probably consider it. They may know that Americans like to get to the point. What they may not know, however, is that the American offer is pretty close to their best offer possible. In fact, almost everywhere in the world except the United States, bargainers leave themselves plenty of room to maneuver. Accordingly, the Chinese or Japanese may counter by asking for a lot, which makes perfect sense, given their cultural perspective. But Americans may react angrily in many cases. This is exactly what happened in a study based on a simulated negotiation session. American negotiators initially asked for a "fair" price—one closer to their final offer—whereas Japanese negotiators initially asked for much higher profit options, a position that upset the Americans.[43]

Despite feelings like these, Americans would probably press on. They may try dealing with one issue at a time. Here they may experience more frustration and anger. For example, the Japanese typically do not like dealing piecemeal with issues—which explains why their concessions are bunched toward the end of the negotiation process. Second, even if Americans are very persuasive, they may get a silent response—which the Americans may interpret as stonewalling. A cultural analysis shows the source of frustration here. The Americans may have used their on-the-spot latitude to grant a concession. But Japanese rarely have the same amount of discretion at their disposal. Instead, the Japanese decision-making style is to take time after hearing an offer to discuss it as a group and, ideally, reach a consensus. Consequently, the Japanese negotiators are not likely to react immediately to an offer.[44]

If they are frustrated enough at this point, Americans may counter with a very aggressive tactic. They might tell the Japanese, "If you can't lower your price, we'll just go with another supplier." This may be the worst thing the Americans could do. The mere directness of this approach might turn off the Japanese. It would be much more appropriate if this option were presented through a third party or, if it must be done directly, then in a completely different way. For example, the American might say, "Lower prices on your part would go a long way toward our not having to consider other options." Additionally, other tactics, like repeating the explanation of your position in more detail, asking questions, playing dumb, or even silence can go a long way.[45]

Stage 4: Agreement   Many negotiations do come to a conclusion where an agreement is reached. Agreements are the culmination of all the concessions and persuasion used in stage 3 and earlier. That said, an agreement is only as good as the follow through. In other words, all the considerable time and effort you invested in the previous three stages (sounding out the other party, trying to understand their culture, traveling, persuading, etc.) could be wasted if both parties don't behave in ways that are consistent with the agreement. Recognizing this fact, many American companies will insist that elaborate formal contracts be signed that bind each party to the agreement. Not unexpectedly, this demand is sometimes viewed as a negative or even something to resist outright. In some parts of the world, negotiators are loath to seal the deal with a final, written contract. Instead, they hope that the ties that they spent so much time building and strengthening in the earlier stages of the process will now pay off. They hope that the general trust established via an extended nontask-sounding phase will allow a much more general agreement to be drafted and acknowledged by each party.[46] Despite this inclination, most foreign firms nowadays expect a lengthy formal contract to be requested if they are negotiating with U.S. companies.

The Chinese have similar views about the form of a good agreement. Instead of a specific contract, they prefer broad agreement about general principles. Some say the Chinese want broad agreements because they believe that if all parties agree to the principles, the details can be worked out later by people of good intention and trust.[47] Of course, Americans and other Westerners often take the position that if trust exists, then the Chinese should be willing to make clear commitments. Who is right probably depends on the specific case. One thing, however, is certain: Americans tend to slight the process of establishing broad principles. To Americans, these principles are similar to the corporate codes that are all the rage these days—they are nice words, but in practice, they can be unimportant, if not meaningless. (Ironically, however, you will recall from Chapter 3 that U.S. firms are more likely to have such codes than their foreign competition.)

What many Americans fail to realize, however, is that these principles are the standards the Chinese use to evaluate future agreements. As result, Americans often agree to them with little input. Ultimately, this may be the right thing to do anyway, since general items can be interpreted to support your position. Nevertheless, experts recommend that Western firms provide serious input into this process, including laying out their ideas on business concepts such as quality products, profit, and shareholder return, instead of just going through the motions.

Whether it is broad or narrow, however, even the very notion of a contract can have different implications across countries. For example, in Russia a party to a contract can only do what is expressly allowed. Generally, in the United States you can do anything that is not prohibited by contract (provided it is legal).[48] Again, an agreement is only good if it is kept. Whether other parties live up to their end of the agreement depends on, at least in part, the potential long-term impact. This impact, in turn, is determined by the trust we have in the other parties and our satisfaction with the agreement. Making sure the other party feels it also got a good deal, therefore, pays off in the long run.[49] Global competition is so fierce today that general principles are probably worth abiding by in order to communicate effectively and negotiate a lasting agreement.

Chapter Summary

Conflict is a common occurrence in international communication, and important causes include differing cultural norms, decision-making styles, and the characteristic cultural tendency to engage in or avoid conflict. We discussed different styles that cultures use to deal with conflict issues once they arise. These approaches balance concern for your own outcomes against concern for the outcomes of others. For instance, Americans tend to use a competitive style. There are also cultural differences in the *accounts* or explanations that people provide once conflict occurs between parties. Cultures that are more collectivist tend to use mitigating accounts (e.g., concessions) while more individualistic cultures often use aggravating accounts (e.g., denials). Likewise, culture can shape how people respond to these accounts. For example, aggravating accounts are likely to be viewed negatively in collective cultures.

An important way to avoid or minimize conflict is through negotiation. We presented two negotiation frameworks. The broader of the two is intended to be used as a general guide to how culture can impact negotiations. It covers five basic factors and includes everything from how people conceptualize issues in negotiations to how the process of negotiation should unfold. The second framework focused on the stages of the negotiation process itself, but it also highlights the importance of preparation. Preparation should include things like learning about the other side in-depth (about their culture and how that impacts negotiation), seeking outside experts when necessary, using translators and a multicultural negotiating team, and generally being willing to spend significant time getting ready.

Once preparation is complete, the actual negotiations typically proceed through four main stages. We showed how different cultures put more or less weight on each stage. For example, Americans tend to undervalue the first stage of negotiating—*nontask sounding*—relative to other cultures. This "getting to know one another" phase is viewed by Americans as best kept brief and perfunctory, whereas it is a relatively long and important stage for some other cultures. The next stage, *task-related exchange of information*, is also typically more important for countries other than the United States (e.g., Japan). In a high-context culture such as Japan, long and in-depth exchange of bargaining positions is expected. *Persuasion* is the third stage, one that is typically seen as the "heart" of negotiation for most Americans. This is the point when modification and persuasion of others' positions unfolds. Yet, for some high-context cultures, it can be less important, and relatively little time is spent in the kind of overt persuasion that Americans are used to. *Agreement* is the final stage, and again some big differences are commonly observed. Americans prefer elaborate contracts that bind parties to the agreement. Others, mostly high-context cultures, rely a great deal on the trust established in earlier stages to truly seal a deal. Throughout the discussion, we examined some of the mistakes that can be made in an international negotiation process as well as some techniques that may result in more beneficial outcomes.

Discussion Questions

1. In discussing conflict, we highlighted negative implications and effects. Can you think of any positive effects that might result from intercultural conflict?

2. How might Asians, Latins, and Americans (U.S.) characteristically deal with conflict? More importantly, what is it about each group's typical style that would create a sense of frustration when dealing with the other groups?

3. Reflect on how an American and a Saudi might move through the four stages of negotiation. How might each stage be approached and what areas might each nationality emphasize?

business.college.hmco.com/students

Up to the Challenge?

Understanding the Mexican and American Negotiation Gap

A T THE BEGINNING OF the chapter, we presented a scenario and part of an exchange between Mexican and American managers from different units in the same company. Their job was to negotiate which unit would buy some computer equipment. Just in case you were wondering, this was an exchange between real managers, part of a training program that the managers were going through on negotiations. So while the stakes involved were simulated, it nevertheless prompted some amazing cross-cultural differences, along with plenty of anger, frustration, and misunderstanding.

In a nutshell, the Mexicans displayed more concern for relationships than their American counterparts during negotiations. The Mexicans tended to use stories and allegories to help support their points, attempted to find collaborative outcomes that were mutually beneficial, and acknowledged the arguments of the other side in the negotiations. Likewise, the Mexicans also tended to be more effusive, though they would respond by rejecting the Americans' arguments and making demands of their own if they felt they were being pushed too far. Americans, in contrast, used interruptions and attacking arguments more than their Mexican colleagues. In short, they were more competitive in their approach. The Americans also tended to focus more on moving things along by making references to time and requesting additional information. That said, Americans were often willing to accommodate Mexican negotiators in the end, preferring to present specific alternatives and work through them, conceding or compromising as necessary. The Mexicans, however, were more concerned with establishing a positive working relationship first and then preferred to explore options jointly rather than consider specific arrangements.

Overall, the Mexicans felt the Americans were too aggressive and confrontational. The Americans, on the other hand, tended, to view the Mexicans as indecisive, weak, and tangential. All of this, from the tactics used to the reactions of each side, may be influenced by cultural differences. In particular, Mexicans tend toward collectivism while Americans tend toward individualism. Americans tend to worry less about relationships and be focused more on "winning" in a negotiation. They may also view conflict and arguing as positives (they "help clear the air"). But to many Mexicans, being respectful, harmonious, smoothing, and empathetic in interactions (*simpatía*), especially with friends and family, is an important aspect of their cultural values (i.e., part of "Mexican collectivism"). In addition, Mexicans tend to be polychronic (high context) while their American counterparts tend to be more monochronic (hence the American emphasis on time, feeling rushed, being exacting with language, etc.).

As we presented it here, this was a negotiation between in-groups of a sort, since everyone was part of the same firm. How might the two sides be impacted as a consequence? Why? In this circumstance, do you have any suggestions about how each side might better respond and adapt to the other, or have been better prepared to do just that? And what if the situation were different? What if each side had to interact with an out-group? For instance, how might negotiation tactics have played out differently for each side had this been a negotiation between companies (say, with an outside supplier)? Why?

As we noted in this chapter, perhaps the biggest mistake a manager can make is to be unfamiliar with the norms and typical behaviors of another culture. If both sides had been better prepared about the potential for "cultural disconnects" during the negotiations, things might have indeed gone more smoothly. And international negotiations these days don't always require a passport. Sometimes it's no farther than a walk across the hall.[50]

International Development

An International Negotiation Scenario

Purpose

To diagnose and assess an international negotiation that has gone wrong, to learn how better to approach this and other cross-cultural negotiations, and to gain self-insight into your own negotiating tendencies and styles.

Instructions

Read the following scenario independently, either inside or outside class. Next, divide into groups of four to six. Discuss the questions posed at the end of the scenario with your group and develop consensus answers if possible (allow 20–25 minutes). Then report your group's answers, followed by a class discussion and wrap-up (20 minutes).

The Scenario

Econ, a rapidly growing electronics retailer located in the Southwest, is currently attempting to negotiate a number of agreements with manufacturers located in Japan and elsewhere in the Far East. Econ has a reputation for selling the newest products at discounted prices and, at the same time, having the largest inventory possible. Its slogan is, "Never be undersold or out of stock." To demonstrate their desire to develop close ties with the new suppliers, management has decided to send Peter Nelson, one of the firm's top purchasing agents, to the Far East. He has been given the responsibility to negotiate a set of contracts that will improve Econ's market share in the Southwest and, at the same time, enhance its reputation as an up-and-coming electronics firm. Accompanying Peter is Reid MacLeod, a technical expert in computer hardware and software.

One organization of particular interest to Econ is Nagaoka, Inc., a Japanese firm that has established itself as a leader in writable disk drives and wireless hardware. Before leaving for Japan, Peter set up a number of meetings with Mr. Washsami, Nagaoka's vice president of sales. These meetings represent the first-time encounter with a Japanese firm for both Peter and Reid. The Americans arrive at the Nagaoka plant as scheduled and are escorted to a well-appointed meeting room. Besides Mr. Washsami, there are three other individuals present. They are Mr. Asakawa, Director of Production, Mr. Matsuata, Mr. Asakawa's assistant, and Mr. Konatshima, the company's interpreter (Mr. Konatshima was asked to attend because only Mr. Washsami speaks English). After several minutes of formal introductions, the two sides sit down to begin discussions. To break the ice, Peter indicates to the interpreter that, since the group will be working together for several days, it would be desirable to use first names. He then repeats his and his colleague's first name. The Japanese nod their heads but continue to use last names. Peter tries a second time but the response is the same. He decides not to push the issue further, but wonders why the Japanese are being so formal.

Peter again takes charge by explaining what he and Reid hope to accomplish and Econ's business philosophy. Peter directs his comments to Mr. Washsami because he is the most senior person on the Japanese team. The interpreter repeats his comments for the benefit of the others. They respond by nodding followed by long periods of silence. Feeling uncomfortable with the silence, Peter begins to explain the specific needs that Econ has to Mr. Washsami. Of particular importance to Econ are discounts for large volumes and a multiyear contract. In response to Peter's comments, Mr. Washsami indicates that it would be difficult to make decisions so soon. He receives accepting glances from his colleagues. Not accepting Mr. Washsami's statements, Reid presses the issue of price. However, the more Peter and Reid press, the more adamant and withdrawn Mr. Washsami becomes and the longer the periods of silence. Finally, Peter and Reid accept Mr. Washsami's unwillingness to discuss price at this time.

Peter turns his attention to important technical specifications for the drives Nagaoka manufactures. In this case, Peter directs his comments to Mr. Asakawa, director of production. Peter assumes that because Mr. Asakawa is the director, he is the person with the technical understanding to answer questions. In response to the questioning, Mr. Asakawa hesitates and, before responding, talks to his assistant. It soon becomes clear to Peter that the person with all the answers is not

Mr. Asakawa, but his assistant. Peter, however, is confused because he does not want to offend the director or place Mr. Matsuata in an awkward position with his boss. Peter attempts to overcome his dilemma by directing his comments to the interpreter without specific reference to either Mr. Asakawa or Mr. Matsuata. Unfortunately, such a strategy only confuses the interpreter and makes the situation worse.

The group has been meeting now for two hours and Peter is becoming anxious about the amount of progress being made. As far as he can see, there has been very little progress. Even worse, the Japanese negotiators' casual and relaxed style, coupled with their reluctance to talk, has given Peter the impression that they are not very interested in doing business with Econ. In a final attempt to salvage something from the meeting, Peter turns his attention to the issues of delivery dates and how long it would take to receive an order once it had been placed. Here again, the Japanese are reluctant to make a commitment on quantities and delivery times. However, sensing some movement by Mr. Washsami, Peter presses on. After about 30 minutes of interpreter-assisted conversation, Mr. Washsami finally says yes to the specific delivery date requested by Reid. Mr. Washsami's yes, however, is followed by a long explanation about why such a date would be difficult to meet and how it would put considerable strain on Nagaoka's production facility.

Believing that he has finally obtained a commitment from Mr. Washsami, Peter decided that this would be a great opportunity to begin writing down points of agreement. Peter continues by suggesting that, since there is agreement on a delivery date, they can begin to write up a tentative agreement between Econ and Nagaoka. At first the interpreter is reluctant to repeat Peter's comments, but finally translates the message. To Peter's surprise, the Japanese look shocked and indicate that there is still not agreement on a delivery date. Peter is totally confused and suggests that they take a luncheon break to reconsider their position. The two sides agree to meet at 2:00 p.m. and leave for lunch together.

1. What do you believe went wrong with the negotiations between Econ and Nagaoka?
2. Who is at fault?
3. What would you have done differently?

Source: From *Skills for Managerial Success,* L.W. Mealiea & G.P. Latham, © 1996 McGraw Hill. Reprinted by permission of the publisher. pp. 166-167, 170-172.

 Tapping into the Global Network

International Negotiation Exercise

Purpose

To explore the difficulties that can occur when negotiating with people from other cultures.

Instructions

Divide into groups of 4-6 people. Your instructor will assign each group one culture to study in order to cover a variety of different countries and cultures. Outside class, do research to find three dominant cultural values and their corresponding negotiation behaviors for your assigned culture. Several websites might be useful in your research. Your instructor might also suggest other sites at which to find information. Consider the following:

- **Negotiation.biz.** This is a site devoted to being a resource for those interested in studying cross-cultural negotiation. The site provides a great deal of country-specific information regarding country characteristics and values that might impact negotiation:

  http://www.negotiation.biz/countries/ Countries.htm

- **U.S. Embassies and Consulates Directory.** This site has an unbelievable amount of information about countries all over the world in which the United States has a consular presence or embassy. An invaluable resource for this assignment and more:

  http://travel.state.gov/links.html

- **U.S. Department of State Country Background Notes.** This is a companion site to that listed above, both maintained by the Department of State. We list it here separately because it can be missed on the above site:

  http://www.state.gov/r/pa/ei/bgn/

- **The Economist Country Profiles.** *The Economist* magazine is well known; its Intelligence Unit—while less well known—is an invaluable resource for anyone interested in international business:

  http://www.economist.com/countries/

  Based on its research, each group should do three things:

1. meet to discuss each cultural value and some of the behavior your assigned country or culture produces.

2. next, make some predictions about how negotiators from that country or culture act as a result.

3. finally, come up with a strategic negotiating response for each of the predicted negotiating behaviors in your assigned country or culture.

.In class, each group will have ten to fifteen minutes to present its research findings and suggested negotiating strategy. The instructor will wrap things up with a discussion of cultural differences and their relationship to international business negotiations.

Source: Adapted from Whatley, A. (1979). *Training for the cross-cultural mind.* Washington, DC: SIETAR. As appeared in *Management international: Cases, exercises, and readings* by Dorothy Marcic and Sheila Puffer. Copyright © 1994 by West Publishing Company, Minneapolis/St. Paul, MN, a division of International Thomson Publishing, Inc.

CASE 3

Grupo Financiero Inverlat

By October 1996, it had been four months since management at the Bank of Nova Scotia (BNS) increased its stake in the Mexican bank, Grupo Financiero Inverlat (Inverlat), from 8.1 percent, to an equity and convertible debt package that represented 54 percent ownership of the bank. A team of Canadian managers had been sent to Mexico to assume management of the ailing financial institution immediately after the deal was struck. Jim O'Donnell, now Director General Adjunto (DGA)[1] of the retail bank at Inverlat, had been there from the beginning.

Jim was a member of the original group that performed the due diligence to analyze Inverlat's finances before negotiations could begin. Later, he and his wife Anne-Marie (also an executive with the bank) were the first Canadians to arrive in Mexico in May 1996. Since then, fourteen additional Canadian managers had arrived, and restructured the four most senior levels within Inverlat. The pace of change had been overwhelming. Jim now wondered how successful his early efforts had been and what could be done to facilitate the remaining restructuring.

A Brief Inverlat History

In 1982, in his last days as leader of the Mexican Republic, President Lopez Portillo announced the nationalization of Mexico's banks. They would remain government institutions for the next eight to ten years. Managers characterized the years under government control as a period of stagnation in which the structure of the Mexican financial institutions remained constant despite substantial innovations in technology and practice in the banking industry internationally.

Many Inverlat managers claimed that their bank had generally deteriorated more than the rest of the banking sector in Mexico. Managers believed that there was no overall strategy or leadership. Lacking a strong central management structure, each of the bank's geographic regions began to function independently, resulting in a system of control one manager described as "feudal." The eight regions developed such a level of autonomy that managers commonly referred to Inverlat not as a bank, but as eight small banks. The fragmented structure made new product development almost impossible. When the central corporate offices developed a new product, they had no guarantee that it would be implemented in the regions and ultimately, the branches. The power struggle within the regions demanded such loyalty that employees often had to say: "I cannot support you (in some initiative) because my boss told me not to."

In 1990, an amendment to the Mexican constitution allowed majority private sector ownership of Mexican commercial banks. Between 1990 and 1992, eighteen banks were privatized by the Mexican government including Inverlat. BNS, looking to expand its interests in Latin America, purchased 8 percent of the company in 1992 for C$154 million.

Richard Ivey School of Business
The University of Western Ontario

Daniel D. Campbell prepared this case under the direction of Professors Kathleen Slaughter and Henry W. Lane solely to provide material for class discussion. The authors do not intend to illustrate either effective or ineffective handling of a managerial situation. The authors may have disguised certain names and other identifying information to protect confidentiality. Ivey Management Services prohibits any form of reproduction, storage, or transmittal without its written permission. This material is not covered under authorization from CanCopy or any reproduction rights organization. To order copies or request permission to reproduce materials, contact Ivey Publishing, Ivey Management Services, c/o Richard Ivey School of Business, The University of Western Ontario, London, Ontario, Canada, N6A 3K7; phone (519) 661-3208, fax (519) 661-3882, e-mail cases@ivey.uwo.ca. Copyright © 1997 Ivey Management Services. One-time permission to reproduce granted by Ivey Management Services on August 1, 2004.

Under the structure of the newly privatized bank, there were three corporate cultures: that of the original bank; that of the Casa de Bolsa, the bank's brokerage house; and that of the new chair of the bank, an executive from Banamex, Mexico's largest financial institution. Many senior Banamex executives were invited to join Inverlat; some even came out of retirement to do so. The Banamex culture soon dominated the organization, as senior management tried to create a "Little Banamex." Inverlat managers without a history in Banamex said that the strategy could never function because Inverlat did not have the clients, technology, or financial resources of Banamex.

Inverlat's leaders did recognize, however, that the years of stagnation under nationalization had created a bank that had failed to create a new generation of bankers to reflect the changing times. They realized that the bank required a rejuvenation, but the managers did not have the knowledge or the capacity to effect the change.

Nowhere was the lack of development more prominent, and ultimately more devastating, than in the credit assessment function. The banks pursued a growth strategy dependent on increased lending but, unfamiliar with the challenges of lending to the private sector, failed to collateralize their loans properly or to ensure that covenants were being maintained. In early 1995, following a severe devaluation of the Mexican peso, Mexico's credit environment collapsed; so did the bank. The Mexican government assumed responsibility for the bank, and BNS was forced to write down its original investment by almost 95 percent to C$10 million.

Negotiations with BNS

Management at BNS chose to view the loss in value of their investment as a further buying opportunity and, in early 1996, they began negotiations with the Mexican government. BNS contributed C$50 million for 16 percent of new stock in the bank and C$125 million in bonds convertible on March 31 in the year 2000 for an additional 39 percent of equity. If, in the year 2000, BNS decided not to assume ownership of the bank, they could walk away without converting the debt and retain a much smaller portion of ownership.

As the majority shareholder until the year 2000, the Mexican government contracted BNS to manage the bank. A maximum of 20 BNS managers would be paid by the Mexican government to manage Inverlat on the government's behalf. If BNS wanted more Canadian managers to work in the bank, BNS would have to pay for them. It was intended that the Canadian managers would remain at Inverlat only until the Mexican managers developed the skills to manage the bank effectively on their own.

With the exception of a handful of the most senior officers in the bank, employees at Inverlat had no direct means of receiving information about the progression of the negotiations with BNS. Instead, they were forced to rely on often inaccurate reports from the Mexican media. As the negotiation progressed, support among Inverlat employees for a deal with BNS was very strong. Inverlat employees did not want to become government bureaucrats and viewed BNS as a savior that would bring money, technology, and expertise.

Employee Expectations

Soon after the deal was completed with BNS, however, the general euphoria was gradually replaced by the fear of actions the Canadians were likely to take as they assumed their management role. Senior managers were worried that they would be replaced by someone younger, who spoke English and had an MBA. Rumors, supported by inaccurate reports in local newspapers, ran rampant. One newspaper reported that as many as 180 senior-level managers would be imported to Inverlat from BNS in Canada.

Anxiety mounted as speculation increased about the magnitude of downsizing that BNS would implement as it restructured the bank in its turnaround. Although BNS had purchased banks in other Latin American countries, few Inverlat employees, including the most senior management, had any knowledge about the strategies that BNS management had used. Inverlat managers felt that their employees viewed BNS as a "gringo" corporation, and expected them to take the same actions that U.S. companies had taken as they restructured companies they had purchased in Mexico. Most believed that if any foreign bank purchased Inverlat, most of the senior management team would be displaced and up to half of the bank staff would be let go. Similarly, very few managers knew the details of the contract that limited the number of managers that could come to the bank from Canada.

Very few of the Mexican employees had had any significant contact with Canadian managers, but the majority expected behavior similar to that of U.S. managers. Only a handful of senior-level managers had been in contact during the due diligence, and the Canadians realized that they required greater insight into the Mexican culture if they were to manage effectively. As a result, the members of the senior team that were going to manage the Mexican bank arrived in Mexico one month in advance to study Spanish. The Canadian managers studied in an intensive program in Cuernavaca, a small city eighty kilometers southwest of Mexico City. During the three-week course, lectures were available on the Mexican culture. Mexican managers were extremely impressed by this attempt by the Canadians to gain a better understanding of the situation they were entering and thought the consideration was very respectful. One manager commented that:

> *At the first meeting, the Canadians apologized because it would be in English, but promised that the next would be in Spanish. The fact is, some are still in English, but the approach and the attempt were very important.*

Four months later, the Canadian team was still undergoing intense tutorial sessions in Spanish on a daily basis with varying levels of success.

Canadian managers said they were trying to guard against putting people into positions simply because they were bilingual. A Canadian manager, expressing his commitment to function in Spanish, commented that:

> *There are sixteen Canadians down here and 10,000 Mexicans. Surely to God, the sixteen Canadians can learn Spanish rather than trying to teach the 10,000 Mexicans English or having people feel that they are being left out of promotions or opportunities just because they don't speak English. This is a Spanish-speaking country and the customers speak Spanish.*

Inverlat and BNS Cultures

In Canada, BNS was considered the bank with the most stringent financial control systems of the country's largest banks. Stringent, not only in deciding not to spend money in nonessential areas, but also in maintaining a tough system of policies and controls that ensured that managers held to their budgets.

Inverlat executives, on the other hand, were accustomed to almost complete autonomy with little or no control imposed on their spending. Very little analysis was done to allocate resources to a project, and adherence to budget was not monitored. Mexican managers believed that greater controls such as the ones used by BNS should be implemented in Inverlat, but they also felt that conflicts would arise.

An early example experienced in the bank was a new policy implemented by BNS management to control gifts received by managers from clients. BNS managers imposed a limit of 500 pesos[2] for the maximum value of a gift that could be received by an executive. Gifts of larger value could be accepted, but were then raffled off to all employees of the bank at Christmas. Some Mexican managers took offense at the imposition of an arbitrary limit. They felt that it was an indication that BNS did not trust their judgment. Managers thought that it would be better if the bank communicated the need for the use of good judgment when accepting gifts and then trusted their managers to act appropriately.

Mandates of BNS

Two months after the arrival of the Canadian executive team, the new bank chairman, Bill Sutton, gave an address to 175 senior executives within Inverlat. The purpose of the address was threefold: to outline management's main objectives in the short term; to unveil the new organizational structure of senior-level managers; and to reassure employees that no staff reductions would be undertaken for the first year. The primary objectives, later printed in a special company-wide bulletin were the following:

1. Identify all non-performing loans of the bank.
2. Develop an organization focused on the client.
3. Improve the productivity and efficiency of all operations and activities.
4. Improve the profitability of the 315 branches.
5. Develop a liability strategy.
6. Improve the integrity of the financial information.

These objectives were generally well received by the Mexican managers. Some criticized them as being too intangible and difficult to measure. Most, however, believed that the general nature of the objectives was more practical, given the type of changes that were being made in the first year. They did agree that the goals would need to be adjusted as planning became more focused during the 1997 budget planning process.

The new management structure differed sharply from the existing structure of the bank. The original eight geographic regions were reduced to four. Managers were pleased to see that the head of each of these divisions was Mexican, and it was generally viewed as a promotion for the managers.

The second change was the nature in which the Canadians were added to the management structure. The senior Canadian managers became "Directores Generales Adjuntos (DGAs)" or senior vice presidents

of several key areas, displacing Mexican managers. The Mexican DGAs not directly replaced by Canadians would now report to one or more of the Canadian DGAs, but this was not reflected in the organization chart (see Exhibit 1). Mexican DGAs retained their titles and formally remained at the same level as their Canadian counterparts.

Mexican managers later reported mixed feelings by employees about whether or not they worked under a Canadian or Mexican DGA. Many felt that a Mexican DGA and his (there were no female DGAs working within the bank) employees were more "vulnerable" than a Canadian; however, senior managers also felt that they had an opportunity to ascend to the DGA position when it was being held by a Mexican. Many felt that Canadian managers would always hold the key positions in the bank and that certain authority would never be relinquished to a Mexican. This was not the message

EXHIBIT 1 *Grupo Financiero Inverlat Organization Chart (Post-reorganization)*

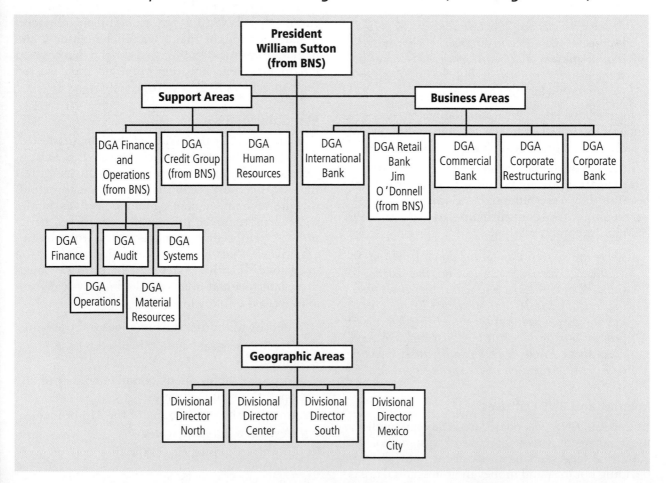

that BNS management wanted to convey. One of Jim O'Donnell's first comments to his employees was that he would only be in Mexico until one of them felt confident that they could fill his shoes.

The last message was the new management's commitment not to reduce staff levels. A policy of "no hires, no fires" was put in place. Employees were able to breathe a sigh of relief. Many had expected the Canadian management team to reduce staff by 3,000 to 5,000 employees during the first several months after their arrival.

The Communication Challenge

Canadian and Mexican managers already experienced many of the difficulties that the two different languages could present. Many of the most senior Mexican managers spoke English, but the remaining managers required translators when speaking with the Canadians. Even when managers reporting directly to them spoke English, Canadians felt frustration at not being able to speak directly to the next level below. One manager commented that "sometimes, I feel like a bloody dictator," referring to the need to communicate decisions to his department via his most senior officers.

Meetings

Even when all managers at a meeting spoke English, the risk of miscommunication was high. A Mexican manager recalled one of the early meetings in English attended by several Mexicans. Each of the Mexican managers left the meeting with little doubt about what had been decided during the meeting. It was only later, when the Mexicans spoke of the proceedings in Spanish, that they realized they each had a different interpretation about what had transpired. What they found even more alarming was that each manager had heard what he had wanted to hear, clearly demonstrating to themselves the effect of their biases on their perception of events.

This problem might have been exacerbated by the way some of the Canadians chose to conduct meetings. Mexican managers were accustomed to a flexible atmosphere in which they were free to leave the room or carry on side-conversations as they saw fit. Canadian managers became frustrated and changed the meeting style to a more structured, controlled atmosphere similar to what they used in Canada. The Mexican managers were told that breaks would be scheduled every two hours and

that only then should they get up from the table or leave the room.

Canadian managers believed that the original conduct of the Mexican managers during meetings was due to a lack of discipline and that the new conduct would lead to higher productivity. The Canadians did not recognize the negative impact that could result from the elimination of the informal interactions that had occurred in the original style.

Beyond Language

Despite the cross-cultural training received in Cuernavaca, some Canadians still felt they had a lot to learn about the cultural nuances that could create major pitfalls. Jim O'Donnell recalled a meeting at which he and several Mexican managers were having difficulty with some material developed by another Mexican not present at the meeting. Jim requested that this manager join them to provide further explanation. Several minutes later, as this person entered the room, Jim said jokingly, "OK, here's the guy that screwed it all up." The manager was noticeably upset. It was not until later, after some explaining, that Jim's comment was understood to be a joke. Jim said it brought home the fact that, in the Mexican culture, it was unacceptable, even in jest, to be critical of someone in front of other people.

This was easier said than done. Often, what the Canadians considered a minor difference of opinion could appear as criticism that Mexican managers would prefer be made behind closed doors when coming from a more senior manager. One Mexican manager commented on the risks of disagreeing with an employee when others were present:

> When someone's boss is not in agreement, or critical of actions taken by an employee and says something during a meeting with other employees present, other managers will use it as an opportunity to also say bad things about the manager. Instead, when a disagreement arises in an open meeting, the senior manager should say, "see me later, and we will discuss it."

To the contrary, the Canadian managers were trying to encourage an environment in which all managers participated in meetings and positive criticism was offered and accepted.

Mexican Communication Style

On verbal communication, one of the original Inverlat managers commented:

> In Mexico, interactions between individuals are extremely polite. Because Mexicans will make every effort not to offend the person they are dealing with, they are careful to "sugar-coat" almost everything they say. Requests are always accompanied by "por favor," no matter how insignificant the request.
>
> Mexicans often speak the diminutive form. For example: Esperame means "Wait for me." Esperame un rato means "Wait for me a moment." A Mexican would more often say Esperame un ratito. "Ratito" is the diminutive form meaning "a very short moment." It is not as direct.
>
> This politeness is extended into other interactions. Every time a Mexican meets a co-worker or subordinate, a greeting such as "Hello, how are you?" is appropriate, even if it is the fourth or fifth time that day that they have met. If you don't do this, the other person will think you are angry with him or her or that you are poorly educated.

One Canadian manager explained that some of the Mexican managers he dealt with went to great lengths to avoid confrontation. He was frustrated when the Mexicans would "tell him what he wanted to hear." Often these managers would consent to something that they could or would not do, simply to avoid a confrontation at the time.

Other Messages: Intended or Otherwise

Due to the high level of anxiety, Mexican managers were very sensitive to messages they read into the actions taken by the Canadians. This process began before the Canadians made any significant changes.

As the Canadians began to plan the new organizational structure, they conducted a series of interviews with the senior Mexican managers. The Canadians decided who they would talk to based on areas where they believed they required more information. Unfortunately, many managers believed that if they were not spoken to, then they were not considered of importance to the Canadians and should fear for their positions. Even after the organizational structure was revealed and many Mexican managers found

themselves in good positions, they still retained hard feelings, believing that they had not been considered important enough to provide input into the new structure.

Similarly, at lower levels in the bank, because of the lack of activity in the economy as a whole, many employees were left with time on their hands. Because many employees feared staff reductions at some point, they believed that those with the most work or those being offered new work were the ones that would retain their jobs.

Communications as an Ongoing Process

When Jim held his first meeting with the nine senior managers reporting to him, he began by saying that none of them would have their jobs in two months. Realizing the level of anxiety at that point, he quickly added that he meant they would all be shuffled around to other areas of the retail bank. Jim explained that this would give them an opportunity to learn about other areas of the bank and the interdependencies that needed to be considered when making decisions.

Jim stuck to his word, and within two months, all but one of the managers had been moved. Some, however, had experienced anxiety about the method by which they were moved. Typically, Jim would meet with an employee and tell him that in two or three days he would report to a new area (generally, Mexican managers gave at least a month's notice). When that day arrived, Jim would talk to them for thirty to forty-five minutes about their new responsibilities and goals, and then he would send them on their way.

For many of the Mexicans, this means of communication was too abrupt. Many wondered if they had been moved from their past jobs because of poor performance. More senior Mexican managers explained that often these managers would come to them and ask why Jim had decided to move them. Most of the Mexicans felt that more communication was required about why things were happening the way they were.

Accountability

Early on, the Canadian managers identified an almost complete lack of accountability within the bank. Senior managers had rarely made decisions outside the anonymity of a committee, and when resources were committed to a project, it was equally rare for someone to check back to see what results were attained. As a result, very little analysis was done before a new project was approved and undertaken.

The first initiative taken by the Canadians to improve the level of analysis, and later implementation, was the use of what they called the "business case." The case represented a cost-benefit analysis that would be approved and reviewed by senior managers. Initially, it was difficult to explain to the Mexican managers how to provide the elements of analysis that the Canadians required. The Mexicans were given a framework, but they initially returned cases that adhered too rigidly to the outline. Similarly, managers would submit business cases of 140 pages for a $35,000 project.

Cases required multiple revisions to a point of frustration on both sides, but it was only when an analysis could be prepared that satisfied the Canadians and was understood by both parties, that it could be certain that they all had the same perception of what they were talking about.

Some of the Mexican managers found the business case method overly cumbersome and felt that many good ideas would be missed because of the disincentive created by the business case. One manager commented that "It is a bit discouraging. Some people around here feel like you need to do a business case to go to the bathroom."

Most agreed that a positive element of the business case was the need it created to talk with other areas of the bank. To do a complete analysis, it was often necessary to contact other branches of the bank for information because their business would be affected. This was the first time that efforts across functional areas of the bank would be coordinated. To reinforce this notion, often Canadian managers required that senior managers from several areas of the bank grant their approval before a project in a business case could move forward.

Matrix Responsibility

Changes in the organizational structure further complicated the implementation of a system of accountability. Senior management had recognized a duplication of services across the different functional areas of the bank. For example, each product group had its own marketing and systems departments. These functions were stripped away and consolidated into central groups that would service all areas of the organization.

Similarly, product groups had been responsible for the development and delivery of their products. Performance was evaluated based on the sales levels each product group could attain. Under the initial restructuring, the product groups would no longer be responsible for the sale of their products, only for their design. Instead, the branches would become a delivery network that would be responsible for almost all contact with the client. As a result, managers in product groups, who were still responsible for ensuring the sales levels, felt that they were now being measured against criteria over which they had no direct control. The Canadian management team was finding it very difficult to explain to the Mexicans that they now had to "influence" instead of "control." Product managers were being given the role of "coaches" who would help the branch delivery network to offer their product most effectively.

As adjustments were made to the structure, the Mexican manager's perception of his status also had to be considered. In the management hierarchy, the Mexican manager's relationships were with the people in the various positions that they dealt with, not with the positions themselves. When a person was moved, subordinates felt loyalty to that individual. As a result, Mexican managers moving within an organization (or even to another organization) often did so with a small entourage of employees who accompanied them.

Staff Reductions

As services within the bank were consolidated, it was obvious that staff reductions would be required. Inverlat staff were comforted by the bank's commitment to retain all staff for the first year, particularly when considering the poor state of the economy and the banking sector; but, even at lower levels of the organization, the need for reductions was apparent. Some managers complained that the restructuring process was being slowed considerably by the need to find places for personnel who were clearly no longer required.

Motivations for retaining staffing levels were twofold. First, BNS did not want to tarnish the image of its foreign investment in Mexico with massive reductions at the outset. When the

Spanish bank, Banco Bilbao Viscaya (BBV), purchased Banca Cremi the previous year, they began the restructuring process with a staff reduction of over 2,000 employees. BNS executives thought that this action had not been well received by the Mexican government or marketplace.

The second reason BNS management felt compelled to wait for staff reductions was that they wanted adequate time to identify which employees were productive and fit into the new organizational culture, and which employees would not add significant value. The problem was, quality employees were not sure if they would have a job in a year, and many managers thought that employees would begin to look for secure positions in other organizations. One Canadian manager commented that even some employees who were performing well in their current positions would ultimately lose their jobs. Many thought action needed to be taken sooner than later. A senior Mexican manager explained the situation:

> Take the worst-case scenario, blind guessing. At least then, you will be correct 50 percent of the time and retain some good people. If you wait, people within the organization will begin to look for other jobs and the market will choose who it wants. But as the market hires away your people, it will be correct at 90 percent of the time and you will be left with the rest.

Until that point, not many managers had been hired away from the bank. Many felt that this was due to the poor condition of the banking sector. As the economy improved, however, many believed that the talented managers would begin to leave the bank if job security could not be improved.

Jim felt that something was needed to communicate a sense of security to the talented managers they could already identify, but he was not certain how to proceed.

Conclusion

Jim felt that the Canadian team had been relatively successful in the early months. Many managers referred to the period as the "Honeymoon Stage." It was generally felt that the situation would intensify as managers looked for results from the restructured organization and as staff reductions became a reality. Jim then wondered how he could best prepare for the months ahead. Much of the communication with employees to date had been on an ad hoc basis. Jim did not feel they could take the risk of starting reductions without laying out a plan. The negative rumors would cause the bank to lose many of its most valued Mexican managers.

Assignment Questions*

1. How would you describe the management values of the Canadians and Mexicans in the case? What cultural differences might these reflect? How are these reflected in the current communications climate at Inverlat?

2. Who are the key stakeholders at Inverlat? What are their communications priorities and needs? Why?

3. What communications decisions must Jim O'Donnell make for the short term and long term to facilitate Inverlat's success? How should he try to bridge cultural issues in doing so?

*Questions not part of original case.

CASE 4

Contract Negotiations in Western Africa: A Case of Mistaken Identity

Peter Janes, a young member of Eurojet's Contracts Department, was on his way to Saheli in French-speaking western Africa to work on the complicated negotiations involved in selling a jet airliner to the Saheli government. He was not altogether thrilled with the assignment and hoped it would be a quick deal, since financing seemed to be available for it. Janes, educated in law, had experience in contract negotiation in India, the Philippines, Saudi Arabia, and, most recently, Australia. At 27, he was one of the younger members of the department but was seen as trustworthy, with a high degree of motivation. If successful, it would be the first deal he had brought to closure on his own. But he had serious doubts about the project's feasibility or desirability. Furthermore, he had no desire to become a Francophone Africa expert within the company. In addition, Janes had left behind what seemed to be the beginning of a great relationship in Australia and he wanted to get back to his girlfriend.

The Company

Eurojet, based in the U.K., was one of the larger diversified aircraft manufacturers. It had developed a special jet for Third World operations, able to operate from hot, high-altitude airfields, including unprepared strips. However, orders were hard to come by because of the difficulties in Third World financing and the poor financial condition of regional airlines. The company was therefore delighted to learn that its regional sales executive in Saheli, Mr. Ali Osaju, had found a potential sale in his country's desire for a presidential aircraft, along with its need for reliable regional air transport.

The sale looked even more likely when it was discovered that the government export/import bank had a substantial budget available for Saheli, making financing of the multimillion-dollar aircraft feasible. It would be necessary to arrange an international commercial bank loan for Saheli as well. The potential of the airliner to earn revenue through regional transport was considered important in securing the loan.

The Negotiating Team

The Saheli government announced that it was ready to begin detailed negotiations. According to Eurojet policy, negotiations were conducted by the Contracts Department in close cooperation with sales and internal specialist functions. Peter Janes, having just spent three months based in Australia working across Southeast Asia on specialist leasing packages, with only four days off in the last six months, was assigned to the team because of his Third World experience and his ability to speak French. He had been with the company for about two years but had no experience in Africa.

Ali Osaju was a highly placed African of Middle-Eastern origin, educated in Europe, with a background in aviation. He had joined the company at about the same time as Janes. Osaju had no previous experience in selling high-tech capital goods but had many good connections. He was seen as invaluable to the company because of his African background combined with his European education. He had been developing local contacts in Saheli by spending a week there every two or three months over the past two years.

The Negotiating Policy

The company's negotiating policy inevitably led to what was referred to as the "two-headed monster approach." The sales representative was responsible for initial discussions and for overall relations

"A Case of Mistaken Identity" prepared by Gordon Anderson, MBA graduate 1988 and Christine Mead, Research Assistant under the supervision of Susan Schneider, as a basis for class discussion rather than to illustrate either effective or ineffective handling of an administrative situation. Copyright © 1993 INSEAD-CEDAP, Fontainebleau, France.

with the customer. The contracts representative was responsible for negotiating concrete offers and signing contracts and finance agreements on behalf of the company. This double approach led to varying degrees of tension between the members of particular teams as well as between the departments in general. Sales was particularly aggrieved that contracts operated on a worldwide basis rather than a regional one.

Working on a team where both parties have important roles to play required considerable sensitivity. In his two years of working at Eurojet, Peter Janes was looked on by the sales people as a considerate and skilled negotiating partner. He was not likely to lose a contract which they had spent years developing because of cultural clumsiness. Nevertheless, he walked a very narrow line, as it was his role to say no to all the wishes of the customer which were not feasible from the company's perspective. As this was to be his first solo contract negotiation and Ali Osaju's first sale with the company, they shared a similar personal motivation for closing the deal.

The Negotiation: The Early Days

Eurojet was not the only company trying to sell a jet-liner to Saheli. The Russians, who had had considerable influence on the country since its independence twenty years earlier, were very much present, trying to sell their aircraft and sabotage the deal with Eurojet. Janes and Osaju frequently received strange phone calls in their hotel rooms and were aware that all their telephone calls were bugged. Once, Janes returned to his room to find that his briefcase had been tampered with. In addition, another European company with a number of contracts in surrounding countries was trying to arrange a deal.

The main negotiating point of the team was to propose that the Sahelis accept one airplane that could be converted from a regional airliner to a VIP presidential jet. The Sahelis had originally wanted a specially designed VIP jet, which would have cost an extra ten million dollars and would never be used other than for the president. The negotiations moved extremely slowly. Janes and Osaju spent hours waiting to see officials and chasing administrative papers from one office to another. They became aware that no one official wanted to be responsible for making the decision, to avoid being blamed should things go wrong.

The two men spent many hours debating strategy in the bar of the hotel. Janes objected to Osaju telling him what to do. Osaju objected to Janes making issues too complicated for the client. The relationship was a very tense one. They both felt they were getting little support from head office. They also thought that the circumstances they were working in were very difficult.

Peter Janes began to feel he was in a no-win situation. He realized that the negotiating process could go on for months, and he knew that another colleague had already begun to take over his activities with multi-order prospects in Australia. Conditions at the hotel were not that comfortable, and both he and Osaju were paid on a salary-only basis. There were no overseas allowances.

The lack of support from headquarters was a problem for both the negotiators. Communications were difficult, as they felt they could not talk freely over the telephone because of being bugged. Furthermore, they did not feel that their contacts at headquarters could begin to understand the finer points of the negotiation difficulties. They did learn from headquarters that they were considered to be moving too slowly in making the deal.

There were constant discussions on finance, spare parts, configuration, certification, and training. All the legal and technical documents had to be translated from English to French, causing many minor but significant misunderstandings. In one case, the standard contract in the U.K. called for the Saheli government to waive its "sovereign immunity" and "contract in its private rather that its public capacity." However, Saheli had adopted the Napoleonic Code from France and had no equivalent legal concepts. The courts in the U.K. had a very limited right to hear actions against the Crown and they assumed that this element of the law held true for all countries. The Saheli negotiators listened with polite disbelief to these explanations and sent a telegram to the president saying "Sahelian sovereignty is being threatened."

Janes and Osaju decided on a very basic strategy of patience and a friendly, open manner. Establishing trust and preserving individual and corporate credibility were recognized as being vital. They placed great emphasis on simplifying the bureaucratic process. Two months of negotiating passed with no commitment in sight.

Eurojet management were beginning to show a lack of confidence in the deal. Peter Janes had committed the company to $1,000,000 of expenditure to fit an airliner to the Sahelis' specifications and deliver it on time, yet saw no formal contract nor any evidence of the loan money. On the Saheli side, there was considerable nervousness about the commercial sovereign loans from the international banks.

Peter Janes had adapted himself to local culture as much as he could. Although his natural inclinations would have been to get things done quickly, deal with business first and make friends later, he was aware that that was not how business deals were made in Saheli. So he had spent many hours making friends, going to people's houses and walking round their businesses and factories. On one such occasion, he was walking round a factory with one of his friends, holding his hand as was the custom for Sahelian male friends to do. To his horror, a group of foreign diplomats came toward them on their tour of the factory. Janes was aware of an almost superhuman effort on his part not to let go of his friend's hand and keep his own relaxed, even as he felt the rest of his body stiffen with tension.

Janes continued to make his daily round of visits to offices and homes, establishing himself as open and trustworthy and trying to express complex legal and technical terms in a simple way. He began to be aware of a warming of perceptions toward him. Up until then he had felt that the Sahelian officials were always guarded, on the defensive in the presence of Eurojet's legal commercial representative. He thought that this was because it was his role to say "no." In the third month of the negotiations, he received an extremely encouraging sign. A source close to the president had recently been quoted as saying "He (Janes) doesn't say 'yes' very often, but when he says 'yes' he means 'yes.'" This was the sign that he and Osaju had been waiting for, a sign that this credibility had been established and they could now begin to deal with some of the more sensitive issues in the negotiation.

Mistaken Identity?

Most meetings in Saheli began with extended conversations about everyone's family and general social subjects. It was not uncommon to go to a meeting and find twenty people in the room, friends and relations of the person who had arranged the meeting. It was considered extremely rude not to go around the room greeting and chatting with everyone, so that even the first stage of saying hello in a meeting could take one or two hours.

On one of these occasions, Peter Janes was introduced to the son of the presidential pilot, a nine-year-old soccer fanatic. Janes had last played soccer at university, but he was a great fan and was amused to find in this nine-year-old extensive knowledge of all the international teams. The father told his son that Janes played soccer himself, which Janes took to be a bit of fun. Thereafter, he was always introduced as "Mr. Janes, the great footballer" and had many affable conversations with the father and son about playing soccer. It soon became clear that the son, having listened with awe to Janes's extensive explanations about the game, decided that he played for Cedex, the international team.

The first inkling Janes had that this matter had gone beyond a family joke was when the head of the local television station sought an invitation to meet him and immediately brought the conversation around to soccer. In order to avoid embarrassment, Janes was careful to sidestep questions—his training as a lawyer was not for nothing—by saying "Cedex is doing fine" or "No, I'm not playing as much soccer as I used to." He was very careful neither to deny nor to affirm the misunderstanding of his playing for Cedex, but the situation began to make him extremely uneasy.

Conversations with complete strangers became increasingly bizarre. Janes at first thought his hosts were having a laugh at his expense, but he then began to suspect that there was something more important at stake than making him feel foolish. The Minister of Protocol invited him to be the guest of honor at the local Cup Final. His new visa was returned to him as a "Visa de Courtoisie" or diplomatic visa. Several times he tried to bring the subject up with the pilot-father, but his attempts were always met with a big guffaw, a slap on the back, and some remark about "the great footballer!"

Janes was increasingly upset about further references to his career as an international soccer player. He did not understand how anyone could take him as a professional player for an international team when he spent all his time negotiating the sale of aircraft with government officials. He imagined daily what it would be like to phone his boss at home to try and justify the loss of the contract by explaining that he had misled people into thinking that he was a famous soccer player.

He was unwilling to embarrass people by saying they were wrong, but he was equally uncomfortable not striking down the myth—perhaps it served some purpose. His status as an international soccer player was apparently much greater than that of a young lawyer, and perhaps he needed that "little extra" to justify his power in negotiating and signing the contract. It was relatively easy to give indirect answers to questions, thus salving his conscience and protecting his strangely acquired status. Nonetheless, alluding to his legal training, Janes had said to Osaju, "I can put my hand on my heart and say 'I have not told a lie' but I don't feel comfortable. We have worked so hard for credibility I would hate a silly issue like this to backfire on us." At the time they had agreed to laugh off the matter, as the people involved were not main players in the negotiations.

The issue came to a head one day when Peter Janes had a chance meeting in the lobby of the hotel with an important Saheli minister and his counterpart from a neighboring country, with whom Eurojet was very keen to do business. To Janes's horror, the two launched into an enthusiastic and serious discussion about potential dates for a tour of West Africa by Cedex. Maybe now, he thought, he had better set the record straight.

Epilogue

Peter Janes continued to make non-committal replies and managed to avoid any further serious problems. Although greatly disturbing to him personally, the soccer question was a non-issue in terms of the negotiations. Fortunately for Janes, he could discuss his feelings about the situation with Ali Osaju and so relieve some of his own tension by laughing about the absurdity of it.

After ten months of intense negotiations, the deal was almost called off by the negotiating team at the last minute. They had spent days of retranslating the French contract back into English and then sitting beside a Sahelian typist who did not speak English saying each word to her phonetically so that she could type it. They both had had very little sleep in order to get the contract finished in time. When they finally went with the Attorney General to the president's office to sign the contract, they were kept waiting for several hours as usual. During that time,

the Attorney General reread the French contract and discovered numerous spelling mistakes in it. He then declared that he could not give it to the president in its present condition and that the signing would have to be delayed for another week.

Osaju and Janes both hit the wall—literally. It was the last straw. While Osaju threw books and papers, Janes strode around the room shouting that unless they signed immediately he was withdrawing Eurojet's approval of the contract. The Attorney General stood his ground, and Osaju and Janes stormed off to the hotel. They could scarcely believe what they had done after almost a year's worth of friendly and meticulous negotiating. Janes went to sleep, exhausted after the last ten days of work and the loss of the contract.

He was woken four hours later to be informed that the Attorney General was waiting to see him. He was escorted to an office across the road where he found the Attorney General in his shirtsleeves sitting at a typewriter, carefully changing all the spelling mistakes himself. He wanted Peter to initial all the changes so that he would feel confident that no substantial changes were being made in the contract. The contract was signed the next day.

Despite Eurojet's advice, the aircraft was not handled by the national airlines but kept under the president's control and thus rarely used. Debt servicing soon became a problem and one year later the aircraft was quietly and informally repossessed. Eurojet offered to resell the aircraft, but the Saheli government balked at authorizing the sale.

Osaju spent one more year in Africa, and was then promoted to the Far East, where he was made Regional Sales Director. Janes was promoted to another project, where he continued to work for the next four years.

Assignment Questions

1. Why did the negotiations described encounter difficulties? What cultural differences might be relevant?

2. How woud you assess the support that headquarters provided for the negotiating team? How could the firm do a better job in this regard?

3. How should negotiators go about building relationships with local contacts in West African countries? What should have been done differently? Why?

PART III

Capitalizing on International Opportunities

8

Taking Stock: Developing International Strategy

Learning Objectives

After reading this chapter, you should be able to:

▸ Describe basic international strategic concepts and the theory of national competitive advantage.

▸ Identify types of international strategies and the firm and industry factors that affect them.

▸ Describe the steps involved in the process of creating international strategy.

▸ Identify the organizational features that help companies develop and implement their international strategies successfully.

INTERNATIONAL CHALLENGE

Jollibee Foods: A Menu for Beating McDonald's in the Philippines

JOLLIBEE FOODS IS a fast-food chain based in the Philippines that began as a family-run ice cream parlor in 1975. Today, Jollibee's major "local" competitor is global giant McDonald's Corporation, a com-pany with over 30,000 restaurants that serve almost 50 million people *daily* in some 120 countries. Of course, McDonald's is one of the best-known companies in the world, with products, like the Big Mac, that often look and taste about the same wherever they are ordered. This, combined with its reputation for high quality, cleanliness, and fast service, makes McDonald's a very tough competitor indeed. Moreover, McDonald's has a track record of picking excellent, high-traffic locations for its stores and successfully pulling in kids—with jungle gyms, signature characters, and licensed toys and novelties.

But Jollibee wasn't intimidated. In fact, Jollibee has thrived in the face of the McDonald's challenge in its home market. Today, Jollibee sits on top of the fast-food heap in the Philippines, with an enviable 55 percent share of the market. Granted, McDonald's has grown in the Philippines over the past several years, but Jollibee has grown faster. From 1996 to 2004, Jollibee went from about 200 outlets to over 900 (an increase of about 250 percent) while McDonald's went from 90 outlets to about 240 (an increase of about 166 percent). During this same time period, Jollibee also embarked on a modest foreign expansion plan of its own. Today, Jollibee has some thirty restaurants in foreign locations, including Hong Kong, Vietnam, and the United Arab Emirates. And Jollibee even invaded McDonald's home turf, opening several outlets in California.

The bottom line is that Jollibee has successfully competed on its home turf against McDonald's, arguably the world's most formidable fast-food retailer, since the 1980s. So here's *your* challenge. What strategic recipe did Jollibee create to beat back McDonald's in the Philippines? How should McDonald's respond to win back some of its Philippines market from Jollibee? As you read through this chapter, you'll come to understand the process of developing international strategy and some of the factors that make for successful forays into foreign markets. If you can, do a little research on the Philippines as part of your evaluation and assessment of both companies. The Philippines has cycled through bouts of political instability and economic weakness over the years, factors that gave foreign companies pause about investing there. While Jollibee took advantage of some of these factors, they don't fully explain its success. Come up with your own strategic assessment for Jollibee. Then take a look at the *Up to the Challenge?* box at the end of the chapter to see what steps Jollibee took to take a bite out of the Big Mac.[1]

▶ *International Strategy: Deciding How to Compete*

As we've seen in previous chapters, companies operating internationally often face a diverse quilt of cultures, values, and practices. In addition, companies typically encounter an array of opportunities (e.g., unexploited markets) and threats in foreign countries (e.g., political risk, possible moves by competitors, management headaches). Consequently, figuring out the best way to operate in various markets around the world can be a very complicated matter. That said, developing an overall plan for competing abroad and choosing market entry options that make sense for the firm can mean the difference between success and failure when operating internationally.[2]

Indeed, deciding how a company should pursue opportunities in foreign markets is a critical part of international strategic management. This chapter will focus on the basic strategies firms can pursue abroad as well as how to develop them (Chapter 9 will address specific foreign market entry options). Generally speaking, the process of formulating international strategy involves developing international goals and then implementing whatever approach to international business the company has adopted. And the stakes are high. Today, companies must be able to anticipate and react quickly to changes in markets and technology or lose their ability to compete effectively. For instance, while multinationals often see China as a fantastic place to make money, many experts consider it the toughest market in the world, with increasingly aggressive and savvy local companies emerging to challenge established firms such as U.S.-based Motorola.[3]

Clearly, advances in communication and transportation have made it easier for all companies to source the best parts, materials, products, and labor from anywhere in the world in ways that best meet their needs. For instance, sending one forty-foot cargo container full of clothes (a container holds about 6,000 items) by boat from Shanghai to New York takes about a month, but costs less than $4,000. This might be perfectly fine if the customer is a retailer like Target or Wal-Mart. On the other hand, sending the equivalent container by air is much more expensive (about $50,000), but only takes a couple of days (which might be key for manufacturing firms that need critical, high-value parts on a just-in-time basis).[4]

Consequently, with the ability to communicate 24/7 and plenty of transportation options, you might think that the importance of location as a competitive weapon isn't what it used to be. After all, if everyone can source globally (e.g., manufacture garments in China because labor is cheap), then there's no unique advantage to doing so. But this overlooks how important it is to figure out where the best places are to manufacture, to innovate, to buy supplies, to sell products, and so on in the first place. Indeed, when it comes to innovation and long-term success, location still matters a great deal.[5] For instance, the world's best consumer electronics firms are based in Japan, the best entertainment firms are located in Hollywood, and the best in leather fashions come from Italy. Understanding how and why these clusters of excellence exist around the world underscores why strategic planning may be the most important task facing international managers.[6] Despite the potential value of having a coherent international strategy, a surprising number of companies enter overseas markets without a clear, well-designed approach. This failure to plan can lead to a variety of problems:

- *An inability to predict accurately the direction of foreign markets* (making it impossible to adapt accordingly)
- *Poor use of resources abroad* (e.g., because of improperly selected investments or bad decisions about how or where to enter foreign markets)
- *Underestimating the resources needed to compete effectively abroad*
- *Failing to anticipate operational problems in foreign environments* (e.g., overlooking the need to stockpile raw materials that can't be reliably obtained from local suppliers)[7]

So what does having an international strategy do for a company? Regardless of the industry in which companies compete or their level of overseas sophistication, all international strategies should provide answers to the same basic questions, including:

- *What products or services will be sold abroad?*
- *Where and how will services be delivered or products made?*
- *What resources are necessary for international competition and how will they be acquired?*
- *How will competitors be outperformed?*[8]

Traditionally, developing international strategy was the exclusive purview of top executives. Today, many firms involve teams of people who are closer to the marketplace in the creation of international strategy. The idea is to react more quickly to specific changes in an evolving international environment. For instance, line managers are often in a better position to spot trends and test new ideas than senior management. If the goal of strategy development is to stay nimble and quickly take advantage of international opportunities, then involving people who understand the marketplace best should help this process.[9]

In fact, some companies like Hewlett-Packard even involve suppliers and customers in strategic planning to help identify new business opportunities. Overall, research suggests that the best strategic planning process is one that builds in flexibility and openness to change. Particularly in rapidly changing environments, companies may have to modify, amend, and tweak their international strategies as they go, or even dump them altogether if conditions warrant.[10]

As we've suggested, the goal of this chapter is to introduce you to basic concepts about strategy and competitiveness. Next, we'll discuss some company level strategies for multinationals and outline the process of strategy development. Along the way, we'll examine some of the special challenges facing small firms when it comes to developing international strategy. Finally, we'll review some of the organizational features that companies should possess to successfully develop and implement their international strategies.

Strategic Concepts for International Competition

Back in Chapter 1 we provided snapshots of the economic powers that are emerging to challenge the dominance of established players such as Japan and the United States. The past several years have seen dramatic increases in the growth of international business, much of it fueled by rapidly developing countries such as China.[11] Another important trend to mention is that small and medium-sized companies have contributed greatly to the growth in international business in recent years. In fact, they actually account for a bigger slice of international trade than large firms. For instance, the fifty biggest American exporters (e.g., Boeing) account for only about a third of exported merchandise, with small and medium-sized firms accounting for most of the rest.[12]

Nevertheless, large multinationals continue to be the focus of research on international strategy because of their enormous influence and impressive global reach. Consider Mitsubishi Corporation. This Japanese giant actually represents a family of over two dozen companies with interrelated ownership. This ownership structure, called **keiretsu**, is relatively common in Japan, although it is slowly fading. One of the family members is usually a trading company (called a *sogo shosa*) that helps market products from the rest of the corporate family to the outside world. In this role, Mitsubishi at one point sold as many as 100,000 products to some 45,000 customers worldwide.[13]

keiretsu
In Japan, a family of companies with interrelated ownership

EXHIBIT 8.1 *Understanding the Value Chain*

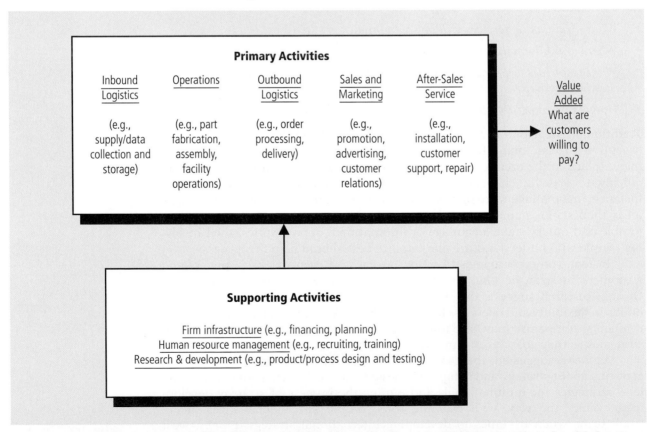

Source: Adapted from Porter, M. E. (1998). Competing across locations: Enhancing competitive advantage through a global strategy. *Harvard Business School Press*, Product #2026, 6.

Basic Business-Level Strategies Of course, this discussion begs the question of how international companies actually compete. Fundamentally, all companies make money through **value creation**, offering products or services that customers want. There are three basic business-level strategies for pursuing this end, either alone or in combination.

One way companies can meet international customer demands is by **differentiating** their products or services from those of competitors. In other words, they provide unique or superior products that customers are willing to pay for. That's the route Mercedes-Benz takes in offering what it believes are the world's best production cars. But a Mercedes isn't cheap. So another way to provide value is through **cost leadership**, offering cheaper products or more efficient services than competitors. For example, Asian computer firms and component manufacturers have done well by combining efficient manufacturing operations and inexpensive labor, allowing them to undercut competitors on price (e.g., Taiwan-based Acer). Finally, firms embracing a **niche strategy** focus on a specific line of products or services relative to competitors who operate more broadly. By serving a specific market segment, firms hope to do a better job of responding to customers and meeting their needs (e.g., on price, differentiation, or both) than do their competitors. Porsche is an example of a firm that traditionally pursued a niche strategy (up until recently, the company focused exclusively on upscale sports cars), one based on providing superior performance compared to competitors (i.e., differentiation).[14]

The Value Chain: Making Choices and Building Competencies Regardless of the basic approach used to attract customers, companies can add value by changing any of their primary activities (e.g., manufacturing products, marketing products) or supporting activities (e.g., procuring raw materials, designing products), either alone or in combination. As Exhibit 8.1 suggests, a firm can be thought of as a linked set of these primary and supporting activities, referred to as a **value chain**. Consequently, a company's international strategy also involves the choices it makes in terms of how value chain activities are *configured* (e.g., where do value chain activities actually happen?) and *coordinated* (e.g., are dispersed activities tightly controlled from headquarters, or do they remain under local control?).

Often companies change value chain activities to improve their **core competencies**, skills that are hard for competitors to imitate. Core competencies can be located anywhere in a value chain and still provide the basis for international competitiveness. For instance, one firm's competitiveness might rest on its outstanding logistical execution (e.g., Wal-Mart's sophisticated distribution system), while another's is based on its ability to innovate (e.g., consider 3M's long history of creating unique products), and yet another's is based on its prowess in manufacturing (e.g., Toyota's track record for quality). If firms have a core competency that helps them outperform competitors (e.g., they attract more customers because they have the best logistics, are the most innovative, or have the highest quality), then they possess a **distinctive competency**.

Since international business should continue to grow over the long term (e.g., as trade barriers continue to fall), one view is that firms compete best by moving different value chain activities to wherever **location economies** exist. For instance, if the cheapest and most productive labor for assembling a particular product is in Vietnam, then that's where a company should locate production operations. If the best product designers are found in the United States, then that's where R&D activities should be located.[15]

---

value creation
The process of offering products or services that customers want

differentiating
The basic strategy of providing unique or superior products to customers

cost leadership
The basic strategy of providing cheaper products or more efficient services than competitors

niche strategy
Focusing on a more specific line of products or services relative to competitors

value chain
The linked set of primary and supporting activities firms use to produce products or services

core competencies
Skills or abilities that are difficult for competing firms to imitate

distinctive competency
A skill or ability that helps firms to outperform competitors

location economies
Places where value chain activities can be performed most cheaply and efficiently

Locating certain value chain activities in places that offer such benefits gives companies a source of competitive advantage compared to firms that fail to do so. For instance, companies that need software development and maintenance may gain an edge over rivals by locating those activities in India, a source of inexpensive and well-trained programmers. And sometimes firms use a complex patchwork of locations for various value chain activities. Consider what Hewlett-Packard does in bringing a new computer server to the market. The concept for a server is hatched by the firm's designers in Singapore, with managers in Houston providing final approval. Next, parts and components are engineered in Taiwan. Final product assembly occurs in a variety of locations (e.g., China, India, Australia), with most of the output staying in those markets.[16] Of course, the advantages associated with dispersing value chain activities to various locations can be offset by various problems (e.g., coordination difficulties driven by cultural differences). So the idea is to capitalize on location advantages while effectively coordinating and integrating operations across those locations. Clearly, that's easier said than done.[17]

On top of that, location economies such as low labor costs or plentiful raw materials only offer a sustainable competitive advantage if it's hard for other firms to follow suit. In other words, there's nothing terribly unique about moving plants to low-wage locations or sourcing materials from certain overseas

EXHIBIT 8.2   *Location Factors That May Offer an International Competitive Advantage*

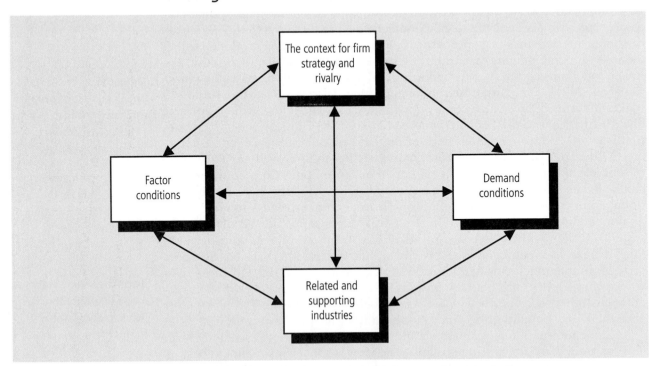

Source: Adapted from Porter, M. E. (1990). The competitive advantage of nations. *Harvard Business Review, 90,* 77.

locations. You may be at a disadvantage if your competitors operate in a low-wage environment and you don't, everything else being equal. But jumping on the low-wage bandwagon won't set you apart. Instead, locations that somehow help companies continually improve their productivity, processes, marketing savvy, or capacity for innovation may do more to provide a competitive advantage over the long haul. Put simply, it's the ability to constantly change and adapt that allows many international firms to outperform competitors.[18]

Locations and Competitiveness This discussion suggests that competitiveness is a complex concept involving both the industries that companies are in as well as the places where they do business. Of course, companies compete. But in a sense, nations also compete to provide goods and services that international markets demand as well as a rising standard of living for their citizens.[19]

This raises the question of how nations become competitive and why certain nations seem to produce firms that are very successful in specific industries. For instance, why do American companies lead in computer software, but Japanese companies lead in consumer electronics? The **theory of national competitive advantage** tries to answer such questions. It argues that four factors shape the context in which nations, and the firms based there, compete. These factors, presented in Exhibit 8.2, represent a combination of national and firm-specific characteristics. Understanding how they interact can help explain why industries and companies succeed or fail in particular locations:

theory of national competitive advantage Theory explaining how nations become competitive and why they produce firms that are very successful in specific industries

1. **Factor conditions.** Does a nation offer the components needed for competitive production in a particular industry, such as abundant raw materials, capital, business infrastructure, and skilled labor? With the right combination of conditions, home-grown competitors can spring up, do well domestically, and eventually become formidable international competitors. For instance, the prime grape-growing land in California and a large pool of expert winemakers are key reasons why the United States is a worldwide leader in this industry.

2. **Demand conditions.** What's the nature of the market in a particular country for an industry's goods or services? Large, sophisticated home markets often force firms to become more innovative, which may foreshadow where international markets are ultimately headed. This early awareness can help firms stay ahead of competitors from other countries. For instance, Americans' desire for convenience and speed has spawned efficient fast-food companies (e.g., McDonald's, Subway), many of which have done well overseas where similar desires have emerged.

3. **Related and supporting industries.** Does a cluster of suppliers or related industries that are internationally competitive exist in a country? If so, they can provide superior and mutually beneficial access to components, technology, and innovation (often thanks to shorter lines of communication and established working relationships). For instance, Italian shoe companies owe much of their overseas success to the close relationships they have developed with local leather suppliers, shoe component manufacturers, and specialized equipment firms.

4. **Firm strategy, structure, and rivalry.** How does the domestic competitive environment, as well as local laws, culture, and business practices, impact the ways in which firms organize and operate in a particular country? Tough domestic competition forces firms to be more innovative, productive, and cost conscious, all characteristics that may serve them well in international markets. For instance, Honda's excellent performance in the U.S. auto market is partially a consequence of its intensive competitive struggles with formidable home-grown rivals in Japan (e.g., Toyota and Nissan). Likewise, management practices can also make it easier or harder for firms in certain countries to compete in specific industries.[20]

As Exhibit 8.2 suggests, the four factors driving national competitive advantage can interact to affect how successful firms are in international markets. For example, just having demanding domestic customers may not be enough to give a firm in a particular country a competitive advantage. But if that firm also faces tough domestic competition and existing conditions support its efforts to develop more innovative products (e.g., the technology infrastructure is excellent), then a competitive advantage may result when the company tries to sell its products in other countries. A combination of factors may help explain why successful American software firms such as Microsoft have also done well abroad. Conversely, a combination of factors may explain why Italian leather and wool goods firms, some with histories dating back several hundred years, have seen their long-running success recently put at risk by upstart Chinese competitors. Being in a cluster of related industries with well-developed relationships and a tradition of craftsmanship helped the Italian firms prosper for many years. However, the local business environment made it difficult for them to respond quickly to the Chinese threat. Specifically, as low-cost but high-quality Chinese companies started winning customers away, the Italian firms were hamstrung by local labor laws that made it difficult to cut employees or move work elsewhere.[21] Overall, the theory of national competitive advantage is useful for thinking about how country-specific factors can affect firms' international competitiveness. That said, questions about the theory remain.[22] For instance, government policies can influence firms' ability to compete. However, the exact nature and extent of that influence isn't completely understood, particularly as it relates to the creation of internationally competitive firms in a country.[23] Moreover, having a positive domestic environment doesn't necessarily mean that a particular industry or company will thrive in a particular location. Conversely, companies have emerged from locations without some of the positive factors specified by the theory and still become formidable international competitors.[24]

Nevertheless, the factors spelled out by the theory of national competitive advantage do seem to impact the international strategies used by certain firms.[25] And that may be the key point. The strategic decisions that firms make given the conditions they face may ultimately play the biggest role in their international performance. In essence, firms need to make strategic choices that can best take advantage of conditions in specific countries. And when firms are operating in a variety of countries in different industries, they need to consider developing international strategies at a corporate level. Put simply, they need to find a way to effectively manage operations that stretch across a diverse array of both products and countries.[26] We'll turn our attention to those corporate-level strategies next.

▸ *Corporate Strategies Used by Multinationals*

The bottom line is that corporate strategies are used by multinationals to guide how their business-level strategies (e.g., to add value based on differentiation or low cost) are executed across countries. Clearly, firms may evolve through several levels of internationalization and be successful competitors in each. Many small companies first enter international markets by exporting and only later establish overseas facilities. Some firms eventually build subsidiaries in dozens of countries and form alliances with other companies.

Foreign market entry decisions are driven by a variety of factors, including the nature of (1) the industry the firm is in, (2) the particular market being entered, (3) the firm's strengths and weaknesses, and (4) the firm's stage of international development. We'll address some of these evolutionary issues in the next chapter when we consider various options for entering foreign markets in more detail. For now, however, we'll examine four common corporate strategies used by large multinationals—firms that already have an extensive international footprint.[27]

Actually, multinationals may use multiple strategies that reflect the needs of various business units or product lines. For example, General Electric offers an astonishing array of products and services that cut across several industries. These include appliances, communication and media services, electrical equipment, financial services, jet engines, lighting, medical diagnostic systems, and plastics (and this isn't a complete list!). Consequently, the degree to which GE tailors its products and services to local customers' needs (versus selling the same product everywhere in the same way at the same price) to compete effectively varies considerably across business units. And that has implications for the international strategies those units need to pursue. It may help to think of diverse multinationals like GE as networks of relationships that exist among many dispersed organizations, each with somewhat different goals, perspectives, and strategies.[28]

The Multidomestic Strategy

Nevertheless, we'll simplify things by treating multinationals as if they used a single strategy to guide all of their international operations. With this in mind, consider that a multinational's international strategy often reflects the nature of the industry in which it competes. For instance, in the commercial banking and beverage industries, multinationals must respond effectively to a diverse set of local preferences and needs. Put simply, in these industries, what will satisfy customers can vary dramatically from country to country. In response, multinationals may need to modify product features, marketing approaches, service delivery methods, and pricing, either alone or in combination.

And in some industries requiring local responsiveness, there's little accompanying pressure for integrating or centralizing operations on a global basis. In fact, differences in local needs may obliterate any advantages that might otherwise be obtained with centralized or integrated operations. For instance, centralizing production of certain food products makes little sense for companies like Nestlé and Unilever (both of which operate hundreds of manufacturing facilities worldwide). Transportation costs would offset any savings from economies of scale, and centralization would make it more difficult to offer an array of products tailored for specific locations (e.g., by size, price, packaging, taste, etc.) in the first place.

As a result, foreign subsidiaries of multinationals in multidomestic industries are often given a high degree of operational independence. In a sense, they operate more or less as intact companies so as to best provide tailored products and services for the local markets that they serve. In short, multinationals taking such an approach are using a **multidomestic strategy**, where goals are developed and implemented independently by units in specific countries.[29]

multidomestic strategy
An approach where business goals are developed and implemented independently for specific countries

The Global Strategy

At the other end of the spectrum are industries in which country-specific tastes are basically few or nonexistent. In these industries, the same standardized products or services can be sold everywhere with relatively few, if any, adjustments. For example, as a key competitor in the production of commercial aircraft, Boeing operates in an industry that has become increasingly global over the years. Consequently, Boeing sells commercial aircraft worldwide with few major differences across countries. This is not to say that no differences exist. Boeing typically offers customers around the world a limited set of variations on a particular plane, usually to accommodate individual airlines' needs (e.g., for passenger capacity, aircraft range, etc.). For instance, potential Japanese customers for Boeing's newest model under development, the 7E7, were said to be interested in shorter-range versions of the plane (given the distances traveled in the Japanese market), while U.S. airlines were reportedly interested in longer-range versions (given the relatively longer distances flown in the American market).[30]

In any case, multinationals operating in industries where requirements for local tailoring are minimal often pursue a **global strategy**—an approach where goals and directions are set on a worldwide basis. Indeed, with a global strategy, company headquarters serves a key integrating and controlling role, maintaining central control over operations worldwide. That said, companies pursuing global strategies may eschew scattering value chain activities around the world. Instead, they often prefer to concentrate important value chain activities such as manufacturing and product development in key places.[31] And that's basically the approach that Boeing takes in competing against Airbus, its European rival. For example, Boeing operates a design center in Moscow, where several hundred employees develop parts for various planes. Boeing also coordinates overseas suppliers (e.g., Xian Aircraft in China and Mexmil in Mexico) that produce parts and partners with firms that both design and manufacture key aircraft components (e.g., Mitsubishi). In essence, Boeing is an exporter of commercial aircraft. All of its planes are assembled in the United States (albeit with an increasing percentage of parts coming from foreign suppliers and partners) and then sold to airlines around the world.[32]

global strategy
An approach where business goals and directions are set on a worldwide basis

The Transnational Strategy

Other companies compete in industries where it is important to both tailor products or services to local market preferences and operate on an integrated basis worldwide. Consequently, these firms may want to move value chain activities to wherever they can be done "best" (e.g., cheapest, most efficiently, with the highest value added, etc.), while still adapting to important local preferences.[33] This approach is the essence of a **transnational strategy**. To some extent, this approach represents a "best of both worlds" blend of global and multidomestic approaches, one in which firms seek economies of scale and location advantages worldwide while still "acting locally" with their products or services out of competitive necessity. It's also an approach with a high potential for conflict and management headaches given the competing demands of local responsiveness and global efficiency.[34]

Consequently, companies that pursue a transnational strategy sometimes want to tilt the balance toward the global side with respect to product standardization. For instance, Procter & Gamble moved to simplify its personal care product lines and formulas worldwide. Today, the firm's Vidal Sassoon hair care products use a single fragrance worldwide. However, to satisfy local tastes, less fragrance is used in places where customers prefer subtlety (e.g., Japan) and more is used where customers like intense scents (e.g., some European countries). Although moving toward similar products or services worldwide simplifies things for companies, going too far risks alienating customers if significant preference differences exist across markets.[35] As a result, firms pursuing a transnational strategy must tweak and juggle the often competing demands for local responsiveness and global integration. Balancing these demands well requires effective management. In fact, multinationals using a transnational strategy must quickly transfer their core competencies throughout their worldwide organization and be prepared to take advantage of new or improved core competencies wherever they are developed.[36]

transnational strategy
An approach whereby a firm moves key activities to wherever they can be done best while still adapting to local product or service preferences

Another Alternative: The Regional Strategy

Despite the hype sometimes associated with them, global and transnational strategies may not be the best approaches for multinationals.[37] Indeed, multinationals sometimes have great difficulty figuring out just how responsive they should be to local preferences. Some products fall into an area where lifestyles and tastes are converging worldwide (favoring global strategies), while others are in an area where customers still hold on to their own unique preferences in specific countries (favoring multidomestic strategies).

Exhibit 8.3 lists factors that tend to favor global versus multidomestic strategies. As you can see, the formation of regional trading blocks (e.g., NAFTA) appears under the multidomestic column. Indeed, some multinationals that compete in supposedly "global" industries might be better off pursuing a **regional strategy**. A regional strategy allows managers in a particular geographic area like South America to make decisions, set goals, and respond to customers' needs. Part of this strategy also involves achieving efficiencies and

regional strategy
An approach that gives managers in a particular geographic area the freedom to make decisions, set goals, and respond to customers' needs

EXHIBIT 8.3   *Some Factors Favoring Global versus Multidomestic Strategies*

Factors Favoring a Global Approach	Factors Favoring a Multidomestic Approach
• Converging income across industrialized nations	• Industry standards remain diverse across nations
• Increasing similarity of consumer lifestyles and tastes worldwide	• Customers continue to demand products/services tailored to local needs
• Rapid advances in technology, communications, transportation; globalized financial markets	• Being seen as a "local" company is often a competitive asset
• Increasing worldwide trade, formation of global alliances	• Global organizations are hard to manage and control
• Reduced trade barriers, more open markets, and privatization of state-dominated economies	• Globalization can undercut unique competencies of foreign subsidiaries
• Emergence of nations with productive, low-cost labor (such as Thailand and Indonesia)	• Formation of regional trading blocks and agreements (e.g., NAFTA, the European Union)

Sources: Adapted from Morrison, A. J., Ricks, D. A., & Roth, K. (1991). Globalization versus regionalization: Which way for the multinational? *Organizational Dynamics, 19,* 17–29; Yip, G. S. (1995). *Total global strategy.* Englewood Cliffs, NJ: Prentice-Hall.

economies by leveraging any location advantages that may exist within the region (e.g., to minimize production costs by locating plants in cheap labor nations within a region).

For instance, French multinational Thomson Consumer Electronics uses a regional strategy for its television lines. Plants in Britain, Spain, Germany, and France each make specific types of televisions for the European market. Thomson's North American operations are run independently and focus on producing televisions with the RCA and GE labels just for that market, largely using regional suppliers of components. While this regional approach lacks the worldwide integration found in a transnational strategy, it offers more local product customization than a global strategy would. That said, a regional strategy does allow more geographic coordination than a multidomestic strategy (where multinationals set up quasi-independent subsidiaries to serve specific national markets). Overall, a regional strategy often represents a good compromise for companies in certain industries.[38] Finally, Exhibit 8.4 summarizes how industry pressures match up to the four corporate-level international strategies we've discussed.

When Strategy Provides a Competitive Advantage

At this point, you may be wondering when a firm's international strategy matters most. Of course, executing a strategy well is important. But the strategy itself can provide an important competitive edge, depending, in part, on the degree of alignment between the industry and the strategies typically used by competitors. For example, a multinational's global strategy may offer a competitive advantage when competitors use a multidomestic approach and the underlying character of the industry actually favors globalization (e.g., where customer preferences are becoming the same everywhere and global economies of scale are possible). In short, if a multinational uses a global strategy in an underglobalized industry (i.e., when competitors rely on strategies that don't fit

EXHIBIT 8.4   *Mapping International Strategy: Responding to Pressures for Local Responsiveness and Global Integration*

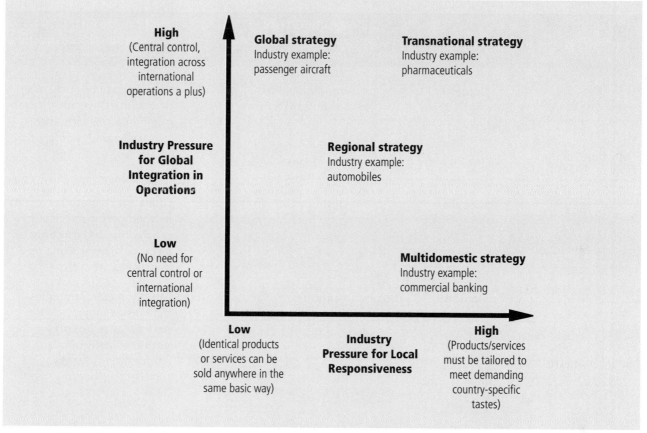

Sources: Adapted from Beamish, P. W., Morrison, A. J., Rosenzweig, P. M., & Inken, A. C. (2000). *International management: Text and cases* (4th Ed.). Burr Ridge, IL: Irwin McGraw-Hill, 143; Daniels, J. D., & Radebaugh, L. H. (2001). *International business: Environments and operations* (9th Ed.). Upper Saddle River, NJ: Prentice-Hall, 529.

the industry's underlying character), it should enjoy a competitive advantage. In fact, research supports the idea that the match or mismatch between the actual strategies used by international competitors in an industry and its underlying potential for globalization affects the relationship between multinational strategy and performance. Exhibit 8.5 summarizes the points we're making here.[39]

The Cultural Backdrop to International Strategy

Clearly, multinationals should develop their international strategies carefully. Of course, that process is shaped by firms' context. For instance, the smaller size of their home markets may help explain why European multinationals, relative to their American and Japanese counterparts, tend to give foreign subsidiaries more autonomy. Indeed, small home market size may also help explain why foreign sales tend to account for a larger percentage of total sales in European multinationals. Conversely, the large U.S. market may be one reason that American multinationals have been slower to internationalize than European and Japanese multinationals.[40]

EXHIBIT 8.5   *When Multidomestic and Global Strategies Matter Most: Taking Advantage of Mismatches between Industry Character and Competitors' Strategies*

Underlying Industry Character	Strategy Generally Used in Industry	Resulting Level of Industry Globalization (and Example)	Implications for Multinational Strategy and Performance
Most global	Domestic	Underglobalized (credit card industry)	Global strategies may offer real competitive advantages and higher performance relative to multidomestic strategies.
	Global	Optimum (ship-building industry)	Global strategies may result in good performance but may not necessarily offer a competitive advantage relative to other firms.
Most domestic	Domestic	Optimum (funeral industry)	Multidomestic strategies may result in good performance but may not necessarily offer a competitive advantage relative to other firms.
	Global	Overglobalized (tire industry)	Multidomestic strategies may offer real competitive advantages and higher performance relative to global strategies.

Source: Adapted from Birkinshaw, J., Morrison, A., & Hulland, J. (1995). Structural and competitive determinants of a global integration strategy. *Strategic Management Journal, 16:* 637–655.

But these patterns also reflect the influence of culture on how managers interpret the "rules of the game" in international business.[41] In essence, managers from different countries may bring different views about time, risks, and goals into the strategic planning process. For example, many Japanese multinationals have a tradition of centralized control, with all roads leading back to Japan. This tradition has been linked to several cultural factors, including Confucian values, the importance of in-group networks, and a desire to avoid uncertainty. Cultural values can also impact the methods used to develop international strategy. For example, when developing their strategies, companies based in countries with high individualism (e.g., the United States) tend to rely more on subjective information than on quantitative data or forecasting methods.[42]

Perceptions about culture matter, too. For example, the wider the perceived cultural gap between headquarters and foreign subsidiaries, the tighter the management control from headquarters tends to be.[43] Likewise, perceived similarity can shape strategy. Firms often make their first forays abroad in countries thought to have similar cultures and business practices. The rationale, of course, is that starting with foreign markets that are similar to the home market is "safer." But when perceptions about similarity are inaccurate, problems result. The high failure rate of Canadian retail firms entering the American market, many of which assumed that the United States was merely a larger version of Canada, is a case in point. Perceptions notwithstanding, real differences in tastes, values, and business practices exist between the two countries.[44]

Finally, culture can impact the ownership positions firms take in their foreign operations. For instance, multinationals based in high power distance, strong uncertainty avoidance countries (e.g., France) are more likely to maintain majority ownership over foreign subsidiaries than multinationals based in low power distance, weak uncertainty avoidance countries (e.g., the United States). And managers with a low power distance perspective tend to be more comfortable sharing control of overseas operations with a partner (e.g., as in a joint venture).[45] Overall, international managers should consider how their values and perspectives shape their strategy development and implementation efforts.

▶ *Winning Big: Small Firms and International Strategy*

That said, thinking about cultural issues can seem like a luxury to small firms (i.e., companies with fewer than 500 employees). For small firms, developing an international strategy is often a struggle.

The Strategy Struggle

Compared to large multinationals, small firms have fewer managerial and financial resources. Certain market entry options (e.g., building costly new plants overseas) may simply be beyond the reach of small firms. On top of that, the strategic planning process in small firms is typically reactive and informal instead of proactive and systematic as is often the case in large multinationals.

Often small firms are preoccupied with their domestic business. And when they do make international contacts or attract attention from potential overseas customers, they may respond poorly, as loads of unanswered e-mails will attest! Consider New York–based MMO Music, a small family-run business that makes the CDs used in karaoke machines. For years MMO lost overseas sales because the firm's president was so busy handling domestic growth that he couldn't respond quickly to foreign clients.[46]

Many small firms also underestimate how much time, money, and talent is needed to develop and execute an international strategy. For example, doing business in China usually means hammering out contracts in person. So a small firm's top management (often all the management there is!) might spend weeks in Beijing, usually after spending months trying to figure out China's opaque business practices and hunting for potential partners. No wonder small firms sometimes let such opportunities pass or have trouble capitalizing on them, despite the potential gains.[47]

Getting Help

That said, help is available for small firms. Even simple export deals can be challenging for small firms if they lack overseas contacts or relevant expertise (e.g., on transportation issues or legal matters). Overcoming these challenges may mean spending money and giving up some control, usually tough things for small firms to do. But once MMO hired an international sales director, its overseas sales tripled. Other small firms use consultants to acquire international business skills or even to sell their products. For instance, California-based Meridian Group can develop an export strategy and even implement it for small firms, managing sales, distribution, and shipping in the process.[48] Yet another option is to partner with a larger firm that can provide expertise, contacts, and technical help. For example, small Japanese companies have jump-started their efforts to sell outside of slow-growth Japan in recent years by teaming up with large Japanese trading companies (e.g., Mitsui).[49]

Government agencies can also help. For instance, the U.S. Department of Commerce's website (**www.doc.gov**) offers help and advice for small firms. Likewise, city or state governments can prove surprisingly helpful. In fact, local governmental agencies charged with promoting international trade often do an outstanding job. Many have grown their services as small firms increasingly moved into international markets.

When Small Firms Succeed Overseas: Finding and Exploiting a Specialized Niche

Interestingly, small firms that have successful international strategies tend to be manufacturers. For many of these companies, their international strategy is built around exporting products with unique features.[50] Indeed, small, highly specialized firms are the most common type of company in the international economy. Many offer unique products for very narrow market segments. Ironically, these specialized firms are often found in global industries. With a specific product, low overhead, accessible management, and quick decision making, small specialists can outperform large multinationals in global industries. For instance, offshore oil drilling equipment is basically a global industry with several large multinational competitors. However, small firms in this industry have done well by providing very specific types of equipment for underwater drilling (e.g., for use in certain water or seabed conditions).[51]

▶ *The Process of Developing International Strategy*

Clearly, firms should develop international strategies that fit their competitive contexts. But how is international strategy developed in the first place? While firms vary to some extent, in many cases management follows a series of five

EXHIBIT 8.6   *The Process of Developing International Strategy*

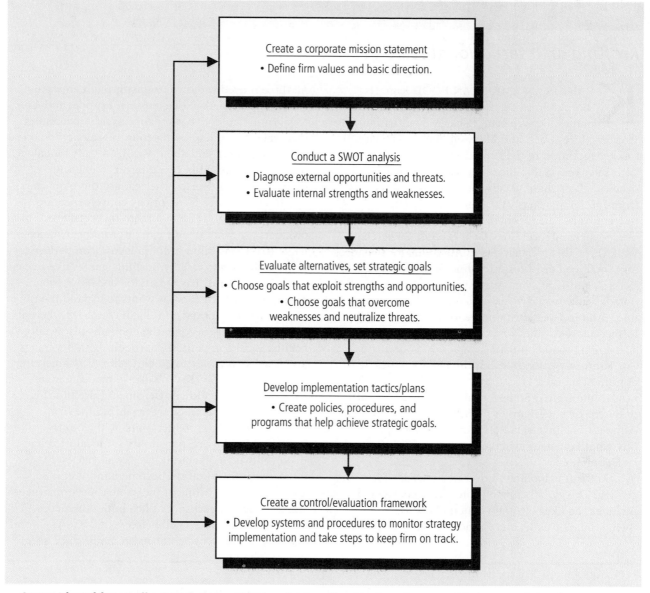

Source: Adapted from Griffin, R. W., & Pustay, M. W. (2005). *International business: A managerial perspective* (4th Ed.). Upper Saddle River, NJ: Prentice-Hall, 322.

basic steps in developing international strategy. These steps are outlined in Exhibit 8.6 and we'll consider them next.

Step 1: The Mission Statement

To clarify direction, many firms start the process of developing an international strategy by creating a **mission statement**. This statement summarizes firm values and its overall purpose. Ideally, the mission statement will express common goals in a way that succinctly captures management's vision for the firm.[52]

mission statement
A statement that summarizes key values and an overall organization purpose

🌐 International Insights

Krafting an International Strategy

KRAFT IS AN AMERICAN FOOD icon. Its more than five dozen brands are household names like Velveeta, Oscar Meyer, Triscuit, Planters, Lifesavers, and Maxwell House. The largest food corporation in the United States, Kraft is a giant, with sales over $30 billion. But Kraft is an also-ran overseas. Less than 30 percent of Kraft's sales come from foreign markets. By comparison, Heinz earns 44 percent of its sales abroad, McDonald's comes in at over 50 percent, and Coca-Cola exceeds 80 percent. Walk through supermarkets in Australia, for instance, and you'll be hard pressed to find Kraft products. Referring to Kraft, one Australian supermarket owner noted, "They would be classified as a slow-moving line." And in Great Britain, one of Kraft's strongest foreign markets, the company only ranks eighth in size among food companies.

Kraft wants to grow, but the United States, its dominant market, is saturated. Indeed, the food business in the United States is cutthroat. Brand loyalty is undercut by supermarket brands and intense price competition. Take salad dressing. Many shoppers just buy what's on sale—whether it's Kraft, Wish-Bone, or Hellmann's.

So Kraft is looking to overseas markets for growth. The global competition is formidable and includes the likes of Anglo-Dutch Unilever, Switzerland's Nestlé, and France's Groupe Danone.

All three moved rapidly into fast-growth emerging markets in Latin America, eastern Europe, and Asia. Nestlé and Unilever both realize over 30 percent of their sales from developing countries alone. In contrast, one expert said about Kraft, "A truly global organization would have a quarter to one-third of their business in North America, not three-quarters."

Indeed, Kraft's forte, pricey convenience foods, often has a tough time in foreign markets where basic products are what people can afford. For instance, while Kraft's visibility in India is low, competitor Unilever has done well by pushing staples like rice and salt. But Kraft has a plan for boosting revenues in emerging markets. First, it wants to expand the range of products and brands it sells in countries where it already operates. Second, the company also wants to acquire local competitors, particularly in beverages and snacks, as a way to quickly enter new emerging markets. Internally, Kraft has also made changes. In 2004, new CEO Roger Deromedi (hired for his international experience) reorganized the firm around five global product units, with country managers holding responsibility for local merchandising efforts. As he put it, the "challenges we face . . . demand that we become a more unified, global company" while at the same time strengthening the "local expertise that has built our success." Whether these moves will help expand Kraft's international reach in the years ahead remains to be seen.[53]

For example, in its mission statement, motorcycle maker Harley-Davidson describes itself as "an action-oriented, international company—a leader in its commitment to continuously improve the quality of mutually beneficial relationships with stakeholders." Other firms eschew mission statements or produce them after much of the strategic planning process is complete.[54]

SWOT analysis
A tool firms use to diagnose their internal strengths and weaknesses and external opportunities and threats

Step 2: Conducting a SWOT Analysis

Assuming a mission statement is developed first, performing a **SWOT analysis** is typically the second step in strategy development. SWOT stands for *strengths*, *weaknesses*, *opportunities*, and *threats*. It involves an assessment of the company's internal circumstances and external environment. A SWOT analysis usually involves **environmental scanning**, a process in which information about the internal and external situation facing the firm is systematically collected and evaluated. The external side of this assessment is known as an **environmental analysis**. Here the company assesses both (1) promising international opportunities for its products or services (e.g., unmet demand or weak competition in certain markets); and (2) any threats in foreign markets that might preclude those opportunities from being fully realized (e.g., inadequate business infrastructure, political instability, onerous government regulations, increasing competition, etc.).[55]

Ideally, firms will examine opportunities and threats at a multinational, regional, or country-specific level. At the multinational level, companies assess how worldwide trends might impact their businesses. For instance, many consumer products companies are optimistic about their long-term prospects for international growth because of rising disposable incomes in developing countries like China.[56] But assessing external opportunities and threats is easier said than done, particularly for companies that have been largely domestic in their orientation. Such firms may lack the staff or expertise to conduct an environmental analysis of international markets. Consequently, these firms may fail to perceive international opportunities or significant foreign threats.

In any case, it may be hard for companies to take advantage of international opportunities because of both internal weaknesses and pressure from competitors. Take a look at the accompanying International Insights about Kraft Foods' international challenges to see what we mean.

Analyzing the environment from a regional perspective involves looking at emerging trends in a geographic area. For example, some South American governments loosened regulations and improved their business infrastructures in recent years, creating opportunities for multinationals specializing in construction, energy, and communications.[57]

Speaking of opportunities, Chinese companies have moved into Africa in a big way in recent years. Of course, many multinationals stay away because of perceptions about the region's poverty, political instability, poor infrastructure, and so on. But Chinese mining, energy, and construction companies see such negatives as opportunities that they can take advantage of. In short, Chinese firms feel they can address needs in Africa that once were concerns in China. As the director of a Chinese well-digging firm put it, "China doesn't need many new water wells. But Africans struggle to find drinking water every day." And Chinese consumer-products firms view Africa as a region where they can avoid tough competition from Japanese, European, and American multinationals. That perception led office-supply company Shanghai Hero Co. to build a new facility in South Africa, giving it easy access to the wider African market.[58]

Finally, environmental analysis can also be country-specific, assessing whether the cultural, legal, economic, and political circumstances in a particular country are opportunities or threats. For example, at one point multinationals wanting to do business in Saudi Arabia had to consider the fact that the Saudi economy was growing twice as fast as its electricity-generating capacity. Multinationals unwilling to risk power interruptions canceled or delayed plans to build new facilities as a result. Others installed generators to keep things running during blackouts.[59]

Before we move on, it's important to note that cultural values and prior experiences shape managers' scanning tendencies. Depending on their backgrounds, managers may pay attention to different things in the environmental

environmental scanning A process in which information about the internal and external situation facing the firm is systematically collected and evaluated

environmental analysis The external side of a SWOT analysis that involves assessing promising external opportunities as well as threats in foreign markets

EXHIBIT 8.7   *The Environmental Scanning Process in a Marketing-Based Multinational*

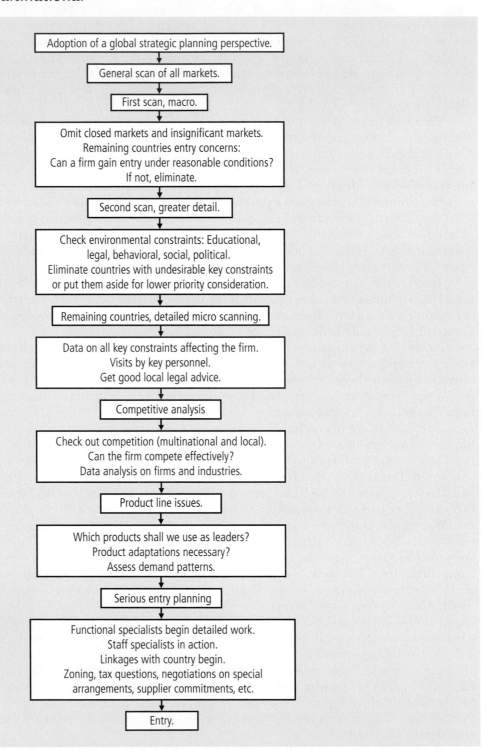

Source: From *International Dimensions of Business Policy and Strategy*, 2nd edition, p. 69 by J. Garland, R.N. Farmer & M. Taylor. © 1990. Reprinted with permission of South-Western College Publishing, a division of Thomson Learning. Fax 800-730-2215.

scanning process. One study found that Nigerian managers paid more attention to governmental issues than their American counterparts while the opposite was true for technology issues. In Nigeria and other developing countries, political instability can drastically affect business. The United States, in contrast, is politically stable, but has a volatile technological environment. Overall, managers coming from these contexts need to adjust their environmental scanning efforts when considering opportunities elsewhere.[60]

At this point, take a look at Exhibit 8.7. It presents the environmental scanning process that a marketing-based multinational (e.g., Procter & Gamble) might use. The process often starts broadly before narrowing to the point where the firm collects specific information in preparation for entry into a particular country. It's also important to note that what multinationals pay attention to in this process is usually driven by internal needs. For instance, a multinational that needs hard-to-obtain materials or highly skilled labor to produce its products will make these issues a priority when assessing where to put a new plant.[61] In short, the evaluation of the external environment often reflects firms' assessment of their internal environment.

Speaking of which, the internal side of a SWOT analysis is known as an **internal resource audit**. This audit involves identifying key business success factors for the firm. For example, in the pharmaceutical industry, business success factors might include product efficacy and patents held, while in the automotive industry, styling, quality, and fuel efficiency might be key factors. In short, business success factors can vary across industries. Business success factors can also vary over time as well as from country to country. In essence, firms want to see how internal resources stack up against the demands they'll face in foreign markets.[62] For instance, an effective distribution system is a key success factor for Wal-Mart. In fact, Wal-Mart's computerized warehouses and its ability to influence suppliers with large orders help it keep prices low in the United States. However, when it first opened stores in Mexico, Wal-Mart's Mexican suppliers wanted to ship smaller orders directly to stores, not warehouses. Wal-Mart initially underestimated the difficulties of creating a Mexican version of its American distribution system and experienced lower initial sales in Mexico as a result.[63]

So the internal resource audit should include an evaluation of both internal strengths (e.g., a skilled workforce, superior technology) and weaknesses (e.g., high debt, poor name recognition, lack of international experience) relative to competitors. Firms typically want to build on distinctive strengths that would be tough for competitors to copy in the short term (i.e., strengths that might provide a sustainable competitive advantage).[64] But if a strength is truly distinctive, then management should be able to answer yes to the following questions:

- Can the strength help the firm exploit opportunities or avoid threats in international markets?

- Is the strength rare or unique, or do competitors possess similar "value-added" capabilities?

- Is the strength extremely difficult or expensive for competitors to duplicate?

- Is the firm organized to take maximum advantage of the competitive potential of a strength?[65]

internal resource audit
The internal side of a SWOT analysis that involves identifying key business success factors inside the firm

For instance, Japanese electronics giant Matsushita built a network of 150 plants across dozens of countries, providing a buffer against currency and economic fluctuations in particular locations. Dispersed manufacturing capability, combined with cutting-edge technology and world-class brands (e.g., Panasonic), gives Matsushita a global reach that few competitors can match.[66]

Step 3: Deciding on an International Strategy and Setting Goals

After the SWOT analysis, the typical next step is for the firm to adopt an international strategy. Ultimately, strategic goals should be set that exploit firm strengths and opportunities while neutralizing competitive threats and internal weaknesses. Goals should reflect decisions about how broad or narrow the breadth and depth of the firm's international operations will be. For instance, will the firm:

- Compete in specific countries or wherever opportunities exist?
- Offer all its products/services abroad or just a subset?
- Own its overseas operations or use other entry options (e.g., licensing)?

Once these general goals are set, more specific objectives can be developed.[67] Goals should be achievable and have a specific time frame for accomplishment.[68] Areas where international goals might be set include:

- **Profitability** (e.g., increase international profit growth 20 percent)
- **Production** (e.g., increase the ratio of foreign to domestic production from 50 percent to 75 percent)
- **Marketing** (e.g., integrate marketing efforts across European countries)
- **Finance** (e.g., minimize foreign exchange losses)
- **Technology** (e.g., successfully transfer technology to foreign subsidiaries)
- **Research and development** (e.g., disperse R&D capability worldwide)

Consider how Mercedes-Benz defined some of it strategic goals. Mercedes is a luxury brand that embodies German craftsmanship and quality. But German labor costs, among other things, made it very difficult for Mercedes to export cars to North America at a profit. So Mercedes decided to move a substantial amount of manufacturing capacity to the United States. Mercedes built an assembly plant in Alabama, allowing the firm to manufacture at lower cost in a key market. Mercedes also bought more components from non-German suppliers. On one hand, achieving these and related strategic goals may dilute Mercedes' image as the embodiment of German craftsmanship, ultimately hurting sales. On the other hand, Mercedes' sales suggest that the risk of being seen as "less German" was worth taking, at least so far.[69]

Step 4: Developing Implementation Tactics and Plans

After strategic goals have been set, companies should develop specific plans and tactics that will deploy corporate resources (material, money, people, etc.) to achieve them. New procedures or processes may also have to be developed to achieve company goals, including specific steps designed to neutralize competitors. Basically, a support system must be in place to actually move the firm from where it is to where it wants to be internationally.[70]

That said, firms often underestimate what's needed to compete effectively abroad. Pepsi's decision in the 1990s to increase international revenues some 300 percent may be a case in point. To achieve this goal, the firm quickly expanded its global presence. Unfortunately, this expansion backfired. By the late 1990s Pepsi was actually losing money overseas and pulled out of some important international markets. And today, small local competitors are giving both Pepsi and Coca-Cola a run for their money in developing markets (e.g., Peru, Mexico). With lower overhead costs, cheaper prices, and local knowledge (that spawned effective guerrilla marketing tactics), small firms like Peru's Kola Real are cutting into the once fat margins of Pepsi and Coke.[71]

This underscores the idea that to secure a competitive advantage abroad, multinationals must carefully design and execute actions that support their international strategies and improve key value chain activities. For example, multinationals can neutralize a common advantage of home-grown competitors—greater understanding of the local market—by developing products tailored to local tastes. In Japan, local soft drink maker Suntory Ltd. introduced "Asian tea" drinks in response to local tastes. But Coca-Cola countered by developing and offering an Asian tea for the Japanese market. Of course, such tactics carry risks. Adapting products for specific markets can increase costs or prove wrongheaded, as restaurant chain TGI Fridays discovered in South Korea. Customers turned up their noses at its adapted menu, which included a variety of local items, because they expected an "American" dining experience. This example underscores the difficulty of teasing out when and how adapting products to local preferences makes competitive sense.[72]

Companies in other industries also face daunting challenges. For instance, Texas Instruments' (TI) semiconductor group wanted to establish a manufacturing and technology presence quickly to better absorb market growth wherever it occurred. That meant getting capital-intensive facilities and plants up and running fast to preempt competitors. To achieve this, TI developed new tactics and practices, including the formation of a ten-person team to facilitate new plant construction worldwide. The team developed procedures (e.g., to cut through red tape quickly, find high-quality local vendors) that enabled TI to bring world-class chip manufacturing plants on line eight months faster than competing firms.[73]

Step 5: Putting Control and Evaluation Procedures in Place

This final step involves the control and evaluation procedures designed to ensure that all the work done to this point isn't wasted and strategy implementation efforts stay on track. This "last" step is also about ensuring that companies can quickly adjust, if not reinvent, their strategies as business circumstances change. Clearly, the development and implementation of international strategy is a dynamic, ongoing process.[74]

For example, in the 1980s and 1990s, Japanese car companies such as Nissan, Honda, and Toyota all built car plants in the United States to meet the needs of the American market. And by 2004, all three had built or were building truck plants in the United States, assaulting a bastion of profitability for both Ford and GM. And when growing export demands needed to be met around the world, Japanese plants in the United States ramped up production in response. As a result, Japanese firms at one point were actually shipping more cars abroad from their American plants than GM, Ford, and DaimlerChrysler combined! This shift in strategy allowed Japanese automakers to take advantage of lower U.S. production costs relative to Japan. Moreover, the type of cars that emerging markets were clamoring for happened to be the ones the Japanese firms were already making in the United States. For instance, Toyota's American plants helped it sidestep import restrictions in Taiwan and South Korea on cars built in Japan. This strategic flexibility is one reason why Japanese car companies have proven to be such formidable international competitors.[75]

We conclude this section with an International Insights on Nokia and its unique approach to international strategy development.

🌐 International Insights

Nokia: Creating International Strategy from the Ground Up

HELSINKI-BASED NOKIA has grown spectacularly in recent years. In 1996, Nokia had 21 percent of the world's mobile phone market. By 2004, Nokia's market-leading share was almost 40 percent, more than second-place Motorola and third-place Ericsson combined. Today, 20 percent of the world's population has mobile phones, with some 450 million units being sold every year. But although China and India, two huge markets, have considerable growth potential left, making good money in the cell phone business is no easy task given the number of competitors and downward pressures on prices.

Consequently, Nokia and its rivals are looking to add new services for cell phone customers as well as exploring new lines of business. Optimists claim the long-term future for Nokia looks bright, thanks to its industry-leading track record in design, marketing, and technological innovation.

Arguably, much of Nokia's success also stems from a strategy development process that has proven adroit at predicting customer preferences. And that process can be traced back to CEO Jorma Ollila. A few months after he became CEO in 1992, Mr. Ollila felt that Nokia should become a global heavyweight in telecommunications and related industries. This basic mission has guided Nokia's strategy to this day. And given the industry's volatility, Mr. Ollila's operating strategy is to react quickly to changes in international markets. For instance, when Nokia overestimated how quickly digital phones would penetrate the United States, Ollila quickly turned loose independent "commando teams" of managers to fix the problem.

Such involvement is also central to Nokia's efforts to anticipate future trends and adapt its strategy to match them. Nokia routinely brings together hundreds of managers from the dozens of countries where it operates. In small groups, they conduct brainstorming sessions to identify emerging trends that represent opportunities for Nokia in various markets (e.g., Nokia believes that the workplace will eventually be completely wireless). The company also drills this captive audience on the need to understand local customers. Nokia feels that involving line managers in this way generates ideas that would never come up otherwise. It uses a "strategy panel" of top managers that sifts through the ideas generated from these brainstorming sessions on a monthly basis. This strategy development approach has resulted in some successful moves for Nokia in recent years (e.g., camera phones) as well as some bold gambles that may yet pay off handsomely (e.g., Nokia's leaps into portable video game consoles, server software, and wireless networks, just to name a few).

But Nokia is also aware of internal weaknesses that it must struggle with. Once asked what the firm's biggest internal threat was, CEO Ollila had a quick, one-word response: "complacency." Such self-awareness helps Nokia's managers stay focused on uncovering new opportunities. We wouldn't bet against them.[76]

▶ *Organizational Requirements for Successful International Strategy*

In this last section, we briefly discuss four organizational features that have important implications for multinationals' ability to successfully develop and implement their international strategies:

- **Corporate structure** (the way reporting relationships and business units are organized)

- **Management processes** (the planning, budgeting, coordination, and performance appraisal activities and systems used to run the firm)

- **Human resources** (the people who staff the firm worldwide)

- **Corporate culture** (the expectations, values, beliefs, and unwritten rules that guide employee behavior in the company)[77]

Multinationals must build characteristics into these organizational features that will support strategy development and implementation. When firm characteristics and strategic demands are aligned, better performance results.[78]

For example, a global strategy requires a corporate structure with some centralized authority to assist global product development and make global decisions. This doesn't necessarily mean that "headquarters" makes all decisions. But some structure must exist to coordinate worldwide operations and make decisions, often with input from local operations. Having all units in a particular business line worldwide report to a global business manager is one way to accomplish this. For instance, GE Canada's lighting unit used to compete at GE headquarters with all other GE business units in Canada for its share of resources. This competition was eliminated by having the unit go directly to a global lighting manager for funding.[79] Chapter 10 considers this and other structural options for international firms in more detail.

Management processes that facilitate coordination and strategic decision making are also critical if companies are to respond quickly to the competitive environments they face. For example, companies can have more success developing and implementing global strategies by using teams of key employees from different countries to make decisions with worldwide implications. Such teams can bridge cultural and geographic barriers to develop and execute complex global strategies effectively.[80]

Likewise, management processes may include specific capabilities that help the firm outperform competitors in areas that are important to customers. In the semiconductor industry this might involve developing cutting-edge chips more quickly than competitors. Identifying and developing capabilities that are complex and diffused through the company (i.e., that cut across functions) and that rely on well-developed interfaces (e.g., sophisticated networks of informal communications) are best because they are tough for competitors to imitate.[81]

The structures and processes designed to support an international strategy are themselves supported by a firm's culture and human resources. For example, cultural values that emphasize global flexibility and responsiveness help give the firm an identity that fosters its ability to execute a global strategy.

EXHIBIT 8.8   *Corporate Features That Support a Global Strategy*

General Area	Specific Corporate Feature Necessary
Corporate Structure	• Centralized global authority • No international division • Strong business dimension
Management Processes	• Global strategy information system • Global strategic planning • Cross-country coordination • Global budgeting
Human Resources	• Global performance review and compensation • Use of foreign nationals • Frequent travel • Statements and actions of leaders
Corporate Culture	• Global identity • Commitment to worldwide employment • Interdependence of businesses

Source: Adapted from Yip, G. S. (1995). *Total global strategy*. Englewood Cliffs, NJ: Prentice-Hall.

Exhibit 8.8 illustrates how corporate structure, management processes, human resources, and corporate culture should be aligned to support a global strategy. Of course, for other strategies, these organizational features will be different. For instance, a corporate structure in which decision authority for products, marketing, and so on is largely delegated to subsidiaries in specific countries makes sense for firms using a multidomestic strategy.

Designing a Fair Strategy Development Process

Finally, companies should pay attention to how strategy is created. It turns out that if the processes used to create strategies are perceived to be fair, then local managers are more likely to implement them. "Due process" in this case means that:

• The managers at headquarters make a serious effort to familiarize themselves with local operations.

• Real two-way communication occurs when strategy is being developed.

• Managers at headquarters are consistent across subsidiaries in making decisions.

• Local employees can challenge headquarters' strategic perspectives and decisions.

• Local employees are given an explanation for the strategic decisions ultimately made.[82]

Chapter Summary

Figuring out how a company should compete abroad is part of international strategic management. Unfortunately, a surprising number of companies enter overseas markets without a clear, well-designed approach. This can lead to problems, such as (1) the inability to accurately predict the direction of foreign markets, (2) the poor use of resources abroad, (3) underestimating the resources needed to effectively compete, and (4) failing to anticipate operational problems in foreign environments. All international strategies should help firms decide (1) what products/services will be sold abroad, (2) where and how services will be delivered or products made, (3) what resources are necessary and how they will be acquired, and (4) how competitors will be outperformed.

At a business level, firms make money through *value creation*, offering products or services that customers want. One way to do that is by *differentiating* products from competitors'. Another tack is the *cost-leadership approach*. Finally, a *niche strategy* involves focusing on a specific line of products or services relative to competitors who operate more broadly. A company can also add value by changing any *primary* or *supporting activities* in its *value chain*. International strategy is ultimately about how value chain activities are *configured* and *coordinated*. *Core competencies* can be located anywhere in the value chain and are the basis for international competitiveness. Firms often compete by moving value chain activities to wherever *location economies* exist.

The *theory of national competitive advantage* explains how specific countries can help companies obtain a competitive edge. *Factor conditions* describe whether a nation has the components for competitive production in an industry. *Demand conditions* describe the markets in a country for certain goods and services. *Related and supporting industries* describe whether competitive suppliers or related industries exist in a country. *Firm strategy, structure*, and *rivalry* describe how the local environment affects firms in a particular country.

Four corporate-level strategies used by multinationals were discussed. *Multidomestic strategies* may be best when local product or service preferences vary considerably and integration pressures in an industry are low. *Global strategies*, in contrast, work best in industries where the same basic products can be sold everywhere and integration pressures are high. A *transnational strategy* may be appropriate when firms need to move value chain activities to wherever they can be done best but still must adapt products to local preferences. A *regional strategy* represents a compromise between global and multidomestic approaches. After presenting these strategies, we discussed how the match or mismatch between international competition in an industry and the industry's underlying character can impact the effectiveness of a firm's strategy. We also discussed how differences in cultural values and perspectives can influence the strategies that managers pursue. Finally, we considered some of the limitations that small firms face in developing international strategies, particularly in terms of their limited financial and managerial resources. Overcoming these limitations often means seeking help (e.g., from consulting firms and government agencies), which is readily available.

Next, we outlined the process of creating international strategy, which consists of five key steps. First, firms often develop a mission statement. Second, companies conduct a *SWOT analysis*. The external side of the equation is an *environmental analysis* that involves the assessment of external opportunities as well as external threats. The internal side of a SWOT analysis is called an *internal resources audit* and involves an assessment of internal strengths and weaknesses. The next step involves the actual selection of a strategy and goals, followed by the development of implementation tactics and plans. Finally, steps have to be taken to monitor strategy implementation on an ongoing basis.

We concluded by pointing out that organizational features such as corporate structure, management processes, human resources, and corporate culture all need to be aligned with a firm's international strategy to maximize performance. Likewise, companies need to realize that if the processes used to develop strategy are perceived to be fair, managers worldwide are more likely to act accordingly. To create fairness, company managers should, among other things, make a serious effort to familiarize themselves with local operations and ensure two-way communication with local employees when developing international strategy.

Discussion Questions

1. What is the value of having a coherent international business strategy?

2. What factors determine national competitive advantage?

3. Explain the differences between global, transnational, and multidomestic strategies. What roles do industry and firm characteristics play in the choice of strategy?

4. What is a SWOT analysis? What do you do with the results?

5. What organizational features are needed to successfully develop and implement a global strategy?

Up to the Challenge?

Jollibee's Strategy for Chewing Up McDonald's

AT THE BEGINNING of the chapter, we asked you to think about how Jollibee has been able to outperform global giant McDonald's in the Philippines. Jollibee decided that it had to copy certain aspects of McDonald's approach that clearly work across borders. Specifically, Jollibee felt it had to offer the same type of clean and speedy service that McDonald's offers worldwide. Jollibee strictly adheres to what it calls its "FSC" standards for excellence ("food, service, cleanliness") in all outlets. Employee training is taken very seriously. Moreover, Jollibee's pay and benefits lead the fast-food industry in the Philippines. Jollibee also makes much of its own food products in two centrally located "commissaries" in the Philippines. In setting up new outlets, Jollibee goes after prime locations. In fact, it often surrounds McDonald's outlets in the Philippines with restaurants of its own. Finally, Jollibee aggressively markets itself to kids with in-store novelties, activities, and signature characters—just like McDonald's.

That said, Jollibee felt that it had to outperform McDonald's in certain areas to gain a competitive advantage. The best way to do that was to "act locally" more than the Big Mac. First, the company incorporated unique aspects of Philippine culture in developing its service delivery model. Anytime a customer approaches a Jollibee counter, employees say, "*Magandang umaga po,* welcome to Jollibee." The first part of this phrase

is a traditional Filipino greeting and is designed to underscore the company's local heritage and create an atmosphere of humble Filipino hospitality. On top of that, Jollibee prices its food lower than comparable items at McDonald's, taking advantage of weak local economic conditions. The firm's "value meals," for instance, cost only $1–$2.

Perhaps most important, Jollibee offers a broader menu than McDonald's, one that also is more geared toward Filipinos' sweet-and-spicy tastes. These flavors are incorporated across Jollibee's entire menu, from chicken to noodles to hamburgers. For example, the Aloha Burger is a Jollibee concoction that includes a layer of pineapple, while Palabok Fiesta is a noodle and meat sauce dish topped with smoked fish, deep fried pork skin, bean curd, and onions. Along with the spicy flavors, Jollibee customers can opt for rice with their meals, another local preference, instead of french fries.

Of course, whether Jollibee can maintain its edge over McDonald's indefinitely remains to be seen. McDonald's, well known for its flexibility, responded to Jollibee's success by spicing up its own menu in the Philippines. Ironically, Jollibee's own foreign expansion exposed it to some of the same difficulties McDonald's has encountered in the Philippines and other international locations. For instance, Jollibee brought only a portion of its menu to the American market in order to test reactions and build a reliable supplier base. Nevertheless, Jollibee found that it still had to make adjustments, including offering larger portions in the United States than it did in the Philippines. Other surprises were more pleasant. Jollibee's foreign outlets tend to be located in areas with large populations of Filipino expatriates. But in California, only 50 percent of Jollibee's customers had connections to the Philippines. In fact, one Jollibee manager said that Americans were acquiring some Filipino tastes. He noted that his non-Filipino customers in California "love the Aloha Burger and they return to the store and order it again and again."

That said, what kinds of challenges might Jollibee face if it continues to expand in foreign markets? How should it respond? What else can Jollibee do to stay on top in its home market and keep McDonald's at bay in the Philippines (see **www.jollibee.com.ph**)?[83]

International Development

Conducting a Company Situation Analysis

Purpose

1. To practice your skills in analyzing and assessing company strategies.
2. To find out more about a company's international business situation relative to competitors.

Instructions

Your instructor will divide the class into groups of three to six people. Each group should interview a senior manager (preferably one with responsibility for a major line of business) at a local company that has some international activity. Ideally, the interview should focus on a specific line of business. For instance, if you interview managers at diversified companies, you should focus on a specific product line sold abroad since strategies are often different across business lines.

The interview should cover the issues listed here. Ideally, the manager should answer questions for the business line he or she is responsible for in the company and also should answer the same questions for two or three major competitors.

1. *The nature of management*
   - Are there foreigners in senior management positions?
   - How extensive is the cross-cultural training for managers?
2. *Company strategy*
   - Is the company's vision global, transnational, regional, or domestic?
   - How willing is the firm to embrace alliances with foreign firms?
   - Do units in different foreign locations operate independently or as a single global company?
   - How important is environmental scanning in the company?
   - To what extent does the home country control key decisions?
3. *Operational issues*
   - Where are the company's major facilities located (in the home country or abroad)?
   - Are product design decisions centralized or decentralized?
   - Are manufacturing decisions centralized or decentralized?

After the interview is completed, each group should make an assessment about the basic strategy employed by the company (and its major competitors). Each group should then develop recommendations about what the company can do to either (1) close the gap with competitors in terms of international practices or (2) maintain the advantages the company already enjoys.

Depending on the class and time available, your instructor may ask you to conduct additional research about the company interviewed and its industry before you come up with group recommendations. These recommendations could be part of your group presentations or even be written up and given to the companies interviewed.

Assuming a more basic assignment, each group should make a 15-minute class presentation about their findings (allow 20 minutes if presentations are to include the group's own recommendations). Your instructor will then lead a class discussion (another 15–20 minutes), focusing on these issues:

- How "globalized" were the companies interviewed? Did they generally tend to be ahead or behind their competition in this regard? Why or why not?
- What industry, firm, or competitive factors might account for the differences or similarities observed across firm practices?

An Alternative Approach

If the class size is too large or other constraints (e.g., time, availability of senior executives) make an interview approach impractical, your instructor may convert this activity into a library research assignment. You may be asked to do an in-depth analysis of the strategic approach taken by a particular international company or even an industry group. If so, you may also be asked to use the interview questions listed to predict the responses that senior managers in the company or industry might make.

 Tapping into the Global Network

Making Moves on a Global Stage

Purpose

To experience making competitive moves in an international context and to anticipate the possible reactions of competitors.

Instructions

Your instructor will divide the class into six groups. Each group will be assigned to analyze one of the following pairs of competitors. The pairs consist of an American multinational and a foreign rival (your instructor may assign other pairs of companies as well):

- General Electric Co. (**www.ge.com**) versus ABB Ltd. (**www.abb.com**)
- Gillette Co. (**www.gillette.com**) versus Bic S.A. (**www.bicworld.com**)
- Motorola Inc. (**www.motorola.com**) versus Nokia Corp. (**www.nokia.com**)
- General Motors Corp. (**www.gm.com**) versus Toyota Motor Corp. (**www.toyota.co.jp**)
- Hewlett-Packard Co. (**www.hp.com**) versus Canon Inc. (**www.canon.com**)
- Kraft Foods Inc. (**www.kraft.com**) versus Nestlé S.A. (**www.nestle.com**)

In particular, each group will be asked to select one product category or product type in which both of their paired companies compete. Next, each group will be asked to assess where the American firm in their pair stands relative to its foreign rival in that product category or type. Specifically, groups will be asked to assess the foreign rival's potential ability to react to increased pressure in that product area (i.e., the level of motivation to defend a position in a product area) as well as the degree of importance of that product area to the American firm. Each group will also assess the relative clout of both firms (i.e., which firm is better able to take strong competitive moves or better defend against the same?). Finally, each group will develop recommendations for how the American firm in their pair can do a better job competing against its foreign rival (e.g., what specific competitive moves might be made and why?).

More details of how each group should go about this competitive assessment, as well as possible competitive moves that might be tried as a result, can be found in this article:

MacMillan, I. C., van Putten, A. B., & McGrath, R. G. (2003). Global gamesmanship. *Harvard Business Review*, May, 62–73.

All groups should read this article before starting in earnest. Specific instructions for how groups can measure product importance, clout, and so on, using publicly available information, can be found at: **www.triad-consultants.com**.

Depending on the class and time available, your instructor may ask each group to write a report summarizing its assessment and recommendations. The scope and length of that report will be defined by your instructor. In addition, your instructor may ask each group to give a 15–20 minute presentation about their findings.

9

Jumping In: Foreign Market Entry and Ownership Options

INTERNATIONAL CHALLENGE

What Price Entry? General Electric Finds That China Drives a Hard Bargain

Learning Objectives

After reading this chapter, you should be able to:

▸ Describe the various stages of international development that firms may pass through and how they relate to foreign market entry.

▸ Describe the strengths and weaknesses of various foreign market entry options that do not require ownership.

▸ Describe the strengths and weaknesses of various foreign market entry options that require some ownership responsibilities.

▸ Understand the different types of strategic alliances between international companies and why they are used.

IT'S NOT THAT GENERAL ELECTRIC IS A NOVICE when it comes to China. Over the last twenty-odd years, GE has been trying to sell everything from power-generating turbines to jet engines to light bulbs in China, often with considerable success. That said, GE's efforts there to sell power turbines illustrates how the rules for market entry have shifted in China in recent years. It also highlights the conundrum faced by many multinationals who eye booming demand in China with relish. This might come as something of a surprise since, on the surface, the competitive context facing GE, at least with respect to modern power turbines, seems relatively straightforward.

Specifically, GE's potential turbine customers in China are a relatively small number of regional utilities and independent energy-producing firms. Today's most advanced power turbines are sophisticated, 80,000-pound pieces of technology that pump out huge amounts of electricity using natural gas to spin their high-tech blades. Consequently, GE's main competitors at the moment are relatively few (i.e., other multinationals, such as Germany's Siemens). In contrast, multinationals in comparatively low-tech industries such as personal care (e.g., shampoo-makers such as Procter & Gamble and Unilever) and beverages (e.g., beer makers SABMiller and Belgium's Interbrew SA) have found that China is really made up of many different local markets (often driven by area-specific preferences). Moreover, in these industries, multinationals may face hundreds, if not thousands, of local competitors that operate cheaply and possess in-depth knowledge about local customers. To put it mildly, China can be a tough place to sell products for foreign multinationals.

But GE faced big challenges of its own recently when it tried to win a contract that could be worth billions to provide power turbines to several regional utilities in China. On the one hand, China represents an attractive growth market for GE's power turbines. Soaring economic development has caused electricity demands in China to skyrocket in recent years. China's 1.3 billion citizens must cope with brownouts and the fact that the country's utilities currently provide less than 90 percent of demand. And speaking of demand, the megawatts needed to power China continue to grow at a 15 percent annual clip. As a result, China needs to spend over $10 billion annually on new power plants well past 2010 to catch up.

On the other hand, in competing against the likes of Siemens and Mitsubishi for the turbine business, GE soon realized that the Chinese authorities charged with negotiating the most favorable deal were asking for more than just a great price: They wanted access to *all* the technology that allowed GE to develop its cutting-edge turbines in the first place. In particular, government officials asked GE to pass along its proprietary technology to a couple of Chinese firms that wanted, at some point in the future, to be able to construct the turbines on their own. This idea is consistent with China's goal of moving away from being a cheap producer of low-tech goods. Instead, China wants its companies to be global players in high-tech manufacturing industries. And there's the rub. China's recent strategy has been to dangle access to its growing internal markets to foreign multinationals in exchange for the transfer of the most critical technologies. Interestingly, when China joined the World Trade Organization in 2001, it signed agreements to dump many of its technology-transfer rules and requirements for multinationals. What China didn't sign, however, were agreements to stop government agencies that were negotiating deals with foreign multinationals from insisting on transfers of technology.

As you might suspect, GE was torn. The firm definitely wanted access to China's high-growth market for power turbines. That said, the Chinese demand for 100 percent access to their technology was hard to swallow, especially since the process of developing its most advanced power turbine cost GE some $500 million. As one GE executive put it, "we're interested in protecting the technology that we made significant financial investment in." Basically, companies like GE face a tradeoff—pursue short-term profits at the risk of creating formidable local competitors in the long run, thanks to transfers of technology, or keep the technology and get shut out of a key market. Indeed, multinationals such as Motorola, Nokia, and Ericsson all either formed joint ventures with local partners or established research and development centers in China as vehicles for responding to Chinese demands for the transfer of technology.

So here's your challenge. What approach do you think GE should take in response to these technology transfer demands? Is there a way that GE can protect itself, at least to some degree, and still gain access to the Chinese market for power turbines? And what might the role of the U.S. government be, if any, in all of this? Think about these questions as you read through this chapter, especially our sections on modes of entry in foreign markets and their associated pros and cons. If you can, do some research on the power turbine industry and the sensitive technologies involved. Then take a look at the *Up to the Challenge?* box at the end of the chapter for a glimpse at how GE actually responded.[1]

▶ *Taking the Plunge*

This chapter examines the options companies have for entering foreign markets. Of course, how a company chooses to proceed is often a direct reflection of its corporate-level international strategy. Other factors that shape the choices a company makes include the pros and cons of the various entry options, the nature of the foreign market, and the firm's level of international development (and how successful it is). We'll consider some of these factors in this chapter.

Stages of International Development

Let's start by examining the stages of international development that many firms evolve through in their international operations. A small company might first dip into foreign markets by exporting. Indeed, exporting is a common option for small firms since large capital outlays are not required (e.g., to build expensive plants overseas). But as companies grow and evolve, they may move from relying on exports to building manufacturing facilities overseas. That said, the international developmental process is anything but exact. Many firms do not evolve in a clear sequence of steps or move in a linear fashion through developmental stages. For instance, companies can jump from exporting to establishing an international division without establishing an overseas sales subsidiary first. Likewise, overseas acquisitions may allow firms to leapfrog some steps.[2]

And consider the dichotomy between service and manufacturing firms. A manufacturer is more likely to go through a gradual series of stages as it expands internationally. Global car giant Toyota is a good example. It began by exporting cars from its home base in Japan, slowly expanding its presence overseas by building local manufacturing capabilities in key markets such as the United States. Today, Toyota is aggressively expanding its manufacturing base in China (new plants came on line in China in 2002 and 2003), where it wants to sell a million vehicles annually by 2010.[3]

In contrast, service companies, such as banks or insurance providers, essentially have to jump in with both feet when they decide to enter foreign markets, often through acquisitions. Unlike manufacturing firms, service companies don't have the luxury of starting out slowly and gaining experience (e.g., by exporting a product overseas) before setting up operations abroad.

For instance, GE Capital, the financial services arm of parent GE, lends money and offers insurance worldwide. Accounting for a big slice of GE's corporate profits, GE Capital has arguably become a master at setting up foreign operations quickly, either building them from scratch or rapidly integrating foreign acquisitions. A few years ago, GE Capital bought troubled Toho Mutual, a Japanese insurance firm. In short order, GE Capital installed its own procedures and accounting methods while scrapping Toho Mutual's seniority-based personnel system.[4] Of course, the success of this approach depends on how well the company executes and the extent to which management and cultural difficulties hamper operations. For instance, Western banks and other financial services firms that barreled into eastern European markets ran into cultural, recruiting, and legal obstacles that ate into potential profits, especially after paying millions to snap up local banks. Indeed, that's exactly what happened in 2003 to Belgian banking and insurance giant KBC Group NV when it experienced multimillion-dollar losses in a variety of eastern European markets.[5]

Nevertheless, many firms evolve through relatively distinct stages as they become more sophisticated in their international operations. Not surprisingly, there are different perspectives about how to define those stages.[6] But most experts assume that companies can be successful in any stage and that the time companies take to progress through internationalization stages varies. Take a look at Exhibit 9.1. It presents a six-stage framework for understanding the process of internationalization.

EXHIBIT 9.1   *Common Stages in the Process of Corporate Internationalization*

Stage 1:	Export
Stage 2:	Sales subsidiary
Stage 3:	International division
Stage 4:	Multinational
Stage 5:	Global or transnational
Stage 6:	Alliances, partners, and consortia

Source: Adapted from Briscoe, D. R. (1995). *International human resource management.* Englewood Cliffs, NJ: Prentice-Hall.

Stage 1: Exporting In stage 1, a domestic company begins internationalizing by exporting its products or services to foreign customers. This stage may include marketing of products or services abroad, perhaps through an export department run by a manager and small supporting staff. Such departments typically are considered ancillary to the firm's domestic sales and marketing activities. In other cases, domestic firms that are new to international business may turn to banks or consulting firms to handle most export-related activities and provide the necessary expertise (e.g., dealing with documents, currency issues, shipping, and letters of credit). Mail-order firm L. L. Bean is an example of a stage 1 firm. The company largely serves the U.S. market but also exports to a variety of countries.[7]

As overseas sales continue to grow, firms may feel it's best to contract with distributors to represent their products abroad (e.g., to promote products, answer questions, provide follow-up service, etc.).

Stage 2: Sales Subsidiary Once a firm decides to open overseas sales offices, it would essentially be moving to stage 2. That point is reached when a firm establishes sales offices or sales subsidiaries in a foreign country. Up until recently, Milwaukee-based motorcycle-maker Harley-Davidson was the quintessential example of a stage 2 firm. Strong growth in foreign markets prompted Harley-Davidson, which exports around 25 percent of its motorcycles, to establish overseas offices for better marketing and sales support.

Stage 3: International Division As you might expect, this stage usually involves the assembly or manufacture of a significant amount of product overseas. Sometimes this stage represents a natural progression from the creation of overseas sales subsidiaries. In other cases, companies move from exporting to an international division in one fell swoop. Regardless, having an international division means that a more sophisticated organizational structure is in place to oversee all foreign business activity and to support future international expansion. Usually, an international division also means that the company has placed a greater emphasis on hiring personnel who are knowledgeable about international business.

For instance, a few years ago Harley-Davidson established its first foreign assembly operation, shipping motorcycle kits to Brazil for final assembly and subsequent sale. So while the vast majority of Harley-Davidson motorcycles are still assembled in the United States, Harley-Davidson is arguably evolving toward stage 3. In many cases, the move to overseas production is accompanied by a decision to create a separate international division that is responsible for monitoring and controlling all overseas operations from the home office.

Stage 4: Multinational Stages 4–6 describe more complex multinational operations that may evolve over time. In stage 4, multinational companies recognize that while headquarters plays a key role in important strategic decisions, foreign operations often do best when staffed by local employees who understand the local environment. In fact, the role of the foreign subsidiary in stage 4 is to serve the needs of the national or regional market where it is located. But achieving the right balance between headquarters control and local fine-tuning isn't easy.

For instance, to enter the Brazilian market, J.C. Penney bought Lojas Renner, a family-run regional department store chain. But rather than turning Lojas Renner into just another J.C. Penney outpost, the company kept things local. After running into trouble in other countries, J.C. Penney realized that successful retailing is often a localized phenomenon. So J.C. Penney wanted to keep the local expertise that was the backbone of Lojas Renner's outstanding reputation for service and value. Consequently, J.C. Penney kept the Lojas Renner name on storefronts in Brazil and kept the local management team in place to run things. Those steps, along with J.C. Penney's financial help, allowed Lojas Renner to grow more than 100 percent in two years.[8]

By comparison, Wal-Mart, the world's biggest retailer, seems to be less willing to project a local image and rely on local expertise than J.C. Penney when operating abroad. Nevertheless, Wal-Mart keeps growing internationally. In 2003, Wal-Mart had over 1,300 stores in foreign locations and plans to open another 130 stores overseas. But critics suggest that Wal-Mart still has a "headquarters knows best" mentality and lacks sufficient international business experience in its top management ranks. They claim that Wal-Mart largely relies on its "American approach" overseas and needs to introduce more local products to its foreign stores. This, so the thinking goes, may explain why Wal-Mart has been criticized for everything from "abusing" local suppliers to cultural snafus in foreign markets. For instance, Wal-Mart had difficulty explaining certain concepts to employees (e.g., its price "rollbacks") and had trouble convincing fussy Japanese customers that it sold high-quality products. Japanese employees also initially resisted Wal-Mart's aggressive "10 foot rule," which pushes employees to offer help to customers who come within 10 feet (in most Japanese stores the norm is to wait for customers to ask for assistance).[9]

In contrast, France's Carrefour, which operates in more than thirty countries, says that over 90 percent of the products in its stores are local in origin. As one Carrefour executive explained, "In China, we are Chinese; in Spain, we are Spanish." Dutch competitor Ahold goes even further, operating under different store names and emphasizing local brands in the more than two dozen countries where it operates. As Ahold's CEO put it, "Everything the customer sees we localize. Everything they don't see we globalize."

Despite its belief that overseas growth will be a profit engine in the future, Wal-Mart lags behind some of its overseas competitors, operating in just ten countries at the end of 2003. Moreover, some of Wal-Mart's recent forays abroad (e.g., in Germany, Indonesia, and Argentina) suffered big losses, at least initially. In Germany, for instance, Wal-Mart didn't fully understand German shoppers, government regulations, and the pervasive role of German unions, much less the competitive landscape. Wal-Mart now aims to have all its overseas retail teams led by locals, is taking steps to be more culturally savvy, and looks for outstanding ideas overseas that can help its domestic operations back in the United States. Overall, it would be wise not to underestimate Wal-Mart over the long haul. Already Wal-Mart is the number one retailer in both Canada and Mexico. The rest of the world may be next.[10]

Stage 5: Global or Transnational Speaking of the rest of the world, it's a more global or *transnational* orientation that marks companies in stage 5. Of course, some companies never reach this stage, perhaps because their industries don't require operational integration worldwide. As we discussed back in Chapter 8, companies that operate on a global or transnational basis try to ignore geographical boundaries in terms of their ongoing operations. In short, they will build product, source materials, or perform services anywhere in the world if doing so somehow minimizes costs and maximizes returns. For instance, computer-peripherals maker Logitech International has dual headquarters (in Silicon Valley and Switzerland) and bases its top manufacturing executive in Taiwan so it can make faster decisions about where it can source product (Taiwan is arguably the hub of low-cost Asian computer component suppliers and manufacturers). Of course, managing this effectively is no easy chore, requiring flexibility, the ability to bridge cultures (and time zones), interdependence across all units, and a global perspective, among other things. However, a transnational orientation also will allow for location-specific tailoring of products or services where necessary, often to a surprising degree. And for large, diverse companies like General Electric, assessing whether the firm operates "globally" or "transnationally" really makes little sense. Instead, each business unit (e.g., plastics, medical imaging, etc.) must decide how local it needs to be to succeed against the competition.[11]

Stage 6: Alliances, Partners, and Consortia Stage 6 highlights the fact that firms are increasingly linking up to leverage their combined resources (such as people, equipment, technology, and research). For many multinationals, partnerships and alliances are a way to access resources that they believe are either too expensive or otherwise impossible to secure alone.[12] So multinationals are rushing to form joint ventures and other types of cooperative alliances. For instance, DaimlerChrysler, Mitsubishi Motors, and Hyundai partnered to jointly develop a new engine. By sharing key technologies and minimizing development costs, the three companies hope to use the engine, in a variety of configurations, in cars sold in Europe, Asia, and the United States. As one auto executive put it, "You collaborate or die. You must achieve economies of scale."[13]

Despite the increasing popularity of such linkages, building trust between partners can be quite difficult, especially when the firms involved are separated by cultural differences. However, even these gaps can be bridged. For instance, one study found that American automotive suppliers developed greater trust with Japanese automakers operating in the United States than with American automakers. One factor that seemed to make a difference was the greater tendency for the Japanese firms to be helpful (e.g., by sending consultants to help American partners for months on end without charge). In short, to build trust in partnerships, you may have to give it first.[14] We'll address these and related human resource management issues in future chapters.

▸ *Foreign Market Entry Options*

Our discussion so far suggests several options when it comes to entering foreign markets. Consequently, this section presents all of the entry options in detail along with their respective pros and cons. One theme that will emerge from our presentation is that the choice of entry mode reflects both the entry barriers that exist in certain foreign markets as well as the resources that firms have to overcome those barriers.[15] Of course, a firm's goals and international strategy, as well as location advantages and opportunities in foreign markets, are all important factors that also shape entry choices.[16] That said, Chapter 10 will explore in more detail some of the factors driving the entry choices companies ultimately make.

Entry without Ownership

First, we'll consider entry options that don't involve ownership of overseas facilities or plants. Next, we'll focus on entry options that involve at least partial ownership of overseas assets. In both cases, we'll evaluate the pluses and minuses of various options and the circumstances that might make them most attractive.

Exporting Exporting involves sending goods or services to other countries where they can be sold. And as we've said, many companies' first exposure to international business is through exporting. Often exporting is a way for companies to increase their revenues. For instance, opportunities in foreign markets may entice firms to begin exporting. Conversely, weakening domestic demand may prompt firms to diversify their markets by exporting, soaking up excess domestic capacity in the process.[17]

One of the advantages of exporting is that it involves no foreign ownership requirements and, as a consequence, is relatively low cost compared to other market entry options. Likewise, exporting allows companies to shield themselves from risks in certain markets, to sidestep foreign investment restrictions, and to shift gears relatively painlessly (export agreements can generally be terminated fairly quickly and inexpensively). Moreover, once companies start exporting to foreign markets, they can use feedback from customers to further tailor their products and increase their overseas business. In fact, quick profits may not be the primary motivation for small firms to begin exporting. Instead, learning about new markets, new technologies, and new ways of doing things may also be motivations.[18]

But cost containment is hardly an issue limited to small firms. Manufacturing or assembling products in one place and then exporting them abroad can help bigger companies, like Boeing, take advantage of economies of scale. On the other hand, by not moving manufacturing or assembly overseas, firms may miss out on foreign location economies that represent long-term advantages, such as cheaper labor.[19]

Of course, exporting does have costs that must be considered. For instance, shipping the product, setting up a distribution system, printing foreign language brochures, and buying advertising in overseas markets can all carry hefty price tags. Some large firms feel they must make substantial direct investments overseas to support their exporting activities. To help sell the cars it exported to Japan, Chrysler at one point spent $100 million to buy Japanese car dealerships, sank another $10 million into a parts distribution center outside Tokyo, and dropped $180 million more to modify its cars for the Japanese market. So much for "cheap" exporting![20]

In fact, exporters grapple with a variety of barriers and challenges. For instance, substantial tariffs on imported products are still in place in many countries. Indeed, Boeing faced that headache when it was trying to sell planes to Russia's Aeroflot a few years ago. As air travel slumped in the wake of the tragic events of September 11, 2001, Boeing scrambled to land new orders. Aeroflot's aging fleet represented a tempting target, with Boeing offering dozens of planes in a deal worth billions. But standing in the way was a steep 40 percent tariff on imported planes, making Boeing products expensive for the cash-strapped Russian carrier. Of course, foreign exporters can also face hurdles in the United States. For example, in 2002 steel companies in Europe and Asia howled about lost export sales to the United States when the American government briefly imposed tariffs as high as 30 percent on a variety of foreign steel products.[21]

Besides tariffs and other import/export regulatory barriers that boost costs, exporters also face two sets of logistical challenges: (1) communications can be difficult because of the distance from customers (e-mail and other communication technology notwithstanding); and (2) certain modes of transportation are too slow, unreliable, or expensive for particular types of exported goods. In many situations, the key to overcoming these drawbacks is to find a foreign distributor who has both the knowledge and resources to market imported products successfully.[22] For another look at how export rules can impact U.S. firms, read the following International Insights.

So what type of firms concentrate on exporting? Clearly, small firms (those with fewer than 500 employees) are well represented. However, small firms run by managers who embrace risk taking and innovation tend to be the most successful exporters. Small firms led by managers who have such "entrepreneurial" attitudes tend to export a higher percentage of their total sales and have higher export growth rates than competitors run by more conservative bosses. A good example might be Frontier Foods, a small food company based in Australia. A few years ago, Frontier began exporting a variety of cheese products to China. This was a daring step because most Chinese at the time had no experience with cheese, were concerned about digestion problems, or disliked the taste. But Frontier's risky move worked, thanks, in part, to a burgeoning middle class that was more open to new tastes as well as the soaring growth of fast-food operators and Western-type supermarkets in China. By the end of 2003, China accounted for 70 percent of Frontier's revenues.[23]

direct exporting
The sale of a firm's products or services directly to foreign customers

indirect exporting
The sale of a domestic firm's product to another domestic firm, which then exports the product after altering it in some way

intracorporate transfer
The sale of a product by a firm located in one country to an affiliated company in another country

Of course, big firms, such as corporate giant Boeing, also export. Indeed, Boeing illustrates the three different types of exporting. When it sells a plane to a foreign airline, Boeing is engaged in **direct exporting**, where sales of a firm's products or services directly involve foreign customers. However, the many U.S. companies that supply Boeing with parts or components are involved in **indirect exporting**. This type of exporting occurs when a domestic firm sells a product to another domestic firm, which then exports the product, often after changing it in some fashion. The final major type of exporting is an **intracorporate transfer**. In this case, a firm located in one country sells a product to an affiliated company in another country. For instance, Ford plants in Mexico produce a variety of products (e.g., fuel tanks) that are then exported to Ford

🌐 International Insights

Trouble Can Start at Home for U.S. Exporters

OPTICAL ASSOCIATES, a small company that makes components for semiconductor firms, was doing well in the exporting game. That is, until the company shipped equipment to an Indian nuclear research facility without obtaining an export license. Federal authorities told the firm that doing so had violated U.S. export restrictions on selling to "forbidden entities." As a result, Optical Associates faced a $500,000 fine. Think that's bad? IBM paid a whopping $8.5-million fine for shipping computers to a Russian nuclear lab. Other penalties can include the loss of export rights and jail time for company officials. For instance, Texas-based Macosia International lost its export privileges for seven years after being found guilty of shipping leg irons and handcuffs to Mexico without the required license.

Of course, some might say that Optical Associates and IBM should have known better. Nevertheless, the number of companies accused of violating U.S. export laws has grown steadily in recent years, with the list of the accused including plenty of household names. So what's going on here? A general rise in international trade, combined with ongoing threats from terrorism and weapons development, has led the U.S. government to step up enforcement of export laws and expand export restrictions to some fifty countries (e.g., India and Pakistan were added to the list in 1998 after performing nuclear tests). Even allies, such as Israel, are subject to restrictions on products like high-speed computers and encryption software. Critics charge that export laws have become too complex and difficult to fathom, costing firms a bundle in lost business and late shipments, not to mention various government-imposed penalties. Plus, the complexity of international business has made it harder for companies to follow the law in the first place. As one manufacturing association executive put it, "When you're sourcing from ten to fifteen countries for a product, or you're part of a supply chain, knowing who your customers are is much more difficult than you think."

Naturally, big companies, particularly those in chemicals, aerospace, or other sensitive industries, tend to have the best resources for coping with the daunting array of export restrictions (e.g., export managers, software to help track and comply with export regulations). But for smaller firms, the complex and cumbersome nature of existing regulations can be intimidating. Most American companies have taken the position, at least in public, that while export restrictions are needed and should be kept in place in many cases, the regulations governing them should be simplified (e.g., less paperwork, shorter approval times for export licenses, etc.). In the meantime, firms that "put their heads in the sand" when it comes to U.S. export laws do so at their own peril.[24]

car assembly plants in the United States.[25] It might surprise you to learn such intracorporate transfers account for about a third of international trade worldwide and about 40 percent of all imports to and exports from the United States. Take a look at Exhibit 9.2 for a breakdown of intracorporate transfers in U.S. imports and exports.[26]

Overall, exporting and importing are deeply woven into the fabric of international business. And exporting is more than just an initial entry option for companies that want to get their feet wet in international business. For firms like Boeing, exporting is a way of life. Moreover, even firms that don't view themselves primarily as exporters often export extensively in conjunction with other market entry options. For instance, a U.S. manufacturer might build an assembly plant abroad, import the needed parts and components from all over the world, and then export finished products to other foreign markets.

Honda is a good example of a company that uses exporting and importing extensively, often in very creative ways. The company operates a variety of facilities in the United States, including a major auto assembly plant in Marysville, Ohio. And Honda makes creative use of its $1-billion trading arm, Honda Trading America Corporation (HTAC). To help supply its American operations, Honda ships parts and components from Japan to the United States. At one point, however, the transport ships involved went back to Japan empty after unloading their cargos in the United States. But thanks to HTAC, those ships now return to Japan fully loaded with everything from scrap metal to frozen salmon to soybeans. Indeed, next to Honda's Marysville auto plant sits a huge warehouse that sorts and packages soybeans grown under contract by over 100 American farmers. Operated by an HTAC subsidiary, soybeans are loaded onto rail cars and sent to California, then put on ships bound for Japan. HTAC exports around 800,000 bushels of American soybeans to Japan, accounting for about 14 percent of the high-end foreign soybeans sold there. Profits from this soybean venture help buffer Honda from downturns in the auto market and have introduced many American farmers to exporting and international business. Sounds like a win-win to us.[27]

licensing
The selling of rights to a company's brand names, patents, manufacturing technology, or any other intellectual property to another firm

Licensing Another relatively inexpensive foreign market entry option is licensing. This option is often used when foreign investment restrictions are in place or firms have limited resources and want to reduce their financial exposure in risky foreign markets. **Licensing** also makes sense when high tariffs make importing goods too expensive or when a high level of product customization is needed that is best done locally. Likewise, when a company in a competitive industry wants to sell a product abroad that's a bit long in the tooth (e.g., an older product or one with dated technology), margins may be slim. In that case, heavy investments in overseas markets make little sense given the potential returns. So licensing often represents a low-cost entry alternative that will allow the firm to still make good money on the product.

Generally speaking, licensing involves selling the right to the company's brand names, patents, manufacturing technology, or any other intellectual property to another firm (the *licensee*). In many cases, the license granted comes with specific restrictions (e.g., licensed products can only be sold in a particular location for a fixed amount of time, usually several years). In an international

EXHIBIT 9.2 *Sources of Intracorporate Transfers in U.S. Imports and Exports*

U.S. Trade Flow	Intracorporate Transfer Source	
	American Multinationals	Foreign Multinationals
Imported goods	Products imported from overseas subsidiaries to U.S. parent firm	Products imported from foreign parent company to a subsidiary in the U.S.
Exported goods	U.S. parent firm exports products to its overseas subsidiaries	Foreign-owned subsidiaries in the U.S. export products to parent firm abroad

Source: Adapted from Koretz, G. (1997). A new twist in trade numbers, *Business Week*, May 12, 24.

context, the firm providing the license (the *licensor*) often obtains quick access to foreign markets and an immediate benefit in the form of royalties or other fees that are paid by the foreign licensee, all without having to set up costly overseas plants. Royalties can be paid up front in the form of a flat fee. They can also be paid as a percentage of sales value or as a flat fee paid per sale.[28]

But licensing also has risks and drawbacks. For example, firms wishing to license their intellectual property to foreign companies should carefully craft the terms, conditions, and boundaries of the licensing contract. The contract should clearly spell out the obligations of both the licensor and the licensee. Typically, the licensor wants the licensee to make narrow or limited use of its intellectual property and to avoid passing trade secrets to competitors. Negotiating such terms is rarely easy since the two sides involved usually have conflicting motives. For instance, the licensor often wants a fairly short-term agreement, especially if it's using licensing as a way to test a market before jumping in with major investments of its own. On the other hand, the foreign licensee often wants a longer agreement, one that will allow it to recoup costs associated with producing and distributing the licensed product.[29]

Even when an equitable licensing deal is struck, there are still major risks. For instance, the licensor gives up considerable control by definition and can be hurt if the licensee produces shoddy goods or behaves in other ways that damage the licensor's reputation. The lack of control also makes it more difficult for licensors to take advantage of location economies. Finally, firms that end up licensing their important technologies and production processes to foreign companies may be "educating" a potential competitor. Indeed, firms often overestimate their ability to control technologies once licensed.[30]

This is a troubling prospect since the management of technology can be the biggest contributor to success or failure in many industries.[31] Nevertheless, multinational firms often find themselves on the horns of a dilemma. Consider Mitsubishi Motors' experience with Hyundai of South Korea back in the mid-1990s. To gain access to fast-growing Asian car markets, Mitsubishi felt it needed to license some of its proprietary technology to help Hyundai build a better car on its behalf. This strategy did help Mitsubishi increase its Asian presence. At the same time, however, Hyundai became a potential rival to Mitsubishi in Asia. Thanks in part to its licensing agreements with Mitsubishi, Hyundai felt it became self-sufficient in most critical technological areas. Today, Hyundai is ahead of Mitsubishi in key markets (e.g., China) and is the fastest-growing Asian car company in others (e.g., Europe).[32]

Licensing technology is especially risky where the legal protection of intellectual property rights is weak. So why did Microsoft license parts of its proprietary computer codes to Chinese firms at bargain-basement rates? Microsoft felt that close ties with Chinese organizations, including those with government connections, would give it more leverage in the fight against software piracy. Roughly 80 percent of the PCs in China use bootlegged copies of Microsoft products. By licensing its technology, Microsoft hoped to develop Chinese versions of its products that could then be sold as upgrades to its bootlegged products.[33]

In fact, multinationals often find themselves pressured into licensing agreements by nations eager to acquire new technology. At one point, for instance, Chrysler refused to license production of components and related technology to Chinese firms. China wanted to export Chinese-made minivans and parts without having to pay Chrysler a licensing fee and refused to include intellectual property protections in any contracts. General Motors, in contrast, signed several production deals after agreeing to Chinese demands to license its technology, betting that the potential was worth the risks. As a consequence, GM was better positioned than many of its global rivals to produce and sell cars in China—a market that some experts predict will soon be the largest in the world. Indeed, by the end of 2003, GM's China Group had the fattest profit margins in the company and announced that it would be bringing out at least one new model annually in China.[34]

Franchising Imagine having a contract that allows you to operate a business using the methods, procedures, products, trademarks, and marketing strategies created by another company. Moreover, that contract may involve longer commitments between the parties involved and require tighter controls as well as stricter adherence to specific operating rules than licensing would. This is the essence of **franchising**.

franchising
The contractual right to operate a business using the methods, procedures, products, trademarks, and marketing strategies created by another company

The company offering the methods, trademarks, products, and so on is the *franchisor*, while the firm that agrees to run the business using those methods and products is the *franchisee*. Service firms, particularly in the food and lodging industries, are most likely to enter foreign markets as franchisors. McDonald's is a good example. The company looks for foreign firms or investors to run its restaurants in a particular country. In exchange for use of company trademarks, operating procedures, products, and various support services (like training and logistics help), the foreign franchisee pays McDonald's a fee. Sometimes the franchisee also has to fork over a portion of revenues to the franchisor. Perhaps the most important aspect about franchising, however, is that franchisees must adhere to strict guidelines about how the business has to be run. That's one reason why McDonald's restaurants look and operate just about the same worldwide.[35]

The greater control franchising offers is a key advantage compared to licensing. Like licensing, franchising also allows the franchisor to shift costs (and risks) to the franchisee. So when a foreign firm signs a deal to run a McDonald's restaurant, that firm often has to come up with the money to start the business. This requirement allows franchisors, especially established ones like McDonald's, to expand quickly worldwide at a relatively low cost.[36] And McDonald's success has led smaller fast-food companies to dip into international markets (they include A&W, Au Bon Pain, Big Boy, Schlotzky's Delicatessen, and Shakey's Pizza, just to name a few). However, smaller franchisors sometimes can't support franchisees to the same extent that bigger firms like McDonald's can (e.g., with global supply networks, extensive employee training programs, etc.). Consequently, franchisees may have to scramble to find suppliers or make necessary menu changes on their own. One Big Boy franchisee in Thailand ended up with a menu oriented toward Thai locals and passing European tourists instead of the chain's trademark "American" hamburgers. As the franchisee put it, "We thought we were bringing American food to the masses. But now we're bringing Thai and European food to the tourists."[37]

That said, franchising also has other challenges that even the biggest firms have to grapple with. For instance, control issues remain a concern. Firms often have high standards that franchisees may not be motivated to duplicate. In fact, a brand name and the expectations that go with it are precious commodities that the franchisor must protect. Customers come to McDonald's, for example, with high expectations of speed, cleanliness, and food quality. Foreign franchisees that do not live up to these expectations can hurt McDonald's reputation.

Sometimes the franchisor will replace weak franchisees by setting up company-owned outlets in foreign countries if local firms can't meet the franchisor's standards. Take a look at the following International Insights on some of the franchise conflicts McDonald's has experienced in Brazil.

Indeed, these control and franchisee management issues are one reason why a few companies in this industry have decided to avoid franchising entirely. Starbucks is a case in point. With over $4 billion in revenue and some 8,000 stores worldwide (over 1,000 in Asia alone), Starbucks is a big company that still is a fraction of the size of McDonald's (with $17 billion in revenue and over 31,000 stores worldwide). Since it doesn't franchise, Starbucks' profit margins are lower than McDonald's and other fast-food chains (without franchisees, Starbucks has to eat higher employee costs). But Howard Schultz, founder and chairman of the Seattle-based coffee chain, says that Starbucks' success is due in large measure to its decision not to franchise. As he put it, "I look at franchising as a way of accessing capital, and I will never make the tradeoff between cheap money and losing control over our stores."[38]

Of course, McDonald's and other firms see this tradeoff differently. To them, too many company-owned outlets are expensive and undercut a major advantage of franchising—that someone else puts up the resources needed to run the business.[39] In fact, because of the high costs of owning foreign facilities, some multinationals have shifted to an even greater reliance on franchising. For instance, after spending billions to battle Coca-Cola globally with new bottling plants and joint ventures, PepsiCo decided to use more franchisees to bottle beverages in overseas markets as a way to reduce costs. Indeed, in 2004 PepsiCo inked a franchise agreement with Baghdad Soft Drink, one of its former bottlers in Iraq. Interestingly, the Middle East is one area where Pepsi has traditionally outsold Coke. Consequently, Pepsi felt that a franchise arrangement could help it recapture the 26-million-customer-strong Iraqi market while mitigating some of the risks involved.[40]

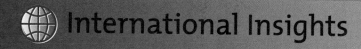

International Insights

McDonald's Moves in Brazil Fry Local Franchisees

McDONALD'S HAS BEEN on a tear in Brazil over the past few years, opening several hundred new restaurants there. Today, the American icon ranks as Brazil's third-largest corporate employer. But some Brazilian franchisees have complaints. They grouse that the rapid expansion of McDonald's, which put new restaurants in the vicinity of old ones, cuts into their sales. Plus, given Brazil's roller-coaster currency, the price of imported items, like ketchup packets, can shoot up unpredictably, further complicating franchisees' profit picture. Some Brazilian franchisees also claim McDonald's is ripping them off, demanding a 17 percent cut of sales as a rental fee (almost twice what U.S. franchisees supposedly pay). In fact, a group of franchisees sued McDonald's in Brazilian court over the disputed fees.

McDonald's rejected these complaints, arguing that Brazilian franchisees were "spoiled" by the easy profits they made earlier. On the rental fee controversy, the company argued that the rental fee helped it recoup the cost of designing and building restaurants in Brazil as well as providing technical help to local franchisees. So far the Brazilian courts have tended to side with McDonald's. But McDonald's Brazilian experience is a reminder that what's under the arches abroad may not always be golden.[41]

Management Contracts In an international management contract, one company provides a foreign organization with specific services, technical help, or managerial expertise for either a flat fee or a percentage of sales or profits. Usually such a **management contract** is for a specific period of time. Like the other entry modes considered so far, this is a relatively low-risk way for a company to increase international revenues since no ownership costs are involved.[42]

management contract
Contract that provides a foreign organization with specific services, technical help, or managerial expertise for either a flat fee or a percentage of sales/profits

To take one example, some years ago Argentinean oil producer Yacimientos Petroliferos Fiscales SA (YPF) used management contracts at its main refinery in La Plata. The technical help that was provided under contract by U.S.-based Hughes Tool Co. helped YPF modernize the plant and cut the cost of oil production in half. Later, Chevron Corp. supplied executives under a management contract with YPF to help run the ongoing operation.[43] Likewise, U.S. Steel's consulting group provided managers and engineers to help Slovakia's Vychodoslovenske zeleziarne AS (or VSZ) modernize and refine its automated steelmaking equipment and capabilities. U.S. Steel later bought VSZ (see our discussion later in this chapter).[44]

turnkey project
Project that typically involves a contract to design and build a facility in a foreign country

Turnkey Projects Sometimes a management contract is a consequence of an international **turnkey project**. These projects usually involve a contract to design and build a facility in a foreign country. When the project is complete, the facility may be run for a short time by the contractor to ensure smooth operations. In many cases, however, an operational facility will eventually be turned over to the company or government issuing the contract. Most international turnkey projects involve building expensive, large-scale facilities such as power plants, dams, airports, oil refineries, and so on.

Some countries lack the internal expertise needed to construct such complex facilities and turn to foreign firms for help. This often provides a forum for local companies to learn about the technology and processes associated with building these facilities. Turnkey projects are especially attractive when more direct forms of foreign investment are impossible or when political or economic instability makes such investments risky. On the other hand, turnkey projects are often limited, one-shot deals that can transfer know-how to potential competitors.[45]

Moreover, sometimes foreign governments scuttle approved projects or take steps that dramatically increase costs. Certain countries have a reputation for putting bureaucratic obstacles in the way of foreign companies. India is just one of many examples. Although free market reforms have been made in the last several years and hundreds of U.S. firms do business in India, a shifting morass of bureaucracies and convoluted regulations remain sources of frustration for multinationals. Foreign companies may have to deal with the central government as well as one or more of thirty-five state governments. For instance, several agreements to build power plants were signed between Indian governments and foreign firms in the early 1990s. A decade later, financing troubles were still being worked out on certain projects, while on other projects some of the American, French, and South Korean firms involved had given up and pulled out. That said, many foreign companies are attracted to opportunities in India. Among other things, India's power grid, telecommunication system, and transportation network (e.g., rail, roads) leave something to be desired. And therein lies plenty of potential business for foreign companies such as U.S. construction giant Bechtel.[46]

Contract Manufacturing An increasingly popular option in recent years, **contract manufacturing** allows companies to outsource their manufacturing operations to other firms, either in whole or in part. The pluses associated with this option are obvious—companies can avoid spending capital to build and maintain expensive plants as well as paying the workforces needed to run them. For instance, shoe companies like Nike and Reebok are able to focus on critical value-added areas, such as marketing and shoe design, because all of their manufacturing is done under contract, mostly in low-wage Asian countries (e.g., China).

contract manufacturing
The outsourcing of one firm's manufacturing operations to other companies, either in whole or in part

On the other hand, contract manufacturing basically means that firms have ceded control for product quality and timely delivery to someone else. Moreover, contract manufacturing may bring unwelcome attention to companies. For instance, Nike has taken public relations hits in recent years because of the alleged mistreatment of workers making its shoes for its contract manufacturers operating in Indonesia and Vietnam. In addition, contract manufacturing is part of the debate about the offshoring of jobs in developed countries such as the United States. Manufacturing workers in a variety of industries in the United States continue to be under pressure thanks, in part, to the rising tide of contract manufacturing in various industries. For example, American furniture makers are increasingly looking to companies in China to produce furniture on their behalf. In the process, dozens of plants in the United States have been closed and thousands of employees terminated, sparking political debates and hurting the images of some firms.[47]

Entry Options Involving Ownership

Many firms progress from nonownership strategies like exporting to those involving ownership of overseas facilities as they become larger and more sophisticated. Moving to ownership may also reflect a desire to make more money abroad, something made easier with the control that ownership affords. Ownership also allows firms to more closely coordinate worldwide operations, something that many multinationals find increasingly attractive. That said, ownership typically entails greater expense and risk.[48]

Wholly Owned Foreign Subsidiaries: The Greenfield Approach One straightforward ownership option for firms, known as the **greenfield approach**, is to enter a foreign market by establishing a wholly owned subsidiary there. Doing that from scratch means scouting for and then buying a piece of property on foreign soil that can accommodate subsidiary operations. Once this site is acquired, construction can begin on the facility. Later, workers can be hired to staff the new operation.

greenfield approach
Entering a foreign market by establishing a wholly owned subsidiary from scratch

The big advantage with this approach is maximum control. A firm can pick a site that maximizes location economies (e.g., being close to target markets or being able to access low-cost local labor) and then put a modern facility on it. Location economies explain why companies spent billions in recent years to build new plants in Mexico near the American border. Such *maquiladora* facilities allow the parent company to pay duty only on the value that local Mexican labor adds to exported products. This arrangement, combined with low Mexican wage rates, proximity to the American market, and access to the U.S. transportation system, lowered overall production costs. For instance, Japanese multinational Sanyo trimmed up to $20 off every $250 TV set it produced in Tijuana, a major savings. Another advantage with the greenfield option is that proprietary technology can be easily protected. And workers can be hired fresh, with no negative prior history to worry about.

But the negatives about the greenfield option are also clear. Building a greenfield facility takes time and is very expensive. And while facilities are under construction, companies may be particularly vulnerable to the whims of the host government (e.g., taxes may be hiked, onerous environmental requirements may be imposed, etc.). Nor does recruiting and training a new workforce just happen overnight, especially in a new culture and legal environment. Unfortunately, firms sometimes ignore these realities and push too fast to set up new foreign subsidiaries. For instance, U.S.-based Lincoln Electric Co. lost money for the first time after the firm built sixteen new plants in eleven countries within a four-year period. The company ended up closing plants in four countries and switched to exporting and alliances as its main international entry modes.[49]

Wholly Owned Foreign Subsidiaries: The Acquisition Approach Multinationals can also establish wholly owned foreign subsidiaries by purchasing foreign companies. This **acquisition approach** usually involves complicated negotiations and financial transactions. There may also be legal or political hurdles to surmount, especially if the multinational is acquiring a foreign company with a strong local reputation or one that is state owned.

In fact, many countries moving toward market-based economies have engaged in **privatization efforts** on a large scale in recent years (i.e., governments selling off state-owned enterprises or assets, either in whole or in part, to private companies or individuals). Indeed, over $700 billion in assets were privatized in the past decade. China is a good case in point. Many of China's state-owned businesses are poorly equipped to survive, particularly when matched against foreign firms. China views privatization as one way to convert state-owned businesses into more effective competitors. Often that means having foreign companies purchase or otherwise invest in state-owned enterprises. But turning around moribund state-owned enterprises is rarely simple or cheap.[50]

And that fact underscores some of the major risks associated with the acquisition approach. When multinationals acquire another firm, either a private or state-owned company, they are also buying all the problems that company had, such as poor labor-management relations, debt, and inferior product quality.[51] On top of that, cultural and managerial differences between the multinational and the foreign firm being acquired can be difficult to overcome.[52] In fact, national culture can affect the way multinationals manage their international acquisitions in the first place.[53]

For instance, U.S. Steel acquired steelmaker Vychodoslovenske zeleziarne AS (VSZ) for $1.2 billion in 2000. U.S. Steel's goal in buying VSZ, a former state-owned enterprise in Slovakia, was to position itself to supply steel to the developing countries of eastern Europe. However, along with the acquisition came antiquated equipment, management corruption, lousy customer service, a bloated workforce of 17,000, and resistance to the "American business culture." Consequently, U.S. Steel expected to spend hundreds of millions over several years to make VSZ a world-class supplier.[54]

And U.S. Steel's experience is hardly unique. For example, Ispat International, a London-based steelmaker, spent $1 billion to buy Kazakhstan's

acquisition approach
Establishing a wholly owned subsidiary abroad by buying an existing plant or facility from a foreign firm

privatization efforts
The selling of state-owned enterprises or assets to private parties

huge Karmet steelmaking complex in 1996. Among the problems Ispat inherited (besides outdated equipment) were twelve former KGB agents who initially refused to leave their gadget-filled spy suite. Chechen fighters also hung around and demanded payoffs from suppliers. And hundreds of workers showed up drunk every day. On top of everything else, Ispat felt that some 40 percent of Karmet's 38,000 employees were unneeded while the local union saw the company as a rich target and wanted a 75 percent wage hike. Over several years, Ispat spent more than $550 million to upgrade the complex.[55] Nevertheless, one advantage that acquisitions typically have over a greenfield approach is speed. The multinational is, in most cases, buying an operational foreign facility that comes complete with workforce, equipment, product, distribution system, brand names, and reputation. That explains Nestlé's acquisition of Polish chocolate maker Goplana. The Swiss giant felt that building a new plant would delay its entry into Poland by two years. Waiting that long would prevent Nestlé from seizing a large share of one of eastern Europe's largest markets.[56]

Multinationals also target foreign companies for acquisition precisely because they have assets, such as successful brands or unique technologies that represent valuable competitive advantages. When added to the multinational's "portfolio," these advantages have the potential to quickly add to international revenues. For instance, in 1996 Coca-Cola acquired Parle Exports, India's number one soft-drink supplier. Doing so allowed Coke to scoop up all of India's local soft-drink brands, plus fifty-odd bottling plants. As a result, Coke owned brands accounting for some 60 percent of the Indian soft-drink market.[57] Conversely, Indian IT firm Wipro bought U.S.-based American Management Systems Inc. and NerveWire Inc. in 2003. Wipro hoped that such acquisitions would give it the expertise needed to more successfully compete in the IT consulting business.[58]

In fact, the ability to enter foreign markets quickly, especially in response to competitors' moves, has become an increasingly attractive option as international competition intensifies and demands for worldwide efficiency rise. This may explain why 48 percent of U.S. manufacturers in one survey said that the best international entry strategy was to acquire existing foreign plants. Only 31 percent said the best bet was to build greenfield facilities.[59]

And as we've suggested, this acquisition trend is not unique to American firms. European multinationals, for instance, have spent hundreds of billions to buy U.S. firms in recent years for similar reasons. This buying pattern is unlikely to disappear anytime soon since European firms continue to want quick access to the large and cohesive American market.[60]

But big cross-border acquisitions may not always be the best way to go. One of the often-stated reasons for doing such deals is that consolidation and size in "global" industries results in greater efficiencies. Nevertheless, the savings that acquisitions are supposed to produce are often overestimated, undercut in many cases by the complexities inherent in cross-border deals. Managers also need to ask themselves whether their industry is really becoming more concentrated on a global basis or if they're just jumping on the proverbial bandwagon. Take a look at Exhibit 9.3. It presents a basic decision matrix for figuring out whether a foreign acquisition is the right move. Of course, as simple as it looks, deciding how global an industry is becoming is hardly child's play. Nevertheless, managers routinely succumb to various types of traps in thinking about these issues (e.g., getting caught up in the hype, wanting to match the "big deals" made by competitors, etc.).[61]

EXHIBIT 9.3   *Will Foreign Acquisitions Pay Off? A Decision Matrix*

		Is your industry really becoming more concentrated globally?	
		Yes	**No**
Is your company pursuing foreign acquisitions as part of an effort to consolidate globally?	**Yes**	Foreign acquisitions are most likely to pay off.	Overexpansion is the likely outcome of foreign acquisition.
	No	Failing to pursue foreign acquisition risks putting the firm at a disadvantage.	Not pursuing a foreign acquisition is appropriate.

Source: Adapted from Ghemawat, P., & Ghadar, F. (2000). The dubious logic of global megamergers. *Harvard Business Review, 78*, 71.

joint ventures
A strategic alliance that involves shared ownership of a business entity by two or more separate companies

Joint Ventures   A cheaper alternative to acquisitions is to pursue various types of alliances and partnerships with other firms. Some alliances, like **joint ventures**, involve shared ownership between companies. But ownership of a foreign operation need not be complete. A joint venture is a specific type of strategic alliance between two companies that is set up as a separate legal entity. Joint venture ownership can be split 50/50 between the parent companies or one firm can have a more dominant stake. Partners that hold more than a 50 percent share usually do so to have tighter control over the joint venture.[62]

In fact, multinationals with sophisticated technology often want a controlling stake in joint ventures, especially if the partner is a local firm whose role is largely to supply expertise about local markets.[63] This is the approach that U.S.-based Whirlpool took to quickly position itself in key Asian markets. In the mid-1990s, Whirlpool parted with $265 million to start joint ventures with four Chinese and two Indian firms. In each case, Whirlpool bought a controlling stake in an effort to balance costs with maximum control. Nevertheless, the expensive nature of this rapid expansion and effective local competitors eventually caused Whirlpool to pursue cheaper alternatives.[64]

Not all international joint ventures involve manufacturing a final product. Sometimes they're designed to procure raw materials, produce components, or deliver services. Creating a joint venture may also involve construction of greenfield facilities, the acquisition of existing firms, or both. Finally, joint ventures may have more than two partners. Clearly, the form and purpose of joint ventures can vary considerably.[65]

That said, a common goal for many international joint ventures is to market, produce, and distribute a product in a particular foreign country or region. Often the partners are a large multinational and a smaller local company, as is the case with Whirlpool and its Asian counterparts. It's easy to see why both parties would be attracted to a joint venture. For example, the multinational might provide product design and technological expertise (something the local company might desire), while the local partner might provide marketing know-how and knowledge of local culture, laws, and business practices (something the multinational might desire). In short, both sides benefit.[66]

Cost, knowledge, and risk sharing are also major reasons for creating joint ventures. This can be especially important for firms that want to be the first to position themselves in risky emerging markets. For instance, United Technologies' (UT) Pratt & Whitney unit signed a joint venture agreement with Russia's Aviadvigatel in 1995 to put engines on Russian-built jets, even though big profits were unlikely in the near future. Likewise, UT's Otis Elevator unit was among the first U.S. firms to enter China in the early 1980s. In fact, Otis started negotiating with eastern European partners just hours after the Berlin Wall fell.[67]

However, joint ventures are not limited to partnerships between large multinationals and small local firms. Increasingly, the costs and risks of entering a particular international market or coming up with a salable product are driving even the biggest multinationals into joint ventures with each other. For instance, several years ago Chrysler and BMW formed a 50/50 joint venture to build a $500-million engine plant. The facility was designed to crank out small engines (under 2.0 liters) for a variety of markets. Building the plant was important to both sides since over 50 percent of the cars sold outside the United States have engine displacements of 1.6 liters or less and neither firm had small engines available. The joint venture setup was attractive because neither firm thought it could sell enough of the new engines alone to recoup the costs of designing and producing it. The joint venture was meant to solve that problem.[68]

Joint ventures can provide access to markets that otherwise would be difficult to penetrate (e.g., China, where joint ventures can be either equity based or contractual in nature). Having a local firm as a partner in such markets can also be a useful buffer against pressures from foreign governments and changes in local regulations.[69] Having a local partner can also allay some of the mistrust that certain countries feel toward foreign multinationals because of fears of exploitation or a history of colonialism. Many developing countries, for instance, are concerned that foreign multinationals will overwhelm local firms. Joint ventures can help allay these fears and teach local firms to be more competitive.[70]

Of course, that could also hurt multinationals if key technologies or know-how is transferred to a local partner. Like licensing, the joint venture may turn local firms into formidable competitors later on. One way to handle this is to have the joint venture agreement expressly forbid the transfer of certain critical technologies. But getting this agreement in the first place can be tough, especially in places like China where technology transfer is encouraged.

In addition, a variety of cultural and managerial conflicts can plague joint ventures. And decisions about selecting a partner, managing the venture, and developing performance appraisal strategies are incredibly thorny in themselves.[71] Nevertheless, resolving such issues is critical if the joint venture is to perform well.[72] One mechanism for minimizing conflict between partners is to manage the joint venture using a **delegated arrangement.** In other words, the partners agree to step back from the management of ongoing operations and instead either hire new executives or reassign executives already working for the partners. As you might suspect, however, this is only a partial solution. Many conflicts can erupt over who will be hired or transferred.[73]

Other disadvantages of joint ventures revolve around control issues. Decisive decision making may be hampered because of the need to consult with the joint venture partner, especially if the partners do not see eye to eye on matters. Joint ventures also may fail to provide the level of control multinationals

delegated arrangement An agreement whereby joint venture partners step back from active management of operations

need to take full advantage of location economies or coordinate worldwide operations. A common way to minimize these disadvantages is for the multinational to have majority control over the joint venture. Of course, foreign companies don't want to play second fiddle in many cases. So finding a partner willing to accept a minority position can be difficult. And while taking a majority position means greater control, it also means more financial risk.[74]

Nevertheless, the additional financial commitment may be worth it. For example, having a dominant position in a joint venture in China can pay big dividends. And U.S. multinationals are finding it easier to acquire larger shares of Chinese joint ventures. This may allow American managers involved in Chinese joint ventures to gain more leverage over:

- Key business decisions.

- How an effective local sales force is developed.

- The strategies used to retain key Chinese personnel.

- How aggressively the local partner lobbies government officials on the joint venture's behalf.

Not surprisingly, American managers tend to feel that Chinese joint ventures are more efficient and profitable when dominant control is maintained.[75]

This sounds like multinationals' ideal joint venture is one where they can run things as usual despite having a local partner. Indeed, multinationals often seem most satisfied with joint ventures where they can ignore the local partner, at least on certain issues, and run operations in their own way. But acting that way may mean that the partner's perspective, and the opportunities for learning that go along with it, is lost. When this happens, it undercuts one of the major benefits of establishing a joint venture in the first place.[76]

Before we move on to the next section, take a look at Exhibit 9.4. It summarizes some of the key pluses and minuses of the market entry options that we have presented. Chapter 10 will explore the challenges associated with joint ventures and other types of strategic alliances in more detail.

Other Types of Strategic Alliances

Speaking of which, joint ventures are just one of many possible strategic alliances. That said, making alliances work well requires trust between the parties, a clear set of shared objectives, and a diplomatic management style, among other things. One success story, at least so far, is the Renault-Nissan partnership. In 1999, France's Renault took a 37 percent equity stake in struggling Nissan. Making this partnership work and moving from losses to profits in the process is arguably thanks in no small measure to Renault's charismatic leader, Carlos Ghosn. His goal is clear. Ghosn wants all Renaults and Nissans to share platforms and basic components by 2010. While the cars produced will look and be marketed differently, Ghosn hopes the savings from sharing will be impressive. Interestingly, part of the alliance's success has been Ghosn's sensitive and effective management of, as he puts it, "the contradiction between synergy and identity." According to Ghosn, each corporate partner must maintain its unique identity ("because it is the basis of motivation") while still embracing common goals.[77]

In any case, other types of alliances are typically narrower in scope, less stable, and shorter in duration than most joint ventures. These alliances may

EXHIBIT 9.4   *Pluses and Minuses of Foreign Market Entry Options*

Entry Mode	Pluses	Minuses
Exporting	• fairly inexpensive • easy foreign access • no ownership risks	• missed location economies • logistical difficulties (transportation/communication)
Licensing	• fairly inexpensive • useful where trade barriers/tariffs preclude exporting • leverages location economies without ownership concerns	• risky where intellectual property protection is weak • control ceded to licensee may inhibit coordination • may help create new competitors
Franchising	• low cost, low risk • offers more control than licensing • builds presence fast	• control still an issue • franchisee may not be motivated to adhere to franchisor's standards
Management contracts	• very inexpensive • low-risk revenue	• no long-term presence • may create competitors
Turnkey projects	• an option if direct investment isn't feasible • lowers risk if long-term instability exists	• no long-term presence • may create competitors • vulnerable to political and legislative changes
Contract manufacturing	• little financial risk • reduces manufacturing costs • allows firm to focus on other value-added areas	• less control (may hamper product quality/delivery) • learning is compromised • public image may suffer
Greenfield subsidiaries	• allows high control • offers location economies • can pick own site, workers, technology	• very expensive to set up • time-consuming to set up • requires considerable international expertise • risky due to ownership
Acquired subsidiaries	• allows high control • rapid market entry • offers location economies	• risky due to ownership • cultural differences may be formidable • may be buying problems
Joint ventures	• less financial risk than subsidiaries • leverages partners' resources, know-how	• risks giving some control or technology to partner • still some ownership risk

Sources: Adapted from Griffin, R. W., & Pustay, M. W. (2004). *International business* (4th Ed.). Upper Saddle Ridge, NJ: Prentice-Hall.

also lack the formal structure and independent legal status found in joint ventures. As such, they are formed when multinationals believe that a cooperative arrangement is the best way to advance their own self-interest in specific areas. For a variety of reasons, including ease of market entry, the sharing of risk, and the ability to realize competitive advantages quickly, the use of strategic alliances has grown dramatically in recent years. Specifically, the number of cross-border connections between firms has been rising at double-digit rates annually over the past decade. And the advantages associated with alliances are especially critical in less developed countries—where deregulation has created more demanding and more competitive markets.[78]

Of course, other entry options provide similar advantages. However, strategic alliances are often a better way for a multinational to learn "invisible skills" from a foreign partner. These skills are informal forms of expertise or know-how that can only be learned through the close observation possible in cooperative relationships. Often, they are quite complex and evolve from a specific cultural context, such as Honda's expertise in developing and producing engines. This expertise has been applied to diverse products (Honda cars, motorcycles, lawn mowers) and reflects a complex blend of know-how in flexible manufacturing, customer service, quality control, product development, and just-in-time materials management.[79]

production alliances
Agreements to manufacture products or deliver services in a shared facility that is either built from scratch or owned by one of the partner firms

Acquiring such expertise is often part of the motivation behind **production alliances**. Such alliances involve firms that agree to manufacture products or deliver services in a shared facility that is either built from scratch or owned by one of the partners. For instance, prior to its acquisition by Boeing, McDonnell-Douglas and Shanghai Aviation Industrial Corp. had a production alliance to assemble jetliners in China using kits shipped over from the United States. The alliance was seen by the Chinese as a way to learn how to develop and build commercial aircraft.[80] Costs can also be part of the equation. H. J. Heinz, for instance, asked food business competitors Unilever and Nestlé to consider sharing production facilities as a way to reduce manufacturing overhead.[81]

research and development alliances
Alliances that involve joint research aimed at the development of new services, products, or technologies

Research and development alliances are another way for multinationals to stay ahead of rapidly changing technology. These alliances involve joint research aimed at the development of new services, products, or technologies. Often partners agree to cross-license any new developments that result from joint research so that all participating firms can equally share in any applications. Hewlett-Packard's cooperative arrangement with Japan's Canon Corp. to develop new printer technology is an example of this type of alliance.

financial alliances
Alliances formed by partners whose primary goal is to reduce the monetary risks of undertaking a particular project

Strategic alliances are popular in other areas as well. **Financial alliances** are formed by partners whose primary goal is to reduce the monetary risks of doing a particular project. Such was the case when IBM and Toshiba entered into an alliance to share the $1-billion cost of developing new computer chip manufacturing facilities.[82]

marketing alliances
Alliances designed to share marketing-related expertise or services

Finally, **marketing alliances** are designed to share marketing-related expertise or services. Such alliances are often formed by firms that want access to the other partner's markets and are willing to pool resources to get it. This has become standard practice in the airline business worldwide. For instance, the SkyTeam alliance binds Delta Airlines, Alitalia, CSA Czech Airlines, and Air France/KLM in a code-sharing agreement that allows the airlines to sell customers "seamless" tickets for flights from American cities to various European destinations and beyond. Likewise, the reverse is true. Such alliances allow airlines to tap into the strength of each other's route structures. For example, to fly

EXHIBIT 9.5   *Beyond Joint Ventures: Other Types of International Strategic Alliances*

Type of Alliance	Purpose
Production alliance	Partners' motivation may include the desire to acquire complex manufacturing expertise and know-how from each other as well as reducing the costs of production.
Research and development alliance	The partners conduct joint research to develop new products, services, or technologies (i.e., pooled resources are more likely to lead to breakthroughs).
Financial alliance	The partners reduce their financial exposure with particularly expensive and risky projects by sharing the costs involved (e.g., jointly building a $1-billion chip manufacturing facility).
Marketing alliance	Partners share services or expertise in marketing-related areas in ways that generate additional profits for both.

from Cincinnati to Rome, a Delta flight will move customers from the United States to Germany, with an Alitalia flight picking up the leg from Frankfurt to Rome. Alitalia does the reverse by tapping into Delta's extensive route structure inside the United States. Exhibit 9.5 summarizes the different types of strategic alliances considered in this section.[83]

Chapter Summary

We began this chapter by considering the *six stages* that companies may go through in their international development. In *stage 1*, a domestic company begins internationalizing by exporting its products or services to foreign customers. Once it has opened overseas offices or sales subsidiaries in a foreign country, a company has moved to *stage 2*. Next, *stage 3* involves the actual production of a significant amount of product overseas. In *stage 4*, a company recognizes the need for headquarters to make strategic decisions, even if local operations are largely staffed by local employees. A more global or transnational orientation occurs in *stage 5*. Finally, *stage 6* highlights the fact that firms are increasingly linking up to leverage their combined resources.

We then considered various options for entering foreign markets, starting with entry modes that don't require ownership of foreign facilities. This includes *exporting*; sending goods or services to foreign countries where they can be sold.

Several types of exporting exist, including: (1) *direct exporting*; (2) *indirect exporting;* and (3) *intracorporate transfers.*

Licensing involves selling the right to use a firm's intellectual property (e.g., brands, technology) to a foreign company (the *licensee*). In many cases, the license granted comes with specific restrictions regarding where products can be sold and for how long. The firm providing the license (the *licensor*) obtains quick access to foreign markets and an immediate benefit in the form of royalties or other fees that are paid by the foreign licensee. Licensing can be a very risky proposition, especially when proprietary technology is involved.

Franchising involves the contractual right to operate a business using the methods, procedures, products, trademarks, and marketing strategies created by another company. The company offering the methods, trademarks, products, and so on is the *franchisor*, while the firm that agrees to run the business using those methods and products is the *franchisee*. Service firms, particularly in the food and lodging industries, are most likely to enter foreign markets as franchisors. *Management contracts* and *turnkey projects* are also examples of entry modes not requiring any ownership responsibilities. Turnkey projects typically involve a contract to design and build a facility in a foreign country. When the project is complete, the facility may be run for a short time by the contractor, often under a management contract, to ensure smooth operations. Finally, *contract manufacturing* allows companies to outsource their manufacturing operations to other firms, either in whole or in part.

We then considered modes of entry involving ownership, like *wholly owned foreign subsidiaries*. This includes subsidiaries whose facilities are built from scratch (the *greenfield approach*) as well as subsidiaries that are purchased from foreign companies (the *acquisition approach*). A greenfield approach offers companies maximum control but is often time consuming and very expensive to execute. Acquisitions typically allow for speedier entry into foreign markets. That said, the acquiring firm is also buying all the problems that the acquired company had, such as poor labor-management relations, debt, and inferior product quality. On top of that, differences in cultural values and management styles can complicate prospects for an acquisition.

A form of entry that only requires partial ownership is the *joint venture*. A joint venture is a specific type of strategic alliance between two companies that is set up as a separate legal entity. Ownership of this entity can be split 50/50 between the parent companies, or one firm can have a more dominant stake. A common goal for many international joint ventures is to market, produce, and distribute a product in a particular foreign country or region. Often the partners are a large multinational and a smaller local company. In these circumstances, the multinational might provide the basic product design and technological expertise, while the local partner might provide knowledge of local culture, laws, and business practices. Of course, a variety of challenges, conflicts, and management hassles often come with joint ventures as well as other types of strategic alliances. Other types of alliances include *production alliances*, *research and development alliances*, *financial alliances*, and *marketing alliances*.

Discussion Questions

1. What are the different stages that companies may pass through as they develop internationally? Can you think of examples of firms that have progressed through all the stages? What about examples of firms that have remained very successful in a particular stage?

2. Compare and contrast the various foreign market entry options that do not involve ownership. Under what circumstances would each option be ideal?

3. Likewise, compare and contrast the various foreign market entry options that involve ownership. Under what circumstances would each option be ideal?

4. Describe the different types of international alliances that may exist between firms. What are some of the major management headaches associated with such alliances?

Up to the Challenge?

General Electric Antes Up (Some) Technology to Gain Market Access in China

BACK AT THE beginning of the chapter we described GE's conundrum in China. Facing a choice between giving up on a potentially lucrative contract to supply high-tech power turbines to Chinese utilities and having to transfer key technologies to potential competitors, GE eventually found the middle ground. And it was a position that allowed it to win the biggest single slice of the turbine deal (a contract to supply thirteen turbines, worth about $900 million).

In essence, GE passed along some, but not all, of the critical technologies (e.g., designs, manufacturing processes, etc.) necessary to produce its most sophisticated power turbines. GE realized that technology transfers were unavoidable if it wanted to compete successfully for at least a piece of the Chinese market. Consequently, in the deal that was struck, GE agreed to set up two joint ventures where it had a majority stake. The first joint venture was with a state-owned firm, Harbin Power Equipment Ltd., which was allowed to assemble the GE turbines in one of its plants. The second joint venture was with Shenyang Liming Aero-Engine Group Corp. It allowed the company to produce certain turbine blades and included the transfer of technologies involving blade metallurgy as well as turbine combustion systems. That said, GE was able to keep some critical technologies secret. For example, GE held on to the cooling system design for the first row of turbine blades as well as their proprietary thermal protective coating. Indeed, the contract called for GE to produce these first-row blades at one of its U.S. plants, sending them to the Harbin plant in China for installation in the final product.

Nevertheless, GE's actions raise the question of creating new, potential competitors by giving up some technologies. It also begs the question of whether the U.S. government played a role, particularly as it relates to GE's ability to protect some of its technology. First, GE reasoned that the threat of creating new competitors by transferring technologies was not imminent. In short, the experience of other multinationals (e.g., Nokia's joint ventures with Chinese firms) suggested that having critical technologies simply wasn't enough to turn Chinese companies into serious global competitors in advanced manufacturing industries. In short, Chinese firms didn't have the technical staff expertise to take full advantage of the technologies to which they were given access. For instance, after their joint ventures with telecom giants like Ericsson and Nokia dissolved, Chinese firms were unable to stand on their own and manufacture state-of-the-art telecommunications equipment (especially given the rapid advances in that area).

Indeed, GE's own experience was similar. In the past, GE had licensed its turbine technology to Chinese companies, figuring they would somehow find ways to access certain technologies anyway. GE also had formed joint ventures with state-owned firms in China during the 1980s to produce small, less sophisticated power turbines. Likewise,

other multinationals in the turbine business formed joint ventures with Chinese firms during the same time frame, all of which involved the transfer of some technology. The net result of all this was that Chinese firms eventually mastered the ability to produce steam-driven turbines—an ability that was, by then, no longer state-of-the-art given the larger, natural gas–driven power turbines subsequently developed by GE. Put simply, the Chinese firms had been unable to keep up with advancing technologies pursued by multinationals like GE and Siemens.

As for the role of the U.S. government, American multinationals such as GE can sometimes use U.S. trade law to protect their technologies. Indeed, the U.S. export regulations are such that GE is prohibited from transferring key aspects of its turbine technology to Chinese firms. Specifically, U.S. law prevents GE from exporting cooling system technologies for turbine blades since they are also applicable to aircraft engine design. Similarly, computer-chip giant Intel used U.S. export restrictions on sensitive technologies to successfully blunt Chinese demands for building a cutting-edge silicon wafer plant in China.

The upshot of all of this is that GE felt it could maintain control over its most critical technology and still land a big chunk of the business. And it plans to continue to develop more advanced and more complex turbines while its Chinese counterparts try to digest and develop enough staff expertise to reproduce GE's current turbines. In essence, GE hopes to keep the potential Chinese competition in its rear-view mirror. For the moment, GE may be right. Chinese officials admit that, at least in the short run, they remain dependent on GE for key imported components and their associated technologies. As one official put it, "The foreigners are now agreeing to tell us how and where to dig a hole, but we still do not know why to dig a hole there."

But is this all a risky pipe dream on GE's part? How long can GE really expect to "have its cake and eat it too"? Isn't there a real risk that Chinese firms will scale the learning curve faster in the future and develop enough internal expertise to actually catch up, if not surpass, multinationals like GE? And doesn't that put enormous pressure on GE to stay out in front, as well as invite the Chinese side to continue to push for even more technology access in the future?[84]

International Development

Critical Incidents in International Strategy

Purpose

To develop strategies and implementation solutions to deal with problems facing various international corporations.

Instructions

Please read all four of the critical incidents that follow and develop a strategy for solving the problems presented (done *before* class). Your instructor will divide the class into groups. Each group should identify the strategic issues in all four incidents and try to achieve some kind of consensus on which strategy to implement (20 minutes).

Your instructor will lead a discussion on strategic issues. Are there some common issues that need to be addressed in international dealings? How can managers be more sensitive to these issues (20 minutes)? As an option, your instructor may ask each group to make a brief presentation on their respective findings (another 20 minutes).

Critical Incidents

Although strategic decision making is often quite complex and filled with many issues, the situations here are simplified examples of composite companies, based on true business cases. The idea is to discuss the few issues in these critical incidents without all the complexity that occurs in longer cases.

1. A clothing manufacturer has been losing business because of a competitor's lower prices and must take some action soon before the balance sheet looks worse. One idea would be to locate a new plant in Mexico, where wages are cheaper. It has been estimated that this could save the company enough to reduce the price of clothing by 15 percent, which would once again make it competitive. However, one of the top managers has mentioned that a shoe factory was just recently relocated to the area in question, and it has been hit with higher turnover and lower productivity than expected. He read that the shoes are expected to cost 12 percent more than former esti-

mates had predicted. Should the company relocate this factory to Mexico? If not, what other strategies could be employed?

2. Equip, Inc. is interested in buying 70 percent of a large heavy machinery company in one of the former Soviet bloc countries. With a purchase price of $40 million and updating costs of $10 million, Equip figures it can realize a profit within three years, with a decent return for investors. However, the government has balked at Equip owning 70 percent; instead, it wants to sell 35 percent at $20 million and expects the company to put in $8 million for renovations. Although it has not been explicitly stated (and no direct answer to questions has been given), the international department expects the company to resist laying off part of the inflated workforce. This would greatly change the profit picture. Still, if the market proceeds as expected, the company could be earning a respectable profit within five years. Inside information suggests that the government will not sell more than 49 percent, no matter what. Yet this is the type of machinery you want to get into, and you know you can develop this market further than almost any other company.

3. Your development and construction company put in a $60-million bid to build the new airport in a South American capital city. The government has decided to privatize the airport. You know the other companies that bid and know that you are the most competent. Your idea is to reduce the number of employees at the airport from 2,000 to 85, with most work being contracted out to small businesses. Calculations show this to be the most efficient way to run the airport. Figures show that this project will mean a net profit of $2 million for the company, assuming no major unforeseen problems. However, a Canadian firm is given the job, a company you know is on the brink of bankruptcy. You also know that the government minister in charge of awarding the contract had spent six months in Canada a couple of years ago. Two years later

you are not awarded the contract, and after the Canadian firm goes under, the government comes back to you and offers you the contract. However, because the Canadian firm made promises to keep the 2,000 employees and to hire several less-than-efficient subcontractors, you are not certain you can make a profit on this venture (it looks quite difficult to get out of those promises). It even looks as if you will lose about $1million. However, you know that several other major governments considering new airports around the world are looking at this project to see who does it and with what quality, and they are also looking at a few other similar projects now under construction by other companies.

4. You run a large mail order and television-ordering business that has enjoyed enormous success in recent years. However, several of your key managers feel it is time to branch out into less developed countries, for there is virtually no competition in these places. They argue that even though profits would be low for several years, your company would have itself firmly established when the market surges (assuming it in fact would). Other managers do not disagree with that. On the contrary, they feel these are strong reasons to enter such markets. What they argue against are basically the problems of low income and uncertain economic futures in these countries, particularly in four of the countries. Two of the eight countries proposed even have some political instability (though admittedly not much). They also argue that these countries have poor phone systems, making it difficult for phone calls to get through, and most of them do not have any capability of an 800-type system, though a few governments are said to be "thinking it over." Two of the countries are in the Pacific Rim region and are projecting tremendous rates of economic growth in the next five years. However, they are not yet consumer societies, and there is some disagreement when and if they will become so. What will you do?

Source: From *International Management Cases and Exercises*, 2nd edition by D. Marcie and S. Puffer, pp. 311–313. © 1994. Reprinted with permission of South-Western College Publishing, a division of Thomson Learning. Fax 800 730-2215.

 Tapping into the Global Network

Using the Global Practices Instrument

Purpose

The goal here is to help you reflect on your company's international operations and hone your ability to assess the internal corporate environment from a strategic perspective. This instrument measures the extent to which corporate practices embrace an international perspective and reflect a clear international strategy. We think it may be particularly useful now that you have read Chapters 8 and 9, which both deal with international strategy issues.

Instructions

Answer the following questions for *your* firm by circling the appropriate number. If you're not employed or the company you work for has no international presence, then find an internationally oriented company that you might be interested in learning more about (alternatively, your instructor may assign a company to you) and do some Internet research to answer the questions. A good place to start if you need to find a suitable company is Hoover's online information service for business, which will allow you to search for companies by industry or location (**www.hoovers. com**). Alternatively, if you're a subscriber, you can pick a company on the Fortune Global 500 list (**http://www.fortune.com/fortune/fortune500**), or, if you're more interested in the international strategies used in fast-growing companies, start with the *Inc.* magazine list of the 500 fastest-growing firms (**http://www.inc.com/inc500/**).

Of course, whether a particular international strategy orientation is appropriate for a specific company is another matter entirely. Likewise, a company may have a reasonable international strategy but may not execute it very well. These are issues that you should consider once all the answers are in.

In other words, how well do you think the company's existing strategy matches what it should be doing? If the match is poor, what recommendations would you have? If the match is good, what suggestions, if any, do you have for improving the firm's execution (e.g., in terms of market entry options or other management-related issues)?

A. *Management Team*

1. The firm's vision and culture is:

Domestic   1   2   3   4   5   Global

2. The senior management team . . .

Doesn't include foreigners   1   2   3   4   5   Includes many foreigners

3. Key jobs in all countries are held by . . .

Home country employees   1   2   3   4   5   Local employees

4. Top managers travel the world . . .

Rarely   1   2   3   4   5   Often

5. Top management familiarity with culture in key markets:

Unfamiliar   1   2   3   4   5   Familiar

6. Number of foreign nationals on company's board of directors:

None   1   2   3   4   5   Three or more

B. *Strategy*

1. Firm strategy for each country, region, or profit center:

Separate, independent   1   2   3   4   5   Governed by one global plan

2. Firm philosophy about alliances or coalitions abroad:

"Go it alone"; relies on controlling subsidiaries or acquisitions in new markets   1   2   3   4   5   "Share to gain"; relies on foreign alliances to meet threats

3. Units in specific foreign locations . . .

Operate as separate companies   1   2   3   4   5   Operate as one global company

4. In the company, environmental scanning of foreign markets is . . .

Somewhat important   1   2   3   4   5   Extremely important

5. The decisions made in the company reflect . . .

Home country concerns and control   1   2   3   4   5   No preferential treatment to any country

C. *Operations and Products*

1. The primary focus of the company is . . .

Exporting   1   2   3   4   5   Full global operations

2. The company's major operating facilities are located:

In the home country   1   2   3   4   5   In North America, Japan, Europe, and elsewhere

3. Production processes and product design decisions are . . .

Decentralized; each major country makes its own decisions   1   2   3   4   5   Centralized, though minor local changes are okay

D. *Scoring*

Add up the points for each area:

    A. Management team (score range is 6–30):
        _____, divide by 6 = _____ average

    B. Strategy (score range is 5–25): _____,
        divide by 5 = _____ average

    C. Operations/Products (score range is
        3–15): _____, divide by 3 = _____ average

To see where the firm is on the continuum between purely domestic and fully global, compare averages with the following scores.

Domestic	Moving toward Global	Approaching Global	Global

←———————————————————————→

  1.0   1.5   2.0   2.5   3.0   3.5   4.0   4.5   5.0

Source: Adapted from Lussier, R. N., Baeder, R. W., & Corman, J. (1994). Measuring global practices: Global strategic planning through company situational analysis. *Business Horizons,* September–October, 58–60.

10

Making It Work: Effective International Operations

INTERNATIONAL CHALLENGE

McDonald's Challenge in France

Learning Objectives

After reading this chapter, you should be able to:

▸ Understand the options available for managing strategic alliances.

▸ Recognize the ways that organizations structure their international operations and the respective strengths and weaknesses of these structures.

▸ Comprehend the various formal and informal approaches to coordination.

▸ Appreciate the value of getting a technological edge and keeping it.

Who better to understand the issues involved in doing business in foreign lands than McDonald's—the prototype of a global company (**http://www.mcdonalds.com/corp/about.html**)? This icon of an American company has operations in over 120 countries from Argentina to Uruguay. In between they have stores in countries such as Croatia, Egypt, India, Japan, Oman, Saudi Arabia, and South Africa among others, and international operations account for about half the total revenue of this Oak Brook, Illinois, company. More than anyone, McDonald's has jumped into foreign markets—often with a proven and familiar operational approach: a good deal of consistency in its menu offerings, a similar appearance of its restaurants, and its renowned quick service.

Most stores are run by local owners who "partner" with McDonald's in the world's largest franchising consortium. In Saudi Arabia, seventy-one stores have opened since 1993, many operated by HH Prince Misha'al Bin Khalid Bin Fahad Al Faisal Al Saud, including two in the holy city of Mecca. Yet, despite this history of experience and understanding of local predilections and tastes, McDonald's has its problems. As the firm's fortunes continue to improve here in the United States, McDonald's faces issues in other countries. For example, in 2004, over one-third of the franchisees in Brazil are suing the company. They are accusing it of gouging the local stores by overcharging for rent and by creating too much competition by opening too many stores that are close to one another.

So, while McDonald's is turning out its best performance in years in the United States, its foreign operations are stagnating. In Europe, for example, sales have been off. Europe accounts for nearly 48 percent of McDonald's operating profit, but poor performance in the United Kingdom and Germany, among other places, has eaten into that bottom line. France presents another such challenge. It's hard to imagine that the country that taught the world about haute cuisine would embrace deep-fried potatoes and greasy burgers. As you read this chapter, and given what you know about France from your reading of earlier chapters, think about how McDonald's might "make it work" in France. Then refer to the *Up to the Challenge?* box at the end of this chapter for some surprises about the Big Mac in France.[1]

▶ *Making It Work: Effective International Operations*

The previous two chapters examined international strategy—the first assessing strategy itself, and the second examining various approaches to implementing the strategy. Once a firm has both assessed and implemented a strategy, its next goal is to stay afloat internationally. Accordingly, we now extend our discussion to the steps firms take to ensure that their international strategies work. First, we'll talk about general challenges in managing strategic alliances. We then turn our attention to a key mechanism through which firms implement their strategy, organizational structure, or the basic pattern of the firms' components, including various forms of organizational design and related coordinating tools. Today, any good strategy and structure must anticipate and incorporate technology. Clearly, it's important to get a technological edge and to keep it once you have obtained it, and this is the subject of the last section of this chapter.

Challenges in Managing Strategic Alliances

Chapters 8 and 9 reviewed the strategic options available to firms and what a firm might do to bring those various strategic options into play. Deciding among options is one thing, but executing and managing them is quite another. In particular, there are many challenges to be faced and considered before venturing into an alliance with a foreign partner, and these are summarized in Exhibit 10.1. First, it must be determined if an alliance is really the best strategic option for a given multinational. This usually involves making judgments about some of the control-benefit tradeoffs we have discussed in earlier chapters. Drawing on partners' capabilities and competencies has strategic advantages, but they often come at the price of dependency, management headaches, and higher costs.

Next comes the thorny issue of selecting a partner. One argument asserts that partners should have similar operating philosophies and management styles. Common ground is often difficult to find in an international context. Instead of similarity, however, partners should have **complementary needs**, goals, and capabilities. For this part of the equation, the KLM-Northwest alliance made considerable sense. KLM has a strong route structure in Europe and Africa, while Northwest offers extensive service within the United States. Joining these complementary strengths creates a formidable service network from which both sides can benefit.

Failure to monitor the partnerships' relationship is one reason why alliances have a low survival rate. Such ongoing fine-tuning can be especially challenging when the multinational has formed several alliances. In fact, some multinationals, such as Corning Glass, have deliberately formed **alliance networks** to build a portfolio of partners who can help provide competitive advantages at a relatively low cost. Managing these networks is very time consuming and creates a potentially dangerous level of dependency. At the same time, the increasing popularity of alliances is also making it harder for multinationals to

complementary needs
The ability of each partner in an alliance to benefit from the expertise and core competencies of the other

alliance networks
A set of alliances formed by one firm with partners who can help provide competitive advantages at a relatively low cost

EXHIBIT 10.1 *Key Issues in Managing Strategic Alliances*

Issue	Description
The logic of collaboration	Identifying when, where, and why to form an alliance; are the costs (less control) worth it?
Selecting partners	Picking partners that maximize benefits and minimize risks (compatible management, trust, and complementary needs and assets)
Structuring alliances	Providing a structure that gives incentives for success (contract or equity based)
Managing alliance dynamics	Being aware of the management adjustments needed as alliances evolve
Managing alliance networks	Creating a system of reinforcing alliances that avoids anarchy
Recognizing alliance limits	Alliances can create organizational constraints, strategic gridlock, and dependence
The role of governments	Understanding the impact of government policies and pressures

Source: Adapted from Gomes-Casseres, B. (1993). *Managing international alliances.* Publication No. 793–133. Boston, MA: Harvard Business School Publishing.

find new partners. Indeed, in the airline industry it is hard to find a firm that is not already in a partnership. Even Midwest Express—a small Milwaukee-based airline that offers luxury travel at coach fares—has a marketing alliance with London-based Virgin Atlantic Airways.

Another management challenge that multinationals need to be aware of is the extent to which governments can affect alliances.[2] For instance, McDonnell-Douglas's agreement with its Chinese partner faltered when the Civil Aviation Administration of China (CAAC) decided to oppose the alliance. The CAAC used its regulatory power to cancel sales of jets assembled in China by the alliance. As a result, McDonnell-Douglas lost ground in a booming market. Despite having a ten-year assembly history in China, McDonnell-Douglas sold only eighty-seven jets to Chinese airlines. In contrast, Boeing, which made a point of cultivating a close relationship with the CAAC, had sold 250 during the same time. Ironically, Boeing's subsequent purchase of McDonnell-Douglas meant that they were no longer competitors in the Chinese market.[3]

Finally, experts suggest that before multinationals get into a strategic alliance, they need to consider how to get out of one. Alliances terminate for a variety of reasons. Partners' goals, opportunities, or financial situations may all change. Our point is that the "divorce" can be a messy, costly, and unfriendly affair. Multinationals can protect themselves by including exit clauses in alliance agreements that clearly spell out (1) the conditions that permit each partner to dissolve the marriage, (2) how alliance assets will be liquidated and divided up, (3) how liabilities will be handled, and (4) how disputes threatening the alliance will be resolved.[4]

degree of control
How much "say" an entry mode offers over strategic and operational decisions

Factors Affecting International Market Entry Choice

Chapter 9 reviewed a variety of foreign market entry options and their pluses and minuses. In many cases, entry decisions come down to judgments about (1) **degree of control** (how much "say" an entry mode provides in terms of strategic and operational decisions), (2) **resource commitment** (the resources required to pursue a particular entry mode), (3) **dissemination risk** (the risks of having proprietary technology or expertise fall into the hands of a foreign partner), and (4) **systemic risk** (economic and political risks present in foreign markets). These judgments are affected by a wide variety of factors. In fact, over twenty different factors have been linked to entry choice, sometimes in an inconsistent fashion.[5] Exhibit 10.2 summarizes what we believe are some key factors influencing entry choice.

For instance, the nature of a firm's core competencies often drives entry choices. Multinationals whose main competitive advantage is proprietary technology may avoid licensing and other entry modes that make controlling technology difficult. If that technology is evolving or in flux, however, then a strategic alliance with another firm may aid in the development of new or improved technologies. In contrast, if competitive advantage is based on management expertise (as in the case of many service firms), then licensing, franchising, or management contracts may represent little risk. In such cases, a brand name often goes with that expertise, something that is reasonably well protected internationally and difficult to duplicate.[6]

International experience also can drive a firm's entry choices. Firms with limited experience often use strategies that allow for complete control. As they gain experience, firms tend to enter more culturally and geographically distant markets where full control is difficult. This, in turn, leads to a heavier reliance on alliances, licensing, and other approaches. However, very experienced multinationals may go back to high-control entry modes (such as acquisitions) in order to coordinate their vast global operations more tightly.[7] Industry characteristics may also affect entry decisions. For firms in global industries, worldwide coordination and control of foreign units is essential. This need may dictate a preference for high control, something that wholly owned subsidiaries provide.[8]

Things get pretty complicated, however, once combinations of entry factors are considered. For instance, research suggests that firm nationality and level of internationalization (the percentage of sales earned abroad) do not affect the entry choices of firms competing in global industries. One explanation is that global industries by definition go beyond national borders and that national culture therefore offers little of value as competition flows across countries.[9]

Other studies suggest that culture and national origin do affect firm entry decisions. For instance, Japanese multinationals are less likely to react to shifting assessments of risk in China by raising or lowering their equity stake in joint ventures than are their American or European counterparts. Likewise, relative to the Japanese and Europeans, U.S. multinationals are less likely to insist on a majority stake in Chinese joint ventures despite the fact that they tend to put more capital into such ventures than their agreed-on equity share calls for. More research is needed to explain exactly why these patterns occur.[10]

Research also suggests that perceptions of cultural distance can affect choice of entry mode.[11] However, the direction of this effect varies across studies. For instance, one study found that U.S. manufacturing multinationals tend to rely more on entry options that involve ownership (such as acquisitions) when the cultural distance with the target country is high. The idea is that ownership allows for more control over key technologies and management practices when they will be used in a culture that is very different. Conversely, lower

resource commitment
The resources required to pursue a particular entry mode

dissemination risk
The risks of having proprietary technology or expertise fall into the hands of a foreign partner

systemic risk
The economic and political risks present in foreign markets

EXHIBIT 10.2 *Factors Affecting Choice of International Entry Mode*

Type of Factor	Examples
Firm factors	International experience Core competencies National culture of home country Corporate culture Firm strategy, goals, and motivation
Industry factors	Industry globalization Industry growth rate Technical intensity of industry
Location factors	Extent of scale/location economies Country risk Cultural distance Knowledge of local market Potential of local market Competition in local market
Venture-specific factors	Value of firm assets risked in foreign location Extent to which know-how involved in the venture is informal (tacit) Costs of making/enforcing contracts with local partners Size of planned foreign venture Intent to conduct research and development with local partners

Source: Adapted from Phatak, A. V. (1997). *International management: Concepts and cases.* Cincinnati, OH: South-Western.

double-layered acculturation
The need for a multinational firm to confront both a strange national culture and a different corporate culture when operating abroad

levels of perceived cultural distance are more likely to result in a preference for licensing and other indirect forms of foreign investment.[12] Research on service firms has reached the opposite conclusion. One study found that in a service environment, increased cultural distance was associated with entry modes that do not require ownership (such as relying on a management contract to run a hotel in a culturally distant location).

Another interesting study found that when the cultural distance between the parent and host country was high, barriers to success were most severe when the foreign venture required **double-layered acculturation**. In other words, success was less likely when a multinational had to confront both a strange national culture and a strange corporate culture. This situation would occur when the multinational entered the market by setting up a joint venture, as opposed to building a brand new and wholly owned facility where only national culture is relevant. Ironically, the results also suggested that joint ventures and foreign acquisitions were the entry modes most likely to improve multinationals' ability to learn about cultural differences. This learning could increase the likelihood of success in subsequent ventures.[13] Overall, these are complex results and it is by no means clear why some of these cultural or national differences exist. This conclusion underscores two basic points: (1) the issue of how nationality and culture impact international strategy implementation needs additional research, and (2) multiple variables may interact to affect entry choice.[14]

Structuring International Business Operations

Once an entry choice is analyzed and taken, a key decision then becomes how to structure international operations. **Structure** refers to the way an organization is set up. It is what the firm uses to allocate resources, coordinate employees, distribute tasks, implement procedures, and gather and transfer information used in decision making. There is no shortage of options for organizations, although some are tied to a specific entry choice. Nevertheless, there are benefits and tradeoffs between various structures. To perform well, however, a firm's organizational structure should match the sophistication of its competitive environment.[15] This implies an evolutionary process. Organizational structure typically changes as firms expand their international operations or modify their strategic approach. Accordingly, we'll begin by examining simple structures and work our way up to more complex versions used by firms pursuing global strategies.

Basic Structures for International Business In most cases, firms new to the international arena start by exporting to foreign markets. Early on, exports will be processed and handled by staff in existing departments, such as marketing. As exports grow, however, this arrangement can prove burdensome or even overwhelming. At that point, firms may consider modifying their structure to better manage export operations. A common first step is to hire an export manager. This individual may also have a small staff. Together, this group is often organized into an export department. If the company has only a few products, the export manager may report to the top marketing executive. This is the approach used by Allen-Edmonds Corporation, a U.S.-based manufacturer of high-quality dress shoes. Export staff involved in the sales and marketing of the company's shoes in Europe and Asia report to the vice president of marketing. If a firm exports a broad range of products, the export manager and his or her staff may report directly to the CEO.[16] These two possibilities are presented in Exhibit 10.3. Either way, we don't mean to imply that these export processes are simple. In fact, these processes can be very complex, as we illustrate in the *Tapping into the Global Network* exercise at the end of this chapter.

As a firm expands further, so do pressures to become more knowledgeable about specific overseas markets. This issue must be confronted once a company starts sending people abroad or begins operating foreign facilities. Generally speaking, a small export department is unlikely to be up to these challenges. In response to these strategic pressures, many firms at this stage turn to an international division structure. This involves splitting the company into domestic and international operations. The international division may report to a senior international executive at company headquarters (such as the vice president of international operations), and it serves as the umbrella under which all international activities are conducted.[17] For many companies, the resulting structure looks something like what you see in the top part of Exhibit 10.4. There, you will see that domestic divisions coordinate different product lines; anything sold overseas is lumped into the international division. The international division, however, may be further subdivided as overseas business expands. As you can see in the lower half of Exhibit 10.4, these subdivisions can be made either by geographic area or by product line. For instance, motorcycle maker Harley-Davidson essentially views international operations in geographic terms, with Europe and Asia treated as separate markets. As a result, different

structure
The decisions the firm makes in regard to how the organization is set up to allocate resources and perform tasks

EXHIBIT 10.3   *Typical Structures for Firms with a Primary Focus on International Exports*

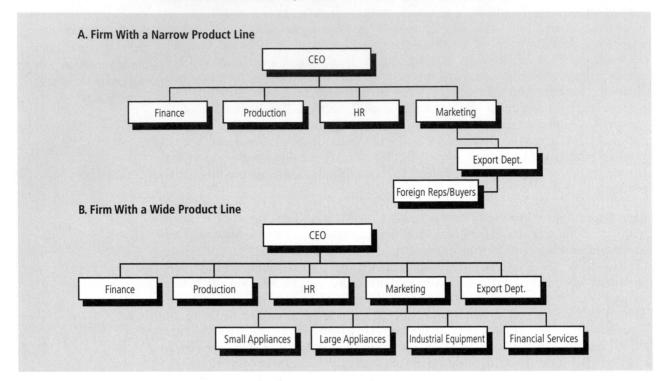

sub-units within the international side of Harley's business handle European and Asian operations.

One advantage of the international division structure is that it concentrates managerial expertise and know-how. It also helps coordinate overseas functions (e.g., purchasing, marketing, and sales). Companies that have a limited range of products, few senior managers with foreign experience, and a relatively small percentage of foreign sales are good candidates for this type of approach. This description fits Harley-Davidson since its domestic U.S. sales are twice that of total foreign sales.

The international division structure also has disadvantages. For one, there is potential for turf battles between the domestic and international divisions, especially as the international division grows and gobbles up more resources. The coordination of domestic and international operations can also prove troublesome, and even a major problem as the firm adopts more global strategies. Transferring information and know-how between international and domestic operations is often difficult as well.[18] Interestingly, while this international division structure is common among U.S. firms, it is not so among European multinationals. Undoubtedly, the main reason for this is that American firms rely more heavily on the domestic front than do corresponding European firms.[19]

Global Organizational Structures As international operations expand, senior executives may start to embrace the idea that foreign markets are a critical part of the corporation. For the first time, managers may feel that the company is

EXHIBIT 10.4 *Examples of an International Division Structure*

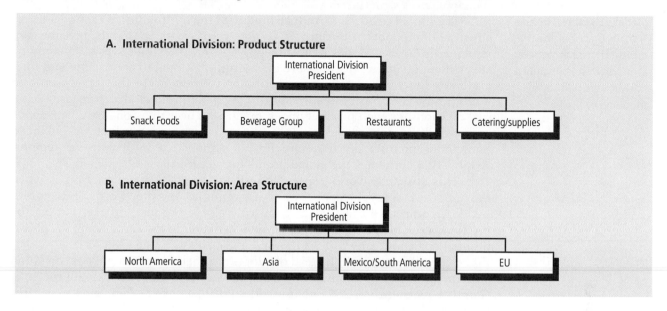

truly international and that the home country is just one of many markets for the firm. Around this time, management sometimes decides that an international division structure has outlived its usefulness.[20] However, the extent to which management actually adopts a more global strategy depends on a wide range of factors (see Chapter 9).

We should point out that for multinationals with a variety of different businesses, a combination of structures may work best. Some of a multinational's businesses may, for example, compete in industries that are low in globalization potential, suggesting that a country-by-country structure would be useful. Other businesses may be subject to restrictions (such as high tariffs) in some countries, a situation that argues for coordination across units in those countries. Still other businesses and countries might need a structure that could provide both global coordination and local responsiveness.[21] Nevertheless, we are going to simplify things by focusing on three global structures commonly found in multinationals: (1) the global area structure, (2) the global product structure; and (3) the global matrix structure.

The **global area structure** is a good choice for multinationals that have relatively few products and that compete in industries where a high degree of local responsiveness is required. This structure divides up the entire world into countries or regions, with each area having a fairly high degree of functional autonomy (they may have their own human resource, marketing, and production functions). Operational and strategic decision making is typically delegated to different regions or countries. The role of headquarters is to maintain overall strategic direction and control the multinational's finances. Of course, the main advantage of this structure is outstanding local responsiveness. Therefore, it is a good option for multinationals that view their businesses as essentially multidomestic. However, if local responsiveness becomes less critical or if location economies are more important (such as being able to chop production costs by moving manufacturing to a specific location), this structure can prove ineffective. The global area structure may also make it difficult to transfer

global area structure
This particular setup divides up operations of a firm into countries or regions, with each area having a fairly high degree of functional autonomy

learning, know-how, and competencies across borders.[22] Exhibit 10.5 illustrates the global area structure.

global product structure
A structure whereby the multinational organizes around what is usually a fairly diversified set of products or businesses

The **global product structure** organizes the multinational around a diversified set of products or businesses. By *diversified* we mean that the products are made with different types of technology and have distinct sets of customers. Diversification often puts pressure on the multinational to coordinate and integrate key functions—such as marketing and production—that are specific to these products or businesses. In short, the global product structure uses separate divisions for each product line or business. These divisions have worldwide responsibilities for all functions associated with the product or business. Sometimes product divisions are further subdivided into areas or regions. Exhibit 10.6 illustrates the global product structure.

This structure works especially well for diversified multinationals when the pressures for local responsiveness are minimal. In other words, if the multinational competes in industries with truly global products (those that can be pretty much sold everywhere in the same form and in the same way), the global product structure can work well. Apparently, this was the case for the merger that created ExxonMobil. Instead of adopting either the existing Exxon or Mobil structures, a new product-based structure was devised.[23] Likewise, Procter & Gamble's *Organization 2005* plan was designed to replace their area structures with global product structures that are tied to specific categories (e.g., paper goods, feminine protection, beauty care).[24]

But a global product structure does create a high level of duplication since each product line or business has to have its own facilities, human resources, and so on. ExxonMobil has dealt with this issue directly with the creation of a global services unit that provides centralized support in information systems, procurement, and human resources. Nevertheless, if local needs change or

EXHIBIT 10.5   *The Global Area Structure*

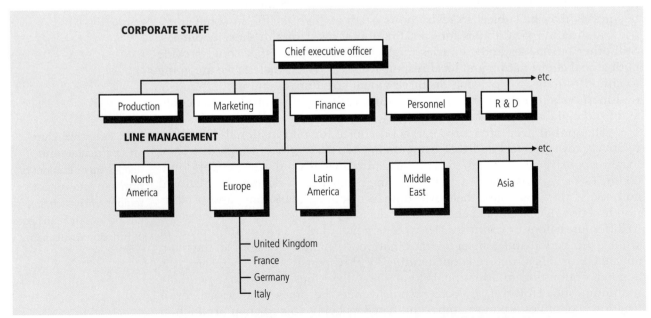

Source: "The Global Area Structure" from *International Dimensions of Management*, 4/e, p. 164, by Arvind V. Phatak, © 1995. Reprinted with permission of South-Western College Publishing, a division of Thomson Learning. Fax 800 730-2215.

become more diverse, this structure is ill-equipped to deal with it. In fact, local managers will often have a hard time even being heard since divisional product managers have more power and tend to focus on markets (often domestic ones) that account for the bulk of sales. Local responsiveness is not a strong point of this setup.[25] Indeed, this was the experience of P&G. Thousands of managers were transferred or reassigned (over 1,000 European staffers to Geneva alone), creating considerable griping among middle and other management levels. These effects, in combination with weak earnings, were partly responsible for the CEO's departure after only a year and a half on the job. P&G has since reverted to some of its original geographic structure in an effort to remain responsive to customers.[26]

Finally, the **global matrix structure** is an option that many multinationals consider, especially those that compete in industries where both global integration and local responsiveness are required. Multinationals are also looking for a structure that will make it easier to take advantage of location economies and transfer learning across country and product lines. The global matrix tries to reconcile these often conflicting goals by having overlapping geographic and product division structures. In effect, decision making is shared between the product managers and geographic managers. In theory, both substructures (product based and geography based) would have equal say; individual managers report to both a product executive and a geographic executive. The global matrix structure is illustrated in Exhibit 10.7.

global matrix structure A structural option that has overlapping geographic and product division structures and in which decision making is shared between product and geographic managers

EXHIBIT 10.6 *The Global Product Structure*

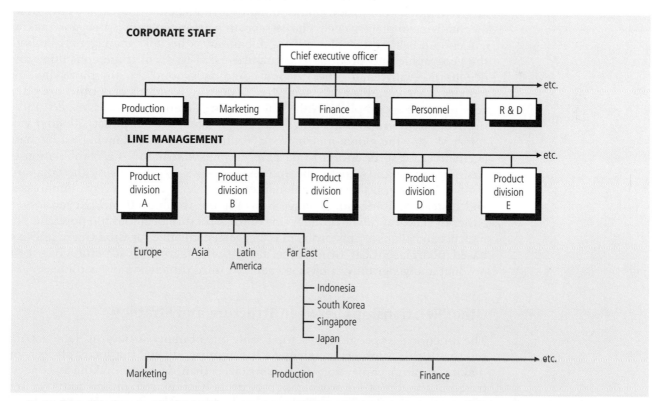

Source: "The Global Product Structure" from *International Dimensions of Management*, 4/e, p. 161, by Arvind V. Phatak, © 1995. Reprinted with permission of South-Western College Publishing, a division of Thomson Learning. Fax 800 730-2215.

EXHIBIT 10.7   *The Global Matrix Structure*

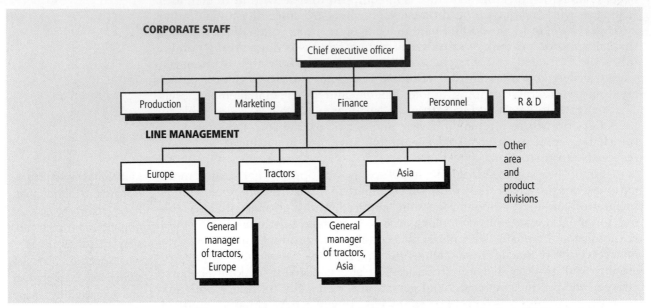

Source: "The Global Matrix Structure" from *International Dimensions of Management*, 4/e, p. 169, by Arvind V. Phatak, © 1995. Reprinted with permission of South-Western College Publishing, a division of Thomson Learning. Fax 800 730-2215.

While this structure has great potential, it is very difficult to implement in practice.[27] By definition, the global matrix blurs lines of authority and can create tremendous confusion and ambiguity if management does not have other mechanisms in place to help clarify reporting arrangements.[28] Decision making can end up being much slower in a global matrix because managers from both the geographic and product substructures need to spend time consulting and negotiating with each other to find common ground. Furthermore, holding managers accountable and staying free of destructive levels of conflict are often very tough to accomplish. With dual reporting arrangements, managers under fire from a geographic executive can always blame the product side and vice versa. Making the global matrix work requires a delicate balancing act by management. Ericsson's efforts to develop its matrix structure—a combination of customer units and geographic entities—were designed to bring the company close to customers. The financial markets, however, were relatively unimpressed and instead had additional suggestions for the troubled firm.[29] Regardless, if either the geographic or product side of the structure becomes too powerful, the matrix can collapse. This problem is a special challenge for Ciba-Geigy, a Swiss-based pharmaceutical firm, since along with its matrix structure based on product and geography, it has also added a third dimension of customer.

Other Relationships between Structure and Strategy

The functional or geographic setup is only one of many structural elements of a multinational. Another key element is *centralization*, or the locus of decision making in an organization. In a centralized firm decision making is concentrated at the top of an organization or at its headquarters/home country. To a degree, the specific way an organization is differentiated (e.g., by products, by geography, etc.) determines the degree of centralization, but there is more to decision making than this. There are differences in the ability of foreign operations or subsidiaries to make decisions.

In an earlier chapter, we referred to various strategies a firm could employ when it goes global, and this is relevant to centralization. For example, a firm could adopt a globalization strategy that emphasizes similarity of products and services in various markets, or it could adopt a multidomestic strategy that focuses on tailoring. Typically, the choice is closely aligned with the amount of control over decisions. In Exhibit 10.8 we show the relationship between various strategies and aspects of structure, including centralization. The exhibit shows that the degree to which decision making is centralized is often associated with the strategy a firm employs. For example, firms that use a multidomestic approach are likely to cede decision making to the national units in which they do business.

Our statements about decision making are general, and many exceptions could be noted. For example, Deutsche Bank did not necessarily use a structure that was based on its strategy. Instead, it used a centralized approach common to German companies in its ill-fated acquisition of Bankers Trust, a U.S. company. Indeed, Deutsche Bank's chairman pointed out, "We don't believe in autonomy. We will continue with our centralized management."[30] Certain businesses may also have a tendency to exercise more control than others, even though their strategy might suggest otherwise. In the pharmaceutical business, for example, where control is critical, and in other technologically complex areas, where quality is of the highest importance (e.g., GE's aircraft engine business), centralization is also used.[31] In contrast, there are also times when firms have adopted a less centralized approach than was necessary. A case in point is BMW's purchase of the British company Rover. At first, to avoid attributions of a heavy-handed German approach to control and to keep its brand as a selling point, BMW gave Rover a relatively free hand. After four straight years of losses and lagging productivity, BMW exercised more centralized control and then sold the operation about a year later.

As the BMW example suggests, the location of decision making within a company can change over time, sometimes dramatically. Likewise, the *formal* decision chain may differ from the *actual* decision mode; moreover, actual decision making is less one-sided that we have implied. In general, all this suggests that a multinational possesses considerable informal structural control, a point we now turn to in greater depth.

Formal and Informal Approaches to Coordination

There is more to strategy implementation than just pure organizational structure. Companies also need mechanisms to coordinate the various pieces of the firm in ways that support its international goals. For instance, corporate culture, management processes, and human resources have to be appropriately aligned with firm strategy for it to be implemented successfully, especially in the case of global strategies (see also Exhibit 10.8 for other such differences across strategies). McDonald's strong corporate culture and well-trained managers are examples of informal coordination mechanisms. These mechanisms support the firm's structure as it pursues its international strategy. More formal coordination mechanisms also exist. For example, some multinationals use teams of managers from different units (either on a permanent or temporary basis) to

EXHIBIT 10.8   *The Relationship between Structural Components and Strategy*

Aspect of Structure	Type of Strategy			
	Multidomestic	International	Globalization	Transnational
Centralization	National/local control	Core functions centralized; others under national control	Centralized at best global point	Combination centralized/ decentralized
Division of labor	Global area	International division	Global product	Global matrix
Need for integrating mechanisms	Low	Medium	High	Very high
Organizational culture	Not important	Important	Important	Very important

Source: Adapted from Hill, C. W., & Jones, E. R. (1995). *Strategic management.* Boston: Houghton Mifflin; Deresky, J. *International management.* Upper Saddle River, NJ: Prentice-Hall.

improve coordination and information exchange across the organization. Others assign individual managers to act as a liaison between a business area and a geographic area. Still other multinationals may initiate policies whereby managers who need information from another unit are encouraged to contact their counterparts directly.[32]

Today, however, many experts are endorsing an interesting type of informal coordination mechanism known as the **lateral communication network**. This network can be defined as the informal set of interpersonal relationships that exists between managers in different units of a multinational. When problems exist in one unit, managers can tap their informal networks for help. The attractiveness of such networks is that they can be a quick, flexible, and effective way to exchange information. These networks are valuable for two reasons: (1) information flow is needed to spread expertise and knowledge throughout a global organization, and (2) the global structures of large multinationals often impede this information flow. In fact, some experts argue that informal interunit networking is even more important than formal structures. This suggests that multinationals should view themselves more as a set of relational networks than as a rigid structure that distributes responsibilities. Research tends to support this idea. One study found that decision-making autonomy of a subsidiary (a structural variable) had little impact on the level of communications (1) between subsidiaries, or (2) between headquarters and subsidiaries. In both cases, however, the level of communications was positively affected by the extent to which managers engaged in informal networking with their peers.[33]

Unfortunately, the informality itself makes building networks difficult by definition. Some multinationals, however, are trying to encourage managers to develop such networks. The idea is to create a patchwork quilt of relationships that will effectively cover and interconnect the entire organization. One way to support the development of informal networks is to encourage managers to use the sophisticated communications technology available to nurture their global contacts (such as electronic mail systems and telephone and video conferencing). Companies that bring people together from around the world for

lateral communication network
The informal set of interpersonal relationships that exists between managers in different units of a multinational

face-to-face interactions and relationship building, including Nokia, SC Johnson, and Unilever among others, have successfully encouraged the formation of informal networks.

The Management of Technology by Multinationals

One advantage of these informal networks is the ability to make better decisions about entering or avoiding a particular country or about scaling back existing operations in risky locations. The issue of risk probably plays a larger role in the area of technology than any other. Today, risk can increasingly be tied to threats to a firm's technological advantage—or lack thereof. Many of the better firms recognize that to survive and succeed, they must continually change and update their technological applications. There have been a number of dramatic technological changes and advances in the twentieth century, particularly in the areas of communications and transportation. And, the rapid development of information technology has made many of these changes possible. On the other hand, some experts have also argued that instead of making strategy obsolete, the Internet actually has the opposite effect. Since it does not provide a proprietary operational advantage, this could make strategy all the more important.[34] Even wildly successful Internet ventures are not necessarily seen as ways to transform a firm, but instead as a way to reinforce their core business. Nonetheless, it is probably fair to say that the competitive advantage offered by factoring technology (such as the Internet) into strategic initiatives can contribute to business success.

Getting a Technological Advantage

If the preceding statement is true, then how do firms develop a technological edge? There are several ways to gain a leg up on the competition. One of the main ways is to develop an advantage entirely on your own. For example, a firm could assemble an in-house group of scientists and engineers to work on developing or altering a technology of importance to the firm. In many global industries, such as computers, biotechnology, communications, and oil/gas development, this is exactly what many firms do. But, this approach is expensive and not all R&D spending results in new, innovative, and marketable products. Nevertheless, the amount of R&D expenses and the percentage of scientists relative to the total number of employees are the main ways that the technology intensity of firms is indexed. Since World War II, the United States on average has devoted a larger percentage of its gross domestic product to R&D than any other country. U.S. firms are still among the forefront in such investments. In 1992, for example, R&D expenditures as a percentage of GDP were 3 percent in Japan, 2.7 percent in Germany, and 1.8 percent in the United States.[35] Exhibit 10.9 presents more recent data in regard to this point for a wide variety of countries.[36] As you can see, the Triad is responsible for most of this investment, with the United States, Japan, and European countries leading the way by a large margin. At the same time, if expenditures come to fruition, then we can anticipate that countries such as Sweden, Korea, and Switzerland, among others, will be producing viable products or ventures based on advanced technology in the near future. Innovation is also not necessarily a direct offshoot of development expenditures, particularly innovation that results in marketable products. One researcher has developed a national innovation score, which is roughly calculated by taking the total number of patents filed multiplied by an index that indicates the value of each country's patents. The United States (at 100) is rated well above its next closest rival Japan (31.3), with Germany (7.2) and other European and Asian countries relatively far behind. There are also national differences within a particular technology. For example, Hong Kong, Denmark, Sweden, and the United States rank at the top among 200 countries in their quality and extent of network infrastructure and network usage, whereas Germany and Japan rank number 17 and 20, respectively.[37]

As these numbers suggest, acquiring a technological edge via in-house research facilities can be very expensive. As a result, even some big firms have decided to cut back on their R&D. This "Lone Ranger" strategy, however, is not the only option. Firms from industries such as semiconductors and telecommunications often decide to cost-share their R&D. Take, for example, Bell

EXHIBIT 10.9 *Rankings of Various Countries on Total R&D Spending*

Rank	Country	Expenditure (US$ millions)	Rank	Country	Expenditure (US$ millions)
1	United States	243,548	25	Russia	1,956
2	Japan	141,694	26	Singapore	1,567
3	Germany	50,262	27	Argentina	1,466
4	France	31,684	28	Poland	1,157
5	United Kingdom	25,750	29	Ireland	1,109
6	Italy	12,219	30	Turkey	935
7	Canada	10,034	31	South Africa	779
8	Korea	10,028	32	New Zealand	734
9	Sweden	8,776	33	Czech Republic	683
10	China	8,201	34	Portugal	660
11	Switzerland	8,083	35	Greece	614
12	The Netherlands	7,630	36	Chile	425
13	Taiwan	5,903	37	Colombia	374
14	Brazil	5,876	38	Hong Kong	354
15	Australia	5,570	39	Venezuela	341
16	Spain	5,383	40	Hungary	329
17	Belgium	4,490	41	Slovenia	300
18	Finland	4,003	42	Malaysia	287
19	Austria	3,786	43	Indonesia	187
20	Denmark	3,461	44	Iceland	162
21	Israel	2,841	45	Thailand	147
22	Norway	2,590	46	Slovak Republic	134
23	India	2,303	47	Philippines	51
24	Mexico	1,997	48	Estonia	30

Source: (2001). Total expenditure on R&D, ranking as of April 24, 2001. **Http://www.imd.ch/wcy/criteria/4301.cfm**

Communications Research (now Telcordia and a division of SAIC)—the large R&D unit that was formed by the seven regional U.S. phone operating companies (Baby Bells) that were created from the AT&T divesture. The consortium was very successful; although there were some problems in information sharing, the cost saving to the consortium was great.

In addition to "building it yourself" and "cost sharing," there is at least one other option for acquiring a technological edge. In some cases, a firm might simply purchase the technology that it needs. Ford, for example, bought a smaller company called Excell Industries that provided it with a better way to make windows using a technology that would have been far more expensive for Ford to develop on its own.[38] This is a common strategy in the high-technology and communications industries. For example, several years ago Acer Computers, Inc., the Taiwanese company that was among the first to make unique-looking PCs (e.g., different colors, rounded shapes, etc.), bought several U.S. firms. Acer's goal was to use the technology developed by several Silicon Valley companies to rapidly accelerate their North American business. This approach turned out to be less effective than they hoped, and in mid-2001, Acer turned from being a manufacturer to a marketing and services provider, making e-business the company's new core focus.[39]

As you have probably already gathered, even though acquiring existing technology may be cheaper (in the long run) than developing it on your own, acquisitions are still expensive. In fact, Acer paid over $100 million for two American companies. In general, technology is just plain expensive, and this makes it extremely difficult for newly developing economies and firms to catch up. At the same time, however, the availability of low-cost but powerful PCs has been a boon for small countries and companies alike.[40] Many areas of the world are seeing growth in sales of PCs far higher than sales growth in the United States. Latin America, for example, saw a 24 percent growth spurt in 2002, up to 2 million machines. Sales in Chile alone have increased over 350 percent in the last several years. While South America has a lot of ground to make up, continued decreases in PC prices worldwide are likely to accelerate this trend.[41]

Using Your Technological Edge

Once a company develops or acquires the technology it needs, it must then decide how to best use it. One way to do this is to try to keep the technology within the firm for its exclusive use. Usually those firms with large R&D units try to keep their critical technology in-house as they apply it to new products and services. Some firms seem to be especially good at new product development. The 3M Company of St. Paul, Minnesota, is particularly well known for its application of technology to new product development.[42] One of the main reasons seems to be that the marketing function of the firm has a close tie to the R&D group. This was certainly the case for the development of the Post-It product for which 3M is famous. Nevertheless, even among the best companies, most new products fail to become successful. In fact, economists estimate that about 80 percent of all new products fail in the marketplace.[43] Once a new product is developed, firms can choose to sell or transfer the technology to others. This can be a good source of revenue for the firm, but also a source of worry, as we will show. Probably the most common transfer of critical technology is from the multinational to one or more of its foreign subsidiaries (usually wholly owned).

Obviously, one of the key advantages of this approach is that the multinational retains control over the important and proprietary technology. However, there are numerous other ways to transfer technology across borders. Since many of these were discussed in Chapter 9, we will only briefly mention them here.

One additional way that technology can be transferred is through franchising. Here a company sells another firm the right to use its products or services and the easily recognized company name. In return for all these benefits, the franchisee usually pays the company a fee based on the volume of business. There are many famous examples of U.S. businesses that transfer their technology in this way, including McDonald's, Holiday Inn, and Avis. Franchising offers less control over critical company technologies (in products or services) than if the multinational operated the business itself. But if the processes can be relatively easily copied anyway (e.g, the Burger King approach), then franchising may be the way to go. As we also know from Chapter 9, licensing and joint ventures are other ways that technological know-how can be shifted across borders. Each of these methods offers even less control by the multinational over important technology. Nevertheless, as we noted earlier, joint ventures are very common. One reason to risk proprietary technology by entering into an agreement with a foreign government is to get access to a market that is otherwise impenetrable. Joint ventures, for example, are a very common way to gain a foothold in China. Companies are stumbling over one another to enter China because of the size of this market, despite the fact that their technology is put at great risk.

Maintaining Your Edge

As we have said, the competitive advantage offered by technology is often a critical factor in the success of a multinational's products and services. Nevertheless, the process of transferring technology can put one's advantage at risk. As a result, many countries have developed laws that help their multinationals protect their technological edge. Although we dealt generally with these issues in Chapter 2, here we can say that there are two main methods by which a multinational can protect its technology from abuse.

patent
A tool that allows the original developer of an invention monopoly rights for a certain period of time (e.g., 17 years in the U.S)

One mechanism that multinationals can use to protect their technology is a **patent**. A patent offers the developer monopoly rights for a certain period of time (e.g, seventeen years in the United States) for a new or substantially enhanced product or process. The justification for such a monopoly is that the originating firm spent a great deal of its time and money on the advancement and, as a result, they should be rewarded for their work. Proponents also argue that new product development would all but dry up if there were no such protection or incentive in the form of patents. At the same time, patent protection is not inexpensive, especially as protection is sought in a number of foreign countries. Another type of protection is the **trademark**. Trademarks are the distinctive product designs, features, or logos that distinguish the product or service from others. Since people often buy a product because the trademark symbolizes an attractive, high-quality product (e.g., Hilfiger jeans, Reebok shoes, etc.), these designs also often receive protection from competition.

trademark
The unique product designs, features, or logos that distinguish the product or service from others

Although patents, trademarks, and other mechanisms do provide protection for the multinational, there are several issues here that make protection much less than complete. For one thing, there are some great differences among countries in how strictly they control the patent and trademark process. Exhibit 10.10, for example, compares these protections across a number of countries. As you will note, there is wide variance in the duration of a patent or trademark across countries as well as the amount of money a multinational can charge another company to use its technology (see "limits on royalties"). Perhaps the most important variable here, however, is whether the country is highly industrialized or in the process of developing. The latter type of country (e.g., Brazil, Egypt) is less likely to provide strong protection for technology than are industrialized countries (see left half of Exhibit 10.10).

Beyond cross-national differences in protection, another issue for multinationals is the ability to prevent misuse of legal mechanisms or the bypassing of them altogether (e.g, illegal pirating of products). Pirating was discussed in an earlier chapter. For now, however, we should point out that misuse of patent and trademark applications is also an issue. By this, we are referring to the

EXHIBIT 10.10 *The Protection of Technology across Borders*

Country	Limit on Royalties	Highest Tax on Royalty (%)	Patent Duration (Yrs.)	Trademark Duration
Canada	None	25	17	15 yrs. renewable
France	6% of sales, unless approved tech	33.3	20	10 yrs. renewable
Germany	10% of sales	25	20	10 yrs. renewable
Italy	None	21	20	20 yrs. renewable
Japan	None, but often 8% of sales	20	20	10 yrs. renewable
United Kingdom	None, but often 7% of sales	25	20	7 yrs. renewable
United States	None	46	17	20 yrs. renewable
Newly Industrialized/ Developing				
Argentina	None	45	5, 10, 15	10 yrs. renewable
Brazil	1–5% of sales to unrelated firms only	25	15	10 yrs. renewable
Egypt	None	40	15, renewable	10 yrs. renewable
Mexico	None, but often 6% of sales	40	14	5 yrs. renewable
Nigeria	1% of sales	15	20	7 yrs. renewable
Singapore	None	32	Only U.K. patents are valid	U.K. or Singapore registered 7 yrs.

Source: Adapted from Business International Corporation. (1990). Copyright © Investing, Licensing, and Trading Conditions. Reproduced by permission of *The Economist* Intelligence Unit.

⊕ International Insights

U.S. Firm Battled a Japanese Giant to Protect Its Technology

STEVEN CASE, founder and chairman of a firm called Cyberoptics, has made a lot of good moves in his business career. But his invitation to Yamaha Motor Co. to visit Cyberoptics was not his best! Although the meeting initially was seen as very positive, their five-year alliance together ended up in U.S. District Court. Cyberoptics was suing Yamaha for contract and patent violations, charging that Yamaha, the maker of motorcycles and other vehicles, used a flood of patent filings to poach the technology Cyberoptics had developed.

A few years ago, it was common for many U.S. companies to worry that Japan would dominate lots of critical technology. Cases like that of Cyperoptics, however, show why worries about large foreign firms may still be warranted. In fact, the sheer number of similar cases a few years ago led the U.S. Trade Representative to raise the practice of "patent-flooding" by Japanese firms, and the Cyberoptics

case in particular, as an issue between countries. This practice caused much conflict in the late 1980s between Tokyo and Washington, and the issue has persisted despite a 1995 treaty designed to stop the practice.

Apparently, patent flooding is common in Japan; in the United States, however, it is often viewed as a questionable and potentially illegal business practice. Flooding occurs when a firm files for many separate but isolated patents that closely resemble a rival's patent that is larger in scope. As a result, the original innovating firm finds it difficult or impossible to bring the patented item to market. If it does, it finds itself slapped with lawsuits by the "flooder" claiming a patent infringement. To avoid all the problems and the costs, many firms (particularly smaller ones) are cornered into exchanging mutual patent rights.

The Cyberoptics case is much like this typical situation. And because of its relatively small size, there

---

legal but improper use of mechanisms like patents. For example, large firms sometimes engage in patent "flooding." This involves applying for many different patents dealing with small variations on technology originally developed by one's competition. This practice handcuffs the innovating firm and ties them to the firm that flooded the patents. The accompanying International Insights provides a specific example of how patent flooding affected a small U.S. firm.

Chapter Summary

In this chapter we extended our discussion of international strategy by considering key ways that firms ensure that their international strategies work. First, we discussed the general challenges involved in managing *strategic alliances*. For example, we reviewed firm, industry, location, and venture-specific factors that can affect the choice of international entry modes. This led to a discussion of a key mechanism through which firms implement their strategy: *organizational structure*—the basic pattern or design of the firm's components.

We also considered the strengths and weaknesses of different types of structures. First, we

discussed the *simple structures* that companies often use when they are first gaining experience in the international arena. These included hiring an export manager or setting up an export department. As international business grows, firms may split into domestic and international operations—the essence of the *international division structure*.

Organizations that see themselves as international companies and that have a substantial portion of their business overseas often turn to *global organizational structures*. We considered three examples: The *global area structure* divides worldwide operations by geography and is a good

business.college.hmco.com/students

was a lot on the line. Mr. Case set up the company after leaving his teaching position at the University of Minnesota. His company makes products such as optical laser sensors and three-dimensional image analysis software that, among other things, help robots operate better. The firm started with three employees but now has over 200, as well as revenues of over $64 million. Prior to this, however, Cyberoptics' problems began when Mr. Case met with Yamaha engineers at an Anaheim, California, hotel. During the meeting, Cyberoptics demonstrated its new product. And Yamaha was impressed; they bought 500 of the systems over the next five years. What followed, however, did not impress an overly trusting and perhaps naive Cyberoptics

Mr. Case said in his court affidavit that during a visit to Yamaha after his demonstration he came up with a way to improve the effectiveness of Yamaha's robots. In fact, he jotted down an outline of his invention right there on a napkin. Yamaha engineers were impressed and told him so. In fact, the napkin is one of the many documents entered into evidence for this case. Mr. Case claims he signed and dated it for patent purposes. Other documents allegedly also support Cyberoptics' claim that Yamaha made only slight

changes to its inventions when they filed patents. Mr. Case says that without informing him, Yamaha filed twenty-six such patents in a number of countries that represent only slight variants of the Cyberoptics product. He claimed this was in violation of an agreement that neither company would file patents on their collaboration without mutual consent. Mr. Case says that he was not even aware of the Yamaha patents until another company pointed them out. The patents included were very similar to those he had sketched out on the napkin and in other places. For Yamaha's part, they denied the allegations. They claimed they informed Cyberoptics of the applications and that the napkin was nothing more than a duplication of existing Yamaha diagrams that their engineers showed Mr. Case. They did not remember seeing the napkin. Yamaha countersued Cyberoptics for defamation, saying that the charges were false and slanderous. The record does show, however, that Yamaha did apply for many related patents, and as early as 1996 Japan was added to the U.S. watchlist of countries with weak patent protection. While the facts were being sorted out in U.S. federal court, Cyberoptics continued to spend a lot of time and money to protect its technology.[44]

---

choice when products need to be responsive to local needs. The *global product structure*, in contrast, divides operations around product or business lines. This is a structure that works well for firms that have highly diversified products that can be sold anywhere in the world with little or no modification. Finally, the *global matrix structure* relies on overlapping product and geographic divisions and tries to balance the needs of global integration with local responsiveness. This structure, while it is very difficult to implement, is useful for firms that compete in global industries but still need to react effectively to local concerns. In addition, we included a discussion of the formal and informal coordination mechanisms—such as *lateral communication networks*—that support a multinational's structure and its international strategy.

Any time you add more complexity to a design or strategy, you open yourself up to potentially greater problems, and this is true in international operations as well. In particular, a firm that takes the international plunge subjects itself to more risk

than others and probably more than many imagine. One of the biggest potential risk factors, and an issue any manager would need to monitor, has to do with technology. Clearly, it is important to get a technological edge (e.g., via R&D) and to keep it once you have obtained it (e.g., by filing patents). We concluded the chapter with a discussion of these important issues.

Discussion Questions

1. What factors shape a foreign entry decision?

2. When might you use a specific organizational structure? How does structure relate to strategy?

3. What structures and processes could help a firm better coordinate among the various international strategies and structures?

4. Describe some of the management challenges involved in protecting one's technological innovations. How might an organizational structure help a firm maintain its technological edge?

Up to the Challenge?

Bon ton roulet: McDos est magnifique!

Even while McDonald's is in the process of closing hundreds of restaurants outside of the United States, business in France is booming—a new outlet opens there every week! And apparently it pays to do so since the average customer in France spends $9 per visit. In the United States this figure is close to $4, even though a Big Mac costs the same. What's McDonald's secret in France (McDos among the French)? Instead of the corporation's usual obsession with operational consistency and efficiency, they seem to be doing the opposite. Unlike in the United States where menus have been streamlined to compete with the rapid service of Wendy's and others, in France the opposite is happening. Many items have been added to the menu, including, for example, a hot ham and cheese sandwich (the "Croque McDo") And, they've spent lavishly to retrofit restaurant interiors and added big screens to show music videos to customers who like to linger over their meals.

Internationally, McDonald's has gone through some rough times. In fact, to head off this slide, the CEO was replaced in early 2003 by the former head of international operations—an area that now shows signs of coming around. France leads the way here, a surprising occurrence for international business observers. Denis Hennequin, the chief executive in France, is leading this change in performance. The challenge for Mr. Hennequin is a big one. After all, historically there is little love lost between the French and the Americans, and this has been heightened by tensions after 9/11. Consider Mr. Hennequin's reaction to the burning of a McDonald's in the south of France by an antiglobalization activist. He decried the act, but later responded with humorous ad copy that portrayed a fat, ignorant American who couldn't understand why McDonald's France used locally produced ingredients that were naturally grown. As Mr. Hennequin observed: "Some of our ads are over the edge, but you have to have a sense of humor."

More substantively, he has made great efforts to redesign the restaurant architecture. Some units in the French Alps include wood and stone interiors that make you think you're in a chalet. Restaurants in Paris look like a Montmartre café that Hemingway would have frequented, and others elsewhere are housed in nineteenth-century buildings with bicycle seats on the barstools. This approach to styling is common in France (in about half of McDonald's 950 French locations), but it is still found only in "funky" U.S. cities such as Ann Arbor, Eugene, and Yellow Springs. As CEO Hennequin has said, "We are upgrading the experience, making McDonald's a destination restaurant." And, it appears that all this is worth the cost. For example, the rise in some store sales in France in 2003 was almost twice that of the worldwide average. Don't make the mistake of thinking the McDonald's model is gone. They have not adapted their food to cater to French tastes—you won't smell any garlic in the air, just Big Macs. Indeed, Hennequin is himself a convert to the McDonald's way. "Please don't give me that nonsense that McDonald's is a threat to the French way of life. Tomorrow's society will be multicultural and it will take more than a burger to kill French culture." He has great respect for the basic value proposition of the corporation: "Who wants to go into a grotty old café where the toilets are dirty and the waiters are rude—that place should be out of business. People don't deserve to be treated as trash simply because they ask for a glass of water."

McDonald's U.S. is toying with this more customized orientation. For example, they are experimenting with a theater-themed restaurant in Times Square—inspired by the French success. While it remains to be seen how all this plays out for McDonald's, the good times roll on in France for McDos.

International Development

A Detailed Look at Managing International Operations

Purpose

To develop your skills in recognizing and identifying operational plans based on particular international strategic alliances.

Instructions

Your instructor will place you in groups of four to six for this exercise. Then, each group should select a company that it is interested in, one that does business internationally. Research the firm on the Internet and through your online library resources, such as ABI Inform or LEXIS/NEXIS. Next, identify the firm's main competitors or the two or three biggest players in that industry. Visit those websites and gather information about those firms as well.

Describe the international strategy used by your target firm and the main competitors in that industry. Do the following for each firm:

- Detail aspects of their international strategy. From your research, discuss the probable reasons for a firm's choice.

- Describe the organizational structure used by each firm to run its international business. Mention and discuss options for structuring international operations in their order of value.

- Evaluate the effectiveness of each firm's strategic approach compared to their competition.

- Provide a brief analysis of the risks faced by these firms using existing rating schemes available on the web (**e.g., http://www.polrisk.com/**).

- Are there any special technological issues or risks that may have determined (a) the particular strategy employed, and (b) the organizational structure used?

If the class is small enough, your instructor may have your group make a brief presentation (10 minutes) about your findings to the class. This could be followed by a discussion about managing international operations. Alternatively, your instructor may make this an individual assignment and ask students to take part in a general class discussion on the issues raised.

Tapping into the Global Network

Exporting Your Technology Products

For this exercise, we want you to imagine that you work for a firm that makes equipment, and software to drive it, that is useful in the chemical and biological industries. Most of your sales are to drug firms, academic institutions, and other research and development labs, and you wish to expand your business overseas. That means you will need to research issues related to the export of your products to other countries. Choose three countries from each continent that might be in a position to purchase your products/services. Your instructor may wish to put the class in groups to complete the project, in which case each person can be responsible for a continent. Once you target your countries, you should prepare a report that addresses the following items:

1. Do you need an export license from the U.S. Bureau of Industry and Security (formerly the Export Administration) for any of your products? (Check with **www.bxa.doc.gov**)

2. To answer question 1, you will need to read a quick tutorial on export controls (**http://www.bxa.doc.gov/licensing/exporting basics.htm**) prior to determining a commodity classification for your product. As it turns out, all commodities, technology, or software subject to the licensing authority of the BXA are included in the Commerce Control List (CCL). So, please go to **http://www.bxa.doc.gov/licensing/index.htm#factsheets**

and begin the classification process for at least two of your products.

3. According to U.S. law, the burden is on all exporters either to classify their products and services and then request a BXA review or to have the BXA do this for you prior to receiving their classification review. Look closely at the guidelines for preparing an export license after you classify your products (see website just above). Then complete the application form (forms are also available on the same website). So this part of the assignment asks you to simulate the required application process (but not to submit it to the BXA). Nevertheless, you can give an oral report of your findings to the class. The other groups will be familiar with these forms because they will also have completed them.

4. What are some examples of countries that are barred from possible exports from the United States? If none of the countries you have

chosen is barred, be sure to note at least one country that is. Conversely, if each of the countries you chose cannot receive your exported product, choose at least two countries that can. (One source for this is: **http://www.treas.gov/offices/eotffc/ofac/sanctions/index.html**, although it is not a complete source.)

5. Finally, show that you have performed due diligence in familiarizing yourself with warning signs and red flags of possible problems with your export transaction partner (**http://www.bxa.doc.gov/enforcement/unauthorizedpersons.htm**)

6. Another resource you might find useful in completing this project is the home page of the Trade Information Center of the U.S. Department of Commerce (**http://www.ita.doc.gov/td/tic/**) as well as the Export-Import Bank of the United States (**http://www.exim.gov/**).

CASE 5

Go Global—or No?

For two years, DataClear has had the data analysis market to itself. But now a British upstart is nipping at its heels. Should DataClear continue to focus on its strong domestic prospects or expand overseas to head off the nascent international threat?

"Why aren't they biting?" wondered Greg McNally as he laid down another perfectly executed cast. He was fly-fishing in the most beautiful spot he had ever seen, on the Alta River in Norway—reputedly the home of Scandinavia's worthiest salmon. And he had plenty of opportunity to admire the view. No fish were getting in the way.

What a difference from the luck he'd had a couple of weeks earlier trout fishing at Nelson's Spring Creek in Montana. It seemed like so much more time had passed since the two-day offsite he had called there, designed to be part celebration of the past, part planning for the future.

Some celebration had definitely been in order. The company, DataClear, was really taking off, fueled by the success of its first software product, ClearCloud. In 1999, its first full year of operation, DataClear's sales had reached $2.2 million. Now, the following September, it was looking like 2000 sales could easily reach $5.3 million. At the all-staff meeting on the Friday before the offsite, Greg had announced the company's success in recruiting two more great executives, bringing the staff to thirty-eight. "I'm more confident than ever that we'll hit our goals: $20 million in 2001 and then $60 million in 2002!"

Clouds on the Horizon

A New Jersey native, Greg held an MSc from Rutgers and then went West to get his Ph.D in computer science from UC Berkeley. He spent the next fifteen years at Borland and Oracle, first as a software developer and then as a senior product manager. He started DataClear in Palo Alto, California, in the spring of 1998.

At that time, Greg realized that companies were collecting information faster than they could analyze it and that data analysis was an underexploited segment of the software business. It was at a seminar at Northwestern University that he saw his opportunity. Two researchers had developed a set of algorithms that enabled analysts to sift through large amounts of raw data in powerful ways without programmers' help. Greg cashed in his Oracle options and, in partnership with the two researchers, created DataClear to develop applications based on the algorithms.

His partners took responsibility for product development and an initial stake of 20 percent each; Greg provided $500,000 in financing in return for 60 percent of the shares and the job of CEO. A year later, Greg offered David Lester, founder of DL Ventures and a former Oracle executive, 30 percent of the company in return for $5 million in additional funding.

In his previous positions, Greg had shown a knack for leading "fizzy" technical teams, and under his leadership, the two researchers came up with a state-of-the-art data analysis package they dubbed ClearCloud (from the clarity the software brought to large data clouds). Two versions, one for the telecommunications industry and the other for financial services providers, were officially launched in September 1998. ClearCloud had a number of immediate and profitable applications.

HBR's cases present common managerial dilemmas and offer concrete solutions from experts. As written, they are hypothetical, and the names used are fictitious.

"Go Global—Or No?" by Walter Kuemmerle. Reprinted by permission of *Harvard Business Review*, June 2001. Copyright © 2001 by the Harvard Business School Publishing Corporation. All rights reserved.

For instance, it could be used to help credit card companies detect fraud patterns more quickly in the millions of transactions that occurred every day. Greg conservatively estimated the annual demand from the U.S. telecommunications and financial services sectors to be around $600 million. The challenge was to make potential users aware of the product.

ClearCloud was an instant hit, and within just a month of its launch, Greg had needed to recruit a dozen sales staffers. One of the first was Susan Moskowski, a former sales rep at Banking Data Systems, who had worked successfully with Greg on several major joint pitches to financial institutions. She had spent two years at BDS's Singapore subsidiary, where she had laid the groundwork for a number of important contracts. She had left BDS to do an MBA at Stanford and joined DataClear immediately on graduating as the new company's head of sales. She was an immediate success, landing DataClear's first major contract, with a large West Coast banking group.

Greg realized that ClearCloud had huge potential outside the telecommunications and financial services industries. In fact, with relatively little product development, Greg and his partners believed, ClearCloud could be adapted for the chemical, petrochemical, and pharmaceutical industries. Annual demand from customers in those sectors could reach as high as $900 million.

But accessing and serving clients in those fields would involve building specialized sales and service infrastructures. Just two months ago, to spearhead that initiative, Greg recruited a new business-development manager who had twenty years experience in the chemical industry. A former senior R&D manager at DuPont, Tom Birmingham was excited by ClearCloud's blockbuster potential in the U.S. market. "The databases can only get bigger," he told Greg and Susan. Greg had asked Tom to put together a presentation for the offsite in Montana on the prospects for expanding into these new sectors.

Just two weeks before the outing, however, Susan burst into Greg's office and handed him an article from one of the leading trade journals. It highlighted a British start-up, VisiDat, which was beta testing a data analysis package that was only weeks away from launch. "We're not going to have the market to ourselves much longer," she told Greg. "We need to agree on a strategy for dealing with this kind of competition. If they start out as a global player, and we stay hunkered down in the U.S., they'll kill us. I've seen this before."

The news did not take Greg altogether by surprise. "I agree we've got to put together a strategy," he said. "Why don't we table the domestic-expansion discussion and talk about this at our offsite meeting, where we can get everyone's ideas? Unlike the rest of us, you've had some experience overseas, so perhaps you should lead the discussion. I'll square things with Tom."

Go Fish

In Montana, Susan kicked off the first session with the story of GulfSoft, a thinly disguised case study of her former employer. The company had developed a software package for the oil and gas exploration business, which it had introduced only in the United States. But at almost the same time, a French company had launched a comparable product, which it marketed aggressively on a global basis. A year later, the competitor had a much larger installed base worldwide than GulfSoft and was making inroads into GulfSoft's U.S. sales. When she reached the end of the story, Susan paused, adding ominously, "Today, we have twenty installations of ClearCloud outside the U.S.—fifteen in the U.K. and five in Japan—and those are only U.S. customers purchasing for their overseas subsidiaries."

At Susan's signal, the room went dark. Much of what followed, in a blizzard of overhead projections, was market research showing a lot of latent demand for ClearCloud outside the United States. The foreign markets in telecommunications and financial services were shown to be about as large as those in the U.S.—that is, another $600 million. The potential in pharmaceuticals, petrochemicals, and chemicals looked to be about $660 million. Taken altogether that meant a potential market of $1.5 billion domestically and $1.26 billion abroad.

In ending, Susan drew the obvious moral. "It seems pretty clear to me that the only defense for this kind of threat is to attack. We don't have any international sales strategy. We're here because we need one—and fast."

She glanced at Greg for any hint of objection, didn't see it, and plunged ahead. "We know we can sell a lot of software in the U.S., but if we want

DataClear to succeed in the long run, we need to preempt the competition and go worldwide. We need a large installed base ASAP.

"I propose that for the afternoon we split into two groups and focus on our two options for going forward. Group A can consider building our own organization to serve Europe. Group B can think about forming alliances with players already established there. Based on what you can come back with tomorrow, we'll make the call."

As the lights came back on, Greg blinked. He was dazzled. But he sensed that he needed to do some thinking, and he did his best thinking knee-deep in the river. After lunch, as the two groups got to work, Greg waded into Nelson's Spring Creek. The fish seemed to leap to his hook, but his thoughts were more elusive and ambivalent.

Money, Money, Money

Greg decided he needed a reality check, and that night he called David Lester to review the day's discussion. Not too surprisingly, Lester didn't have a lot of advice to give on the spot. In fact he had questions of his own. "Instead of focusing on foreign markets in our core industries, what if we focus on developing ClearCloud for the domestic pharmaceutical, chemical, and petrochemical industries and capitalize in the $900-million U.S. market?" he asked. "How much would that cost?" Greg offered a best guess of $2 million for the additional software-development costs but hadn't yet come up with a number for marketing and sales; the industries were so different from the ones DataClear currently focused on. "Whatever the cost turns out to be, we're going to need another round of financing," Greg allowed. "Right now we're on track to generate a positive cash flow without raising any additional capital, but it won't be enough to fund a move beyond our core industries."

"That's not where I was headed," Lester replied. "What if we went out and raised a lot more money and expanded the product offering and our geographic reach at the same time?"

Greg swallowed hard; he was usually game for a challenge, but a double expansion was daunting. He couldn't help thinking of the sticky note he'd posted on the frame of his computer screen a few days after he started DataClear. It clung there still, and it had just one word on it: "Focus."

Lester sensed Greg's hesitation: "Look. We're not going to decide this tonight. And really, at the end of the day it's up to you, Greg. You've done the right things so far. Keep doing them." Hanging up, Greg was reminded how pleased he was with Lester's hands-off approach. For the first time, he wondered what things would be like if he had a more hands-on venture capitalist as an investor—maybe one with some experience in international expansion.

Greg was also reminded of his own lack of international management experience. Eight years earlier, he had politely turned down an opportunity to lead a team of fifty Oracle development engineers in Japan, primarily because he had been unwilling to relocate to Tokyo for two years. His boss at the time had told him: "Greg, software is a global business, and what you don't learn early about cross-border management will come back to haunt you later."

Options on the Table

At ten o'clock the next morning, Group A took the floor and made their recommendation right off the bat: DataClear should immediately establish an office in the U.K. and staff it with four to six salespeople. Britain would be a beachhead into all of Europe, but eventually there would also be a sales office somewhere on the Continent, maybe in Brussels. They had even drafted a job description for a head of European sales.

Greg was impressed, if a little overwhelmed. "Any idea how much this would cost us in terms of salaries and expenses over the first year?" he asked.

"Conservatively, about $500,000 a year, probably more," the group leader replied. "But cost is not so much the point here. If we don't make this move, we'll get killed by VisiDat—or some other competitor we don't even know about yet. Imagine if SAP introduced a similar product. With their marketing machine, they would just crush us."

Tom Birmingham started to object. "Where are we going to find local staff to install and support the product?" he wanted to know. "I mean, this is not just about setting up an office to sell: ClearCloud is a complex product, and it needs a service infrastructure. We'd have to translate the interface software, or at least the manuals, into local languages. We'd need additional resources in business development and product support to manage all this. Selling ClearCloud in Europe is going to cost a lot more than $500,000 a year . . ."

Susan was quick to jump in. "Good point, Tom, and that isn't all we'll need. We also have to have somebody in Asia. Either Singapore or Tokyo would be an ideal base. Probably Tokyo works better because more potential clients are headquartered there than in the rest of Asia. We need at least four people in Asia, for the time being." Tom frowned, but, feeling that Susan had the momentum, decided to hold his fire.

After lunch, it was Group B's turn. They suggested using autonomous software distributors in each country. That would help DataClear keep a tight grip on expenses. Greg spoke up then. "What about teaming up with some local firm in Europe that offers a complementary product? Couldn't we get what we need through a joint venture?"

"Funny you should mention that, Greg," said the presenter from Group B. "We came up with the idea of Benro but didn't have time to pursue it. They might be willing to talk about reciprocal distribution." Benro was a small software shop in Norway. Greg knew it had about $5 million in sales last year from its data-mining package for financial services companies. Benro was very familiar with European customers in the financial services sector but had no experience with other industries. "Working with Benro might be cheaper than doing this all on our own, at least for now," the presenter said.

Susan chose that moment to speak up again. "I have to admit I'm skeptical about joint ventures. I think it will probably take too long to negotiate and sign the contracts, which won't even cover all the eventualities. At some point we will have to learn how to succeed in each region on our own."

That's when Greg noticed Tom studying Susan, his eyes narrowing. So he wasn't surprised—in fact he was a little relieved—when Tom put the brakes on: "I guess I don't see how we can make that decision until we gather a little more input, Susan," Tom said. "At the very least, we need to have a conversation with Benro and any other potential partners. And I know I'd want to meet some candidates to lead a foreign sales office before I'd be comfortable going that route. But my real concern is more

fundamental. Are we up to doing all this at the same time we're building our market presence in the U.S.? Remember, we don't yet have the capability to serve the chemical and pharmaceutical industries here. There are still only thirty-eight of us, and I estimate that building the support infrastructure we need just for domestic expansion could cost as much as $2 million—on top of product development."

Before Susan could object, Greg struck the compromise. "Tell you what. Let's commit to making this decision in no more than three weeks. I'll clear my calendar and connect with Benro myself. At the same time, Susan, you can flush out some good candidates for a foreign sales office and schedule them to meet with Tom and me."

Casting About

And that's how Greg McNally found himself up a creek in Norway that Sunday morning. Benro's CEO had been interested; Greg was confident that the meeting with him on Monday would yield some attractive options. And once the trip was booked, it didn't take Greg long to realize that he'd be near some fabled fishing spots.

He also realized it would be a great chance to pick the brain of his old Berkeley classmate, Sarah Pappas. A hardware engineer, Sarah had started her own company, Desix, in Mountain View, California, in 1993. The company designed specialty chips for the mobile communications industry. Within seven years, Desix had grown into one of the most successful specialized design shops around the world, with about 400 employees. Like Greg, Sarah had received funding from a venture capitalist. Since a lot of demand for Desix's services was in Scandinavia and to a lesser degree in Japan as well, Sarah had opened subsidiaries in both places and even decided to split her time between Mountain View and Oslo.

Greg arrived in Oslo on Thursday morning and met Sarah that evening at a waterfront restaurant. They spent the first half-hour swapping news about mutual friends. Sarah hadn't changed much, thought Greg. But when the conversation turned to potential geographic expansion and he asked about her experience, Greg saw her smile grow a little tense. "Ah, well," she began. "How much time do you have?"

"That bad?"

"Actually, to be honest, some things were easier than we thought," she allowed. "Recruiting, for example. We never expected to get any great engineers to leave Nokia or Hitachi to join us, but we ended up hiring our Oslo and Tokyo core teams without much trouble. Still, some things turned out to be hard—like coordinating the three sites across the borders. There were so many misunderstandings between Oslo and Mountain View that at first our productivity went down by 40 percent."

The story got worse. Sarah explained how, in 1998, her venture capitalist sought to exit its investment. Since an IPO seemed inadvisable for various reasons, the parties agreed to sell the company to Pelmer, a large equipment manufacturer. Sarah agreed to stay on for three years but couldn't do much to keep the engineers in her Oslo and Tokyo subsidiaries from leaving. No one had fully anticipated the clash between Pelmer's strong U.S. culture and Desix's local cultures in Oslo and Tokyo. By this point, Sarah felt, the merger had destroyed much that had gone into making Desix a small multinational company.

"I can tell I've been a real buzz killer," she laughed apologetically, as Greg picked up the check. "But if I were you, given what I've been through, I'd stay focused on the U.S. for as long as possible. You might not build the next Oracle or Siebel that way, but you'll live a happier life."

"So you think you made the wrong choice in expanding internationally?"

"Well, no," said Sarah, "because I don't think we had a choice. You, on the other hand, can sell much more product in the U.S. than we could have."

Up to His Waist

The next day brought its own worries, as Greg met with Pierre Lambert, a candidate for head of European sales, whom Susan had identified through a headhunter. Lambert had graduated from the Ecole des Mines in Paris and then worked for four years at Alcatel and five years at Lucent. As they talked, it occurred to Greg that he had no experience in reading résumés from outside the States. Was Ecole des Mines a good school? He

noted that Lambert had worked only in France and the U.S. How successful would he be in the U.K. or Germany? As he wrapped up the interview, Greg figured he would need to see at least five candidates to form an opinion about the European labor market. And Asia would be even harder.

That evening, he compared notes with Tom, who had interviewed Lambert by phone the previous day. Tom expressed some doubts: he suspected Lambert wasn't mature enough to deal with the level of executives—CIOs and chief scientists—that DataClear would be targeting. That call only just ended when the cell phone rang again with Susan on the line. "Greg—I thought you would want to know. VisiDat just made its first significant sale—to Shell. The deal is worth at least $500,000. This is huge for them."

And now, two days later, here he stood in the glorious, frustrating Alta. He could see the salmon hanging out under the surface. He cast his line again, an elegant, silvery arc across the river and maneuvered the fly deftly through the water. Nothing.

Greg slogged back to shore and peered into the box housing his extensive collection of hand-tied salmon flies. Was it just that he was so preoccupied? Or were the conditions really so different here that none of his flies would work? One thing was for sure: it was a lot chillier than he'd expected. Despite the liner socks, his feet were getting cold.

Assignment Questions

1. What dilemma or strategic threat is DataClear facing?

2. Would you recommend that DataClear expand into international markets at this point in time? Either way, fully explain the basis for your recommendation.

3. If your answer to question 2 was yes, lay out specific recommendations for exactly how DataClear should proceed to "go global" in the near term. If the answer to question 2 was no, what specific steps should DataClear take to position itself for possible future expansion overseas?

CASE 6

Trouble in Paradise

From Mike Graves's tall windows, which were draped in red velvet, the view of Shanghai was spectacular: the stately old Western-style buildings, the riot of modern skyscrapers, the familiar needle of the TV tower. But today Mike barely noticed it. Clenching a copy of his Chinese partner's proposal for another acquisition—it would be the company's fourth—he paced the floor and replayed in his mind that morning's unsettling phone call.

He had called his boss, Bill Windler, at headquarters in Ohio, hoping to get a nice quote to inject into the brief remarks he was to make at that day's banquet celebrating the joint venture's tenth anniversary. But as he gave Windler a quick rundown of what he intended to say—mostly about the joint venture's progress toward "world-class quality"—Mike could sense his boss's growing frustration. About five minutes into the call, Windler cut Mike off in midsentence, saying, "Don't throw your shoulder out patting yourself on the back."

Windler reminded Mike about the margins he was looking for across all of Heartland Spindle's businesses. "A 4 percent ROI is pathetic," Windler said. "We've been in there ten years, Mike. The numbers should look better by now." He said he was looking for a 20 percent ROI, adding that such a number could surely be achieved through greater efficiency and more automation. And in Windler's view, the company had at least 1,200 employees too many. "That needs to be fixed, fast," he said.

Mike knew his boss wouldn't take no for an answer, but he had also learned that his Chinese partners would never agree to drastic moves such as the layoffs suggested by Windler. It was beginning to look as though the five good years he had spent here as general manager might be destined to come to a painful end. Mike couldn't help but wonder if those harsh words from Ohio were a warning that his contract might not be renewed in six months.

Then, to top things off, just as Mike had extricated himself from the phone conversation, this latest acquisition proposal had arrived from deputy general manager Qinlin Li. The top executive on the Chinese side of the joint venture, Qinlin had been with the JV since its inception. As before, there would be almost irresistible pressure to go along with the deal. The Chinese side would make it clear yet again that the delicate partnership depended on Mike's support for continuous expansion and protection of jobs. The timing couldn't have been worse: the last thing Windler would want was more growth initiatives eating into the profits.

A knock on the heavy teak door snapped him out of his musings. Feng Chen, Mike's assistant and translator, informed him that his car was waiting.

Enhance Friendly Cooperation

As the car pulled up outside the Shangri-La Hotel, Mike forced himself to smile at the red carpet lined with dozens of lavish flower baskets sent by local government officials, business partners, suppliers, customers, and even competitors. A marching band in full uniform stood at the hotel entrance, and above it stretched a bright red banner that said, in Chinese and English: "Enhance Friendly Cooperation and Ensure Mutual Growth" and "Celebrate the Tenth Anniversary of Zhong-Lian Knitting Co. Ltd."

HBR's cases, which are fictional, present common managerial dilemmas and offer concrete solutions from experts.

"Trouble in Paradise," Katherine Xin et al., *Harvard Business Review*, Aug. 2003, Vol. 81, Issue 8. Copyright © 2003 by the Harvard Business School Publishing Corporation. Reprinted by permission of Harvard Business School Publishing. All rights reserved.

Mike exchanged greetings with Qinlin, who had been there for an hour already and was still seeing to last-minute details. In the ballroom, an elegant young woman in a red silk qi-pao, a traditional dress for formal celebrations, escorted Mike to the round table that was front and center. Two Chinese senior executives, Qinlin's immediate subordinates, stood up and nodded their greetings.

There was a burst of excited applause, and cameras flashed. Qinlin was accompanying three important government officials into the room. They approached Mike's table and politely bickered for several minutes over who should enjoy the most prominent seat at the table, as required by Chinese custom. At last, the eldest and most highly placed official accepted the seat of honor. Qinlin stepped up to the podium, above which hung a huge Chinese knot of red silk, the symbol of cooperation. There was an expectant hush as he tapped the microphone.

"Ladies and gentlemen," Qinlin began, "thank you for joining me to celebrate the tenth anniversary of Zhong-Lian Knitting Company Limited. Those who were with the company at the beginning remember the hardships we endured and the hard work we put in. Since the establishment of Zhong-Lian as a 50/50 joint venture between Suzhou First Textile Company and our U.S. partner, Heartland Spindle Company, Zhong-Lian has faced many difficulties and obstacles. But we succeeded." Mike was listening to the translator's words, but he could hear the passion in Qinlin's voice. "We turned a money-losing company into a money-making company, and we made great headway as a result of support from our government, efforts on the part of both parent companies, and all our managers and employees."

Mike hadn't been there during the early days, but he knew the stories. He was the fourth GM sent by Heartland in ten years. His two most recent predecessors had left before their three-year assignments were complete, one for family reasons—his wife couldn't adapt to China—and the other for a better job offer (allegedly). Mike, a veteran manager with twenty years of international experience, had lived and worked in Japan, Hong Kong, and Australia before Heartland sent him to Shanghai.

Mike's toughest challenge at the outset was the language barrier. He wouldn't have survived without Feng Chen's help. It didn't take long for Mike to learn what cha-bu-duo meant: "almost okay!" He hated that word! It was baffling to him: even though his Chinese partners were intelligent and willing to work hard, they weren't exactly obsessed with quality. They cut corners and hardly ever followed operating procedures to the letter. Buttons often fell off sweaters before the garments were even shipped out of the factory. Cha-bu-duo is why Mike insisted on introducing Total Quality Management to Zhong-Lian—and TQM was probably why the JV had been so successful. Mike had also felt a small sense of satisfaction when he taught his Chinese colleagues a new term: Six Sigma.

Cha-bu-duo wasn't the only expression Mike heard all too often. He also quickly got used to yan-jiu-yan-jiu, which means "Let's review and discuss!" When he proposed a new system to deal with sewage disposal three months after he started (he was astonished that his Chinese partner hadn't updated it already), his counterparts said, "Okay, yan-jiu-yan-jiu." Two months later, after Mike's repeated prodding, the proposal made it onto a meeting agenda. But at the meeting, the Chinese managers seemed reluctant to discuss the matter, and no one wanted to assume responsibility for solving the problem. When Mike asked managers for feedback individually, they all had ideas, many of them excellent. He couldn't imagine why the managers hadn't spoken up at the meeting.

It didn't make sense to him until months later, when Mike heard someone say, "Keeping silent in a group is safer. You won't get in trouble if you don't do anything. But you will get in trouble if you make a mistake. We are experienced under this system, and we know how it works." At any rate, Mike was relieved when the equipment was set up—even though it took two years and outside pressure from the provincial Environment Protection Bureau to make it happen.

There was another burst of applause. Qinlin's voice reverberated through the room. "We have acquired three money-losing state-owned enterprises and managed to earn an annual profit of between 5 percent and 6 percent," he said. "The number of employees increased from 400 to 2,300 in the past decade. Given the slump of the textile industry in these years, Zhong-Lian's achievement is remarkable. In the coming years, we will further enhance the company and maintain our growth momentum."

Qinlin paused, and his eyes sparkled. "Let me tell you another piece of good news" he said. "We are preparing our fourth acquisition, which is expected to raise our production capacity by 40 percent. The number of our employees will grow to nearly 3,500. And all this will help us launch our next initiative: building our own national brand."

What little appetite Mike had for the celebration vanished. He had long been trying to quash that kind of talk. Heartland, he knew, would never support launching an apparel brand that would eat up resources and limit profits for years. Qinlin knows this well, Mike thought, so why is he raising expectations in such a public way?

Qinlin thanked the vice mayor and the other government officials without whose "wise supervision," in his effusive words, the joint venture would not have made such great progress. The vice mayor rose to speak and returned the compliments, praising Zhong-Lian's contribution to the local economy —especially to maintaining employment levels— and calling the joint venture a flagship among the city's enterprises.

When it was Mike's turn, he too voiced the expected praise for the officials—it was a ritual whose airy forms and steely seriousness had become almost second nature to him. But throughout his little speech, he felt he was hardly doing more than going through the motions. He was preoccupied by Qinlin's plans and what they would mean for profitability.

Later, the lazy Susan at each table was filled with eight cold dishes, eight hot dishes, and two showpiece dishes: a whole suckling pig and a whole braised mandarin fish in the shape of a squirrel. Qinlin, as the host of his table, proposed a toast. Then he emptied his glass as a sign of his sincerity and joy. Glasses clinked; champagne and Coke bubbled. But Mike had become so attuned to the subtleties of these gatherings that he immediately noticed the response of the officials: instead of emptying their glasses, they merely took sips. Mike supposed that they must have heard about his opposition, muted though it had been, to the expansion ideas.

Living in Style

Sitting in the backseat of the company car, Mike felt his tension ease when his driver, Lao Li, turned into his neighborhood. The car slipped by a row of cypresses and passed a perfectly manicured golf course. Designed in European country style, the elegant Green Villa was an ideal residence for expatriates. Mike loved this village—its extensive recreational amenities, its first-class service. At very little cost, for example, Mike's family had hired a live-in domestic helper who happened to be a superior cook. His wife, Linda, played golf three times a week with her friends in the village, and she had recently taken up yoga. The company paid $7,800 a month to rent the family's home; it also paid for a chauffeur, a nanny, and the children's education at Concordia International School (the best in Shanghai). Life here was easy and comfortable—a world away from what it would have been like back in Ohio.

But Mike's tension returned when he thought about his meeting the next morning with the people at Hua-Ying, the potential acquisition. He wouldn't be living in Green Villa much longer if he signed off on that deal.

Over dinner, Mike told Linda about the conversation with Windler.

"Don't they understand that the Chinese way of doing business is different from the American way?" Linda asked him sympathetically. "It's not all about squeezing the most out of your workers here. They value stability and long-term employment. You'd think Heartland would've been prepared for this sort of performance. It's not like you're losing money, like so many JVs here do. Just last week on the course, Christie and Maya told me that their husbands' businesses hadn't turned a profit yet."

"I know, but that doesn't seem to be good enough any more," Mike said. He recounted Bill's suggestions about layoffs and investing in more automated equipment. He knew that he would soon have to broach these subjects with his Chinese partners.

Mike's biggest problem was that he could see both sides. Heartland wanted to reposition itself in the U.S. market—selling at discount stores wasn't profitable enough. But to enable Heartland to make the jump to high-end retailers, the joint venture would have to meet much higher standards of quality. Those old dyeing machines, for instance, would have to go; they had cost the company a lot of money over the last few years, not just in shipping and handling charges for returned products but also in terms of the company's reputation. New machines would fix that problem, but they'd create another one: many jobs would disappear.

The Chinese partners were much more concerned with creating jobs and keeping government officials happy than with improving quality. They wanted to keep growing into new provinces and buying up unprofitable companies, even if turning them around took years. But expansion would require significant additional resources that Heartland Spindle clearly wasn't ready to commit. And now there would be pressure to create a new company to market a national brand, again a drain on cash.

"So what do you think you're going to do?" Linda asked.

"I'm meeting with executives from Hua-Ying tomorrow morning. Maybe they'll surprise me with an operation that won't take forever to turn around—that'd be the best case," Mike said. "After that, I'll have to talk to Qinlin and the others about Heartland's concerns. But I know how that conversation will play out. They'll say Heartland is being shortsighted and that the JV's history of turning around money-losing businesses should prove that we just need to be more patient.

"I wish Bill and the rest back in the States had a better understanding of how things work here. I was skeptical myself at the beginning. Remember when we first got here and I was fuming at the business expenses? Seemed like every executive on the payroll was wining and dining some key partner or contact. And Robert O'Reilly, our controller, came to me shouting that our Chinese partner spent money like water. But, gradually, we both figured out that those expenses were paying off for us. The Chinese ritual of sharing food—nurturing guanxi—is so powerful in making deals that it became one of our hidden assets. I'm afraid we won't get those kinds of results if we focus only on cutting costs and laying off workers, as Ohio wants us to do."

PowerPoint and Green Tea

The chief executive of Hua-Ying, Genfa Wang, sent his own limousine to pick up Mike and Qinlin as a symbol of his sincerity and hospitality. Genfa and his top managers were waiting at the gate when the car pulled up, and one of the men stepped forward to open the car door. Genfa greeted Mike, Qinlin, and Feng Chen with, "My honor! My honor! It is a great pleasure to have you here with us."

The first building they entered looked fairly clean, but the conference room carpet was pocked with cigarette burns. Not exactly a high-class operation, Mike thought. Up on the third floor, there was a disagreeable odor—no flush. He could just imagine the state of the plumbing. And hadn't leaky pipes been responsible for the initial spread of SARS into cities like Hong Kong? He was sure he had read something like that. His unease grew. What other hidden risks were lurking in this facility? There was no way he was going to be able to agree to this acquisition, he thought.

But he was pleasantly surprised to see seven cups of Bi Luo Chun tea, one of the best Chinese green teas, on an elegant redwood table. And a minute later, Genfa pulled out a laptop and began making his presentation using PowerPoint slides. Mike was shocked. He hadn't expected such sophistication from a company this size, especially a company that seemed to lack modern sanitary facilities. Genfa, sensing Mike's reaction, said proudly, "My nephew gave me training on this high-tech stuff. He is a college graduate, a vice GM of our company in charge of technology and engineering."

Great, Mike thought with exasperation. There were probably a few relatives on the board, too. But his mood swung back during Genfa's forty-minute presentation as the CEO spoke precisely and clearly about the numbers—it was obvious he was shrewd about the market. Mike was intrigued.

At the second building, his earlier impressions were reinforced: the machines in here looked old and shabby. Some workers were busy, but others were idly waiting for a product delivery. Bales of goods were stacked high in one corner, and Mike stumbled over a box as he picked his way through the dim light. When he noticed that the record sheets on the desk and walls were handwritten, his heart sank: So much for high tech.

On his way home that night in his own company's car, Mike gazed out the window, trying to figure out what to do next. Should he recommend the acquisition to Bill? Should he propose rejecting the deal and thus probably bring an end to the partnership? The idea of buying out the JV had occurred to him, but it clearly wouldn't work, not with the Chinese partner dreaming of a national brand. When the Audi came to a stop outside Mike's house, he hadn't reached any conclusions. He knew he was going to have another sleepless night at Green Villa.

Assignment Questions

1. How do Heartland Spindle's goals and objectives dovetail (or not) with its Chinese partners?

2. Are Heartland Spindle's goals realistic or not in your opinion? If not, what implications does this have for its Chinese partnership?

3. Describe some of the options that Mike might consider here for dealing with the Chinese partners and the joint venture. Which would you recommend and why?

4. Assess Mike as a manager here . . . has he been effective or not? Explain.

PART IV

Managing People in the International Arena

11

Motivating and Leading across Cultures

INTERNATIONAL CHALLENGE

Winning over the Bear: How Should Western Firms Motivate Russian Employees?

Learning Objectives

After reading this chapter, you should be able to:

▶ Understand that motivation principles may need to be adapted to be applicable across cultures.

▶ Understand how effective cross-cultural motivation strategies can be developed.

▶ Understand how a leader's behavior, power sources, and influence tactics can be modified to be more effective across international environments.

▶ Grasp the challenges facing international managers in multinationals and understand how effective international leaders can be developed.

RUSSIA CONTINUES THE PROCESS of transforming itself into a market-based economy. Indeed, the Russian economy has been booming in recent years. And you don't have to look hard to find the trappings of Western consumerism. In many Russian cities, new shopping malls, supermarkets, and movie theaters present an image that would not be out of place in America.

Of course, appearances can be deceiving. Underneath Russia's emerging façade is a long history of paternalism and autocracy that's proven hard to shake. As one American ambassador put it, "Russia seems more similar to our culture than it really is." There's little doubt that most Western firms operating in Russia would agree with this assessment. Many of these firms have faced a variety of challenges in trying to apply Western management and motivation practices with Russian employees. If anything, those challenges have increased in recent years as more foreign companies set up shop in Russia. Generally speaking, foreign firms, including such American household names such as Coca-Cola and Pizza Hut, prefer local employees to expensive expatriates.

So which Western motivation tactics can best serve foreign companies in Russia? This question was put to the test by researchers who pitted three Western motivation programs against each other in a Russian cotton mill.

- **Program 1 was based on the reinforcement concept of providing contingent rewards**. It involved giving Russian employees extrinsic rewards (e.g., valued American consumer goods, bonuses) in exchange for improvements in performance.

- **Program 2 was also based on reinforcement ideas but focused instead on behavior management tactics**. These tactics were used to shape employee behavior using verbal feedback. For instance, Russian supervisors were trained to praise workers when they improved their performance and to offer corrective suggestions when negative behaviors were displayed.

- **Program 3 used a job enrichment approach that relied on employee participation.** Here the researchers asked employees for suggestions about how their jobs and work might be changed and improved, without Russian supervisors being present. For instance, employees were asked to provide their ideas for improving work procedures, increasing worker autonomy, and developing additional skills. Employees also were empowered to implement their suggestions, with the idea that doing so would improve their motivation and subsequent performance.

So here's your challenge. Which of these programs would work best to improve the motivation and performance of Russian employees? Why? If you can, do some research on how Russian history and culture might affect employee motivation. For answers about the research team's findings, take a look at the *Up to the Challenge?* box at the end of the chapter.[1]

▶ *Motivating and Leading Abroad: Are All Bets Off?*

Most American managers think that business success requires motivated employees. That said, *how* to motivate employees remains a frustrating and difficult process for many managers. And adding cross-cultural issues to the mix makes the question of employee motivation all the more complex. For example, what motivates employees and how they respond to feedback may vary dramatically depending on cultural factors, all the talk about "globalization" and "value convergence" notwithstanding.[2] In fact, cultural values (such as the value placed on hard work and thrift) may affect employee motivation in ways that can help explain different economic growth rates across nations.[3] Overall, cultural values may influence what kind of "psychological contract" employees have with their employers. For example, is work simply viewed as an economic "money for effort" transaction, an inherent good in itself, or does it provide an important social role (e.g., an opportunity to be part of something important, something larger than yourself)? How employees view their relationship with employers may have important implications for motivation.[4]

Consequently, in the first part of this chapter we explain how culture can limit the applicability of American approaches to motivation. To be effective, managers need to know which motivation strategies are applicable across cultures and which require culture-specific approaches or adaptations.[5] Motivation appears to have relatively few cross-cultural "universals." For instance, managers in most cultures would prefer to rely less on formal authority to motivate their employees.[6] Likewise, employees everywhere want to be trusted by their superiors and fairly compensated. But *how* managers can best go about delegating authority, building trust, and defining "fair pay" may vary considerably from place to place.[7] Indeed, cultural values often have a big impact on leadership styles, a motivation-related topic we'll tackle later in this chapter. Overall, universally applicable approaches to motivation are rare because there are relatively few shared values across all cultures.[8] International managers must therefore work to understand how cultures and values can shape employee motivation in particular countries. On top of that, international managers also face the possibility that important regional differences in values exist *within* a country, which impact both motivation and business performance. For instance, research shows that regional subcultures in Brazil have distinct motivational tendencies, which, in turn, have implications for company performance.[9]

▶ *Motivation Concepts and Their Applicability to Other Cultures*

In this section we'll examine the cross-cultural applicability and limitations of several motivation theories.[10] Maslow's hierarchy of needs and Herzberg's two-factor theory both focus on the basic needs that energize employees. In contrast, equity theory, reinforcement theory, and expectancy theory all examine the process by which employees are motivated to pursue various needs.

Maslow's Hierarchy of Needs

Maslow said that people have five needs that are triggered in a hierarchical fashion.[11] The most basic are *physiological needs* (e.g., food and shelter). If these are met (e.g., through adequate wages), then employees are motivated to satisfy *safety needs*. Benefits such as life insurance help provide safety. Next up are *social needs*. These are satisfied when employees feel they "belong." *Esteem needs* are met when employees have self-respect and confidence. Finally, **self-actualization** needs are motivating after all other needs have been met and reflect employees' desire to reach their maximum potential. Overall, research shows that needs aren't always triggered in the exact order specified by Maslow's hierarchy.[12]

self-actualization
The highest-order need that reflects desire to reach your maximum potential

Cross-cultural Applicability Nevertheless, we might expect employees' motivation to pursue higher-order needs (e.g., self-actualization) to be strongest in highly industrialized countries, with lower-order survival needs more prominent in less developed countries. In other words, many workers in poor countries may not have the luxury of pursuing self-actualization if their survival or safety is in question.[13]

That said, research suggests a more complex pattern. For instance, cooperative co-workers and other social needs may rank above self-actualization for some Chinese employees.[14] Other studies find that employees in individualistic societies (e.g., the United States) are more likely to be interested in pursuing personal accomplishment than employees in more collective societies (e.g., Japan).[15] Likewise, Germans raised in the formerly communist eastern part of the country may still focus more on existence needs and be less concerned with personal achievement than Germans raised in the western half of the country. For over forty years, subservience to the state was taught in schools and organizations in East Germany. This had a huge impact on work-related values. Despite being discredited and abandoned for well over a decade now, the effects of these teachings will take some time to completely disappear.[16]

In any event, these research findings are inconsistent with the idea that needs operate in a fixed hierarchy across borders.[17] Indeed, some experts feel that Maslow's hierarchy is a philosophy that reflects *American* values. Its emphasis on higher-order growth needs is especially popular in the United

EXHIBIT 11.1   *Sources of Work Motivation in Zambia*

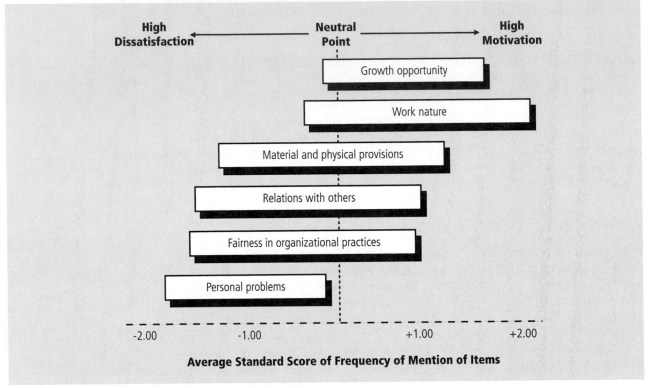

Source: Figure from "Work Motivation in a Developing Country" P.D. Machungwa & N. Schmitt, *Journal of Applied Psychology*, Vol. 68, p. 41, 1983. Copyright © 1983 by the American Psychological Association. Reprinted with permission.

States because American culture strongly values individualism and risk taking. Underscoring this is the fact that "achievement" is extremely difficult to translate into other languages.[18]

Herzberg's Two-Factor Approach

Herzberg claimed that without adequate *hygiene factors* such as good working conditions and pay, employees will be unhappy and unmotivated. But to produce highly motivated and satisfied employees, Herzberg said that *motivators* such as challenge, responsibility, autonomy, and accomplishment are also necessary. Providing motivators is referred to as **job enrichment**.[19]

job enrichment
Injecting motivators such as autonomy and challenge into the job setting

Cross-cultural Applicability One study found that workers in Zambia generally matched Herzberg's two-factor approach, with growth needs and other intrinsic factors associated with high motivation and poor relationships and bad working conditions associated with dissatisfaction.[20] These results are summarized in Exhibit 11.1.

That said, in another study, British managers were more interested in responsibility and autonomy than their French counterparts. The French, on the other hand, were more interested in security, fringe benefits, and good working conditions than their British colleagues. Generally speaking, these results imply that job enrichment efforts will be easier to implement in Britain than in France.[21] In fact, when employees value individualism, risk taking (weak uncertainty avoidance), and performance (masculinity), Herzberg's motivators may be viewed as a way to enhance individual achievement. Many, if not most, employees in the United States and Britain fit this description. On the other hand, in Sweden many employees embrace individualism but are also very relationship-oriented (femininity). In these circumstances, Herzberg's motivators may be seen as helping to improve interpersonal harmony.[22] For example, years ago Sweden's Volvo pioneered the idea of putting workers into small, semiautonomous teams to build cars. This job enrichment tactic was designed to increase cooperation among employees.[23]

But how might job enrichment efforts fare in developing countries such as Indonesia and Pakistan? It could prove a tough sell. These countries tend to be collectivist, strong in uncertainty avoidance and high in power distance, and low in masculinity. In strong uncertainty avoidance cultures, some workers may be reluctant to make decisions because of the ambiguity inherent in doing so. Employees in collectivist cultures may also react negatively to efforts aimed at enriching jobs on an individual basis. High power distance discourages autonomous decision making. In feminine cultures, job enrichment efforts that focus on the job itself, without concern for personal relationships, may fail since employees' obligations to family or community are often paramount.[24] Nevertheless, there is clearly a worldwide trend toward increasingly complex or "enriched" jobs and the responsibility and control that go with them. But the ability of people to cope with such jobs may depend, at least in part, on the culture context in which they work.[25]

Taking that into account, many experts believe that the obstacles to implementing job enrichment efforts, particularly those aimed at empowering employees to make decisions and operate more autonomously, can be overcome with some effort and attention. Specifically, managers in multinational firms should take care to learn about the local cultural environment in depth before attempting any job enrichment effort. Once they understand how local values may impact job enrichment, managers can take steps to blunt the obstacles represented by local values while leveraging others to improve employee motivation.[26]

For instance, French electronics giant Thomson was able to improve the motivation and performance of the workforce at a components plant in Morocco by convincing employees to take on more responsibilities and embrace autonomous decision making. Along the way, openness and trust were increased dramatically. On the surface, this sounds like a typical "Western" job enrichment effort. But *how* these motivation changes were accomplished was not. Indeed, it was done in a culture-specific way. The company was operating in a high power distance context, one where senior executives were expected to wield authority in a supreme and often arbitrary manner. Consequently, top management decided to lead by example, using a culturally appropriate leverage point to do so. In essence, management described their efforts to improve motivation as part of a new moral code, one that management as well as employees would live by. Moreover, this new code was linked to the values of Islam, a major cultural force in Moroccan life. For example, management encouraged employees to embrace greater responsibility as a way of living Islamic values at work (e.g., being open and honest, respecting the contributions of others).[27]

Before leaving our discussion of Herzberg's ideas, we want to note that hygiene factors alone can sometimes prove highly motivating to employees. For instance, job security and pay (hygiene factors) often behave as motivators in

EXHIBIT 11.2   *Where Are the (Un)happiest Employees?*

Country	Employees Claiming They Are Very Satisfied with Their Current Job (%)
The Top Five	
Denmark	61
India (middle and upper classes only)	55
Norway	54
United States	50
Ireland	49
The Bottom Five	
Estonia	11
China	11
Czech Republic	10
Ukraine	10
Hungary	9

Source: "Nothing is Rotten in Denmark" M. Boyle, *Fortune*, Feb. 19, 2001, p. 242. Copyright ©2001 Time, Inc. All rights reserved.

developing countries.[28] But the same may be true in many industrialized nations. For example, Jorma Ollila, CEO of Finland's Nokia lobbied national leaders to reduce income taxes. Apparently, Mr. Ollila was concerned that high taxes made it harder for Nokia to recruit key professionals.

Along the same lines, Exhibit 11.2 lists the countries with the highest and lowest percentage of employees who say that they're very satisfied with their jobs. Employees in Denmark may rank so highly because of outstanding relations between labor and management (including good pay, another hygiene factor). Ironically, this theme of getting along is reflected in toymaker Lego, one of Denmark's best-known companies. The firm's name is derived from two Danish words that mean "play well." On the other hand, few employees in Hungary appear to be very satisfied with their jobs. Once again, hygiene factors—in this case lousy wages and poor labor relations—may explain why Hungarian employees are a lot less happy than their Danish counterparts.[29] For another look at how a hygiene factor, money, is a big motivator for some Russian women, read the following International Insights.

Equity Theory: You Should Get What You Deserve

equity theory
Theory predicting that when employees feel they've been unfairly treated, they are motivated to restore fairness in a number of ways

Equity theory contends that when employees perceive that they've been treated unfairly, they are motivated to restore a sense of fairness.[30] This happens when employees compare themselves against other people in terms of *job outcomes* (e.g., pay, benefits) and *job inputs* (e.g., effort, skills). When the comparison of outcomes to inputs is in balance, employees should feel satisfied. If it isn't, employees often try to restore the balance somehow.[31]

Applying Equity Concepts in Other Cultures That said, how different cultures define, interpret, and assess fairness can vary considerably, often in ways that are poorly understood.[32] Nevertheless, at the risk of generalizing, existing

International Insights

Money Drives Russian Women Working for Mary Kay

DALLAS-BASED Mary Kay Cosmetics has been successful in Russia for years. Thanks to burgeoning demand for cosmetics, Russia ranks near the top of Mary Kay's more than two dozen foreign operations. But a big key to Mary Kay's success is its sales force of Russian women.

Most of these women are clearly motivated by money. Mary Kay provides sales training and sells its products to its Russian sales representatives at a 60 percent discount to retail prices. Typically, the Russian sales representatives then sell their Mary Kay products at full price, preferably to small groups of customers. On average, the women in Mary Kay's sales force make several hundred dollars a month. But Mary Kay's best Russian performers rake in thousands monthly. And some even have their own offices and secretaries. Compare this to the low average monthly wage in Russia and you can see why turnover among Mary Kay's Russian sales force is so small.

Mary Kay is attractive to Russian women because it offers financial independence, something that is still relatively rare in Russia. Women sometimes feel that Russia's developing market economy has left them behind. Two-thirds of Russia's unemployed are women, and some Russian organizations still reserve certain jobs for men. When they are employed, women in Russia are often trapped in low-paying positions and are the first to be laid off. Ironically, these same attitudes toward gender in Russia help make being a Mary Kay sales representative a socially acceptable job for Russian women—one that can pay well.[33]

research suggests some important principles and implications that managers ought to consider. For instance, cultures that value individualism tend to embrace equity concepts. In such cultures, individual performance is important (inputs) and should be rewarded accordingly based on deservingness (outcomes). On the other hand, in collectivist cultures rewards are more likely to be distributed equally, regardless of performance, to preserve group harmony and cohesiveness.[34] In fact, as the following International Insights suggests, rewarding superior performance may sometimes create problems in China.

However, the link between culture and equity-based rewards is complex. In one study, for example, Americans and Chinese evaluated hypothetical members of a work group. Although both Americans and Chinese tended to distribute rewards based on equity, the Chinese used a weaker equity standard to avoid creating conflict in the group. These results seem to confirm that employees in collectivistic cultures are less likely to apply equity concepts when distributing rewards than employees in individualistic cultures.[35] Other experts, however, suggest that employees in collectivistic cultures may use equity norms most when rewarding efforts to promote group cohesiveness.[36]

Another study illustrates how social changes may affect reward distribution preferences. In recent years, many Americans have become more concerned with cooperation and less concerned with wealth. The opposite trend is happening in China as it moves away from traditional egalitarian practices. In the study, Chinese and American managers had to distribute rewards among hypothetical employees. Two types of rewards were examined—material rewards (e.g., pay raises) and socio-emotional rewards (e.g., more supportive managers). Overall, Chinese managers preferred to use equity-based rules (e.g., performance) to distribute both types of rewards. Americans, however, based

International Insights

Jacket Gesture Backfires in Shanghai

AMERICANS SOMETIMES forget that their approaches to motivation reflect American values. In one joint-venture plant in Shanghai, American managers gave leather jackets to a small group of Chinese employees. The idea was to recognize and encourage employee initiative. And this group had come up with the best suggestions for improving operations after being encouraged to do so.

But instead of serving as an example to the rest of the plant, one designed to promote employee initiative, the jacket gesture prompted a backlash. Once they found out about the jackets, many Chinese employees in the rest of the plant wanted to know why they didn't get one. Management's explanation, that the jackets were a reward, went nowhere. Chinese employees continued their complaints, asking for equal treatment. At one point, the firm started getting calls from local officials about the issue. After deciding things were getting a bit out of hand, the Americans caved in and gave every Chinese employee a jacket (over 700 employees!).

Historically, Chinese employees expect to be taken care of by their bosses and offer loyalty and obedience in return. Tying rewards to performance was rarely part of that equation. Chinese companies also typically gave workers benefits such as housing and food in addition to job security. Until recently, foreign companies that fired employees for lousy performance would be grilled by local officials concerned about the "social problems" caused by displaced workers. While China is changing and the use of performance-based rewards is rising, vestiges of the old "iron rice bowl" approach remain. And that's something to consider when it comes to motivating Chinese workers.[37]

material rewards on performance but distributed socio-emotional rewards equally. This result supports the idea that America is becoming less individualistic while China is moving in the opposite direction. Other studies suggest even more complex processes at work, with the pace of change in reward distribution preferences varying considerably across transition economies as a consequence of local circumstances. For instance, there is evidence to suggest that managers in China are actually moving more slowly in adopting "Western" equity rules to distribute material rewards than their counterparts in Russia.[38]

So what do these complex findings on an equity approach to motivation mean for international managers? Our advice is that managers should: (1) think through how their own cultural values might affect their willingness to use equity rules in doling out rewards; and (2) take the time needed to understand how their subordinates' cultural values might affect their motivation when equity rules are used. What's more, the world isn't a static place. As countries evolve, traditional values and practices may change in ways that affect how rewards should be allocated. Again, China may be a case in point. In recent years, coastal firms in China could keep workers from the interior reasonably satisfied with little or no pay raises. Why? Because outside coastal cities, job prospects were slim. As one production worker who had earned the same pay (about $60 per month) for three years put it, "What would I do back home?" But growing labor unrest in China is causing some to predict that this kind of reaction may not last forever. Indeed, many low-paid employees in China already feel pangs of inequity, particularly if they compare themselves to others who seem better off.[39]

The Reinforcement Approach: Connecting Behavior and Consequences

The **reinforcement approach** views motivation in terms of consequences. Clearly linking valued consequences to desired behaviors should motivate employees to produce those behaviors.[40] For example, managers can improve employee performance by applying *positive reinforcers* (e.g., big bonuses). Conversely, poor performance can be eliminated by carefully applying *punishment* (e.g., a pay cut).[41]

reinforcement approach The theory that rewards and punishments are central to guiding work behavior

Cultural Factors and Reinforcement But managers need to know what employees value to use positive reinforcement effectively. However, this isn't as simple as it seems. For example, in South Africa many black employees are more motivated when their firm makes a real effort to help remove the social inequalities left over from apartheid (e.g., the inferior housing still plaguing much of the black majority). This connection between work and life outside of work also reflects African cultural values that emphasize the importance of community and family. Such values are seldom seen in Western management approaches.[42]

Culture may also affect how employees interpret performance-related feedback. For instance, American employees tend to prefer positive feedback, while Japanese employees tend to embrace more critical feedback. The reasons may have to do with culture. Americans often like to revel in their triumphs, especially individual ones. Failure tends to be threatening to individual self-worth. In Japan, however, critical evaluations may help people maintain a humble posture toward the wider group as well as offer suggestions for improving overall group performance.[43]

Along the same lines, American and Mexican workers may react differently when a supervisor gives positive performance feedback.[44] Americans may see praise as suggesting that even better performance is possible, while Mexicans may see it as an acknowledgment that their current performance is good. Mexican workers are also less likely to exceed the informal performance norms of their work groups regardless of the feedback they receive from a supervisor. Compared with Americans, Mexicans tend to be more collectivist and, as such, are likely to pay close attention to group norms.[45]

Cultural values can also present other hurdles for reinforcement strategies. For instance, performance-based pay may not motivate workers in strong uncertainty avoidance cultures because a portion of pay is put at risk. Similarly, in highly collective cultures, individual merit pay may be less effective than pay based on group performance. Using large bonuses or hefty pay increases alone may also prove difficult in feminine cultures since loyalty to the boss, company, or co-workers is prized above performance. India is an example of a country where cultural values may sometimes limit reinforcement strategies. In fact, pay systems in some Indian companies violate reinforcement principles. For example, compensation may reflect employee seniority as opposed to being contingent on behavior. Performance appraisal can be rudimentary and not timed to coincide with key tasks, making "merit pay" seem arbitrary. And this perception may reinforce many Indians' socialization experiences with family, religion, and other institutions. These experiences may lead some Indians to embrace a resigned fatalism and indifference to good performance (a state referred to as *chalega*). Instead, effort may be directed to activities aimed at strengthening relationships with supervisors who offer valued rewards.[46]

Overall, research on the effective use of reinforcement strategies suggests that managers need to consider how culture affects what employees find motivating as well as how employees react to them in the work context. These factors will help determine what motivators will work best in a culture and what strategies will be most effective for using them. Once again, this assumes that managers are willing and able to scale what is often a formidable learning curve to best understand what works in a particular culture. As we've said, this doesn't necessarily mean that international managers have to "give up" Western approaches to motivation. However, to be accepted by employees, they may have to modify those approaches to fit local sensibilities.[47]

The Expectancy Approach

expectancy approach
An approach to motivation that emphasizes the conscious decisions employees make to maximize their outcomes

The **expectancy approach** to motivation subsumes many of the concepts we've discussed so far. In a nutshell, the expectancy approach assumes that three factors determine employee effort in a given situation.[48] First, employees must believe that working hard will result in good performance. If, for example, employees feel it's impossible to hit production goals, they won't exert much effort. Second, employees must believe that rewards are associated with good performance. If this isn't the case, then motivation will suffer. Finally, motivation and effort will also suffer if the rewards available to employees are unimportant to them.

Cultural Assumptions As you've probably guessed, the expectancy approach makes some now-familiar cultural assumptions. It emphasizes individualism and has a masculine orientation since the focus is on tasks rather than on relationships. The expectancy approach also assumes that individual workers can control their lives to a great extent by manipulating effort. These assumptions fit American culture quite well. But many Chinese believe that fate helps determine events. Similarly, many Mexicans feel that being from the appropriate family is a real key to success. Likewise, many Saudi Arabians believe that what happens at work is a reflection of God's will. In each case, external forces are important.[49]

By saying that rewards have to be valued to produce motivation, the expectancy approach implicitly suggests that reward systems must be designed with cultural values in mind. One study of American, French, and Dutch managers helps make this point. The Americans felt that bonuses should be tightly connected to performance. This fits the expectancy assumption that people are achievement-oriented and can tolerate the ambiguity that comes with fluctuating bonuses. In contrast, French and Dutch managers were less interested in money and were skeptical about linking pay and performance. The bonuses earned by French and Dutch managers were smaller and varied less than did the Americans'. These differences are predictable. Compared with their American counterparts, the Dutch tend to have a more feminine orientation and are less individualistic. As a consequence, Dutch managers are less likely to use pay as a way to "keep score" of individual achievement. Similarly, managers in strong uncertainty avoidance cultures, such as France, may shy away from highly variable performance bonuses for executives.[50]

These cultural differences may help explain why the "outrage threshold" for executive compensation packages is generally much lower in Europe than in the United States. For instance, the nearly $7-million pay package for the CEO of European grocery chain Ahold NV provoked outcry about "excessive compensation." Such a sum is unlikely to provoke as big a fuss in the United States. Even so, pay packages for U.S. executives will produce outrage if they seen "exorbitant" by American standards and are not perceived to be strongly linked to performance (such as the outrage produced in 2003 by the revelation that the chairman of the New York Stock Exchange had retirement clauses in his pay package worth over $187 million).[51]

Of course, values and sensibilities often change and evolve. Indeed, some of the outrage that we've seen in Europe about "huge" executive pay packages reflects a shift toward American-style compensation. For instance, rank and seniority once were all that mattered in German banks. Performance bonuses were unknown. But when German banks started losing talent to American and British rivals in recent years, they began fighting back with a common American tactic—bonuses in exchange for performance. Now banks such as Deutsche Bank and Bayerische Vereinsbank have bonus plans in place that can increase total compensation by 50 percent or more. Yet German banks aren't just copying American-style bonus plans. Many German banks remain uneasy about using big bonuses to publicize individual achievements.

So German banks tend to offer smaller bonuses than American banks for comparable positions. In a good year, for instance, currency traders in a U.S. bank might earn bonuses equal to 700 percent of their salaries. But Germans may feel that such huge bonuses prompt unnecessary risks and foster destructive competition among employees. As a consequence, some German banks try to encourage cooperation and teamwork by making part of the bonus contingent on an employee's ability to work well with colleagues. Nevertheless, Deutsche Bank and other German financial services firms seem to be moving toward the more aggressive pay-for-performance approaches found in U.S. banks.[52] For a closer look at how performance-reward linkages may be evolving in Japan, read the International Insights on the next page.

As interesting as this Japanese restaurant example is, major shifts in attitudes about motivation won't happen overnight. For instance, in recent years Japanese have been seeking out foreign companies for employment in ever-increasing numbers. In most cases, this attraction is based on the belief that foreign firms are more likely to pay for individual performance, encourage creativity, and promote based on personal achievement than Japanese firms. That said, the percentage of Japanese in the workforce who are employed by foreign companies is small (2.3 percent) and trails the percentage in other industrialized nations by a considerable margin (e.g., over 5 percent in both the United States and Germany). So while change is occurring, we need to consider both the starting point and the rate of change.[53] In general, the perceived link between effort and performance remains stronger for Americans than for Japanese. The longer history of performance-contingent reward systems in the United States may help explain this. Finally, Americans still tend to see pay increases, promotions, and personal recognition as more desirable than do their Japanese counterparts. Cultural values that emphasize individual performance and achievement in the United States and group cohesion in Japan may account for this difference in perception. Consequently, how fast and to what extent Japanese society will become more individualistic remains to be seen. But the government apparently wants to move in that direction. A few years ago, Japan launched a new education policy designed to encourage children to adopt a more independent and individually oriented mindset. Only time will tell whether this controversial policy has any significant impact in Japan.[54]

🌐 International Insights

Japanese Restaurant Chain to Employees: Perform or You're Chopped Liver

AMERICA'S "CUTTHROAT CAPITALISM" is a tough sell for many Japanese. Contentious disputes about pay and performance are virtually unknown in Japan, at least in traditional companies. But Japanese firms like Global Dining may provide a peek into the future. This restaurant chain embraced three innovations that are shocking for many Japanese—plenty of conflict, do-or-die competition between employees, and brutally honest individual performance feedback.

How brutal? One cook sat in front of a group of bosses and peers to demand a big pay increase. They immediately shouted out criticisms, including that his cooking was uneven and sales on his shift weak. A quick vote was taken, with the humiliated cook being rebuffed on his raise request. In fact, all employees, from senior leaders to dishwashers, are evaluated against performance criteria in such face-to-face meetings. Employees who miss their performance targets get no bonuses. Managers who foul up are quickly demoted or fired. On the flip side, excellent performers are rewarded incredibly well. One young restaurant manager made over $150,000, considerably more than a typical mid-career executive working for a large Japanese firm. Global Dining's CEO summed up the system's philosophy this way: "Just as sharks need to keep swimming to stay alive, we only want people who are constantly craving challenges."

The willingness to embrace such a demanding approach is part of a broader debate in Japan about traditionally cushy relationships between employees and big firms that often had little to do with performance (e.g., lifetime employment, seniority-based raises, etc.). Of course, Japan's prolonged economic challenges have been driving that debate. And Global Dining isn't alone. Companies such as Sony, clothing chain Fast Retailing, and machine parts firm Misumi Corporation are among the big Japanese companies that have brought in younger managers willing to live with the ups and downs of tough pay-for-performance schemes. Thanks to bonuses, one young Misumi manager pulled in almost $530,000, a sum that eclipsed the pay of the company president.

But some workers at Global Dining worry about the pressure of life under such a ruthless performance management system. Even waiters watch each other closely since everyone votes on pay raises and bonuses for everyone else (one performance marker—how long it takes waiters to notice that a customer needs another drink). That said, Global Dining employees may have the last word since the system actually encourages criticism of superiors, right up to the CEO. In fact, at one point, employees complained to the CEO that the bonus formula made it too easy to get nothing at all. Eventually, employees demanded a vote on the issue; the CEO lost, and the formula was modified. One manager who left Global Dining to start his own restaurant said that while performance management was a good thing, his system would be less ruthless. As he put it, "There's a saying, 'too much is as bad as too little.'"[55]

Conclusions about Motivation across Cultures

Overall, we suggest that international managers explicitly take cultural variables into account when designing and implementing motivation strategies abroad.[56] Granted, this is a tall order, one that is complicated by the fact that cultural values are a moving target. Plus, international managers may not recognize how their own values and biases affect the motivation strategies they use.[57] We embrace the idea that whatever motivational strategy is adopted, it should be *culturally synergistic*. In other words, motivation efforts should complement rather than conflict with the various cultures involved. Developing such a motivation strategy involves four basic steps:

1. **Describe the motivation situation**. How does the manager view the motivation issues? What perspectives do subordinates have? The purpose of this first step is to discover whether different motivational perspectives exist and whether they create conflict.

2. **Identify cultural assumptions about motivation**. The next step is to uncover the cultural values that help explain why different perspectives on motivation exist. The goal is to be able to reverse perspectives and see things from another culture's point of view.

3. **Generate culturally synergistic alternatives**. Once cultural assumptions have been identified, the next challenge is to develop motivation strategies that blend elements of the cultures involved or even go beyond them.

4. **Select and implement a synergistic strategy**. The final step involves picking what appears to be the best motivation strategy and implementing it. A key here is to have all parties observe the strategy from their own cultural perspective. The chosen strategy may need to be fine-tuned based on any feedback received.

Accomplishing these steps may require a series of extended conversations with foreign employees as well as their involvement in the development of specific motivation strategies. Moreover, to develop and successfully implement such strategies, managers and employees must both possess cultural self-awareness (i.e., awareness of your own values and biases) and cross-cultural awareness (i.e., awareness of others' values and perspectives). Having both types of awareness increases the odds that the chosen strategy can be implemented in a way that reflects the specific cultural dynamics involved. But to reach that point, underlying values and cultural frames of reference must be identified first. Doing so should create an appreciation for alternative perspectives, something that can then be used in generating motivational approaches that accomplish management goals in ways that are sensitive to local cultural values.[58]

▶ *What Constitutes Effective Leadership in an International Context?*

We've said that cultural values may affect employee behavior in ways that have implications for how companies should design work, manage performance, and provide rewards. We'll tackle these issues from management's perspective in this section.

Effective leadership in international companies requires incredible openness and an ability to appreciate a wide variety of cultural differences. But it also requires an ability to bridge differences quickly, to develop, as we described in the previous section, culturally synergistic solutions to international management challenges.[59]

However, defining "leadership" in the first place becomes more complex when borders are crossed. Back in Chapter 4, we discussed how different cultures define leadership and the characteristics that effective leaders possess. Nevertheless, important questions remain. For instance, do managers behave differently across cultures in leadership roles? Do certain situations require similar leadership behaviors, regardless of culture? Can corporate culture override or weaken other cross-cultural effects with respect to leadership? This section will offer some answers to these questions.

International Insights

The Evolving Russian Leadership Style

AMERICANS OFTEN feel that managers need motivation, drive, and self-confidence to be effective. So how do Russian business leaders compare? Exhibit 11.3 provides some answers for Russian managers across three time periods.

Leadership Motivation

For hundreds of years, village elders were the absolute authority in rural Russia. This autocratic leadership carried over into the Soviet system, with managers avoiding blame and refusing to take action without approval. But in a more open economy, Russian managers must shift from being authoritarian to being authoritative, providing vision, and encouraging initiative. Although autocratic attitudes persist, many Russian managers now take responsibility and make strategic decisions on their own.

Leadership Drive

Russian villages focused on the community and treated individual achievement with contempt. They valued tenacity, hard work, and caution. These values helped Russians survive in a climate with short growing seasons and brutally cold winters. Under communism, Soviet managers focused on following rules, making connections, and demonstrating loyalty instead of developing new products or services. Today, most formal restrictions on individual ambition are gone and many Russians have started their own businesses. However, some Russians still see entrepreneurs and managers as immoral people who exploit others for personal gain.

The Honesty and Integrity of the Leader

A dichotomy exists in the area of corruption and integrity. Russians may feel it is acceptable to deceive strangers in business deals. But deceiving trusted friends is unethical. Russians may also use personal connections to obtain favors. For centuries, Russian villagers offered food to landowners in exchange for protection. These traditional values were reflected in the way Soviet managers operated. Stealing state property and deceiving superiors was acceptable because it helped Soviet managers protect their resources. Using personal connections to cut red

When in Rome: Leader Behavior across Cultures

Leader behavior can vary dramatically across cultures, and effective international managers are aware of this. But leadership concepts, values, and styles continue to evolve around the world. This evolutionary process is most noticeable in nations that have undergone social and economic upheaval, such as Poland, the eastern half of Germany, and other parts of the old Soviet bloc.[60] For a closer look at how social changes have affected leadership in Russia, read the accompanying International Insights.

In any case, research in the United States reveals two basic types of leader behavior. **Task-oriented behavior** includes clarifying performance expectations and specific procedures to be followed. Other examples include planning, scheduling, providing technical help, and goal setting. **Relationship-oriented behavior** includes showing concern for subordinates' feelings, needs, and well-being. Other examples include expressing empathy, warmth, encouragement, consideration, and trust to subordinates. But which type of leader behavior produces the best performance? In which countries? There's no simple answer. Depending on the circumstances, leaders may need to use different combinations of task-oriented and relationship-oriented behaviors to be effective.[61]

task-oriented behavior
Leader behavior that is focused on clarifying work procedures and performance expectations for employees

relationship-oriented behavior
Leader behavior that expresses concern for subordinates' feelings, needs, and well-being

tape was common under communism and persists to this day. Indeed, corruption increased with the collapse of the Soviet system. Today, some Russian entrepreneurs pay protection money to criminals just to stay in business.

The Leader's Self-Confidence

Russians have been described as both self-confident and fatalistic. Soviet leaders were sensitive to criticism about their product quality yet took great pride in running huge manufacturing plants. Today, some Russian leaders vacillate between believing that they can't accomplish anything without foreign help to making grandiose promises to foreign partners.

Guidelines for Leading in Russia

Based on this evolutionary snapshot, here are some leadership guidelines for firms that want to do business in Russia:

- **Don't assume that Russian leadership is the same as leadership in the West**. Encourage blended leadership approaches that take into account Russian history, character, and the changes that have taken and are continuing to take place.

- **Avoid hubris and present a nonexploitative image**. Avoid actions that appear to exploit Russians to make money or that make managers appear too powerful. Instead, attempt to cultivate a caring and attentive leadership style.

- **Work to build trust**. To overcome Russians' traditional ambivalence to authority, strive to share information (including bad news) and encourage dissent. But recognize that building trust is a slow process that requires patience.

- **Work to form strong personal relationships with Russian business partners**. Making an effort to develop personal relationships will improve the odds of being treated with trust and respect.

- **Instill respect for ethical practices in business**. Russians should be shown that Western business practices can protect against the excesses of Russia's developing market economy.

- **Involve Russians in joint problem solving and action planning**. To overcome low self-confidence, involve Russian managers in problem solving. Likewise, Russian managers' expertise can be developed by involving them in the creation of action plans aimed at achieving business goals.[62]

In India, for example, a **nurturant style**, which mixes empathy and concern for subordinates with an emphasis on getting the job done, often works best.[63] And in Japan, the **PM leader** is often most effective, especially when subordinate achievement motivation is high. This leader combines concern about problem solving and motivation of group performance (Performance leadership) with behavior designed to promote interdependence, avoid conflict, and maintain harmony within the group (Maintenance leadership). These behaviors resemble the distinction between task- and relationship-oriented behaviors drawn by U.S. researchers.[64]

But lumping everything into two behavioral dimensions can mask important cross-cultural differences. For instance, the relationship-oriented behavior described by Western scholars is colder and more egalitarian than the paternalistic Indian version.[65] In fact, international managers may get themselves into trouble by thinking about leadership in terms of "task-oriented" and "relationship-oriented" behaviors. This dichotomy may simply be inappropriate in many cultures.[66]

A study of Iranian employees illustrates this point nicely. The Iranians filled out a questionnaire that measured whether their immediate supervisor showed task-oriented and relationship-oriented behaviors. The results revealed

nurturant style
A leadership style that mixes empathy and concern for subordinates with an emphasis on getting the job done

PM leader
An approach to leadership that combines concern about problem solving and work group performance with behavior designed to promote harmony within the group

EXHIBIT 11.3   *Russian Leadership across Three Eras*

Leadership Trait	Village Elder (1400–1917)	Soviet Manager (1917–1991)	Market-Oriented Manager (1991–present)
Motivation			
Power	Autocrat	Centralized leadership	Moving to power sharing
Responsibility	Centralized	No action without permission	Learning to take responsibility
Drive			
Achievement	Don't make waves	Pawns of system	Unlimited potential
Ambition	Equal poverty for all	Serve party, collective good	Overcoming the sin of success
Initiative	Caution stressed	Follow rules, show loyalty	Fighting old values
Tenacity	Struggle to live	Struggle to accomplish anything	Struggle to accomplish something new
Honesty/Integrity			
Dual ethics	Deception in business, honesty with friends	Deceive bosses, personal integrity	Lawless capitalism, personal trust
Connections	Making deals with landowners	Cutting red tape of the state	Greasing palms, learning business practices
Self-confidence	Helplessness vs. bravado	Inferior quality vs. "big is best"	Need foreign help vs. over-promising

Source: Adapted from Puffer, S. M. (1994). Understanding the bear: A portrait of Russian business leaders. *Academy of Management Executive, 8,* 41–54.

that Iranian supervisors who acted in a benevolent and paternalistic way had the best performance ratings from subordinates. But forcing the Iranian data into task- and relationship-oriented factors produced no significant relationships with leader performance or subordinate satisfaction. This suggests that American definitions of leader behavior may make little sense in Middle Eastern cultures. In Iran, the boundary between work and family relationships is often ambiguous. The warm but firm father figure who plays such a prominent role in Iranian society translates into the supervisor who is directive but still shows respect for subordinates.[67]

Clearly, culture can impact how employees perceive leader style and behavior. Leaders also must express their behavior in culturally specific ways to be effective. In essence, leadership style must be understood in terms of both its general underlying structure as well as its particular expression in certain cultures. For example, American and Japanese leaders might agree that being supportive (i.e., a relationship-oriented behavior) is important for success. In the individualistic United States, a manager might express support by showing respect for subordinates' ideas. In collectivistic Japan, however, a manager might express support by spending more time with subordinates as a group.[68]

In fact, one study comparing managers from America, Britain, Japan, and Hong Kong found that while there was agreement on basic aspects of leadership style, the specific expression of these behaviors varied across the four countries.[69] These differences can explain the problems that managers run into when placed into foreign contexts. For instance, American and Japanese managers often encounter enormous difficulties leading in each other's "home" environment. Overcoming this may require a blending of leadership strategies that's akin to our synergistic recommendations on motivation.[70]

Culture and the Impact of Leader Behavior Culture also affects the impact of leader behavior on employee commitment and performance. In collectivist, high power distance cultures such as Taiwan, task-oriented behavior may have a stronger positive impact on employees than in individualistic, low power distance cultures such as the United States.[71] For instance, the criticism that Japanese managers often aim at subordinates would be viewed as punitive by most Americans, even though it works well in Japan. In their high power distance, collective context, Japanese managers usually balance criticism with plenty of supportive behaviors and go to great lengths to minimize status symbols. On the other hand, Americans are more likely to use status symbols (e.g., a fancy office) to project authority.[72]

What happens, however, when American subordinates are exposed to Japanese leadership in a facility located in the United States? In one study, Japanese managers had less impact on American than Japanese subordinates and had less influence overall than American supervisors. However, American subordinates performed better when a Japanese supervisor was friendly and supportive but worse when an American supervisor did basically the same thing. So supervisors' nationalities may affect how their behavior is *interpreted* by subordinates. Friendliness by an American supervisor may imply weakness, while the same behavior from a Japanese supervisor may be seen as a desire to get things done. But can different leader behaviors have the same positive effects across cultural contexts? Yes, at least according to experts applying Likert's **System 4 approach**.[73] Likert argued that four basic systems of leadership exist. In an *exploitative authoritative* (System 1) organization, decision making is confined to upper management, communication is top-down, and punishments are used to motivate. A *benevolent authoritative* (System 2) organization is also autocratic. However, managers are more paternalistic, are interested in employees' needs, and may give employees limited decision-making freedom. In a *consultative* (System 3) organization, employees are even more involved in communicating, decision making, and working with managers. Still, management usually reserves the right to make the final decision. Finally, the *democratic* (System 4) organization involves employees heavily in decision making in everything from problem solving to setting performance goals. Supervisors are supportive, the use of teams is widespread, and employees communicate laterally as well as vertically.

System 4 approach
A model which predicts that four main styles of leadership exist that determine effectiveness

Likert's approach argues that all companies should move toward System 3 and 4 leadership because a participative style results in the highest performance and morale. Studies with American firms show that as companies move closer to System 4, various indicators of performance also increase.[74] These results aren't surprising since a participative approach like System 4 is a good match for a low power distance culture like the United States. By the same token, shouldn't an autocratic leadership approach fit better and yield workers who are equally productive in a high power distance culture?

A comparison of managers in two manufacturing plants (one in Mexico, one in the United States) owned by an American firm suggests the answer may be yes. Both plants produced the same product and were virtually identical. Interestingly, Mexican managers were more autocratic as leaders than their

American counterparts. Overall, the Mexicans used System 2 (benevolent authoritative), whereas the Americans used System 3 (consultative). Nevertheless, both plants were equally productive and efficient, probably because the more autocratic Mexican style was a good match for the high power distance culture in Mexico. Likewise, the more participative System 3 approach was a good fit for the U.S. plant and its American values.[75]

The broader implication here is that foreign plants can match the level of performance attained in U.S. plants without having to use a strictly "American" approach to leadership. Let's consider the U.S.-Mexico comparison in more detail. Many of the initial production problems facing American-owned plants in Mexico are traceable to American management techniques that are inconsistent with Mexican cultural values. These differences surface when U.S. multinationals send Americans to manage Mexican workers, often with insufficient preparation. Exhibit 11.4 describes the different management expectations that may separate Americans and Mexicans. Not surprisingly, Mexican workers sometimes appear passive to U.S. managers. In part, this may reflect a tradition that emphasizes jobs over profits. Moreover, compared to the United States, Mexico is less individualistic but higher in power distance and stronger in uncertainty avoidance. Many Mexicans embrace the view that conformity, respect, and personal loyalty to supervisors are important and should be rewarded. Indeed, the family may be the best analogy for the Mexican view of organizations. Just like in a family, people should work cooperatively but within a prescribed role. The value Americans place on individual achievement and power sharing may strike Mexican employees as inconsistent with their embrace of interdependence.

American managers also need to be sensitive about how they interact with Mexican employees. For instance, honoring status is part of Mexican business rituals. At one U.S.-owned plant in Mexico, the ranking union leader was insulted when the American plant manager failed to introduce him to visiting executives. The American saw the union leader as just another employee. The union leader, however, had a status that, under Mexican law, is equal to that of management. Formality is another way that Mexicans recognize status differences. Americans tend to be informal managers. One American manager

EXHIBIT 11.4   *Great Expectations: The Gap between American and Mexican Managers*

Leadership Issue	Management Expectations and Attitudes	
	American Managers	Mexican Managers
Valued employee behaviors	Initiative, achievement	Obedience, harmony
Key evaluation	Performance	Personal loyalty
Leadership style	Loose/informal, communicative, power sharing possible	Close/formal, empathetic, use of directives, no power sharing
Basis of discipline/justice	Uniform application of rules and procedures	Personal relations
Work environment model	Competitive team	Cooperative family

Source: Adapted from de Forest, M. E. (1994). Thinking of a plant in Mexico? *Academy of Management Executive, 8,* 33–40.

in Mexico tried to break down status differences by wearing blue jeans and dispensing with titles. Mexicans thought he was unsophisticated. Distance between management and labor is expected.

Overall, many Mexican workers respond best to formal but empathetic supervisors. Traditionally, responsibility and autonomy aren't that important. Close supervision is expected, but leaders should also be personal and sensitive. Not surprisingly, American managers' efforts to share power and encourage problem solving are often confusing to Mexican workers, although this can be overcome with training, patience, and by using the concept of family to encourage change (e.g., "we are all brothers and sisters in this together").[76] Mexican supervisors are often used to being obeyed without question. In fact, having to explain why an order is necessary can be seen as a weakness.

At the same time, American managers may feel that Mexican workers are undisciplined. Policies are sometimes loosely followed in Mexico. The problem is that Americans and Mexicans often view discipline differently. To many American managers, discipline results when policies are applied equally to all workers. To Mexicans, however, discipline is embodied in the form of loyalty to an authority figure, not a policy manual. One American plant manager learned this lesson the hard way. To prevent labor unrest, the American manager put together an elaborate grievance system. Later, the manager was shocked when the entire workforce walked off the job without using the new system to air their complaints. Resolving worker grievances in Mexico may require a relationship-oriented approach, one where managers empathize with workers' needs in exchange for personal loyalty.[77]

Adapting Leader Behavior to the Cultural Context   Another implication of this discussion is that to be effective, international managers may need to adapt their leadership style to match cultural expectations in specific countries. For instance, consider a cultural mistake that American managers sometimes make in Japan. American managers may give pieces of a project to different individuals, feeling that giving clear assignments to each employee is the best way to organize work. In Japan, however, a better strategy would be to give the entire project to subordinates as a group and allow them to tackle it as they see fit. This would be more consistent with the Japanese view that interaction among employees provides the structure for organizing work.[78]

Nevertheless, many Americans continue to believe that if they are good managers in Los Angeles they can act the same way everywhere and succeed. One clever study debunked this idea by comparing Americans managing in Hong Kong and the United States on twelve different leader behaviors. As expected, the American managers behaved similarly in both places. But the relationship between behavior and performance was quite different. While eight of the leader behaviors were correlated with overall performance for Americans managing in the United States, only one behavior was correlated with performance for the Americans in Hong Kong. So the same behaviors that "worked" in the United States had no impact on performance in Hong Kong.[79]

Of course, American managers aren't the only ones who can have trouble adapting their leadership approaches to foreign contexts. Consider some of the challenges German giant Siemens has encountered in trying to run its U.S. subsidiaries and 70,000 American employees. One of the complaints from the American side is that German leadership is too autocratic, inflexible, and bureaucratic, with many decisions requiring approval from Germany.[80]

The Cross-Cultural Applicability of Transformational Leadership

transformational leadership
A type of leadership that inspires intense loyalty and outstanding performance among employees, usually in a crisis

In this section we consider **transformational leadership**, an increasingly popular perspective. In general, the transformational leader is able to galvanize employees and help turn poorly performing companies into winners. In essence, this happens when the transformational leader creates an emotional bond with followers, one that inspires intense loyalty and outstanding performance. This bond is the result of the leader's

- **Charisma:** The leader arouses intense emotions among followers based on absolute faith in and identification with the leader.

- **Use of inspirational appeals:** The leader communicates a clear and compelling vision for the future, one that entails extremely high performance expectations.

- **Intellectual stimulation:** The leader challenges subordinates to think about new ways to run the business, overcome problems, design products, and so on as they pursue the leader's vision.

- **Individualized consideration:** The leader gives subordinates personal attention, empathizes with their concerns, and communicates with them as individuals.[81]

Studies of American employees show that transformational leaders can have positive effects on subordinate effort, performance, and satisfaction. That said, employees must want to follow a charismatic leader. Usually this requires a willingness to cede control to the leader, something that's more likely when subordinates feel vulnerable (e.g., during a business downturn). Small wonder that transformational leaders have the greatest impact when a firm faces a crisis.[82] So, is the world of international business, with its rapid changes and competitive threats, tailor-made for transformational leadership? Some experts say yes, arguing that the most successful international managers are transformational leaders.[83] They point to studies showing the positive impact of transformational leadership in places as diverse as Israel, New Zealand, Germany, and Singapore.[84] Still, broad statements about the "global" value of transformational leadership should be treated cautiously.[85] For instance, the appeal of transformational leadership may be somewhat limited in collective cultures where group harmony is highly prized. In countries like Japan, for instance, a charismatic leader who tries to galvanize individual performance could be seen as destructive to group cohesiveness. Nevertheless, Nissan CEO Carlos Ghosn arguably is a charismatic leader who has succeeded in Japan. Viewed as a heroic leader by many Japanese, Ghosn came from Renault to oversee the successful turnaround of a struggling Nissan. Of Lebanese decent, Ghosn was born in Brazil but brought up in France. Regardless, he has done well at the helm of Nissan with a combination of vision, tough performance expectations, and empathy. Ghosn's bold moves include shuttering unproductive plants and laying off employees (decisions that still raise eyebrows in Japan), paired with a push for bold, if not audacious, new product designs. Indeed, Ghosn's words on product design speak volumes about his inspirational vision and ability to intellectually stimulate employees, both hallmarks of transformational leaders: "You don't build your character by doing what everybody else is doing. We are unleashing the imagination of our designers as part of our strategy for the market. You are going to see revolutionary designs from Nissan."[86]

Whether Ghosn reflects shifting Japanese views about leadership or is merely the exception that proves the rule is unclear at this point. Nevertheless, what we can say is that everything else being equal, implementing a transformational approach to leadership is still more difficult in Japan than in the United States.

Toward Cross-Cultural Leadership: Adapting Path-Goal Ideas

It's probably clear by now that there's no shortage of approaches about how best to lead under different conditions. Unfortunately, when it comes to a comprehensive framework that can account for a variety of situational factors, including culture, we still have a long way to go. That said, one leadership model that we can adapt to include cultural variables is the **path-goal leadership approach**.[87] This approach says that there are four basic leadership styles:

path-goal leadership approach
A model that predicts that a leader's effectiveness is contingent on how well leadership style aligns with various aspects of the situation

- **Directive:** The leader provides clear procedures, guidelines, and rules for subordinates to follow when doing their jobs.

- **Supportive:** The leader focuses on subordinates' needs and overall well-being to maintain positive relationships.

- **Participative:** The leader consults with subordinates, solicits their opinions, and otherwise involves them in decision making.

- **Achievement-oriented:** The leader focuses on maximizing subordinate performance by setting lofty goals, providing challenges, and emphasizing excellence.

To be most effective, leaders should use the style that best fits the demands of a particular situation. In fact, several contingency factors may shape which style produces the highest motivation and performance among employees. For example, tasks that are poorly defined or unpredictable may require more directive leadership, everything else being equal. On the other hand, tasks that are well defined, with clear guidelines for performance may be a better fit for participative leadership. Similarly, employees who have few skills and who lack experience may benefit from directive leadership, while employees who have well-developed skills and plenty of experience may benefit from achievement-oriented leadership.

As it stands, path-goal theory is "culture free." But introducing Hofstede's cultural dimensions as a set of possible contingencies suggests some basic applications. In general, participative leadership should work best in low power distance cultures, while directive leadership should work best in high power distance societies. Countries with moderate levels of power distance may find leadership that combines participation with some supportive behavior most attractive. A paternalistic style combining both supportive and directive behaviors should work best in collective societies (remember that collectivism is often associated with high power distance). Individualistic societies, which are often associated with low power distance, should embrace participative leadership. Finally, strong uncertainty avoidance cultures may prefer directive leadership, while in cultures more tolerant of ambiguity, participative and achievement-oriented styles might be better received. We've summarized these applications in Exhibit 11.5.

Obviously, these are generalizations. A major goal for future research is to discover how important cultural values are relative to other contingency factors

EXHIBIT 11.5   *Introducing Cultural Contingencies into Path-Goal Theory:*
Identifying Compatible Leadership Styles

Culture	Country Example	Most Compatible Leadership Style			
		Directive	Supportive	Participative	Achievement
Small PD*	Sweden			X	
Large PD	France	X			
Moderate PD	United States		X	X	
Collectivist	Taiwan	X	X		
Individualist	Denmark			X	
Moderate IND	Argentina			X	
Strong UA	Greece	X			
Weak UA	England			X	X
Moderate UA	Germany			X	X

*PD = Power Distance, UA = Uncertainty Avoidance, IND = Individualist
Source: Adapted from Rodrigues, C. (1990). The situation and national culture as contingencies for leadership behavior: Two conceptual models. *Advances in international comparative management*, vol. 5, ed. B. Prasad (Greenwich, CT: JAI Press), 51–68.

(e.g., task structure) in determining what type of leadership will be most effective in specific cultural contexts.[88]

Leadership Issues in Multinationals

In this last section, we want to underscore the difficulties that multinationals face with cross-cultural leadership issues. Just consider all the possible combinations. Managers and employees who are from the country where the multinational is headquartered, a host country where the multinational operates, or a third country may all have to interact. Likewise, these interactions may happen in the headquarters country, in a host country, or in a third country.

Some multinationals hope that the increasing similarity of companies around the world in terms of structure, technology, and strategy will weaken or overcome cross-cultural differences. However, while companies around the world may look increasingly alike with respect to these factors, leader behavior may continue to be influenced by cultural values. As we've said, this implies that leaders must take cultural values into account to be effective.[89] In fact, some American, European, and Japanese multinationals have created comprehensive programs to develop more effective international managers. General Electric, Unilever, Nokia, and Sony Corporation are just such examples.[90]

Other multinationals want to substitute their corporate values for the local values that they encounter in various countries. These multinationals believe that by emphasizing corporate values, a more homogeneous international workforce can be created. This would allow managers to use similar leadership strategies everywhere, even if the multinationals operate in dozens of countries and have thousands of foreign employees. This assumes, of course, that employees are willing to accept corporate values at the expense of their own.

EXHIBIT 11.6   *Comparing Transnational and Traditional Skills for International Managers*

Transnational Skills	Transnationally Competent Managers	Traditional International Managers
Global perspective	Understand worldwide business environment from a global perspective.	Focus on a single foreign country and on managing relationships between headquarters and that country.
Local responsiveness	Learn about many cultures.	Become an expert on one culture.
Synergistic learning	Work with and learn from people from many cultures simultaneously.	Work with and coach people in each foreign culture separately or sequentially.
	Create a culturally synergistic organizational environment.	Integrate foreigners into the headquarters' national organizational culture.
Transition and adaptation	Adapt to living in many foreign cultures.	Adapt to living in a foreign culture.
Cross-cultural interaction	Use cross-cultural interaction skills on a daily basis throughout one's career.	Use cross-cultural interaction skills primarily on foreign assignments.
Collaboration	Interact with foreign colleagues as equals.	Interact within clearly defined hierarchies of structural and cultural dominance.
Foreign experience	Transpatriation for career and organization development.	Expatriation or inpatriation primarily to get the job done.

Source: "Managing Globally Competent People" by N.J. Adler and S. Bartholomew, *Academy of Management Executive*, Vol. 6, p. 54, 1992. Copyright © 1992 Academy of Management Review. Used with permission.

The attraction of this strategy is that it would make life a lot simpler. But building a global workforce with a common set of values is very difficult. Just working for a multinational may accentuate cultural values. In one study, cultural differences were more pronounced among employees working for a multinational than for employees working in their own countries for a local firm. So Italians acted more "Italian" when they worked for a foreign firm than when they worked for an Italian company. The same was true for the other nationalities in the study.[91]

Resistance can also occur when multinationals pressure foreign employees to accept corporate values that conflict with local values. For example, an American multinational's attempts to encourage participative decision making among its European managers backfired. In fact, the multinational's indoctrination efforts only underscored the differences between corporate and local values. Opposition from European managers was the result.[92]

The Skills Needed for International Leadership   As we've suggested, the best option for multinationals may be training and career development programs aimed at building international leadership skills throughout the corporation.[93] But that's just part of the story. Companies need to identify their aspiring international managers early, using valid and reliable methods.[94] And once that happens, it will take managers time to acquire the skills they need to be effective international leaders. As the CEO of one international search firm put it, "cultural sensitivity doesn't always come naturally, so developing global executives often requires helping people to see their own biases." And doing that means more than simply plopping managers into a foreign outpost and leaving it at that. Indeed, rotating people through international assignments is just one part of a systematic and proactive effort by the firm to design a career plan that takes managers' experience and skills, as well as the company's needs, into account.[95] Generally speaking, international managers should have a perspective on cultural issues that is not limited to a particular country or region. The continuing internationalization of business is increasing the frequency and variety of cross-cultural relationships that managers have to contend with. As a result, a country-based or regional set of experiences and skills is insufficient over the long haul. Ultimately, managers need transnational skills to be effective (these are listed in Exhibit 11.6).

At this point, however, relatively few multinationals have made a sustained effort to develop transnational leadership skills in their managers. Fortunately, leadership development programs are being implemented that can overcome the limitations inherent in the modest efforts undertaken by most firms.[96] Chapter 12 will consider international employees in more detail and illustrate how firms can link leadership development to the business objectives they pursue abroad. For now, we'll leave you with some general suggestions for a transnational leadership development strategy. These are summarized in Exhibit 11.7. Companies that are serious about preparing their managers for international leadership challenges should take these ideas to heart.[97]

EXHIBIT 11.7   *Suggestions for Developing Leaders with Transnational Skills*

Suggestion	Description/Explanation
Place a premium on experience.	Research suggests that work experience is often the best way to develop international managers.
Make sure leadership development and other human resource practices are aligned.	Building international skills into performance appraisal and establishing target assignments helps reinforce the importance of international executive development.
Create support mechanisms to help the development process.	Develop methods for tracking career moves and the outcome of various developmental activities.
Ensure that senior executives take responsibility for international leadership development.	Easier said than done, top management should work to monitor careers and plan assignments as a way of building visible and influential support for development efforts.
Educate top management about developmental information.	If top management understands how development activities and evaluations work, they'll be more likely to support them.
Managers need to know how they are viewed and what their next career moves will be.	Letting leaders with potential know that top executives are paying attention helps retain them and underscores their value to the firm.

Source: Adapted from Conner, J. (2000). Developing the global leaders of tomorrow. *Human Resource Management, 39,* 147–157.

Chapter Summary

In this chapter, we combined a discussion of motivation and leadership across cultures and countries. A key point that we made early on is that if managers need to know which motivational techniques work well overseas, then what passes for common wisdom in the United States may be inappropriate in other countries. In fact, we reviewed some motivational approaches that are popular in the United States (e.g., Herzberg's two-factor approach, the use of equity and reinforcement principles, and the expectancy approach) and assessed their cross-cultural applicability.

Overall, there are relatively few universal approaches when it comes to motivation. Even if the underlying principles being used are the same, how they are framed and presented needs to reflect local values to be effective, at least to an extent. For instance, something as "simple" as feedback designed to reinforce good performance can have very different effects when applied elsewhere. For example, employees in Mexico may react differently when a supervisor gives positive performance feedback. While Americans generally are positively energized to improve on their already good performance, Mexican employees may interpret the feedback as meaning that their current level of effort is adequate.

We suggested that managers explicitly take cultural variables into account in designing their reward systems and motivational strategies. Specifically, we suggested a series of four action steps that international managers can take to develop synergistic solutions to motivation issues. These steps involve efforts by managers to understand their own value systems, as well as employees', before tackling motivation issues. Identifying underlying values and cultural frames of reference should create an appreciation for alternative perspectives, something that can then be used in generating motivational approaches that accomplish management goals in ways that are sensitive to local cultural values and dynamics.

Similar conclusions were reached about what makes for effective leadership in an international context. In the process of reviewing different approaches to leadership (e.g., Likert's System 4 approach), we concluded that leader behavior can vary dramatically across cultures and that a manager's international effectiveness can be increased by awareness of this fact. Indeed, what constitutes *effective* leadership behavior and style also differs across cultures to some degree. A take-charge, aggressive style may work well in many situations in the United States, whereas in the Netherlands it may be less successful. Next, we turned our attention to a modified version of the *path-goal approach* to leadership. In a nutshell, this approach suggests that to be most effective, leaders should use the style that best fits the demands of a particular situation and culture. Specifically, when combined with Hofstede's cultural dimensions, the path-goal approach can be used to suggest which of four basic leader styles might generally prove to be a good fit in a particular culture.

We concluded the chapter by examining cross-cultural leadership issues from a corporate perspective. In particular, we suggested that multinationals really need leaders with transnational skills throughout their ranks. Moreover, we offered some suggestions for how such leaders can be developed.

Discussion Questions

1. What difficulties might each of the motivation approaches discussed in this chapter encounter when used abroad? What specific concerns might come up if managers were trying to motivate Japanese employees? Mexican employees?

2. What steps would you take to develop a culturally synergistic approach to motivation challenges? What difficulties might you encounter in trying to implement those steps?

3. Describe Likert's System 4 approach. How can it explain why different leader behaviors can have the same positive effects across cultures?

4. How can corporations identify and develop managers with transnational leadership skills?

business.college.hmco.com/students

Up to the Challenge?

Motivating Russian Employees

At the beginning of the chapter we described a study that put three American motivational approaches to the test with Russian mill workers. To refresh your memory, the first approach gave workers valued extrinsic rewards (e.g., consumer goods, cash bonuses) in exchange for improvements in performance. The second approach involved behavioral management, with Russian supervisors trying to shape employee behavior with praise for good performance and corrective suggestions when performance was below par. The third approach borrowed from job enrichment ideas and relied on participative management tactics to improve motivation and performance. In a nutshell, employees were asked for suggestions about how to change their jobs and allowed to implement them.

Your challenge was to predict which of these three motivational approaches would work best with Russian employees. The research team felt that both the extrinsic reward and behavioral management approaches would work well. Extrinsic rewards linked to performance complement the emphasis Russians place on hard work that is connected to material gains. And behavioral management lines up pretty well with Russian human resource management traditions that encourage feelings of accomplishment and taking responsibility for the common good.

But participative management was expected to encounter tough sledding, mainly because of Russian tradition and values. Although these values are changing and individualism is slowly rising, many Russians have worked for years in a traditional, "keep your mouth shut" environment. Asking questions and challenging authority was, and to some extent still is, a recipe for trouble in Russia.

The Russian tradition of hard work was implemented in a communal context where power distance was high and strong, autocratic leadership expected. In this tradition, employees were often very loyal to their work groups and colleagues while looking to management for approval and guidance on even trivial issues. Moreover, many Russian employees distrust outsiders and are hesitant to share information. So the research team believed that participative management, which requires employees who are willing to take the initiative, challenge the status quo, and communicate openly, would be hard for many Russians to swallow, at least in the short term. In essence, participative management tactics would undercut employees' traditional relationships with their bosses rather than motivate them.

To test these predictions, the researchers designed a clever real-life experiment. They randomly assigned Russian production employees to one of the three motivation approaches. Before the approaches were applied, baseline performance data per worker (i.e., amount of cotton fabric produced) was collected for two weeks. Then the motivation approaches were used in each group for the next two weeks, after which performance was measured again. Once the approaches were stopped, performance was measured a final time after another two weeks. The idea was to see if performance improved after an approach began, but then slid back to baseline levels after it ended. If that happened, the obvious conclusion would be that using the approach had caused the spike in performance.

The research team's predictions were on target. Production improved after extrinsic rewards were introduced but slid back after they were removed. The same basic pattern was seen for the behavioral management approach. But the participative management approach actually caused performance to drop. These results highlight both the benefits and risks associated with using Western motivation tactics in Russia, especially without extensive preparation and training. The extrinsic reward and behavioral management interventions appeared to work because they were consistent with Russian traditions and values, unlike participative management.

Consistent with these findings, reports from the field suggest that money and other extrinsic rewards are often powerful motivators for many Russian employees. And Russian employees tend to discuss pay and perks among themselves to a greater extent than their Western counterparts, perhaps because of communal traditions. Consequently, Western managers should expect an earful if they pay and reward Russian employees differently without clearly explaining the reasons for doing so. Today, many Western companies operating in Russia offer employees merit-based raises and bonuses plus a full slate of perks and benefits, such as health care and pension plans, and, in a nod to the Soviet-era practice of providing cheap meals for employees, free lunches.

But as the Russian economy evolves and begins to offer wider opportunities for employees, are there any risks and dangers for Western companies from a motivation standpoint? For instance, there appear to be significant generational differences across the Russian workforce. Specifically, there are (1) older workers with excellent technical skills but no real understanding of Western business models; (2) Russians who have traveled abroad for business training if not business degrees and who may have extensive experience working for international firms; and (3) younger employees who are inexperienced but quite open minded and willing to learn. Which type of employee would you want to hire if you were an international company setting up shop in Russia? And if you had all three types of employees on the payroll, how would you motivate them? Would your tactics vary across the three groups? If so, how?[98]

International Development

Testing Your Cross-Cultural Motivation Skills

Purpose

The goal of this exercise is to consider the challenge of motivating people from different cultures. Six short situations are presented about Egyptian, Chinese, Japanese, and American subordinates, along with alternative possibilities for motivating them.

Instructions

You can think about and select an answer for each situation either ahead of time or in class. Your instructor may ask you to break into small groups of four to eight and come up with a consensus answer for each example in class. Your group can then make a brief presentation (5 minutes) about your answers and rationales. In either case, your instructor can then lead a discussion about the most appropriate answers for each situation.

Motivation Situations

1. You would like to have a Saudi Arabian colleague's help so that you can finish a major assignment. You are most likely to get that help if you say:
   a. "In the name of God, please help me."
   b. "If you help me, I'll buy you dinner."
   c. "My friend, I need your help."
   d. "Let's be the first to finish this assignment."

2. You are a department manager in China. Which of the following would probably work best to motivate your production supervisor to improve performance?
   a. "If our department increases output by 20 percent, you'll get a 5 percent bonus."
   b. "I'm planning to reorganize the department and I'm thinking of promoting you if production increases."
   c. "If your team doesn't meet the quotas, you're fired."
   d. "Why don't you put in some overtime to help make the production quotas?"

3. You are a manager about to conduct a series of performance appraisals on your American subordinates. To motivate them, you will probably want to focus on recognizing the Americans'
   a. promptness.
   b. creativity.
   c. directness and openness.
   d. accomplishments.

4. Last month your Japanese team hit all production targets. Which of the following would be the best way to acknowledge their achievement?
   a. Treat them to a dinner where you give special recognition to the team leader.
   b. Don't mention it, because meeting targets is their job.

c. Call the oldest team member aside and thank him or her.

d. Thank the group at your next meeting and ask them to increase production even more.

5. You are managing a factory in Egypt. One supervisor's group is not meeting your production expectations. Which of the following might be the best way for you to draw the supervisor's attention to this problem?

   a. "Increase your group's productivity or you're fired."

   b. "Do you need any help with your group?"

   c. "You'd better take care of your group, or I may have to move you to another job."

   d. "Why don't you hold a meeting with your group to find out what's wrong?"

6. You are a manager in a large international company and are about to begin an important project. Mr. Hiro has been assigned to work for you on this project. Because Mr. Hiro is Japanese, which of the following is likely to motivate him?

   a. Being part of a strong, leading international firm.

   b. A good raise in his annual salary.

   c. A promotion to group leader and a better title.

   d. A trip to Hawaii for him and his wife after the project is completed.

Source: From *Multicultural Management: New Skills for Global Business,* F. Elashmawi & P.R. Harris, pp. 148-151, © 1993 Butterworth-Heinemann. Reprinted by permission.

Tapping into the Global Network

Leadership Transitions in Emerging Market Economies

Purpose

The goal here is to conduct a detailed analysis of the type of leadership certain countries relied on when they were state dominated and the type of leadership they are now moving to embrace in a more market-oriented environment. Your instructor will assign specific countries to research.

This chapter discussed some of the leadership challenges facing Russian managers in their transition process. Other countries are going through similar transformations. These include China, Vietnam, and the countries in eastern Europe that were once part of the Soviet Union (e.g., Poland, Hungary, Romania).

Instructions

Your instructor will place you into small groups (ideally 3–5) to do research on the basic approach to leadership used in a specific country that is transitioning to a market economy. This research effort should be done outside of class and focus on: (a) the approaches to leadership used when the state controlled the economy; (b) the type of leadership and management practices needed if the country in question is to become a globally competitive market economy; (c) an assessment of progress made to date; and (d) suggestions for how the remaining barriers to change can be overcome (including how changes in leadership values and management practices can be encouraged).

Your instructor may ask each group to make a presentation (20 minutes) about its findings to the class. This could be followed by a discussion about common and unique leadership themes in these transitioning economies as well as the role of cultural values. If your instructor decides to make this an individual assignment, be prepared to take part in a general class discussion on the issues raised.

To get started with your research, you may want to consult the websites below for background information and profiles about countries undergoing economic transition. These websites should help you refine your research efforts and act as a gateway to articles, reports, and other websites about leadership issues and management practices in specific countries undergoing economic transition:

The CIA World Factbook
www.cia.gov/cia/publications/fact book/

International Monetary Fund Country Information page
www.imf.org/external/country/index.htm

Organisation for Economic Co-operation and Development's page
www.oecd.org/topic/0,2686,en_2649_37445 _1_1_1_1_37445,00.html

U.S. Agency for International Development
www.usaid.gov/
The World Bank Group
www.worldbank.org

12 Building an Effective International Workforce

Learning Objectives

After reading this chapter, you should be able to:

▸ Explain why having an international human resource management strategy is critical for achieving a firm's international business goals.

▸ Identify options for staffing international operations as well as their pros and cons.

▸ Discuss how cultural factors impact the selection and development of international employees.

▸ Understand how firms can manage equal opportunity and diversity issues in their international operations.

▸ Identify the major factors associated with the effective use of expatriates.

INTERNATIONAL CHALLENGE

Using Human Resources Strategically: Making the China Gambit Pay

CHINA PRESENTS MANY CHALLENGES for foreign companies. Among other things, corruption is fairly widespread and the long-term viability of China's political system is unclear. Nevertheless, many foreign high-tech firms believe that China is a huge growth market for electronics. For instance, demand for mobile communications equipment and services has soared in China, now the biggest cell phone market on the planet. In 2003, local and foreign firms competed for over 200 million Chinese cell phone subscribers. On top of that, China is also a cheap export platform, thanks in part to its enormous supply of inexpensive labor. The combination of low-cost production and high growth prospects is what prompts foreign companies to take the risks that come with investing in China. And the biggest risk taker among Western firms is U.S.-based Motorola. By 2003, Motorola had invested $3.4 billion in China, and announced that the firm, along with some partners and suppliers, planned to spend billions more in the country through 2007. One of its biggest investments, the Motorola Tianjin Integrated Semiconductor Manufacturing Complex, began operating in the summer of 2001.

Already the biggest foreign investor in China when it comes to electronics, Motorola's $560-million Tianjin plant underscored the firm's strategic desire to manufacture near the growing Asian markets it wanted to serve. China alone already accounts for some 20 percent of Motorola's total sales. Overall, Motorola has dozens of factories and sales offices in China that collectively employ over 6,000 people.

Nevertheless, Motorola has found that operating in China meant responding to some unique (and evolving) human resource management issues. Here's a partial list:

- While China's workforce lags behind other industrialized countries in terms of education and skills, its catch-up efforts are starting to pay off in some important areas. Chinese universities, for instance, are churning out some half-million engineering and science graduates annually. Likewise, efforts have been made to ramp up China's vocational education system. Chinese officials also believe that co-ownership speeds up the transfer of training, technology, and management know-how. That explains why China prefers that foreign firms establish joint ventures with local companies.

- While fading, vestiges of China's tradition of lifetime employment and extensive benefits for workers remain. Although wages remain quite low by Western standards, employers typically provide benefits including child care, housing subsidies, and medical coverage. This traditional "iron rice bowl" system is less flexible than many foreign companies, especially those from the United States, are used to.

- Wage increases in state-owned companies are often small, infrequent, and not directly connected to individual or company performance. Likewise, promotions may be based on seniority or connections (*guanxi*) rather than performance. The Chinese government frets that such approaches can stifle initiative and creativity. On the other hand, Chinese officials also are unlikely to do anything that might significantly boost wages, fearing that it could slow foreign investment. In any case, the upshot for foreign companies is that they often feel pressure to modify the incentive-laden human resource management practices that they use in other countries (e.g., the United States).

- Although regulations have been loosened considerably in recent years, a complicated and centralized labor structure exists where the government has leverage over wages, labor movement, training regulations, and firing of workers. The Chinese government, however, continues to take steps to streamline the system.

Overall, Motorola has made some interesting moves to respond to the human resource challenges it faces in China. If you had been advising Motorola, what recommendations would you have made to shape the firm's human resource management strategy in China? More specifically, what advice would you have offered for effectively hiring, developing, and retaining Chinese employees? Keep in mind that as far back as 1989, Motorola's goal was to manufacture its high-technology products inside China to world-class standards. Think about some options for Motorola as you read through this chapter. If you can, do some research about the company as well as Chinese human resource practices. And keep the big picture in mind. In the end, Motorola's approach to human resource management, in China or elsewhere, needs to be aligned with its business strategy. Then read the *Up to the Challenge?* box at the end of the chapter to learn about the key elements of Motorola's human resource management approaches in China and how its strategy has evolved.[1]

▸ *A Strategic Look at International Human Resource Management*

In Chapter 11 we considered the motivation and leadership challenges facing managers in international business. This chapter takes things to the next level by considering the broader role that **human resource management** plays in an international context. Traditionally, human resource management involves activities that help select, train, develop, appraise, and reward employees. However, international human resource managers must also be able to contribute to the overall international strategic planning process for the business and think strategically within their own functional area if the firm is to achieve its international goals.[2] Ideally, human resource executives should be involved in all phases of the development and implementation of a company's international goals.[3]

human resource management
Activities that help select, train, develop, appraise, and reward employees

But why is a strategic perspective on international human resource management so critical? In a nutshell, companies with a highly trained, flexible, and motivated international workforce may have an advantage over competitors, especially if that workforce directly supports corporate goals.[4] As Michael Porter put it (we covered his theory of national competitive advantage back in Chapter 8), "Human resource management affects competitive advantage in any firm, through its role in determining the skills and motivation of employees."[5] What's more, developing an effective international workforce is much more difficult for a competitor to emulate than buying technology or securing capital.[6] Indeed, how well companies manage their human resources around the world can mean the difference between success and failure. If you're still not convinced, consider the fact that compared to their competitors, firms that effectively manage their international human resources typically:

- do a better job of identifying new international business opportunities and are better equipped to adapt to changing conditions worldwide.

- are less likely to violate local cultural norms and values (and are less likely to lose business as a result).

- do a better job of spreading learning throughout the firm and identifying innovative ideas wherever they exist.

- do a better job of coordinating and integrating subsidiary operations worldwide.

- have a satisfied and committed overseas staff with low turnover.[7]

And as we've seen, companies are more likely than ever to find themselves doing business in places with diverse cultural, legal, economic, and political perspectives. The challenge for many firms is how to balance the need to coordinate units scattered around the world against the need for individual units to have the control necessary to deal effectively with local issues.[8]

By definition, this balancing act becomes more difficult to pull off as the level of diversity firms are exposed to increases. For example, consider a situation where the parent firm's national culture differs dramatically from the cultures that prevail in its foreign subsidiaries. In this case, it may be harder for the parent firm to share information, technology, and innovations between the home office and foreign outposts. Likewise, it may prove more difficult to promote needed organizational changes and manage any conflicts that come up between employees in different countries. Fortunately, human resource management strategies can overcome such problems.[9] For instance, international human resource managers can take steps to ensure that top executives understand the different cultures within the company workforce and around the world. They can also offer advice about how the firm can coordinate functions across boundaries and help develop outstanding cross-cultural skills in employees (e.g., through various training programs and career paths that involve significant overseas exposure).[10]

Of course, these are very general suggestions and a wide range of human resource practices might be used to implement them. As a starting point, companies should develop an international human resource philosophy that describes corporate values and attitudes about human resources. This philosophy will help shape the core international human resource policies that define how employees all over the world should be treated. In other words, these policies will provide a broad outline of what constitutes acceptable international human resource practices. Under this broad umbrella, individual units can then fine-tune and select specific practices that best fit their local conditions.

However, executing this won't be easy, especially for firms operating in dozens of countries. Such firms might find it extremely difficult, for example, to design a compensation system that is sensitive to cultural differences yet still meets general guidelines of being seen as fair and equally motivating by employees everywhere. On top of that, how benefit packages are constructed, as well as the hiring, firing, and promotion practices used, can all be impacted by culture and local human resource management practices.

Despite those difficulties, selecting the right human resource management strategy can pay off for firms, particularly in difficult foreign markets. Consider multinationals wanting to quickly enter transition economies (i.e., economies that are moving from being state-dominated to being market-based, such as China and countries in the former Soviet Union). Certain market entry options, such as buying local firms, building greenfield plants, or setting up joint ventures may create human resource challenges that undercut firm perfor-mance in such transition economies.

To meet these challenges, multinationals need to adopt an appropriate human resource management strategy. Exhibit 12.1 presents three possible strategies that might be used in transition economies. For example, Exhibit 12.1 describes both a social welfare approach (e.g., a "womb to tomb" perspective on employees that was once characteristic of many state-dominated economies) as well as a cost-containment approach (e.g., characteristic of U.S. firms that believe in quickly downsizing or otherwise minimizing employee costs in the face of changing business conditions). However, an invest-in-employees approach may have the best chance of positively impacting firm performance in transition economies. This may be especially true in transition economies where strong uncertainty avoidance prevails and a strong desire for stability exists (e.g., as in the Ukraine). After all, the invest-in-employees approach, like the social welfare approach, does offer some stability to employees—provided they perform and live up to their end of the bargain. In essence, implementing this strategy involves using a package of human resource practices that reflect the idea of "investing" in the workforce (see Exhibit 12.1). Consequently, this is something that multinationals entering transition economies may want to move toward, at least over the long term. Still, the degree to which multinationals should pursue this approach depends on local conditions. Put simply, one size does not fit all—some combination of the strategies in Exhibit 12.1 may be the best bet, depending on the circumstances in specific transition economies.[11]

Once again, this caution underscores the idea that developing an effective human resource management system that both reflects broad principles and allows for local flexibility is a tall order.[12] Then there's the question of how that system gets developed in the first place. Our earlier suggestion to establish a corporate-wide philosophy first implies that corporate headquarters makes basic policy decisions, but gives units around the world some say over what human resource practices are actually implemented. In reality, however, a variety of developmental processes exist across firms. Some firms run virtually all international human resource functions out of corporate headquarters. Others centralize only general policy making and ask foreign units for advice about how to implement policies locally. Some firms use what they feel are the most effective human resource practices on a worldwide basis, regardless of origin. In

EXHIBIT 12.1   *Human Resource Management (HRM) in Transition Economies: Three Possible Strategies*

HRM Issue	Social Welfare Approach (e.g., used in former Soviet Union)	Cost-Containment Approach (e.g., used in U.S. firms with a "downsizing mentality")	Invest-in-Employees Approach (e.g., used in Western firms with a high-commitment perspective)
Employee training and development efforts	Narrow-training tends to be technology-specific	Reduce training expenditures to the extent possible	Provide wide range of developmental training for new, existing employees
Monetary incentives	Pay is determined on a collective basis and is generally not performance-driven	Individual performance drives pay levels	Both individual bonuses/incentives and unit/firm-based profit-sharing systems are used
Employee health and welfare provisions	Provide direct, extensive subsidies for housing, health, child care, and other social concerns	Divestiture from social environment, cut back or eliminate subsidies for employee welfare	Slowly phase out direct subsidies not directly linked to employee performance
Employee job security	Offer high job security	No job security offered	Medium job security offered
Expected HRM link to firm performance	Negative—may result in poorer performance	Negative—may result in poorer performance	Positive—may result in better performance

Source: Adapted from Buck, T., Filatotchev, I., Demina, N., & Wright, M. (2003). Inside ownership: human resource strategies and performance in a transition economy. *Journal of International Business Studies, 34,* 530–549.

other cases, international human resource activities are divided up among corporate headquarters, regional areas, and individual subsidiaries, with each having specific responsibilities.[13]

Finally, some firms organize international human resource functions around the type of employee. For instance, some multinationals centralize human resource functions for parent-country nationals (PCNs) and third-country nationals (TCNs), but delegate decisions about host-country nationals (HCNs) to local units.[14] We'll have more to say about different types of employees in the next section. But first, take a look at the following International Insights box. As you'll see, just screening job candidates is anything but simple when foreign prospects are involved.

▸ *Basic Options for Staffing Foreign Operations*

In this section, we'll begin our exploration of international human resource management approaches by examining the options for staffing international operations. Next, we'll investigate how firms can develop employees with global management skills. We'll wrap up the chapter by considering issues surrounding the use of expatriates.

⊕ International Insights

Hiring the Best and Brightest from Abroad Means Going the Extra Mile

IN MANY FIELDS such as computers, pharmaceuticals, and aerospace, finding the best employees with critical skills means scouring the world for talent. Consequently, American household names like Hewlett-Packard, Microsoft, Texas Instruments, and Pfizer have hired foreigners to fill key positions in the United States in recent years. And that's happened even in the face of visa hurdles that must be cleared to legally bring foreigners into the United States to work.

But just screening potential foreign hires presents special issues and challenges. For instance, being able to assess educational credentials is important regardless of where the job candidate is from. But what about foreign job candidates whose educational credentials were obtained outside the United States?

Clearly, many overseas universities provide a superior education. The problem is that figuring out what's "superior" is rarely easy for American human resource professionals. Foreign universities usually have different standards, courses, and grading systems than their American counterparts, making a direct comparison difficult. Some U.S. firms use their own in-house tests to evaluate foreign applicants' education, skills, and abilities. A more common approach is to rely on consulting firms, such as New York–based World Education Services Inc. (**www.wes.org**), to assess the educational credentials of foreign job candidates.

And the challenge doesn't stop there. Assessing the work experience of foreign job applicants can also prove difficult, as does conducting background checks for criminal behavior. Once again, many U.S. firms use consultants who have the expertise and overseas contacts necessary to size up foreign candidates' work experiences and how they compare against American candidates with similar backgrounds. Moreover, language barriers often come into play when contacting foreign references or "gatekeepers" (e.g., administrative assistants, secretaries) who don't speak English. So whoever is conducting background checks must be fluent in the relevant language.

When it comes to screening for past criminal behavior, the problem is that laws and legal systems vary. Consequently, what might be considered crimes in the United States aren't necessarily viewed as such in other countries. For instance, foreigners hired to work in the United States often seek permanent resident status. In order to do so, foreigners must present documents from their home countries that describe whether or not they have a criminal history. This procedure could cause an American firm to lose a foreign hire. In addition, foreigners with clean records from their home countries may be barred from working in the United States because they've admitted behavior that is illegal under American law. A related problem is that criminal records may be inadequate in certain countries, making background checks more difficult.

Cultural differences can also make screening foreign candidates a challenge. Communication styles, expectations about performance feedback, and work values may all vary across countries. American human resource professionals should explain the company's values to foreign job candidates and do their homework about the candidate's culture before the interview takes place. This preparation will make it easier to assess whether the foreign job candidate can successfully adapt to the American work environment. For instance, you might be surprised to learn that British employees in the United States appear to have higher rates of failure than foreign employees from any other country. This fact runs counter to most Americans' perceptions about the similarity of British and American work cultures.[15]

As we've suggested, the strategic choices firms make to compete in the global economy should be supported by their international human resource practices.[16] For instance, a company that has significant interests and deep roots abroad should be led by senior executives who have substantial international experience, including a firsthand understanding of foreign markets, cultures, and business practices. Indeed, U.S. multinationals have focused more in

EXHIBIT 12.2   *Why Use Expatriates? Possible Benefits for Companies and Employees*

Possible Benefits for Companies	Possible Benefits for Employees
Key skills and expertise transferred to the foreign operation to address important issues	Skill development (e.g., culture, language, flexibility, adaptability)
Employee retention and commitment	Recognition, rewards, advancement
Know-how about local markets and practices transferred back to the parent company	Greater commitment to firm
Development of senior management team (building a broader international experience base)	Travel opportunities
Better overall performance of the foreign operation	Greater job and work life satisfaction

Source: Adapted from Downes, M., & Thomas, A. S. (2000). Managing overseas assignments to build organizational knowledge. *Human Resource Planning, 20,* 33–48.

recent years on hiring and promoting top managers with international experience as well as offering international development opportunities to managers lower in the ranks. A good example is Richard Waggoner, who was instrumental in putting GM's South American operations back on track. That foreign experience was a key reason why GM eventually named Waggoner CEO.[17]

But staffing international operations can be complex, with human resource managers facing a potentially confusing array of choices. For example, a traditional option is to recruit **parent-country nationals** (PCNs) for top management and important technical positions in foreign subsidiaries. PCNs have citizenship in the country where the hiring company is headquartered.

Once abroad, PCNs are usually referred to as **expatriates**. The reasons for using expatriates or PCNs could include one or more of the possible benefits summarized in Exhibit 12.2. As you can see, the expatriate function offers some pluses for both the company and employees.[18] But the two most common reasons for sending a PCN on an expatriate assignment are the perceived lack of appropriate expertise (e.g., technical, managerial) in a foreign subsidiary and/or the belief that a PCN is the best option for effectively monitoring and controlling foreign operations.

On the other hand, sending a PCN abroad is typically the most expensive option. Adding to the expense is the fact that failure rates for expatriate assignments (i.e., the expatriate returns prematurely or otherwise fails to achieve desired objectives) may be high. Although estimates for failure rates vary considerably (from 15 percent to over 50 percent), a rough rule of thumb is that around 25 percent of expatriate postings end in some kind of failure.[19] We'll say more later about expatriates. In many cases, however, the biggest drawback with PCNs is their limited grasp of local cultures and business practices, especially early on in a foreign assignment.[20] To offset this, some firms recruit immigrants, or their adult children, for positions in foreign subsidiaries back in their ancestral homes. But as the following International Insights suggests, this option isn't as simple as it seems.

Consequently, many companies turn to **host-country nationals** (HCNs), especially to fill lower- and middle-level management jobs. HCNs are individuals from the foreign country where a multinational has set up operations. Some firms are reluctant to put HCNs in top management positions overseas, feeling

parent-country nationals Employees who have citizenship in the country where the hiring company is headquartered

expatriates A parent-country national who works overseas for an extended period of time

host-country nationals Individuals from the foreign country where a multinational has set up operations

🌐 International Insights

Ethnic Expatriates: Straddling Cultural Boundaries

Here's a good idea. Recruit ethnic expatriates, people who immigrated to the United States or who lived there for years, and send them "home" to run your foreign operations there or to provide professional expertise in critical areas. What better way to fill important openings in markets that require both technical skills and a keen understanding of the local context? And many companies have found it to be an effective international human resource strategy.

For instance, firms as diverse as Hertz, Home Depot, Marriott, McDonald's, and Payless Shoes have all sent highly trained and well-educated immigrants who are comfortable straddling cultural boundaries back to their home countries to staff operations or provide service support to foreign franchisees. Consider Payless Shoes manager Roxana Oreliana as a specific case in point. Ms. Oreliana fled the civil war in her native El Salvador when she was 15. Reaching the United States, Ms. Oreliana eventually became an American citizen, only to find herself—by choice—back in her homeland at age 35. Managing a store for Payless Shoes as part of its booming business in Central America, Ms. Oreliana is part of a company growth wave that saw some 200 stores open in the region by 2004 and prospects for hundreds more. As a store manager, Ms. Oreliana helps promote the Payless Shoes brand in El Salvador, a role that is well served by her mastery of Spanish and knowledge of local culture.

But the outcomes aren't always so rosy. Ethnic expatriates sometimes overestimate their ability to understand their native cultures, especially after spending years in the United States. Or they may be seen as having betrayed corporate headquarters by "going native." And local employees may find ethnic expatriates' attempts to "act locally" as flimsy impersonations that betray foreign influences, highlighting their status as overpaid interlopers.

For instance, after twenty-two years in the United States Seiji returned to Japan to lead Apple Computer's Japanese subsidiary. He left after a year. Part of the reason was that his American colleagues saw him as too Japanese, while his Japanese co-workers saw him as too American. Tanya immigrated to the United States at the age of 9. When she returned to her native Russia as a management consultant, she had an American MBA to go with her fluent Russian. But in less than two years, she was back in America, weary of Russian women who were put off by her ambition. Moreover, her local employees simply ignored the work deadlines she set. Danny spent almost three decades in the United States before returning to his birthplace, Taiwan, to lead Taiwan Aerospace. The move was a nightmare. Danny's Taiwanese colleagues saw him as an intruder. Like the others, Danny soon gave up and returned to the United States.

So what can firms do to improve ethnic expatriates' chances of success? One option is to hire locals as cultural translators to assist ethnic expatriates. Another is to provide catch-up cross-cultural training for ethnic expatriates. For instance, after working in Mexico as a manager for Levi Strauss, Grace Canepa, a Peruvian educated in the United States, learned that Mexicans thought she was rude when she failed to use professional titles to address them. Unfortunately, less than 20 percent of ethnic expatriates receive any cross-cultural training.[21]

it would dilute their control over foreign operations or make it tougher to maintain a unified corporate culture. Nevertheless, HCNs offer some potential advantages over PCNs. Not surprisingly, HCNs typically have a better grasp of the local culture, business practices, and language. HCNs also tend to be cheaper for the company since expatriates usually entail expensive relocation costs and higher salaries. Finally, hiring locals to staff foreign operations can bring public relations benefits and relieve government pressures to "go local" when staffing subsidiary operations.[22]

third-country nationals
Employees who enjoy citizenship in a country other than that of the foreign subsidiary where they work or the country where the parent company is based

Another increasingly popular option is to use **third-country nationals** (TCNs) in foreign subsidiaries. As the name implies, TCNs enjoy citizenship in a country other than the foreign subsidiary where they work or the country where the parent company is based. Say a company wants someone with expertise in local culture and business practices to fill a management position in a foreign subsidiary. PCNs may have plenty of management experience but may lack local knowledge. Likewise, while HCNs may understand local conditions, they may lack relevant technical skills. A TCN may be the best option, especially if the goal is to groom someone for top management positions in foreign subsidiaries or to effectively run operations in countries that lack home-grown management talent. For instance, an American firm setting up manufacturing operations in Costa Rica may find appropriate candidates in Mexico, a country with a large pool of Spanish-speaking management talent.

international cadre
A talented group of managers, maintained by a firm, who can be plugged into any country and successfully represent the company's values

Although PCNs, HCNs, and TCNs represent three major staffing categories, they don't describe all the possibilities. For instance, large multinationals often want a talented **international cadre** of managers who can be plugged into any country and successfully represent the company's values. Doing this means selecting managers based on potential and ability, regardless of nationality, and then exposing them to a variety of international experiences. Managers in the international cadre spend their careers jumping from one foreign assignment to the next. For example, during a visit to China, we met an American executive in S.C. Johnson & Son's Shanghai plant who had been continuously working in various overseas subsidiaries for over twenty years! Building an international cadre seems to pay dividends. According to one study, multinationals that use regional transfers and TCNs extensively to build their international cadres tend to perform better than multinationals that rely more on traditional expatriates.[23]

permanent expatriate
An employee who stays on at one or more foreign subsidiaries for an extended period of years

By the same token, PCN doesn't really describe the **permanent expatriate**, an employee who stays on at a particular foreign subsidiary for an extended period. And how about an American who is hired directly by the French subsidiary of a U.S. multinational? Is the American a PCN or HCN? Neither, really. Finally, consider a promising Chinese employee working in Beijing for an American firm. The Chinese employee is sent to the United States to fill a temporary position at corporate headquarters. Such employees are sometimes referred to as *inpatriates*. Sending foreign employees to the home country is often done to develop skills and strengthen commitment to the parent firm. Likewise, companies can take advantage of what inpatriates can teach them about doing business in particular countries.[24]

Exhibit 12.3 illustrates some of this staffing complexity. It outlines the potential movement of employees between a firm's home country, countries hosting its foreign subsidiaries, and a country where no operations exist. Interestingly, some experts urge international firms to strive for heterogeneity in their staffing composition—in short, to have PCNs, HCNs, TCNs, and other types of employees working side-by-side wherever possible. The basic idea is that creating this kind of diverse working environment should improve innovation and learning, outcomes that ultimately improve subsidiary performance. The role for international human resource management professionals in such a context would be to ensure that the advantages of staffing heterogeneity would not be overwhelmed by its accompanying disadvantages (e.g., more conflict, more difficulty coordinating operations). This could be accomplished via appropriate socialization and training efforts (e.g., to make employees aware of staffing goals, improve conflict management skills, etc.).[25]

EXHIBIT 12.3   *Types of International Staff and Their Potential Movement across Locations*

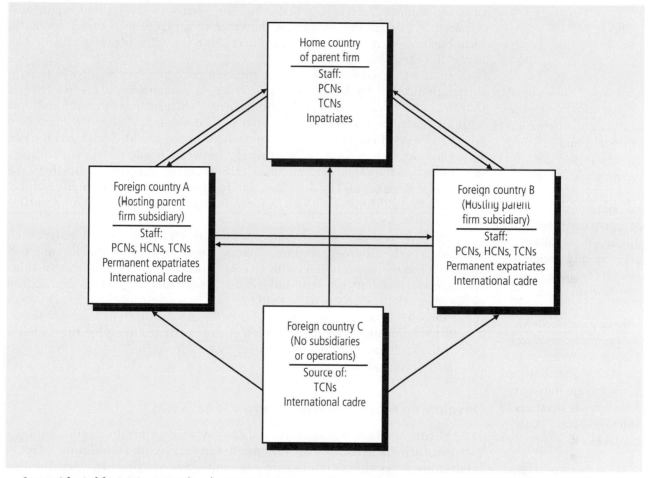

Source: Adapted from Briscoe, D. R. (1995). *International human resource management.* Englewood Cliffs, NJ: Prentice-Hall.

▸ *Selecting and Developing International Employees*

At this juncture, you're probably wondering how firms decide which staffing option is best for a particular job in a particular location. Ideally, such decisions should be directly tied to the company's international business strategy and its competitive environment. In many cases, selection approaches also are shaped by the sophistication of overseas operations and the firm's level of internationalization. Likewise, factors such as firm size, market, industry, and culture can impact selection approaches.[26]

Research underscores this complexity. For instance, one study examined why the proportion of American expatriates staffing foreign positions for a U.S. bank varied across countries. It turned out that overseas branches with higher proportions of American expatriates offered more complex services and were in countries that were culturally distinct from the United States. In these circumstances, expatriates may have more insights about complex services used in the

United States and can provide more continuity with the home office than their local counterparts.

In contrast, bank branches in foreign countries with fierce local competition for financial services relied more on locals (HCNs) than expatriates. Apparently, in such circumstances the value of an HCN who understands the local business scene and has good connections to local firms outweighs the positives that expatriates possess.[27]

In any case, companies often embrace a particular philosophy in making international staffing decisions. For instance, a **geocentric philosophy** means that the firm stresses ability and performance when selecting international staff, without regard to nationality. The goal is to develop and socialize managers who can be good corporate citizens anywhere in the world. Standards for performance are determined collaboratively between headquarters and foreign operations. At the other extreme is an **ethnocentric philosophy**. In this case, headquarters makes all key decisions and foreign subsidiaries have little autonomy or input. All important jobs at headquarters and in all foreign operations are held by PCNs.

In between these two extremes are two other philosophies. A **polycentric philosophy** gives human resource management control to the foreign subsidiary, although headquarters still makes broad strategic decisions. In other words, each subsidiary is a semi-independent entity that controls its own staffing needs. As a result, HCNs usually hold top jobs in foreign subsidiaries. However, these same HCNs rarely move beyond their local subsidiary to headquarters or other foreign locations. Similarly, with a **regiocentric philosophy**, most foreign employees will not move into headquarters positions. Nevertheless, employees can move from country to country in a particular region.[28]

Developing Managers with International Skills

Many firms embrace a geocentric philosophy as they become more sophisticated in their international operations. It can take years to build an effective international workforce, one where key employees are flexible, open minded, and expert in several cultures and languages. Since big multinationals operate in dozens of countries, virtually all aspects of the business involve international contact. Such firms can no longer rely on just a handful of managers with international experience to succeed. In short, all employees must be able to recognize cultural differences that affect business communications and working relationships.[29] Take a look at Exhibit 12.4 for a summary of the skills that international managers need to succeed. Then read the accompanying International Insights on the travel challenges facing today's international managers.

But how should firms go about developing employees with appropriate international skills? While there's no precise recipe, many companies rotate promising managers through different types of foreign assignments over several years. This strategy produces managers with experience across a variety of countries and organizational circumstances, such as managing a start-up operation, an ongoing joint venture, a restructuring, and so on. Another option is to recruit foreign students who want to work in their home country after graduation—where their language and cultural skills can be put to good use. Likewise, some firms will focus on potential employees who are fluent in multiple languages, open to other cultures, and willing to tackle overseas assignments.

---

geocentric philosophy
An approach that stresses ability and performance when selecting international staff, without regard to nationality

ethnocentric philosophy
An approach where headquarters makes all key decisions and foreign subsidiaries have little autonomy or input

polycentric philosophy
An approach that places human resource management control in the hands of the foreign subsidiary, although headquarters still makes broad strategic decisions

regiocentric philosophy
An approach that expects foreign employees to move from country to country in a particular region, rather than into headquarters positions

EXHIBIT 12.4   *Do You Measure Up? The Skill Profile for International Managers*

Skill	Managerial Implications
Multidimensional perspective	Extensive multi-functional, multi-country, and multi-environment experience
Line management proficiency	Successful track record in overseas projects/assignments
Effective decision making	Successful in making strategic decisions
Resourcefulness	Skilled in becoming known and accepted by host country's government and business elite
Culturally adaptive	Quick and easy to adapt to foreign cultures, with diverse cross-cultural experience
Culturally sensitive	Can effectively deal with people from a variety of cultures, races, nationalities, and religions
Team-building skills	Able to create culturally diverse working groups that achieve organizational goals
Mental maturity	Endurance for the rigors of foreign posts
Negotiating skills	Track record of conducting successful business negotiations in multicultural environments
Change agent skills	Track record of successfully initiating and implementing organizational changes
Visionary ability	Quick to spot and respond to political or economic threats and opportunities in the host country

Source: Adapted from Howard, C. G. (1992). Profile of the 21st-century expatriate manager. *HR Magazine*, June, 93–100.

Finally, some U.S. companies have had success with training programs that bring high-potential managers from all over the world to work together on a variety of projects in a simulated environment. Such programs build cross-national relationships and improve cross-cultural problem-solving skills. For example, Motorola annually puts hundreds of up-and-coming international managers through a business simulation that can last weeks. As one manager who went through the simulation said, "It's surprising how realistic and demanding it is." And using such tools can save firms money. French food giant Danone SA cut its failure rate among expatriate managers from 35 percent to 3 percent in three years by using simulations to evaluate international talent.[30]

In fact, some firms with extensive overseas operations have developed global training programs for employees. Sometimes, this includes training for expatriates going to specific countries (which we'll discuss later). However, global training programs are mainly aimed at broader goals, such as developing overall cultural awareness, working effectively in cross-cultural teams, and building cross-cultural communication skills. Procter & Gamble, Intel Corporation, and Eastman Kodak are examples of U.S. firms that have successfully implemented global training programs.[31]

🌐 International Insights

Globetrotting Lessons in International Management

INTERNATIONAL MANAGERS are adaptable people who can cope with frequent overseas travel. Sound glamorous? Maybe. But the pace can be frenetic and exhausting. In fact, the tendency to send managers on short-term trips (i.e., less than a year) instead of traditional expatriate assignments (which typically last several years) has been accelerating recently. According to one survey of 500 global companies, nearly 80 percent expect to increase their use of shorter overseas assignments in the future. Another survey found that short-term assignments were the fastest-growing type of overseas experience. The reasons for this trend include lower costs and the success that companies feel they've had in developing "global managers" with broad international skills. In other words, companies often feel that their best managers can work effectively anywhere in the world. So why park them in one place for three years?

Short-term assignments mean that international managers often end up flitting around the world on brief, grueling trips. Even jaunts that used to last weeks or months are now crammed into a few days. Also common are compressed overseas trips that include several stops. One manager's four-day itinerary out of New York included visits to Helsinki, London, and São Paulo. Total frequent flyer miles earned: 17,000.

And don't assume that the allure of flashy cities like Paris or Hong Kong will help you overcome jet lag. As international markets expand, managers are increasingly finding themselves in underdeveloped and sometimes risky locations where they face dirt roads, lousy hotels, scary diseases (e.g., SARS), and the occasional hair-raising event. One American manager ended up using buckets of sea water for washing (and flushing) in Papua New Guinea after the hotel's water main was blown up by local guerrillas. Another American manager on the way to a Cairo business meeting found himself in the middle of 500,000 chanting Egyptians conducting a huge protest march about U.S. involvement in Iraq.

Indeed, in the post-9/11 environment, many companies are reserving travel for only the most important tasks or relationship-building efforts.

Still, travel will remain an important part of international business. That said, companies these days may pay more attention to the reasons for international travel as well as to employee safety and security.

In any case, on top of safety-related concerns are the personal and family hardships associated with frequent international travel. Consider Peter McAteer, an executive at Boston-based Giga Information. Three out of four weeks, Mr. McAteer is away from home, mostly out of the country. When asked what he wanted for Christmas, Mr. McAteer's son replied that he wanted his father to be home. Likewise, John Aliberti's wife says that "China has taken over our lives." His two children miss their father and endure the taunts of schoolmates about the dad who is never around. Why? Because Mr. Aliberti makes up to ten trips to China every year to drum up business for his firm, Pittsburgh-based Union Switch & Signal.

Of course, there are positives associated with all this short-term globetrotting. Mr. Aliberti thrives on the feeling he gets of being "on the frontier" in China. Another big plus for Aliberti is that he can act like a CEO in China, signing contracts and making decisions on the spot. The Chinese also fuss over Aliberti, providing limousines, luxury hotels, and respect.

Nevertheless, balancing the positives and negatives of frequent international travel requires enormous flexibility and adaptability. Consider Joaquin Carbanel. He had to adapt early when his Cuban parents sent him to live in the United States at the age of nine. After earning a law degree, Mr. Carbanel joined BellSouth Corporation and subsequently spent much of his time shuttling between Atlanta and various South American countries. Mr. Carbanel says that being able to adapt your style to whatever culture you're in today is essential for survival as an international manager. Over time, Mr. Carbanel learned to handle big differences in business styles across three continents. Also important are foreign language skills, having a mentor to keep you "tuned in" at company headquarters, and resistance to jet lag. After all of his experiences, Mr. Carbanel says that "you feel at home wherever you are."[32]

Cultural Differences in Selection and Development Procedures

Earlier we suggested that cultural values shape how firms select and develop their international staff. For instance, among large multinationals, American and British firms use somewhat different procedures to select and manage expatriates than German and Japanese firms.[33] But perhaps the best illustration of this effect occurs when cultures collide. Consider what American Thomas Dimmick experienced when he was hired by Samsung, the South Korean electronics company, to help set up a plant in New Jersey:

"The hiring process was unique. Many people attended the interviews. Side conversations in Korean were the norm. Decision making inched forward as consensus was painstakingly achieved. The senior people did not commit themselves to a position until their respective staffs had fully and freely expressed their support or concerns for my candidacy. Personal issues were critical. Those items went beyond my wife and me. They penetrated into realms of what my father had done for a living, whether or not my mother worked outside of the home, and what my brothers and sister were doing. They all seemed to have a significance I could not fathom."[34]

Mr. Dimmick was dumbfounded because this hiring process differed dramatically from what usually happens in American firms. Plus, as Mr. Dimmick admitted, his own ignorance of Korean culture and hiring practices prevented him from understanding what was happening. Likewise, Samsung's Korean managers were obviously unaware that Americans would be shocked by the personal questions they asked. In the United States, such questions are off limits and are perceived as irrelevant, discriminatory, or both. In fact, simply asking some of these questions is illegal in the United States. Nonetheless, foreign managers may be unaware of these legal and cultural restrictions or simply find them hard to grasp. Korean managers may feel that a good hire can't be made without understanding candidates' home life, religious orientation, and family.[35]

Fortunately, selection procedures can be modified. For example, traditional American selection and job analysis procedures can be adapted to better fit some of the cultural values that Japanese firms often want to reinforce in their U.S. plants. How? It isn't easy. In one auto parts plant, the Japanese management wanted to stress team skills, consensus building, harmonious relationships, and other "Japanese values" when hiring American workers. But these values make the U.S. practice of openly comparing individual applicants an uncomfortable event for some Japanese. In contrast, American managers generally feel that it's their responsibility to pick the best candidate for a particular job, making comparisons between individuals difficult to avoid. Clearly, the American and Japanese approaches to selection are different. Fortunately, the selection system developed at the American plant cleverly blended Japanese and American approaches.

Under this blended system, groups of job applicants are asked to assemble windshield wiper motors. Individuals' performance within groups is then graded by a group of trained assessors who arrive at a final score for each person using a consensus decision process. All applicants who reach a predetermined cutoff score are considered qualified and hired as needed to staff the plant. This system combined individual assessment (American) with consensus decision making for overall evaluation (Japanese). It also allowed Japanese managers to assess what for them were critical issues, such as the ability of an applicant to work well in teams.[36]

Finally, the success of any selection or training program depends on whether it matches the culture of the employees being trained. For American managers, self-focused training does more to improve performance than group-focused training. The opposite is true for Chinese managers. To Americans, information about their capability to succeed at a task (self-focused training) seems more "useful" than information about the capability of a group that they belong to (group-focused training). Self-focused information is valued in individualistic cultures since performance is often defined in terms of a single person's actions. In contrast, Chinese managers may pay more attention to information that describes how a group that they belong to should approach a task. In collectivistic cultures, people view themselves as members of a group first and as individuals second. As a result, "performance" is defined in terms of shared responsibilities, making information about group performance more valuable. The upshot is that firms should take the cultural values of the audience into account when designing training programs.[37]

Managing Equal Opportunity and Organizational Diversity

In this section, we consider the challenges international companies face in managing diversity. Cultural norms, for example, can make it difficult for American firms to provide equal opportunities for potential expatriates, despite the legal requirement to do so. Consider the 1991 Civil Rights Act, which made it illegal for American firms to discriminate against U.S. citizens working abroad on the basis of color, sex, race, religion, or national origin. American firms can sidestep this requirement only if complying with U.S. law means a local law will be violated. For instance, if a foreign country's laws prohibit women from being managers, then U.S. civil rights laws don't apply to American firms doing business there.[38]

Usually, however, American companies face cultural rather than legislative hurdles. The American view that everyone deserves equal opportunity in the job market is a cultural value not shared everywhere. U.S.-based Colgate-Palmolive found this out when Brazilian employees asked to fill out a survey about "equal opportunity" in the firm had no idea what it meant. The wording of the survey was changed as a result.[39]

Actually, some believe that sending women or minorities into certain cultural environments overseas precludes their ability to be effective and sends a message that American firms want to export their human resource management philosophies. Granted, some Saudi Arabian men would not seriously consider doing business with Saudi women. And aspiring businesswomen in Saudi Arabia face the fact that it's illegal for women to drive cars.[40] Likewise, women have traditionally been viewed as subordinate to men in many African countries.[41] In Russia, about 75 percent of the unemployed are female and relatively few women have reached senior management.[42]

Japan is also a country where women often are expected to be subordinate to men, although this situation is changing.[43] Women occupy nearly half of the managerial positions in the United States, compared to less than 10 percent in Japan.[44] According to one survey, nearly 60 percent of Japanese women feel that men should provide income while women should take care of the house and children. The percentage of women with such views is much lower in North America and western Europe. For instance, only 24 percent of American women feel that men should be the breadwinner.[45]

In any case, American firms operating in places like Japan and Saudi Arabia sometimes refrain from sending female expatriates so as not to provoke local sensibilities. But American firms may lose lawsuits if they exclude women or minorities from overseas posts to avoid clashing with local cultural norms.[46] Of course, sexism may explain the reluctance of some U.S. companies to send women on overseas assignments. And this is hardly a phenomenon unique to American firms. European women also face discrimination that makes it harder for them to land expatriate assignments than for male counterparts of similar background and skills.[47]

The percentage of North American expatriates who are women ranges from 10 percent to 20 percent, underscoring the possible role of gender discrimination in expatriate selection. Some experts, however, predict that the percentage will rise as women continue to move slowly but surely into management ranks. Nevertheless, some women undoubtedly lose out on overseas opportunities simply because their superiors incorrectly assume that they're less interested in international careers than men are. Companies also may overstate the risks of sending women or minorities into supposedly hostile environments. The reality is that women posted abroad are usually seen as foreigners first and women second. Consequently, they're less likely to encounter the problems experienced by local women. Actually, gender may be an advantage to women in a foreign environment because it makes them more visible. Many women in overseas postings say that their foreign counterparts were curious about them. The fact that they were women made them more memorable and gave them greater access to important people.[48]

So how can firms help women expatriates succeed overseas? Consider these suggestions:

- **Hiring:** Give women serious consideration for overseas assignments. This helps root out inaccurate perceptions about the "handicaps" women face and underscores that women are more likely to succeed than men in certain situations.

- **Pre-departure training:** Firms can train women to take advantage of cultural attitudes about gender and to use their unique position in certain countries to increase their effectiveness. Women also need to be educated about how to respond to sexist remarks and forms of harassment they may encounter in certain countries.

- **On-site support:** Training on cultural and gender issues should continue for the first several months overseas. Among other things, this provides a forum for discussing any unexpected difficulties that may occur abroad. Firms can also help female expatriates by providing clear job titles and duties. Ambiguity in these areas can undercut a woman's credibility, especially in countries like Japan.

- **Role modeling after repatriation:** After they return, female expatriates should serve as visible role models for other women considering international careers. The idea is to show other women that it's possible to succeed as an expatriate, even in a "hostile" environment.[49]

But how do multinationals juggle diversity issues across dozens of countries? In essence, companies face two basic types of diversity issues. First, they have to effectively manage *cross-national diversity* (i.e., interactions between PCNs, HCNs, and TCNs). Then there's the challenge of managing **intranational diversity**—interaction between employees from a specific country who represent

intranational diversity Interaction between employees from a specific country who represent different races or ethnic groups

different races, ethnic groups, and so on. In fact, the continuing flow of immigrants into the U.S. job market has increased the intranational diversity challenges American firms face.[50]

There are four approaches for dealing with both cross-national and intranational diversity issues. The most functional approach, **multiculturalism**, involves being open to the positive aspects of all cultures. These cultural elements can then be used to create new ways of interacting and doing business. The least functional approach, **separation**, involves the rejection of all cultural values save your own. As you might expect, this strategy makes it virtually impossible for people from different cultural backgrounds to work together without conflict. The other two approaches fall between these extremes. **Assimilation** requires that subordinate groups (e.g., foreign-born employees working in a U.S. firm) conform to the values of the dominant group (e.g., the firm's American managers) to get along. This approach can produce distrust in the long run if the firm makes no effort to understand the values of the subordinate group. The last approach, **deculturation**, is really a benign form of separation. It occurs when each group maintains its own values without trying to influence anyone else (e.g., the expatriate who doesn't understand the host country's culture and has no desire to).[51]

But if multiculturalism is the best approach, how is it actually implemented? The first step is to embrace a broader view of cultural diversity. Consider Colgate-Palmolive (yes, the firm with the Brazilian survey problem). Clearly the stakes are high for Colgate-Palmolive. With operations in over 200 countries, roughly 75 percent of the company's revenues come from outside of North America. Colgate-Palmolive's approach centers on respect. All managers experience *Valuing Colgate People*, a program that shows how valuing differences can help achieve organizational goals. The program initially focuses on the firm's global values (e.g., caring for employees, teamwork). Later, issues in specific countries are examined. For managers in the United States, this means looking at things like racial, gender, and age discrimination. Elsewhere, the issue might be religious or class discrimination. The idea is to focus on the problems in each location that make it difficult for employees to respect each other. The final goal of the program is to examine whether firm procedures and systems support respect. For example, managers' performance evaluations include their efforts to model respect to their subordinates. Eventually, Colgate-Palmolive wants to extend the program to all employees worldwide.[52]

multiculturalism
An approach that involves being open to the positive aspects of all cultures

separation
An approach that involves the rejection of all cultural values except your own

assimilation
An approach requiring subordinate groups to conform to the values of the dominant group in order to get along

deculturation
An approach that allows each group to maintain its own values without trying to influence anyone else

▸ *The Case of Expatriates*

In this last section, we consider selection and development issues for expatriates. Clearly, American multinationals are relying on traditional expatriate assignments much less than before, thanks in no small measure to rising expenses and heightened security concerns in the post-9/11 environment. Indeed, U.S. companies are increasingly substituting for expatriates by hiring more locals, sending people on short-term overseas trips, and using technology (e.g., teleconferencing, e-mail).[53] Plus, it's important to remember that expatriates represent only a small slice of most firms' overseas workforce in any case (usually 1–2 percent).[54]

Nevertheless, there's no doubt that expatriates remain important to many U.S. multinationals. Moreover, the trend toward fewer expatriates and shorter assignments is not universal. For example, in one recent survey, Japanese firms were the most likely to report that they were actually moving toward longer expatriate stints overseas.[55] The bottom line is that expatriates often fulfill a variety of critical roles for multinationals, ranging from technical expert to subsidiary manager to relationship builder (perhaps as part of an informal coordination effort), either alone or in combination. Overall, there's simply no substitute for a long-term international assignment in many cases.

And on a broad scale, the number of Americans who work outside of the United States or travel overseas on business is staggering. Roughly 6 million Americans work overseas, with another 7.5 million embarking on foreign business trips every year. U.S. multinationals alone employ about 1.3 million expatriates of one kind or another. Also, roughly 80 percent of expatriates have a spouse or partner. Then throw children into the mix. Of the 70 percent of expatriate managers who are dual-career couples, some 60 percent have kids under 18. Taken together, a reasonable estimate might be that upwards of 3 million people are directly impacted by expatriate assignments—just in American multinationals. And some large multinationals do use expatriates extensively. Consider energy giant Royal Dutch/Shell. Although the firm uses local talent a great deal, it also has nearly 5,600 expatriates in some 120 countries.[56]

Of course, you may not find a three-year foreign assignment appealing. Perhaps you'd worry about terrorism, political upheavals, or your personal safety in general. Indeed, the perception is that the world has become a more dangerous place in recent years. Today, nearly 30 percent of some 240 foreign locations are ranked as high risk, compared to just over 20 percent in 1998.[57]

But maybe you're not the sort of person who would thrive in a challenging foreign environment in any case. Nevertheless, U.S. multinationals increasingly want their managers to have extensive foreign experience.[58] Despite that, using expatriates is a dicey proposition in many respects. When companies make mistakes in selecting and managing their expatriates, the consequences can be disastrous. Exhibit 12.5 summarizes these consequences.

Simply put, expatriates are very expensive even when things go well. Add up all the extras (e.g., higher pay, airfare for family members, moving expenses, housing allowances, education benefits for the kids, company car, taxes, home leave, extensive training, etc.) and the first year abroad can end up costing 300 percent of the expatriate's base salary. The bill for an overseas stay of three years can easily top $1 million per expatriate (Chapter 13 discusses expatriate costs in more detail). Next, we'll examine the factors that affect expatriate success and how companies can use this information to better manage expatriate assignments.[59]

Selecting Expatriates

When selecting expatriates, American companies often overemphasize technical skills, managerial qualifications, and the desire to quickly snuff out problems overseas. Indeed, European and Scandinavian companies tend to stress cross-cultural skills more and use a larger number of evaluation tools than American firms. This suggests a more strategic selection process for European and Scandinavian firms, one in which viable candidates are matched with the goals and requirements of a specific foreign assignment. Relatively few American firms systematically link their strategic goals to expatriate selection. Moreover, psychological factors (e.g., open-mindedness, curiosity, sociability) and family dynamics (e.g., the spouse or partner's willingness or ability to adapt to the foreign context) are often the most important predictors of expatriate success, particularly in certain locations.[60]

EXHIBIT 12.5   *Expatriates: The Consequences of Failure*

Consequence	Description/Implication
Premature return	Estimates of the percentages of expatriates who fail and are asked to come home (or request it), vary considerably (from 15–50%, depending on the type of assignment or the expatriate's situation). Regardless, a premature return potentially jeopardizes the firm's ability to compete effectively.
Wasted relocation costs	Sending an expatriate abroad (plus a partner, spouse, or children in most cases), not to mention belongings, is very expensive. Round-trip costs for a premature return can easily top $100,000.
Wasted preparation costs	A failed assignment means that the firm loses both the direct (e.g., support training expenses, overseas pay premiums, housing allowances) and indirect costs (e.g., not getting the job done) spent on preparing and supporting expatriates.
Other indirect costs	Failure hurts the career and confidence of the expatriate and damages relations with local employees, officials, customers, and suppliers (all of which will take time to repair).
Ineffective performance	Even if expatriates stick out their assignments, up to 50 percent may not be performing well (e.g., making poor decisions, hurting local relations).
Turnover after repatriation	Some 25% of expatriates quit within one year of returning from a foreign assignment, which leaves the firm with no return on its $1-million-plus investment for a typical three-year posting. Such turnover may reflect the fact that 75% of expatriates fail to receive a higher-level position upon their return.
Negative momentum	As word spreads of the problems that expatriates have (e.g., failure rates, "out-of-sight, out-of-mind" issues, lousy prospects after repatriation, etc.), recruiting new expatriates becomes harder, making it more difficult to coordinate foreign operations and capitalize on overseas opportunities.

Sources: Adapted from Birdseye, M. G., & Hill, J. S. (1995). Individual, organizational/work and environmental influences on expatriate turnover tendencies: An empirical study. *Journal of International Business Studies, 41,* 787–806; Black, J. S., Gregersen, H. B., & Mendenhall, M. E. (1992). *Global assignments: Successfully expatriating and repatriating international managers.* San Francisco, CA: Jossey-Bass; Carpenter, S. (2001). Battling the overseas blues. *Monitor on Psychology,* July/August, 48–49; Hauser, J. (1999). Managing expatriates' careers. *HR Focus,* February, 11–12; Poe, A. C. (2000). Destination everywhere. *HR Magazine,* October, 67–75.

In any event, how do multinationals evaluate candidates for foreign assignments? Clearly, practices vary. However, interviews (sometimes including spouses and partners), personality tests (e.g., measuring adaptability, emotional maturity), performance in training exercises, and an assessment of past accomplishments are typical screening tools used to select expatriates. Interviews are almost always used by American firms in the selection process. Beyond job-specific qualifications, these interviews often focus on individual factors that predict expatriate success. Other relevant success factors include aspects of the foreign location or the firm itself. As Exhibit 12.6 suggests, the list of potentially important factors is formidable.[61] A key, however, is to focus on achieving a good person-job fit when selecting expatriates for specific assignments. And that means assessing how individual, location, and firm-specific issues may interact—a tall order in many cases.[62]

EXHIBIT 12.6 *Expatriate Assignments: Factors That May Contribute to Success . . . or Failure*

Firm Factors	Assignment Location Factors	Individual Factors
Nature and extent of cross-cultural training provided	Extent of cultural differences with "home" environment	Tolerance, flexibility, ability to integrate headquarters and host country business practices
Communication/coordination mechanisms available to assist expatriates	Level of development (e.g., poverty, infrastructure, markets)	Coping skills, social orientation, ability to re-establish social networks
Nature of the assignment (e.g., how clear, how difficult)	Climate and stability (e.g., level of political/business risk)	Language knowledge, prior international experience
Career development plan (e.g., for repatriation)	Government regulation (e.g., of product content, labor use)	Education, functional expertise
Incentives offered	Proximity to home country	Family dynamics
Mentor availability	Attitudes toward foreigners	Management skills

Source: Adapted from Downes, M., & Thomas, A. S. (2000). Managing overseas assignments to build organizational knowledge. *Human Resource Planning, 20,* 33–48.

Indeed, the constellation of factors that produce successful expatriate assignments isn't the same for everyone. For instance, American, Japanese, and European expatriates may adjust and adapt to foreign assignments in different ways. These differences reflect variations in expatriates' home cultures and the human resource management practices used by their companies.[63]

But even if these complexities are taken into account in the selection process, the person chosen may not accept. The financial package will need to be attractive. In addition, safety, family, and career issues are often concerns. For instance, spouses and partners may have to quit their jobs to follow the expatriate. Some spouses and partners may veto the foreign assignment if they can't work or pursue educational opportunities in the host country. And there's good reason to worry about career issues since more expatriates are actually demoted than are given a higher-level job after returning. Many firms simply place returning expatriates in whatever positions happen to be open at the time. Ideally, companies should be explicit about how foreign assignments will help develop the expatriate's career. According to one survey, however, most companies make no firm promises regarding the job expatriates will have when they return.

But many companies are responding to the evolving concerns of potential expatriates (though bigger firms are most likely to offer help). For instance, about 25 percent of firms with expatriates now take the loss of spouse or partner income into account in constructing expatriate packages. In doing so, these firms offer job search, résumé preparation, or career counseling to spouses and partners. Likewise, roughly 90 percent of firms with expatriates permit location visits before a foreign assignment is accepted, and about 50 percent offer language training to family members accompanying expatriates. Extraordinary measures, at least by historical standards, are also being taken by some companies to recruit and protect expatriates, particularly in unsafe or unstable locations. For example, in 2003 one American construction firm offered expatriates willing to work in Iraq a $75,000 tax-free "hardship" bonus per year, a sum

EXHIBIT 12.7   *A Recommended Process for Selecting Expatriates*

Step	Description
1.	Create selection team.
2.	Define purpose of foreign assignment.
3.	Assess the foreign assignment context.
4.	Establish appropriate selection criteria.
5.	Recruit good candidates.
6.	Use multiple selection and evaluation methods.
7.	Interview expatriate and spouse/partner.
8.	Make foreign assignment offer.
9.	Transition expatriate into training program.

Source: Black, J. S., Gregersen, H. B., & Mendenhall, M. E. (1992). *Global assignments: Successfully expatriating and repatriating international managers* (San Francisco, CA: Jossey-Bass), 83. Copyright © Jossey-Bass Inc. By permission of the publisher.

nearly 60 percent of the average expatriates' base salary. Other companies now require extensive security briefings prior to departure (e.g., covering emergency procedures, personal safety advice, security risks, and the local political situation) and provide more secure living arrangements in risky places (e.g., walled housing with round-the-clock security staff).[64]

Overall, firms need a clear and coherent process for selecting expatriates (see Exhibit 12.7). First, companies should create a selection team consisting of home-country, host-country, and human resource managers. The human resource management role here is to identify potential candidates and to ensure that valid selection tools are used. Likewise, the home- and host-country managers should ensure the needs of both the parent company and foreign subsidiary are met. The next steps involve clarifying the purpose of the assignment and assessing how important cross-cultural skills will be in the foreign location. Once the first three steps are complete, the selection team can develop criteria for success in the position. The team can then use these criteria to identify good candidates (e.g., through referrals, job postings). Next, candidates should be screened using a portfolio of tools (e.g., interviews, exercises, tests). Throughout this process, the team should encourage expatriate candidates and their families to think about whether the assignment is really a good fit for them. The idea is to put the decision squarely where it belongs—with the potential expatriate.

Once the candidate pool has been narrowed, more in-depth interviews can take place that lay out the assignment in detail. These interviews should include what expatriates can expect to find in the host country and the ramifications of the assignment for their careers. Especially important at this stage is to conduct interviews with spouses, partners, and other family members. Preassignment visits may also help family members develop a better sense of what life in the foreign location will be like. Any concerns expressed by the candidate or family members about the location or assignment should be taken seriously and discussed in depth. Finally, the selection team can offer the position to the candidate with the best chances of success and, once accepted, take additional steps to prepare the expatriate.[65]

Training, Preparation, and Adjustment of Expatriates

But what constitutes effective preparation for an overseas assignment? Generally speaking, training and preparation should be part of an ongoing process, with rigorous efforts made before, during, and after repatriation (expatriates often experience a culture shock at the beginning of their foreign assignment and again once they return home). All training programs should have two basic goals: (1) to help employees be effective in their overseas jobs as quickly as possible; and (2) to minimize any adjustment problems expatriates and their families have in their new environment as well as after they return.[66]

But the unfortunate reality is that many firms give expatriates no cross-cultural training prior to departure (nearly 40 percent of all firms with expatriates fall into this category according to some estimates). And when it comes to small- to mid-sized companies, the figure may be closer to 90 percent. This flies in the face of evidence suggesting that cross-cultural training can improve the ability to adjust to new cultural environments as well as boost job performance.[67]

So what should training look like and what should it include? Learning from cross-cultural training involves a three-step process. The first step involves *paying attention to cultural differences* that explain why foreigners think and behave the way they do. Next, expatriates *must retain knowledge about behavior that is culturally appropriate*. In other words, expatriates must think about the new cultural knowledge they receive and use it to develop a mental framework for their own behavior. Such a framework helps expatriates remember how to behave in foreign settings and the consequences of mistakes. The last step involves *practicing culturally appropriate behavior* that is consistent with expatriates' mental frameworks. This trying-it-out process helps expatriates fine-tune culturally appropriate behaviors and increases their confidence when interacting with foreign colleagues, clients, and suppliers.[68]

The training itself can range from superficial activities that can be covered in a few days to extremely rigorous efforts requiring substantial time and effort. In fact, some intensive training efforts may take months. Exhibit 12.8 displays the range of training rigor possible and some associated activities. Determining the right mix of rigor and activities is critical. In making this determination, firms must assess how important the assignment is, how long it will last, and the extent to which an expatriate must interact with the local population. For instance, if an expatriate's job requires extensive interactions with locals and communication norms in the foreign country are different, then more rigorous

EXHIBIT 12.8 *Levels of Cross-Cultural Training Rigor*

Level of Rigor	Time Duration	Activities Included
Low	4–20 hours	Lectures, films, books, area briefings
Moderate	20–60 hours	Everything above, plus role plays, cases, survival-level language training
High	60–180 hours	Everything above, plus assessment centers, simulations, field trips, in-depth language training

Source: Black, J. S., Gregersen, H. B., & Mendenhall, M. E. (1992). *Global assignments: Successfully expatriating and repatriating international managers* (San Francisco, CA: Jossey-Bass), 97. Copyright © Jossey-Bass Inc. By permission of the publisher.

cultural toughness
The extent to which a foreign culture is different from a person's home environment, making adjustment more difficult

training in communication is advisable. This example also underscores the importance of assessing **cultural toughness**. In other words, how different is the assignment location's culture from the home culture of the expatriate? Everything else being equal, the greater the difference from the home culture, the more difficult the expatriate's adjustment process in a foreign country will be. Consequently, more rigorous training is needed for expatriates headed to countries that, to them, are high in cultural toughness. For instance, Americans typically have more trouble adjusting in African, Middle Eastern, and Far Eastern countries than they would in western European countries. In essence, the cultural values Americans encounter in Kenya may seem more "foreign" than those encountered in Germany. Overall, cultural toughness shows up repeatedly as a factor that negatively affects expatriates' adjustment and even their willingness to accept a foreign assignment in the first place.[69]

Trends in Expatriate Preparation Some multinationals are going to great lengths to create sophisticated training programs for expatriates. Royal Dutch/Shell, for instance, sent surveys to 17,000 former, current, and potential expatriates, as well as family members, to systematically assess the issues confronting employees in foreign assignments. The company used the results to develop better training and career-management programs.[70]

Many training programs now try to improve open-mindedness by challenging expatriates' prejudices, assumptions, and attitudes about different cultures. This goes beyond the short, superficial courses on business etiquette overseas often used in the past. Today, firms are more likely to emphasize understanding and respecting all cultures in their training approaches. That's what Motorola had in mind when it built a cultural training center in Illinois. Among other things, the center implemented courses designed to help company managers become more effective in whatever cultural context they found themselves.[71] But how well such extensive efforts actually work is open to debate. One expert put it this way: "We have a pretty good handle on what the skills and traits are that are necessary to do well in a cross-cultural environment, but we still don't really know whether we can effectively train people in those skills."[72]

Earlier we noted that many firms are doing more to address safety, family, and dual-career couple issues. In part, that's because many of these issues are already causing problems and are unlikely to go away (they may well get worse). For instance, 88 percent of Fortune 500 firms in one survey said that dual-career problems will create more expatriate selection and performance headaches in the years ahead. Indeed, the expatriate's family situation is often the most important predictor of success or failure—even more important than cultural skills, adaptability, or job knowledge.[73]

The good news is that involving spouses, partners, and children in predeparture cultural training can improve the adjustment of expatriates and their families, especially when combined with other forms of assistance (e.g., help with spouse/partner job searches or lost income replacement).[74]

Nevertheless, when it comes to training and preparation, expatriates would be wise to look out for themselves. As one expert observed, "It would still be rare to find a company that is utilizing everything that research has shown us about selecting, training, developing, and supporting expatriates."[75]

Consequently, expatriates may want to take steps on their own to prepare for overseas assignments. That might mean signing up for college courses to help build skills and abilities not included in company training. Expatriates may also find it worthwhile to seek independent advice from firms that specialize in cross-cultural training (e.g., Chicago-based Cendant Intercultural: **www. cendantintercultural.com**). Soliciting insights from people who have been posted to the country where the expatriate will be sent may be another good option. Finally, if not already provided by the employer, a predeparture visit to the host country (with the family) could prove very useful and help ease the settling-in process. Once abroad, expatriates can also seek out an impressive network of groups that offer support, advice, and, in some cases, camaraderie. Many of these groups were founded by expatriates and can be easily accessed on line (two such examples are **www.anamericanabroad.com** and **www.tales mag.com**).[76]

Returning Home: Repatriation Issues

Unfortunately, the need for preparation, planning, and training doesn't end when expatriates leave for some exotic foreign locale. A host of potential problems also await expatriates when they return. These **repatriation** problems explain the high turnover rate among expatriates after they return home. Consider these common repatriation challenges:

repatriation
The return and adjustment of expatriates to their home country after an extended stay overseas

- Changes in the home country and in the expatriate's values after several years abroad make the home environment seem foreign.

- Changes in the home company require major adjustments and new learning upon return.

- Experiencing a new job after return is often difficult (e.g., it may be a demotion, a role disconnected from the overseas assignment, or a job not on a clear career track).

- Having to reorient to living conditions in the home country that are quite different from those encountered abroad.

- Feeling unappreciated by the firm after performing well overseas.

- Having to adjust to a lower standard of living after returning home (no more foreign service premiums or fancy benefits).[77]

Many companies now realize how expensive it is to neglect repatriation issues and some address repatriation issues before the expatriate leaves. For instance, Monsanto, the pharmaceutical, chemical, and agricultural giant, started a repatriation program to combat high turnover among its expatriates. In large part, expatriates' dashed expectations for promotions and advancement on return were causing the turnover problem. Monsanto now does predeparture planning for the jobs expatriates will have when they return. The firm also gives returning expatriates opportunities to showcase their overseas accomplishments publicly and provides counselors to help with any readjustment problems. Such programs can improve the performance and adjustment of employees after an overseas assignment.[78]

Attacking the "out of sight, out of mind" problem is also a key issue. Some companies deliberately bring back expatriates several times a year to give them visibility and thank them for their work. Expatriates can meet with important managers and, ideally, a designated expatriate mentor. Return trips home serve to jump-start the adjustment process. And the longer expatriates are away, the more difficult they will find it to return. To combat this effect, firms can increase the frequency of home visits as the final return date approaches, especially for employees gone for more than two years.

For example, Coherent, Inc., a U.S.-based manufacturer with several overseas offices, brings expatriates home for short stints of a few months before their final return. During this time, expatriates complete modest projects. They then return to their foreign postings to conclude their affairs before coming home for good. This months-long period in the United States helps reacquaint expatriates with the office, their colleagues, and ongoing projects. It also gives expatriates an extended taste of life back home. Overall, the program has helped cut down the repatriation adjustment period. Exhibit 12.9 lists some additional steps that firms can take to ease the repatriation process.

EXHIBIT 12.9 *Steps for Improving the Repatriation Process*

Time Frame	Steps/Description
Before departure	• Clearly communicate reentry job options. • Establish career development plan. • Appoint home and host country mentors to support expatriate. • Arrange home visits for visibility.
Six to nine months before return	• Narrow list of reentry job options. • Send expatriate job openings/listings. • Ask expatriate to polish résumé. • Conduct home office visits to facilitate adjustment and schedule job interviews.
Three to six months before return	• Conduct briefings with employee and family about what they've learned. • Brief employee and family on changes in the home country that may impact their return. • Ask employee to list personal/professional expectations about the return to minimize misunderstandings and correct mistaken assumptions. • Explain firm's moving policies and repatriation programs—especially those dealing with financial issues.
Immediately upon return home	• Assign employee and family to a welcome-home group consisting of former expatriates. • Match employee with a home sponsor who will cover changes in company structure, policy, technology, or products/services. • Provide returning spouse with career-related assistance (e.g., job-hunting help). • Offer counseling for more serious problems. • Show that the firm cares about overseas experiences.
Three to six months after returning home	• Provide training that addresses reentry shock, pace of any negative feelings about the return. • Assess how employee's new skills and experience can be better used by the firm (ask employee for suggestions). • Re-assess adjustment process to identify outstanding problems and offer assistance.

Sources: Adapted from Shilling, M. (1993). How to win at repatriation, *Personnel Journal* (September); Solomon, C. M. (1995). Repatriation: Up, down, or out? *Personnel Journal*, January, 28–37.

Chapter Summary

We began this chapter by discussing the strategic value of international human resource management. However, developing specific human resource practices that support firm goals may require that companies develop an *international human resource philosophy* that will help shape *core international human resource policies* as well as human resource strategies used in specific markets. For instance, multinationals wanting to quickly enter transition economies may want to adopt an invest-in-employees strategy, particularly if they are using market entry options that typically create human resource challenges (e.g., buying local firms, building greenfield plants, or setting up joint ventures).

We also pointed out that the selection and development of international staff is a complex issue. In doing so, we examined the skills that international managers need to be successful.

Next, we considered the basic options for staffing foreign operations. These include *PCNs*, *HCNs*, and *TCNs*. Some firms are trying to develop an *international cadre* of managers who can be sent anywhere in the world. Companies are increasingly using *inpatriates*, foreign employees brought to the home country for various developmental assignments, to increase commitment.

Sometimes firms embrace a particular selection philosophy in making staffing decisions. At one extreme is a *geocentric* approach—where ability is all that matters. An *ethnocentric* approach, in contrast, means that only PCNs will be posted in key overseas positions. *Polycentric* and *regiocentric* approaches fall between these two extremes. In a polycentric approach, human resource management control is in the hands of the foreign subsidiary, although headquarters still makes key decisions. Likewise, under a regiocentric approach, most foreign employees will not move into headquarters positions. However, employees can move from country to country in a particular region.

This chapter also examined the broader issue of managing both *cross-national* and *intranational diversity* in organizations. For instance, firms are sometimes reluctant to send women to certain countries because of local biases. But such concerns are usually overstated. Indeed, in certain foreign locations, women may actually be more likely to succeed than men because of local attitudes.

Finally, we considered several issues associated with *expatriates*. Clearly, the consequences of failed expatriate assignments are often severe. Therefore, companies need to use selection criteria that accurately predict expatriate success. Of course, expatriates also need to be prepared to deal with all the cultural and lifestyle changes that will be encountered abroad. The exact nature and level of training needed should be driven, in part, by the *cultural toughness* of the foreign location. Preparation is also needed if employees are to be successfully *repatriated* back to their home countries. Fortunately, companies are moving toward more sophisticated repatriation programs that kick in before the expatriate has even begun the foreign assignment. Such programs can have a positive impact on employees' adjustment and performance after returning home.

Discussion Questions

1. Why is having an international human resource management strategy important for companies?

2. What are some of the pros and cons associated with using PCNs, TCNs, and HCNs?

3. How does culture impact the selection and development of international employees?

4. What are some of the major approaches that companies can take to managing diversity? Which approach has the best chance of success in your view?

5. What should the basic elements of a successful program to select, prepare, and repatriate employees destined for foreign assignments look like? How can cultural toughness, family issues, and concerns about gender be managed effectively?

business.college.hmco.com/students

Up to the Challenge?

Motorola's Moves in China

AT THE BEGINNING of this chapter, we asked how Motorola might have responded to human resource management challenges in China, especially given its large investment there. Clearly, Motorola has taken a variety of successful steps to adapt to the Chinese human resource management environment, one where practices continue to evolve as China becomes a more competitive economy in the global marketplace.

Initially, Motorola had two major human resource problems in China. First, Motorola needed a local workforce that could meet the firm's world-class quality standards. Motorola felt that the local labor pool lacked the skills and the obsessive approach to quality it desired. The company realized that it could intensively train workers in all aspects of its operations if it had 100 percent ownership of its Chinese plants. So when Motorola began negotiating with China in 1989, 100 percent ownership was something it bargained for and eventually won. Motorola also realized that building training programs around existing corporate slogans like "Six Sigma" (meaning factories should have no more than four defects per million products shipped) would appeal to Chinese employees. Sloganeering is something that generally works well in China. And sure enough, it only took new Chinese employees at one Motorola plant six months to hit the Six Sigma quality target. As one expatriate managing a Motorola cell phone plant in China put it, "We can do anything here that we do anywhere else. The learning curve is a fast ramp."

The second major challenge for Motorola was to hold on to its highly trained Chinese workforce, an expensive investment that could be lost to competing companies' hiring forays. Indeed, thanks in large part to rapid economic growth (and the bidding wars for talent that come with it), Chinese supervisors and managers voluntarily leave firms in China at an astounding rate (over 40 percent a year in some management classifications). To stem this tide, Motorola pays its employees extremely well by Chinese standards. Plus, in a nod to China's "iron rice bowl" tradition of housing subsidies, Motorola built several hundred condos for their Chinese workforce, offering a cut-rate ownership deal to employees who could come up with a down payment.

Although Motorola's investment gamble and Chinese human resources practices seemed to work well for several years, they were expensive. Moreover, Motorola competes in a volatile set of industries that change and evolve rapidly. This combination of expensive operations and heavy competitive pressure (including challenges from upstart Chinese firms), caused Motorola to pull back in late 2003. In essence, Motorola felt it could no longer afford its "own and staff" approach.

Specifically, Motorola dumped its Tianjin chip manufacturing plant, selling a majority stake to a local contract manufacturing firm, Semiconductor Manufacturing International Corp. A slowdown in the chip sector caused Motorola to rethink the wisdom of continuing to equip the Tianjin plant, a facility that had already cost the company $1 billion. Indeed, Motorola decided to move toward an "asset light" approach that relied more on contract manufacturers to produce chips and other components. The logic was that having other firms build and run high-tech plants (which means that the other firms assume all the HR challenges and headaches) was simply cheaper for Motorola, particularly when it was being squeezed by competitors. Despite that, Motorola isn't completely out of the Chinese manufacturing game yet—the firm continues to run another chip-making plant close to the Tianjin facility in which it retains full ownership.

Overall, Motorola's success with its HR policies in China could not overcome fundamental business challenges that put pressure on its bottom line. That was particularly true in China itself as multinational and local competitors increasingly made life difficult for the firm. An irony in all of this is that China's government continues to take steps that should cut down some of the benefits-related expenses incurred by multinational employers. For instance, proposals to make it easier for Chinese to buy homes should reduce the pressure on companies to provide employees with expensive housing benefits. Moreover, while China's interior provinces are still overregulated and hamstrung by state-instituted controls, they remain a source of cheap labor. These regions represent the next frontier in China as foreign companies that have hugged the comparatively wealthy eastern coast of China move inland.

So what would you advise Motorola at this point? Hang it up completely and get out of the expensive business of owning plants in China? Or concentrate on owning fewer plants and building an effective Chinese workforce that: (1) gives Motorola the control and high-quality production it desires; and (2) is reasonably immune to talent raids from other firms? If you lean toward the latter option, what else might Motorola do to attract, motivate, and retain its Chinese employees? Needless to say, Motorola and other foreign companies still face plenty of challenges as they cope with the evolving business and human resource management scene in China.[79]

International Development

What Is Your International Orientation?

Purpose

The goal here is to develop self-insight regarding your level of experience with and interest in other countries and cultures. This may provide some indication as to whether you might be attracted to and succeed in a foreign work environment.

Instructions

The following sample items are taken from the International Orientation Scale. Answer each question and give yourself a score for each dimension. The highest possible score for any dimension is 20 points.

Dimension 1: International Attitudes

Use the following scale to answer questions Q1 through Q4, placing the appropriate number next to each question.

5	4	3	2	1
Strongly agree	Agree	Not sure	Disagree	Strongly disagree

Q1. _____ Foreign language skills should be taught as early as elementary school.

Q2. _____ Traveling the world is a priority in my life.

Q3. _____ A year-long overseas assignment from my company would be a fantastic opportunity for my family and me.

Q4. _____ Other countries fascinate me.

_____ Add up total score for Dimension 1

Dimension 2: Foreign Experiences

Q1. _____ I have studied a foreign language.

1 = Never
2 = For less than a year
3 = For a year
4 = For a few years
5 = For several years

Q2. _____ I can speak another language.

1 = I don't know another language.
2 = I am limited to very short and simple phrases.
3 = I know basic grammatical structure and speak with a limited vocabulary.
4 = I understand conversation on most topics.
5 = I am very fluent in another language.

Q3. _____ I have spent time overseas (traveling, studying abroad, etc.).

1 = Never
2 = About a week
3 = A few weeks
4 = A few months
5 = Several months or years

Q4. _____ I was overseas before the age of 18.

1 = Never
2 = About a week
3 = A few weeks
4 = A few months
5 = Several months or years

_____ Add up total score for Dimension 2

Dimension 3: Comfort with Differences

Use the following scale for questions Q1 through Q4, placing the appropriate number next to each question.

5	4	3	2	1
Extremely different	**Quite different**	**Somewhat different**	**Mostly similar**	**Quite similar**

Q1. _____ My friends' career goals, interests, and educations are . . .

Q2. _____ My friends' ethnic backgrounds are . . .

Q3. _____ My friends' religious affiliations are . . .

Q4. _____ My friends' first languages are . . .

_____ Add up total score for Dimension 3

Dimension 4: Participation in Cultural Events

Use the following scale to answer questions Q1 through Q4, placing the appropriate number next to each question.

5	4	3	2	1
Always	**Often**	**Some- times**	**Rarely**	**Never**

Q1. _____ I eat at a variety of ethnic restaurants (e.g., Greek, Indian, Thai, German).

Q2. _____ I watch the major networks' world news programs.

Q3. _____ I attend ethnic festivals.

Q4. _____ I visit art galleries and museums.

_____ Add up total score for Dimension 4

Self-Assessment Discussion Questions

Would you like to improve your international orientation? If so, what could you do to change various aspects of your life?

Is an overseas assignment something that is attractive to you? Why or why not? Are there specific places in the world that you would be interested in going to as an expatriate? Places that you would not? Why?

———————

Source: This exercise was prepared by Paula Caligiuri, School of Management and Labor Relations, Rutgers University. Used with permission. As appeared in *Management international: Cases, exercises, and readings* by Dorothy Marcic and Sheila Puffer. Copyright © 1994 by West Publishing Company, Minneapolis/St. Paul, MN., a division of International Thomson Publishing, Inc. Reprinted by permission.

 Tapping into the Global Network

Learning More about International Human Resource Management in Specific Firms

Purpose

This exercise has two basic goals: (1) to learn more about the human resource management issues facing companies in overseas subsidiaries and other international cooperative relationships; and (2) to compare how different companies try to cope with the international human resource management challenges they face.

Instructions

Your instructor will divide the class into groups of three to six people. Each group should interview at least two managers (preferably oncs with some human resource management responsibility) at a local company engaging in international business activity that requires staff abroad. Examples of activities requiring overseas staff (i.e., expatriates, local employees, or third-country nationals, either alone or in combination) include:

- having offices in foreign countries to help market and sell products or services.
- running foreign subsidiaries that deliver services or manufacture products.
- having joint ventures abroad.
- being part of an international alliance to develop technology, build a product, share information, or make international deals.

The purpose of the interviews should be to assess the international human resource challenges facing the company and to determine what strategies the company is using to resolve them. You may want to include the following general questions in your interviews:

- What is the nature of your involvement in international business operations?

- What are the key human resources challenges facing your company in its international operations (e.g., staffing foreign operations, not having enough control to deal with local issues)? Why do these challenges exist? To what extent do they reflect cultural, legal, or political differences across countries?

- What human resource strategies, policies, and practices have been developed to overcome these challenges? Have they been successful? Why or why not?

You may wish to develop other, more specific questions on your own that are tailored to particular companies. Likewise, your instructor may ask you to research specific international human resource management issues and develop questions aimed at examining how local companies have responded.

To conclude the exercise, each student group should make a 15-minute class presentation about their findings. If using small groups is impractical, your instructor may set up this activity as an individual assignment. Likewise, if interviewing managers is impractical, your instructor may treat this activity as an Internet research assignment designed to answer the questions raised.

There are a variety of information sources available, many of them on the Internet, for doing outside research on international human resource management issues. For instance, you may find the following websites useful in your research efforts (either for generating questions, better understanding the employee side of international human resource management issues, or learning more about specific company practices):

- **www.expatriates.com/** (a website with an extensive directory of expatriate-oriented links).

- **www.hrspectrum.com/articles_pres. htm** (a consulting-firm website with some useful tidbits about international human resource management issues).

- **www.hrvillage.com/** (a website aimed at helping firms and individuals respond to human resource management issues).

- **www.shrm.org/** (website of the Society for Human Resource Management, a professional organization that provides a wealth of information and links).

- **www.workindex.com/exthome.asp** (basically a meta-site with thousands of links and listings about human resource management issues and tools).

After all groups have made their presentations, your instructor will lead a class discussion (another 15–20 minutes) that focuses on three issues:

- To what extent do the human resource challenges reported reflect the type of international operations companies are engaged in?

- To what extent do the human resource challenges reported reflect country-specific factors (e.g., cultural differences)?

- Assess the quality and appropriateness of the human resource strategies being pursued by various companies. Are there any suggestions for improvement?

13

Evaluating and Rewarding International Employees

Learning Objectives

After reading this chapter, you should be able to:

▸ Identify problems in appraising performance and then providing feedback about performance levels to people in different cultures.

▸ Realize that compensation is one of the main reasons to evaluate performance and that this means *more* than just level of pay.

▸ Appreciate the fact that compensation has different inherent meaning across cultures.

▸ Understand the different models that are available for compensating expatriates and apply the best method.

INTERNATIONAL CHALLENGE

Receiving a Performance Evaluation Overseas

You have been assigned by your firm to the People's Republic of China for an extended work assignment. You have never been to China before, but you feel your company did a very good job preparing you to live and be a manager in this new culture. You have learned a few words of Mandarin and you think you will even get the tones correctly so that others will understand you. And despite getting sick the first two weeks of the assignment, you have bounced back quickly, working hard and avoiding the usual homesickness. After your first six months on assignment, you are evaluated. The evaluation, however, is very puzzling. You have done a good deal of reading and you are aware that China is a group-oriented (collective) culture. So during your first few months as manager, you tried some group involvement techniques. In particular, you tried to get your employees to participate in decision making about the production line setup and supply ordering system. In cases where this did not work out too well, you gave the team and its leaders quick and direct feedback in an effort to be useful. Apparently, these techniques backfired miserably, and you received a neutral or ambiguous evaluation by your host-country boss. Although you didn't realize it until months later, this evaluation turned out to be a very bad thing, likely to be a setback for potential promotions when you return to the United States. On top of this, you didn't realize how expensive good housing is in Shanghai. Your salary, while adjusted upward for this overseas assignment, does not make up for the high cost of living. All this makes you wonder if you should have done what your peer group of managers did—turn down an assignment in China! This, in turn, has you wondering about your old peer group. What are they doing and how are they positioned for future roles in the company? What is your future role? All this has you further pining for the comforts and clarity of home. What went wrong here and how might you stop this downward spiral? Think about possible explanations as you read this chapter. We will discuss our interpretations in the *Up to the Challenge?* box at the end of this chapter.

▸ *Performance Appraisal*

Performance evaluation is one of the most controversial (and probably hated) events for most employees. Likewise, if you ask a group of practicing managers what they dislike most about their jobs, the task of evaluating employees is often at the top of their list. The annual (or more frequent) **performance appraisal** is usually despised by everyone. Partly this distaste results from a general reluctance to provide employees with direct feedback about their performance. Few managers enjoy this process, especially when the performance feedback is negative. Furthermore, the process itself is inherently difficult.

performance appraisal
The provision of feedback about performance on the job

Giving an Evaluation

Put yourself into the typical evaluation situation. Let's say you have six people who report directly to you and your job is to determine how well they performed their jobs. Unless you took extensive notes on each employee as the year unfolded, this task—at a minimum—requires a good memory. You have to recall the accomplishments and the limitations of each person. Then you might need to sum these pluses and minuses across the year-long evaluation period accurately, trying not to be overly influenced by recently occurring events or overly salient events. For some jobs (like sales), this process may be easier than it is for others (research and development). Nonetheless, you must then compare these summed and appropriately weighted evaluations across your six people. If you don't distinguish the six people from one another, your boss may wonder why you don't have the fortitude to give someone a negative evaluation. Further, your pool of rewards is very limited, so you have to rank your people from first to sixth. As if all of this isn't tough enough, now comes the hard part. You may have to meet with each person to give them the feedback and tell them what level of rewards you think they deserve. No wonder people dislike this whole process!

Now, however, imagine that your job is to evaluate one of your people who is on foreign assignment. You may have visited the foreign location during the year, but you did not have a chance to see and evaluate the manager's performance in the way that you are used to. Further, you have limited understanding of the environment she works in and the larger cultural and country impediments to her performance. In other words, we could take the usual level of dislike for performance evaluations and multiply it by two or three to gauge the difficulty in evaluating expatriate performance. The first half of this chapter details the problems and pitfalls that can occur when conducting performance evaluations of expatriates and foreign nationals that you may be working with. The second half of the chapter reviews the intricacies of compensation for these groups of people.

Performance Evaluation for Expatriates

As we said, many companies are recognizing the importance of a global perspective. In particular, they understand the value of learning and using new motivation methods, negotiation techniques, and more. In order to do this, however, they must often send managers abroad to gain that global perspective. Research has shown that this technique is often successful.[1] In one study, 150 expatriate managers were surveyed about the expertise they developed overseas. These managers reported that an overseas experience resulted in the following changes in their skills:

- An increased ability to manage cultural differences.

- A better ability to understand the multinational firm and relations between domestic and international operations.

- A more open mind about different problem-solving methods.

- A more flexible approach to dealing with human resources.

These are all valuable skills for the employee and positive outcomes for the company, but for a number of reasons they may not be realized or even recognized by a particular firm. One reason is that few of these skills are usually assessed in a normal (domestic) performance appraisal. Second, even if the dimensions are considered, they are very difficult to evaluate. For example, how would you decide whether your employee has an "open mind" or can "better manage for cultural differences"? Third, "open-mindedness" almost has to be seen to be evaluated—often through repeated interactions with others. Fourth, people from different cultures give and take appraisal feedback in very different ways. One culture, for example, may value loyalty and commitment to the firm very highly, whereas others may not. Likewise, some cultures do not give feedback publicly, even if that feedback is positive. So, not only is evaluation an unwanted but necessary part of the job for a manager to start with, more problems emerge when they are conducted from a distance—either a geographic distance or a cultural one.

Despite these problems, most multinationals evaluate the performance of their expatriates, regardless of their country of origin or their assignment. The remainder of this section will deal with several important questions about performance appraisal: (1) *Who* should evaluate the performance of the expatriate? (2) *When* or how often should they be evaluated? and (3) *What* in the performance of an expatriate manager should be evaluated?

Who Should Evaluate Performance?

A company has a large number of options for evaluating domestic or expatriate employees. In addition to a traditional supervisor evaluation, performance could also be judged by one's peers, subordinates, and/or customers. In a global setting, however, there are often two different sources for each of these evaluators. For example, while an American manager assigned to the Netherlands may have a Dutch boss, he or she may still have a boss in the United States. There is much controversy about which evaluation source is better—the evaluation by the host manager or the evaluation by the home office manager. We will discuss the pros and cons of each of these sources in turn.

Evaluations by Host/Local Managers An expatriate will often have to be evaluated by local management. That manager may be familiar with the expatriate's culture, and may be a national of that country as well. Alternatively, the manager could be from virtually anywhere in the world. Regardless, that manager will probably appraise the expatriate's performance from his or her own cultural perspective. In a very large sense, this is a good thing. After all, the expatriate was sent overseas to do a good job in that foreign country. And the quality of the expatriate's job in large part may revolve around how culturally aware and savvy he or she is. So a manager who is from the Netherlands and thus is familiar with local cultural values and behaviors may be in a very good position to judge whether or not the expatriate is aware of those cultural norms and is using them to advantage. Likewise, having a **host-country evaluation** takes advantage of the host manager's knowledge of the expatriate's performance that is based on daily interactions. The manager has seen more of the expatriate's performance than nearly anybody, and almost certainly more than the home office manager, who may be back in the United States.

Using host-country managers to conduct appraisals, however, is not without problems. One source of the problems is the very thing we mentioned above as a possible advantage—the host managers' use of their own cultural frames of reference. A story about an American working in India illustrates this point.[2] Following the current rage in the United States, this American manager tried to use some participative management by asking his Indian subordinates to provide input and new ideas about a project. While this technique may have worked well in the United States, it did not in India. As we noted earlier in the book, Indian culture is high in power distance and more autocratic leadership is expected. Accordingly, the Indians felt that the U.S. manager did not know what he was doing. A good manager should not have to ask his employees for ideas. One result of this situation was that the expatriate received very negative performance evaluations from his host manager. And later, upon his return to the United States, this incident had a lingering effect on his career—it was one of the reasons he was denied a promotion.

You could say that that manager's problem performance deserved a negative evaluation. After all, if you are going to be an expatriate manager, then you should be aware of one of the primary cultural values embodied in the country to which you've been assigned. Perhaps the blame could also be placed on the home office for having failed to provide cultural training for this manager. Regardless of where the blame lies, however, this can be an issue with the use of host-country nationals as the source of an appraisal. If the home office manager had conducted the evaluation, the performance rating might not have been nearly so negative.

There are other potential problems associated with a host manager's performance evaluation. There is always the language problem; the manager may not be able to clearly communicate feedback to the expatriate. Also, the dimensions of performance that are evaluated may be different for the host manager and the home office. Some things may just be more salient or important to the host manager and therefore may carry unusually heavy weight in the evaluation. An expatriate in China, for example, may learn over time to show considerable restraint in sharing her feelings, even if she is upset at one of her subordinates. This trait may count positively in an evaluation by a host Chinese manager. For a U.S. evaluator, however, this "restraint" may count negatively. Finally, an appraisal by a host-country manager may not be tied closely to the company's overall global strategy. So if the expatriate acts in a way that may not directly benefit the foreign subsidiary but does benefit the corporation as a whole, she or he may still receive a negative performance evaluation. In a case like this, we hope that the home office would recognize the overall benefit of the expatriate's performance, but they may not. Instead, they may simply focus on the easier piece of information to gather and digest—the appraisal by the host manager. Overall, then, the use of host-country managers to conduct appraisals has both

host-country evaluation Performance appraisals provided by managers from the country where the multinational has located a facility

pluses and minuses. A multinational may, therefore, want to consider using home office personnel for performance evaluations.

home-country evaluations
Performance appraisals provided by managers in the home office to employees stationed overseas

cultural identity
When an evaluator shares many of the same cultural values and beliefs of the employee being evaluated

Evaluations by Home Office Management There are clear advantages to **home-country evaluations**, in which a home office manager conducts a performance evaluation. For one, this person may be familiar with your work or pattern of work. The new information provided by your expatriate experience could be integrated and evaluated in this context. Second, this person presumably speaks the same language and thus could have a leg up on a host-country manager in communicating feedback. Third, this person probably shares many of the same cultural values and beliefs that you have. This **cultural identity** provides the capability for much to be shared and learned from a performance appraisal. Collectively, these characteristics appear to provide distinct advantages to the home office manager as the provider of performance evaluations.

On the other hand, however, there are also some disadvantages associated with using the home-country manager as the evaluator. Again, these problems result from the very thing that offer advantages to home-country managers—the fact that they are geographically and psychologically distant from the employee who works at a foreign location. Specifically, a home-country manager typically receives very little feedback or information about the employee to be evaluated. And considering that the home office manager has little if any opportunity to observe the employee, there can be problems with the quality of the evaluation. In fact, in the study of overseas employees described earlier, expatriates reported that they did not have much contact at all with the home office during their overseas assignment. And what little contact that did exist was often not with their direct supervisor. It was the rare expatriate who had home office contact more than several times a year. Even worse yet, this sporadic contact was usually initiated by the expatriate. One can only presume that this contact resulted from encountering a significant problem that required intervention by the home office. While this situation has probably changed for the better due to the availability of improved and cheaper technology, mere contact does not equate with understanding. In fact, another potential problem with the use of home office appraisals is these managers' relative lack of familiarity with the intricacies of the expatriates' foreign posting. These evaluators may not have any experience working in the country where the employee is assigned. As a result, they may not understand the pressures the expatriate faces and the standard to use when evaluating their performance. Again, what is worse is the fact that about 67 percent of upper managers in U.S. corporations have no international experience whatsoever, let alone experience in the country in question.[3]

What's the solution? Some firms have tried to capitalize on the strengths offered by both host- and home-country evaluations by getting both types of managerial evaluations on the same employee. For example, firms such as AT&T and 3M Corporation have developed a "career sponsor" program to link the expatriate to the corporate office. The sponsor's job is to keep the expatriate in touch with what is going on at home and to act as a mentor. Many times, these sponsors will conduct performance evaluations using the cultural perspective of the home office, and assessments of such programs show them to be successful.[4] Likewise, research on U.S. multinational firms show that a balanced set of raters from both the home and host country relates positively to the accuracy of performance evaluations.[5]

When Should Performance Be Evaluated?

As for domestic evaluations, the question of *when* to do performance evaluations is not easily answered. In the United States, the most common interval used between evaluations is six months, while a nearly similar percentage conduct appraisals on an annual basis. As usual, however, when it comes to the international stage, things get considerably more complex. On one hand, it seems premature to conduct an appraisal after six months on a foreign assignment—even if the complete overseas assignment is only designed to last one year. After all, as we discussed in the previous chapter, expatriates need time to adjust to their very new and different surroundings. Likewise, considerable time is necessary for family adjustment. Thus, six months would appear to be too soon to conduct the first appraisal. On the other hand, if it is obvious that things are not going well, it would behoove management—in either the host or home country—to let the expatriate know as soon as possible. It seems inappropriate to let the problems fester for yet another six months before giving any feedback.

So what is the answer here? At first blush the answer would seem obvious—use a compromise strategy where expatriates get some informal feedback early on in their assignment period and wait until the end of the first year for the formal appraisal. The problems with this compromise have been detailed earlier. For one, home office contact with the expatriate is not that frequent as it is; accordingly, even the compromise strategy is difficult to execute. Additionally, for the host-country manager, such informal feedback may be culturally difficult or inappropriate to deliver. As a result, that manager may be constrained to wait until the formal evaluation is scheduled. Finally, a six-month period that covers the necessary adjustment time may just not be enough time to see any effects of the expatriate's performance. So, as with domestic appraisals, the question of timing is not easily answered. As unsatisfying as it may be, the answer is probably a fuzzy one—that is, evaluate at the "right" time for the particular assignment.

What Should Be Evaluated?

In some ways the questions of "who" and "when" are much easier to answer than the issue of *what* should be evaluated.

Variables that Affect the "What" Question   Whether you choose a host- or home-country evaluator and regardless of when and how often the appraisal is conducted, exactly *what* should be evaluated? This is an extremely complicated question, and one for which there is also no single answer. A sales job may involve different skills than may be required in financial or production management. Beyond this general blanket statement, however, there are some very important considerations to keep in mind when you are evaluating performance. There seem to be at least three important variables that can affect an expatriate's performance and should be taken into account when constructing and delivering a performance appraisal: (1) the *environment* in which the job is done, (2) the *task* or tasks themselves, and (3) the *personality* of the expatriate.[6]

Environmental Variables   The circumstances under which any job is performed can be more or less demanding. Working in a mine is more difficult than working in an office. This notion of **environmental variables**, however, expands

environmental variables
The extent to which the environment in which an employee works presents special challenges that might be recognized in a performance evaluation

greatly when we consider a cross-cultural performance appraisal. That is, working for a mining company in Zimbabwe is probably more difficult than working for one in Montana. In general, some environments are easier to work in than others, and this fact may determine the performance level of an expatriate manager. Given the little time that is spent communicating with the expatriate, however, we assume that the full impact of these environmental variables will not be appreciated. For example, experts point out that you should probably not give an expatriate manager in Mexico a negative evaluation if the productivity of his employees is only half the average productivity of an American plant.[7] Although this result seems indicative of poor managerial performance, it must be tempered and benchmarked in light of the Mexican work environment. In particular, if that performance level was observed, it would show that the expatriate manager actually has employees working at a level that is about four times higher than the usual Mexican plant! In short, we must appreciate that the expatriate manager is dealing with the constraints of working in Mexico, not the relative advantages of managing in the United States, Germany, or Japan.

task variables
The extent to which the job itself presents special challenges to an employee

Task Variables A second set of variables—**task variables**—deals with the actual tasks themselves that are being undertaken. Close attention should be paid to the duties or types of job assignments that may affect performance levels.[8] Certain tasks require a greater amount of interaction with others. Being adept in the area of cultural "awareness" is much more important in these tasks than it would be for other assignments. A software engineer, for example, is less likely to need these cultural skills to be successful than would a production manager. The latter must interact with a large number of foreign nationals in order to be successful. Likewise, during foreign assignments, middle-level managers might be responsible for interacting with local and regional government officials. In the United States, this function is usually reserved for the highest officers in the organization.[9] Thus, there are differences in the types of tasks expatriates and nationals perform in general, let alone the task variations across different foreign assignments. The manager who performs the appraisal might not fully appreciate these task differences.

personality variables
The degree to which people differ in their ability to handle the difficulty and ambiguity inherent in a foreign assignment

Personality Variables Finally, there are simply inherent differences among individuals in their abilities to handle a foreign assignment. These are **personality variables**. In Chapter 12 we described research that looks at who may do better in a foreign assignment than others. In fact, otherwise good performers may be poor ones if their personality leads them to be closed to change or not sensitive to others. Clearly, traits like these could negatively impact their performance and perhaps derail a career that would have been otherwise successful without the foreign assignment. Since the choice of the person for the overseas assignment is one of the few variables that firms have a great deal of control over, personality predictors of adjustment should be considered important.

Problems in Cross-Cultural Evaluations

Even if your firm has considered these three important constraints on performance overseas, they still may run into some problems with an appraisal system. Perhaps the biggest obstacle may be exactly what to measure about an employee's performance. You may say, "No problem. If the expatriate is a reasonably high-level manager, we could use a variety of financial measures to index their performance. After all, the reason we set up a foreign operation was to make money, not to break some culture barrier." Well, even with this straightforward logic in mind, things are not as easy as they seem. For one, most financial performance data are subject to a conversion problem, including sales revenue and some other important measures. Worse yet, some currencies are not convertible to other (foreign) currencies. As several authors pointed out, the fact that you made nearly 300 million yuan on your operations in China may be not that meaningful if it's not possible to bring that money out or if there are constraints on doing so.[10]

A second reason to look closely at financial performance measures is that many multinationals use a variety of techniques to minimize their taxes and to avoid possible losses from fluctuations in the value of the foreign currency. Accordingly, the true contribution of the foreign subsidiary to the overall financial performance of a firm is often masked via these techniques. Experts recommend, therefore, that many traditional financial measures of performance not be used as the primary determinant of an expatriate's performance evaluation because they are cruder than similar values measured domestically. If you still wish to use financial yardsticks to evaluate an expatriate's performance, some experts recommend that a second set of measures be calculated that purifies the influence of the financial differences across borders. Given that we already know that the home office maintains little contact with the expatriate, it seems unlikely that most companies would find the time and money to do this. Instead, a variety of other general guidelines should probably be considered in evaluating an expatriate's performance.

Guidelines for Expatriate Evaluation

We have said a lot about the problems and pitfalls involved in a performance appraisal for an expatriate. What are some of the practical implications of all this? What in the way of guidelines can we suggest for better appraisals of performance?

Rating an Assignment One suggestion is to do a thorough assessment of the general difficulty of the foreign assignment faced by the expatriate.[11] Then, a difficulty score could be used to weight the normal performance appraisal process. For example, if the expatriate has received a very difficult assignment, her usual evaluation could be multiplied by 2.0. If the foreign posting is only moderately difficult, then the process could be weighted by 1.5, and so on. Of course, the challenge for human resource personnel is to figure out which assignment is more difficult than others.

Factors that Determine Assignment Difficulty Experts point to at least three things that probably play a crucial role here. First, the extent of language adjustment—if any—would certainly add to assignment difficulty. An expatriate with Holiday Inn could have some assignments where the language of use is English (e.g., India), whereas for other assignments (e.g., Tibet) they may need several languages from the Sino-Tibetan family. Since Chinese and Tibetan are extremely difficult languages to speak, let alone write, this would certainly add to the difficulty of an assignment in Lhasa, Tibet. Although strongly related to language usage, the degree of *cultural toughness* can also affect difficulty of assignment. Clearly, an assignment in London or even Amsterdam would be easier for most American expatriates than would one in Quito, Ecuador, or Jakarta, Indonesia.

Finally, *economic and political stability* are factors that would determine difficulty. We discussed these issues in detail in Chapter 2. For now, however, we simply note that the political and economic problems in any one country can be very difficult for an expatriate manager to overcome. Those who do well in such environments are probably performing at very high levels. For example, one set of authors relates a story of a relatively high-ranking American expatriate who was instrumental in stopping a strike in the firm's Chilean plant. This strike would have shut down the plant and soured relations with the home office. They pointed out that stopping the strike was a very large accomplishment for an American, especially in a country that is used to such strikes. Clearly, the expatriate manager must have demonstrated a good deal of cultural acumen and insight. Because of the volatility in exchange rates in Chile, however, demand for the plant's product temporarily decreased by 30 percent. Rather than recognizing the excellent performance of the expatriate in averting the strike, the home office focused on the negative sales figures. As a result, the expatriate received an undesirable, lackluster performance evaluation.[12]

General Guidelines Beyond rating the difficulty of the assignment, an evaluator can also do the following:

- Place somewhat more weight on evaluations performed by home-country managers; all in all, they are more familiar with actual performance of expatriates than are host-country managers.

- If the home office has responsibility for the evaluation, they should try to involve another person with expatriate experience in the same country in the appraisal process.

- If the host country has responsibility for the evaluation, those managers might be well advised to seek input from the home office manager before conveying it to the expatriate employee.

Issues Involved in Evaluating Foreign-Born Employees

Until now, we have focused on the important task of completing a performance appraisal on an employee assigned overseas. You may also be asked to evaluate the performance of a foreign expatriate, perhaps based in the United States. For example, a Chinese national may be assigned to work in one of your company's U.S. plants. Likewise, even if you are assigned overseas, it may be your job to conduct an evaluation of the performance of the foreign nationals working with you.

Under each of these circumstances, things get even more complex. Beyond all the issues we discussed above, you'll also have to grapple with exactly how you should deliver feedback—regardless of whether it is good or bad news. There are very wide differences in the way that employees get feedback. For example, one study looked at the form of appraisal systems in five Arab countries.[13] It was found that the systems themselves were basically informal, with little evidence of forms, files, and documents that we are used to in the United States. As a result, feedback in Arab countries is largely subjective and informal, with an emphasis on the interpersonal aspects of performance on the job. It is unlikely, therefore, to see papers change hands or written evaluation documents enter a file for future reference. This presents an interesting situation because many multinational firms simply export their formal and explicit performance appraisal forms to their foreign subsidiary.[14] As a result, there is great potential for a culture clash when an implicit and informal culture meets an explicit and formal evaluation system.

Even the feedback itself is likely to be moderated by culture. For example, given that we know Japan to be a collectivist culture, we should not be surprised to find that performance appraisal is likely to be done in a group setting. Of course, such a venue for delivering feedback is rare in the individualistic United States. While some might say that the popularity of team approaches in the United States has many firms thinking about group evaluations, they certainly are not the major way evaluations are conducted.[15] Further, the effects of various types of praise or criticism—whether delivered in a group or alone—vary considerably among cultures.

Perhaps the best way to illustrate these differences is to consider England—a country that has all the appearances of being culturally similar to the United States. One study did just that by looking at how performance feedback would affect the behavior of the Americans and the English.[16] It found that Americans became more productive after receiving either praise or criticism. In general, the more feedback they received, the higher their subsequent performance. This finding was observed for the English *only* after they received praise for their behavior; they did not respond well to criticism.[17] In fact, criticism is a type of feedback that is not often delivered effectively in England. Apparently, German workers are similar on this count—in general, they are often resentful of feedback because they believe it makes them admit failures and shortcomings.[18] Likewise, other research showed there can be wide differences in reactions to performance appraisals among Asian countries (e.g., Indonesia, Malaysia, the Philippines, and Thailand), even though we may be tempted to group these cultures together.[19]

So feedback is not equally effective in different cultures. Exhibit 13.1 presents an analysis of these and other differences one is likely to see in performance appraisal systems and feedback across three different cultures. This figure shows that there is wide variance in how an appraisal is conducted and what is (and is not!) said during the appraisal. In the United States, for example, the emphasis in the appraisal is on evaluation, not on development or improvement per se. Criticism is direct, with little eye toward saving the face of the person receiving the evaluation. In other cultures, however, the process of providing the feedback is monitored much more carefully for its effect on the recipient. In Korea, for example, feedback is very indirect, with great concern for saving face. Despite this admonition to pay close attention to cultural differences, even among apparently similar countries there are some general things to keep in mind when delivering performance feedback. The following International Insights provides some very general guidelines that are probably instructive for all of us, even if there are specific differences among cultures.

▶ *Compensation of International Employees*

One of the main reasons that companies spend time conducting appraisals and developing their unique cultural approaches is the effect the appraisal has on **compensation**. And often one's compensation is tied to one's future with the company. Thus, we will discuss a number of important issues about

compensation
The set of ways that employees are recognized for their performance, including pay, vacation time, stock options, and more

International Insights

Giving Performance Feedback to Foreign Employees

IN THE UNITED STATES, managers are often told to reward in public and criticize in private. This advice, however, may not always be the best for your foreign employees. One expert provides the following specific recommendations for crafting feedback that you might deliver through a performance evaluation. Although this advice does not always hold true for every foreign national, the following suggestions are very good starting points for the American manager:

- **Give feedback through a third party:** In many cultures, direct feedback—even if it is positive in form—can be very uncomfortable. If you belong to a collectivistic culture, being singled out for feedback can be very disconcerting. Accordingly, feedback may often be best delivered (even in individualistic cultures) through a trusted third party.

- **Communicate to the whole group:** In addition to this suggestion, another way to blunt the effect of direct feedback is to gather the work group together. One can then provide the set of feedback you wish to communicate to the gathering as a whole. Since some work today is team based, this method is probably a good technique for individualistic cultures as well.

- **Change the form of the feedback:** Almost always there are several ways of saying the same thing. Try several different approaches, even if the employee gives the appearance of understanding what you are saying.

- **Simplify the feedback:** This recommendation applies to feedback for any employee, but especially a foreign one. And it refers to the fact that we can almost always simplify and clarify what we mean. For example, you can eliminate or replace needless words. For example, the phrase "in spite of the fact that . . ." could be simplified to *though* or simply *although*. (Other examples: "the reason why is that" to *because*; "This is a subject that" to *this subject*.)

- **Avoid slang:** Phrases like "the bottom line," "they'll eat this one up," "the home stretch," "I'm all ears," and "let's get rolling" are difficult to interpret. Although these phrases are so common to us that they are obvious, consider the perspective of someone from another culture.[20]

---

compensation across borders and cultures. As you will see, there is a wide disparity across countries in pay levels—for workers and executives alike. This alone is an important area to study, but it is further complicated when it involves a cross-national assignment. Wage and benefit differences across countries present a set of practical problems for international human resource personnel. We will discuss these issues in the last half of this chapter.

Compensation Systems

Probably the first (and only) thing most people think of when they hear the word *compensation* is their level of pay. However, we are compensated for our work in many ways beyond pay level alone. For one, health insurance coverage is one of the relatively hidden parts of our paycheck. Health care costs represent a large and increasing cost to firms, especially those with an international presence. Additionally, pension plans, vacation and personal time off,

EXHIBIT 13.1   *Differences in Performance Evaluation Systems across Three Countries*

Appraisal Characteristic	United States	Saudi Arabia	Korea
General emphasis	Evaluation	Evaluation/coaching	Coaching
Amount of feedback	High	High	Low
Delivery method	Individual	Individual	Individual
Emphasis on face saving	Low degree	High degree	High degree
Level of employee involvement	Medium to high	High	Low
Type of feedback	Criticism is direct	Criticism less direct	Criticism very indirect
Level of formality	Formal; probably written	Informal; not written	Informal; not written
Determinant of positive appraisal	Visible performance criteria	Seniority/connections	Seniority

Source: Harris, P. R., & Moran, R. T. (1991). *Managing cultural differences* (3rd Ed.). Houston, TX: Gulf. Reprinted by permission.

recreation facilities, and more are all other sources of substantial cost to firms. And there is considerable variation in compensation methods across jobs within our culture, let alone across cultures. How do companies in other countries and cultures compensate their employees, including the leaders of their firms?

The Meaning of Compensation

One issue to contemplate before considering differences in various types of compensation is the meaning of compensation across cultures. Compensation in the United States is thought of as the swap of effort and output for wages and benefits. This "exchange" model of compensation is common among many Western individualistic cultures. But even among these cultures, compensation may mean more than just exchange. In Germany, for example, the word for compensation implies achievement. Apparently, the word originated among shoemakers who custom-fit shoes to the buyer's feet. Shoes that "measured up" were ones that deserved compensation.[21] The Japanese word for compensation suggests a protection or safety net. The notion of trust inherent in this perspective makes the more paternalistic Japanese employment system easier to understand. These examples suggest that compensation as a simple exchange may be specific to the United States and similar cultures. Accordingly, topics such as entitlement and obligation may play a more important role when compensation is delivered across cultures. Surely, you are bound to encounter some of these expectations about the employment relationship when doing business across borders.

Pay Levels across Countries

Wage levels vary across countries and cultures. In fact, it is common to read about companies that have or are considering moving their facilities offshore because of wage differentials. Beyond any social issues raised by such practices, we presume that these moves are intended to save (or make) money. We used to live in Milwaukee, Wisconsin, and while there we saw several companies fold up their operations and move elsewhere. For instance, Briggs & Stratton, the company that makes small engines for lawnmowers, moved some of their operations in Wisconsin to Mexico, where labor costs—pay levels in particular—are lower. And Wisconsin is hardly alone as firms look closely at labor costs in other countries.

Data show that there are many countries with labor costs that are similar (e.g., Canada, France, the United Kingdom) or even higher (e.g., Belgium, Germany, the Netherlands, and Sweden) than those in the United States. Germany, for example, has costs that are approximately 152 percent of the costs for U.S. production workers. While these data do not paint the complete cost picture for a firm that is considering a relocation, they are instructive. Cost differences partly explain why some foreign firms have built factories in the United States (e.g., BMW, Honda, Nissan, Toyota) and why some firms, such as Briggs & Stratton, are leaving the United States. The Bureau of Labor Statistics (BLS) reported that Mexican labor costs in the late 1990s were only 25 percent of those in the United States. Certainly, this figure can explain in large part why thousands of U.S. firms have established *maquiladoras*—plants set up just across the U.S. border within Mexico.[22]

We should note that these data are rough estimates; there are large differences within countries in compensation rates (witness some companies moving from Michigan and Wisconsin to Kentucky). Likewise, the in-country data are also subject to some further interpretation. For example, while the BLS estimates that Mexican wages are only 25 percent of U.S. costs, other estimates put this ratio at closer to 40 percent. Nevertheless, even the higher estimate produces an effective labor cost of $6/hour in Mexico relative to $16.70 in the United States.[23] Apparently, the difference in these figures results from extra-production costs that are not reflected in the BLS estimates. It is customary in Mexico, for example, to pay a Christmas bonus of one month's pay. Likewise, it is common and expected that Mexican workers receive 80 percent of their base pay for vacation bonuses in addition to bonuses paid for being punctual. Also, the Mexican government requires that firms distribute 10 percent of pretax profits to employees. Although this can be unequally distributed among workers, an estimate of the average cost per employee can be built in to these estimates. Finally, Mexican law mandates that workers be paid 365 days a year.[24]

CEO Compensation across Countries

Cross-national differences also emerge when we consider the compensation of managers and CEOs of U.S. firms relative to executives of foreign companies.[25]

Relative Compensation Exhibit 13.2 presents data regarding the average compensation of CEOs from various countries for firms with annual revenue of $500 million or more.[26] The figures show the compensation of CEOs relative to average workers. Some that claim the high base salaries paid to U.S. executives is misleading. Indeed, U.S. CEOs do have very high base salaries—they are the highest in the world. But the total compensation package also far and away favors United States executives. The CEO of Computer Associates, Charles Wang, took home a base salary of (only) $4.6 million in 2000, but he pocketed over $650 million in long-term compensation. It may be that the marginal tax rates in the United States lead Americans to be cash crazy, but they don't explain the massive CEO–average worker pay discrepancy.[27]

Perks and Other Compensation The compensation policies of many firms recognize the bite taken by taxes and as a result firms try to reimburse their CEOs in nontaxable ways. One common way is by providing **perks**. For example, consider the package received by a Portuguese executive who may be earning a mere $35,000 a year. This person may have a maid, a gardener, and a washerwoman. In addition, he or she will probably be given a company car (with gas), housing, a monthly expense allowance (about $500), and his/her utilities will be paid. Likewise, a Mexican executive with a base pay of $30,000 will receive a company-supplied car and chauffeur along with a certain amount of groceries and liquor delivered to his or her home twice a month.[28] Because of tax rates, the Japanese executive may receive among the best set of perquisites. In fact, a Japanese firm often pays up to 50 percent of mortgage interest for all employees, and as they move up, they get much more. Managers may also get a car/chauffeur, a bigger expense account, and paid memberships in exclusive golf and social clubs (known in Japan as "castles"). In fact, an American working in Japan said this about one of his Japanese colleagues: "Each time he got promoted, he moved to a better house. And as his expense account grew, the bars he'd visit would get better."

perks
Compensation extras not ordinarily given to typical employees (e.g., chauffeur/driver, cook, gardener, etc.)

Total Compensation In spite of the higher level of perks paid to executives in most other countries, the overall package clearly favors Americans. In fact, in terms of total compensation, American CEOs far outpace those from the other countries listed in Exhibit 13.2. A comparable Italian executive receives only a

EXHIBIT 13.2   *Oceans Apart: CEO Compensation Ratios across Countries*

Country	CEO Pay*	Country	CEO Pay*
United States	475	Italy	20
Venezuela	50	Canada	20
Brazil	49	Belgium	18
Mexico	47	Spain	16
Singapore	44	Netherlands	16
Argentina	44	France	14
Malaysia	42	New Zealand	13
Hong Kong	41	Sweden	12
United Kingdom	24	Germany	12
Thailand	24	Switzerland	11
Australia	23	Japan	11
South Africa	22	South Korea	8

*Average CEO pay is reported as a multiple of average manufacturing employees' pay.
Source: Adapted from ———. (2000). Chief executives' pay. *The Economist,* September 30, 110.

fraction of the compensation that an American CEO receives on average. Also, there is much greater emphasis in the United States on variable forms of compensation. Bonuses and incentives based on performance account for about 50 percent or more of the total compensation of U.S. executives, whereas for the other countries this percentage reached a high of only about 23 percent. All in all, we see a dramatic difference that favors U.S. chief executives.[29]

Vacation Time

Exhibit 13.2 does not include one other very important part of a compensation package—vacation time. Perhaps you've heard about the vaunted vacation time received by many European workers and executives. Exhibit 13.3 shows that there are indeed large differences in the number of paid vacation days per year across countries. As with our discussion of how CEO compensation is driven by tax codes, vacation time is also affected by legal regulations. For example, whereas Sweden mandates a minimum of thirty paid vacation days per year, Hong Kong only requires seven paid days and there is no minimum at all in the United States or the United Kingdom. Likewise, there is some variation in the number of holidays observed in various countries. Collectively, this shows that the typical number of paid vacation days ranges from a low of about thirty in the United States to a high of forty-six or forty-seven in France, Germany, and Hong Kong.

All these figures suggest that one needs a complete understanding of a country's laws and customs to fully understand the compensation costs associated with doing business there. We do not, however, wish to overstate the impact of the laws and customs of each individual country. Indeed, some evidence suggests that there is increasing similarity in compensation practices (e.g., in wages, benefits, and other legally required compensation) among countries with similar cultures. In fact, one study analyzed the effect of both country and cultural categorization on compensation practices.[30] These researchers found that cultural grouping (e.g., Asian, Latin, European, etc.) explained compensation patterns much better than country-level customs and laws.

The Basis for Compensation across Countries

We know from the foregoing that there are differences in compensation across both countries and cultures. On what basis do various countries and cultures provide compensation? The study just discussed suggests that cultural practices are important to consider. To answer this question fully, however, we refer back to our earlier discussion of the meaning of compensation across cultures. Some countries, such as the United States, refer to compensation as an exchange. This label suggests that the notion of *equity* is a major basis for determining level of compensation. Equity prescribes that those who contribute more are deserving of greater compensation. As we discussed in Chapter 11, U.S. firms are more likely to operate on this equity principle than perhaps firms in any other country.

This equity standard, however, is not the only one used to determine compensation levels. Consider the French as an example. Like most European countries, their traditional bonus system is not tied closely to performance. In fact, in France it is common for many employees to receive an extra month's salary before their traditional vacation time in July or August and once again before

EXHIBIT 13.3   *Paid Vacation Days in Various Countries*

Country	Lawfully Required Number of Days	No. of Days Usually Given	Legal Holidays	Total Paid Vacation Days
Canada	10	20	11	33
France	25	25–30	16	46
Germany	15	30	16	46
Hong Kong	7	20–30	17	47
Japan	19	20	16	36
Mexico	14	15–20	19	39
Sweden	30	30	14	44
United Kingdom	0	25–30	9	39
United States	0	20	10	30

Source: Milkovich, G. T., & Newman, J. M. (1999). *Compensation.* Chicago: Irwin. Reprinted by permission.

Christmas. This pattern leads many French to think in terms of net pay. In fact, when they are offered a monthly salary, the French quite automatically ask, "Is it net or gross?" and "How many times a year do I get this salary?"[31] As a result, the French have gotten very used to these bonuses, so much so that they really consider them as part of their base pay. In fact, there have been cases of companies that introduced additional equity-based pay opportunities but then quickly regretted it. In one French company, for example, a performance-based bonus was paid for two straight years because the company did well. The third year, however, saw a drop in performance and no such bonus was paid. The Works Council (a union-like organization in France), however, did not accept this and threatened to close down the plant. Apparently, the "bonus" had become viewed as an entitlement and strong feelings were expressed. As a result, the company paid the bonus. Mexico carries this practice a step further by systematizing worker acquisition of compensation extras. In particular, Mexico has an "acquired rights" law that mandates that if a bonus or benefit is given out at least two years in a row, it becomes the employee's right to receive it in the future.[32]

The Japanese view of compensation is paternalistic—one that implies rewards for loyalty and commitment. So one would predict that performance is determined by these more long-term concerns and is indexed by things like ability to get along with others, longevity, and seniority. As a result, Japanese firms are more likely to compensate their employees for seniority than are U.S. firms. One study, for example, examined the pay raise decisions of a group of Japanese and American managers.[33] These managers were asked to allot pay raises to a group of employees, including people described as low and high performers. The results were consistent with what we might expect. The U.S. managers gave much higher raises to the high performers and much lower raises to the poor performers than did the Japanese managers. For example, the Japanese gave about twice as much of a raise to low performers than did the Americans. Likewise, they gave about 80 percent less to high performers than did the U.S. managers. Thus, there appears to be a much higher link between performance and pay decisions for U.S. than Japanese managers.

🌐 International Insights

Hiroshi Okuda—A Nail That Stuck Out at Toyota

THE PRESIDENT OF TOYOTA (and until recently Chairman) was Hiroshi Okuda, and apparently he stood out in a crowd. For one thing, his appearance was different from that of most Japanese executives—he is over six feet tall and stood out in a crowd whether he was in Detroit or Tokyo. More importantly, he was very outspoken and frank. An example was a dinner he held with American journalists, where he more than held his own in English. One question about his competition prompted Mr. Okuda to say, "I don't understand why Ford chose that kind of styling for the Taurus; it is too round. In Japan that styling was popular four or five years ago." Similarly frank comments about the

superiority of Toyota's Lexus operation in Japan over that in Kentucky also drew attention. Toyota's own PR department muttered off record that if you stick out all over the place, you are going to get banged. Even a friend said of Okuda, "He sticks out all over the place."

There is no doubt that he stuck out at Toyota. For one thing, Okuda was the first person outside the Toyoda family to run the company. Technically he was not the CEO—that position during his tenure was still held by 71-year-old Shoichiro Toyoda. Everyone knew who was in charge, however—Mr. Okuda. He changed many things about the company, much of which appeared to be for the better. Toyota was due for a

---

Although these findings are probably true of many Asian firms that share the Confucian tradition, that tradition may be in the process of changing. Results of a survey of 1,900 Japanese human resource officers shows that the relative impact of seniority to merit in determining pay raises had changed over the last 20 years. While Japanese firms do indeed use seniority as a major mechanism to determine a pay raise, the weight placed on ability/merit (54 percent) relative to seniority (46 percent) changed over the last two decades. The weight given to seniority dropped over the period covered by the survey. One can only guess that the current rate is significantly less than the 46 percent reported in this study.[34] The accompanying International Insights suggests that if Toyota is any indicator, then the change may be even more dramatic. It also shows, however, that Japanese who openly advocate equity as the basis of compensation can still attract considerable notice and resistance.

Other research also reports that the number of British firms that have implemented equity compensation systems had increased by a factor of about five in the past few decades.[35] Additionally, that research also showed that international compensation systems are becoming more and more similar.[36] Nevertheless we still see differences. In fact, Exhibit 13.4 presents expected differences in compensation methods across three of Hofstede's most important cultural dimensions.[37]

Expatriate Compensation

So far we have reviewed differences among countries and cultures in various types of compensation. It is also important, however, to consider the compensation packages and necessities of an *expatriate* employee.

shakeup, given its erratic performance before Mr. Okuda's arrival. Beyond the many problems with the Japanese economy, Toyota was also dealing with a common problem for family-run companies. Sometimes a family member whose time has come to lead just isn't up to the task. Apparently, this was the case when Tatsuro Toyoda ascended to Toyota CEO in 1992. A close company observer said, "Tatsuro was very civilized but a lousy businessman." Toyota by then had become big and lethargic. Mr. Okuda was brought in to change entrenched management attitudes. He believed that only younger executives had the vigor and imagination to run a big company like Toyota. Accordingly, he announced a new policy that took titles away from general managers at age 55 and managers at age 50. They were allowed to stay on with the firm, but with seriously reduced responsibilities.

With these and other actions, Mr. Okuda completely overhauled Toyota's traditional seniority-based promotion system and remodeled it with a new emphasis on merit. "I had no choice," he said. "Employing young people is vital to any company." Mr. Okuda also cleared away the deadwood from the board of directors and retired about a third of Toyota's top executives. Although the normal retirement age is 60 in Japan and most of these people were over that age, it is still unusual, because of the Japanese reverence for seniority, to force such guidelines on top management. Nevertheless, younger men were put in their place, some jumping several grades with one promotion—again, a highly unusual move in Japanese corporations. In a *Fortune* interview a few years ago, Mr. Okuda said, "So far we have not been able to rejuvenate the workforce as I had hoped. The general impression is that Toyota is old and conservative." Apparently, more than the traditional seniority system will change at Toyota in the future.[38]

Expatriate Costs As we discussed in Chapter 10, when U.S. multinationals establish a presence overseas, they often send over their managers to run that unit. And, simply stated, the use of expatriates is expensive! The average annual **expatriate cost** to send an employee overseas is about $300,000.[39] In fact, this figure is about five times as high as a domestic relocation. One firm estimated that a $100,000 executive could cost at least a million dollars to post overseas for three years.[40] What accounts for all these costs? There are the usual things involved in a move, including interviewing and actual moving costs themselves. And each of these factors is more expensive for an expatriate than for a domestic relocation. A majority of companies, however, go well beyond this by providing a large number of costly benefits. These can include financial allowances and assistance with acclimating to the foreign culture. Exhibit 13.5 presents some examples of additional costs that could be incurred with an expatriate.

expatriate costs
The total costs necessary to send and support an employee to work out of the country on an extended assignment

Although many companies are aware of the many additional costs faced by expatriates, a surprisingly high percentage (77 percent) of those who return from an assignment are dissatisfied with the compensation they received.[41] This unhappiness can make expatriates less willing to adjust to a new culture, less productive, and more willing to leave the firm after they return from their foreign assignment. Accordingly, it is worth looking at the main goals and components of the expatriate compensation package in order to improve on expatriate satisfaction and performance.

Models for Compensating Expatriates As detailed in Chapter 12, an expatriate assignment can be difficult. There are cultural, language, and environmental adjustments, among others, to be made. These difficulties are no secret to the potential expatriate. Accordingly, a firm must design a compensation plan that will be enough of an incentive to attract good people. There are a variety of ways to classify the methods that multinationals use to devise such plans. One main

EXHIBIT 13.4   *Predicted Compensation Practices across Cultures*

Cultural Dimensions	Sample Countries	Characteristics of Compensation System
Individualism–Collectivism		
Individualist	United States Canada New Zealand United Kingdom	Performance-based compensation schemes; equity for distribution; rewards given for individual efforts
Collectivist	Indonesia Japan Korea Singapore	Extra performance variables; group compensation scheme likely to be successful; equality/need rule important
Power Distance		
Low	United States United Kingdom Denmark Australia	Wage gap between lower and higher job, jobs not often great; profit sharing/gain sharing likely to be successful
High	Malaysia Mexico Philippines Spain	Hierarchical compensation; compensation tied to one's place in the social structure; large salary gap between workers and management
Uncertainty Avoidance		
Weak	Singapore Sweden Canada United States	Lots of variable/contingent compensation; bonuses/pay at risk, dependent on performance
Strong	Greece Japan Korea Portugal	Highly structured, lock-step compensation plans; centralized decision making and evaluation; discretionary pay minimized

Sources: Adapted from Gomez-Mejia, L. R., & Welbourne, T. (1991). Compensation strategies in a global context. *Human Resource Planning, 14,* 29–41; Hodgetts, R. M., & Luthans, F. (1993). U.S. multinationals' compensation strategies for local management: Cross-cultural interpretations. *Compensation and Benefits Review,* 42–48.

ad hoc compensation method
A method by which an expatriate will negotiate with his or her firm for covering the costs inherent in a foreign assignment

method is the *ad hoc* **approach**, in which individual employees negotiate with their firm for covering the costs inherent in a foreign assignment.[42] While this approach has some merit, the drawbacks include the potential for unequal treatment of expatriates and a lack of country-specific knowledge (e.g., taxes, cost of living, etc.) on the part of both the firm and the employee. Although a firm may be able to successfully negotiate down its costs with an expatriate, several experts have pointed out that this strategy may be shortsighted. The employee who takes the foreign assignment may quickly find out that the compensation (in total or part) is inadequate or is different from that of others. This discovery can lead to an early termination of an expatriate assignment, which in turn is expensive for a firm (see Chapter 12).

EXHIBIT 13.5 *Potential Sources of Costs Associated with Expatriation*

Direct Payments/Reimbursements	Support for Adjustment to Foreign Assignment
Tax reduction/equalization	Home leave (4–6 weeks)
Housing allowance	Emergency leave
Furnishing allowance	Personal security
Education allowance	Car/driver
Hardship/foreign service premium	Domestic help
Currency protection	Spouse employment
Goods and services differential	Child care provider
Temporary living allowance	Language/translation services
Car/transportation allowance	Cultural training
Assignment completion bonus	Repatriation assistance
Extension bonus	Social club fees
Help renting U.S. home	Imported food and other goods

Source: Adapted from Milkovich, G. T., & Newman, J. M. (1999). *Compensation.* Chicago: Irwin.

Another more systematic approach is called the **localization method.** Basically, this approach involves paying the expatriate the same as the local nationals in similar positions. This approach may be especially useful when an employee is going to be a career internationalist, because the permanent expatriate probably does not keep the home country standard in evaluating his or her compensation. The model is also used for the more typical expatriate as well. Localization, however, is much easier to apply when an expatriate moves to a country with a higher standard of living. It is difficult to accept a lower level of compensation because the standard of living is less expensive in Mexico than in the United States. The localization approach is rarely used without adjustments being made (base pay, allowances, etc.), but it still has serious limits.[43]

localization method
A more systematic method of compensation that involves paying the expatriate essentially the same as local nationals in similar positions

The Balance Sheet Method By far the most popular approach is called the **balance sheet method.** The philosophy behind this approach is that the expatriate should not suffer a loss as a result of a transfer. This general goal of trying to "keep the expatriate whole" is the stated objective of many multinational companies, as found in a recent survey.[44] Accordingly, it is a system that is designed to keep expatriates' standard of living on a par with that of their contemporaries at home. Although Exhibit 13.5 shows that there are many potential costs associated with expatriation, the balance sheet approach commonly divides expenses into four categories. Beyond the base salary, major expenses are usually considered in the categories of housing, income taxes, goods/services, and a reserve or discretionary component. First, however, let's consider the issue of base salary. Using this balance sheet approach, salary would be determined in the same way as for domestic employees. That is, if domestic employees receive average raises of about 5 percent, then so do the expatriates. The particular economic conditions in the foreign posting are not germane to the expatriate's base salary.

balance sheet method
The most popular approach to compensation; based on the belief that expatriates should not suffer a loss as a result of an international assignment

Likewise, it is common for a multinational to pay a premium or incentive to the expatriate for taking the foreign assignment. As we mentioned here and earlier in Chapter 12, there are some distinct disadvantages of expatriation—not the least of which are a "career interrupt" and the hardship of living in a foreign country. Firms often make compensation adjustments to account for this hardship. These adjustments can represent a sizable cost to a firm. In fact, many companies pay a foreign service premium, and these often range from 10 to 30 percent of base pay.[45] Some companies go beyond this amount to pay a hardship allowance as well for locations that are undesirable because of extreme weather, safety concerns, or limited access to goods or medical services. An American expatriate assigned to Amsterdam, for example, would receive a lower allowance than for an assignment in Tehran, Iran (where some still celebrate Death to Americans as a holiday).[46] So, whereas the monthly allowance for an assignment in Seoul might be $300, the same allotment for Chengdu could be as much as $1,000. It is difficult to make such hardship judgments, even for firms that have considerable experience with the international domain. Accordingly, many look to easily available rating schemes, such as the U.S. Department of State's *Hardship Post Differential Guidelines* and *The Economists' Hardship Rating Assessment*.[47] Both of these guides are updated periodically to reflect the degree of hardship experienced by foreign service personnel and are used by many multinationals for the same purpose.

Hardship Post Differential Guidelines
The U.S. Department of State's guidelines for determining any cost differentials that might be granted to expatriates because of the difficulty of a particular assignment

Purchasing Power and the Balance Sheet   Beyond these base payments, however, the balance sheet approach is mainly concerned with a set of expenses that are common in any family budget. The main purpose of the balance sheet approach is to protect or equalize expenses in the foreign country relative to the home country for each category, and Exhibit 13.6 depicts this approach.[48] The first column of this figure presents the base costs in the home country—say, the United States. Of course, the home country purchasing power changes depending on one's income, family size, and other variables. But for purposes of discussion, let us consider how purchasing power at home might be translated into purchasing power abroad. As shown in column 2 of this figure, most categories of costs tend to be higher overseas than at home. The goal of this approach is to provide **purchase power parity**.

purchase power parity
The degree to which an expatriate's money will purchase the same items in a foreign locale

Housing Costs   Housing, for example, usually involves considerably higher expenses than you might think, even in what might be considered a generally low-cost country. There are several reasons for this. For one, housing is typically rented and this is often covered by a shorter-term lease, which drives up costs. Second, Americans expect larger and more luxurious digs than their counterparts in a foreign country (unless those Americans are from Manhattan or San Francisco!). In fact, some human resource personnel have noted that it is sometimes impossible even to find comparable housing for a U.S. expatriate in a city like Tokyo or Beijing, let alone pay for it!

The costs for housing expatriates around the world can vary dramatically. Exhibit 13.7 presents some estimates of housing costs in various cities in the world. As you can see in the figure, housing in many cities is outrageously expensive. Even Chicago or New York, which some Americans might consider expensive, looks like a real bargain when compared with some foreign cities. Column 2 of Exhibit 13.7 reflects the fact that host-country housing costs are often more expensive than at home for U.S. expatriates. With the balance sheet

EXHIBIT 13.6   *The Balance Sheet Approach to Expatriate Compensation*

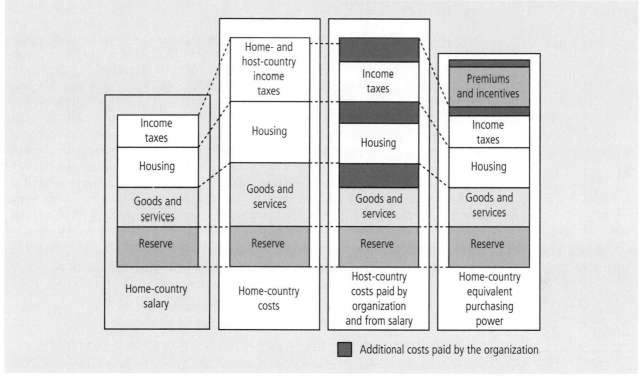

Source: Reynolds, C. (1994). Compensation basics for North American expatriates: Developing an effective program for employees working abroad. *American Compensation Association.* Reprinted from ACA Building Block #15. 1994 with permission from the American Compensation Association (ACA). 14040 N. Northsight Blvd., Scottsdale, AZ. U.S.A. 85260; © ACA.

EXHIBIT 13.7   *Expatriate Housing Costs in Ten Foreign Cities**

Location	Estimated Yearly Housing Costs
Beijing	$158,400
Hong Kong	$156,000
Tokyo	$153,600
Shanghai[2]	$120,000
Moscow	$108,000
Seoul	$102,000
London	$93,600
Ho Chi Minh City	$86,400
Singapore	$85,200
New York	$72,000

*This figure presents an estimate of the average yearly housing costs for a typical expatriate family of four. Estimates are taken from a sample of comparable homes or apartments that would be available to rent. These costs are based on rents for a home/apartment with 3–4 bedrooms, in safe and accessible neighborhoods, and they include costs for utilities, insurance, maintenance, and taxes.
[2]Estimate for three-bedroom apartment, since that is the only reasonably available housing source.
Source: Adapted from ———. (1997). Housing costs in foreign cities. *The Wall Street Journal*, January 24, B8.

approach, if we assume your housing costs are about $6,000 per month in Chicago and about $12,800 in Tokyo, the company would make up the $6,800 difference per month.[49]

Taxes A second major category of expatriate expenses is taxes, which is also reflected in the balance sheet approach in Exhibit 13.6. This area of compensation is among the most technical and difficult for a multinational to deal with. In part, this is a consequence of the large number of tax, securities, and currency control rules both in the United States and in foreign countries.[50] Exhibit 13.8 presents only one such complication—the different corporate and marginal income tax rates in several countries where U.S. expatriates are commonly sent. As you can see, the marginal tax rates of these countries vary markedly: Britain and Ireland are quite low, whereas France and the Netherlands are relatively high. The United States has tax-equalization agreements with some thirty-five countries around the world which recognize the payments made to one's home country. France and Belgium, for example, are leaders in making "totalization" agreements in their laws. France has included the following items in their laws regarding expatriates:

- An agreement that companies with an office in France can avoid French taxation of an expatriate's housing, schooling, and other allowances.

- Provisions to eliminate taxes (in France) of expatriate income from sources such as dividends, interest, and capital gains.

- A totalization agreement to eliminate social security taxes in France.

- A system to greatly reduce French taxes on income from stock options.[51]

However, even when foreign tax rates are lower (e.g., in Canada), the total tax burden for an expatriate may be higher. This is the case for several reasons. For one, many countries tax not only income but also all allowances, adjustments, and incentives. Worse yet, the United States is among the very few countries in the world (the only industrialized one!) to tax expatriate income, beyond an exempted amount.[52] So even if a company executive is paying relatively low

EXHIBIT 13.8 *Selected Tax Rates around the World*

Country	Corporate Tax Rate*	Top Marginal Income Tax Rate
France	40	57
Germany	50	52
Ireland	29	44
Italy	41	46
Japan	42	49
Netherlands	38	60
Spain	37	48
Sweden	28	58
Switzerland	30	57
United Kingdom	30	40
United States	40	40

*Includes local and state taxes.
Source: Adapted from ———. (2000). Whose burden is heaviest? *The Economist,* September 9, 53–54.

taxes while on an Irish assignment, he or she will probably also have a tax due in the United States (income below an exempted amount is excluded). If you are an Irish expatriate working in the United States, however, you may not be taxed by your government. Therefore, with the balance sheet approach, the firm will either pay a differential to the expatriate to account for the increased tax burden (protection), or it will pay directly to the other country an amount that ensures equivalent purchasing power for the expatriate (equalization). Regardless of how these additional costs are paid out, the goal is to make up the difference in costs incurred by the expatriate.

Living Expenses   A final but important category of expenses typically included in the balance sheet approach is living expenses—the goods and services that you will buy when living in a foreign country. Some of these expenses include food, transportation, clothing, and entertainment items, among many others. This category of expenses may be the most difficult to estimate since this category shows more fluctuation in price than any of the others. Additionally, the currency exchange rate is more likely to be felt here than in other expatriate expense categories. In housing, for example, one often signs a year-long lease with the annual price predetermined.

   Despite these difficulties, we can still get estimates of the difference in prices of a collection of goods and services. Various companies publish a survey of these costs in many cities, data that are regularly collected all around the world. Exhibit 13.9 shows what an expatriate might face while spending a year or two in Tokyo or Hong Kong. Clearly, the cost of goods and services in Japan and many other Asian cities is high. On the other hand, some other cities on this list are surprisingly inexpensive (e.g., Frankfurt, Prague, Manila). Johannesburg, for example, is a relatively cheap place to live; an expatriate's living expenses here are about 60 percent below those of the Big Apple.[53]

   If this list is hard to swallow for an expatriate, consider the Big Mac economic index that is reported annually by *The Economist* magazine.[54] Their rationale—partly tongue in cheek—is to provide a quick and easily digestible (even if you think the product is not) method that can be used to compare costs across countries (see Exhibit 13.10). While this is hardly a perfect index of purchasing power parity, it certainly is food for thought.[55] Regardless of what index you use, it appears that a basket of goods and services in some countries is expensive, whereas in others it may be relatively cheap.[56] What is especially interesting is that even in those countries that have inexpensive goods and services, purchases by expatriates end up being higher anyway. One expert points out that most expatriates keep their relatively high-living home-country consumption tastes even in a foreign country. They are willing and anxious to buy expensive imports from their home country, a habit that in turn drives up the expense index much higher than the estimates.[57]

   Presumably, expatriates would receive an adjustment to their average domestic living expenses while on foreign assignment. If the readily available adjustment indexes are not appropriate (perhaps because expatriates want to import goods they are used to at home), then a firm may wish to conduct its own cost survey. Nonetheless, the survey results could rapidly become useless because of inflation or changes in exchange rates. This is a case where a firm would probably wish to pay the employee allowance in local currency and at monthly intervals.[58]

EXHIBIT 13.9   *Cost Estimates for Goods and Services in Various World Cities*

City	Cost of Living*	City	Cost of Living*
Tokyo	140	Rome	84
Osaka	138	Tel Aviv	79
Oslo	126	Mexico City	77
Zurich	121	Toronto	74
Hong Kong	115	Prague	72
Copenhagen	113	Jakarta	71
Paris	112	Warsaw	66
London	108	Kuala Lumpur	63
New York	100	Johannesburg	61
Singapore	99	Bangkok	58
Stockholm	97	Cairo	52
Seoul	96	Buenos Aires	50
Frankfurt	94	São Paulo	40
Beijing	92	Manila	38
Moscow	88		

*The ratings, using New York City as the base rating of 100, were estimated using the average price of over 100 goods and services that you would commonly buy (these include food, clothing, entertainment, and transportation costs).
Source: Adapted from ———. (2003). Cost of living index. *The Economist*, August 9, 2003.

The Balance Sheet on Balance   All in all, you can see that the major goal of the balance sheet approach is to treat the expatriate fairly. Certainly, the effect of many of the adjustments is to make a foreign posting less of a hardship for an employee; sometimes they may even help to make expatriation a pleasure. This is not to say, however, that the balance sheet approach is without its problems. For one, the approach is difficult for a firm to administer and is complex to explain. As suggested, the balance sheet approach often requires either collecting or buying sets of data on cost of living and housing. Likewise, the transfer of payments for the various adjustments is also difficult both to explain to the expatriate and to monitor fiscally.

Some practical problems could also emerge. Earlier, we implied that expenses in the three major categories will be greater for the overseas employee. What if costs are less for an expatriate who transfers, say, to Mexico? Should the payments to the employee be reduced to reflect a lower cost of living in Mexico? While the balance sheet system would function to eliminate such "windfalls" to the employee, many firms do not do so.[59] Indeed, most balance sheet users are now using some modified version that makes these adjustments.[60] But in principle, the balance sheet would allow for the reduced compensation to the expatriate in a low-cost country. Along the same lines, others have noted a significant change in the number of companies that even consider a foreign assignment as something deserving of a special premium.[61] In fact, the number of firms that do not pay any incentive premium at all to work overseas has nearly doubled in recent years.[62] So although firms may adjust compensation for the increased cost of overseas living, increasingly they feel that some of the best jobs are there.

EXHIBIT 13.10   *Do You Want Fries with That Foreign Assignment?*
The Big Mac in Various Countries

Country	Cost of Big Mac (in US$)	Working Time Needed to Purchase (in min.)*
Argentina	1.40	30
Brazil	1.64	45
Chile	1.95	53
Czech Rep.	1.91	45
Mexico	2.14	76
Philippines	1.23	66
Poland	1.56	46
South Africa	1.74	35
Thailand	1.37	50
United States	2.54	10
Venezuela	2.32	76

*Estimate of the number of minutes average worker in various countries must work to buy a Big Mac.
Source: Adapted from ———. (2003). *The Economist*, April 26th, p. 68; _____ *The Economist*, September 13th, p. 98; and Williams, F. (2003). Price of a Big Mac. *Financial Times*, August 21, p. 4.

With increasing globalization, their rationale is that employees should relish an opportunity to work overseas. If a firm makes the foreign assignment a real part of the career track for its management, this is probably a reasonable position to take. All this has led some experts to claim that days of the "champagne lifestyle" of expatriate compensation and windfall perks are numbered.[63] Time will tell on this point. For now, however, we encourage you to complete the hands-on exercise at the end of this chapter. There we ask you to put together a fair compensation package for expatriate employees in several different foreign assignments. We think you will find that this is no easy task.

Compensating Foreign Country Nationals

One of many things management has to think about is the specific mix of U.S., local, and third-country nationals in the staffing of a foreign office or plant. The strategic issues involved in these and other decisions have been discussed earlier (Chapters 8, 9, and 12), but for now we can certainly remind you that there are many good reasons for hiring local nationals. Obviously, there would be minimal relocation costs for such personnel. And many of the adjustment problems resulting from cultural differences would be averted. Likewise, if the operation is a joint venture—as, say, many enterprises are in the People's Republic of China—you may earn the approval of that government by hiring their citizens.[64]

Compensation Methods   Regardless of the reason they are hired, it is clear that many local and third-country nationals are employed by U.S. multinationals. And there are a variety of different models for compensating those employees. For one, a company could peg salaries at the level of the U.S. expatriate with whom they may work side by side. As it turns out, few U.S. firms use this

⊕ International Insights

Chinese Managers Know Their Way around the Labor Market

COMPANY-PAID APARTMENTS and houses, 20 percent or more salary increases, food and clothing allowances, fully paid maternity leave, paid day care, retirement, saving, and medical benefits . . . even a laundry allotment. We know what you're thinking—who can I call, and where can I send my résumé? As it turns out, you would not be calling a Silicon Valley company. Unfortunately, you'd have to make a very long-distance call, and even then they don't want your résumé! What we've described is actually a typical compensation package provided to Chinese citizens who work for joint ventures of foreign-owned businesses in the People's Republic of China.

These data are based on a survey of human resource personnel from fifty-eight offices throughout China.[65] The main reason for these very attractive compensation packages is the immense amount of competition for well-educated and savvy Chinese nationals, many of whom speak very good English. These types of people make excellent managers in joint-venture operations. For one, their dual language skills represent an excellent asset—one that few American businesspersons have. While some firms provide Chinese language training, the demands of the job and the relatively short time frame for the assignment make mastery of the difficult Chinese language nearly impossible. Additionally, they are obviously privy to the home culture and often have more than a passing familiarity with U.S. culture—many having been educated here. Third, the Chinese government mandates the hiring of a percentage of their nationals in these joint ventures. Finally, these people are just plain smart. This combination of skills makes

approach.[66] More often than not, salaries of local nationals are set to their prevailing country standards. In general, local nationals receive the fewest elements of compensation of the three groups (U.S. vs. local vs. third-country nationals).[67] This does not necessarily mean that it will always be cheaper for the U.S. firm to hire local nationals. For example, the firm may save money using an expatriate in Belgium and France because of savings earned by avoiding the social security premiums that are necessary for their citizens. Conversely, the high tax equalization and other costs for expatriates in Britain and Germany may make a local national a relative bargain.[68] In some countries, however, this situation is changing dramatically, and it is therefore necessary for the human resources professional to stay abreast of the current employment situation. Surprisingly, China appears to be one of these countries where compensation may be more complex (and fluid) than you think, as shown in the accompanying International Insights.

Despite these examples, there will certainly be many times when the multinational will employ an expatriate and a local national in the same position where they will work closely with each other. It is inevitable that these groups of personnel will compare their compensation packages, and sometimes the difference will be all too apparent (chauffeured car, etc.). Since locals average lower compensation, this situation appears destined to have problems. A survey of 225 human resource managers and directors of U.S. multinationals looked at the problems they have experienced in compensating their international managers.[69] A variety of different problems were mentioned, but the single most important one was the discrepancies among compensation programs for expatriates, local nationals, and third-country nationals. These were identified as the source of significant or very significant problems for 80 percent of the sample!

them a hot commodity among the many U.S. and other foreign companies that have established joint ventures in China. We recently visited the Shanghai plant of a major U.S. personal products manufacturer, SC Johnson & Son (sometimes known as "Johnson Wax"). Many of their Chinese managers fit this profile. We spent some time with one manager and got a chance to speak with him (in English). As it turns out, he had been employed with several similar firms in the last several years, including some of SC Johnson's competitors in China, such as Procter & Gamble, Kimberly Clark, and others. He said it was not uncommon to receive multiple offers at any one time.

Now, despite what seem like generous pay raises and perquisites, pay in China is definitely low by U.S. standards. The typical manager working for a joint venture office gets about $7,000 a year (including allowances). The average industrial worker for a state factory earns only $500 per year (not including state subsidies). "Pay and benefits packages reflect a mixture of old ways and emerging capitalism," says Paula DeLisle, a consultant in Hong Kong for the Wyatt Co. International, based in Washington, D.C. Indeed, this appears to be the case, because in the shadow of this services-to-the-highest-bidder phenomenon, there are some legal guidelines on wage payments. Although the Provisions for Labor Management stipulate that compensation is at the discretion of the board of directors, there are also more direct regulations on wages. Article 8 of the Sino-Foreign Joint Ventures Provisions sets wage levels at 120 to 150 percent of the real wages of local staff and workers in similar state enterprises. Later, however, Article 39 of this document states that the salary and bonus system should adhere to principles of "each according to his work" and "more pay for more work." It remains to be seen what happens in the interplay between these two objectives—market and bureaucratic regulations. They may continue to function side by side. As Ms. DeLisle says, "On one hand, the paternalistic employer will earmark specific allowances, and on the other the free market enterprise uses discretionary bonuses to motivate performance."[70]

The *Wall Street Journal* recently reported that 100 percent of a sample of forty-five large U.S. multinationals reported that different compensation levels were their biggest international problem. Incidentally, third-country nationals (e.g., a Dutch manager working in Britain for a U.S. firm) typically fare better in terms of total compensation than local nationals. These people may need a salary and living adjustment to attract them to a different location, whereas the local national is already there. Once there, all have to work together because it is common to mix these three groups of employees in any one location. The issues of how this cultural diversity of groups and teams mix together and the problems they might present, are the topics of our next and last chapter.

Chapter Summary

Few people enjoy conducting performance evaluations on their employees, and adding foreign employees into the mix only makes the task more distasteful for management. There are many problems associated with the appraisal of the expatriate's performance, and they are not easily overcome. These basic questions loom large: *who* will evaluate the expatriate, *how often* will the evaluation be done, and most importantly, *what* will be evaluated and how. The "who" question involves tradeoffs between whether the evaluation is conducted by a local manager or the home office. We detailed some of the problems faced by both parties and presented general guidelines for delivering feedback in an international context (the what/how question).

One main reason to evaluate is eventually to compensate. We also dealt with this topic in detail, pointing out along the way that compensation means more than just pay level. Nevertheless, there are differences in pay levels across countries. American CEOs seem to have the best deal, with their pay far outstripping that of typical workers, and that of CEOs in all other countries.

We also discussed the complex issues involved in compensating expatriate employees. The *balance sheet* approach to compensation is among the most popular. Its goal is to maintain the same lifestyle for the foreign employee as she or he would enjoy at home. This is difficult to do because adjustments for housing, taxes, and goods and services, among other things, need to be considered. Firms will often pay a consulting firm for data on housing costs as well as living and other expenses that vary over time. Expatriation is a large expense for an employer, but the benefits of having a cadre of managers and executives with international experience may prove to be worth the cost.

business.college.hmco.com/students

Discussion Questions

1. What are some of the problems in evaluating employee performance, and how are these problems complicated by an international setting?

2. How might cultural beliefs about the basis for compensation affect your approach to rewarding expatriates and host-country/ third-country nationals in the same firm?

3. What are some of the ways that employees and executives alike can be compensated for their international service?

4. How should expatriates be compensated? What is the best approach and why?

Up to the Challenge?

Performance Evaluation Overseas

At the start of this chapter, we asked you to put yourself in place of an expatriate assigned to the People's Republic of China. You tried to use your management knowledge about employee participation techniques in an effort to improve performance on one of the production lines for which you are responsible. Unfortunately, this and several related techniques, such as providing rewards for good performance, did not work well. Because of the language barrier, you have not made much headway in terms of diagnosing what went wrong. At your six-month review, you received a decent evaluation, although it was somewhat neutral and open to interpretation.

What you should know now is that language is probably not the only problem. Even if you spoke Mandarin well, the Chinese would probably not give you direct feedback about the cause of the problems with your implementations. As we know from Chapter 5, such feedback to a superior may cause that person to lose face. In fact, this effect is probably the source of the problem with the participation and feedback techniques that were tried. The Chinese employees are unlikely to provide suggestions for improving the production process because it could have the related effect of showing you (the manager) up. In cultures like these, the manager is presumed to have the necessary expertise, and attempts to show otherwise often result in loss of face. Incidentally, this may also be the reason you received an ambiguous evaluation rather than a more direct and somewhat negative appraisal. If a local or third-country national delivered the feedback, that person would also be reluctant to provide the direct feedback that you as an American might be used to. As we saw in this chapter, preferences for feedback and ways that it is provided differ a good deal among cultures. This is why a further evaluation provided by one's home-country manager might yield valuable information for the expatriate. Finally, as we found out in the second half of this chapter, China can be a surprisingly expensive place for an expatriate to live. If your firm did not use the balance sheet model of compensation, then you may suffer financial as well as performance problems. So what solutions might exist in this particular case? How should your company appraise performance and compensate expatriates posted to China?

International Development

Giving Negative Feedback across Cultures

Purpose

The goal here is to explore the managerial task of giving performance feedback to employees; to consider how to make feedback useful, especially across cultures; and to practice the skills of giving helpful feedback.

Instructions

This year your company, after careful consideration, has instituted a 360-degree feedback performance evaluation system. It was agreed that one of your jobs as a manager would be to meet with each employee individually to go over his or her results.

You are about to meet with Chris Damone, a line supervisor who has been with the company for seven years. A review of Chris's past performance evaluations indicates an employee who has been reliable and has had above-average productivity. Results from Chris's 360, however, have a definitely negative consistency, i.e., he avoids trying new ideas, uses coercion with peers and subordinates, doesn't listen well, ignores feedback, often fails to return phone calls or other inquiries, blames mistakes on others or tries to cover them up, and is often unavailable when questions arise. In addition to this feedback, you are aware that Chris has been an outspoken opponent of the company's affirmative action policy and was particularly angry to have been passed over for a recent promotion in favor of a minority employee.

Part A: Evaluations of Americans

Prepare an action plan regarding this situation (15 minutes). Working in groups of three to five, prepare a plan that will help Chris improve. It might be useful to assign someone in your group to be the spokesperson who will eventually summarize your plan to the class.

Consider some or all of these questions as you work on the plan:

1. What could the manager have done differently, if anything, to clearly present the problems with Chris's behavior? Did the manager check frequently with Chris to be sure that the message being sent was the one being received?
2. Were Chris and the manager able to listen to one another without becoming confrontational or defensive?
3. Are the goals of the action plan clear and helpful?
4. How should the manager proceed as the goals set with Chris are met or fail to be met?

Part B: Cross-Cultural Evaluation

Now prepare your plan to help present feedback to an employee in the Middle East. Consider the situation regarding Chris to apply here. As you prepare your action plan and recommendations, consider some or all of these questions:

1. What could/should the manager have done differently with this employee from the Middle East?
2. What are the key differences between this plan and the one you devised for the U.S. employee?
3. What were the cultural differences that led you to make changes in the plan here?

Source: French, W. (1998). *Human resources management* (4th Ed.), 362–363. Boston: Houghton Mifflin. This exercise was originally prepared by Janet W. Wohlberg, The Rappay Group, 1075 Main Street, Williamstown, MA 01267. Used with permission.

Tapping into the Global Network

Assembling an Expatriate Compensation Package

Purpose

The goal here is to improve your understanding of how salary, tax, and living cost differentials across countries make it very difficult to put together an expatriate compensation package.

Instructions

This exercise involves completing a report that summarizes your research on the compensation of expatriates assigned to different countries. Depending upon your instructor's directions, this exercise can be completed in small groups or as an individual exercise. Regardless, imagine that an American firm has plans to send a manager on an expatriate assignment to one of two foreign countries and would like your advice about how to structure a compensation package. Your instructor will indicate which pairs of cities and countries are being considered for the expatriate's posting. Unless your instructor specifies otherwise, you can assume that the potential expatriate is based in Chicago, is married with two school-age children, and has a base salary of $150,000. Of this amount, approximately 60 percent is spent on living expenses, about 30 percent goes to cover various taxes, and the remaining 10 percent is allotted to savings.

As noted in the chapter, living expenses are complex and vary dramatically from country to country. Your report will certainly have to account for transportation, clothing, housing, food, and many other elements that could play a role in this category. Remember that the tax situation for many foreign assignments is complex, and this will have to be factored into your report. All in all, how should the compensation packages differ across the two countries (if at all)? Along the way, be sure to describe why there are differences across countries (or why not) in the specific aspects of the

package. In addition to the text and other reference sources, you may find many of the websites below useful for completing your report:

The U.S. Department of State Foreign Per Diem Page

www.state.gov/m/a/als/prdm/

This site provides cost estimates for living in almost every country in the world. A related site presents more detail on indexes of living costs, cost differentials, housing, and more.

STAT-USA/Internet (a service of the U.S. Department of Commerce)

www.stat-usa.gov/tradtest.nsf

Here you'll find country and market research information as well as detailed summaries of general background information on most countries in the world.

International Tax and Accounting Site Directory

www.taxsites.com/international. html#countries

This is an international tax site directory, with country-specific information.

OECD Data Site, Purchase Power Parity

www.oecd.org

This site presents data that allow one to compare the cost of a basket of consumer goods and services across a number of countries.

Global Relocation Survey (sponsored by GMAC and SHRM)

www.windhamint.com/Surveys.asp

A nearly eighty-page report on trends and costs in relocating personnel all over the globe.

14 Managing Groups across Cultures: From Work Teams to Labor Unions

INTERNATIONAL CHALLENGE

Teams at BP

Learning Objectives

After reading this chapter, you should be able to:

▸ Recognize the impact of groups in a cross-cultural environment.

▸ Be aware of the promise and pitfalls presented by diversity in and among groups.

▸ Understand the various forms and effects of unions across a large number of countries.

▸ Identify various forms of employee decision-making input, beyond unions.

LIKE MANY FIRMS headquartered in the European Union, British Petroleum (BP) has to be concerned with how teams of workers from different countries and cultures get along with each other. In BP's finance center in Brussels, the firm asked forty professionals from thirteen different countries to work closely together. Prior to this, these professionals had been working autonomously within their own countries, providing finance and accounting services internally. BP had successfully experimented with a multicultural group in its London operations and wished to extend this effort to serve its European operations. Rob Ruijter, a Dutchman, was appointed team leader. Mr. Ruijter, an experienced expatriate, knew that the going would not be easy. He recognized that there were opportunities offered by diversity, and he wished to capitalize on them. He also knew that cultural differences could create problems and reduce group productivity. He wanted to avoid this potential disaster by making sure the team became close knit as soon as possible. As you read this chapter, think about some of the practical things that Mr. Ruijter and BP could do to avoid problems and to capitalize on the possibilities offered by group diversity. Then read the *Up to the Challenge?* box at the end of the chapter for some of the steps BP took to improve its international teams.[1]

Groups are the basic building blocks of organizations. A group is defined as two or more people who interact together in order to pursue common goals. This broad definition applies to everything from a small group of friends who interact socially to an international labor union with thousands of members. Indeed, this captures the scope of Chapter 14, which we will approach in two parts. First, we'll focus on small work groups and the impact that culture may have on the way that they function. The second half of this chapter, while still concerned with how groups operate across cultures, will focus on the larger issue of relations between groups of workers and management. We'll examine differences in labor relations across borders. One of the most important group issues in labor relations is the connection between management and unions. In some countries, maintaining this link has been a smoother and more successful process than in others. We'll also look at different forms of employee participation around the world (sometimes referred to as "industrial democracy") and their relative effectiveness. Finally, we'll examine how frequently conflict, such as strikes and lockouts, can occur in different countries.

▶ *Managing Groups across Cultures*

Groups are important to the life of most firms—multinational or not. There are task forces, cross-functional teams, self-directed work teams, special committees, boards, production crews, and many other groups aimed at accomplishing particular goals. Why do we have so many different types of groups? One major reason is that groups offer extraordinary opportunities to get something done. Groups offer the potential for pooling knowledge, making better decisions, and more—the result can be a harder-working, smarter, and more productive set of people.

Many of us, of course, have had lousy experiences in groups. The real challenge for the manager is to set the stage so that the promise of groups can be realized. As we noted in earlier chapters on communication, training, and performance appraisal, the challenge that a manager ordinarily faces in these areas is magnified several fold in multicultural groups. Consequently, we'll review cultural differences in the ways groups typically operate and then outline techniques that allow managers to build more effective work groups in an international context.

Differences in Group Behavior across Cultures

First, we'll consider differences across cultures regarding the importance of groups in everyday life.

Individuals and Collectivists As you may remember from Chapter 4, one of the most important cultural distinctions is the difference between individualism and collectivism. Examples of individualistic countries include the United States, Britain, Netherlands, and Belgium, while collectivistic countries include Taiwan, Mexico, the Philippines, Japan, and many South American countries. In collectivistic countries, people see group goals as more important than individual goals while in individualistic countries, people are expected to take care of themselves and the emphasis is on autonomy, individual achievement, and privacy. People in individualistic cultures tend to apply the same value standards to everyone, while collectivists apply different standards to their **in-groups** and **out-groups**.[2]

in-groups
Groups that people identify with closely and pattern their behavior after, particularly in collective cultures

out-groups
Groups of secondary importance, especially to people in collective cultures

In-groups and Out-groups Indeed, collectivists put great emphasis on the needs of the in-group over those of the individual—they value cooperation with in-group members over their own self-interest. But for collectivists, all groups are not the same. Some, for example, place their family first (e.g., many Chinese), while others place their organization first (e.g., many Japanese). Regardless of how the in-group is defined, collectivists draw sharper boundaries between their own in-group and out-groups than do individualists. The distinction between family and neighbors is large in collectivistic cultures and relatively small in individualistic cultures. As we discussed in an earlier chapter, the self-attitudes of collectivists tend to be more influenced by their standing in groups than is true for individualists. When asked to describe themselves, collectivists are more likely to use group-based descriptions (e.g., "I am happy when I work with friends") than are individualists ("I am a happy person").

Nevertheless, it's easy to underestimate the pervasive effect of collectivist norms on the lives of people. We don't mean to imply that individualists can't work well in groups to accomplish tasks. Clearly they do. But when people get together, the process of group interaction differs substantially when individualists and collectivists are involved. And people apparently learn early how group processes are supposed to proceed. One study, for example, looked at group interaction patterns of 10- to 12-year-old Chinese and American children who worked on the same task.[3] The Chinese children approached the task in a cooperative, group-enhancing way, while the American kids chose strategies that reflected self-enhancing, competitive motives. This pattern underscores both the individualistic and achievement-oriented upbringing most Americans experience as well as the traditional Chinese saying, "Friendship first and competition second."[4]

Group Productivity across Cultures

So how might groups affect the process, quality, and quantity of work done in various cultures? We'll consider some general answers to this question next.

Social Loafing In research done in the United States, people are more productive working alone than when working with others in groups. This phenomenon is known as **social loafing**. Apparently people loaf because they assume the group will get the job done and because they can then redirect their effort toward their own goals—even if that just involves relaxing. Similar results have been found in over fifty different studies, encompassing many different types of jobs and organizations but comprising mostly American workers.[5]

social loafing
The tendency to be more productive when working alone than when working with others in groups, especially when individual performance is not easily distinguished

But is social loafing a uniquely American effect? There is good reason to believe it is, since U.S. culture emphasizes individuality and Americans often have trouble with teamwork. Other cultures (e.g., Japan) tend to be more team oriented, with the workplace being organized accordingly. Indeed, research shows that in contrast to Americans, Japanese perform better in groups than when working alone.[6] Likewise, studies show that social loafing occurs among Americans (individualists) but not among Chinese (collectivists).[7]

In-groups and Social Loafing The social loafing research that we have discussed so far only compared people who were working alone versus those in groups.[8] Moreover, "group" effects do not always favor collectivists. For example, there may be surprisingly poor communication among collectivistic employees who work for the same company but who are members of different in-groups.[9] Likewise, another study found that collectivists were actually more competitive than individualists when facing members of out-groups.[10] Indeed, the type of group appears to impact social loafing, particularly among collectivists. In general, collectivists are more likely to loaf when they participate in a group that is of no special significance to them (i.e., an out-group).

In one study examining this issue, managers from China, Israel, and the United States were asked to work by themselves, while others were placed in two different group situations.[11] An in-group situation was created by leading

International Insights

The Best Care in the Air Might Be Cross-Cultural

ONE ACTIVITY THAT is group oriented is the operation of large commercial jet aircraft. The flight crew of some modern aircraft can exceed twenty people. Interestingly, an analysis of commercial aviation accidents showed that flight crew behavior, rather than technical failures, have been the cause of about 70 percent of all accidents. Consequently, communication, leadership, and decision making have been studied in an attempt to reduce problems that lead to accidents. And as we have documented, many of these interpersonal issues are affected by culture.

Following this reasoning, one study looked at the attitudes of flight crews from a variety of countries, including the United States and several Asian nations.[12] Commercial aviation is a highly regulated industry, and as a result, flight crews perform very similar tasks in very similar environments. So, because their job differences are minimized across cultures, any differences in attitudes noted among these workers are probably culturally based. The researchers asked all crew members, including pilots and flight attendants, to complete a questionnaire about optimal behavior on the flight deck. The results were very interesting. For one, Asian pilots and flight attendants were more similar in their attitudes than were these same American groups. This finding might reflect the now familiar need for social harmony

managers to believe that they shared a number of similar characteristics that usually lead to close friendships. An out-group condition was created by telling managers that other group members had very different characteristics and that they came from very different backgrounds. In all cases, the managers worked on simulated management tasks such as rating job applications. Chinese and Israelis were chosen to participate because they came from collectivist cultures, and Americans were chosen to represent an individualistic culture.

The findings were interesting. Once again, there was a reduction in group performance (loafing) for Americans but not for the Israeli or Chinese managers. But the collectivists also showed social loafing when they worked with an out-group. The collectivists (from China and Israel) were likely to reduce their input into a work team when that group held few ties of any importance to them. When the collectivists worked with an in-group, however, their performance was not reduced.

Implications of Social Loafing Research What does this all mean for international managers? First, management strategies based on individual performance may be less effective in collectivist cultures. For example, the belief that individually based incentives would be maximally effective in China or Israel fails to recognize the impact and importance of groups to these cultures. Using a pay-for-performance approach in China, for example, may be counterproductive. That said, care must also be taken when adopting a group incentive plan in a collective culture. The type of group in which collectivists work may affect their performance. Consequently, forming a group around a natural collection of individuals (i.e., an in-group) may be the best bet for improving performance in a collectivist culture.[13]

Based on this reasoning, a manager might be wise, for example, to employ group-based incentive schemes in a place like China (see Chapter 11, where we discussed motivation). Nevertheless, workforce diversity appears to be increasing among collectivist cultures. As a result, there was more consistency in attitudes among the Asian flight crews.

Moreover, the results showed that American flight attendants preferred a captain who encouraged their questions but who also took charge in any emergency. American pilots actually stood out from all the other groups, including American flight attendants. They generally showed highly individualistic attitudes, reflective of the solo flyer of the old days of aviation. In the Asian cultures, however, both the attendants and pilots preferred to see an autocratic but communicative captain in almost all circumstances.

These differences present problems for the most common training method for today's flight crews. This approach, called *crew resource management* (CRM), emphasizes recognition, acceptance, and the free flow of information among the crew. Accordingly, CRM appears to reflect collectivism and low power distance. As such, the technique may create problems

or be an advantage, depending upon the culture of the crew being trained. Highly individualistic American pilots are asked to forgo their "flyboy" images and work more in teams. Although this may be tough for them, CRM training can also capitalize on the American orientation toward low power distance—via their natural tendency to share flight information. And although Asian crews appear to be more team oriented and therefore compatible with CRM training, their high power distance orientation may discourage the open sharing of information. Indeed, CRM training in forceful action by junior officers may be too foreign for a Chinese flight crew to adopt. At the same time, the CRM concept of group input may be too difficult for American pilots to accept. So in an emergency both groups have assets and liabilities to fall back on. The challenge for crew resource management is to make sure all aspects of the training sink in to crews from all cultures.

in many rapidly developing economies like India and China as work and travel patterns change in response to job opportunities. In China, for example, although people need a work permit to move from the countryside to big cities like Shanghai, there is still remarkable (albeit, illegal) movement of the labor force. As a result, managers will have to be especially clever and insightful when they introduce group performance strategies in such settings.[14]

Finally, consider the use of group-based management schemes in the highly individualistic United States. Team-based approaches have been increasing in the United States, with about 10 percent of all employees in American firms now organized into self-directed work groups.[15] Given the emphasis on individualism in American culture, making team-based approaches work well in the United States can prove a challenge. On the other hand, the United States is becoming less culturally homogeneous, thanks, in part, to a steady flow of immigrants. So another challenge for American managers—as well as foreign expatriate managers—is to understand and match methods and tasks in an increasingly diverse U.S. workforce. One area where this cultural mix has already taken place is among flight crews of commercial airlines. The accompanying International Insights illustrates some of the challenges such groups represent.

Diversity: When Different Cultural Groups Come into Contact

Until now, we have talked about differences in group behavior across cultures. Yet there are many circumstances under which international managers have to deal with diversity as they effectively lead groups of workers, including home-country nationals, third-country nationals, and expatriates. And staying at home is no escape from diversity issues. Managers in many developed countries, including the United States, are often faced with leading groups consisting of foreign nationals, immigrants, and members of racial and ethnic minority populations.

EXHIBIT 14.1   *Philosophies about Diversity*

Common and Misleading Assumptions	Uncommon but More Applicable Assumptions
Homogeneity: The melting pot. We are all the same.	**Heterogeneity:** Cultural complexity. There are many different cultural groups; people have similarities to and differences from me.
Parochialism: There is only one way. We don't entertain other ways of working or doing things.	**Compound:** Our way is not the only way. There are many culturally different ways of reaching the same goal and living life.
Ethnocentrism: There is one best way. Our way is the best way and all other ways are not as good as ours in reaching a goal.	**Contingency:** Our way is one possible way. There are many other different but equally good ways to reach the goal.

Source: Adapted from Adler, N. J. (1991). *International dimensions of organizational behavior.* Boston: PWS-Kent.

Assumptions about Diversity If anything, the United States may be behind other developed countries in dealing with diversity issues. This could reflect the philosophy or assumptions many Americans hold about the topic. Exhibit 14.1 presents a set of assumptions about diversity that are common, but misguided.[16] The exhibit also presents more appropriate assumptions that better characterize the impact of diversity. It's common in the United States (and other countries as well) to assume similarity in behavior and attitudes (see the first column of Exhibit 14.1). For instance, in response to a story about how we were befriended on a recent trip to China by a local resident, one American noted, "It just goes to show you that people are the same everywhere."

While this statement may be partially correct, it nevertheless represents the **homogeneity** perspective. Applied to multicultural groups, homogeneity suggests that with enough interaction, the group would blend its many different perspectives into one. (The *E pluribus unum* motto that appears on U.S. currency illustrates this philosophy—it means "out of many, one.") But this could prove to be a very misleading assumption if widely and uniformly applied.[17] A less commonly held assumption, but probably a more appropriate one, is that of **heterogeneity**. This refers to a situation of cultural pluralism. Even if homogeneity eventually does result in your particular multicultural group, it's probably best to assume heterogeneity to start with. Likewise, issues of **parochialism** and **ethnocentrism** can also be problematic and are best approached by more open and different paths to a goal.

Minuses and Pluses of Diversity As Exhibit 14.1 suggests, managers who are responsible for building work groups that are composed of people from different cultures have their hands full. In fact, beyond any philosophical perspective, a large number of practical problems need to be overcome in order for groups to run smoothly and effectively. Exhibit 14.2 lists some of these road blocks. Some could be predicted simply from a consideration of the word *diversity* itself. Our dictionary defines the word as "varied, dissimilar, and divergent." In general, these three adjectives mean heavy sledding for a manager. In fact, international executives have an easier time listing multiple disadvantages associated with cultural diversity in groups than coming up with even one advantage. As a

---

homogeneity
Applied to diversity issues, it refers to a view that people everywhere are basically the same

heterogeneity
The belief in cultural complexity; that people are both similar to and different from one another

parochialism
The belief that there are few ways to act; the inability to recognize or entertain other ways of working

ethnocentrism
The belief that there is one best way and that is our way of doing things; all other ways are inferior

EXHIBIT 14.2   *Cultural Diversity in Groups: Advantages and Disadvantages*

Advantages	Disadvantages
Better understanding of foreign employees	Increased ambiguity/confusion about norms and leadership
More effective work relations with foreign clients	Greater potential for miscommunication
Better marketing ability to foreign customers	More time needed to manage cultural differences
More creative ideas produced over time	Potential for lower group cohesion
Decisions stand the test of time and location	Harder to agree on specific decisions

Source: Adapted from Adler, N. J. (1991). *International dimensions of organizational behavior.* Boston: PWS-Kent.

French executive put it, "I have been involved in many situations over the years, but I can't think of one made easier because it involved more than one culture."

Perhaps one reason that disadvantages are easy to recall is that they are so salient. Exhibit 14.2, for example, points out that communication itself is more problematic in such groups. Likewise, the potential confusion and conflict that can emerge with cross-cultural groups stands out and is easy to remember. In contrast, the benefits associated with group diversity take longer to manifest and are more difficult to observe.

Imagine two different types of groups, each working on developing a new type of computer chip. One group consists of about twenty-five American scientists, mostly men, who are working on the project. Will there be problems among these relatively homogenous project team members? Yes, undoubtedly. There are the usual problems we are all familiar with when we work closely with other people. Now, however, consider the same project, but with a change of players. Let's say that this project is being tackled as a cooperative alliance among three multinationals—German, Japanese, and American. As shown in column 2 of Exhibit 14.2, now we can expect many more problems. For one, we know from our discussion of communication in Chapter 6 that there will be difficulties in this area. Likewise, each culture has different ways of working and of leading the work that is done. Finally, sorting out all these things will take more time since the people involved have different norms and don't speak the same language. On the other hand, the diversity brought to the computer chip project offers the potential for creative and inventive design solutions. The many different perspectives brought to the problem offer a kind of built-in brainstorming—the very kind of activity that can lead to creative ideas.[18] The accompanying International Insights, in fact, presents more detail about this real situation—one faced by Siemens, Toshiba, and IBM.

Using Diversity to your Advantage   Overall, the particular composition of a diverse group does impact its performance. Across multiple ways of defining diversity (gender, age, culture), the more varied a group is, the more difficult time they have—at least initially.[19] More diverse groups have more trouble communicating, have more difficulty building unit cohesion, and take longer to set up an effective structure than do more homogenous groups.[20] Nevertheless, once an understanding and structure are put in place, the diverse group becomes as effective as the homogenous group. And because of their ability to

International Insights

Cross-Cultural Teams Open in the Catskills

SOME YEARS AGO, three companies that ordinarily competed with each other formed a strategic alliance to develop a revolutionary computer chip. The Triad (as they called themselves) was composed of employees from Siemens AG of Germany, Toshiba of Japan, and IBM of the United States who were put to work in upstate New York at an IBM facility. Nearly 100 scientists were formed into teams to represent the three companies (and three continents) in this project. Initially, the project's managers worried that the teams' diverse cultural backgrounds might create problems. It turns out that they had reason for concern.

Take, for example, the Toshiba scientists. The Germans were shocked to find them closing their eyes and apparently sleeping during important meetings. This, however, is a common practice for overburdened Japanese workers when the discussion doesn't center on them. The Japanese themselves, who ordinarily work in large teams, found it very difficult to sit in small, individual offices and speak English. As a result, they often withdrew whenever possible to the more comfortable confines of all-Japanese groups. Further undercutting any team synergy were the feelings of the American scientists. They felt that the Germans planned way too much and that the Japanese—who typically prefer to review proposals constantly—wouldn't make a specific or clear decision. The Germans and the Japanese complained that their American counterparts didn't spend enough time getting to know them, either at work or at social events.[21] Unfortunately, all this led to a climate of misunderstanding and mistrust. There were even some suspicions that information and progress were being held back from the group by various company cliques.

In theory, the pooling of a diverse and intelligent group of people together to design new advanced technology should pay creative dividends. The reason this didn't work in the Triad project, at least initially, was that people were able to stay in their separate groups. In analyzing the situation, the lack of attention to group interaction and team building was seen as the culprit. Although there was great effort on the technical and logistical side of things, there was little if any attention paid to understanding different approaches to work. Instead, the three companies gave their employees short briefings on working and living abroad. One human resources executive for Toshiba said, "We should have done more cooperative efforts with HR people from Siemens and IBM to develop joint training programs." Siemens also briefed their employees on living abroad and a bit on what they called the American "hamburger style of management." Americans, they said, start their criticism gently. They start with "how's the family" small talk; that's the "top of the hamburger bun." Then they go right to the meat, namely, the criticism, topped off with more bun (words of encouragement). With Germans, in contrast, it's all meat, and with Japanese you have to learn to smell the meat. Despite all the obstacles, Triad members said they learned a lot from their experiences—both about technology and about cooperating with different groups of people from around the world.[22]

bring a variety of perspectives to the table, diverse groups may perform best over the long run. This is particularly the case when the group is working on projects requiring creativity and problem solving rather than simple routine tasks.[23] This is exactly what one study of top management teams found—that cultural diversity was responsible for higher team performance and that when conflict did occur, it was also more functional.[24]

Indeed, other studies have found that while homogeneous teams (i.e., with members who have similar demographic characteristics) outperformed diverse groups at first, over time the performance of highly heterogeneous teams improved and equaled that of the less diverse teams.[25] Interestingly, teams defined as "moderately" heterogeneous did not perform nearly as well as the other two types of teams. Apparently, the multiple subgroups present in highly heterogeneous teams don't allow people to fall back so easily on the comfort of their familiar in-group. Gradually, people move their focus from their individual group to that of a larger whole.[26]

So how can you manage diversity to your advantage? Below are guidelines that should be considered if you are to get the most out of multicultural teams.[27]

- **Choose appropriate tasks:** It would be a mistake to choose members of a multicultural team based solely on their ethnicity. Instead, members who have similarly high ability levels but diverse attitudes and perspectives should be chosen.

- **Explicitly recognize differences:** Instead of minimizing or overlooking cultural differences, members should be encouraged to recognize and describe those differences. This will push team members toward understanding those differences. Hopefully, the group can then start to be open to what team members of different cultures can contribute. A corresponding disadvantage of this technique is that it may accentuate existing differences and create "fault lines" within the group. So this must be done carefully.

- **Develop a vision/mission:** Because multicultural teams come from diverse backgrounds, they often have difficulty agreeing on how to focus their efforts. Accordingly, specific meetings and time spent on hashing out a broad goal that goes beyond individual differences will go a long way toward making the multicultural team effective.

- **Give team members equal status:** Unequal status or power differences among team members can be a problem. Under these circumstances, the potential creativity of a multicultural team could be stifled because of pressures (implicit or otherwise) from more powerful members. It is common among international teams to make someone from the parent company the leader of the team. While there may be good reason to do so, the parent culture may end up dominating the proceedings. This kind of domination is more likely to happen if the team is composed of people from high power distance cultures. Although the team may have a lot to contribute, the strong norm of deferring to the leader in most matters will suppress their potential contribution.

- **Provide feedback:** Culturally diverse teams have difficulty agreeing on the benefit of various ideas—perhaps because the methods they use to gauge the benefits are so different. Accordingly, to develop similar judgment criteria, give frequent feedback to members on their ideas. This should produce greater cohesion and help speed along the process of developing ideas.[28]

Clearly, managing diversity on multicultural teams is difficult. Nevertheless, there is the promise that, managed correctly, such teams have much to contribute. That said, it's important to recognize that these teams are only one part of the equation when it comes to managing groups across cultures. Next, we'll turn our attention to the broader picture—the challenge of managing labor relations across cultures.

▶ *Labor Relations in and across Cultures*

Working with small multicultural teams is tough enough. But when labor unions and labor regulations are involved, the management challenges may cut across entire companies, industries, or countries. In the most general sense, the field of **labor relations** deals with employee-employer relationships—which can vary dramatically across countries. For example, the regulations and practices of labor relations are very different in France than they are in neighboring Spain. To address these topics, we will first outline the perspectives of management and workers. We will then discuss agreements or structures that have been devised for soliciting employee input or control. These methods include not only labor unions, but also many other agreements and mechanisms that companies have devised or been forced to adopt. Despite the best intentions of firms, unions, and governments, there are times when conflicts arise. Sometimes agreement just can't be reached and the conflict reaches the point where action is taken, either by workers (strikes) or by management (lockouts). We will discuss each of these topics in turn.

labor relations
A field focused on understanding the nature and quality of employee-employer relationships

Management and Worker Perspectives on Labor Relations

Workers in many different countries are concerned with their pay, job security, benefits, and working conditions. They often join labor unions in order to have power over these important work outcomes.[29] And they often wish to extend this power to have a say in important decisions facing the firm. In other cases, complex laws control firms in ways that effectively serve the function of a union—even when no organized labor groups exist.

Either way, groups of workers have basically one main method of getting their way on key issues—by threatening to reduce work output or stop it all together. This threat may be less credible, however, when the employer is a multinational. A large multinational has many resources at its disposal and, as a result, may be able to outlast a union strike (e.g., by simply absorbing losses at a particular location). Or, if the multinational is flexible enough, it may be able to increase production temporarily at another facility to offset losses at facilities experiencing labor unrest. The multinational may also threaten to move its operations to another country in response to a strike. Consequently, multinationals typically have considerable power—more than a domestic firm—over employees.

Hyster Corporation of Portland, Oregon, is a case in point. This firm had a forklift-truck plant in Irvine, Scotland, with 500 employees. Thanks to a grant from the British government, Hyster was ready to invest $60 million in the Irvine plant, creating another 100 jobs. The big catch, however, was that the resulting increase in production would create overcapacity in Hyster's European operations. Consequently, enlarging its Scottish plant meant that Hyster would have to cut back production at its factory in the Netherlands. But moving Hyster's Dutch production capacity to Irvine would mean that Scottish workers had to take a 14 percent pay cut. Hyster gave the workers forty-eight hours to accept the deal.

As if this weren't enough, the next day each employee got a letter from the company. The letter said, "Hyster is not convinced at this time that Irvine is the best of the many alternatives open to it. It has not made up its mind. The location of the plant to lead Europe is still open." At the bottom of the page, employees were asked to vote for or against consolidation of production at the Irvine plant and the pay cut that went with it. Facing potential job loss, only eleven employees voted no. Employees complained that they had had no warning and no real input into the company's decision process. And while Hyster's employees were not unionized, many felt it wouldn't have made a difference: "It was an industrial rape," "It was do-or-else," said some employees.[30]

To combat this power of multinationals, unions and other employee groups have tried to use legal means to increase their control. For instance, French unions have begun coordinating lawsuits by members to seek redress for alleged breaches of contract about unemployment benefits.[31]

Many countries have also enacted permanent employment laws, partially in response to union lobbying and pressure. Such laws offer generous protections for workers (e.g., in France, thirty-five hours is the legal weekly work limit for all employees) and make it very difficult to fire anyone after a probationary period has passed. And even if the required termination conditions are met, the employee is often due large amounts of severance pay. In Europe, for example, there are extensive laws and requirements regarding termination. The average laid-off worker in the United States gets one week's severance pay for every year of service. German workers, however, get more than four times as much on average—ranging from one month of pay for every year of employment on up. When you add in other mandated benefits such as relocation and retraining that are available in Germany, costs in the United States seem modest. Of course, this even assumes that you are permitted to let a worker go in Germany. As one executive recruiter in Germany put it, "U.S. firms that establish themselves here are shocked by the termination rules. The possibility of firing someone quickly without cause is impossible."

Colgate-Palmolive ran into some of these rules after it announced plans to close its factory in Hamburg and eliminate the 500 jobs there. Colgate initially offered German employees about $40,000 each—a severance plan costing the company over $20 million. Colgate argued that the plan was similar to or better than what other firms in the area had recently provided. However, German law gives the union an opportunity to approve such decisions, and the union felt the offer was far too low given that the Hamburg operation was profitable for Colgate. The union attracted a good deal of public attention to their plight, including stories in local papers about how employees and their families had worked for Colgate for three generations. Eventually, the mayor of Hamburg publicly condemned the company for its move and the union threatened to drag out the negotiation process. Eventually, Colgate raised its offer and agreed to a settlement.[32]

Likewise, in Belgium an employee making $50,000 a year would be entitled to termination benefits of nearly $100,000 (see Exhibit 14.3).[33] Companies operating in Europe must obey a variety of nationally mandated rules regarding treatment of employees. As a result, sometimes firms become very creative to avoid costly employee severance rules and protracted discussions with unions. For instance, when Dutch IT firm PinkRoccade NV wanted to shed 700 employees, it terminated people in batches of nineteen—a process that took almost a year. The reason? Dutch law requires firms to enter negotiations with unions and other groups representing employees (to justify and obtain approval for layoffs) if more than twenty employees are let go at a time. Other Dutch firms have simply placed unneeded, but perfectly healthy, employees on disability to dump

EXHIBIT 14.3   *Severance Payments Required for European Employees*

Country	Payments (US$) by Seniority of Employee	
	Younger Employee*	Middle-Aged Employee*
Italy	45,000	130,000
Spain	56,000	125,000
Belgium	40,000	95,000
Portugal	38,000	83,000
Greece	28,000	67,000
Germany	15,000	25,000
United Kingdom	12,000	19,000
Ireland	8,000	13,000

*Younger employee assumes age 35, fifteen years' service, earning $30,000; Middle-aged employee assumes age 45, twenty years' service, earning $50,000. Each country may require additional benefits that are not specified here.
Source: From "Employee Dismissals Can Prove Costly for Companies in Europe" *HR Focus*, August 1992, p. 18. Reprinted by permission © IOMA's HRfocus August 1992. 212/244-0360. http//www.ioma.com

them, shifting the cost to the government. Ironically, Dutch labor laws are more flexible in many respects than their counterparts in countries such as Germany and France.[34]

That said, the influence of unions and restrictive labor laws may be waning across western Europe, thanks, in part, to the ability of multinationals to quickly shift production to lower-wage locations in the east. For instance, Volkswagen AG was able to persuade union members at one of its plants in Spain to accept a 5 percent pay cut by threatening to move production (and jobs) to Slovakia, where wages are 50 percent less. Indeed, as the European Union expanded eastward, thousands of union jobs have followed. To preserve jobs, unions in western Europe have been increasingly willing in recent years to give in to multinational demands on pay raises, more flexible work rules, and greater use of temporary and contract employees.[35]

Labor Unions across Countries

We have shown that both unions and multinationals have ways to exert influence over each other. Still, multinationals have the upper hand, with greater overall influence than any employee group or union.[36] However, this influence varies among countries. Accordingly, we'll review some of the differences among countries in the structure of employee input and control.

As suggested, there are many mechanisms by which employees try to wrest control from management. Of course, a common approach is a union. Unions in the United States were originally established to bring about reform in the workplace before laws existed to protect worker interests and rights. Now, American unions have a relatively high profile, and that profile isn't always positive. In fact, national surveys indicate a relatively negative view of unions by Americans. Perhaps this attitude can partly explain why union membership in the United States has been steadily declining in recent years. In fact, today union members make up less than 15 percent of the total American workforce.

While other industrialized countries have also seen a general decline in union membership, the overall percentage is still higher elsewhere.[37] Exhibit 14.4 presents data on union density rates in a large number of countries. As you can see, the percentage of workers who are unionized varies greatly across countries. The oldest and most well-developed union systems occur in the EU countries. Even among these countries, however, there are differences in the percentage of workers covered by unions. France, for example, has only about 9 percent of its workforce covered by unions, while Britain has a relatively large percentage of workers who are union members (nearly 33 percent). These national differences have been tied to a number of factors, including the political leanings of the government, how wages are determined, and the size of the public employment sector.[38]

It is important to note that these **union density rates** should not be taken completely at face value. For one thing, the raw percentage of union members is not all-important. Often, the bargaining agreements reached by the union and management end up covering many more employees than just union members.[39] More importantly, a high union density does not necessarily mean that unions are more effective or influential. In fact, in some cases, a relatively low density rate (e.g., France at less than 10 percent) may belie the true degree of union influence. Also, in some countries, labor may be represented by a political party, which also increases union influence. Clearly, however, not all unions across borders are structured the same nor are they equally influential. We will discuss the impact of unions in a number of important countries around the globe. This discussion is more detailed about Western countries, reflecting the fact that they were industrialized before other areas and, as a result, have had greater opportunity for employee groups to form unions.

union density rate
The percentage of workers that are unionized in any one country

Unions among EU Countries

Because the concept of union influence is mostly indexed by perceptions, there is some debate about which unions are influential and why. Nevertheless, it appears, at least among EU countries, that union power, while diminished in recent years, is still a force to be reckoned with.[40]

Unions in Germany Unlike the United States, where union contracts are negotiated on a company-by-company basis, Germany relies on a centralized system in which some 60,000 contracts are set using industry-wide bargaining. Unions will typically bargain with a group or federation of employers in an industry. There is only one union for workers in most major industries, and membership in that organization is entirely voluntary. As in the United States, the contract will include most major work issues, including pay, benefits, and conditions of employment. As such, the main goals of the union are economic in form, as opposed to some of the more politically motivated union activity found in countries such as France or Italy.

The relationship between unions and management has been fairly cooperative over the last twenty years or so, with just a handful of days lost to strikes every year. One reason is that workers have a number of avenues of input into how the business is run, including representation on the board of directors. Indeed, all companies in Germany with over 2,000 employees are required to give 50 percent of supervisory board seats to worker representatives. This situation, unique to Germany, is called **codetermination**. This policy, set up by

codetermination
A system that provides worker input to the board of directors in German companies

International Insights

Germans Think Americans Work Too Hard

ANGIE CLARK AND Andreas Drauschke have similar managerial jobs for similar pay (about $33,000 a year) in department stores in Washington and Berlin. Apparently, however, the comparison ends there. Mr. Drauschke's job is contractually set at a 37-hour workweek with six weeks annual paid leave. His store closes at 2 P.M. on Saturday, is never open on Sunday, and stays open one night (Thursday) each week. "I can't understand that people go shopping at night in America . . . logically speaking, why should someone need to buy a bicycle at 8:30 P.M.?" (He manages the auto and bicycle division of the store.)

Ms. Clark, on the other hand, works at least forty-four hours a week, including evening shifts and weekend stints. She often brings work home and has never taken off more than one week at a time. While most Americans admire the stereotypic German industriousness, Ms. Clark—a frequent visitor to Germany—has a different view. American workers average about 20 percent more working hours per week than Germans. And the disparity has increased in recent years, with Americans working just over 1,800 hours annually compared to about 1,450 hours for Germans. "Germans put leisure first and work second," said Ms. Clark. Many of her colleagues at the store hold second jobs and rack up sixty hours or more per week of work. Mr. Drauschke, however, has no interest in working beyond the mandated thirty-seven hours per week, even for more money. "Free time can't be paid for," said the German. He finds the American penchant for holding multiple jobs simply unthinkable.

Apparently, the long and irregular work hours come at a price for Americans. Turnover at the German store is nearly zero, while it pushes 40 percent a year in the American store. Likewise, because of the long apprenticeships they serve, German workers know their products inside and out. Training for Ms. Clark's U.S. workers is about two days. Despite these advantages, the German government worries that the short weeks, many holidays, and other perks are crimping Germany's competitiveness.[41]

EXHIBIT 14.4   Union Density Rates around the World

Country	Density (%)*	Change Last Decade (%)	Country	Density (%)*	Change Last Decade (%)
Australia	35.2	-35.2	South Korea	18.0	—
Belgium	51.9	-0.2	Mexico	26.0	—
Canada	37.4	1.8	Netherlands	25.6	-11.0
Denmark	80.1	2.3	Poland	33.8	-42.5
France	9.1	-37.2	Singapore	17.0	—
Germany	28.9	-17.6	Spain	18.6	62.1
Greece	24.3	-33.8	Sweden	91.1	8.7
Iceland	83.3	6.3	Switzerland	22.5	-21.7
Ireland	48.9	-12.6	United Kingdom	32.9	27.7
Italy	44.1	27.4	United States	14.2	-22.1
Japan	24.0	216.7	Venezuela	25	—

*Rates are estimates of the percentage of wage and salary workers who are union members.
Source: Adapted from ———. (1999). Human Development Report, 1999: United Nations Development Program, Profile of People in Work (www.undp.org).

the Allies after World War II, was designed to prevent industrial might from lining up completely with a potentially threatening government, as had happened before the war. The system is most predominant in the steel and coal industries, sectors that were critical pre- and postwar enterprises. Here, unions select five board members, shareholders select another five members, and this body then selects an eleventh member. Outside of steel and coal, union membership on boards varies by industry size.[42]

As we've said, in recent years German unions have been willing to trade concessions on working conditions and pay for job security. For example, the giant German union IG Metall has thrown in the towel on certain issues— such as fighting for shorter work weeks. Nevertheless, the accompanying International Insights box elaborates on the German concern with free time— something American workers often feel they have precious little of. Overall, attitudes in Germany toward labor unions have hardened, with unions being blamed for higher unemployment, expensive wage rates, rigid labor laws, and weakening German competitiveness. Consequently, union participation rates continue to drift downward.[43]

Unions in the United Kingdom The union movement in the United Kingdom has a very long history—among the longest of any country. British unions are also relatively powerful, although their influence has waned in the last several years. The union movement can be seen as political in Britain, although not as political as some other countries, such as France. In fact, the desire for unions to push their political agenda led to the formation of the Labour Party in Britain in 1883. Since then, the trade unions have played a significant role in this political party and to this day provide the vast majority of financial support for the party.

Union density in the United Kingdom is about 2.5 times that of the United States. Union participation, however, has seen a big dip. At the height of its influence in 1979, membership was around 57 percent; in comparison, the density rate now is around 33 percent. There are several reasons for the drop in participation in unions, but perhaps the biggest reason has to do with the political environment, with the government passing legislation that reduced the power of the unions. Additionally, the economy fared reasonably well in recent years, further reducing the appeal of union membership.[44] Nevertheless, unions still wield considerable power and influence. Since a large firm may negotiate with several unions, the process is complex. Cross-union dealings can be fractionated. This situation has played into the hands of companies that have successfully pushed collective bargaining down from a national to a business level. Likewise, many new businesses have tried to maintain a nonunion status consistent with the "enterprise culture" of recent governments.[45]

Unions in France French unions have been dominated by five main national unions. As in Japan, most large employers also have a company union. These unions are among the most political in the world. In fact, the chief distinction among these unions is not the industry or occupations they cover, but their political/social leanings.[46] The development of these five confederations can be clearly traced to ideological issues and conflicts, and they reflect the pattern of social division in France.[47] These five major confederations have competed with one another for membership, and it is common for all five to be present in any one work setting. Employees may choose to join one or the other depending on their political viewpoint.

Membership in any of these unions is not large by the standards of other countries. The largest union—the CFDT (Confédération Démocratique Française du Travail), a largely industry/public service union with a communist leaning—has only about 890,000 members. In general, France, at under 10 percent, has among the lowest levels of union density of all industrialized countries (see Exhibit 14.4). Partly, this low density reflects the fact that unions really don't have to push for new members. For much of the time since the mid-1970s, the French government has embraced the idea of protecting, if not enhancing, the rights of employees. Likewise, there has been a long government tradition of extending collective agreements to companies and industries that were not party to the accord. Consequently, a worker could benefit from the union's influence without having to be a union member. As a result, union influence is much greater than the 9 percent density figure would suggest. That said, French unions, like their German counterparts, have been under pressure in recent years to cooperate in government efforts to reform onerous labor laws and regulations.[48]

Other European Unions As mentioned earlier, the extent of union structures and activities in Europe runs the gamut. Because Europe was the first continent to industrialize, there is great complexity and variety of union representation. In the Netherlands, for example, trade unions were initially formed and developed by religious and political groups. A good case in point is the largest union in Holland, the FNV; it is a merger between a socialist union and a Catholic union. These unions are not as ideological as French unions and have participated with the government in many initiatives—including the formation of the Dutch welfare state. Unions are important in the Netherlands, and several experts have claimed that their influence is much greater than their 26 percent density rate suggests.[49] Likewise, Dutch employees can exert control over the workplace via other unique outlets, as we discuss later in the chapter.

Unions in Sweden, as in most other European countries, began as a socialist movement among manual workers. And because of a largely friendly government, they flourished in a mutually cooperative environment. This can perhaps account for why Sweden has such a high density rate (91 percent). Although there has been some hostility between government and the unions in recent years, union membership rates have been relatively steady.[50] In fact, unions have been in the forefront of recognizing global competitive pressures. As a result, they have embraced many management initiatives to improve productivity, such as technological advances.[51] Belgium, too, has a relatively high union density rate (about 52 percent). It might be even higher, however, if there were fewer laws governing labor relations. In fact, the workplace in Belgium is one of the most highly controlled in the world. We have already pointed out that there are a large number of laws governing compensation, severance pay, and other human resource issues in Belgium. Despite the fact that the most important unions are organized around religious or political bases, there is a "culture of compromise" in their interactions.[52] Spain is perhaps on the other end of the regulated spectrum. Recently, there has been more unified union activity, especially in response to the great financial gains made by corporations.

In general, the long history of union organizing has left many full-time, permanent European workers covered by an extensive set of regulations and protections, especially by American standards. Many multinationals have long complained about this state of affairs, and there are signs that European countries will slowly roll back many of these expensive protections. In the meantime, however, firms are coping with the current state of affairs by relying on contract, temporary, and part-time workers—in short, workers with fewer legal protections. For instance, in the Netherlands, part-time workers occupy about one-third of all jobs, compared to less than 15 percent in the United States.[53]

Indeed, if you're willing to take temporary, contract, or part-time work, many firms in western Europe are hiring. In France, for example, temporary employment has risen by 50 percent since the late 1980s. Of course, most workers would much prefer full-time, permanent employment, but part-time or temporary work is certainly better than nothing. Many firms point out that such work keeps many off the public dole—especially young workers, among whom unemployment is a big problem. Governments are going along with this trend, if only begrudgingly. In Germany, for instance, a legal ban on temporary agencies was lifted only in 1994. Spain also exemplifies this trend—seven out of every ten jobs created in the mid-1990s were for temporary workers. This is easily understood when you consider that employers can be required to pay those thrown out of work for up to three and a half years afterward.

Many experts predict that the increasing use of temporary and part-time workers will continue in western Europe unless there is a major shift in workplace legal regulation. And some reforms have been enacted. In Spain, for example, the government cut severance pay nearly in half.[54] Sweden is starting to cut the dole as well. While workers have traditionally been guaranteed 80 percent of their last net pay—indefinitely—a new law reduces benefits after a worker refuses a job referral and removes them altogether after three refusals. The law also specifies that after 300 days of jobless benefits, the person must enter a skills-training course full time until he or she gets a job. France recently enacted a similar law, and Dutch law cuts all benefits if one job referral is refused. Finally, Denmark also cut its benefit time to three months down from eighteen months.

Unions in Asia

Unions also exert influence in Asia, although this varies from country to country.

Japanese Unions There are over 60,000 unions in Japan, the vast majority of which are called **enterprise unions**.[55] That is, while there are some large national unions in the public and private sectors (e.g., Municipal Workers; Iron & Steel Workers' Union; Railway Workers' Union), nearly 95 percent of all unions are enterprise, or in-house, unions. The tradition has been to follow the principle of "one company, one union." In other words, these in-house unions represent only the employees of their respective companies. Membership in these unions is limited to regular and permanent employees. A large number of workers in any given company are part time or temporary and are covered neither by unions nor by the human resource practices that are often associated with Japanese firms (e.g., lifetime employment, etc.).

As might be expected from our many discussions of Japanese culture, the relationship between union and management is largely harmonious. This wasn't always the case. In fact, after World War II, many Japanese unions were both militant and violent. The labor movement was often led by radical and militant union organizers whose agendas frequently included socialist revolution.

enterprise unions
The tendency for unions in Japan to be associated with one company, rather than an industry or trade across companies

One of the worst strikes—called the 100-day strike—occurred in 1953 at Nissan. Management locked employees out of plants for over three months. Finally, after many long and backbreaking strikes, Japanese employers basically struck a deal with their unions: they provided lifetime employment and good benefits in exchange for no labor strife.

Both groups have largely kept the bargain. Indeed, there is relatively little labor strife in Japan. This is partially the case because junior-level managers often occupy union leadership roles. In fact, the training received in such union positions is viewed favorably by management and is taken into account for future promotions.[56] Observers often criticize this relationship as being too cozy; they maintain that Japanese unions are essentially a management control mechanism rather than a way to represent workers. It has been pointed out that even when Japanese unions go out on strike, they do so for very short periods of time—often a half day or less.

For example, a union leader at the Japanese subsidiary of Royal Dutch/Shell claimed that the union was getting "tough" with management over wages: "We went on strike the day before yesterday. We stayed out for forty-five minutes. Yesterday we struck again for fifteen minutes." The next day, the workers struck briefly again (for higher wages) at lunchtime so that the demonstrators would not have to miss any work. This attitude characterizes most Japanese unions. The average Japanese employee strikes about five minutes a year, a rate far below that for the United States. As the head of the Nissan's union said, "Union members want to protect their jobs and preserve their livelihood. The best way to do that is to cooperate with the company." What's more, strikers often work full shifts after walking a picket line. On top of that, productivity often shows no change during a strike. Finally, there is some limited cross-union cooperation in Japan. For instance, several enterprise unions coordinate their bargaining activities during a traditional *shunto*, or Spring Wage Offensive, to establish a national pattern or rate of wage increases. The individual enterprise unions then use this rate as a standard for their own bargaining.[57]

shunto
The efforts of enterprise unions in Japan to coordinate bargaining activity to establish a national pattern of wage increases

🌐 International Insights

Unions in the Middle Kingdom—Not Forbidden, But Not That Useful, Either

NOT ALL THAT LONG AGO, China ordered all foreign-funded companies to enroll their workers in official trade unions. And many felt that this order was overdue given the rising number of fatal accidents, layoffs, and labor conflicts in China. In foreign-funded factories employing millions of Chinese, accidents abound and worker treatment is poor. In some factories, workers are strip-searched, cheated out of their pay, and even forbidden to use the bathroom during work hours. At a foreign-owned factory in Fujian province, forty workers had fingers crushed by obsolete machines. According to official reports, in the booming Guangdong province alone

there are over 45,000 industrial accidents annually and thousands of deaths.

According to one Chinese union representative, over 80 percent of foreign companies operating in China effectively have no unions. This is in spite of the fact that joint venture contracts require union representation. Consequently, even the normally passive (by Western standards) unions are upset. The government got a taste of worker anger recently in Heilongjiang (a northeastern province), where some 2 million workers have lost their jobs since the mid-1990s. Western sources say that over 100,000 workers took to the streets in the province's major

Unions in China As in many other aspects of business, China is unlike any other country. One of the traditional hallmarks of China's labor relations approach was full employment. This employment orientation has been referred to as the *iron rice bowl*. In the past, employees could expect that their needs and jobs were taken care of—they were secure and permanent. An employee could not be fired, and pay and housing were guaranteed. As you might imagine, such a situation was not conducive to what foreigners might consider good service. And, this was not because of a lack of staffing. A visit to any department store in Hangzhou or Changsha would certainly convince you of this. Full employment meant that even in small departments, like the baby section of a store, one person will be responsible for diapers, another person two feet away will be responsible for formula, and yet another not three feet away will get you baby food.

But in recent years, particularly after China joined the WTO, things have begun to change. While vestiges of the old iron rice bowl system persist, workers can now be laid off (made "redundant"). The law provides for treatment of laid-off workers and also provides a system for arbitrating any disputes that occur in this process.[58] And there are unions in China. As you might suspect, however, they play a supporting role when they play any role at all. Communist ideology is consistent with the notion of union activity in that it dictates that "workers are masters of the house."[59] And although unions are ostensibly the link between the party and the masses, they are often ridiculed as unnecessary (*pao loong tau*—"a body to fill a temporary vacancy"). Although China's late leader Deng Xiaoping once said that economic changes have resulted in unions "no longer being the unnecessary organizations that some believe," they are unlikely to replace the influence exerted by the party. After all, the union movement is officially obligated to work with management and the party to resolve disputes and problems.[60]

Things may be a bit different in joint ventures owned by the central government and a foreign enterprise. Generally, management is supposed to "positively support" the work of trade unions in joint ventures. In fact, joint

cities to protest pay cuts and job losses. Although the provincial governor was sacked as a result, workers continued their protests with work slowdowns and unpublicized strikes (which are illegal in China).

The central government is in a difficult position as its growth policies have fostered business activity but have also raised concerns about working conditions, accident rates, and labor strife. On the one hand, the government worries about unions becoming an organizing platform for unified worker dissent, something that could pose a threat to the Communist Party's control over the country. On the other hand, China's leaders also worry about the reactions of foreign investors to aggressive moves to deal with labor-related concerns. For example, an unnamed executive with an American company in Shanghai said, "I don't consider it an appetizing prospect. We've been here for years without any union demands, and now they're telling us we have to start negotiating pay with the Communist party." In response, the Chinese government has moved to assure foreign business that unions won't become overly burdensome while at the same time taking action to suppress unions and labor activists that take unified action. For example, 120 labor leaders who signed a worker protection charter were recently arrested. The government has also taken steps recently to redirect worker complaints with employers. Since the mid-1990s, workers have had the ability to directly challenge employers thanks to a variety of new laws that, among other things, established a system of offices to dispense free legal advice and allowed workers to sue companies themselves. Indeed, since the late 1990s, the number of lawsuits and labor arbitration claims against firms in China has more than doubled, with some 200,000 new cases being filed annually. How these changes will all play out in the years ahead—and what it means for unions in China—remains to be seen.[61]

ventures are required to set aside a percentage of wages paid to help fund programs to educate and train union members. Further, unions have the right to sit on the board of directors to air opinions and complaints. They do not, however, have the right to vote. Still, unions can deal directly with the foreign partners of the joint venture to solve their mutual problems. Perhaps because of their inexperience and lack of negotiating skills, however, unions often don't do very well in this direct relationship. The International Insights on the previous pages highlights some of the resulting problems faced by Chinese workers involved in joint ventures.

Unions in Other Asian Countries Countries such as India, Indonesia, the Philippines, Thailand, and Vietnam are examples of economies—and labor relations—in a state of transition. Hong Kong, which was returned to China in 1997, has little unemployment and very low levels of union activity. Despite Hong Kong's Confucian tradition, many have characterized the attitude of Hong Kong workers as "everyone for himself"—an attitude not likely to foster union participation.[62] Of course, the long-term effect of the return to China on Hong Kong's highly skilled and comparatively well-off workforce will be interesting to follow.

The other so-called "Asian Tigers," the countries of Singapore, South Korea, and Taiwan, have become major influences in the world economy. Although a good deal of government and multinational control is exerted on workplaces in these countries, there are big differences in the state of their labor relations.[63] Labor issues in Singapore and, to a lesser extent, Taiwan have been relatively calm. In contrast, labor relations in South Korea have been more confrontational. A particularly well-publicized strike against Hyundai several years ago illustrates this high level of union activity.[64] The length of the strike and the poor manner in which it was handled by the company was reminiscent of the infamous Homestead strike in Pittsburgh around the turn of the century. Many predict that relations between firms and workers may not improve significantly anytime soon.[65] More recent events at Daewoo seem to support this prediction.[66] Korean workers violently resisted GM's initial efforts to make a bid for the troubled Korean car firm. As one Daewoo worker put it, "Selling the company to GM would mean handing over a piece of Korea to the United States."

Central/South American Unions

Since the passage of the North American Free Trade Agreement, much attention has been focused on Mexico. A variety of federal laws govern labor relations in Mexico, many of which favor labor—including wage and benefit guarantees. As a result, Mexico is a country with a relatively high degree of union participation. In fact, only twenty employees are necessary in order to form a union in Mexico. Consequently, Mexican firms are used to negotiating with many different unions within one unit or factory. If the official union declares a strike, all personnel—including management—must vacate the premises. Flags are stationed at each locked entrance signifying that the plant is under strike. Union members receive pay during the time they're out on a (legal) strike.[67] Unions have won a large number of worker rights, mostly through federal legislation rather than direct union activity. On the other hand, the Labor Secretariat has considerable discretionary power to allow strikes. And in the *maquiladoras* near the U.S. border, companies are often free to choose submissive, government-affiliated unions for their factories.[68] Other major Latin American economies (Brazil, Argentina) have varying levels of government input into labor relations activity.

African Unionism

Overall, union activity in Africa is somewhat like the continent itself—underdeveloped. Nevertheless, there are differences across countries, ranging from the relatively compliant approach in Kenya to the more activist unions in South Africa.[69]

South African labor relations are especially interesting. In the 1970s, when apartheid was at its height, white groups were permitted to form unions and allowed to engage in collective bargaining agreements. Blacks, the vast majority of citizens, however, were denied similar rights. In 1980, black groups gained limited union rights, and the number of union members nearly tripled in five years. Despite the fact that apartheid still existed, the power of the black unions grew quickly. Strike activity increased greatly in the 1980s, some of it very violent. The effect of this organizing was dramatic. In fact, one study showed that the increased wage effects for black workers due to union membership approached the percentage gains realized by American workers, and these gains were greater than for European workers.[70] The main gains were among poorer, low-skill workers, whose minimum wages increased much more than those of any other category of employees. So while future South African President Nelson Mandela was still in jail, black union workers were winning concessions of dramatic size.

Once he became president, Mr. Mandela's challenge was to balance the increasingly strident demands made by both unions and businesses—especially foreign ones. Several years ago, the country's big national union federation (COSATU) staged a one-day nationwide strike against a provision in the new constitution that allowed companies to lock out striking workers. President Mandela appeared with workers wearing COSATU colors and the provision was deleted. Many businesses and foreign investors felt that the incident underscored their concern that South African unions had too much influence over government policies. They argued that if South Africa was to be more competitive globally, government needed to adopt more flexible labor rules and dump state-run enterprises. The unions countered that such moves would create more unemployment and that many of apartheid's inequities (such as low pay and poor living conditions for black citizens) still needed to be addressed. Today, current South African President Thabo Mbeki continues to try and balance such competing demands.[71]

International Employee Unions

As we've noted, unions around the world have had varying degrees of membership and success in recent years. Perhaps the largest challenge to domestic unions, however, is the multinational itself. As we've said, one of the main cards multinationals can play is the threat to move some or all of their operations to another country. Since unions almost always represent workers in one country, they are relatively powerless in the face of this threat.[72]

There have been a variety of responses by unions to this perceived weakness. The most noteworthy has been the development of international organizations of workers and their interests. In fact, as far back as 1919, the League of Nations, as part of the peace agreement ending World War I, created the *International Labor Organization (ILO)*. The ILO is composed of representatives from employees, employers, and governments, with each group having a say in policies that are developed.[73] There are now about 174 member states in this organization. The ILO has mainly been responsible for developing guidelines and standards for labor conditions and treatment. These guidelines, however, have the same legal status as an international treaty. Accordingly, they must be ratified and agreed to on a nation-by-nation basis. Given the controversial issues that the ILO deals with (equal pay, child labor, discrimination against various groups, etc.) and this ratification scheme, many countries fail to embrace all the guidelines. Even if countries ratify a guideline, making sure they comply with its stipulations is even tougher.[74] In many ways, the ILO operates like its larger parent organization, the United Nations. Other important international organizations also have similar goals, including arms of the European Union and the *Organization for Economic Cooperation and Development (OECD)*.

There is also a group of unions with international membership. One of the most important of these is the *International Confederation of Free Trade Unions (ICFTU)*. Its goal is to help national unions in their dealings with multinationals. The membership of the ICFTU is concentrated in North America and Europe and is a force to be reckoned with by firms. Closely associated with these groups are *International Trade Secretariats (ITSs)*, which often cover major industry types (e.g., the International Metal Workers Federation). There are also some ITSs at the company level, such as the General Motors Council, which includes union members from GM plants around the globe. Regardless of the form these organizations take, their general goal is to emulate the organization of a multinational and, in so doing, to develop a transnational bargaining system.

That said, most observers suggest that international unions have been largely ineffective.[75] There are a number of complex reasons for this fact, including the unique laws of various countries and multinational opposition. One of the most insidious reasons, however, has been the ability of multinationals to effectively play one country and its unions against another. There are some examples of cross-border coordination among unions, such as the financial support provided by German union IG Metall to striking workers at British Aerospace.[76] Also, the United Electrical Workers union in the United States recently supported a Mexican union's efforts to organize a General Electric plant in Mexico.

These events, however, are unusual. Many powerful unions within countries are, in effect, political groups and, as a result, are more concerned with national issues, not international labor organizations. In fact, it's common for a union in one country to gain jobs by dealing with a multinational that is having labor trouble in another country. This competitive attitude is summed up by a Canadian union member: "An American union is not going to fight to protect Canadian jobs at the expense of American jobs."[77] For example, some years ago Hoover Appliances (owned by Maytag Corporation) announced plans to close a 600-employee factory in Dijon, France, and move its operations to Glasgow, Scotland. Hoover's Scottish workers traded changes in work conditions for job security and the 400 new jobs that would result. The French were outraged and took to the streets to protest. They also crossed the channel to take part in a TV debate, during which they accused their Scottish colleagues of taking their jobs. British union leaders were rather quiet about the incident, except to say that "we have nothing to be ashamed of."[78]

It's clear that most workers probably see their foreign counterparts as competitors, rather than as allies in the same struggle. This is a large obstacle that international unions will have to overcome to be successful.[79] Nevertheless, several American unions have recently begun to join forces with their European and international counterparts. The AFL-CIO, for example, has made connections with European unions, something it rarely has done, and has also taken nontraditional positions (e.g., supporting immigration amnesty in the United States).[80]

Other Forms of Employee Control/Input

Of course, unions aren't the only means by which employees can obtain desired outcomes. There are a variety of mechanisms by which employees can glean benefits, both within and beyond union structures. These methods are known by different terms, including *industrial democracy*, *self-management*, and *worker participation*. The last term is probably most appropriate here, since we are referring to methods by which workers participate in the management of the firm. This participation can include many different forms of input, ranging from having no say at all to having the right to veto management action. Although there are many forms of worker participation in management (including unions themselves), we will discuss three different varieties: (1) joint consultation committees (JCCs), (2) works councils, and (3) board membership.[81]

Joint Consultation Committees   First, **joint consultation committees (JCCs)** are common in many Western countries. As the name implies, these are groups of workers who sit on a committee that deals with topics of mutual interest to workers and management. Their charge can range from concerns about product quality (such as quality circles) to working conditions, plant safety, and even the general quality of work life (as in Sweden). Typically, committee members make suggestions that may or may not be taken up by management. In turn, management is often expected to keep workers informed about developments via the committee. Obviously, the effectiveness of such committees depends on the goodwill and intentions of a firm and is most likely to be successful in paternalistic companies with relatively good employee relations.[82]

joint consultation committees
Groups of workers who sit on committees that deal with topics of mutual interest to workers and management

Works Councils   **Works councils** are another form of worker participation and are common in many European countries (e.g., Belgium, France, Germany, the Netherlands). These groups are similar to JCCs in many ways, but the essential difference is that works councils often have significant power to block management decisions and actions. Often, these councils exist as a result of national laws that mandate their creation—a step often seen as necessary because of a perceived societal obligation to seek employee input (rather than as a way to improve competitiveness or the bottom line).[83]

In the Netherlands, for example, Dutch law requires that any firm with thirty-five or more employees must create a works council. The council consists of members who are elected by employees and must be consulted in decisions of importance to the organization. These issues are often related to personnel policy (e.g., safety and training programs, pay and benefits issues, relocation of work, plant closures, etc.). If a firm has 100 or more employees, this consultation could include major financial decisions (e.g., new capital investments, business acquisitions, etc.). Theoretically, the works council should represent the interest of employees. Members of the council, however, may be managers or production employees. In reality, councils can be co-opted by management via this and other means.[84]

works councils
Another form of worker participation, common in many European countries, that often have significant power to combat management decisions and actions

In powerful works councils, as in Germany, an employee may effectively hold two jobs—their regular job and their job as council representative. As a result, it's not uncommon to have a second office and perhaps even two staffs, right on company grounds. The council representative may be similar to a shop steward in the U.S. union environment. The difference is that the former has more real input into company decisions.

Board Membership Board membership is a third, less common mechanism by which workers have input into the business. In this case, input is often extensive. In seven European countries (Austria, Denmark, France, Germany, Luxembourg, Norway, and Sweden) law dictates that workers must have some kind of representation on the board of directors of firms. In most cases, these boards are supervisory boards—the group that selects the management board which is responsible for running day-to-day operations. We have already talked about the notion of codetermination in Germany—this is an example of a board membership method. Typically, workers have only a minority membership on the board (the exception being large German firms). And despite what appears to be such a radical idea, research shows that board memberships for workers generally have relatively little effect on the business one way or another. Typically, boards meet very infrequently (often just a few hours a year), and equally often, when talk does turn to substantive issues, worker representatives may be at a disadvantage. Many feel they lack the background to fully evaluate the complex information (e.g., finances) discussed in these meetings. Nevertheless, workers often provide valuable input that has changed health, safety, and investment decisions by the firm. At the minimum, boards appear to provide a symbolic function for workers, with some unions (e.g., in Sweden) viewing them as a valuable source of information rather than as a lever for wielding power.

Putting Agreements into Practice

As we have discussed, there are many ways that agreements between management and workers can evolve. Unfortunately, there are also a variety of ways that disagreements can come about. The result may be conflict and strife between management and labor.

Relations between Management and Labor Multinational firms typically consider the general state of relations between management and employees before they choose to invest in a foreign subsidiary. And these relations show great variability. Exhibit 14.5 ranks thirty-seven countries on the degree of productive relations between management and employees. On a 1 to 10 scale, there are only three countries in this survey with ratings over 8—Japan, Denmark, and Singapore. While there certainly are good reasons not to locate a plant in these and other countries (e.g., Sweden, Norway, and Switzerland), poor employee relations is not one of them. As you can see, the United States tied for twenty-second place out of thirty-seven countries, a relatively low showing, but perhaps not that surprising.

EXHIBIT 14.5   *Rankings of the General Climate of Industrial Relations in Thirty-Seven Countries*

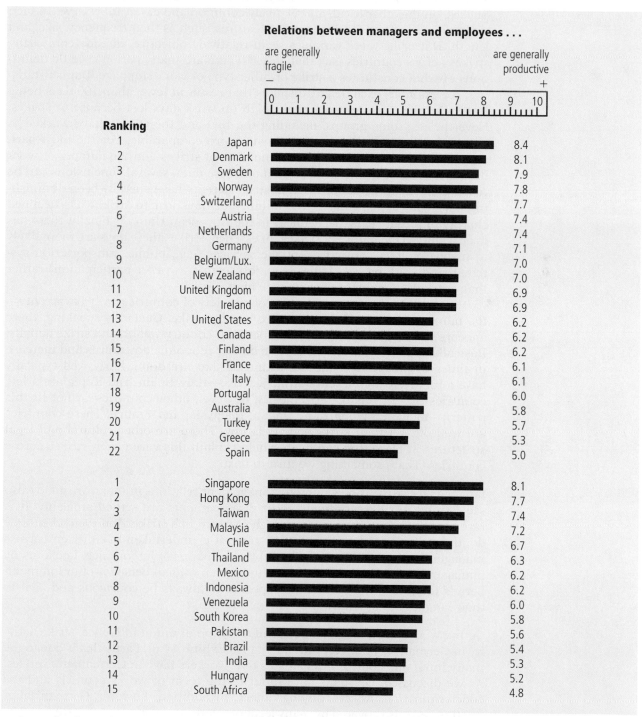

Relations between managers and employees . . .

		are generally fragile –	are generally productive +

Ranking

1	Japan	8.4
2	Denmark	8.1
3	Sweden	7.9
4	Norway	7.8
5	Switzerland	7.7
6	Austria	7.4
7	Netherlands	7.4
8	Germany	7.1
9	Belgium/Lux.	7.0
10	New Zealand	7.0
11	United Kingdom	6.9
12	Ireland	6.9
13	United States	6.2
14	Canada	6.2
15	Finland	6.2
16	France	6.1
17	Italy	6.1
18	Portugal	6.0
19	Australia	5.8
20	Turkey	5.7
21	Greece	5.3
22	Spain	5.0
1	Singapore	8.1
2	Hong Kong	7.7
3	Taiwan	7.4
4	Malaysia	7.2
5	Chile	6.7
6	Thailand	6.3
7	Mexico	6.2
8	Indonesia	6.2
9	Venezuela	6.0
10	South Korea	5.8
11	Pakistan	5.6
12	Brazil	5.4
13	India	5.3
14	Hungary	5.2
15	South Africa	4.8

Source: "Rankings of General Climate of Industrial Relations in 37 Different Countries." *World Competitiveness Report 93*, IMD/WEF, Switzerland.

Deterioration of Relations Sometimes labor-management relations can deteriorate to the point where work slowdowns, sabotage, and even violence occur. These events, however, are either difficult to track or are not all that common. Strikes, on the other hand, are relatively common and easier to observe. In fact, strikes have some easily documented features, such as their frequency, size, and length. But while these variables seem relatively objective, directly comparing strikes across countries isn't that easy.[85] There are many nation-specific definitions of what constitutes a strike or other type of work stoppage. Danish statistics, for example, exclude any disputes that result in fewer than 100 days being lost.[86] Despite this, Denmark ranks high on work days lost because of strikes. Nevertheless, some groups, including the ILO and the OECD, have worked to clarify definitions and make strike data more comparable. For the most part, strike data are usually based on the number of strikes and the number of work days lost because of the strike. Based on these data, several conclusions can be reached about strike action.[87] First, strike activity has generally been diminishing since the 1970s. Indeed, the number of days lost to strikes has declined sharply in recent years, particularly in the European Union.[88] Finally, there has been a shift in the nature of strikes. In essence, strikes these days are more likely to involve political objectives, public services (e.g., public transportation systems), and work process issues (e.g., job security, worker participation) rather than workplace outcomes per se (e.g., higher pay).

Exhibit 14.6 presents a ranking of a variety of countries on strike activity—the number of working days that are lost by strike. Generally speaking, there appears to be a general relationship between country wealth and strike activity. Basically, is seems that strikes decline during economic downturns and increase in times of prosperity.[89] Indeed, countries that are doing fairly well typically have a relatively high level of strike activity—Italy, Spain, and Korea are a few countries that fit this pattern. Clearly, however, other countries do not fit this pattern—including Hong Kong, Japan, Malaysia, and France. These countries are well off, yet their strike activity is low. There are other cultural and legal structures in place that can further help explain this variance in strikes across countries. That's something we turn to next.

Japan As we've mentioned, union-management relations in Japan are good (also see Exhibit 14.5). Accordingly, most disagreements are settled amicably. It is rare for relations to get caustic enough to result in a strike. And even when they do, the strike is brief and not bitter—often it is undertaken to either embarrass management or to bring to their attention a matter of importance. Lockouts by management are very rare. In fact, although emotional behavior of union members is tolerated, management is expected to always be courteous and civil in their language and behavior.[90]

Germany Despite a long and powerful tradition of union influence, strike activity in Germany is relatively infrequent (see Exhibit 14.6). Partly this is due to the many input and control mechanisms that workers have in German enterprises. As we discussed, Germans have input in the form of works councils and the codetermination process, among others. In addition, however, German labor relations are also covered by many legal regulations, making more extreme steps like strikes and lockouts less necessary. For example, laws prohibit either strikes or lockouts when a contract is in effect. Consequently, strikes usually occur when contracts have expired and negotiations are ongoing. In the 1980s, German unions struck with an existing contract in place. During this period of

EXHIBIT 14.6   *Strike Activity in a Variety of Countries*

Country	Days Lost to Strike*	Country	Days Lost to Strike*
Iceland	554	Sweden	30
Spain	250	New Zealand	25
Canada	180	Belgium	25
Denmark	175	United Kingdom	24
Italy	140	Portugal	22
Finland	110	Netherlands	20
France	90	Germany	4
Norway	85	Switzerland	3
Ireland	75	Japan	1
Australia	74	Austria	1
United States	45		

*Entries reflect the number of working days lost per 1,000 employees, annual average from 1993 to 2002.
Source: Adapted from ———. (2004). Labor disputes. *The Economist*, April 24, 108.

high inflation, workers wanted their wages to keep up with this inflation. These situations, however, are rare in Germany.

The United Kingdom As Exhibit 14.6 shows, strike activity in the United Kingdom is not that high. The reason for this might be the government's traditionally "hands-off" approach to labor relations. This approach has resulted in fewer legal constraints on labor action relative to many other EU countries. For example, labor contracts do not prohibit strikes. This may provide an implicit advantage to unions, forcing management to settle. Strikes usually occur during a deadlock in negotiations, although no one type of strike (in terms of frequency or style) seems to predominate in Britain.[91]

The United States By comparison, Exhibit 14.6 shows that the United States has a higher amount of strike activity. American labor contracts typically prohibit strikes during the period of the agreement. So once a contract is in place, a strike (called a **wildcat strike**) is rare and usually not authorized by the union. As in Germany, once a contract expires and a new one is not yet approved, a strike becomes a viable option—an option that is exercised relatively frequently. Employees may sometimes choose to continue to work during the negotiation period, while threatening a strike. Lockouts by management are not unheard of, but they are relatively rare.

wildcat strike
A strike that is called despite the fact that a union has a contract with a company in force

Effect of Unions on Strikes

An important question from management's perspective is the overall effect of having a unionized workforce. Many managers find dealings with unions, regardless of where they are, to be challenging. Nevertheless, there are some benefits from a unionized workforce, including a structured bargaining system and clear contractual obligations that must be fulfilled.

Perhaps a more subtle benefit of union membership, however, is that it may quell more extreme and militant worker action. For instance, the data presented in Exhibit 14.7 show the relation between overall level of worker militancy and union density in twelve EU countries. Militancy is defined as a combination of variables that are indicative of labor strife and unrest. In general, the exhibit shows a negative relationship between militancy and union density. In other words, higher union density is associated with a lower incidence of violence. For example, the five countries on the right portion of Exhibit 14.7 (the United Kingdom, France, Greece, Italy, and Spain) all have high levels of militancy and a relatively low percentage of workers who are unionized. The left side of this graph shows the opposite for several countries (e.g., the Benelux countries). So despite all the management resistance to unions, there may be a silver lining. Organized employee input—perhaps in many forms—may actually make management-worker relations smoother than would otherwise be the case.

EXHIBIT 14.7 *The Relationship between Worker Militancy and Union Representation**

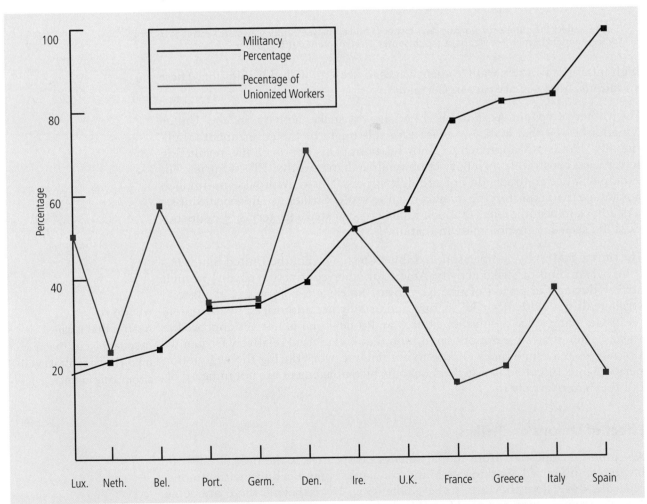

*Spanish labor relations were considered the most militant and are therefore assigned 100%; other countries' rankings are reported relative to this figure.
Source: Adapted from Sparrow, P., and Hiltrop, J. M. (1994). *European human resource management in transition.* New York: Prentice-Hall.

Chapter Summary

In this chapter we looked at the value and influence of *groups*—both small and large—across cultures. First, we examined smaller work teams and considered the impact of culture on how they function. We reviewed research that shows that national and cultural differences have the potential to be both problematic and promising. For example, groups are more important in collectivist countries than they are in individualistic ones. But even in a collectivist culture, in-groups and out-groups vary dramatically in their value. Social loafing, a common effect in individualistic countries, also tends to occur among collectivists but only in groups that are unimportant to them (out-groups). Collectivistic employees are likely to pitch in whole-heartedly when working in groups that are important to them (in-groups).

We also raised the general issue of diversity in cross-cultural groups. Among other things, diversity in groups means that group members bring sometimes widely differing ways of doing things to the table. These differing styles can be a hindrance to group effectiveness if not recognized and managed correctly. We discussed specific cases of diverse cross-cultural teams and offered suggestions for managers who want to capitalize on the promise of diversity.

In the second half of the chapter, we shifted our discussion to larger labor relations issues. We focused on the relations between two important groups—management and employees. There are many differences across countries in both the presence and influence of unions. Nevertheless, employee interests are often represented to management by unions. That said, the percentage of workers who are union members varies across countries.

One reason for the variance is that worker interests can be served by a variety of mechanisms besides unions (e.g., legal methods or other forms of worker input). Indeed, a variety of forms of worker input exist, ranging from mild forms—such as having some say or input into work procedures—to having a de facto veto over important firm decisions. Of course, despite unions and a variety of communication and input methods, sometimes management and employees just can't agree. Labor strikes are one response to a lack of agreement. Once again, the nature and prevalence of strike activity or other forms of employee response to labor-management discord can vary across countries.

Discussion Questions

1. What are the effects of groups on productivity likely to be in various countries? What would increase productivity for American, Chinese, or German groups?

2. What factors could explain why a multicultural group might experience difficulty solving problems in a creative fashion?

3. Why might multinational companies have the upper hand in dealing with workers, even if those workers are unionized and spread across a variety of countries?

4. What are some of the differences between how American, European, and Asian unions operate? Why might those differences exist?

5. What is the relationship between the presence of unions and the level of worker militancy? Explain why this is the case.

Up to the Challenge?

Cultural Diversity among Work Teams at BP

WHEN PEOPLE FROM different cultural traditions come into contact—as they do in the work teams created by BP—many of the issues we have discussed in this book come into play. Communication becomes critical, perception plays a role, decision-making styles can produce conflict, and more. Mr. Ruijter's challenge was to gain the trust and commitment of the team members so that he could capitalize on their strengths. One of the first things he did was to organize a two-day seminar on team building. All team members attended and were encouraged to participate via techniques that would uncover their own approach to groups. Indeed, the seminar led off with an exercise designed to uncover beliefs and philosophies that each member had about cultural differences. Next, team members completed a series of more specific exercises designed to help them better understand their group preferences and those of others. Communication techniques were then practiced in order to make this understanding concrete.

Along the way, the various groups learned many things. For example, early on the Dutch group was concerned with the style of management that would be employed. They were used to an open style that allowed for free expression and sharing of opinions. The Germans, on the other hand, were very concerned that proper operational procedures be put into place quickly. Even minor differences were discovered and discussed. For example, the Americans were surprised that the French shook hands with everyone in their team every morning. Discussion revealed that the French saw this as a sign of friendliness and infor-

mality. The Americans, in contrast, felt that a handshake was a relatively formal sign of politeness. Likewise, the Germans did not wish to be addressed by their first names (even if you knew them well), whereas the Scandinavians wanted to be addressed by last name only. Many of these cultural differences were brought out in the open during the seminar. It appeared that all participants were eager to share the aspects of their culture which they thought were valuable.

As this experience suggests, if there is one thing that goes a long way toward building team cohesion, it's bringing differences out in the open and discussing them fully. This is not, however, as easy as it sounds. BP did it well and their Brussels team developed a set of ground rules for interacting. Some of these rules include the following:

- Do not prejudge people, functions, or cultures.
- Create a climate in which people aren't afraid to ask questions.
- Try not to make assumptions—but if you do, verify and check them for accuracy!
- Discuss and talk out all issues.
- Agree on a common objective and keep it in mind during periods of disagreement.[92]

International Development

Japanese Decision-Making Exercise

Purpose

1. To give students the opportunity to work through a meaningful task using the Japanese approach to consensual decision making.
2. To compare students' own experiences with group decision making with the Japanese approach.

Instructions

Your instructor will explain the processes of Ringi and Nemawashi and will set up the structure of the exercise. Group composition includes leaders (Kacho) and student managers (Bucho). Next, your instructor will divide the class into groups of four to six members. Your group will design a final exam format that is likely to be a valuable learning tool and appropriate basis of evaluation for your class (20 minutes).

After that, your instructor will divide the class into new groups of four to six members (the Kacho groups). In your new group you will continue with the task, using the results of the first group as a starting point. After this meeting, groups can choose their own venue for future meetings. Your instructor will give advice during one or two open-ended class sessions. Outside class meetings will occur at the initiation of the group and student leaders (20 minutes).

Next, the whole class will generate a Ringi document that specifies the content of the exam. This document must be signed by all students in the class. Your instructor will discuss what problems, if any, the Ringi document might cause.

Finally, the whole class will discuss the following questions:

How much did your experience resemble the descriptions of Ringi and Nemawashi provided by your instructor? What difficulties did you encounter? Were those difficulties likely to be present in the Japanese context? If so, how would they probably be managed?

Source: Japanese Decision-Making Exercise by Bill Van Buskirk in *Management International: Cases, Exercises, & Readings* by Dorothy Marcic and Sheila Puffer. Exercise © 1994 by Bill Van Buskirk. Used by permission.

Tapping into the Global Network

The Blanchworth China Company

Purpose

1. To illustrate some of the complexities involved in dealing with labor and unions across borders.
2. To highlight the specific issues facing a British company and its union as it contemplates shifting production to eastern Europe.

Background

For background information on labor unions in the United Kingdom, visit the Trades Union Congress (TUC) website at **www.tuc.org.uk**. The TUC provides links to specific unions as well as information about trade union history, union activity, and employment law in the U.K., among other things. For information about the evolving labor union environment in Eastern Europe, visit the Solidarity Center's website at **www.solidarity center.org**. The Solidarity Center aims to promote workers' rights and help labor unions throughout Central and Eastern Europe.

The Company and the Situation

The Blanchworth China company was founded in the British Isles in the eighteenth century and has established a worldwide reputation for premium quality china designed and handcrafted in the United Kingdom. The china always has sold well in the United States and in the early 1980s, fueled by a strong dollar, it experienced an explosive growth in sales. However, as the dollar went into a long decline through the middle and late 1980s, sales of Blanchworth china dropped by 25 percent in the United States. This decline is particularly important to Blanchworth because the U.S. market accounts for approximately 90 percent of the company's output.

The premium quality china market is roughly divided into two segments based on price: the high

segment is priced from US$75 to US$300 per plate, while the lower segment ranges from US$25 to US$75 per plate. Blanchworth has always dominated the high segment with approximately 85 percent market share, but the company had no presence in the lower segment. Unfortunately, it was the high segment of the market that decreased by 25 percent in sales dollars in the late 1980s, while the lower segment had grown by 50 percent during the same period. It was clearly a worldwide trend, not only in Blanchworth's market, but also for most other discretionary income items.

In addition to the falling value of the U.S. dollar and the shrinking market for higher-priced china, several other factors helped to create a severe financial crisis for Blanchworth by the end of the 1980s. During the "good times" of the 1980s, when demand and profits were high, Blanchworth's skilled workers' union made heavy wage and work-rule demands. The company's managers acceded to these demands in order to avoid any work stoppages. As a result, Blanchworth's crafters became some of the highest-paid skilled workers in the British Isles. Workers' salaries increased from 60 percent of the cost of product to nearly 80 percent by the late 1980s. These high labor costs, coupled with debt incurred by its acquisition of a premium crystal manufacturer, prevented Blanchworth from lowering prices when U.S. demand decreased.

In 1988, management was forced to propose immediate cost-reducing measures in order to save the company. Among other things, they determined to reduce their labor force by 25 percent and to purchase new equipment that would make the remaining workers more productive. After heated encounters between management and union leaders, the union finally became convinced that the labor force cuts were necessary in order to save the company. The union also agreed to rescind work rules that had worked to preclude higher worker productivity. The union made these concessions in order to prevent the company from declaring bankruptcy and to save the most union jobs.

After a year of operation with the new equipment, Blanchworth management found that increases in productivity were offset by the larger than expected number of senior crafters taking advantage of the early retirement package. This package was offered as one means of reducing the labor force by the targeted 25 percent. Profits continued to slide after the workforce reduction, and Blanchworth management finally decided the company would have to enter the lower segment of the premium quality china market. While Blanchworth managers realized it would face many more competitors in this lower segment of the market than in the high-price segment, they believed the company's well-respected name and marketing strengths would allow it to make a quick entry into this segment.

In late 1990, Blanchworth introduced a new line of products that were lighter in weight and less ornate than its original china place settings. This entire product line is produced in eastern Europe at a fraction of the labor cost associated with the Blanchworth U.K. plant. Preliminary market research showed that this line has stronger appeal for the younger, first-time china buyers who see themselves as more contemporary and value conscious than traditional Blanchworth customers; moreover, these younger buyers are generally less brand loyal. Blanchworth called its new line *Krohn China*.

Krohn is carried by the same distribution channel as Blanchworth, but it has its own logo, package design, advertising agency, and display case. Management felt that the name Blanchworth associated with the name Krohn would help to establish an image of high quality, but, at the same time, the name Krohn would differentiate the new line from traditional Blanchworth china. This name association has helped to gain the reseller support necessary in making the new line readily accessible to a large market.

As a result of Blanchworth management's decision to locate its new operations in eastern Europe, members of the union and residents of the community in which the Blanchworth factory is located felt betrayed. Union leaders were never informed about the new product line that could have meant rehiring many Blanchworth skilled workers. In addition, the move to eastern Europe has caused ill-will among many consumers throughout the United Kingdom and has resulted in some critical editorial articles in the local and national press.

The union contends that most U.S. customers are brand loyal to Blanchworth because it is made by skilled workers in the United Kingdom. They argue that this loyalty stems from the fact that many Americans trace their ancestry to one or more countries in the United Kingdom. Management countered that Blanchworth had never been sold as a U.K. product and that most U.S. buyers neither know nor care where their china products are made. Although many bitter feelings arose between management and the union, no work stoppages occurred during 1991.

In early 1992, management announced that after the first year of sales, Krohn generated twice as much profit per plate as Blanchworth. Also, they asserted that Blanchworth employees in the United Kingdom were still not productive enough to offset the high wages these workers earned. As a result, management representatives opened discussions with union leaders about how to solve the continuing low-profit problem. Management suggested that the only solution was a further reduction in wages and benefits, as well as another major change in work rules. The union disagreed with this perspective and countered that the low level of profitability actually resulted from poor management, rather than "overpaid, unproductive workers" as suggested by management.

Although never openly stated, union leaders suspect that management may be considering moving all Blanchworth operations to eastern Europe. The union continues to argue that U.S. customers will not accept Blanchworth china that is not made by U.K. crafters. They cite the fact that 100,000 tourists tour the U.K. plant each year and that at least half of these tourists are Americans. Many of these American tourists purchase over US$1,000 in china products during their visit to the plant. The union contends that the tourists who come to the plant feel a strong affinity for Blanchworth china because it is a product of the United Kingdom, and most of these on-site sales would be lost if the plant were moved to eastern Europe. To further strengthen this argument, the union cites the U.S. Census Bureau statistics giving the following breakdown of U.S. citizens by U.K.

ancestry: England 32.6 million, Scotland 5.4 million, Ireland 38.7 million, and Wales 2.0 million.

Instructions

You are a business consultant who has been brought in to assist Blanchworth's top management with strategic decision making in several areas. During the briefing you are given additional information:

- Management is seriously considering moving all Blanchworth factory operations to eastern Europe while keeping its other functions in the United Kingdom. They make it clear that the design and quality assurance operations would remain in the United Kingdom. The concern is about how quickly the new eastern European plant and workers could achieve full quality production, especially if workers strike at the British plant before the new plant is on line.

- Management is concerned about political instability in eastern Europe. If they move both Krohn and Blanchworth, their entire production could be compromised, with little chance of reopening a plant in the United Kingdom.

- Sales of Krohn in the United Kingdom are extremely sluggish, but are doing well on the continent. Krohn does seem to be gaining acceptance slowly in the United States, mostly among young couples buying it for themselves rather than receiving it as gifts from parents or friends and relatives.

- The union and the community have threatened to discredit the firm if it moves to eastern Europe by taking their case directly to the U.K and U.S. customers.

Answer the following questions about this case:

1. Management believes its foreign sales will be unaffected by moving all operations to eastern Europe. What research should be done before making this decision? Which research methodology do you recommend?

2. Try to anticipate the ways in which the union and the community could discredit the company name if it leaves the United Kingdom. Will Americans boycott the company after the move? Will Americans voice their disapproval in large numbers before the move? How will you get these answers?

3. What specific measures can management take to "inoculate" the firm against the union actions that you anticipated in question 2? Should it take these steps rather than dealing with the problem after it is a reality?

4. Should management ask for concessions in order to keep the firm in the United Kingdom? Make a list of possible concessions and tell who should provide them, for example, the union, community, national government, and so on. Concentrate on the long-term solutions when sketching out a plan for how a win-win situation can be reached in this case.

Source: From *International Business Cultural Sourcebook and Case Studies,* 2nd edition by L.B. Catlin & T.F. White, © 2001, pp. 47–50. Reprinted with permission of South-Western College Publishing, a division of Thomson Learning. Fax 800-730-2215.

CASE 7

The Case of the Floundering Expatriate

At exactly 1:40 on a warm, sunny Friday afternoon in July 1995, Frank Waterhouse, CEO of Argos Diesel, Europe, leaves his office on the top floor of the Argos Tower, overlooking the Zürichsee. In the grip of a tension headache, he rides the glass elevator down the outside of the mirrored building.

To quiet his nerves, he studies his watch. In less than half an hour, Waterhouse must look on as Bert Donaldson faces the company's European managers—executives of the parts suppliers that Argos has acquired over the past two years. Donaldson is supposed to give the keynote address at this event, part of the second Argos Management Meeting organized by his training and education department. But late yesterday afternoon, he phoned Waterhouse to say he didn't think the address would be very good. Donaldson said he hadn't gotten enough feedback from the various division heads to put together the presentation he had planned. His summary of the company's progress wouldn't be what he had hoped.

It's his meeting! Waterhouse thinks, as the elevator moves silently down to the second floor. How could he not be prepared? Is this really the man who everyone at corporate headquarters in Detroit thinks is so fantastic?

Waterhouse remembers his introduction to Donaldson just over a year ago. Argos International's CEO and chairman, Bill Loun, had phoned Waterhouse himself to say he was sending the "pick of the litter." He said that Donaldson had a great international background—that he had been a professor of American studies in Cairo for five years. Then he had returned to the States and joined Argos. Donaldson had helped create the cross-divisional, cross-functional teams that had achieved considerable cost reductions and quality improvements.

Loun had said that Donaldson was just what Argos Europe needed to create a seamless European team—to facilitate communication among the different European parts suppliers that Waterhouse had worked so hard to acquire. Waterhouse had proved his own strategic skills, his own ability to close deals, by successfully building a network of companies in Europe under the Argos umbrella. All the pieces were in place. But for the newly expanded company to meet its financial goals, the units had to work together. The managers had to become an integrated team. Donaldson could help them. Together they would keep the company's share of the diesel engine and turbine market on the rise.

Waterhouse deserved to get the best help, the CEO had said. Bert Donaldson was the best. And later, when the numbers proved the plan successful, Waterhouse could return to the States a hero. (Waterhouse heard Loun's voice clearly in his head: "I've got my eye on you, Frank. You know you're in line.")

Waterhouse had been enthusiastic. Donaldson could help him reach the top. He had met the man several times in Detroit. Donaldson seemed to have a quick mind, and he was very charismatic.

But that wasn't the Donaldson who had arrived in Zürich in August 1994 with his wife and two daughters. This man didn't seem to be a team builder—not in this venue. Here his charisma seemed abrasive.

"The Case of the Floundering Expatriate" by Gordon Adler. Reprinted by permission of *Harvard Business Review*, July/August 1995. Copyright © 1995 by the Harvard Business School Publishing Corporation. All rights reserved.

The elevator comes to a stop. Waterhouse steps into the interior of the building and heads toward the seminar room at the end of the hall.

Waterhouse keeps thinking of his own career. He has spent most of his time since Donaldson's appointment securing three major government contracts in Moscow, Ankara, and Warsaw. He has kept the ball rolling, kept his career on track. It isn't his fault that Donaldson can't handle this assignment. It isn't his fault that the Germans and the French still can't agree on a unified sales plan.

His thoughts turn back to Donaldson. It can't be all Bert's fault, either. Donaldson is a smart man, a good man. His successes in the States were genuine. And Donaldson is worried about this assignment; it isn't as though he's just being stubborn. He sounded worried on the phone. He cares. He knows his job is falling apart and he doesn't know what to do. What can he return to at Argos in the States if he doesn't excel here in Europe?

Let Donaldson run with the ball—that's what they said in Detroit. It isn't working.

Waterhouse reaches the doorway of the seminar room. Ursula Lindt, his executive assistant, spots him from the other side. Lindt is from a wealthy local family. Most of the local hires go to her to discuss their problems. Waterhouse recalls a few of her comments about Donaldson: Staff morale on the fifth floor is lower than ever; there seems to be a general malaise. Herr Direktor Donaldson must be having problems at home. Why else would he work until midnight?

Waterhouse takes a seat in the front row and tries to distract himself by studying the meeting schedule. "Managing Change and Creating Vision: Improving Argos with Teamwork" is the title. Donaldson's "vision" for Argos Europe. Waterhouse sighs. Lindt nears him and, catching his eye, begins to complain.

"A few of the managers have been making noises about poor organization," she says. "And Sauras, the Spanish director, called to complain that the meeting schedule was too tight." Her litany of problems continues: "Maurizio, the director in Rome, came up to me this morning and began to lobby for Donaldson's replacement. He feels that we need someone with a better understanding of the European environment." Seeing Waterhouse frown, Lindt backs off. "But he's always stirring up trouble," she says. "Otherwise,

the conference appears to be a success." She sits down next to Waterhouse and studies her daily planner.

The room slowly fills with whispers and dark hand-tailored suits. Groups break up and reform. "Grüss Gott, Heinz, wie geht's?" "Jacques, ça va bien?" "Bill, good to see you . . . Great." Waterhouse makes a perfunctory inspection of the crowd. Why isn't Donaldson in here schmoozing? He hears a German accent: "Two-ten. Ja ja. Amerikanische Pünktlichkeit." Punctuality. Unlike Donaldson, he knows enough German to get by.

A signal is given. The chitchat fades with the lights. Waterhouse turns his gaze to the front as Donaldson strides up to the podium.

Donaldson speaks. "As President Eisenhower once said, 'I have two kinds of problems, the urgent and the important. The urgent are not important, and the important are never urgent.'" He laughs, but the rest of the room is silent save for the sound of paper shuffling.

Donaldson pauses to straighten his notes and then delivers a flat ten-minute summary of the European companies' organizational structure. He reviews the basics of the team-building plan he has developed—something with which all the listeners are already familiar. He thanks his secretary for her efforts.

Then he turns the meeting over to Waterhouse, who apologizes for not having been able to give the managers any notice that this session would be shorter than planned. He assures them that the rest of the schedule is intact and asks them to take this time as a break before their 4 p.m. logistics meeting, which will be run by the French division head.

The managers exchange glances, and Waterhouse detects one or two undisguised smiles. Walking out of the seminar room, he hears someone say, "At least the meeting didn't run overtime." Waterhouse fumes. He has put in four years of hard work here in Europe. This is the first year of his second three-year contract. He is being groomed for a top management position back in the States. The last thing he needs is a distraction like this.

He remembers how Detroit reacted when, a little over a month ago, he raised the issue of Donaldson's failure to adjust. He had written a careful letter to Bill Loun suggesting that

Donaldson's assignment might be over his head, that the timing wasn't right. The CEO had phoned him right away. "That's rubbish, Frank," his voice had boomed over the line. "You've been asking for someone to help make this plan work, and we've sent you the best we've got. You can't send him back. It's your call—you have the bottom-line responsibility. But I'm hoping he'll be part of your inner circle, Frank. I'd give him more time. Make it work. I'm counting on you."

More time is no longer an option, Waterhouse thinks. But if he fires Donaldson now or sends him back to Detroit, he loses whatever progress has been made toward a unified structure. Donaldson has begun to implement a team-building program; if he leaves, the effort will collapse. And how could he fire Donaldson, anyway? The guy isn't working out here, but firing him would destroy his career. Bert doesn't deserve that.

What's more, the European team program has been touted as a major initiative, and Waterhouse has allowed himself to be thought of as one of its drivers. Turning back would reflect badly on him as well.

On the other hand, the way things are going, if Donaldson stays, he may himself cause the plan to fail. One step forward, two steps back. "I don't have the time to walk Donaldson through remedial cultural adjustment," Waterhouse mumbles under his breath.

Donaldson approaches him in the hall. "I sent a multiple-choice survey to every manager. One of them sent back a rambling six-page essay," he says. "I sent them in April. I got back only seven of forty from the Germans. Every time I called, it was 'under review.' One of them told me his people wanted to discuss it—in German. The Portuguese would have responded if I'd brought it personally."

Waterhouse tells Donaldson he wants to meet with him later. "Five o'clock. In my office." He turns away abruptly.

Ursula Lindt follows him toward the elevator. "Herr Direktor, did you hear what Herr Donaldson called Frau Schweri?"

Bettina Schweri, who organizes Donaldson's programs, is essentially his manager. She speaks five languages fluently and writes three with style. Lindt and Schweri have known each other since childhood and eat lunch together every day.

"A secretary," Lindt says, exasperated. "Frau Schweri a secretary? Simply not to believe."

Back in his office, Waterhouse gets himself a glass of water and two aspirin. In his mind, he's sitting across from Donaldson ten months earlier.

"Once I reach a goal," Donaldson says, "I set another one and get to work. I like to have many things going at once—especially since I have only two years. I'm going for quick results, Frank. I've even got the first project lined up. We'll bring in a couple of trainers from the Consulting Consortium to run that team-skills workshop we talked about."

Waterhouse comes back to the present. That first workshop hadn't gone too badly—at least he hadn't heard of any problems. But he, Waterhouse, had not attended. He picks up the phone and places a call to Paul Janssen, vice president of human resources for Argos Europe. Paul is a good friend, a trusted colleague. The two men often cross paths at the health club.

A few seconds later, Janssen's voice booms over the line. "Frank? Why didn't you just walk down the hall to see me? I haven't seen you at the club in weeks."

Waterhouse doesn't want to chat. "Donaldson's first training weekend, in February," he says. "How'd it go? Really."

"Really. Well, overall, not too bad. A few glitches, but nothing too out of the ordinary for a first run. Bert had some problems with his assistant. Apparently, Frau Schweri had scheduled the two trainers to arrive in Zürich two days early to prepare everything, recover from jet lag, and have dinner at the Baur au Lac. They came the night before. You can imagine how that upset her. Bert knew about the change but didn't inform Frau Schweri."

Waterhouse has the distinct impression that Janssen has been waiting for a chance to talk about this. "Go on," Waterhouse says.

"Well, there were a few problems with the workshops."

"Problems?"

"Well, yes. One of the managers from Norway—Dr. Godal, I believe—asked many questions during Bert's presentation, and he became rather irascible."

"Bert?" Waterhouse asked.

"Yes. And one of the two trainers wore a Mickey Mouse sweater—"

"Mickey Mouse?" Waterhouse laughs without meaning to.

"A sweater with a depiction of Mickey Mouse on the front."

"What on earth does that have to do with Bert?"

"Well, Bert offered them a two-year contract after Frau Schweri advised him not to. He apparently told her he was satisfied with the trainers and, so far as he was concerned, questions about their personal habits and clothing weren't worth his time."

"Yes, and—"

"Well, there were complaints—"

"They all went to Frau Schweri?" He is beginning to see.

"One of the managers said the trainers provided too much information; he felt as though they were condescending to him. A bombardment of information, he called it. Other managers complained that Bert didn't provide enough background information. The French managers seemed to think the meeting was worthwhile. But Bert must think that because his style works with one group, the others will fall into place automatically. And everyone was unhappy with the schedule. The trainers always ran overtime, so everybody was displeased because there weren't any coffee breaks for people from various offices to network. Oh, and the last thing? All the name cards had first names and last names—no titles."

"No titles," Waterhouse says, and lets out a sigh. "Paul, I wish you'd told me all this earlier."

"I didn't think you needed to hear it, Frank. You've been busy with the new contracts." They agree to meet at the club later in the week, and they hang up. Waterhouse stares down at Donaldson's file.

His résumé looks perfect. He has a glowing review from the American University in Cairo. There, Donaldson earned the highest ratings for his effectiveness, his ease among students from forty countries, and his sense of humor. At Argos in the United States, he implemented the cross-divisional team approach in record time. Donaldson is nothing short of a miracle worker.

Waterhouse leans back in his swivel-tilter and lets the scuttlebutt on Donaldson run through his mind. Word is that he's an *Arbeitstier*. "Work animal" is the direct, unflattering translation. He never joins the staff for a leisurely lunch in the canteen, preferring a sandwich in his office. Word is he can speak some Arabic from his lecturing days in Cairo but still can't manage a decent "good morning" in Swiss German. Word is he walks around all day—he says it's management by walking around—asking for suggestions, ideas, plans, or solutions because he can't think of any himself.

Waterhouse remembers an early conversation with Donaldson in which he seemed frustrated. Should he have paid more attention?

"I met with Jakob Hassler, vice president of human resources at Schwyz Turbines," Donaldson had said, pacing the office. "I wanted some ideas for the training program. Schwyz is the first company we acquired here; I wanted to show Hassler that I don't bite. When I opened the door, he just stood there. I offered him a chair beside the coffee table, told him to call me Bert. He nodded, so I asked him about his family and the best place to buy ski boots, and he answered but he acted so aloof. I took a chair across from him, listened to ten minutes of one-word answers, and then I finally asked him how things were going in general, to which he said, 'Everything is normal.' Can you beat that, Frank? I told him I was interested in his ideas, so he pushed his chair back and said, 'Please let me know what you expect.' I reminded him that we're all on the same team, have only two years for major change, gave him a week to get back to me with a few ideas, and you know what he said? He said, 'Ja ja.'"

At the time, Donaldson's frustration seemed to stem from the normal adjustment problems that expatriates face. But he never did adjust. Why doesn't he just give Hassler what he needs to know and get out? Waterhouse knows this; why hasn't Donaldson figured it out?

His phone rings—the inside line. It's Ursula Lindt. "Frau Direktor Donaldson just called. She said Herr Direktor Donaldson was expected home at 4. I told her you had scheduled a meeting with him for 5." She waits. Waterhouse senses that there is more to her message. "What else did she say, Frau Lindt?"

"I inquired after her health, and she said she's near the end of her rope. Bored without her work. She said they thought Zürich would be a breeze after Cairo. Then she went into a tirade. She said that they're having serious problems with their eldest daughter. She'll be in grade 12 at the international school this fall. She's applying to college. Frau Donaldson said her daughter's recommendations from her British teachers are so understated that they'd keep her out of the top schools, and she keeps getting C's because they're using the British grading scale. She reminded me that this is a girl with a combined SAT score of over 1350."

Lindt is done. Waterhouse thanks her for the information, then hangs up. Julie Ann is usually calm, collected. She has made some friends here. Something must have pushed her over the edge. And their daughter is engaging, bright. Why is this all coming to a head now?

Waterhouse recalls his most recent meeting with Donaldson, a couple of days before Donaldson's vacation in May.

"I've tried everything, Frank. I've delegated, I've let them lead, I've given them pep talks." Waterhouse remembers Donaldson sinking deep into his chair, his voice flat. "No matter what I do—if I change an agenda, if I ask them to have a sandwich with me at my desk—someone's always pissed off. We're talking about streamlining an entire European company and they're constantly looking at their watches. We run ten minutes overtime in a meeting and they're shuffling papers. I tell you, Frank, they're just going to have to join the rest of us in the postindustrial age, learn to do things the Argos way. I worked wonders in Detroit . . ."

The clock in Waterhouse's office reads 4:45. What can he do about Donaldson? Let him blunder along for another year? And take another twelve months of . . . he closes the door on that thought. Send him back and forget? Morale on the fifth floor will improve, the Europeans will be appeased, but with Donaldson will go the training program, such as it is. Corporate will just think that Waterhouse has forgotten how to play the American way. They'll think that he mistreated their star. Can he teach Donaldson cultural awareness? With the Ankara, Moscow, and Warsaw projects chewing up all his time? You can't teach cultural savvy. No way.

He hears Donaldson enter the outer office. A hanger clinks on the coat tree. How can he work this out?

Assignment Questions

1. Assess the mistakes Donaldson has made. Why have they occurred? Whose responsibility are they? What are the implications of not satisfactorily dealing with the Donaldson problem?

2. What should Waterhouse do with Donaldson? Be specific and develop an action plan.

3. What could the company have done to better prepare Donaldson?

4. What does this case suggest about the company's current policy for recruiting and preparing expatriates? Make policy suggestions.

CASE 8

In a World of Pay

She's an American superstar who wants to work in Europe. He's the CEO of a German company who wants her pizzazz. But can Typware AG pay Anne Prevost anything like what she expects?

Renate Schmidt, the head of human resources, stood frowning in front of her office window, gazing across the Stuttgart hills and the green Swabian Alps from her lofty perch on the fifteenth floor of Typware's headquarters. It was late afternoon, and the gathering humidity lay over the hills. Thunderheads were threatening in the distance. Those clouds look like I feel, she thought. About to burst.

She walked back to her desk and sat down in the cool leather chair, glaring at the telephone. The problem she faced was like a huge knot—and every time she tried to unravel it, the knot grew tighter.

Jürgen Mehr, Typware's European head of marketing, had just called to voice his displeasure about a prospective new hire—the very candidate he had most favored. Anne Prevost was the director of marketing at an American software company, Xon Technologies, that had lately been making inroads into many of Typware's worldwide markets. As the brains behind Xon's 2002 advertising campaign, Anne had engineered a huge uptick in sales nearly single-handedly, much to Typware's dismay. Now she was ready to jump ship, provided the German software giant made her a good offer. She would be, without a doubt, a brilliant catch.

But when Jürgen heard what the company was considering offering her, he lost his temper. "Renate, 244,000 is simply exorbitant!" he spat. "It's almost as much as I make. This isn't fair, and it's humiliating. What is it with these eigennützige Amerikaner, anyway? Selfish billionaire CEOs. Big armies. Economic hegemony. Do they think they're entitled to everything? I will speak to Thomas Gutschein about this."

Renate took a deep breath, bracing herself for an argument. "Jürgen, please," she began. "Think about this. She already has another offer from that startup, Seistrand Systems. It includes a lot of stock options. I'm sure she would rather come with us, but we have to take that into account. Our global head of marketing's eager to hire her, and I think Thomas will say that we should consider what she's worth to our business—and how costly it would be to have her go to a competitor. You're the one who said that this is a critical role. Anne is the best possible candidate for it."

It was true. Jürgen—like every other senior executive—had been very impressed with Anne. She demonstrated finesse and a deep understanding of the global software industry. An intelligent, careful strategist, Anne had made her mark working in the cutthroat ERP software business, eventually reporting to a famously tough CEO. Along the way, she had garnered armloads of accolades, not only for her marketing creativity but also for her division's performance under brutal economic conditions. She spoke excellent German, having studied in Hamburg during her junior year abroad and worked for a German multinational in the early 1990s. During a dinner on the evening before Anne departed for the United States, Thomas, the CEO, had told Renate and Jürgen that Anne would be a fine addition to the company.

"I know she is good," Jürgen continued, sighing into the receiver. "But this salary is too high."

"We're trying to match the value of the stock options that Seistrand is offering," Renate explained. "The amount is not so out of line when you consider the cost-of-living difference. Things are much more expensive in Europe than they are in the U.S. Is it a fair market price for someone with her experience? It's difficult to say. But I tell you, she's a real professional. She knows what she's doing."

Jürgen was silent. Ever mindful of Typware's shifting bottom line, he was notoriously conservative about salaries, particularly in international negotiations. Renate secretly believed that Anne's stipulations were on the audacious side, but she also believed in following the CEO's direction.

"I understand your concerns" Renate continued. "I have trouble approving it myself." There was a long pause. "Still, you know our strategy is to increase our international revenues by 10%. This position is strategic. Thomas will say we have to pay what it takes."

"Remind me why she is so interested in joining us?" Jürgen grumbled.

"Xon can't promote her. She says there's no more upward mobility for her at the company, and she's not satisfied with the lateral position she has been offered. Seistrand wants her, but the company is small and its stock is highly leveraged, so that presents risks. And she's very interested in the idea of raising her sons in Europe. Wonderful educational opportunity and so on."

"And her husband? Is he being transferred here?" Jürgen asked.

"No husband." Renate let it stand at that, as she imagined Jürgen's eyebrows rising.

"All right, Renate," Jürgen said finally. "I still intend to speak to Thomas about this. And I can't say I support this decision, even given this woman's credentials." He hung up with a loud click.

The View from the Top

Renate massaged her forehead, then pushed her hand through her thick hair. She rose and reached again for the telephone receiver, its earpiece still warm. She called Thomas's assistant and asked whether he was available for coffee that afternoon. He wasn't, the assistant replied. But his lunch appointment the next day had just cancelled.

Precisely at noon, Renate and Thomas stepped from their building and walked to the Königstraße, the upscale retail district in the center of the city. The long, colorful street, closed to traffic and lined with a row of emerald-leafed trees, was crowded with shoppers, students, and people out for a long Mittagspause. Guided to a table at the back of a comfortable Spanish restaurant, Thomas and Renate sat down—Renate first glancing around to make sure no other Typware employees were there.

"You want to talk with me about the American hire—Anne Prevost," Thomas began.

Renate nodded. "Jürgen spoke with you?" she asked.

Thomas responded with a curt nod of his own. "I told him I would consider his comments. I also pointed out that we have been looking for the right person to fill this position for a very long time. We can't wait much longer. I understand she is getting impatient. And I know that she needs to be compensated correctly if we are to relocate her here."

"True," said Renate. "But this salary request is for nearly as much as Jürgen himself makes. If we pay a person who is just coming into the company that much, it will make others who have been with us for a long time feel that we don't care about them."

"Well, Renate, in this case, there is much to consider," Thomas explained. "Prevost is probably trying to figure in differences in tax rates, inflation, benefits, floating currencies, and other items. She probably has stock options and a bonus package that she would give up to come here. And, as you know, the United States does not have subsidized health care or educational support. That's why they have very high salary expectations."

"Yes, Thomas," Renate said impatiently, "I understand. But I am concerned that too many people are already asking for much more than the job warrants. I've told you before that our salary system is really out of order. Everyone should be paid the same for doing equal work, don't you think?" She paused, having introduced the real subject she wanted to discuss.

"I know you feel strongly about that," Thomas replied calmly. "And in theory, it's true enough. But certain jobs are just not ever going to follow the rules, especially at a company in our position." He paused. "I'd like you to do some research, Renate.

Come up with a salary and benefits recommendation that you think you—and this woman—can both live with."

Sensing she would get no further, Renate allowed the conversation to drift. She reported on other personnel matters of interest to Thomas. Only after lunch, when they were parting ways at the office, did Thomas return to the Prevost matter. And even then it was merely to remind Renate of his request. He thanked her for her company and said, "I'll expect your recommendation by tomorrow afternoon."

What's Fair?

Back at her desk, Renate pulled out her Anne Prevost file and glanced over the notes she had jotted down during her phone call with Jürgen the day before. It struck her suddenly how similar his complaints were to ones she had heard six months earlier, when the company's German CIO stormed into her office, threatening to quit. "I just found out what the CIO in Japan makes," he had announced. "It's twice as much as what I make, but we both do the same work. This is completely unfair! I'm going to speak to Thomas."

Renate had privately agreed with him. But despite her discomfort, she did her best to explain that Typware had no choice but to pay market rates for labor. "You've been to Tokyo," she noted. "A cup of coffee there costs double what it does in Stuttgart. Four times what it costs in Chicago!" Even so, it took some time to calm him down; in the end, he got a 100% raise.

"Things were never this complicated at Lesom," she thought. Her previous employer had had a very strict, albeit generous, pay grade system; salaries did not vary substantially from country to country. There was never any debate about what the market supposedly paid or which geographical regions were most expensive. If an employee was not satisfied, he or she simply got a job elsewhere.

Typware was the opposite. Pay was not rationalized at all, and Renate had noticed increasingly troublesome salary and benefit disparities among the managerial ranks. She had also discovered that female and minority employees made less than their white male counterparts. Was that also to be explained by market forces? While Thomas had agreed to rectify the most glaring disparities, he

had seemed uninterested in stabilizing salaries in general. Typware's market was much too competitive, and gaining a strong toehold in international markets too important, he had argued, to apply any kind of monolithic pay scale. Besides, in his experience, such systems just didn't work.

Renate swiveled around to her computer, entered a series of passwords, and pulled up Typware's HR information.

Of the company's 4,800 employees, 85% were in Germany and were paid according to fairly well understood market rates. But since 1996, Typware had ventured aggressively into international markets—not only in France, Spain, Britain, and the Netherlands, but in North and South America, China, India, Russia, Australia, and Japan. The consultants that had helped to negotiate salaries and benefits for overseas employees had recommended a variable set of standards depending on the employee's location. Most expatriates received the equivalent of their German salary plus enrollment in local health care programs, as well as contributions to their German social security and retirement plans. In most cases, the salary had been more than sufficient, given Germany's high cost of living.

Nevertheless, individual expatriate packages had become increasingly complicated over the years. Per diem expenses varied according to country; each case was "special." Two years before, Colombia's country manager had insisted on a 15% "danger pay" salary increase after learning of a kidnapping attempt on an expatriate acquaintance. He had also wanted more money for a German-Spanish private school and around-the-clock bodyguard protection for his twins. He made the case for more household help, given the level of required at-home entertaining. And he pointed out that, after two years, his base salary increases were not keeping pace with Colombian inflation. Renate had tried to hold firm, but Thomas—eager to retain experienced managers and Typware's hard-won global advantage—had given in.

Since then, it seemed that exceptions for expatriates had spiraled out of control, despite Renate's efforts to apply a modicum of consistency. Moscow's manager of operations had insisted on a chauffeur. The Chicago regional director required college tuition fees for his son, making the argument that universities were paid for in Germany. The manager based in India complained that health care there was insufficient compared with German standards and wanted compensation for premium care. As a result of these exceptions, some expatriates had boosted their total salary and benefits by more than 30% while others had seen their compensation fall behind.

"Now this American will complicate things further," Renate worried, as she continued scanning various managers' salary files.

All Good Questions

Typware had never hired a foreign executive to work at headquarters. With no history to guide her, Renate felt completely at a loss. She had not used a recruiting consultancy to assist with this hire, so she had no help from that quarter. Now, hoping her past business would have earned her a favor, she picked up the phone and called Rainer Barth, her contact at the consulting firm she routinely engaged.

"Hier ist Barth," he answered.

"Rainer," Renate began, "I would be very grateful for some advice." She described the situation.

Rainer listened, then started asking questions. "What kind of retirement plan does she have in the U.S.?"

"I don't know," Renate replied. "American social security, of course. And Xon probably contributes to a plan."

"She will not be able to contribute to her U.S. social security if she comes here," Rainer mused. "And she may not qualify for a German social security plan. So you will want to offer her a pension plan that allows her to generate an equally meaningful benefit." He then asked, "Is Anne married? Does she have any children?"

"She is divorced and has two sons. Seven and 11," Renate said.

"And they will enroll in a German school?"

"I assume so. Unless they go to a private German-American school."

"It would be free if they enrolled in a German school. If she prefers a private school, or if they go to college in the U.S., she may want you to contribute something to their tuition. Does she have other family obligations—older parents, for example? If she pays for a retirement or rest home, you must consider that, too; it costs very little here. She may want some help for that."

Renate groaned. "And what else?"

"She probably has executive medical coverage," Rainer added, "which we do not have here. Find out whether anyone in the family has a special health condition. U.S. medical care is generally superior to what we offer here. If there is a condition, you may want to compensate additionally for care."

"Rainer," Renate said, "there's a big problem with all of this. I understand that she wants to be paid fairly to keep up with German salaries, but these extra things will mean she is paid more in the end than her peers and perhaps even than her boss. We do not want resentment. Some managers are already complaining."

Rainer thought for a minute. "Yes, it is complicated." He paused, "Can you contact this woman tonight?"

"Of course."

"Call her and find out her answers to my questions. I will do some research on what my other clients have done. We'll talk in the morning, and you will have your report done by the afternoon."

"Danke schön, Rainer."

"Bitte sehr, Renate. Don't worry. We can make this work."

Past the Eleventh Hour

At midnight, Renate phoned Anne in New York, hoping she would be home from work by then. One of Anne's sons picked up. "Maaawm," he shouted so loudly that Renate winced and pulled the receiver from her ear. "Some lady with an accent is on the phone!"

When Anne came on, Renate immediately remembered why she had been so impressed. There was something calming, genteel—almost European—in her voice. Not like that son, Renate thought.

Renate explained that she was working on a compensation package for Anne and ran through the questions that Rainer had given her. Anne said she had assumed her children would attend a German gymnasium. Renate breathed a silent sigh of relief; at least there would be no additional education costs for now. But Anne added that she was paying the bulk of the $3,000-per-month fee for an assisted living facility for her mother and was concerned about receiving good health care for her seven-year-old son, who suffered from asthma and various allergies.

Renate tried to be conciliatory. "Anne, you know we are very interested in hiring you, but you understand that developing a compensation package is quite complicated," she said. "We hope that you will be willing to compromise on some issues and to be patient for a little while longer."

Anne's voice remained pleasant but took on a firmer tone. "Yes, of course," she replied. "But I have another very good offer and can't keep them waiting forever. You understand. When do you think I can expect to hear from you?"

"Soon," Renate demurred. "Sometime this week."

Anne thanked Renate for calling, and Renate hung up, exhausted. "Meine Güte," she thought as she headed up to bed, "this is not getting any easier."

No Easy Answers

As promised, Rainer called the next morning. But the information he had was not very helpful. "It seems no one here has come up with a solution to the exact situation you are facing," he said apologetically. "So I am pulling together a quick benchmark analysis on your broader issue, which my assistant will e-mail to you later this morning. Of the five largest multinationals based here, three have uniform pay scale systems like the one you had at Lesom. A fourth currently has its international salary system under review, so I was not able to discover anything very specific about its policies. I am still hopeful of getting information about the last one."

Renate sighed. "Well, thank you for trying, Rainer," she said. "It looks as if I'll have to sort this out myself."

"I wish I could be of more help," Rainer said. He sounded as though he were anxious to get off the phone. The thought occurred to Renate that, as a client, Typware might be more trouble than it was worth. "I'll keep researching this problem if you want."

"No, thank you," Renate said. "I need to get this report to the CEO very soon. I'll figure something out, I'm sure."

Assignment Questions

1. How far should Typware go to hire Anne, the American executive? On what points should the company hold firm? Be willing to compromise? Why?

2. How does the situation with Anne relate to Typware's other difficulties putting together fair expatriate compensation packages for the employees it sends abroad? How can Typware better manage these challenges?

3. Are there strategic implications here? How can expatriate compensation be structured to better align with the goals and strategic objectives Typware has . . . or should have? How can the situation with Anne be used as an opportunity to clarify Typware's international objectives?

Chapter Endnotes

Chapter 1

1. Bernstein, A. (2001). Low-skilled jobs: Do they have to move? *Business Week*, February 26, 94–95; Pope, J. (2004). Athletic shoemaker creates new path. Dayton Daily News, February 23, D1, D4.

2. Engardio, P. (2000). The barons of outsourcing. *Business Week*, August 28, 177–178.

3. Baker, S. (2004). Jobs go overseas—under water. *Business Week*, April 5, 13; Friedman, T. (2004). The incredible shrinking world. *Dayton Daily News*, March 6, A8.

4. ———. (2000). Globalization: Threat or opportunity? An IMF issues brief. **(www.imf.org/external/np/exr/ib/ 2000/042100.htm)**

5. Gleckman, H., & Carney, D. (2000). Watching over the World Wide Web. *Business Week*, August 28, 195–196.

6. King, N., Samor, G., & Miller, S. (2004). WTO rules against U.S. cotton aid. *The Wall Street Journal*, April 27, A2.

7. ———. (2001). China and the WTO: Ready for the competition? *The Economist*, September 15, 35–36; ———. (2001). Playing by the rules. *The Economist*, July 28, 67; Cooper, H. (2001). U.S., E.U. end trans-Atlantic banana war. *The Wall Street Journal*, April 12, A2; Winestock, G., & Leggett, K. (2001). China to enter WTO; Dispute on insurance to be first test. *The Wall Street Journal*, September 17, A16, A17; Wonacott, P. (2001). China braces for changes ahead of WTO. *The Wall Street Journal*, July 23, A12.

8. Hutzler, C. (2004). U.S.-China talks fuel high hopes. *The Wall Street Journal*, April 16, A2.

9. ———. (2000). A different, new world order. *The Economist*, November 11, 83–85; Bernstein, A. (2000). Backlash: Behind the anxiety over globalization. *Business Week*, April 24, 38–44.

10. ———. (2001). When the economy held its breath. *The Economist*, September 15, 65–66.

11. Carpenter, M. A., & Fredrickson, J. W. (2001). Top management teams, global strategic posture, and the moderating role of uncertainty. *Academy of Management Journal*, 44, 533–545.

12. ———. (2001). Let the bad times roll. *The Economist*, April 7, 63; Champion, M. (2004). CEOs' worst nightmares. *The Wall Street Journal*, January 21, A13; Oyama, D. (2001). Cisco aims to train 100,000 workers in India by 2006. *The Wall Street Journal*, January 16, A19.

13. Edmondson, G., Capell, K., Moore, P. L., & Burrows, P. (2000). See the world, erase its borders. *Business Week*, August 28, 113–114.

14. ———. (2001). The cutting edge. *The Economist*, February 24, 80.

15. Engardio, P. (2001). America's future: Smart globalization. *Business Week*, August 27, 132–137.

16. ———. (2003). World trade. *The Economist*, December 6, 94; Wonacott, P., & King, N. (2003). Chinese wield quiet clout at trade talks. *The Wall Street Journal*, September 15, A18.

17. Sachs, J. D. (2003). Welcome to the Asian century. *Fortune*, December 29, 53–54.

18. Deans, B. (2001). Popular resistance barrier to trade pact. *Dayton Daily News*, April 22, 16A.

19. ———. (2001). Trade in the Americas: All in the familia. *The Economist*, April 21, 19–22.

20. ———. (2000). Emerging market indicators: Trading partners. *The Economist*, December 2, 106; Wysocki, B. (1996). Imports are surging in developing nations. *The Wall Street Journal*, July 8, A1.

21. Farrell, C. (1994). The triple revolution. *Business Week*, November 19, 16–25.

22. Cooper, J. C., & Madigan, K. (2004). The economy is showing real muscle. *Business Week*, May 3, 33–34; **http://www.nationmaster.com.**

23. Engardio, P. (2001). America's future: Smart globalization. *Business Week*, August 27, 132–137.

24. Baglole, J. (2004). Citibank takes risk by issuing cards in China. *The Wall Street Journal*, March 10, C1, C2.

25. Barrett, A. (1995). It's a small (business) world. *Business Week*, April 17, 96–101.

26. Dempsey, D. (2001). YSI: Blending business, nature. *Dayton Daily News*, April 22, F1.

27. ———. (2003). Between rivalry and co-operation. *The Economist*, November 29, 33–35; Sarmiento, S. (2004). Critics aside, NAFTA has been a boon to Mexico. *The Wall Street Journal*, January 9, A11; Smith, G., Malkin, E., Wheatley, J., Magnusson, P., & Arndt, M. Betting on free trade: Will the Americas be one big market? *Business Week*, April 23, 60–62.

28. King, N. (2004). U.S. reaches a trade agreement with 4 Central American nations. *The Wall Street Journal*, December 18, A1, A8.

29. ———. (2001). Trade in the Americas: All in the familia. *The Economist*, April 21, 19–22; Whalen, C. J., Magnusson, P., & Smith, G. (2001). NAFTA's scorecard: So far, so good. *Business Week*, July 9, 54–56.

30. ———. (1999). A survey of Canada: Holding its own. *The Economist*, July 24, 1–18; Thomas, G. S. (2001). Asia, Canada comprise bulk of U.S. trade deficit. *Dayton Business Journal*, April 20, 16; **http://canadian economy.gc.ca/english/economy/gdp.cfm; http:// www.census.gov/foreigntrade/top/dst/2003/12.**

31. ———. (2000). A survey of Mexico: After the revolution. *The Economist*, October 28, 1–16; Whalen, C. J., Magnusson, P., & Smith, G. (2001). NAFTA's scorecard: So far, so good. *Business Week*, July 9, 54–56.

32. ———. (2000). A survey of Mexico: After the revolution. *The Economist*, October 28, 1–16; Friedman, T. (2004). For Mexico, that sound is in stereo. *The Wall Street Journal*, April 3, A10; Luhnow, D. (2004). Mexico's economy shows signs of revival, boosted by U.S. industry. *The Wall Street Journal*, January 13, A12; Millman, J. (2000). The world's new tiger on the export scene isn't Asian, it's Mexico. *The Wall Street Journal*, May 9, A1, A10; Stevenson, M. (2003). 10 years after NAFTA, Mexico still waiting for jobs, higher wages. *Dayton Daily News*, December 14, AA1.

33. Borrus, A., & Smith, G. (2001). Spotlight on the border. *Business Week*, September 10, 40–43; Millman, J.

(2000). A new future for Mexico's workforce. *The Wall Street Journal*, April 14, A15, A16.

34. ———. (2001). Slowing economy, quickening politics. *The Economist*, May 19, 33–34; ———. (2000). A survey of Mexico: After the revolution. *The Economist*, October 28, 1–16; Millman, J. (2001). Mexico braces for drop-off in auto sector. *The Wall Street Journal*, January 23, A17, A18; Smith, G., & Lindblad, C. (2003). Mexico: Was NAFTA worth it? *Business Week*, December 22, 66–72; **http:// www.census.gov/foreign-trade/top/dst/ 2003/12.**

35. ———. (2002). The economy: On steroids. *The Economist*, January 26, 51–52; ———. (2001). When the economy held its breath. *The Economist*, September 15, 65–66; ———. (2001). United States: The kiss of life? *The Economist*, April 21, 23; Becker, G. S. (2004). How the skeptics missed the power of productivity. *Business Week*, January 12, 26; Miller, R. (2004). Business burns rubber. *Business Week*, February 2, 34–35; Porter, M. E. (2001). Japan: What went wrong. *The Wall Street Journal*, March 21, A22; Sapsford, J., & Barta, P. (2002). Despite the recession, Americans continue to be avid borrowers. *The Wall Street Journal*, January 2, A1, A20.

36. ———. (2001). Survey of corporate finance: The party's over. *The Economist*, January 27, 1–20; ———. (2003). Global 500: The world's largest corporations. *Fortune*, July 21, 106; **http://www.newsmax.com/archives/ articles/2004/2/13/230957.shtml.**

37. ———. (2002). Is Latin America losing its way? *The Economist*, March 2, 11; Baker, S., Weiner, E., Smith, G., Charters, A., & Jacobson, K. (1992). Latin America: The big move to free markets. *Business Week*, June 15, 50–55; Johnson, M. (1996). Untapped Latin America. *Management Review*, 85, 31–34.

38. Brady, R. (2004). The Latin chill may get even frostier. *Business Week*, January 26, 63.

39. ———. (2004). Latin America's economies: Life after debt. *The Economist*, April 3, 37–38.

40. ———. (2000). Latin America: The slow road to reform. *The Economist*, December, 23–26; Casey, M. (2004). Does Argentine recovery have legs? *The Wall Street Journal*, April 9, A7; Smith, G., Goodman, J., Lindblad, C., & Robinson, A. (2002). Argentina: A wrong turn? *Business Week*, January 21, 42–44; Goodman, J. (2001). Beyond the default drama. *Business Week*, September 3, 49; Larroulet, C. (2001). Look to Chile for an answer to the Latin malaise. *The Wall Street Journal*, August 24, A9; Moffett, M. (2001). Argentina pins all its hopes on harsh plan. *The Wall Street Journal*, July 23, A10; Moffett, M., & Bussey, J. (2001). The Argentine economy: A tough nut for a tough man. *The Wall Street Journal*, April 4, A17.

41. Karp, J. (2002). Brazilian growth is below expectations. *The Wall Street Journal*, March 1, A11; Jordan, M. (2001). Auto makers slow production in Brazil. *The Wall Street Journal*, July 23, A10; Karp, J. (2001). Signs point to interest-rate rise in Brazil. *The Wall Street Journal*, April 17, A15; Wheatley, J. (2004). Lula: Battling his way toward growth. *Business Week*, April 5, 42.

42. ———. (2001). Another blow to Mercosur. *The Economist*, March 31, 33–34; Harbrecht, D., Smith, G., & DeGeorge, G. (1994). Ripping down the walls across the Americas. *Business Week*, December 26, 78–79.

43. ———. (2001). In praise of rules: A survey of Asian business. *The Economist*, April 7, 1–18; ———. (2000). Asian economies: Happy neighbors. *The Economist*,

August 26, 63; Weidenbaum, M. (1996). The Chinese family business enterprise. *California Management Review*, 38, 141–156.

44. Bremner, B., Balfour, F., Shari, M., Ihlwan, M., & Engardio, P. (2001). Asia: The big chill. *Business Week*, April 2, 48–50.

45. ———. (2004). Behind the mask: A survey of business in China. *The Economist*, March 20, 3–19; Barnathan, J., & Roberts, D. (1996). A hard "soft" landing: China's state industries are sputtering. *Business Week*, October 21, 50–51; Biers, D. (1996). Weaker Asian exports are prompting lower forecasts for region's economy. *The Wall Street Journal*, August 7, A8; Biers, D. (1996). Asian exports show signs of reviving as global demand for electronics rises. *The Wall Street Journal*, December 26, 8; Engardio, P. (1996). Is the East Asian juggernaut sputtering? *Business Week*, August 26, 44; Engardio, P., Moore, J., & Hill, C. (1996). Time for a reality check in Asia. *Business Week*, December 2, 58–67.

46. ———. (2004) Behind the mask: A survey of business in China.

47. ———. (2004) Behind the mask: A survey of business in China; ———. (2001). China's economic power: Enter the dragon. *The Economist*, March 10, 23–25; Schlevogt, K. A. (2000). The business environment in China: Getting to know the next century's superpower. *Thunderbird International Business Review*, 42 (January–February), 85–111.

48. ———. (2004). Behind the mask: A survey of business in China; Higgins, A. (2004). As China surges, it also proves a buttress to American strength. *The Wall Street Journal*, January 30, A1, A8; Schlevogt, The business environment in China: Getting to know the next century's superpower.

49. ———. (2001). In praise of rules: A survey of Asian business. *The Economist*, April 7, 1–18; ———. (2004). China's economic power: Enter the dragon; Brown, O., & Chang, L. (2002). China says growth slowed to 7.3% in 2001. *The Wall Street Journal*, March 1, A7; Clifford, M., Roberts, D., Engardio, P., & Webb, A. (2001). China: Coping with its new power. *Business Week*, April 16, 28–34; Schlevogt, The business environment in China: Getting to know the next century's superpower.

50. Bremner, B., Roberts, D., & Balfour, F. (2004). China: Headed for a crisis? *Business Week*, May 3, 36–44; Dolven, B. (2004). China grooms global players. *The Wall Street Journal*, February 25, A12; Hutzler, C., Western, L., & Kuhn, A. (2004). China's economy likely to outpace official estimates. *The Wall Street Journal*, February 25, A12.

51. Clifford, M. L., & Roberts, D. (2001). Downturn? What downturn? *Business Week*, April 9, 44; Clifford, Roberts, Engardio, & Webb, China: Coping with its new power; Wonacott, P. (2001). China plans a more market-oriented economy. *The Wall Street Journal*, March 6, A10.

52. ———. (2004). India's shining hopes. *The Economist*, February 21, 1–20; Das, G. (2004). Is India Shining? *The Wall Street Journal*, May 3, A20; Wessel, D. (2003). India could narrow its economic gap with China. *The Wall Street Journal*, July 24, A2.

53. ———. (2004). India's shining hopes; Einhorn, B., Kripalani, M., & Engardio, P. (2001). India 3.0. *Business Week*, February 26, 44–46; Kripalani, M., & Clifford, M. L. (2000). India wired. *Business Week*, March 6, 82–91.

54. Moffett, S., & Dvorak, P. (2004). As Japan recovers, an unlikely source gets credit: China. *The Wall Street Journal*, May 4, A1, A12.

55. ———. (2004). (Still) made in Japan. *The Economist*, April 10, 57–59; ———. (2001). Japan's economy: Another false dawn? *The Economist*, March 24, 79–81; Belson, K. (2001). Japan: This time it could get nasty. *Business Week*, January 15, 52; Bremner, B. (2004). Japan: This looks like the real thing. *Business Week*, April 26, 54–55; Porter, Japan: What went wrong.

56. ———. (2002). Economics focus: checking the slumpometer. *The Economist*, March 2, 72; Porter, Japan: What went wrong.

57. Bremner, B., & Belson, K. (2001). Dark before dawn? *Business Week*, March 19, 54–55; Dvorak, P., Guth, R. A., Singer, J., and Zaun, T. (2001). Frayed by recession, Japan's corporate ties are becoming unraveled. *The Wall Street Journal*, March 2, A1, A6; Ono, Y., & Zaun, T. (2001). Wall Street intensifies Japan's woes, but they all trace back home. *The Wall Street Journal*, March 16, A1, A6.

58. Porter, Japan: What went wrong; Schoenberger, K. (1996). Has Japan changed? *Fortune*, August 19, 72–82.

59. ———. (2001). China's man pushes out Hong Kong's woman. *The Economist*, January 10, 35; ———. (2000). Meddling in Hong Kong. *The Economist*, September 30, 22; ———. (2000). Hong Kong: Atonement day. *The Economist*, February 26, 50; Balfour, F., & Clifford, M. L. (2001). Hong Kong: A city under siege. *Business Week*, July 23, 48–49; Clifford, M. (2001). Hong Kong: Another body blow to the rule of law? *Business Week*, January 29, 55.

60. Flannery, R. (2000). Taipei eases stance on China business. *The Wall Street Journal*, August 3, A9; Roberts, D., Webb, A., Clifford, M., & Hannon, B. (2000). Uneasy collaborators. *Business Week*, August 14, 52–55.

61. ———. (2003). The changing of the guard: A survey of Malaysia. *The Economist*, April 5, 1–16; ———. (2001). Singapore: Death by a thousand cuts. *The Economist*, September 15, 38; ———. (2000). A survey of Southeast Asia: The tigers that changed their stripes. *The Economist*, February 12, 1–16; Shari, M. (2003). Malaysia after Mahathir. *Business Week*, September 29, 58–60.

62. ———. (2003). Keeping the lights on: A survey of South Korea. *The Economist*, April 19, 1–19.

63. ———. (2001). South Korea: Entrepreneurial fresh air. *The Economist*, January 13, 60; Ihlwan, M. (2001). So long, corporate reform. *Business Week*, January 22, 52–53; Booth, J. (2002). South Korean economy gets more diverse. *The Wall Street Journal*, February 7, A14; Bremner, B., & Ihlwan, M. (2002). Cool Korea. *Business Week*, June 10, 54–58.

64. ———. (2000). A survey of South-east Asia: The tigers that changed their stripes; ———. (2001). Indonesia: The odd couple. *The Economist*, February 17, 27–30; ———. (2001). After the B movie, a new main attraction for Filipinos. *The Economist*, January 27, 37–38; Frank, R. (2000). In Subic Bay's decline, Filipinos see return of familiar problems. *The Wall Street Journal*, September 20, A1, A6; Schuman, M. (2001). Indonesia's economy is now sputtering. *The Wall Street Journal*, April 17, A17; Shari, M. (2001). Indonesia: Will rising chaos cripple the economy? *Business Week*, March 26, 66.

65. ———. (2001). Business pains in Vietnam. *The Economist*, March 24, 48; Cumming-Bruce, N. (2001). Vietnam party congress could produce new leadership. *The Wall Street Journal*, April 18, A19; Shari, M. (2003). Thaksin's Thailand. *Business Week*, July 28, 48–50.

66. ———. (2003). When east meets west: A survey of EU enlargement. *The Economist*, November 22, 1–16; ———. (2001). Europe: The Balkan jigsaw. *The Economist*, April 28, 47–48; Chazan, G. (2001). A Ukraine in deepening turmoil stands at a crossroads—and takes a step to the east. *The Wall Street Journal*, March 6, A18; Child, J., & Czegledy, A. P. (1996). Managerial learning in the transformation of eastern Europe: Some key issues. *Organizational Studies*, 17, 167–179; Luthans, F., & Riolli, L. T. (1997). Albania and the Bora Company: Lessons learned before the recent chaos. *Academy of Management Executive*, 11, 61–72.

67. ———. (2001). The Swiss say no. *The Economist*, March 10, 22; Costin, H. (1996). *Managing in the global economy: The European Union*. Fort Worth, TX: Dryden Press.

68. ———. (2001). A survey of European enlargement: Europe's magnetic attraction. *The Economist*, May 19, 1–16; ———. (2001). Permanent revolution for Europe's union? *The Economist*, February 3, 49–50; ———. (2001). The European central bank: The terrible twos begin. *The Economist*, January 6, 63–66; ———. (2000). The Nice summit: So that's all agreed, then. *The Economist*, December 16, 25–28; Hofheinz, P. (2002). One currency, many voices: Issues that still divide Europe. *The Wall Street Journal*, January 2, A6; Mehring, J. (2004). The newbies will set the pace. *Business Week*, May 3, 34.

69. Ewing, J. (2004). Is Siemens still German? *Business Week*, May 17, 50–51.

70. ———. (2001). The world economy: Waiting for growth. *The Economist*, April 28, 76; ———. (2000). Europe's economies: Stumbling yet again? *The Economist*, September 16, 77–80; Rhoads, C., & Sims, T. (2001). Why Europe may resist the economic bug. *The Wall Street Journal*, March 29, A10, A11; Fairlamb, D. (2001). Back from the depths. *Business Week*, January 8, 52–53.

71. ———. (2001). Unwelcome to Iberia. *The Economist*, February 10, 51–52; Edmondson, G., & Malkin, E. (2000). Spain's surge. *Business Week*, May 22, 73–80.

72. ———. (2004). The club in need of a new vision. *The Economist*, May 1, 25–27; ———. (2001). Will western Europe receive the great unwashed—one day? *The Economist*, April 21, 43–44; ———. (2000). Poverty in eastern Europe: The land that time forgot. *The Economist*, September 23, 27–30.

73. ———. (2004). How to pep up Germany's economy. *The Economist*, May 8, 65–67; ——— (2001). More cash, please. *The Economist*, May 12, 55; ———. (2000). Togetherness: A balance sheet. *The Economist*, September 30, 25–28; Ewing, J. (2000). What Germany can teach the rest of Europe. *Business Week*, October 16, 72.

74. ———. (2001). Investment in Eastern Europe. *The Economist*, November 17, 102; Michaels, D. (1996). Booming economy in Poland brings jobs, wealth and apathy. *The Wall Street Journal*, November 25, A1, A10; Miller, K. L., Simpson, P., & Schiller, Z. (1996). Piling into central Europe. *Business Week*, July 1, 42–44.

75. Fairlamb, D., & Turek, B. (2004). Poland and the EU. *Business Week*, May 10, 54–56.

76. ———. (2002). Emerging market indicators: Russia. *The Economist*, February 23, 110; ———. (2001). The smell test. *The Economist*, February 24, 71; ———. (2000). The Russian economy: Boom and gloom. *The Economist*, November 25, 97; Banerjee, N. (1996).

Russian economy showing signs of life as some major firms post hefty profits. *The Wall Street Journal*, June 5, A11; Starobin, P., & Tavernise, S. (2000). A new home for Russian capital—Russia. *Business Week*, March 6, 58.

77. Starobin, P., & Kravchenko, O. (2000). Russia's middle class. *Business Week*, October 16, 78–84; Starobin, P., & Kravchenko, O. (2000). So far, the mobility is all upward. *Business Week*, July 24, 85.

78. ———. (1999). Crime without punishment. *The Economist*, August 28, 17–19; ———. (1999). A krisha over your head. *The Economist*, August 28, 17; Bush, J. (2003). A big chill for business? *Business Week*, November 10, 60–61; Starobin & Belton, Russia: Cleanup time; Belton, C. (2000). The friends of Vladimir. *Business Week*, December 4, 56–58; Starobin, P., & Belton, C. (2000). Tycoon under siege. *Business Week*, July 24, 48–50.

79. ———. (2001). Investment in Eastern Europe. *The Economist*, November 17, 102; ———. (2001). A survey of Russia: Putin's choice. *The Economist*, July 21, 1–16; Bush, J. (2003). Can Putin contain the fallout? *Business Week*, November 24, 58; Jack, A., & Wagstyl, S. (2003). Russian financial crisis five years on. *Financial Times*, August 18, 9; Starobin, P., & Belton, C. (2002). Russia: Cleanup time. *Business Week*, January 14, 46–47.

80. ———. (2003). Peace through industrial parks. *The Economist*, September 20, 66; ———. (2001). Economic pain, unequally spread. *The Economist*, August 11, 35–36; ———. (2001). Appendix 1: Regional economic prospects (in World Bank's *Prospects for Development*: **www.worldbank.org**); ———. (2001). Pink hotels on Syria's hills. *The Economist*, March 24, 54; Reed, S. (2004). Saudi Arabia: Is the kingdom out of the doldrums? *Business Week*, March 22, 74; Rivers, S. T. (2004). Tourism spurs Libya evolution. *The Wall Street Journal*, February 27, A7.

81. ———. (2001). Africa's elusive dawn. *The Economist*, February 24, 17; Holmes, K. R., & Kirkpatrick, M. (1996). Freedom and growth. *The Wall Street Journal*, December 16, A16.; Lansner, T. R. (1996). Out of Africa. *The Wall Street Journal*, December 10, A22; O'Reilly, B. (2000). Death of a continent. *Fortune*, November 13, 259–274.

82. ———. (2004). How to make Africa smile: A survey of sub-Saharan Africa. *The Economist*, January 17, 1–16; ———. (2004). Emerging market indicators. *The Economist*, January 3, 74; ———. (2004). Emerging market indicators. *The Economist*, May 8, 98; Thurow, R. (2003). Once a breadbasket, Zimbabwe today can't feed itself. *The Wall Street Journal*, December 24, A1, A2; Turner, M. (2003). African nations 'off track' in reducing poverty. *Financial Times*, July 9, 3

83. ———. (2004). Trade and Africa: Emerging deals. *The Economist*, February 21, 73; ———. (2001). Afrabet soup. *The Economist*, February 10, 77; ———. (2001). Africa's elusive dawn. *The Economist*, February 24, 17.

84. ———. (2001). Africa's plan to save itself. *The Economist*, July 7, 44; ———. (2001) Africa's elusive dawn; Zachary, G. P. (2001). African leaders stress benefits of self-reliance, *The Wall Street Journal*, February 7, A22.

85. ———. (2001). Appendix 1: Regional economic prospects (in World Bank's *Prospects for Development*: **www.worldbank.org**); Cooper, H. (2002). Can African nations use duty-free deal to revamp economy? *The Wall Street Journal*, January 2, A1, A4; Drum, B. (1993).

Privatization in Africa. *The Columbia Journal of World Business*, Spring, 145–149; Greenberger, R. S. (1996). New leaders replace yesteryear's "big men," and Tanzania benefits. *The Wall Street Journal*, December 10, A1, A15.

86. Reed, J. (2003). South Africa's 'cappuccino effect': Will economic empowerment do more than create a sprinkling of black tycoons? *Financial Times*, November 5, 13.

87. ———. (2004). Face value: Getting Africa moving. *The Economist*, April 17, 64; ———. (2004). Cars in South Africa: Revving up. *The Economist*, February 14, 62–63.

88. ———. (2004). How to make Africa smile: A survey of sub-Saharan Africa; ———. (2000). From apartheid to welfare state. *The Economist*. April 1, 42–43; ———. (2000). South Africa: Pay packets. *The Economist*, July 29, 45–46; ———. (2000). South Africa: The left kicked into touch. *The Economist*, September 16, 56–57; ———. (2001). Africa's great black hope: A survey of South Africa. *The Economist*, February 24, 1–16; Fine, A. (1994). The color of money is starting to change. *Business Week*, March 14, 42; Thurow, R. (2000). South Africans who fought sanctions now scrap for investors. *The Wall Street Journal*, February 11, A1, A4.

89. ———. (2001). When the economy held its breath. *The Economist*, September 15, 65–66; Phillips, M. M. (2001). Global economy appears to be facing 'most challenging' environment in years. *The Wall Street Journal*, April 18, A4.

90. ———. (2003). Digital access index. *The Economist*, November 29, 98; ———. (2001). Geography and the net: Putting it in its place. *The Economist*, August 11, 18–20; ———. (2000). The global battle: Technology and innovation. *The Wall Street Journal*, September 25, R6; Koretz, G. (2001). The net hauls in a big catch. *Business Week*, March 12, 32.

91. Hitt, M. A., Keats, B. W., & DeMarie, S. M. (1998). Navigating in the new competitive landscape: Building strategic flexibility and competitive advantage in the 21st century. *Academy of Management Executive*, 12, 22–42.

92. ———. (2004). Competitive sport in Boca Raton. *The Economist*, February 7, 65–68; Glasgall, W. (1995). Hot money. *Business Week*, March 20, 46–50; Luhnow, D. (2001). Mexican peso holds its own against U.S. dollar. *The Wall Street Journal*, April 12, A14; Schlesinger, J. M. (1996). IMF drafts plan to avert another Mexico. *The Wall Street Journal*, December 31, A4.

93. Phillips, M. M. (2001). Financial contagion knows no borders. *The Wall Street Journal*, July 13, A2; Glasgall, W. (1995). Hot money. *Business Week*, March 20, 46–50.

94. ———. (2004). Tested by the mighty euro. *The Economist*, March 20, 61–62; Cooper, H., & Blumenstein, R. (1996). As U.S. firms gain on rivals, the dollar raises pesky questions. *The Wall Street Journal*, August 16, A1, A4; Miller, R., Arndt, M., Capell, K., & Fairlamb, D. (2003). The incredible falling dollar. *Business Week*, December 22, 36–38.

95. Bianco, A., & Moore, P. L. (2001). Downfall: The inside story of the management fiasco at Xerox. *Business Week*, March 5, 82–90.

96. **http://investor.colgatepalmolive.com/annual_highlights_02.cfm**

97. ———. (2004). Currency hedging: Holding back the flood. *The Economist*, February 21, 72; ———. (2004). Tested by the mighty euro. *The Economist*, March 20, 61–62; Sparks, D. (2000). Business won't hedge the euro

away. *Business Week*, December 4, 157; Zaun, T. (2001). As the yen weakens, Japan's car makers smile. *The Wall Street Journal*, April 10, A15, A19.

98. Katz, I. (2000). Adios, Argentina—hello, Brazil. *Business Week*, January 17, 56.

99. Aeppel, T. (2002). The dollar's strength tests the ingenuity of U.S. manufacturers. *The Wall Street Journal*, January 22, A1, A10; Cooper, C. (2000). Euro's drop is hardest for the smallest. *The Wall Street Journal*, October, 2, A21, A24.

100. ———. (2000). A survey of the new economy: Knowledge is power. *The Economist*, September 23, 27; Siekman, P. (2000). The big myth about U.S. manufacturing. *Fortune*, October 2, 244C–244E.

101. Ante, S. E., & Hof, R. D. (2004). Look who's going offshore. *Business Week*, May 17, 64–65.

102. Ante, S. E. (2004). Shifting work offshore? Outsourcer beware. *Business Week*, January 12, 36–37; Thurm, S. (2004). Lesson in India: Some jobs don't translate overseas. *The Wall Street Journal*, March 3, A1, A10.

103. ———. (2004). The great hollowing out myth. *The Economist*, February 21, 27–29; Bridis, T. (2004). Firms want freedom to move jobs overseas. *Dayton Daily News*, January 8, D1; Haberman, S. (2004). Software: Will outsourcing hurt America's supremacy? *Business Week*. March 1, 84–94; Nussbaum, B. (2004). Where are the jobs? *Business Week*, March 22, 36–52; Schlender, B. (2004). Peter Drucker sets us straight. *Fortune*, January 12, 115–118; Schroeder, M. (2004). Outsourcing may create U.S. jobs. *The Wall Street Journal*, March 30, A2.

104. Kripalani, M., & Engardio, P. (2003). The rise of India. *Business Week*. December 8, 66–78; Teves, O. (2003). Philippines latest to feel jobs surge. *Dayton Daily News*, December 6, D1, D4.

105. ———. (2001). Outsourcing to India: Back office to the world. *The Economist*, May 5, 59–62; Lavin, D. (2002). Globalization goes upscale. *The Wall Street Journal*. February 1, A18; Clifford, M., & Kripalani, M. (2000). Different countries, adjoining cubicles. *Business Week*, August 28, 182–184; Koretz, G. (2000). Solving a global growth enigma. *Business Week*, November 20, 32.

106. Clifford & Kripalani, Different countries, adjoining cubicles.

107. Borrus, A. (2000). Give me your tired, your poor—and all your techies. *Business Week*, November 13, 48; Koretz, G. (2000). The economy's Achilles' heel? *Business Week*, November 13, 42.

108. Baker, S., & Armstrong, L. (1996). The new factory worker. *Business Week*, September 30, 59–68.

109. Kripalani, M., Hamm, S., & Ante, S. (2004). Scrambling to stem India's onslaught. *Business Week*. January 26, 81–81; Montgomery, C. (2002). Chief: No delivery from labor pains. *Dayton Daily News*, March 2, 1E, 8E; Sasseen, J. A. (1994). Which country has the most qualified workforce? *Business Week*, October 17, 92–93.

110. Ewing, J., Carlisle, K., & Capell, K. (2001). Help wanted: Germany starts wooing skilled workers. *Business Week*, September 17, 52–53; Valbrun, M. (2000). Immigrants find economic boom brings more than higher pay. *The Wall Street Journal*, August 16, B1, B4.

111. Coy, P. (2000). The creative economy. *Business Week*, August 28, 76–82.

112. Grow, B. (2004). Hispanic nation. *Business Week*, March 15, 59–67; Malpass, A. (1998). Ready for that job on the street? *Business Week*, March 16, 118.

113. Gentile, M. C. (1996). *Managerial excellence through diversity*. Chicago, IL: Irwin; Joplin, J. R. W., & Daus, C.

S. (1997). Challenges of leading a diverse workforce. *Academy of Management Executive*, *11*, 32–47.

114. Robinson, G., & Dechant, K. (1997). Building a business case for diversity. *Academy of Management Executive*, *11*, 21–31.

115. Phatak, A. V. (1997). *International Management*: Concepts and Cases. Cincinnati, OH: South-Western College Publishing.

116. Stanek, M. B. (2000). The need for global managers: A business necessity. *Management Decision*, *38*, 232–242; Roberts, K., Kossek, E. E., & Ozeki, C. (1998). Managing the global workforce: Challenges and strategies. *Academy of Management Executive*, *12*, 93–106.

117. Murray, M. (2001). As huge companies keep growing, CEOs struggle to keep pace. *The Wall Street Journal*, February 8, A1, A6; **http://www.hoovers.com.**

118. Dwyer, P., Engardio, P., Schiller, Z., & Reed, S. (1994). Tearing up today's organization chart. *Business Week*, November 18, 80–90; Stanek, M. B. (2000). The need for global managers: A business necessity. *Management Decision*, *38*, 232–242, Roberts, Kossek, & Ozeki, Managing the global workforce: Challenges and strategies.

119. Birkinshaw, J., & Hood, N. (2001). Unleash innovation in foreign subsidiaries. *Harvard Business Review* (March), *79*, 131–138; Shrader, R. C. (2001). Collaboration and performance in foreign markets: The case of young high-technology manufacturing firms. *Academy of Management Journal*, *44*, 45–60; Harris, T. G. (1993). The post-capitalist executive: An interview with Peter Drucker. *Harvard Business Review* (May–June), *71*, 115–122; Hitt, Keats, & DeMarie, Navigating in the new competitive landscape: Building strategic flexibility and competitive advantage in the 21st century.

120. Hofstede, G. (1993). Cultural constraints in management theories. *Academy of Management Executive*, *7*, 81–94; Triandis, H. C. (1996). The psychological measurement of cultural syndromes. *American Psychologist*, *51*, 407–415.

121. Melloan, G. (2004). Feeling the muscles of the multinationals. *The Wall Street Journal*, January 6, A19.

122. Hordes, M. W., Clancy, J. A., & Baddaley, J. (1995). A primer for global start-ups. *Academy of Management Executive*, *9*, 7–11.

123. Bernstein, A. (2001). Low-skilled jobs: Do they have to move? *Business Week*, February 26, 94–95; Pope, J. (2004). Athletic shoemaker creates new path. *Dayton Daily News*, February 23, D1, D4; Schlender, B. (2004). Peter Drucker sets us straight. *Fortune*, January 12, 115–118.

Chapter 2

1. Yatsko, P. (2000). Knocking out the knockoffs. *Fortune*, October, 2, 216.

2. Yatsko, Knocking out the knockoffs, 213–218; Behar, R. (2000). Beijing's phony war on fakes. *Fortune*, October 30, 189–208; ———. (1996). Chinese piracy: A case for copying. *The Economist*, November 23, 73; Faison, S. (1996). Copyright pirates prosper in China despite promises. *The New York Times*, February 20, 1996, Kraar, L. (1995). The risks are rising in China. *Fortune*, March 6, 179–180.

3. Richards, E. L. (1994). *Law for global business*. Boston, MA: Irwin.

4. Czinkota, M. R., Ronkainen, I. A., Moffett, M. H., & Moynihan, E. O. (1995). *Global business*. New York: Dryden Press.

5. Czinkota, Ronkainen, Moffett, & Moynihan, *Global business*.

6. Richards, *Law for global business*.

7. Tillinghast, E. (1992). A survey of the legal profession. *The Economist*, July 18, 1–18.

8. Ball, D. A., McCulloch, W. H., Frantz, P. L., Geringer, J. M., & Minor, M. S. (2004). *International Business: The challenge of global competition*. New York: McGraw-Hill/Irwin.

9. Schaffer, R., Earle, B., & Agusti, F. (1993). *International business law and its environment*. Minneapolis, MN: West.

10. ———. (1992). Islam's interest. *The Economist*, January 18, 33–34; see also **www.islamic-banking.com** for information about this topic.

11. Rao, N. V. (1992). Islamic interest rule threatens Pakistan's bid for aid. *The Journal of Commerce*, January 29, 2A.

12. Brown, K. (1994). Banking on laws of Islam: Interest-free loans, investments grow. *Houston Chronicle*, April 10, B4; ———. (1996). Islamic finance: Turning the Prophet's profits. *The Economist*, August 24, 58–59.

13. Cullison, A. E. (1991). Product-liability claims hard to win in Japan. *Journal of Commerce*, August 9, 2A.

14. Darlin, D. (1989). Foreign lawyers in Japan chafe under restrictions. *The Wall Street Journal*, February 7, B1; Flom, J. (1991). Home court is best advantage. *Financial Times*, June 27, 10; Work, C. P., Peterson, S., & Tanakadate, H. (1985). Two air disasters, two cultures, two remedies. *U.S. News and World Report*, August 26, 25–26.

15. Batchelor, C., & Roberts, A. (2003). Sharia-compliant financing starts to take off. *Financial Times*, August 13, 27.

16. Albrecht, K. (1998). Turning the Prophet's words into profits. *Business Week*, March 16, 46.

17. Richards, *Law for global business*.

18. Zamet, J. M., & Bovarnick, M. E. (1986). Employee relations for multinational companies in China. *Columbia Journal of World Business*, 21, 13–19.

19. Chen, K. (2003). A see-through China? Leaders aim at transparency. *The Wall Street Journal*, August 13, A8.

20. Pincus, L. B., & Belohlav, J. A. (1996). Legal issues in multinational business strategy: To play the game, you have to know the rules. *Academy of Management Executives*, 10, 52–61

21. Pincus & Belohlav, Legal issues in multinational business strategy.

22. Richter, I. (2000). Legal colossus may be forged between U.K., German firms. *The Wall Street Journal*, April 10, A25; ———. (2000). Lawyers go global: The battle of the Atlantic. *The Economist*, February 26, 79–81.

23. Wessel, D. (2001). The legal DNA of good economies. *The Wall Street Journal*, September 6, A1.

24. ———. (2001). Unprofitable policies: Insurance in Asia. *The Economist*, August 11, 57–58.

25. De Jonquieres, G. (2003). Modest goals in Cancun: Trying to achieve liberalization in a group of 146 countries is well-nigh impossible. *Financial Times*, September 4, 11.

26. Zachary, G. P. (2000). Who's holding the strings? A reckoning for the WTO. *The Wall Street Journal*, October 5, A21; Roberts, D. (2002). Clear sailing for pirates: For now, the WTO can't stop mainland counterfeiters. *Business Week*, July 15, 53; Roberts, D., &

Magnusson, P. (2002). The tricks of trade: WTO neophyte China is learning fast. *Business Week*, July 15, 52–53.

27. King, N., & Miller, S. (2003). Post Iraq influence of U.S. faces test as new trade talks. *The Wall Street Journal*, September, 9, A1, A10; ———. (2003). Disputes between rich and poor kill trade talks. *The Wall Street Journal*, September 15, A1, A10; Newman, M. (2003). So many countries, so many laws: The Internet may not have borders, but the legal system certainly does. *The Wall Street Journal*, April 28, R8.

28. Phillips, M. M. (2000). Can World Bank lend money to Third World without hurting poor? *The Wall Street Journal*, August 14, A1, A8.

29. Newman, So many countries, so many laws.

30. Dichtl, E., & Koeglmayr, H. G. (1986). Country risk ratings. *Management International Review*, 26, 4–11.

31. Kobrin, S. J., & Punnett, B. J. (1984). The nationalization of oil production. In D. W. Pearce, J. Siebert, & I. Walter (Eds.), *Risk in the political economy of resource development*. London: MacMillan.

32. Richards, *Law for global business*.

33. Richards, *Law for global business*.

34. Harbrecht, D. (1996). Dodging danger while doing business abroad. *Business Week*, May 27, 151.

35. Harbrecht, D. (1996). Dodging danger while doing business abroad. *Business Week*, May 27, 151.

36. Timmons, S. (2000). Doing business among the body snatchers. *Business Week*, July 31, 22–23.

37. Bray, R. (1997). Busy execs can be easy targets. *Financial Times*, February 6, xii.

38. Fifield, A. (2003). War on terror creates unlikely allies. *Financial Times*, August 18, 4.

39. Griffin, R. W., & Pustay, M. W. (2000). *International business: A managerial perspective*. Reading, MA: Addison Wesley.

40. ———. (2003). Political and economic stability. *The Economist*, May 17, 90; ———. Political and economic stability. *The Economist*, August 16, 82.

41. Kahn, J. (1996). China's "greens" win rare battle on river: For now, many factories are closed on putrid Huai. *The Wall Street Journal*, August 2, A8.

42. Richards, *Law for global business*.

43. U.S. Department of State. (1995). U.S. Exports: Non-proliferation and foreign policy controls. *U.S. Department of State Fact Sheet*, December 6, 1995, 1–2.

44. Hufbauer, G. C., & Schott, J. J. (1984). Economic sanctions: An often used and occasionally effective tool of foreign policy. In M. R. Czinkota (Ed.), *Export controls*. New York: Praeger.

45. Schaffer, Earle, & Agusti, *International business law and its environment*.

46. Bandler, J. Ports in a storm: U.S. probes whether shipper acted to bust trade embargoes. *The Wall Street Journal*, May 20, A1, A14.

47. Burton, T. M. (1992). Baxter made cut-rate deal with Syria to escape blacklist, US probe finds. *The Wall Street Journal*, December 22, A3, A4; ———. (1993). How Baxter got off the Arab blacklist and how it got nailed. *The Wall Street Journal*, March 23, A1; Shellenbarer, S. (1990). Did hospital supplier dump its Israel plant to win Arabs' favor? *The Wall Street Journal*, May 1, A1, A10.

48. Richards, *Law for global business*.

49. This paragraph is based on Chazan, G. (2003). Facing Israeli, Arab obstacles: How a Palestinian stone maker handles crackdowns and boycotts. *The Wall Street Journal*, June 20, A6.

50. Pesta, J. (2001). India braces for brave new drug world. *The Wall Street Journal*, March 7, A17.

51. Johnson, K., & Fuhrmans, V. (2002). Spain's generics are a headache for drug firms. *The Wall Street Journal*, December 11, B1, B2.

52. Kraar, The risks are rising in China.

53. Kraar, The risks are rising in China.

54. Fowler, G. A. (2003). Pirates in China move fast to pilfer toy makers' ideas: turning to stealth marketing. *The Wall Street Journal*, January 31, B1, B4.

55. ———. (1996). Chinese piracy: A case for copying. *The Economist*, November 23, 73; Faison, S. (1996). Copyright pirates prosper in China despite promises. *The New York Times*, February 20, 1996; Kraar, The risks are rising in China.

56. Adler, C. (2003). Copied coffee? *Fortune*, September 29, 48.

57. Spaeth, A., & Naj, A. K. (1988). PepsiCo accepts tough conditions for the right to sell cola in India. *The Wall Street Journal*, September 20, 44.

58. Kahn, G. (2002). A sneaker maker says China partner became its rival: New Balance, other brands claim suppliers flood market with extra goods. *The Wall Street Journal*, December 19, A1, A8.

59. Seyoum, B. (1996). The impact of intellectual property rights on foreign direct investment. *Columbia Journal of World Business*, *31*, 51–59.

60. Greenberger, R. S. (1996). Software theft extends well beyond China. *The Wall Street Journal*, May 20, 1996, A1.

61. Barnes, W. (2003). Thai TV group battles pirates. *Financial Times*, August 20, 17; ———. (2003). Imitating property is theft. *The Economist*, May 17, 51–54.

62. Lehman, B. A. (1996). Intellectual property: America's competitive advantage in the 21st century. *Columbia Journal of World Business*, *31*, 7–16.

63. Gregory, A. (1989). Political risk management. In A. Rugman (Ed.), *International business in Canada*. Scarborough, ON: Prentice-Hall.

64. Kunreuther, H. (2003). The pitfalls of an interdependent world: Businesses can reduce their exposure to the risk of catastrophic events by co-operating with others. *Financial Times*, August 28, 9.

65. Bennett, J. (2001). Small businesses abroad get a big hand from OPIC. *The Wall Street Journal*, May 14, B10.

66. Federgruen, A., & Van Ryzin, G. (2003). New risks put scenario planning in favour. *Financial Times*, August 19, 7.

67. Gadiesh, O., & Pean, J. M. (2003). Think globally, market locally. *The Wall Street Journal*, September 9, B2.

68. Rugman, A. M., & Verbeke, A. (1990). *Global corporate strategy and trade policy*. New York: Routledge; Yoffie, D. B. (1988). How an industry builds political advantage. *Harvard Business Review*, May–June, 82–89.

69. Frank, R. (2001). Thai food for the world: Government of Thailand plans to open 3,000 restaurants to promote nation abroad. *The Wall Street Journal*, February 6, B1, B4.

70. Marsh, D. (1992). The European market: Political worries fail to deter western investors. *Financial Times*, October 12, 3.

71. Yatsko, Knocking out the knockoffs, 213–218.

Chapter 3

1. Wilke, J. R. (2003). Two silicon valley cases raise fears of Chinese espionage: Authorities try to tie alleged thefts of secrets to government-controlled companies. *The Wall Street Journal*, January 15, A4.

2. King, N., & Bravin, J. (2000). Call it mission impossible Inc.—Corporate-spying firms thrive. *The Wall Street Journal*, July 3, B1, B4; Crock, S., Smith, G., Weber, J., Melcher, R. A., & Himelstein, L. (1996). They snoop to conquer. *Business Week*, October 28, 172–176.

3. Wood, D. J. (1991). Corporate social performance revisited. *Academy of Management Journal*, *16*, 691–718.

4. Gottlieb, J. Z., & Sanzgiri, J. (1996). Towards an ethical dimension of decision making in organizations. *Journal of Business Ethics*, *15*, 1275–1285.

5. Amba-Rao, S. C. (1993). Multinational corporate social responsibility, ethics, interactions and third-world governments: An agenda for the 1990s. *Journal of Business Ethics*, *12*, 553–572.

6. L'Etang, J. (1995). Ethical corporate social responsibility: A framework for managers. *Journal of Business Ethics*, *14*, 125–132; Reidenbach, R. E., & Robin, D. P. (1990). Toward the development of a multidimensional scale for improving evaluations of business ethics. *Journal of Business Ethics*, *9*, 639–653; Velasquez, M. (1995). International business ethics: The aluminum companies in Jamaica. *Business Ethics Quarterly*, *5*, 865–881; Wood, Corporate social performance revisited.

7. Cohen, J. R., Pant, L. W., & Sharp, D. J. (1992). Cultural and socioeconomic constraints on international codes of ethics: Lessons from accounting. *Journal of Business Ethics*, *11*, 687–700; Schlegelmilch, B. B., & Robertson, D. C. (1995). The influence of country and industry on ethical perceptions of senior executives in the US and Europe. *Journal of International Business Studies*, *26*, 859–879.

8. ———. Business ethics: Doing well by doing good. (2000). *The Economist*, April 22, 65–67.

9. DeGeorge, R. T. (1993). *Competing with integrity in international business*. New York: Oxford University Press.

10. Buller, P. F., Kohls, J. J., & Anderson, K. S. (1991). The challenge of global ethics. *Journal of Business Ethics*, *10*, 767–775; Frederick, W. C. (1991). The moral authority of transnational corporate codes. *Journal of Business Ethics*, *10*, 165–177; Velasquez, International business ethics: The aluminum companies in Jamaica.

11. Donaldson, T. (1989). *The ethics of international business*. New York: Oxford University Press.

12. Jackson, K. T. (1994). Jurisprudence and the interpretation of precepts for international business. *Business Ethics Quarterly*, *4*, 291–320.

13. Jackson, K. T. (1994). Jurisprudence and the interpretation of precepts for international business.

14. Borrus, A., Javetski, B., Parry, J., & Bremner, B. (1996). Change of heart. *Business Week*, May 20, 48–49; Cooper, H., and Bahree, B. (1996). World's best hope for global trade topples few barriers. *The Wall Street Journal*, December 3, A1, A8.

15. Baron, D. P. (1996). *Business and its environment*. Upper Saddle River, NJ: Prentice-Hall.

16. Hinson, H. (1990). Movie stars. *Esquire*, December, 120–126.

17. Kaltenheuser, S. (1995). China: Doing business under an immoral government. *Business Ethics*, May/June,

20–23; Kelly, M. (1996). Is Pizza Hut Burma's keeper? *Business Ethics*, July/August 73–75.

18. Sethi, S. P. (1993). Operational modes for multinational corporations in post-Apartheid South Africa: A proposal for a code of affirmative action in the marketplace. *Journal of Business Ethics*, *12*, 1–12.

19. Kaltenheuser, China: Doing business under an immoral government.

20. Kelly, Is Pizza Hut Burma's keeper?

21. Bardacke, T. (1997). PepsiCo joins list of groups quitting Burma. *Financial Times*, January 28, 1, 18.

22. Kazmin, A. (2003). Burma's timber may blunt impact of sanctions. *Financial Times*, October 5, 3.

23. Shari, M. (2001). Staying the course. *Business Week*, September 24, 112; Bernstein, A. (1999). Sweatshop reform: How to solve the standoff. *Business Week*, May 3, 186–190; Friedland, J., & Pura, R. (1996). Troubled at home, Asian timber firms set sights on the Amazon. *The Wall Street Journal*, November 11, A1, A; ———. (1996). The fun of being a multinational. *The Economist*, July 20, 51–52; ———. (1996). Who's next? *The Economist*, July 13, 48–49; ———. (1999). Sweatshop wars. *The Economist*, Feb. 27, 62–63.

24. Silver, S. (2003). Social responsibility: Kraft blends ethics with coffee beans. *Financial Times*, October 7, 10; See also: Maitland, A. (2003). Customers forced Timberland to change our boots. *Financial Times*, October 6, 6.

25. Mackintosh, J. (2003). GM takes new green credentials for a test-drive. *Financial Times*, October 7, 2.

26. Schlegelmilch & Robertson, The influence of country and industry on ethical perceptions of senior executives in the US and Europe.

27. Becker, H., & Fritzsche, D. J. (1987). A comparison of the ethical behavior of American, French, and German managers. *Columbia Journal of World Business*, *22*, 87–95.

28. Borrus, A., Toy, S., & Salz-Trautman, P. (1995). A world of greased palms: Inside the dirty war for global business. *Business Week*, November 6, 36–38; ———. (1997). Enron and on and on. *The Economist*, June 14, 74; Jordan, M. (1996). Indian leader Rao quits post to face charges. *The Wall Street Journal*, September 23, A17; Steinmetz, G., & Greenberger, R. S. (1997). US embassies give American companies more help overseas. *The Wall Street Journal*, January 21, A1, A6.

29. Dolecheck, M. M. (1992). Cross-cultural analysis of business ethics: Hong Kong and American business personnel. *Journal of Managerial Issues*, *4*, 288–303; Dubinsky, A. J., Jolson, M. A., Kotabe, M., & Lim, C. U. (1991). A cross-national investigation of industrial salespeople's ethical perceptions. *Journal of International Business Studies*, *22*, 651–670; Kennedy, E. J., & Lawton, L. (1996). The effects of social and moral integration on ethical standards: A comparison of American and Ukrainian business students. *Journal of Business Ethics*, *15*, 901–911; McCabe, D. L., Dukerich, J. M., & Dutton, J. (1993). Values and moral dilemmas: A cross-cultural comparison. *Business Ethics Quarterly*, *3*, 117–130.

30. Husted, B. W., Dozier, J. B., McMahon, J. T., & Kattan, M. W. (1996). The impact of cross-national carriers of business ethics on attitudes about questionable practices and form of moral reasoning. *Journal of International Business Studies*, *27*, 391–411.

31. Moore, R. S., & Radloff, S. E. (1996). Attitudes towards business ethics held by South African students. *Journal of Business Ethics*, *15*, 863–869.

32. ———. (2000). Business ethics: Doing well by doing good. *The Economist*, April 22, 65–67.

33. Langlois, C. C., & Schlegelmilch, B. B. (1990). Do corporate codes of ethics reflect national character? Evidence from Europe and the United States. *Journal of International Business Studies*, Fourth Quarter, 519–539.

34. Langlois & Schlegelmilch, Do corporate codes of ethics reflect national character?

35. Langlois & Schlegelmilch, Do corporate codes of ethics reflect national character?; Schlegelmilch, B. B. (1989). The ethics gap between Britain and the United States: A comparison of the state of business ethics in both countries. *European Management Journal*, 7, 57–64.

36. DeGeorge, *Competing with integrity in international business.*

37. Feder, B. J. (1994). Honeywell's route back to South Africa market. *The New York Times*, January 31, C1, C4; Templin, N. (1988). They're getting out of South Africa. *USA Today*, June 14, 7B.

38. Feder, Honeywell's route back to South Africa market.

39. Sethi, Operational modes for multinational corporations in post-Apartheid South Africa: A proposal for a code of affirmative action in the marketplace.

40. McFarlin, D. B., Coster, E. A., & Mogale-Pretorius, C. (1999). Management development in South Africa: Moving toward an Africanized model. *Journal of Management Development*, July, 33–41.

41. Rossouw, G. J. (1998). Establishing moral business culture in newly formed democracies. *Journal of Business Ethics*, *17*, 1563–1571.

42. Kaltenheuser, China: Doing business under an immoral government, 20–23.

43. Vance, C. M., & Paderon, E. S. (1993). An ethical argument for host country workforce training and development in the expatriate management assignment. *Journal of Business Ethics*, *12*, 635–641.

44. Kaltenheuser, China: Doing business under an immoral government.

45. Beaver, W. (1995). Levi's is leaving China. *Business Horizons*, *38*, 35–40.

46. Beaver, Levi's is leaving China.

47. Zachary, G. P. (1994). Levi's tries to make sure contract plants in Asia treat workers well. *The Wall Street Journal*, July 28, A1, A6.

48. Buller, P. F., Kohls, J. J., & Anderson, K. S. (2000). When ethics collide: Managing conflict across cultures. *Organizational Dynamics*, *28*, 52–66.

49. Clifford, M. L. (1996). Keep the heat on sweatshops. *Business Week*, December 3, 90; Holmes, S. (2003). Free speech or false advertising: Nike's sweatshop statement case hits Supreme Court. *BusinessWeek*, April 28, 69–70.

50. Singer, A. W. (1996). Levi Strauss' global sourcing guidelines come of age. *Ethikos*, May/June, 4–12.

51. Ortega, B. (1995). Conduct codes garner goodwill for retailers, but violations go on. *The Wall Street Journal*, July 3, A1, A4.

52. Stein, N. (2003). No way out: Competition to make products for Western companies has revived an old form of abuse: debt bondage. *Fortune*, January 20, 102–108;

53. Edmondson, G., Carlisle, K., Resch, I., Anhalt, K., & Dawley, H. (2000). Workers in bondage. *Business Week*, November 27, 146–162.

54. Bernstein, A. (2003). Sweatshops: Finally, airing the dirty linen. *BusinessWeek*, June 23, 100–102.

55. Donaldson, T. (1994). Global business must mind its morals. *The New York Times*, February 13, E11.
56. Noonan, J. (1984). *Bribes*. New York: Macmillan.
57. Jacoby, N. H., Nehemkis, P., & Eells, R. (1977). *Bribery and extortion in world business: A study of corporate political payments abroad*. New York: Macmillan.
58. Jacoby, Nehemkis, & Eells, *Bribery and extortion in world business*.
59. Jacoby, Nehemkis, & Eells, *Bribery and extortion in world business*.
60. Schaffer, Earle, & Agusti, *International business law and its environment*.
61. Borsuk, R. (2003). In Indonesia, a new twist on spreading the wealth: Decentralization of power multiplies opportunities for bribery, corruption. *The Wall Street Journal*, January 29, A16.
62. Transparency International website (2003), **www. transparency.de.**
63. ———. (2000). Shenanigans in France. *The Economist*, November 4, 53; ———. (1996). Who's next? *The Economist*, July 13, 48–49; Toy, S. (1996). Under suspicion: Le tout business elite. *Business Week*, January 22, 58; Toy, S., Edmondson, G., & Javetski, B. (1995). Will les affaires lead to reform in la France? *Business Week*, February 27, 56–57.
64. ———. (2003). Comparative corruption: Different standards of probity across the continent pose a problem for the European Union. *The Economist*, May 17, 47.
65. Kamm, T., Rohwedder, C., & Trofimov, Y. (2000). Europe can't decide whether dirty money in politics is a problem. *The Wall Street Journal*, February 9, A1; –. (2000). Stopping the rot in public life. *The Economist*, September 16, 41–43; ———. (2000). Bill, borrow and embezzle. *The Economist*, February 17, 48; Reed, J., & Portage, E. (1999). Bribery, corruption are rampant in Eastern Europe, survey finds. *The Wall Street Journal*, November 9, A21.
66. ———. (2001). Another bad apple in Japan. *The Economist*, January 27, 39; Bremner, B. (1996). How the mob burned the banks. *Business Week*, January 29, 42–47.
67. Ward, A. (2003). South Korea's mixed messages over corruption clampdown. *Financial Times*, October 1, 20; Ward, A. (2003). Transparency should by now be a given in Korea: The fraud at one of the country's most powerful industrial groups raises doubts about how far reform has really advanced. *Financial Times*, July 9, 11. See the following references for an earlier, similar scandal: Lee, C. K. (1996). Unfinished business: Kim sends the chaebol a message. *Business Week*, September 9, 56–57; Nakarmi, L. (1995). The slush fund that's shaking up Seoul. *Business Week*, November 13, 60.
68. Cartledge, S. (2003). China's leaders ignore graft at their peril. *Financial Times*, July 7, 13.
69. Pope, H. (2000). Corruption stunts growth in ex-Soviet states. *The Wall Street Journal*, July 5, A17; Galuszka, P., & Brady, R. (1996). The battle for Russia's wealth. *Business Week*, April 1, 50–52.
70. ———. (1990). Hey, America, lighten up a little. *The Economist*, July 28, A5.
71. Czinkota, Ronkainen, Moffett, & Moynihan, *Global business*.
72. Singer, A. W. (1991). Ethics: Are standards lower overseas? *Across the Board*, 28, 31–34.
73. DeGeorge, *Competing with integrity in international business*.
74. Cohen, J. A. (1976). Japan's Watergate. *The New York Times Magazine*, November 21, 104–119.
75. Kotchian, C. A. (1977). The payoff: Lockheed's 70-day mission to Tokyo. *Saturday Review*, July 9, 7–16.
76. Boulton, D. (1978). *The grease machine*. New York: Harper & Row.
77. Kim, S. H., & Barone, S. (1981). Is the Foreign Corrupt Practices Act of 1977 a success or failure? A survey of members of the Academy of International Business. *Journal of International Business Studies*, 12, 123–126.
78. Fadiman, J. A. (1986). A traveler's guide to gifts and bribes. *Harvard Business Review*, July/August, 122–136; Singer, Ethics: Are standards lower overseas?
79. Graham, J. L. (1984). The foreign corrupt practices act: A new perspective. *Journal of International Business Studies*, 15, 107–121.
80. Graham, The foreign corrupt practices act: A new perspective.
81. Vogel, T. T. (1997). Foreigners rang early alarm on Ecuador. *The Wall Street Journal*, February 10, A14.
82. Engardio, P., & Shari, M. (1996). The Suharto empire. *Business Week*, August 19, 46–50.
83. Singer, Ethics: Are standards lower overseas?
84. Donaldson, Global business must mind its morals; Schlegelmilch, B. (1989). The ethics gap between Britain and the United States: A comparison of the state of business ethics in both countries. *European Management Journal*, 7, 57–64.
85. ———. (1996). Operating an ethics hotline: Some practical advice. *Ethikos*, March/April, 11–13.
86. Graham, G. (1993). US seeks OECD foreign bribes ban. *Financial Times*, December 6, 3; Keatley, R. (1994). U.S. campaign against bribery faces resistance from foreign governments. *The Wall Street Journal*, February 4, A6.
87. LeVine, S. (2003). U.S. bribery probe looks at Mobil: Firm's role in payments to high Kazak officials is under investigation. *The Wall Street Journal*, April 23, A2.
88. ———. (2003). Bribery index. *The Economist*, May 18, 104.
89. Dunne, N. (2000). Bribery helps win contracts in developing world. *Financial Times*, January 21, 6; Graham, U.S. seeks OECD foreign bribes ban; Keatley, U.S. campaign against bribery faces resistance from foreign governments; Milbank, D., & Brauchli, M. W. (1995). How U.S. concerns compete in countries where bribes flourish. *The Wall Street Journal*, September 29, A1, A14; Greenberger, R. S. (1995). Foreigners use bribes to beat U.S. rivals in many deals. *The Wall Street Journal*, October 12, 3; Steinmetz, G., & Greenberger, R. S. (1997). US embassies give American companies more help overseas. *The Wall Street Journal*, January 21, A1, A6.
90. Quench, J., & Austin, J. (1993). Should multinationals invest in Africa? *Sloan Management Review*, Spring, 107–118.
91. Miffed, S. (1996). Asia stinks. *Fortune*, December 9, 120–132; Devraj, R. (2000). Development India: Thousands of jobless question green concerns. *Interpress Service*, December 29, 7–8.
92. Litvin, D. (2003). Coca-Cola is not the real thing for India's activists. *Financial Times*, August 15, 11.
93. ———. (2003). Priceless: A survey of water. *The Economist*, July 19, 1–16.
94. Dyer, G. (2003). A drugs deal for the world's poorest: Now the fight over patents and cheap medicine is in middle-income countries. *Financial Times*, September 2, 11.
95. Cooper, H., Zimmerman, R., & McGinley, L. (2001). Patents pending—AIDS epidemic traps drug firms in a vise. *The Wall Street Journal*, March 2, A1; Block, R.

(2001). Big drug firms defend right to patent on AIDS drugs in South African courts. *The Wall Street Journal*, March 6, A1.

96. King, N., & Miller, S. (2003). Disputes between rich and poor kill trade talks: Global effort collapses as developing countries object to U.S., EU goals. *The Wall Street Journal*, September 15, A1, A10.

97. ———. (1996). The global poverty trap. *The Economist*, July 20, 34.

98. Fath, J. (1994). Industrial policies for countries in transition? *Russian and East European Finance and Trade, 30*, 38–77; Godfrey, M. (1995). The struggle against unemployment: Medium term policy options for transitional economies. *International Labour Review, 134*, 3–15; O'Leary, C. J. (1995). Performance indicators: A management tool for active labour programmes in Hungary and Poland. *International Labour Review, 134*, 729–753.

99. Woodruff, D. (1996). East Germany is still a mess—$580 billion later. *Business Week*, June 17, 58.

100. Friedland, J. (1996). Latin America resists reform backlash. *The Wall Street Journal*, August 5, A8.

101. Quench & Austin, Should multinationals invest in Africa?

102. Smith, C. S., & Brauchli, M. W. (1995). Despite rapid growth of China's economy, many are suffering. *The Wall Street Journal*, October 18, A1, A16.

103. Chen, K. (1995). As millions of Chinese try to get rich quick, values get trampled. *The Wall Street Journal*, May 2, A1, A16.

104. ———. (2003). Poverty in Africa. *The Economist*, July 13, 90; Engardio, P., Walsh, D., & Kripalani, M. (2003). Global poverty. *BusinessWeek*, October 14, 108–118.

105. Roberts, D. (2000). The great migration: Chinese peasants are fleeing their villages to chase big-city dreams. *Business Week*, December 18, 176–188; Chen, K. (1996). A teenager's journey mirrors inner migration that's changing China. *The Wall Street Journal*, October 29, A1, A4.

106. Singh, J. B., & Carasco, E. F. (1996). Business ethics, economic development and protection of the environment in the new world order. *Journal of Business Ethics, 15*, 297–307.

107. Kirkpatrick, D. (2001). Looking for profits in poverty. *Fortune*, February 5, 176–177.

108. Ball, D. A., & McCulloch, W. H. (1999). *International business: The challenge of global competition*. Burr Ridge, IL: Irwin McGraw-Hill; King & Bravin, Call it mission impossible Inc.

109. King & Bravin, Call it mission impossible Inc.

110. Girard, K. (2003). Snooping on a shoestring: Competitive intelligence doesn't go away during a down market—it just gets that much more competitive. *Business 2.0*, May, 64–66.

Chapter 4

1. Filipczak, B. (1992). Working for the Japanese. *Training, 26*, 23–29; Linowes, R. G. (1993). The Japanese manager's traumatic entry into the United States: Understanding the American-Japanese cultural divide. *Academy of Management Executive, 7*, 21–40.

2. Hofstede, G. (1993). Cultural constraints in management theories. *Academy of Management Executive, 7*, 81–94; Triandis, H. C. (1996). The psychological measurement of cultural syndromes. *American Psychologist, 51*, 407–415.

3. Adler, N. J. (2002). *International dimensions of organizational behavior* (4th Ed.). Cincinnati, OH: South-Western; Thomas, D. C., Au, K., & Ravlin, E. C. (2003). Cultural variation and the psychological contract. *Journal of Organizational Behavior, 24*, 451–472; Shenkar, O. (2001). Cultural distance revisited: Towards a more rigorous conceptualization and measurement of cultural differences. *Journal of International Business Studies, 32*, 519–535.

4. Granato, J., Inglehart, R., & Leblang, D. (1996). The effect of cultural values on economic development: Theory, hypotheses, and some empirical tests. *American Journal of Political Science, 40*, 607–631.

5. Earley, P. C., & Singh, H. (2000). New approaches to international and cross-cultural management research. In P. C. Earley & H. Singh (Eds.), *Innovations in international and cross-cultural management*, 1–14. Thousand Oaks, CA: Sage.

6. Begley, T. M., & Tan, W. L. (2001). The socio-cultural environment for entrepreneurship: A comparison between East Asian and Anglo-Saxon countries. *Journal of International Business Studies, 32*, 537–553.

7. Newman, K. L., & Nollen, S. D. (1996). Culture and congruence: The fit between management practices and national culture. *Journal of International Business Studies*, Fourth Quarter, 753–779.

8. Gupta, A. K., & Govindarajan, V. (2002). Cultivating a global mindset. *The Academy of Management Executive, 16(1)*, 116–126.

9. Morris, M. W., Podolny, J. M., & Ariel, S. (2000). Missing relations: Incorporating relational constructs into models of culture. In P. C. Earley & H. Singh (Eds.), *Innovations in international and cross-cultural management*, 52–90. Thousand Oaks, CA: Sage; Sampson, E. E. (2000). Reinterpreting individualism and collectivism. *American Psychologist, 55*, 1425–1432.

10. Schneider, S. C., & Barsoux, J. L. (2003). *Managing across cultures* (2nd Ed.). Harlow, England: Pearson Education Ltd.

11. Shenkar, Cultural distance revisited: Towards a more rigorous conceptualization and measurement of cultural differences.

12. Osland, J. S., & Bird, A. (2000). Beyond sophisticated stereotyping. Cultural sensemaking in context. *Academy of Management Executive, 14*, 65–79.

13. Trompenaars, F. (1993). *Riding the waves of culture*. London: Brealey.

14. Ronen, S., & Shenkar, O. (1985). Clustering countries on attitudinal dimensions: A review and synthesis. *Academy of Management Review, 10*, 435–454.

15. Shenkar, Cultural distance revisited: Towards a more rigorous conceptualization and measurement of cultural differences.

16. Alston, J. P. (1989). Wa, Guanxi, and Inhwa: Managerial principles in Japan, China, and Korea. *Business Horizons*, March–April, 26–31.

17. ———. (2002). Japanese careers: Show me the money. *The Economist*, January 26, 56; ———. (2000). In search of the new Japanese dream. *The Economist*, February 19, 59–63; ———. (2000). Child's play. *The Economist*, February 19, 60; ———. (2000). Survey of the young: Tomorrow's child. *The Economist*, December 23, 11–14; Meek, C. B. (1999). Ganbatte: Understanding the Japanese employee. *Business Horizons*, January–February, 27–35; Ono, Y., & Spindle, B. (2000). Japan's long decline makes one thing rise: Individualism. *The Wall Street Journal*, December 29, A1, A4.

18. Alston, Wa, Guanxi, and Inhwa: Managerial principles in Japan, China, and Korea; Bond, M. H. (1991). *Beyond the Chinese face*. Hong Kong: Oxford University Press; Chen, M. (1995). *Asian management systems: Chinese, Japanese and Korean styles of business*. London: Routledge.

19. Chen, *Asian management systems: Chinese, Japanese and Korean styles of business*.

20. Bass, B. M. (1990). *Stogdill's handbook of leadership: A survey of theory and research*. New York: Free Press; McFarlin, D. B., Sweeney, P. D., & Cotton, J. C. (1992). Attitudes toward employee participation in decision-making: A comparison of European and American managers in a U.S. multinational. *Human Resource Management, 31*, 363–383.

21. Lenartowicz, T., & Johnson, J. P. (2003). A cross-national assessment of the values of Latin American managers: Contrasting hues or shades of gray? *Journal of International Business Studies, 34(3)*, 266–281.

22. Adler, *International dimensions of organizational behavior*, Cox, T., & Blake, S. (1991). Managing cultural diversity: Implications for organizational competitiveness. *Academy of Management Executive, 5*, 45–56.

23. Kumbula, T. S. (1993). As apartheid falls, black education becomes (at last) a serious issue. *Black Issues in Higher Education, 10*, September 23, 15–18.

24. McFarlin, D. B., Coster, E. A., & Mogale-Pretorius, C. (1999). Management development in South Africa: Moving toward an Africanized framework. *Journal of Management Development, 18*, 63–78; Thomas, A., & Bendixen, M. (2000). Management implications of ethnicity in South Africa. *Journal of International Business Studies, 31*, 507–519.

25. Sivakumar, K., & Nakata, C. (2001). The stampede toward Hofstede's framework: Avoiding the sample design pit in cross-cultural research. *Journal of International Business Studies, 32*, 555–574.

26. Hofstede, G. (1980). Motivation, leadership, and organization: Do American theories apply abroad? *Organizational Dynamics*, Summer, 42–63; Hofstede, G. (2001). *Culture's consequences* (2nd Ed.). Thousand Oaks, CA: Sage; Hofstede, G. (1984). *Culture's consequences*. Newbury Park, CA: Sage; Hofstede, Cultural constraints in management theories; Hofstede, G. (1991). *Cultures and organizations: Software of the mind*. London: McGraw-Hill U.K.; Hofstede, G. (1996). An American in Paris: The influence of nationality on organization theories. *Organizational Studies, 17*, 525–537.

27. Morris, Podolny, & Ariel, Missing relations: Incorporating relational constructs into models of culture.

28. Hofstede, G. (2001). *Culture's Consequences* (2nd Ed.) Thousand Oaks, CA: Sage Publications; Hofstede, G. (1993). Cultural constraints in management theories.

29. Bond, *Beyond the Chinese face*; Hofstede, Cultural constraints in management theories.

30. Dowling, P. J., & Nagel, T. W. (1986). Nationality and work attitudes: A study of Australian and American business majors. *Journal of Management, 12*, 121–128.

31. van Oudenhoven, J. P. (2001). Do organizations reflect national cultures? A 10-nation study. *International Journal of Intercultural Relations, 25*, 89–107.

32. Used by permission. (Company to remain anonymous.)

33. Hofstede, G., Van Deusen, C. A., Mueller, C. B., Charles, T. A., & The Business Goals Network. (2002). What goals do business leaders pursue? A study in fifteen countries. *Journal of International Business Studies 33(4)*, 785–803.

34. Trompenaars, *Riding the waves of culture*; Trompenaars, F., & Hampden-Turner, C. (1998). *Riding the waves of culture: Understanding cultural diversity in global business* (2nd Ed.). New York: McGraw-Hill.

35. Ali, A. (1988). A cross-national perspective of managerial work value systems. In R. N. Farmer & E. G. McGoun (Eds.), *Advances in international comparative management*, vol. 3, 151–170. Greenwich, CT: JAI Press; Trompenaars, *Riding the waves of culture*.

36. MOW International Research Team (1987). *The meaning of working*. London: Academic Press.

37. Meek, Ganbatte: Understanding the Japanese employee; Zimmerman, M. (1985). *How to do business with the Japanese*. New York: Random House.

38. Lincoln, J. R. (1989). Employee work attitudes and management practice in the U.S. and Japan: Evidence from a large comparative survey. *California Management Review, 32*, 89–106; Meek, Ganbatte: Understanding the Japanese employee.

39. Brady, D. (2002). Rethinking the rat race. *Business Week*, August 26, 142–143.

40. Grant, L. (1997). Unhappy in Japan. *Fortune*, January 13, 142; Meek, Ganbatte: Understanding the Japanese employee; Schaefer, G. (2003). Abusive bosses fuel hot line complaints in Japan. *Dayton Daily News*, June 30, D8.

41. MOW International Research Team, *The meaning of working*.

42. Sherer, P. M. (1996). North American and Asian executives have contrasting values, study finds. *The Wall Street Journal*, March 6, B11.

43. Hofstede, Cultural constraints in management theories.

44. See Greenberg, J., & Baron, R. A. (2000). *Behavior in organizations* (7th Ed.). Englewood Cliffs, NJ: Prentice-Hall; Yukl, G. (2002). *Leadership in Organizations* (5th Ed.). Upper Saddle River, NJ: Prentice Hall

45. Hofstede, G. (1993). Cultural constraints in management theories.

46. Laurent, A. (1983). The cultural diversity of western conceptions of management. *International Studies of Management and Organization, 13*, 75–96.

47. Ali, A. (1988). A cross-national perspective of managerial work value systems. In R. N. Farmer & E. G. McGoun (Eds.), *Advances in international comparative management*, vol. 3, 151–170. Greenwich, CT: JAI Press; Bass, B. M. (1990). *Stogdill's handbook of leadership: A survey of theory and research*. New York: Free Press.

48. Ayman, R., Kreicker, N. A., & Masztal, J. J. (1994). Defining global leadership in business environments. *Consulting Psychology Journal, 46*, 64–73; Dorfman, P. (1996). International and cross-cultural leadership. In B. J. Punnett & O. Shenkar (Eds.), *Handbook for international management research*, 267–350. Cambridge, MA: Blackwell.

49. Yeung, A. K., & Ready, D. A. (1995). Developing leadership capabilities of global corporations: A comparative study in eight nations. *Human Resource Management, 34*, 529–547.

50. Okechuku, C. (1994). The relationship of six managerial characteristics to the assessment of managerial effectiveness in Canada, Hong Kong, and People's Republic of China. *Journal of Occupational and Organizational Psychology, 67*, 79–86.

51. Geppert, M. (1996). Paths of managerial learning in the east German context. *Organization Studies, 17*, 249–268; Kostera, M., Proppe, M., & Szatkowski, M. (1995). Staging the new romantic hero in the old

cynical theatre: On managers, roles and change in Poland. *Journal of Organizational Behavior, 16,* 631–646.

52. Hofstede, G., et al. (2002). What goals do business leaders pursue? A study in fifteen countries.

53. Marks, M. (2003). In search of global leaders. *Harvard Business Review,* August, 43.

54. Osland & Bird, Beyond sophisticated stereotyping: Cultural sense-making in context.

55. Filipczak, B. (1992). Working for the Japanese. *Training, 26,* 23–29; Linowes, R. G. (1993). The Japanese manager's traumatic entry into the United States: Understanding the American-Japanese cultural divide. *Academy of Management Executive, 7,* 21–40.

56. Gutner, T. (1996). Never give a Mandarin a clock and other rules. *Business Week,* December 9, 192; Murphy, K. (1999). Gifts without gaffes for global clients. *Business Week,* December 6, 153.

Chapter 5

1. Webb, J. (2000). History proves Vietnam victors wrong. *The Wall Street Journal,* April 28, A19; ———. (2000). Vietnam then and now. *The Wall Street Journal,* April 8, A18.

2. Smith, E. D., & Pham, C. (1996). Doing business in Vietnam: A cultural guide. *Business Horizons, 39,* 47–51.

3. Smith & Pham, Doing business in Vietnam.

4. McArthur, L. Z., & Brown, R. M. (1983). Toward an ecological theory of social perception, *Psychological Review, 90,* 215–238.

5. Bond, M. H., & Forgas, J. (l984). Linking person perception to behavioral intention across cultures. The role of cultural collectivism. *Journal of Cross-Cultural Psychology, 15,* 337–353.

6. This comment applies equally to cultures that may share fundamental similarities, such as the United States and Australia. Simply sharing characteristics does not imply that one culture understands the other, as is apparently the case with the United States. Bryson, for example, shows that Australia has a very low profile among Americans and they generally know little of the country. (Bryson, B. [2000]. The down where? *The Wall Street Journal,* September 15, A18.)

7. Bond, M. H., Wan, K. C., Leung, K., & Giacalone, R. A. (1985). How are responses to verbal insult related to cultural collectivism and power distance? *Journal of Cross-Cultural Psychology, 16,* 111–127.

8. Forgas, J. P., & Bond, M. H. (1985). Cultural influences on the perceptions of interaction episodes. *Personality and Social Psychology Bulletin, 11,* 75–88.

9. Research cited from Nisbett, R. (2003). The geography of thought: How Asians and Westerners think differently . . . and why. Cited in Begley, S. (2003). East vs. West: One see the big picture, the other is focused. *The Wall Street Journal,* March 28, B1.

10. Hall, E. T. (1983). *The dance of life.* Garden City, NY: Anchor Press; Hall, E. T., & Hall, M. R. (1990). *Understanding cultural differences.* Yarmouth, ME: Intercultural Press.

11. Gudykunst, W. B., & Ting-Toomey, S. (1988). Culture and affective communication. *American Behavioral Scientist, 31,* 384–400; Scherer, K. R., & Wallbott, H. G. (1994). Evidence for universality and cultural variation of differential emotion response patterning. *Journal of Personality and Social Psychology, 66,* 310–328.

12. Sweeney, P. D., & McFarlin, D. B. (2002). *Organizational behavior: Solutions for management.* Burr Ridge, IL: McGraw-Hill Irwin.

13. LaFrance, M., & Mayo, C. (1978). Cultural aspects of nonverbal communication: A review essay. *International Journal of Intercultural Relations, 2,* 71–89; Ramsey, S. J. (1979). Nonverbal behavior: An intercultural perspective. In M. Asante et al. (Eds.), *Handbook of intercultural communication.* Newbury Park, CA: Sage.

14. Archer, H. (2001). Doing business in Japan: The secrets of meishi. **www.shinnova.com/part/99-japa.**

15. Hall, E. T. (1976). *Beyond culture.* Garden City, NY: Anchor Press; Hall & Hall, *Understanding cultural differences.*

16. Levine, R. V., & Wolff, E. (1985). Social time: The heartbeat of culture. *Psychology Today,* March, 28–35.

17. Levine, R. V., & Bartlett, K. (1984). Pace of life, punctuality, and coronary heart disease in six countries. *Journal of Cross-Cultural Psychology, 15,* 233–255.

18. Hall, *The dance of life.*

19. Hall & Hall, *Understanding cultural differences.*

20. Usunier, J-C. G. (1991). Business time perceptions and national cultures: A comparative survey. *Management International Review, 31,* 197–217.

21. Hall, E. T. (1960). The silent language in overseas business. *Harvard Business Review,* May–June, 87–96.

22. Chandler, T. A., Sharma, D. D., Wolf, F. M., & Planchard, S. K. (1981). Multi-attributional causality: A five cross-national samples study. *Journal of Cross-Cultural Psychology, 12,* 207–221; Choi, I., Nisbett, R. E., & Norenzayan, A. (1999). Causal attribution across cultures: Variation and universality. *Psychological Bulletin, 125,* 47–63.

23. Kashima, Y., & Triandis, H. C. (1986). The self-serving bias in attributions as a coping strategy: A cross-cultural study. *Journal of Cross-Cultural Psychology, 17,* 83–97.

24. Smith, S. H., Whitehead, G. I., & Sussman, N. M. (1990). The positivity bias in attributions: Two cross-cultural investigations. *Journal of Cross-Cultural Psychology, 21,* 283–301.

25. Smith, Whitehead, & Sussman, The positivity bias in attributions.

26. Bond, M. H., Leung, K., & Wan, K. (1982). The social impact of self-effacing attributions: The Chinese case. *Journal of Social Psychology, 118,* 157–166.

27. Morris, M. W., & Peng, K. (1994). Culture and cause: American and Chinese attributions for social and physical events. *Journal of Personality and Social Psychology, 67,* 949–971.

28. Begley, S. (2003). East vs. West: One sees the big picture, the other is focused. *The Wall Street Journal,* March 28, B1.

29. Barnum, C., & Wolniansky, N. (1989). Taking cues from body language. *Management Review,* June, 59–60.

30. Miller, J. G. (1988). Bridging the content-structure dichotomy: Culture and self. In M. H. Bond (Ed.), *The cross-cultural challenge to social psychology,* vol. 11. Beverly Hills, CA: Sage.

31. Weisz, J. R., Rothbaum, F. M., & Blackburn, T. C. (1984). Standing out and standing in: The psychology of control in America and Japan. *American Psychologist, 39,* 955–969.

32. Markus, H. R., & Kitayama, S. (1998). The cultural psychology of personality. *Journal of Cross-Cultural Psychology, 29,* 63–87; ———. (1991). Culture and the self: Implications for cognition, emotion, and motivation. *Psychological Review, 98,* 224–253.

33. Bond, M. H., & Cheung, T. (1983). College students' spontaneous self-concept. *Journal of Cross-Cultural Psychology*, June, 153–171.

34. Triandis, H. C. (1989). The self and social behavior in differing cultural contexts. *Psychological Review*, 96, 506–520.

35. See also Cousins, S. D. (1989). Culture and self-perception in Japan and the United States. *Journal of Personality and Social Psychology*, 56, 124–131.

36. Schweder, R. A., & Bourne, E. J. (1982). Does the concept of the person vary cross-culturally? In R. A. Schweder & R. A. Levine (Eds.), *Culture theory: Essays on mind, self, and emotion*. New York: Cambridge University Press (158–199).

37. Miller, J. G. (1984). Culture and the development of everyday social explanation. *Journal of Personality and Social Psychology*, 46, 961–978. See also a study by Stipek, D., Weiner, B., & Li, K. (1989). Testing some attribution-emotion relations in the People's Republic of China. *Journal of Personality and Social Psychology*, 56, 109–116. Based on a carefully done study, these researchers concluded that there is little support for characterizations of Chinese as being particularly other oriented and of Americans as being relatively more self-focused. The difference in results is difficult to explain. We can only say that this study is the newest of the lot and thus may reflect some of the recent changes occurring in China, particularly among the young and educated. Regardless, the general pattern of findings we present in this section appears to reflect some differing views of the self, perhaps reflective of a Western independent self and a non-Western interdependent self.

38. Mabe, P. A., III, & West, S. E. (1982). Validity and self-evaluation of ability: A review and meta-analysis. *Journal of Applied Psychology*, 42, 280–297.

39. Farh, J. L., Dobbins, G. H., & Cheng, B-S. (1991). Cultural relativity in action: A comparison of self-ratings made by Chinese and U.S. workers. *Personnel Psychology*, 44, 129–147.

40. Kelly, L., Whatley, A., & Worthley, R. (1993). Self-appraisal, life goals and national culture: An Asian-Western comparison. *Asia Pacific Journal of Management*, 7, 41–58.

41. Yu, J., & Murphy, K. R. (1993). Modesty bias in self-ratings of performance: A test of the cultural relativity hypothesis. *Personnel Psychology*, 46, 357–363.

42. Sweeney & McFarlin, *Organizational behavior: Solutions for management*. Originally based on Reeder, J. A. (1987). When West meets East: Cultural aspects of doing business in Asia. *Business Horizons*, January–February, 69–74.

43. Redding, S. G., & Ng, M. (1983). The role of "face" in the organizational perceptions of Chinese managers. *International Studies of Management & Organization*, 13, 92–123.

44. Reeder, When West meets East: Cultural aspects of doing business in Asia.

45. Furnham, A., Bond, M., Heaven, P., Hilton, D., Lobel, T., Masters, J., Payne, M., Rajamanikam, R., Stacey, B., & Daalen, H. V. (1992). A comparison of Protestant work ethic beliefs in thirteen nations. *Journal of Social Psychology*, 133, 185–197.

46. Furnham et al., A comparison of Protestant work ethic beliefs in thirteen nations.

47. Lynn, R. (1991). *The secret of the miracle economy: Different national attitudes to competitiveness and money*. Exeter, UK: Social Affairs Unit.

48. Furnham, A. (1992). Just world beliefs in twelve societies. *Journal of Social Psychology*, 133, 317–329.

49. Reeder, When West meets East: Cultural aspects of doing business in Asia.

50. Hymowitz, C. (2000). U.S. executives reply to criticism leveled by foreign counterparts. *The Wall Street Journal*, September 19, B1; ———. (2000). Companies go global, but many managers just don't travel well. *The Wall Street Journal*, August 15, B1.

51. Neff, R. (1989). Japan's hardening view of America. *Business Week*, December 18, 62–64.

52. ———. (2003). Living with a superpower. *The Economist*, January 4, 17–20.

53. Stening, B. W., Everett, J. E., & Longton, P. A. (1981). Mutual perception of managerial performance and style in multinational subsidiaries. *Journal of Occupational Psychology*, 54, 255–263.

54. Almaney, A. J. (1982). How Arabs see the West. *Business Horizons*, September–October, 11–17.

55. Sheehan, J. G. (1978). The Arab: TV's most popular villain. *Christian Century*, December 3, 1214–1218.

56. ———. (1980). The other anti-semitism. *New Republic*. March 6, 22.

57. Almaney, How Arabs see the West.

58. Hastings, E. H., & Hastings, P. K. (1993). *Index to international public opinion* 1992–1993. Westport, CT: Greenwood Press.

59. Oreskes, M. (1990). Poll detects erosion of positive attitudes toward Japan among Americans. *The New York Times*, February 6, B7.

60. Bizman, A., & Amir, Y. (1982). Mutual perceptions of Arabs and Jews in Israel. *Journal of Cross-Cultural Psychology*, 13, 461–469; Brofenbrenner, U. (1961). The mirror image in Soviet-American relations: A social psychologist's report. *Journal of Social Issues*, 17, 45–56.

61. Berrien, F. K. (1969). Familiarity, mirror imaging and social desirability in stereotypes: Japanese vs. Americans. *International Journal of Psychology*, 4, 207–215; Haque, A., & Lawson, D. L. (1980). The mirror image phenomenon in the context of the Arab-Israeli conflict. *Journal of Intercultural Relations*, 4, 107–115; Shari, M. (2000). Wages of hatred: Indonesia's hostility of a minority costs the country dearly. *Business Week*, October 9, 71–74.

62. White, E. (2003). Europeans take a satiric jab at the U.S. *The Wall Street Journal*, August 28, B1.

63. Lee, Y. T., & Ottati, V. (1993). Determinants of in-group and out-group perceptions of heterogeneity: An investigation of Sino-American stereotypes. *Journal of Cross-Cultural Psychology*, 24, 298–818.

64. Iwao, S., & Triandis, H. C. (1993). Validity of auto- and heterostereotypes among Japanese and American students. *Journal of Cross-Cultural Psychology*, 24, 428–444; Vassiliov, V., Triandis, H. C., Vassiliov, G., & McGuire, H., (1972). Interpersonal contact and stereotyping. In H. C. Triandis (Ed.), *The analysis of subjective culture*. New York: Wiley (pp. 89–115).

65. Omens, A. E., Jenner, S. R., & Beatty, J. R. (1987). Intercultural perceptions in United States subsidiaries of Japanese companies. *International Journal of Intercultural Relations*, 11, 249–264.

66. Bond, M. H. (1986). Mutual stereotypes and the facilitation of interaction across cultural lines. *International Journal of Intercultural Relations*, 10, 259–276.

67. Lee & Ottati, Determinants of in-group and out-group perceptions of heterogeneity.

68. Bond, Mutual stereotypes and the facilitation of interaction across cultural lines.

69. Fowler, G. A. (2003). Marketers take heed: The macho Chinese man is back. *The Wall Street Journal*, December 18, B1.

70. Khanna, S. R. (1986). Asian companies and the country stereotype paradox: An empirical study. *Columbia Journal of World Business*, Summer, 29–38.

71. Guth, R. A. Chang, L. (2002). Sony finds it's a small world. *The Wall Street Journal*, December 18, B1.

72. Shimp, T. A., & Sharma, S. (1987). Consumer ethnocentricism: Construction and validation of the CETSCALE. *Journal of Marketing Research*, 24, 280–289.

73. Archer, R. (1992). Want to "buy American"? It's a lot easier said than done. *The Arizona Republic*, March 2, 1992, A6.

74. Dunne, N. (2003). Plugging into European job no easy task: American executives may find cultural differences a barrier to workplace success abroad. *The Financial Times*, August, 22, 7.

75. Lincoln, J. R., (1989). Employee work attitudes and management practice in the U.S. and Japan: Evidence from a large comparative survey. *California Management Review*, Fall, 89–106; Lincoln, J. R., & Kalleberg, A. L. (1990). *Culture, control, and commitment: A study of work organization and work attitudes in the U.S. and Japan*. Cambridge: Cambridge University Press; Near, J. P. (1986). Work and nonwork attitudes among Japanese and American workers. *Advances in International Comparative Management*, vol. 2, 57–67; Near, J. P. (1989). Organizational commitment among Japanese and U.S. workers. *Organization Studies*, 10, 281–300.

76. Azumi, K., & McMillan, C. J. (1976). Worker sentiment in the Japanese factory: Its organizational determinants. In L. Austin (Ed.), *Japan: The paradox of progress*, 215–229. New Haven, CT: Yale University Press; Cole, R. E. (1979). *Work, mobility and participation*. Berkeley: University of California Press; Lincoln, J. R., Hanada, M., & Olson, J. (1981). Cultural orientations and individual reactions to organizations: A study of employees of Japanese-owned firms. *Administrative Science Quarterly*, 26, 93–115; Lincoln, J. R., & McBride, J. (1987) Naoi, A., & Schooler, C. (1985). Occupational conditions and psychological functioning in Japan. *American Journal of Sociology*, 90, 729–752; Pascale, R. T., & Maguire, M. (1980). Comparison of selected work factors in Japan and the United States. *Human Relations*, 33, 433–455.

77. Kunungo, R., Wright, R. (1983). A cross-cultural comparative study of managerial job attitudes. *Journal of International Business Studies*, 14, 115–129.

78. Hui, C. H., Yee, C., & Eastman, K. L. (1995). The relationship between individualism-collectivism and job satisfaction. *Applied Psychology: An International Review*, 44, 276–282.

79. Randall, D. M. (1993). Cross-cultural research on organizational commitment: A review and application of Hofstede's value-survey module. *Journal of Business Research*, 26, 91–110.

80. Luthans, F., McCaul, J. S., & Dodd, N. G. (1985). Organizational commitment: A comparison of American, Japanese, and Korean employees. *Academy of Management Journal*, 28, 213–219.

81. Lincoln & Kalleberg, *Culture, control, and commitment.*

82. England, G. W., & Misumi, J. (1986). Work centrality in Japan and the United States. *Journal of Cross-Cultural Psychology*, 17, 399–416.

83. Gomez-Mejia, L. R. (1984). Effect of occupation on task-related, contextual, and job involvement orientation: A cross-cultural perspective. *Academy of Management Journal*, 27, 706–720.

84. Gomez-Mejia, Effect of occupation on task-related, contextual, and job involvement orientation.

Chapter 6

1. Dawson, C. (2001). What Japan's CEOs can learn from Bridgestone. *Business Week*, January 29, 50; Kunii, I., & Foust, D. (2000). 'They just don't have a clue how to handle this.' *Business Week*, September 18, 43; Zaun, T., Dvorak, P., Shirouzu, N., & Landers, P. (2000). Bridgestone boss has toughness, but is that what crisis demands? *The Wall Street Journal*, September 12, A1, A18.

2. Adair, C. (2000). Don't get into cultural hot water. *The Toronto Star*, August 9, G6.

3. Jandt, F. E. (2001). *Intercultural communication: An introduction*. Thousand Oaks, CA: Sage. Tung, R. L. (1984). How to negotiate with the Japanese. *California Management Review*, 26, 62–77.

4. Adair, Don't get into cultural hot water.

5. ———. (1999). Chinese whispers. *The Economist*, January 30, 77–79.

6. Dulek, R. E., Fielden, J. S., & Hill, J. S. (1991). International communication: An executive primer. *Business Horizons*, 34, 20–25.

7. ———. (2001). Multilingual website widens the way to a new online world. *The Financial Times*, February 7, 1.

8. Fox, J. (2000). The triumph of English. *Fortune*, September 18, 209–212.

9. Daniels, J. D., Radebaugh, L. H., & Sullivan, D. P. (2004). *International Business: Environments and operations*. Upper Saddle River, NJ: Pearson Prentice Hall.

10. ———. (2001). Experts: English language faces increasing corruption. *Miami Herald*, March 25, 21A.

11. ———. (2001). English is still on the march. *The Economist*, February 24, 50–51; ———. (2001). You have ways of making us talk. *The Economist*, February 24, 50; Fox, The triumph of English.

12. Halpern, J. W. (1983). Business communication in China: A second perspective. *Journal of Business Communication*, 20, 43–55; Ling, C. (2001). Learning a new language. *The Wall Street Journal*, March 12, R18; Zong, B., & Hildebrandt, H. W. (1983). Business communication in the People's Republic of China. *Journal of Business Communication*, 20, 25–32.

13. ———. (2001). Tongue-tied. *The Economist*, April 7, 83.

14. Fixman, C. S. (1990). The foreign language needs of U.S.-based corporations. *The Annals of the American Political and Social Science Association*, 511, 25–46.

15. Dulek, Fielden, & Hill, International communication: An executive primer.

16. Glain, S. (1994). Language barrier proves dangerous in Korea's skies. *The Wall Street Journal*, October 4, B1.

17. Clark, D. (1996). 'Hey, #!@*% amigo, can you translate the word 'gaffe'?' *The Wall Street Journal*, July 6, B6.

18. ———. (1987). Viewpoint: Letters. *Advertising Age*, June 29, 20; Ricks, D. A. (1983). *Big business blunders: Mistakes in multinational marketing*. Homewood, IL: Dow Jones Irwin.

19. Victor, D. A. (1992). *International business communication*. New York: HarperCollins.

20. Koide, F. (1978). Some observations on the Japanese language. In J. C. Condon & M. Saito (Eds.), *Intercultural encounters with Japan. Communication—contact and conflict*, 173–179. Tokyo, Japan: Simul Press; Weitz, J. R., Rothbaum, F. M., & Blackburn, T. C. (1984). Standing out and standing in: The psychology of control in America and Japan. *American Psychologist, 39*, 955–969.

21. Barnlund, D. C. (1989). Public and private self in communicating with Japan. *Business Horizons, 32*, 32–40; Tung, How to negotiate with the Japanese.

22. Barnlund, Public and private self in communicating with Japan; Haneda, S., & Shima, H. (1982). Japanese communication behavior as reflected in letter writing. *Journal of Business Communication, 19*, 19–32.

23. Imahori, T. T., & Cupach, W. R. (1994). A cross-cultural comparison of the interpretation and management of face: American and Japanese responses to embarrassing predicaments. *International Journal of Intercultural Relations, 18*, 193–219; Sueda, K. & Wiseman, R. L. (1992). Embarrassment remediation in Japan and the United States. *International Journal of Intercultural Relations, 16*, 159–173.

24. Barnlund, D. C., & Yoshioka, M. (1990). Apologies: Japanese and American styles. *International Journal of Intercultural Relations, 14*, 193–206.

25. Tata, J. (2000). Toward a theoretical framework of intercultural account-giving and account evaluation. *The International Journal of Organizational Analysis, 8*, 155–178.

26. Barnlund, D. C., & Araki, S. (1985). Intercultural encounters: The management of compliments by Japanese and Americans. *Journal of Cross-Cultural Psychology, 16*, 9–26.

27. Dvorak, P. (2000). Japanese dairy pours on the apologies: Snow Brand puts humility first after big recalls. *The Wall Street Journal*, July 12, A21.

28. Almaney, A., & Alwan, A. (1982). *Communicating with Arabs*. Prospect Heights, IL: Waveland Press, cited in Nelson, G. L., El Bakary, W., & Al Batal, M. (1993). Egyptian and American compliments: A cross-cultural study. *International Journal of Intercultural Relations, 17*, 293–313.

29. Copeland, L., & Griggs, L. (1985). *Going International*. New York: Random House.

30. Copeland & Griggs, *Going International;* Victor, *International business communication*.

31. Gudykunst, W. B., Gao, G. E., Nishida, T., Bond, M. H., Leung, K., Wang, G., & Berraclough, R. A. (1989). A cross-cultural comparison of self-monitoring. *Communications Research Reports*, 7–14.

32. Hymowitz, C. (2000). Flooded with e-mail? Try screening, sorting, or maybe just phoning. *The Wall Street Journal*, September 26, B1.

33. Kilpatrick, R. H. (1984). International business communication practices. *Journal of Business Communication, 21*, 33–44.

34. Varner, I. I. (1988). A comparison of American and French business correspondence. *Journal of Business Communication, 25*, 55–65.

35. Haneda, S., & Shima, H. (1982). Japanese communication behavior as reflected in letter writing. *Journal of Business Communication, 19*, 19–32; Johnson, J. (1980). Business communication in Japan. *Journal of Business Communication, 17*, 65–70.

36. Kilpatrick, R. H. (1984). International business communication practices. *Journal of Business Communication, 21*, 33–44.

37. Sullivan, J. J., & Kameda, N. (1983). The concept of profit and Japanese-American business communication problems. *Journal of Business Communication, 19*, 33–39.

38. Rajan, M., & Graham, J. L. (1991). Nobody's grandfather was a merchant: Understanding the Soviet commercial negotiation process and style. *California Management Review*, Spring, 223–239.

39. Stewart, T. A. (2000). Knowledge worth $1.25 billion. *Fortune*, November 27, 302–303.

40. Knapp, M. (1980). *Essentials of nonverbal communication*. New York: Holt, Rinehart and Winston.

41. Barnlund, D. C. (1975). *Public and private self in Japan and the United States: Communication styles of two cultures*. Tokyo: Simul Press; Barnlund, Public and private self in communicating with Japan.

42. Collett, P. (1971). Training Englishmen in the nonverbal behavior of Arabs: An experiment on intercultural communication. *International Journal of Psychology, 6*, 209–215.

43. Lee, H. O., & Boster, F. J. (1992). Collectivism-individualism in perceptions of speech rate: A cross-cultural comparison. *Journal of Cross-Cultural Psychology, 23*, 377–388.

44. Peng, Y., Zebrowitz, L. A., & Lee, H. K. (1993). The impact of cultural background and cross-cultural experience on impressions of American and Korean male speakers. *Journal of Cross-Cultural Psychology, 24*, 203–220.

45. We thank an anonymous reviewer for these comments and insights.

46. Limaye, M. R., & Victor, D. A. (1991). Cross-cultural business communication research: State of the art and hypotheses for the 1990s. *Journal of Business Communication, 28*, 277–299.

47. Haneda & Shima, Japanese communication behavior as reflected in letter writing.

48. Kume, T. (1985). Managerial attitudes toward decision-making: North America and Japan. In W. B. Gudykunst, L. P. Steward, S. Ting-Toomey (Eds.), *Communication, culture, and organizational processes*, 231–251. Beverly Hills, CA: Sage.

49. Elliot, S., Scott, M. D., Jensen, A. D., & McDonough, M. (1982). Perceptions of reticence: A cross-cultural investigation. In M. Burgoon (Ed.), *Communication Yearbook 5*. New Brunswick, NJ: Transaction Books.

50. Triandis & Albert, Cross-cultural perspectives.

51. Victor, *International business communication*.

52. Zaun, T. (2001). Bridgestone lets Firestone be Firestone. *The Wall Street Journal*, May 24, A14.

Chapter 7

1. Heydenfeldt, J. A. G. (2000). The influence of individualism/collectivism on Mexican and U.S. business negotiation. *International Journal of Intercultural Relations, 24*, 383–407.

2. Saner, R., Yiu, L., & Sondergaard, M. (2000). Business diplomacy management: A core competency for global managers. *Academy of Management Executive, 14*, 80–92.

3. Thomas, K. W., & Schmidt, W. H. (1976). A survey of managerial interests with respect to conflict. *Academy of Management Journal, 10*, 315–318.

4. Ricks, D. A. (1983). *Big business blunders: Mistakes in multinational marketing*. Homewood, IL: Dow Jones Irwin.

5. Thomas, K. W. (1976). Conflict and conflict management. In M. D. Dunnette (Ed.), *Handbook of industrial and organizational behavior*, 889–935. Chicago: Rand McNally.

6. Prunty, A. M., Klopf, D. W., & Ishii, S. (1990). Argumentativeness: Japanese and American tendencies to approach and avoid conflict. *Communication Research Reports*, 7, 75–79.

7. Klopf, D. W. (1991). Japanese communication practices: Recent comparative research. *Communication Quarterly*, 39, 130–143.

8. Ting-Toomey, S., Gao, G., Trubinsky, P., Yang, Z., Kim, H. S., Lin, S. L., & Nishida, T. (1991). Culture, face maintenance, and styles of handling interpersonal conflict: A study in five cultures. *International Journal of Conflict Management*, 2, 275–296; Tse, D. K., Francis, J., & Walls, J. (1994). Cultural differences in conducting intra- and inter-cultural negotiations: A Sino-Canadian comparison. *Journal of International Business Studies*, Autumn, 537–555; Trubisky, P., Ting-Toomey, S., & Lin, S. L. (1991). The influence of individualism-collectivism and self-monitoring on conflict styles. *International Journal of Intercultural Relations*, 15, 65–84.

9. Kirkbride, P. S., Tang, S. F. Y., Westwood, R. I. (1991). Chinese conflict preferences and negotiating behavior: Cultural and psychological influences. *Organization Studies*, 12, 365–386; Tang, S. F. Y., & Kirkbride, P. S. (1986). Developing conflict management skills in Hong Kong: An analysis of some cross-cultural implications. *Management Education and Development*, 17, 287–301.

10. Kozan, M. K. (1989). Cultural influences on styles of handling interpersonal conflicts: Comparisons among Jordanian, Turkish, and U.S. managers. *Human Relations*, 42, 787–799.

11. Leung, K., & Iwawaki, S. (1988). Cultural collectivism and distributive behavior. *Journal of Cross-Cultural Psychology*, 19, 35–49.

12. Victor, D. A. (1992). *International Business Communication*. New York: HarperCollins.

13. Tata, J. (2000). Toward a theoretical framework of intercultural account-giving and account evaluation. *International Journal of Organizational Analysis*, 8, 155–178.

14. Pornpitakpan, C., & Giba, S. (1999). The effects of cultural adaptation on business relationships: Americans selling to Japanese and Thais. *Journal of International Business Studies*, 30, 317–338; Tata, Toward a theoretical framework of intercultural account-giving and account evaluation.

15. Weiss, S. E. (1996). International negotiations: Bricks, mortar, and prospects. In B. J. Punnett & O. Shenkar (Eds.), *Handbook for international management research*, 209–265. Cambridge, MA: Blackwell.

16. Stoever, W. A. (1981). *Renegotiations in international business transactions*. Lexington, MA: Lexington Books; Weiss, S. E. (1996). International negotiations: Bricks, mortar, and prospects. In Punnett & Shenkar, *Handbook for international management research*, 209–265.

17. Yang, N., Chen, C. C., Choi, J., & Zou, Y. (2000). Sources of work-family conflict: A Sino-U.S. comparison of the effects of work and family demands. *Academy of Management Journal*, 43, 113–124.

18. Graham, J. L. (1983). Brazilian, Japanese, and American business negotiations. *Journal of International Business Studies*, 14, 47–62; Weiss, International negotiations: Bricks, mortar, and prospects.

19. Thomas, G. S. (2001). Asia, Canada comprise bulk of U.S. trade deficit. *Dayton Business Journal*, April 20, 16; Van Zandt, H. F. (1970). How to negotiate in Japan. *Harvard Business Review*, November–December, 45–56.

20. Gulbro, R., & Herbig, P. (1996). Negotiating successfully in cross-cultural situations. *Industrial Marketing Management*, 25, 235–241.

21. ———. (2003). Avoid the trap of thinking everyone is just like you. *Financial Times*, August 29, 7.

22. Graham, J. L., & Herberger, R. A. (1983). Negotiators abroad—Don't shoot from the hip. *Harvard Business Review*, July–August, 160–168.

23. Gulbro & Herbig, Negotiating successfully in cross-cultural situations; Tung, R. L. (1984). How to negotiate with the Japanese. *California Management Review*, 26, 62–77; Van Zandt, H. F. (1970). How to negotiate in Japan. *Harvard Business Review*, November–December, 45–56; Volkema, R. J. (1999). Ethicality in negotiations: An analysis of perceptual similarities and differences between Brazil and the United States. *Journal of Business Research*, 45, 59–67.

24. Tung, How to negotiate with the Japanese; Van Zandt, How to negotiate in Japan.

25. Grindsted, A. (1994). The impact of cultural styles on negotiation: A case study of Spaniards and Danes. *IEEE Transactions on Professional Communication*, 37, 34–38. Pornpitakpan & Giba, The effects of cultural adaptation on business relationships: Americans selling to Japanese and Thais.

26. Ghauri, P., & Fang, T. (2001). Negotiating with the Chinese: A socio-cultural analysis. *Journal of World Business*, 36, 303–309; Graham, J. L., & Lam, N. M. (2003). The Chinese negotiation. *Harvard Business Review*, October, 82–91.

27. Gulbro & Herbig, Negotiating successfully in cross-cultural situations; Tse, Francis, & Walls, Cultural differences in conducting intra- and inter-cultural negotiations: A Sino-Canadian comparison. Volkema, R., & Fleury, M. (2002). Alternative negotiating conditions and the choice of negotiation tactics: A cross-cultural comparison. *Journal of Business Ethics*, 36, 381–397.

28. Graham, J. L., & Sano, Y. (1986). Across the negotiation table from the Japanese. *International Marketing Review*, 3, 58–71.

29. Graham, J. L., & Mintu-Wimsat, A. (1997). Culture's influence on business negotiations in four countries. *Group Decision and Negotiation*, 6, 483–502; Li, J., & Labig, C. E. (2001). Negotiating with Chinese: Exploratory study of relationship building. *Journal of Managerial Issues*, 13, 342–348.

30. Herbig, P. A., & Kramer, H. E. (1992). Do's and don'ts of cross-cultural negotiations. *Industrial Marketing Management*, 21, 287–298.

31. Banthin, J., & Steizer, L. (1988/89). "Opening" China: Negotiation strategies when East meets West. *Mid-Atlantic Journal of Business*, 25, 1–14; Tung, R. L. (1982). U.S.-China trade negotiations: Practices, procedures, and outcomes. *Journal of International Business Studies*, Fall, 25–37.

32. Campbell, N. C. G., Graham, J. L., Jolibert, A., & Meissner, H. G. (1988). Marketing negotiations in France, Germany, the United Kingdom, and the United States. *Journal of Marketing*, 52, 49-62; Tung, How to negotiate with the Japanese

33. Trompenaars, F., & Hampden-Turner, C. (1998). *Riding the waves of culture*: *Understanding diversity in global business*. New York: McGraw-Hill.

34. Campbell, Graham, Jolibert, & Meissner, Marketing negotiations in France, Germany, the United Kingdom, and the United States; Graham, J. L., Mintu, A. T., & Rodgers, W. (1994). Explorations of negotiation behaviors in ten foreign cultures using a model developed in the United States. *Management Science, 40,* 72–95.

35. Graham, J. L. (1983). Brazilian, Japanese, and American business negotiations. *Journal of International Business Studies, 14,* 47–62; Tung, How to negotiate with the Japanese.

36. Graham, J. L. (1988). Negotiating with the Japanese: A guide to persuasive tactics (Part I & II). *East Asian Executive Reports, 10,* Nov. v. 6, 19–21; Dec. v. 8, 16–17.

37. Barnum, C., & Wolniansky, N. (1989). Why Americans fail at overseas negotiations. *Management Review,* October, 56–57.

38. Volkema, R. J. (1999). Ethicality in negotiations: An analysis of perceptual similarities and differences between Brazil and the United States. *Journal of Business Research, 45,* 59–67.

39. Stewart, S., & Keown, C. F. (1989). Talking with the dragon: Negotiating in the People's Republic of China. *Columbia Journal of World Business, 24,* 68–72.

40. Weiss, J. (1988). The negotiating style of the People's Republic of China: The future of Hong Kong and Macao. *Journal of Social, Political and Economic Studies, 13,* 175–194.

41. Herbig & Kramer, Do's and don'ts of cross-cultural negotiations.

42. Graham & Herberger, Negotiators abroad—Don't shoot from the hip.

43. Graham, J. L. (1985). The influence of culture on the process of business negotiations: An exploratory study. *Journal of International Business Studies, 16,* 81–96; Graham & Herberger, Negotiators abroad—Don't shoot from the hip.

44. Graham, Negotiating with the Japanese: A guide to persuasive tactics (Part I & II); Graham & Herberger, Negotiators abroad—Don't shoot from the hip.

45. Graham, Negotiating with the Japanese: A guide to persuasive tactics (Part I & II).

46. Oh, T. K. (1984). Selling to the Japanese. *Nation's Business,* October, 37–38.

47. Banthin & Steizer, "Opening" China: Negotiation strategies when East meets West.

48. Pettibone, P. J. (1990). Negotiating a joint venture in the Soviet Union: How to protect your interests. *Journal of European Business, 2,* 5–12; Choi, C. J. (1994). Contract enforcement across cultures. *Organization Studies, 15,* 673–682.

49. Adler, N. J., Graham, J. L., & Gehrke, T. S. (1987). Business negotiations in Canada, Mexico, and the United States. *Journal of Business Research, 15,* 411–429.

50. Heydenfeldt, The influence of individualism/collectivism on Mexican and U.S. business negotiation.

Case 3

1. Director General Adjunto is the Mexican equivalent of an executive vice president.

2. In late 1996, one Mexican peso was valued at approximately US$0.0128.

Chapter 8

1. Bainbridge, A. (2001). Jollibee reports 3.3% income drop. *Philippine Daily Inquirer,* February 17; ———. (2002). A busy bee in the hamburger hive. *The Economist,* March 2, 62; Filman, H. (1996). Happy meals for a McDonald's rival. *Business Week,* July 29, 77; Marozzi, J. (1997). Jollibee disappoints despite 12% climb. *Financial Times,* January 31, 26; Prasso, S. (1999). Hamburgers, they appeal to any culture. *Business Week Online International Edition,* June 14; Visaya, M. G. (2000). Jollibee opens 5th branch in California. *Asian Journal Online,* July 10–13; **www.jollibee.com.ph; www.mcdonalds.com.**

2. Hitt, M. A., Ireland, R. D., & Hoskisson, R. E. (2005). *Strategic Management: Competitiveness and Globalization* (6th Ed.). Cincinnati, OH: South-Western.

3. Chang, L. (2003). Making money in China. *The Wall Street Journal,* June 17, A15.

4. King, N. (2004). Panama Canal at crossroads. *The Wall Street Journal,* January 7, B1, B6.

5. Ghemawat, P. (2001). Distance still matters: The hard reality of global expansion. *Harvard Business Review,* September, 137–147.

6. Byrne, J. A. (1996). Strategic Planning. *Business Week,* August 26, 46–52; Porter, M.E. (1998). Clusters and the new economics of competition. *Harvard Business Review,* November–December, 77–90.

7. Phatak, A. V. (1995). *International dimensions of management* (4th Ed.). Cincinnati, OH: South-Western.

8. Gary, L. (2001). Strategy as process. *Harvard Management Update,* July, 8; Griffin, R. W., & Pustay, M. W. (1996). *International business: A managerial perspective.* Reading, MA: Addison-Wesley; Porter, M. E. (1990). The competitive advantage of nations. *Harvard Business Review, 90,* 73–93.

9. Hamel, G. (2001). Innovation's new math. *Fortune.* July 9, 130–131.

10. Byrne, J. A. (1996). Strategic planning. *Business Week,* August 26, 46–52; Brews, P. J., & Hunt, M. R. (1999). Learning to plan and planning to learn: Resolving the planning school/learning school debate. *Strategic Management Journal, 20,* 889–913.

11. ———. (2001). Economic size. *The Economist,* May 12, 110.

12. Mehta, S. N. (1994). Small companies look to cultivate foreign business. *The Wall Street Journal,* July 7, B2; Rose, R. L., & Quintanilla, C. (1996). More small U.S. firms take up exporting, with much success. *The Wall Street Journal,* December 20, A1, A11.

13. Smith, L. (1995). Does the world's biggest company have a future? *Fortune,* August 7, 124–126.

14. Hitt, Ireland, & Hoskisson, *Strategic Management: Competitiveness and Globalization;* Porter, The competitive advantage of nations.

15. Hill, C. W. L. (1998). *International business: Competing in the global marketplace* (2nd Ed.). Burr Ridge, IL: Irwin/McGraw-Hill.

16. Buckman, R. (2004). H-P outsourcing: Beyond China. *The Wall Street Journal,* February 23, A14.

17. Porter, M. E. (1998). Competing across locations: Enhancing competitive advantage through a global strategy. *Harvard Business School Press,* Product #2026.

18. Porter, Competing across locations.

19. Lodge, G. C., & Bell, M. (1995). Is the United States competitive in the world economy? *Harvard Business School* (Publication 9-795-129). Boston, MA: Harvard Business School.

20. Porter, The competitive advantage of nations.

21. Rhoads, C. (2003). Threat from China starts to unravel Italy's cloth trade. *The Wall Street Journal*, December 17, A1, A10.

22. See Grant, R. M. (1991). Porter's "competitive advantage of nations": An assessment. *Strategic Management Journal*, 12, 535–548; Luo, Y., & Park, S. H. (2001). Strategic alignment and performance of market-seeking MNCs in China. *Strategic Management Journal*, 22, 141–155; Mueller, F. (1994). Societal effect, organizational effect and globalization. *Organization Studies*, 15, 407–428; Murtha, T. P., & Lenway, S. A. (1994). Country capabilities and the strategic state: How national political institutions affect multinational corporations' strategies. *Strategic Management Journal*, 15, 113–129.

23. Spencer, J. W. (2003). Global gatekeeping, representation, and network structure: A longitudinal analysis of regional and global knowledge-diffusion networks. *Journal of International Business Studies*, 34, 428–442.

24. Daniels, J. D., & Radebaugh, L. H. (2004). *International business: Environments and operations* (10th Ed.). Upper Saddle River, NJ: Prentice-Hall.

25. Li, P. P. (1993). How national context influences corporate strategy: A comparison of South Korea and Taiwan. In S. B. Prasad & R. B. Peterson (Eds.), *Advances in international comparative management* (vol. 8, pp. 55–78). Greenwich, CT: JAI Press.

26. Hitt, Ireland, & Hoskisson, *Strategic Management: Competitiveness and Globalization*.

27. Craig, C. S., & Douglas, S. P. (1996). Developing strategies for global markets: An evolutionary perspective. *Columbia Journal of World Business*, Spring, 70–81.

28. Ghoshal, S., & Bartlett, C. A. (1990). The multinational organization as an interorganizational network. *Academy of Management Review*, 15, 603–625; Malnight, T. W. (1996). The transition from decentralized to network-based MNC structures: An evolutionary perspective. *Journal of International Business Studies*, 27, 43–65.

29. See Bartlett, C. A., & Ghoshal, S. (1989). *Managing across borders: The transnational solution*. Boston, MA: Harvard Business School Press; Hout, T., Porter, M. E., & Rudden, E. (1982). How global companies win out. *Harvard Business Review*, September–October, 9–108; Lovelock, C. H., & Yip, G. S. (1996). Developing global strategies for service businesses. *California Management Review*, 38, 64–85; Luo, Y. (2001). Determinants of local responsiveness: Perspectives from foreign subsidiaries in an emerging market. *Journal of Management*, 27, 451–477; Prahalad, C. K., & Doz, Y. L. (1987). *The multinational mission: Balancing local demands and global vision*. New York: The Free Press; Tomlinson, R. (2000). Can Nestlé be the very best? *Fortune*, November 13, 353–360.

30. Lunsford, J. L. (2003). Boeing may risk building new jet despite a lack of U.S. customers. *The Wall Street Journal*, October 15, A1, A13.

31. Hitt, Ireland, & Hoskisson, Strategic Management: Competitiveness and Globalization; MacMillan, I. C., van Putten., A. B., & McGrath, R. G. (2003). Global gamesmanship. *Harvard Business Review*, May, 62–73.

32. Holmes, S. (2003). A plane, a plan, a problem. *Business Week*, December 1, 40–42; ———. (2002). Boeing's high-speed flight. *Business Week*, August 12, 74–75.

33. Prahalad & Doz, *The multinational mission: Balancing local demands and global vision*; Wheelen, T. L., & Hunger, J. D. (1995). *Strategic management and business policy* (5th Ed.). Reading, MA: Addison-Wesley.

34. Hitt, Ireland, & Hoskisson, *Strategic Management: Competitiveness and Globalization*; Morrison, A. J., Ricks, D. A., & Roth, K. (1991). Globalization versus regionalization: Which way for the multinational? *Organizational Dynamics*, 19, 17–29.

35. Schiller, Z., Burns, G., & Miller, K. L. (1996). Make it simple: That's P&G's new marketing mantra—and it's spreading. *Business Week*, September 9, 96–104.

36. Luo, Y. (2003). Market-seeking MNEs in an emerging market: How parent-subsidiary links shape overseas success. *Journal of International Business Studies*, 34, 290–309; Bartlett & Ghoshal, *Managing across borders: The transnational solution*.

37. Birkinshaw, J., Morrison, A., & Hulland, J. (1995). Structural and competitive determinants of a global integration strategy. *Strategic Management Journal*, 16, 637–655.

38. Hitt, Ireland, & Hoskisson, *Strategic Management: Competitiveness and Globalization*; Morrison, Ricks, & Roth, Globalization versus regionalization: Which way for the multinational?

39. Birkinshaw, Morrison, & Hulland, Structural and competitive determinants of a global integration strategy.

40. Johansson, J. K., & Yip, G. S. (1994). Exploiting globalization potential: U.S. and Japanese strategies. *Strategic Management Journal*, 15, 579–601; Yip, G. S. (1995). *Total Global Strategy*. Englewood Cliffs, NJ: Prentice-Hall.

41. Mosakowski, E. (2000). Strategic colonialism in unfamiliar cultures. In P. C. Earley & H. Singh (Eds.), *Innovations in international and cross-cultural management*, 311–337. Thousand Oaks, CA: Sage Publications; Rosenstein, J., & Rasheed, A. (1993). National comparisons in strategy: A framework and review. In S. B. Prasad & R. B. Peterson (Eds.), *Advances in international comparative management*, vol. 8, 79–99. Greenwich, CT: JAI Press.

42. Haley, G. T., & Tan, C. T. (1999). East vs. West: Strategic marketing management meets the Asian networks. *Journal of Business & Industrial Marketing*, 14, 91–101; Jain, S. C., & Tucker, L. R. (1995). The influence of culture on strategic constructs in the process of globalization: An empirical study of North American and Japanese Multinationals. *International Business Review*, 2, 19–37; Wacker, J. G., & Sprague, L. G. (1998). Forecasting accuracy: Comparing the relative effectiveness of practices between seven developed countries. *Journal of Operations Management*, 16, 271–290.

43. Horning, C. (1993). Cultural differences, trust and their relationships to business strategy and control. In Prasad & Peterson (Eds.), *Advances in international comparative management*.

44. O'Grady, S., & Lane, H. W. (1996). The psychic distance paradox. *Journal of International Business Studies*, 27, 309–333.

45. Erramilli, M. K. (1996). Nationality and subsidiary ownership patterns in multinational companies. *Journal of International Business Studies*, 27, 225–248; Tse, D. K., Pan, Y., & Au, K. Y. (1997). How multinationals choose entry modes and form alliances: The China experience. *Journal of International Business Studies*, 28, 779–803.

46. Mehta, Small companies look to cultivate foreign business.

47. Moffett, S., & Chang, L. (2003). For ailing Japan, a prescription made in China. *The Wall Street Journal*, August 29, A1, A10.

48. Mehta, Small companies look to cultivate foreign business; Rose & Quintanilla, More small U.S. firms take up exporting, with much success.

49. Moffett & Chang, For ailing Japan, a prescription made in China.

50. Baird, I. S., Lyles, M. A., & Orris, J. B. (1994). The choice of international strategies by small businesses. *Journal of Small Business Management, 32,* 48–59.

51. Mascarenhas, B. (1996). The founding of specialist firms in a global fragmenting industry. *Journal of International Business Studies, 27,* 27–42.

52. Yukl, G. (2002). *Leadership in organizations* (5th Ed.). Englewood Cliffs, NJ: Prentice Hall.

53. Ball, D. (2003). Nestlé craves fatter profits. *The Wall Street Journal,* August 19, B5; Ellison, S. (2004). Kraft CEO to revamp company; Holden gets a new global post. *The Wall Street Journal,* January 9, A9; Ellison, S. (2003). Kraft's stale strategy. *The Wall Street Journal,* December 18, B1, B6; Forster, J., & Gaylord, B. (2001). Can Kraft be a big cheese abroad? *Business Week,* June 4, 63–64.

54. Atwater, L. E., & Atwater, D. C. (1994). Strategies for change and improvement. In B. M. Bass & B. J. Avolio (Eds.), *Improving organizational effectiveness through transformational leadership,* 146–172. Newbury Park, CA: Sage Publications.

55. Griffin, R. W., & Pustay, M. W. (2005). *International business: A managerial perspective* (4th Ed.). Upper Saddle River, NJ: Prentice-Hall.

56. Jacob, R. (1994). The big rise. *Fortune,* May 30, 74–90; Phatak, *International dimensions of management.*

57. Friedland, J. (1996). In this "great game," no holds are barred: U.S. power companies seek to dominate Latin gas markets. *The Wall Street Journal,* August 14, A10; Vogel, T. T. (1996). Foreign funds buoy Colombian leader. *The Wall Street Journal,* August 20, A6.

58. Kahn, J. (1996). China finds a promising market in Africa. *The Wall Street Journal,* July 19, A9.

59. Pearl, D. (1996). Saudis, of all people, find industry hobbled by a lag in electricity. *The Wall Street Journal,* August 20, A1, A8.

60. Sawyer, O. O. (1993). Environmental uncertainty and environmental scanning activities of Nigerian manufacturing executives: A comparative analysis. *Strategic Management Journal, 14,* 287–299.

61. Garland, J., Farmer, R. N., & Taylor, M. (1990). *International dimensions of business policy and strategy* (2nd Ed.). Boston, MA: PWS-Kent.

62. Phatak, *International Dimensions of Management.*

63. Ortega, B. (1994). Wal-Mart is slowed by problems of price and culture in Mexico. *The Wall Street Journal,* July 29, A1, A5.

64. Griffin & Pustay, *International business: A managerial perspective;* Phatak, *International dimensions of management.*

65. Barney, J. B. (1995). Looking inside for competitive advantage. *Academy of Management Executive, 9,* 49–61.

66. Schlender, B. R. (1994). Matsushita shows how to go global. *Fortune,* July 11, 159–166.

67. Phatak, *International dimensions of management.*

68. Griffin & Pustay, *International business: A managerial perspective.*

69. Choi, A. (1995). For Mercedes, going global means being less German. *The Wall Street Journal,* April 27, B4; Taylor, A. (2000). Bumpy roads for global automakers. *Fortune,* December 18, 278–292.

70. Griffin & Pustay, *International business: A managerial perspective.*

71. Luhnow, D., & Terhune, C. (2003). A low-budget cola shakes up markets south of the border. *The Wall Street Journal,* October 27, A1, A18.

72. Gupta, A. K., & Govindarajan, V. (2001). Converting global presence into global competitive advantage. *Academy of Management Executive, 15,* 45–56.

73. Burrows, P., Bernier, L., & Engardio, P. (1995). Texas Instruments' global chip payoff. *Business Week,* August 7, 64–66.

74. Phatak, *International dimensions of management.*

75. Bremner, B., & Dawson, C. (2003). Can anything stop Toyota? *Business Week,* November 17, 114–122; Brown, S. F. (2004). Toyota's global body shop. *Fortune,* February 9, 120B–120F; Naughton, K., & Borrus, A. (1996). America's no. 1 car exporter is . . . Japan? *Business Week,* February 26, 113; Taylor, A. (2001). Imports to Detroit: Eat our dust. *Fortune,* June 11, 150–154.

76. ———. (2003) Beyond the bubble: A survey of telecoms. *The Economist,* October 11, 3–22; ———. (2001). Nokia succumbs. *The Economist,* June 16, 65; ———. (2000). A Finnish fable. *The Economist,* October 14, 83–85; Baker, S. (2001). Outsourcing alone won't save Nokia's rivals. *Business Week,* February 12, 38; Baker, S., Shinal, J., & Kunii, I. M. (2001). Is Nokia's star dimming? *Business Week,* January 22, 66–72; Capell, K., Echikson, W., & Elstrom, P. (2001). Surprise! Nokia doesn't walk on water. *Business Week,* June 25, 49; Edmondson, G., Elstrom, P., & Burrows, P. (1996). At Nokia, a comeback—and then some. *Business Week,* December 2, 106; Pringle, D. (2003). How Nokia thrives by breaking the rules. *The Wall Street Journal,* January 3, A1, A9; Reinhardt, A. (2004). Can Nokia capture mobile workers? *Business Week,* February 9, 80; Reinhardt, A., Sylvers, E., & Kunii, I. M. (2003). Nokia's big leap. *Business Week,* October 13, 50–52.

77. Yip, *Total global strategy.*

78. Johansson & Yip. Exploiting globalization potential: U.S. and Japanese strategies.

79. Yip, *Total global strategy.*

80. Snow, C. C., Snell, S. A., Davison, S. C., & Hambrick, D. C. (1996). Use transnational teams to globalize your company. *Organizational Dynamics, 24,* 50–67.

81. Bartmess, A., & Cerny, K. (1993). Building competitive advantage through a global network of capabilities. *California Management Review, 35,* 2–27.

82. Kim, W. C., & Mauborgne, R. A. (1991). Implementing global strategies: The role of procedural justice. *Strategic Management Journal, 12,* 125–143; ———. (1993). Making global strategies work. *Sloan Management Review,* Spring, 11–25.

83. Bainbridge, A busy bee in the hamburger hive; Bainbridge, Jollibee reports 3.3% income drop; Filman, Happy meals for a McDonald's rival; Marozzi, Jollibee disappoints despite 12% climb; Prasso, Hamburgers, they appeal to any culture; Visaya, Jollibee opens 5th branch in California; www.jollibee.com.ph; www.mcdonalds.com.

Chapter 9

1. Kahn, G., Bilefsky, D., & Lawton, C. (2004). Burned once, brewers return to China—with pint-size goals. *The Wall Street Journal,* March 10, A1, A8; Kranhold, K. (2004). China's price for market entry: Give us your technology, too. *The Wall Street Journal,* February 26, A1, A6.

2. Negandhi, A. (1987). *International management*. Boston, MA: Allyn & Bacon; Welch, L. S., & Luostarinen, R. (1988). Internationalization: Evolution of a concept. *Journal of General Management, 14,* 55–71.

3. Shirouzu, N. (2003). As Toyota pushes hard in China, a lot is riding on the outcome. *The Wall Street Journal,* December 8, A1, A12.

4. Rohwer, J. (2000). GE digs into Asia. *Fortune,* October 2, 165–178.

5. Walker, M. (2003). Banking on Europe's frontier. *The Wall Street Journal,* November 25, A14.

6. Milliman, J., Von Glinow, M. A., & Nathan, M. (1991). Organizational life cycles and strategic international human resource management in multinational companies: Implications for congruence theory. *Academy of Management Journal, 16,* 318–339.

7. Black, J. S., Gregersen, H. B., & Mendenhall, M. E. (1992). *Global assignments: Successfully expatriating and repatriating international managers*. San Francisco: Jossey-Bass.

8. Landers, P. (2001). Penney blends two business cultures. *The Wall Street Journal,* April 5, A15, A17.

9. Bianco, A., & Zellner, W. (2003). Is Wal-Mart too powerful? *Business Week,* October 6, 100–110; Smith, G. (2002). War of the superstores. *Business Week,* September 23, 60; Zimmerman, A., & Fackler, M. (2003). Wal-Mart's foray into Japan spurs a retail upheaval. *The Wall Street Journal,* September 19, A1, A6.

10. ———. (2001). Wal around the world. *The Economist,* December 8, 55–57; Ellison, S. (2001). Carrefour and Ahold find shoppers like to think local. *The Wall Street Journal,* August 31, A5; Zellner, W., Schmidt, K. A., Ihlwan, M., & Dawley, H. (2001). How well does Wal-Mart travel? *Business Week,* September 3, 82–84.

11. Hamm, S. (2003). Borders are so 20th century. *Business Week,* September 22, 68–72; Rohwer, J. (2000). GE digs into Asia. *Fortune,* October 2, 165–178.

12. Tse, D. K., Pan, Y., & Au, K. Y. (1997). How MNCs choose entry modes and form alliances: The China experience. *Journal of International Business Studies, 28,* 779–803.

13. Briscoe, D. R. (1995). *International human resource management*. Englewood Cliffs, NJ: Prentice-Hall; Ball, J., Zaun, T., & Shirouzu, N. (2002). Daimler explores idea of "world engine." *The Wall Street Journal,* January 8, A3.

14. Dyer, J. H. (2000). Examining interfirm trust and relationships in a cross-national setting. In P. C. Earley & H. Singh (Eds.), *Innovations in international and cross-cultural management,* 215–244. Thousand Oaks, CA: Sage.

15. Bogner, W. C., Thomas, H., & McGee, J. (1996). A longitudinal study of the competitive positions and entry paths of European firms in the U.S. pharmaceutical market. *Strategic Management Journal, 17,* 85–107.

16. Daniels, J. D., Radebaugh, L. H., & Sullivan, D. P. (2004). *International business: Environment and operations* (10th Ed). Upper Saddle River, NJ: Pearson Prentice Hall.

17. Griffin, R. W., & Pustay, M. W. (2005). *International business* (4th Ed.). Upper Saddle River, NJ: Pearson Prentice Hall.

18. Burpitt, W. J., & Rondinelli, D. A. (2000). Small firms' motivations for exporting: To earn and learn? *Journal of Small Business Management, 38,* 1–18; Daniels, Radebaugh, & Sullivan, *International business: Environment and operations*.

19. Hill, C. W. L. (1994). *International business: Competing in the global marketplace*. Burr Ridge, IL: Irwin.

20. Updike, E. H., & Vlasic, B. (1996). Will Neon be the little car that could? *Business Week,* June 10, 56.

21. ———. (2002). Steel: Rust never sleeps. *The Economist,* March 9, 61–62; Holmes, S., & Belton, C. (2001). Boeing: In search of a big bear hug. *Business Week,* November 12, 71.

22. Griffin & Pustay, *International business*.

23. Wong, M. (2000). Law's land mines trip up exporters. *Dayton Daily News,* September 17, 1F, 4F.

24. Barringer, B. R., Macy, G., & Wortman, M. S. (1996). Export performance: The role of corporate entrepreneurship and export planning. *Journal of International Management, 2,* 177–199; Buckman, R. (2003). China's determined 'cheeseman' no longer stands alone. *The Wall Street Journal,* December 11, B1, B7; Dosoglu-Guner, B. (2001). Can organizational behavior explain the export intention of firms? The effects of organizational culture and ownership type. *International Business Review, 10,* 71–89.

25. Griffin & Pustay, *International business*.

26. Koretz, G. (1997). A new twist in trade numbers, *Business Week,* May 12, 24.

27. Montgomery, C. (2001). This car company knows (and grows) beans. *Dayton Daily News,* December 9, 1F, 8F.

28. Daniels, Radebaugh, & Sullivan, *International business: Environment and operations*; Hill, *International business: Competing in the global marketplace*.

29. Griffin & Pustay, *International Business*.

30. Hill, *International business: Competing in the global marketplace*.

31. Price, R. M. (1996). Technology and strategic advantage. *California Management Review, 38,* 38–55.

32. Edmondson, G., & Bremmer, B. (2003). The Asian invasion picks up speed. *Business Week,* October 6, 62–64; Mackintosh, J., & McGregor, R. (2003). A leap over the cliff: Are the big profits to be made in China blinding foreign carmakers to the risks ahead? *Financial Times,* August 25, 13; Updike, E. H., & Nakarmi, L. (1995). A moveable feast for Mitsubishi. *Business Week,* August 28, 50–51.

33. Engardio, P., & Roberts, D. (1996). Microsoft's long march. *Business Week,* June 24, 52–54.

34. Clifford, M. L., Roberts, D., Trinephi, M., & Kerwin, K. (1996). Where's that pot of gold? *Business Week,* February 3, 54–58; Naughton, K., Engardio, P., Kerwin, K., & Roberts, D. (1995). How GM got the inside track in China. *Business Week,* November 6, 56–57; Shirouzu, N., & Hawkins, L. (2003). Ford, GM fight over brightest auto market. *The Wall Street Journal,* October 17, A9; Templeman, J., Woodruff, D., Roberts, D., & Engardio, P. (1995). How Mercedes trumped Chrysler in China. *Business Week,* July 31, 50–51.

35. Hill, *International business: Competing in the global marketplace*.

36. Griffin & Pustay, *International business*.

37. Frank, R. (2000). Big Boy's adventures in Thailand. *The Wall Street Journal,* April 12, B1, B4.

38. Serwer, A. (2004). Hot Starbucks to go. *Fortune,* January 26, 60–74.

39. Hill, *International business: Competing in the global marketplace*.

40. Deogun, N. (1997). PepsiCo draws new battle plan to fight Coke. *The Wall Street Journal,* January 27, B1, B10; Frank, R. (1996). PepsiCo's critics worry the glass is still half empty. *The Wall Street Journal,* September 30, B10; Tannenbaum, J. A. (1996). Franchisees see

opportunity in PepsiCo restructuring. *The Wall Street Journal*, October 15, B2; Terhune, C. (2004). PepsiCo to relaunch its cola in Iraq. *Wall Street Journal*, January 7, B4.

41. Jordan, M. (2000). McDonald's strikes sparks with fast growth in Brazil. *The Wall Street Journal*, October 4, A23.

42. Griffin & Pustay, *International business*.

43. Solis, D., & Friedland, J. (1995). A tale of two countries. *The Wall Street Journal*, October 2, R19, R23.

44. Matthews, R. G. (2000). U.S. Steel's plunge into Slovakia reflects urgent need to grow. *The Wall Street Journal*, October 12, A1, A10.

45. Hill, *International business: Competing in the global marketplace*.

46. ———. (2001). Red tape and blue sparks. *The Economist*, June 2, 9–10; ———. (2001). India's economy: Unlocking the potential. *The Economist*, June 2, 13; Kumar, S., & Thacker-Kumar, L. (1996). Investing in India: Strategies for tackling bureaucratic hurdles. *Business Horizons*, 39, 10–16.

47. Griffin & Pustay, *International business*; Morse, D. (2004). In North Carolina, furniture makers try to stay alive. *The Wall Street Journal*, February 20, A1, A6.

48. Yip, G. S. (1995). *Total global strategy*. Englewood Cliffs, NJ: Prentice-Hall.

49. Lublin, J. S. (1995). Too much, too fast. *The Wall Street Journal*, September 26, R8, R10.

50. ———. (2001). Red tape and blue sparks; Wonacott, P. (2001). China's privatization efforts breed new set of problems. *The Wall Street Journal*, November 1, A15.

51. Hill, *International business: Competing in the global marketplace*.

52. Schweiger, D. M., Csiszar, E. N., & Napier, N. K. (1993). Implementing international mergers and acquisitions. *Human Resource Planning*, 16, 53–70.

53. Calori, R., Lubatkin, M., & Very, P. (1994). Control mechanisms in cross-border acquisitions: An international comparison. *Organizational Studies*, 15, 361–379; Olie, R. (1994). Shades of culture and institutions in international mergers. *Organizational Studies*, 15, 381–405.

54. Matthews, R. G. (2000). U.S. Steel's plunge into Slovakia reflects urgent need to grow. *The Wall Street Journal*, October 12, A1, A10.

55. Allen, M. (1995). What is privatization anyway? *The Wall Street Journal*, October 2, R4; Barkema, H. G., Bell, J. H. J., & Pennings, J. M. (1996). Foreign entry, cultural barriers, and learning. *Strategic Management Journal*, 17, 151–166; Filatotchev, I., Hoskisson, R. E., Buck, T., & Wright, M. (1996). Corporate restructuring in Russian privatizations: Implications for U.S. investors. *California Management Review*, 38, 87–105; Ramamurti, R. (2000). A multilevel model of privatization in emerging economies. *Academy of Management Journal*, 25, 525–550; Pope, K. (1996). A steelmaker built up by buying cheap mills finally meets its match. *The Wall Street Journal*, May 2, A1, A6; **www.ispat.com.**

56. Steinmetz, G., & Parker-Pope, T. (1996). All over the map: At a time when companies are scrambling to go global, Nestlé has long been there. *The Wall Street Journal*, September 26, R4, R6.

57. Clifford, M. L., Harris, N., Roberts, D., & Kripalani, M. (1997). Coke pours into Asia. *Business Week*, October 28, 72–80.

58. Kripalani, M., & Einhorn, B. (2003). Global designs for India's tech king. *Business Week*, October 13, 56–58.

59. Chilton, K. (1995). How American manufacturers are facing the global marketplace. *Business Horizons*, 38, 10–19.

60. Baker, S. (2001). Why Europe keeps gobbling up U.S. companies. *Business Week*, June 18, 56.

61. Ghemawat, P., & Ghadar, F. (2000). The dubious logic of global megamergers. *Harvard Business Review*, 78, 64–72.

62. Griffin & Pustay, *International business*.

63. Blodgett, L. L. (1991). Partner contributions as predictors of equity share in joint ventures. *Journal of International Business Studies*, 22, 63–73.

64. Ghemawat & Ghadar, The dubious logic of global megamergers; Rose, R. L. (1996). For Whirlpool, Asia is the new frontier. *The Wall Street Journal*, April 25, B1, B4.

65. Phatak, A. V. (1997). *International management: Concepts and cases*. Cincinnati, OH: South-Western.

66. Hill, *International business: Competing in the global marketplace*.

67. Ingrassia, L., Naj, A. K., & Rosett, C. (1995). Overseas, Otis and its parent get in on the ground floor. *The Wall Street Journal*, April 21, A6.

68. Henderson, A. B. (1996). Chrysler and BMW team up to build small engine plant in South America. *The Wall Street Journal*, October 2, A4.

69. Phatak, *International management: Concepts and cases*.

70. Afriyie, K. (1988). Factor choice characteristics and industrial impact of joint ventures: Lessons from a developing economy. *Columbia Journal of World Business*, 23, 51–62.

71. Geringer, J. M. (1991). Strategic determinants of partner selection criteria in international joint ventures. *Journal of International Business Studies*, 22, 41–62.

72. Weiss, S. E. (1987). Creating the GM-Toyota joint venture: A case in complex negotiations. *Columbia Journal of World Business*, 22, 23–38; Yan, A., & Gray, B. (1994). Bargaining power, management control, and performance in United States-China joint ventures: A comparative case study. *Academy of Management Journal*, 37, 1478–1517.

73. Griffin & Pustay, *International business*; Hill, *International business: Competing in the global marketplace*.

74. Phatak, *International management: Concepts and cases*.

75. Newman, W. H. (1992). Launching a viable joint venture. *California Management Review*, 35, 68–80; Osland, G. E., & Cavusgil, S. T. (1996). Performance issues in U.S.-China joint ventures. *California Management Review*, 38, 106–130.

76. Blumenthal, J. (1995). Relationships between organizational control mechanisms and joint-venture success. In *Advances in global high-technology management*, vol. 5, part B, 115–134. Greenwich, CT: JAI Press.

77. ———. (2001). Halfway down a long road. *The Economist*, August 18, 51–53; ———. (2001). Just good friends. *The Economist*, August 18, 53.

78. Blumenthal, Just good friends; Gillespie, K., & Teegen, H. J. (1995). Market liberalization and international alliance formation: The Mexican paradigm. *Columbia Journal of World Business*, 30, 59–69; Serapio, M. G., & Cascio, W. F. (1996). End-games in international alliances. *Academy of Management Executive*, 10, 62–73.

79. Hamel, G. (1991). Competition for competence and inter-partner learning within international strategic alliances. *Strategic Management Journal*, 12, 83–103.

80. Kahn, J. (1996). McDonnell Douglas' high hopes for China never really soared. *The Wall Street Journal*, May 22, A1, A10.

81. Baker, S. (1996). The odd couple at Heinz. *Business Week*, November 4, 176–178.
82. Bremner, B., Schiller, Z., Smart, T., & Holstein, W. J. (1996). Keiretsu connections: The bonds between the U.S. and Japan's industry groups. *Business Week*, July 22, 52–54.
83. Done, K. (2003). New bonding could mean altered shape for alliances. *Financial Times*, October 1, 18.
84. Kranhold, K. (2004). China's price for market entry: Give us your technology, too. *The Wall Street Journal*, February 26, A1, A6.

Chapter 10

1. This box is based on a number of articles about McDonald's Corporation. Chief among these was Matlack C., & Gogoi, P. (2003). What's this: The French love McDonald's? *Business Week*, January 13, 50; Jordan, M., & Leung, S. (2003). McDonald's faces revolt in Brazil, declining sales abroad. *The Wall Street Journal*, October 21, A17, 18; Josephs, J. (2004). Monsieur McDonald's. **www.jeremyjosephs.com.**
2. Gomes-Casseres, B. (1993). *Managing international alliances*. Publication No. 793–133. Boston, MA: Harvard Business School Publishing.
3. Kahn, J. (1996). McDonnell Douglas' high hopes for China never really soared. *The Wall Street Journal*, May 22, A1, A10; Reinhardt, A., Browder, S., & Engardio, P. (1996). Booming Boeing. *Business Week*, September 30, 118–125; Reinhardt, A., Browder, S., & Stodghill, R. (1996). Three huge hours in Seattle. *Business Week*, December 30, 39–39.
4. Serapio, M. G., & Cascio, W. F. (1996). End-games in international alliances. *Academy of Management Executive*, 10, 62–73.
5. Hill, C. W. L., Hwang, P., & Kim, W. C. (1990). An eclectic theory of the choice of international entry mode. *Strategic Management Journal*, 11, 117–128; Phatak, A. V. (1997). *International management: Concepts and cases*. Cincinnati, OH: South-Western.
6. Hill, C. W. L. (1994). *International business: Competing in the global marketplace*. Burr Ridge, IL: Irwin.
7. Erramilli, M. K. (1991). The experience factor in foreign market entry behavior in service firms. *Journal of International Business Studies*, 22, 479–501.
8. Phatak, *International management: Concepts and cases*.
9. Roth, K., & Ricks, D. A. (1994). Goal configuration in a global industry context. *Strategic Management Journal*, 15, 103–120.
10. Pan, Y. (1996). Influences on foreign equity ownership level in joint ventures in China. *Journal of International Business Studies*, 27, 1–26.
11. Kogut, B., & Singh, H. (1988). The effect of national culture on the choice of entry mode. *Journal of International Business Studies*, 19, 411–432.
12. Shane, S. (1994). The effect of national culture on the choice between licensing and direct foreign investment. *Strategic Management Journal*, 15, 627–642.
13. Barkema, H. G., Bell, J. H. J., & Pennings, J. M. (1996). Foreign entry, cultural barriers, and learning. *Strategic Management Journal*, 17, 151–166.
14. Contractor, F. J., & Kundu, S. K. (1996). Choosing the best organizational mode: The quest for optimal ownership and control in foreign operations. Paper presented at the meeting of the Academy of Management, Cincinnati, OH.
15. Ghoshal, S., & Nohria, N. (1993). Horses for courses: Organizational forms for multinational corporations. *Sloan Management Review*, Winter, 23–34.
16. Griffin, R. W., & Pustay, M. W. (1996). *International business: A managerial perspective*. Reading, MA: Addison-Wesley; Phatak, A. V. (1995). *International dimensions of management* (4th Ed.). Cincinnati, OH: South-Western.
17. Hill, *International business: Competing in the global marketplace*; Phatak, *International dimensions of management*.
18. Hill, *International business: Competing in the global marketplace*.
19. Daniels, J. D., & Radebaugh, L. H. (2001). *International business: Environments and operations*. Upper Saddle River, NJ: Prentice-Hall.
20. Phatak, *International management: Concepts and cases*.
21. Yip, G. S. (1995). *Total global strategy*. Englewood Cliffs, NJ: Prentice-Hall.
22. Hill, *International business: Competing in the global marketplace*; Phatak, *International dimensions of management*.
23. Moore, What's new and better about ExxonMobil?
24. Lublin, J. S. (2001). Place vs. product: It's tough to choose a management model. *The Wall Street Journal*, June 27, A1, A4; Aeppel, T. (2003). Three countries, one dishwasher. *The Wall Street Journal*, October 6, B1.
25. Griffin & Pustay, *International business: A managerial perspective*; Hill, *International business: Competing in the global marketplace*.
26. Lublin, Place vs. product: It's tough to choose a management model; Ansberry, C., & Aeppel, T. Surviving the onslaught. *The Wall Street Journal*, October 6, B1.
27. Hunt, J. W. (1998). Is matrix management a recipe for chaos? *Financial Times*, January 12, 10.
28. Hunt, Is matrix management a recipe for chaos?
29. Latour, A. (1998). Ericsson unveils big overhaul of its structure. *The Wall Street Journal*, October 1, B9; Lelvor, G., & Burt, T. (1998). Ericsson's behavior wins it no friends in the markets. *Financial Times*, October 9, 20.
30. Rhoads, C. (1998). Deutsche Bank to give BT no autonomy. *The Wall Street Journal*, December 1, A3, A4, cited in Sanyal, R. N. (2001). *International management: A strategic perspective*. Upper Saddle River, NJ: Prentice-Hall.
31. Ghoshal & Nohria, Horses for courses: Organizational forms for multinational corporations, 23–26.
32. Hill, *International business: Competing in the global marketplace*.
33. Ghoshal, S., Korine, H., & Szulanski, G. (1994). Interunit communication in multinational corporations. *Management Science*, 40, 96–110.
34. Porter, M. E. (2001). Strategy and the Internet. *Harvard Business Review*, March, 62–78.
35. Farrell, C. (1992). Industrial policy. *Business Week*, April, 6, 70–75.
36. ———. (2001). Total expenditure on R&D, 1999. From **www.imd.ch/wcy/criteria/4301.cfm.**
37. Marsh, P. (2003). In search of the world's hotbeds of innovation. *Financial Times*, May 19, 8; ———. (2002). The mobile telecommunications and internet index, 2002. *The Economist*, September 21, 96.
38. Kelly, K., Port, O., Treece, J., DeGeorge, G., & Schiller, Z. (1992). Learning from Japan. *Business Week*, January 27, 52–60.
39. Cited on Acer Worldwide, Inc. website: **http://global.acer.com.**

40. Buckman, R. (2004). Computer giant in China sets sights on U.S. *The Wall Street Journal*, January 11, B1, B4.

41. ———. (2000). A survey of government and the internet: Net neighbourhoods. *The Economist*, June 24, 4; McCartney, S., & Friedland, J. (1997). Computer sales sizzle as developing nations try to shrink PC gap. *The Wall Street Journal*, June 29, A1, A4.

42. ———. (2000). A survey of e-management: Inside the machine. *The Economist*, November 11, 5–6; Vickery, L. (2001). "Cultural portal" could translate way to profit. *The Wall Street Journal*, February 12, B6.

43. Mansfield, E. (1981). How economists see R&D. *Harvard Business Review*, November–December, 98–106.

44. Peters, T. J., & Waterman, R. H. (1982). *In search of excellence*. New York: Harper & Row.

45. Glain, S. (1996). Little U.S. firm takes on Japanese giant: Yamaha accused of "patent flooding" to gain advantage. *The Wall Street Journal*, June 5, A10.

Chapter 11

1. Cooley, M. (1997). HR in Russia: Training for long-term success. *HR Magazine*, December, 98–106; Starobin, P. (2003). The enigma of Russia. *Business Week*, August 4, 40–46; Welsh, D. H. B., Luthans, F., & Sommer, S. M. (1993). Managing Russian factory workers: The impact of U.S.-based behavioral and participative techniques. *Academy of Management Journal*, 36, 58–79.

2. Communal, C., & Senior, B. (1999). National culture and management: Messages conveyed by British, French, and German advertisements of managerial appointments. *Leadership and Organizational Development Journal*, 20, 26–35.

3. Granato, J., Inglehart, R., & Leblang, D. (1996). The effect of cultural values on economic development: Theory, hypotheses, and some empirical tests. *American Journal of Political Science*, 40, 607–631.

4. Thomas, D. C., Au, K., & Ravlin, E. C. (2003). Cultural variation and the psychological contract. *Journal of Organizational Behavior*, 24, 451–471.

5. Rodrigues, C. (1990). The situation and national culture as contingencies for leadership behavior: Two conceptual models. In B. Prasad (Ed.), *Advances in international comparative management*, 5, 51–68. Greenwich, CT: JAI Press.

6. Bass, B. M. (1990). *Stogdill's handbook of leadership: A survey of theory and research*. New York: Free Press.

7. d'Iribarne, P. (2002). Motivating workers in emerging countries: Universal tools and local applications. *Journal of Organizational Behavior*, 23, 243–256.

8. Hofstede, G. (1993). Cultural constraints in management theories. *Academy of Management Executive*, 7, 81–94.

9. Lenartowicz, T., & Roth, K. (2001). Does subculture within a country matter? A cross-cultural study of motivational domains and business performance in Brazil. *Journal of International Business Studies*, 32, 305–325; Perlaki, I. (1994). Organizational development in Eastern Europe: Learning to build culture-specific OD theories. *Journal of Applied Behavioral Science*, 30, 297–312.

10. Hofstede, G. (1996). An American in Paris: The influence of nationality on organization theories. *Organizational Studies*, 17, 525–537.

11. Maslow, A. H. (1970). *Motivation and personality* (2nd Ed.). New York: Harper & Row.

12. Greenberg, J., & Baron, R. A. (2001). *Behavior in Organizations* (7th Ed.). Englewood Cliffs, NJ: Prentice-Hall.

13. Bhagat, R. S., & McQuaid, S. J. (1982). Role of subjective culture in organizations: A review and directions for future research. *Journal of Applied Psychology*, 67, 653–685.

14. Shenkar, O., & Von Glinow, M. A. (1994). Paradoxes of organizational theory and research: Using the case of China to illustrate national contingency. *Management Science*, 40, 56–71.

15. Sagie, A., Elizur, D., & Yamauchi, H. (1996). The strength and structure of achievement motivation: A cross-cultural comparison. *Journal of Organizational Behavior*, 17, 431–444.

16. Borg, I., & Braun, M. (1996). Work values in East and West Germany: Different weights, but identical structures. *Journal of Organizational Behavior*, 17, 541–555; Frese, M., Kring, W., Soose, A., & Zempel, J. (1996). Personal initiative at work: Differences between East and West Germany. *Academy of Management Journal*, 39, 37–63.

17. Adler, N. J. (2002). *International dimensions of organizational behavior* (4th Ed.). Cincinnati, OH: South-Western; Ronen, S., & Shenkar, O. (1985). Clustering countries on attitudinal dimensions: A review and synthesis. *Academy of Management Review*, 10, 435–454.

18. Hofstede, G. (1984). *Culture's consequences*. Newbury Park, CA: Sage.

19. Herzberg, F. (1966). *Work and the nature of man*. Cleveland, OH: World.

20. Machungwa, P. D., & Schmitt, N. (1983). Work motivation in a developing country. *Journal of Applied Psychology*, 68, 31–42.

21. Kanungo, R. N., & Wright, R. W. (1983). A cross-cultural comparative study of managerial job attitudes. *Journal of International Business Studies*, 14, 115–129.

22. Hofstede, *Culture's consequences*; Hofstede, Cultural constraints in management theories.

23. Rehder, R. R. (1992). Building cars as if people mattered: The Japanese lean system vs. Volvo's Uddevalla system. *Columbia Journal of World Business*, 27, 56–70.

24. Mendonca, M., & Kanungo, R. N. (1994). Motivation through participative management. In R. N. Kanungo & M. Mendonca (Eds.), *Work motivation: Models for developing countries*, 184–212. Thousand Oaks, CA: Sage; Robert, C., Probst, T. M., Martocchio, J. J., Drasgow, F., & Lawler, J. J. (2000). Empowerment and continuous improvement in the United States, Mexico, Poland, and India: Predicting fit on the basis of the dimensions of power distance and individualism. *Journal of Applied Psychology*, 85, 643–658.

25. Schaubroeck, J., Lam, S. S. K., & Xie, J. L. (2000). Collective efficacy versus self-efficacy in coping responses to stressors and control: A cross-cultural study. *Journal of Applied Psychology*, 85, 512–525.

26. Randolph, W. A., & Sashkin, M. (2002). Can organizational empowerment work in multinational settings? *Academy of Management Executive*, 16, 102–115.

27. d'Iribarne, Motivating workers in emerging countries: Universal tools and local applications.

28. Mendonca, M., & Kanungo, R. N. (1994). Motivation through effective reward management in developing countries. In Kanungo & Mendonca, *Work motivation: Models for developing countries*, 49–83.

29. ———. (2002). A survey of management: The return of von Clausewitz. *The Economist*, March 9, 18–20; Boyle, M. (2001). Nothing is rotten in Denmark. *Fortune*, February 19, 242.

30. Adams, J. S. (1965). Inequity in social exchange. In L. Berkowitz (Ed.), *Advances in experimental social psychology*, vol. 2, 267–299. New York: Academic Press.

31. McFarlin, D. B., & Frone, M. R. (1990). Examining a two-tier wage structure in a non-union firm. *Industrial Relations*, 29, 145–157; Sweeney, P. D., & McFarlin, D. B. (2002). *Organizational behavior: Solutions for management*. Burr Ridge, IL: Irwin/McGraw-Hill.

32. Morris, M. W., & Leung, K. (2000). Justice for all? Progress in research on cultural variation in the psychology of distributive and procedural justice. *Applied Psychology: An International Review*, 49, 100–132.

33. Banerjee, N. (1995). For Mary Kay sales reps in Russia, hottest shade is the color of money. *The Wall Street Journal*, August 30, A8.

34. Hofstede, *Culture's consequences*; Hofstede, Cultural constraints in management theories.

35. Bond, M. H., Leung, K., & Wan, K. C. (1982). How does cultural collectivism operate? The impact of task and maintenance contribution on reward distribution. *Journal of Cross-Cultural Psychology*, 13, 186–200.

36. Kim, K. L., Park, H. J., & Suzuki, N. (1990). Reward allocations in the U.S., Japan, and Korea: A comparison of individualistic and collectivistic cultures. *Academy of Management Journal*, 33, 188–198.

37. Bond, M. H. (1991). *Beyond the Chinese face*. Hong Kong: Oxford University Press; Shenkar & Von Glinow, Paradoxes of organizational theory and research: Using the case of China to illustrate national contingency.

38. Giacobbe-Miller, J. K., Miller, D. J., Zhang, W., & Victorov, V. I. (2003). Country and organizational-level adaptation to foreign workplace ideologies: A comparative study of distributive justice values in China, Russia, and the United States. *Journal of International Business*, 34, 389–406.

39. Wonacott, P. (2002). China's secret weapon: Smart, cheap labor for high-tech goods. *The Wall Street Journal*, March 14, A1, A6; Chen, C. C. (1995). New trends in rewards allocation preferences: A Sino-U.S. comparison. *Academy of Management Journal*, 38, 408–428.

40. Skinner, B. F. (1969). *Contingencies of reinforcement*. New York: Appleton-Century-Crofts.

41. Sweeney & McFarlin, *Organizational behavior: Solutions for management*.

42. Mangaliso, M. P. (2001). Building competitive advantage from Ubuntu: Management lessons from South Africa. *The Academy of Management Executive*, 15, 23–33; McFarlin, D. B., Coster, E. A., & Mogale-Pretorius, C. (1999). Management development in South Africa: Moving toward an Africanized framework. *Journal of Management Development*, 18, 63–78.

43. Bailey, J. R., & Chen, C. C. (1997). Conceptions of self and performance-related feedback in the U.S., Japan, and China. *Journal of International Business Studies*, 28, 605–625.

44. Podsakoff, P. M., Dorfman, P. W., Howell, J. P., & Tudor, W. D. (1986). Leader reward and punishment behaviors: A preliminary test of a culture-free style of leadership effectiveness. In R. N. Farmer (Ed.), *Advances in international comparative management*, 2, 95–138.

45. Hofstede, *Culture's consequences*.

46. Mendonca & Kanungo, Motivation through effective reward management in developing countries.

47. d'Iribarne, Motivating workers in emerging countries: Universal tools and local applications.

48. Porter, L. P., & Lawler, E. E. (1968). *Managerial attitudes and performance*. Homewood, IL: Irwin; Vroom, V. H. (1964). *Work and motivation*. New York: Wiley.

49. Adler, *International dimensions of organizational behavior*; Shenkar & Von Glinow, Paradoxes of organizational theory and research: Using the case of China to illustrate national contingency.

50. Pennings, J. M. (1993). Executive reward systems: A cross-national comparison. *Journal of Management Studies*, 30, 261–279.

51. Reilly, D., Ball, D., & Ascarelli, S. (2003). Europe's low pay-rage threshold. *The Wall Street Journal*, September 10, A8, A9.

52. Steinmetz, G. (1995). German banks note the value of bonuses. *The Wall Street Journal*, May 9, A18; Stewart, M. (1996). German management: A challenge to Anglo-American managerial assumptions. *Business Horizons*, 39, 52–54; Walker, M. (2002). Deutsche Bank finds that it has to cut German roots to grow. *The Wall Street Journal*, February 14, A1, A10.

53. ———. (2002). Foreign firms in Japan: Finding hidden talent. *The Economist*, October 26, 58.

54. Dubinsky, A. J., Kotabe, M., Lim, C. U., & Michaels, R. E. (1994). Differences in motivational perceptions among U.S., Japanese, and Korean sales personnel. *Journal of Business Research*, 30, 175–185; Ono, Y. (2002). Rethinking how Japanese should think, *The Wall Street Journal*, March 25, A12, A14.

55. Ono, Y. (2001). A restaurant chain in Japan chops up the social contract. *The Wall Street Journal*, January 17, A1, A19.

56. Gomez-Mejia, L. & Welbourne, T. (1991). Compensation strategies in a global context. *Human Resource Planning*, 14, 29–41.

57. Schneider, S. C., & Barsoux, J. L. (2003). *Managing across cultures* (2nd Ed.). Harlow, England: Pearson Education.

58. Adler, *International dimensions of organizational behavior*.

59. Gupta, A. K., & Govindarajan, V. (2002). Cultivating a global mindset. *Academy of Management Executive*, 16, 116–126.

60. Geppert, M. (1996). Paths of managerial learning in the east German context. *Organization Studies*, 17, 249–268; Kostera, M., Proppe, M., & Szatkowski, M. (1995). Staging the new romantic hero in the old cynical theatre: On managers, roles and change in Poland. *Journal of Organizational Behavior*, 16, 631–646.

61. Yukl, G. (2002). *Leadership in organizations* (5th Ed.). Englewood Cliffs, NJ: Prentice-Hall.

62. Banai, M., & Teng, B. S. (1996). Comparing job characteristics, leadership style, and alienation in Russian public and private enterprises. *Journal of International Management*, 2, 201–224; Kets De Vries, M. F. R. (2000). A journey into the "Wild East": Leadership style and organizational practices in Russia. *Organizational Dynamics*, 28, 67–81; Puffer, S. M. (1994). Understanding the bear: A portrait of Russian business leaders. *Academy of Management Executive*, 8, 41–54; Puffer, S. M., McCarthy, D. J., & Zhuplev, A. V. (1996). Meeting of the mindsets in a changing Russia. *Business Horizons*, 40, 52–59.

63. Sinha, J. B. P. (1980). *The nurturant task leader: A model of effective executive.* New Delhi: Concept; Sinha, J. B. P. (1984). A model of effective leadership styles in India. *International Studies of Management and Organization, 14,* 86–98.

64. Dorfman, International and cross cultural leadership; Misumi, J. (1985). *The behavioral science of leadership: An interdisciplinary Japanese research program.* Ann Arbor, MI: University of Michigan; Peterson, M. P., Brannen, M. Y., & Smith, P. B. (1994). Japanese and United States leadership: Issues in current research. In S. B. Prasad (Ed.), *Advances in international comparative management,* vol. 9, 57–82. Greenwich, CT: JAI Press.

65. Sinha, A model of effective leadership styles in India.

66. Bhagat, R. S., Kedia, B. L., Crawford, S. E., & Kaplan, M. R. (1990). Cross-cultural issues in organizational psychology: Emergent trends and directions for research in the 1990s. In C. L. Cooper & I. T. Robertson (Eds.), *International Review of Industrial and Organizational Psychology, 5,* 59–99.

67. Ayman, R., & Chemers, M. M. (1983). Relationship of supervisory behavior ratings to work group effectiveness and subordinate satisfaction among Iranian managers. *Journal of Applied Psychology, 68,* 338–341.

68. Doktor, R. H. (1990). Asian and American CEOs: A comparative study. *Organizational Dynamics, 18,* 46–57.

69. Smith, P. B., Misumi, J., Tayeb, M., Peterson, M., & Bond, M. (1989). On the generality of leadership style measures across cultures. *Journal of Occupational Psychology, 62,* 97–109.

70. Tolich, M., Kenney, M., & Biggart, N. (1999). Managing the managers: Japanese strategies in the U.S.A. *Journal of Management Studies, 36,* 587–607.

71. Dorfman, P. W., & Howell, J. P. (1988). Dimensions of national culture and effective leadership patterns: Hofstede revisited. In R. N. Farmer & E. G. McGoun (Eds.) *Advances in International Comparative Management, 3,* 127–150.

72. Peterson, Brannen, & Smith, Japanese and United States leadership: Issues in current research.

73. Morris, T., & Pavett, C. M. (1992). Management style and productivity in two cultures. *Journal of International Business Studies,* First Quarter, 169–179.

74. Bass, B. M. (1990). *Stogdill's handbook of leadership: A survey of theory and research.* New York: Free Press; Likert, R. (1967). *The human organization.* New York: McGraw-Hill.

75. Morris & Pavett, Management style and productivity in two cultures.

76. d'Iribarne, Motivating workers in emerging countries: Universal tools and local applications.

77. de Forest, M. E. (1994). Thinking of a plant in Mexico? *Academy of Management Executive, 8,* 33–40; Gowan, M., Ibarreche, S., & Lackey, C. (1996). Doing the right things in Mexico. *Academy of Management Executive, 10,* 74–81; Stephens, G., & Geer, C. R. (1995). Doing business in Mexico: Understanding cultural differences. *Organizational Dynamics, 24,* 39–55.

78. Keys, J. B., Denton, L. T., & Miller, T. R. (1994). The Japanese management theory jungle revisited. *Journal of Management, 20,* 373–402; Maruyama, M. (1992). Changing dimensions in international business. *Academy of Management Executive, 6,* 88–96.

79. Black, J. S., & Porter, L. W. (1990). Managerial behaviors and job performance: A successful manager in Los Angeles may not succeed in Hong Kong. *Journal of International Business Studies,* First Quarter, 99–112.

80. Karnitschnig, M. (2003). For Siemens, move into U.S. causes waves back home. *The Wall Street Journal,* September 8, A1, A8.

81. See Yukl, *Leadership in organizations.*

82. Bass, *Stogdill's handbook of leadership: A survey of theory and research*; Likert, *The human organization;* Yukl, *Leadership in organizations.*

83. Bass, B. M., & Avolio, B. J. (1992). Developing transformational leadership: 1992 and beyond. *Journal of European Industrial Training, 14,* 21–27.

84. Brodbeck, F., Frese, F., & Javidan, M. (2002). Leadership made in Germany: Low on compassion, high on performance. *Academy of Management Executive, 16,* 16–30; Koh, W. L., Steers, R. M., & Terborg, J. R. (1995). The effects of transformational leadership on teacher attitudes and student performance in Singapore. *Journal of Organizational Behavior, 16,* 319–333; Popper, M., Landau, O., & Gluskinos, U. (1992). The Israeli Defence Forces: An example of transformational leadership. *Leadership and Organization Development Journal, 31,* 3–8; Singer, M. S. (1985). Transformational versus transactional leadership: A study of New Zealand company managers. *Psychological Reports, 57,* 143–146.

85. Rossant, J. (2002). The fast fall of France's celebrity CEOs, *Business Week,* April 1, 48; Yukl, *Leadership in organizations*; See also Chapter 9 discussion about Carlos Ghosn.

86. Taylor, A. (2003). Nissan shifts into higher gear. *Fortune,* July 21, 98–104.

87. House, R. J. (1971). A path-goal theory of leader effectiveness. *Administrative Science Quarterly, 16,* 321–339; House, R. J., & Mitchell, T. R. (1974). Path-goal theory of leadership. *Contemporary Business, 3,* 81–98.

88. Dorfman, International and cross-cultural leadership.

89. Child, J. (1981). Culture, contingency, and capitalism in the cross-national study of organizations. In L. L. Cummings & B. M. Staw (Eds.), *Research in organizational behavior,* vol. 3, 303–356. Greenwich, CT: JAI Press; Ronen, *Comparative and multinational management.*

90. Ayman, R., Kreicker, N. A., & Masztal, J. J. (1994). Defining global leadership in business environments. *Consulting Psychology Journal, 46,* 64–73; Gupta & Govindarajan, Cultivating a global mindset; Tichy, N. M. (1993). Global development. In V. Pucik, N. M. Tichy, & C. K. Barnett (Eds.), *Globalizing management: Creating and leading the competitive organization,* 206–226. New York: Wiley.

91. Laurent, A. (1983). The cultural diversity of Western conceptions of management. *International Studies of Management and Organization, 13,* 75–96.

92. McFarlin, D. B., Sweeney, P. D., & Cotton, J. C. (1992). Attitudes toward employee participation in decision-making: A comparison of European and American managers in a United States multinational company. *Human Resource Management, 31,* 363–383.

93. Adler, N. J., & Bartholomew, S. (1992). Managing globally competent people. *Academy of Management Executive, 6,* 52–65.

94. Spreitzer, G. M., McCall, M. W., & Mahoney, J. D. (1997). Early identification of international executive potential. *Journal of Applied Psychology, 82,* 6–29.

95. Meiland, D. (2003). In search of global leaders. *Harvard Business Review,* August, 44–45.

96. Tichy, N. M., Brimm, M. I., Charan, R., & Takeuchi, H. (1993). Leadership development as a lever for global transformation. In V. Pucik, N. M. Tichy, & C. K.

Barnett (Eds.), *Globalizing management: Creating and leading the competitive organization*, 47–60. New York: Wiley.

97. Conner, J. (2000). Developing the global leaders of tomorrow. *Human Resource Management*, *39*, 147–157.

98. Cooley, M. (1997). HR in Russia: Training for long-term success. *HR Magazine*, December, 98–106; Elenkov, D. S. (1998). Can American management concepts work in Russia? *Academy of Management Review*, *40*, 133–156; Starobin, P. (2003). The enigma of Russia. *Business Week*, August 4, 40–46; Welsh, D. H. B., Luthans, F., & Sommer, S. M. (1993). Managing Russian factory workers: The impact of U.S.-based behavioral and participative techniques. *Academy of Management Journal*, *36*, 58–79.

Chapter 12

1. Wonocott, P. (2001). Mobility in China: Off to the city. *The Economist*, September 1, 36; ———. (2000). Motorola China adds $1.9 billion investment. Press release, August 21, **www.motorola.com/news_center**; ———. (2000). Strategic focus: Motorola annual report, **www.motorola.com/general/financial/annual_report/2000/focus/index.html**; Einhorn, B., Roberts, D., & Crockett, R. O. (2003). Winning in China. *Business Week*, January 27, 98–100; Gross, A., & Dyson, P. (1996). The iron rice bowl cracks. *HR Magazine*, July, 84–88; Hutzler, C., & Leggett, K. (2001). For China's premier Zhu, a critical home stretch. *The Wall Street Journal*, August 29, A6, A10; Nyaw, M. K. (1995). Human resource management in the People's Republic of China. In L. F. Moore & P. D. Jennings (Eds.), *Human resource management on the Pacific rim: Institutions, practices, and attitudes*, 187–216. Berlin: Walter de Gruyter; Shenkar, O., & Nyaw, M. K. (1994). How to run a successful joint venture in China. In S. Stewart & N. Campbell (Eds.), *Advances in Chinese industrial studies: Joint ventures in the People's Republic of China*, 273–284. Greenwich, CT: JAI Press; Wonacott, P. (2002). China's secret weapon: Smart, cheap labor for high-tech goods. *The Wall Street Journal*, March 14, A1, A6.

2. Miller, E. L., Beechler, S., Bhatt, B., & Nath, R. (1991). The relationship between the global strategic planning process and the human resource management function. In M. Mendenhall & G. Oddou (Eds.), *International human resource management*, 65–82. Boston, MA: PWS-Kent Publishing; Schuler, R. S., Fulkerson, J. R., & Dowling, P. J. (1991). Strategic performance measurement and management in multinational corporations. *Human Resource Management*, *30*, 365–392; Truss, C., & Gratton, L. (1994). Strategic human resource management: A conceptual approach. *International Journal of Human Resource Management*, *5*, 662–686.

3. Briscoe, D. R. (1995). *International human resource management*. Englewood Cliffs, NJ: Prentice-Hall; Roberts, K., Kossek, E. E., & Ozeki, C. (1998). Managing the global workforce: Challenges and strategies. *The Academy of Management Executive*, *12*, 93–106.

4. Carpenter, M. A., Sanders, W. G., & Gregersen, H. B. (2000). International assignment experience at the top can make a bottom-line difference. *Human Resource Management*, *39*, 277–285; Taylor, S., Beechler, S., & Napier, N. (1996). Toward an integrative model of

strategic international human resource management. *Academy of Management Review*, *21*, 959–985.

5. Porter, M. E. (1985). *Competitive advantage: Creating and sustaining competitive advantage*. New York: Free Press, 43.

6. Sparrow, P., Schuler, R. S., & Jackson, S. E. (1994). Convergence or divergence: Human resource practices and policies for competitive advantage worldwide. *International Journal of Human Resource Management*, *5*, 267–299.

7. Gong, Y. (2003). Toward a dynamic process model of staffing composition and subsidiary outcomes in multinational enterprises. *Journal of Management*, *29*, 259–280; Minbaeva, D., Pedersen, T., Bjorkman, I., Fey, C. F., & Park, H. J. (2003). MNC knowledge transfer, subsidiary absorptive capacity, and HRM. *Journal of International Business Studies*, *34*, 586–599; Odenwald, S. (1993). A guide for global training. *Training and Development*, July, 23–31.

8. Schuler, R. S., & Florkowski, G. W. (1996). International human resources management. In B. J. Punnett & O. Shenkar (Eds.), *Handbook for international management research*, 351–401. Cambridge, MA: Blackwell.

9. Fey, C. F., & Bjorkman, I. (2001). The effect of human resource management practices on MNC subsidiary performance in Russia. *Journal of International Business Studies*, *32*, 59–75; Wright, P. M., McMahan, G. C., & McWilliams, A. (1994). Human resources and sustained competitive advantage: A resource-based perspective. *International Journal of Human Resource Management*, *5*, 301–326.

10. Briscoe, *International human resource management*.

11. Buck, T., Filatotchev, I., Demina, N., & Wright, M. (2003). Inside ownership, human resource strategies and performance in a transition economy. *Journal of International Business Studies*, *34*, 530–549.

12. Roth, K., & O'Donnell, S. (1996). Foreign subsidiary compensation strategy: An agency theory perspective. *Academy of Management Journal*, *39*, 678–703; Schuler & Florkowski, International human resources management.

13. Beechler, S., & Yang, J. Z. (1994). The transfer of Japanese-style management to American subsidiaries: Contingencies, constraints, and competencies. *Journal of International Business Studies*, *25*, 467–491.

14. Bartlett, C., & Ghoshal, S. (1989). *Managing across borders: The transnational solution*. Boston: Harvard Business School Press; Schuler & Florkowski, International human resources management; Schuler, R. S., Fulkerson, J. R., & Dowling, P. J. (1991). Strategic performance measurement and management in multinational corporations. *Human Resource Management*, *30*, 365–392; Taylor, Beechler, & Napier, Toward an integrative model of strategic international human resource management.

15. Bachler, C. J. (1996). Global inpats—don't let them surprise you. *Personnel Journal*, June, 54–64; Greengard, S. (1996). Gain the edge in the knowledge race. *Personnel Journal*, August, 52–56; West, L. A., & Bogumil, W. A. (2000). Foreign knowledge workers as a strategic staffing option. *The Academy of Management Executive*, *14*, 71–84.

16. Cascio, W., & Bailey, E. E. (1995). International human resource management: The state of research and practice. In O. Shenkar (Ed.), *Global perspectives of human resource management*, 15–36. Englewood Cliffs, NJ:

Prentice-Hall; Dowling, P. J., & Schuler, R. S. (1990). *International dimensions of human resource management*. Boston: PWS-Kent Publishing; Hymowitz, C. (2003). European executives give some advice on crossing borders. *The Wall Street Journal*, December 2, B1.

17. Carpenter, Sanders, & Gregersen, International assignment experience at the top can make a bottom-line difference.

18. Downes, M., & Thomas, A. S. (2000). Managing overseas assignments to build organizational knowledge. *Human Resource Planning, 20*, 33–48.

19. Hsieh, T. Y., Lavoie, J., & Sarnek, R. A. P. (1999). Are you taking your expatriate talent seriously? *McKinsey Quarterly, 3*, 71–83.

20. Briscoe, *International human resource management*; Phatak, A. V. (1995). *International dimensions of management* (4th Ed.). Cincinnati, OH: South-Western.

21. Lublin, J. S. (1996). Is transfer to native land a passport to trouble? *The Wall Street Journal*, June 3, B1, B5; Millman, J., & Zimmerman, A. (2003). 'Repats' help Payless Shoes branch out in Latin America. *The Wall Street Journal*, December 24, B1, B2; Millman, J. (2000). Exporting management savvy. *The Wall Street Journal*, October 24, B1, B18; Solomon, C. M. (1994). Global operations demand that HR rethink diversity. *Personnel Journal*, July, 40–50.

22. Phatak, *International dimensions of management*.

23. Latta, G. W. (1998). Global staffing: Are expatriates the only answer? *HR Focus*, July, S1, S2; Woodruff, D. (2000). Distractions make global manager a difficult role. *The Wall Street Journal*, November 21, B1, B18.

24. Adler, N. J. (2002). *International dimensions of organizational behavior* (4th Ed.). Cincinnati, OH: South-Western; Briscoe, *International human resource management*; Schneider, S. C. (1991). National vs. corporate culture: Implications for human resource management. In M. Mendenhall & G. Oddou (Eds.), *International human resource management*, 13–27. Boston: PWS-Kent.

25. Gong, Toward a dynamic process model of staffing composition and subsidiary outcomes in multinational enterprises.

26. Jeanquart-Barone, S., & Peluchette, J. V. (1999). Examining the impact of the cultural dimension of uncertainty avoidance on staffing decisions: A look at U.S. and German firms. *Cross-Cultural Management: An International Journal, 6*, 3–12; Peterson, R. B., Sargent, J., Napier, N. K., & Shim, W. S. (1996). Corporate expatriate HRM policies, internationalization, and performance in the world's largest MNCs. *Management International Review, 36*, 215–230.

27. Boyacigiller, N. (1990). The role of expatriates in the management of interdependence, complexity, and risk in multinational corporations. *Journal of International Business Studies, 21*, 357–381.

28. Dowling & Schuler, *International dimensions of human resource management*.

29. Roberts, K., Kossek, E. E., & Ozeki, C. (1998). Managing the global workforce: Challenges and strategies. *Academy of Management Executive, 12*, 93–106; Solomon, C. M. (1995). Navigating your search for global talent. *Personnel Journal*, May, 94–101; Stanek, M. B. (2000). The need for global managers: A business necessity. *Management Decision, 38*, 232–242.

30. Inkson, K., Arthur, M. B., Pringle, J., & Barry, S. (1997). Expatriate assignment versus overseas experience: Contrasting models of international human resource development. *Journal of World Business, 32*, 351–366;

Solomon, C. M. (1995). Navigating your search for global talent. *Personnel Journal*, May, 94–101; Woodruff, D. (2000). Distractions make global manager a difficult role. *The Wall Street Journal*, November 21, B1, B18.

31. Odenwald, S. (1993). A guide for global training. *Training and Development*, July, 23–31.

32. ———. (2000). International assignments: Nasty, brutish and short. *The Economist*, December 16, 70–71; Greising, D. (1994). Globe trotter: If it's 5:30, this must be Tel Aviv. *Business Week*, October 17, 102; Kaufman, J. (1996). Tethered to Pittsburgh for years, an engineer thrives on trips to Asia. *The Wall Street Journal*, November 19, A1, A8; Miller, L. (1996). Pace of business travel abroad is beyond breakneck. *The Wall Street Journal*, May 31, B1, B6; Lublin, J. S. (2003). No place like home. *The Wall Street Journal*, September 29, R7; Miller, L. (1996). Why business travel is such hard work. *The Wall Street Journal*, October 30, B1, B2; Silverman, R. E. (2001). Global crossings. *The Wall Street Journal*, January 16, B12; Weber, T. E. (2001). After terror attacks, companies rethink role of face-to-face. *The Wall Street Journal*, September 24, B1.

33. Peterson, R. B., Napier, N. K., & Shul-Shim, W. (2000). Expatriate management: Comparison of MNCs across four parent countries. *Thunderbird International Business Review, 42*, 145–166.

34. Dimmick, T. G. (1995). Human resource management in a Korean subsidiary in New Jersey. In Shenkar, *Global perspectives of human resource management*, 63–70.

35. Cascio, W., & Bailey, E. E. (1995). International human resource management: The state of research and practice. In Shenkar, *Global perspectives of human resource management*, 15–36.

36. Love, K. G., Bishop, R. C., Heinisch, D. A., & Montei, M. S. (1994). Selection across two cultures: Adapting the selection of American assemblers to meet Japanese job performance demands. *Personnel Psychology, 47*, 837–846.

37. Earley, P. C. (1994). Self or group? Cultural effects of training on self-efficacy and performance. *Administrative Science Quarterly, 39*, 89–117.

38. Feltes, P., Robinson, R. K., & Fink, R. L. (1993). American female expatriates and the Civil Rights Act of 1991: Balancing legal and business interests. *Business Horizons*, March–April, 82–85.

39. Solomon, C. M. (1994). Global operations demand that HR rethink diversity. *Personnel Journal*, July, 40–50.

40. Feltes, Robinson, & Fink, American female expatriates and the Civil Rights Act of 1991: Balancing legal and business interests; Scheibal, W. (1995). When cultures clash: Applying Title VII abroad. *Business Horizons*, September–October, 4–8.

41. Erwee, R. (1994). South African women: Changing career patterns. In N. J. Adler & D. N. Izraeli (Eds.), *Competitive frontiers: Women managers in a global economy*, 325–342. Cambridge, MA: Blackwell Publishers; Hollway, W., & Mukurasi, L. (1994). Women managers in the Tanzanian civil service. In Adler & Izraeli, *Competitive frontiers: Women managers in a global economy*, 343–357.

42. Kishkovsky, S., & Williamson, E. (1997). Second-class comrades no more: Women stoke Russia's start-up boom. *The Wall Street Journal*, January 30, A12.

43. Dunung, S. P. (1995). *Doing business in Asia: The complete guide*. New York: Lexington Books.

44. Thomas, P. (1995). United States: Success at a huge personal cost. *The Wall Street Journal*, July 25, B1, B12.

45. Reitman, V. (1995). Japan: She is free, yet she's alone in the world. *The Wall Street Journal*, July 26, B1, B12.

46. Scheibal, When cultures clash: Applying Title VII abroad.

47. Linehan, M. & Walsh, J. S. (2000). Beyond the traditional linear view of international managerial careers: A new model of the senior female career in an international context. *Journal of European Industrial Training*, 24, 178–189.

48. Adler, N. J. (1994). In Adler & Izraeli, *Competitive frontiers: Women managing across borders*, 22–42; Adler, *International dimensions of organizational behavior*; Jordan, M. (2001). Have husband, will travel. *The Wall Street Journal*, February 13, B1, B12; Taylor, S., & Napier, N. (1996). Working in Japan: Lessons from women expatriates. *Sloan Management Review*, Spring, 76–84.

49. Linehan & Walsh, Beyond the traditional linear view of international managerial careers: A new model of the senior female career in an international context; Taylor & Napier, Working in Japan: Lessons from women expatriates.

50. Ante, S. E., & Magnusson, P. (2003). Too many visas for techies? *Business Week*, August 25, 39.

51. Tung, R. L. (1993). Managing cross-national and intra-national diversity. *Human Resource Management*, 32, 461–477.

52. **www.colgate.com**; Solomon, C. M. (1994). Global operations demand that HR rethink diversity. *Personnel Journal*, July, 40–50.

53. Lublin, No place like home.

54. ———. (2004). Expatriates and your global workforce. January 4, **http://www.hrspectrum.com/insightofweek.htm.**

55. ———. (2004). 2002 worldwide survey of international assignment policies and practices. January 4, **http://www.orcinc.com/surveys/wws2002.html.**

56. Lublin, No place like home; Harvey, M. (1997). Dual-career expatriates: Expectations, adjustment and satisfaction with international relocation. *Journal of International Business Studies*, 28, 627–659; Hsieh, Lavoie, & Sarnek, Are you taking your expatriate talent seriously?; Harzig, A. (2001). Of bears, bumble-bees, and spiders: The role of expatriates in controlling foreign subsidiaries. *Journal of World Business*, 36, 366–379; Shaffer, M. A., & Harrison, D. A. (2001). Forgotten partners of international assignments: Development and test of a model of spouse adjustment. *Journal of Applied Psychology*, 86, 238–254.

57. Lublin, No place like home.

58. Carpenter, Sanders, & Gregersen, International assignment experience at the top can make a bottom-line difference; Harris, N. (2002). Tools to protect traveling employees. *The Wall Street Journal*, March 11, R8.

59. Engen, J. R. (1995). Coming home. *Training*. March, 37–40; Hauser, J. (1999). Managing expatriates' careers. *HR Focus*, February, 11–12; Latta, G. W. (1999). Expatriate policy and practice: A ten-year comparison of trends. *Compensation and Benefits Review*, 31, 35–39; Poe, A. C. (2000). Destination everywhere. *HR Magazine*, October, 67–75; Wederspahn, G. M. (1992). Costing failures in expatriate human resources management. *Human Resource Planning*, 15, 27–35.

60. Black, J. S., Gregersen, H. B., & Mendenhall, M. E. (1992). *Global assignments: Successfully expatriating and repatriating international managers*. San Francisco, CA: Jossey-Bass; Carpenter, S. (2001). Battling the overseas blues. *Monitor on Psychology*, July/August, 48–49; Hsieh, Lavoie, & Sarnek, Are you taking your expatriate talent seriously?; Klaus, K. J. (1995). How to establish an effective expatriate program: Best practices in international assignment administration. *Employment Relations Today*, Spring, 59–70.

61. Adler, *International dimensions of organizational behavior*; Black, Gregersen, & Mendenhall, *Global assignments: Successfully expatriating and repatriating international managers*; Briscoe, *International human resource management*; Carpenter, Battling the overseas blues; Downes & Thomas, Managing overseas assignments to build organizational knowledge; Garonzik, R., Brockner, J., & Siegel, P. A. (2000). Identifying international assignees at risk for premature departure: The interactive effect of outcome favorability and procedural fairness. *Journal of Applied Psychology*, 85, 13–20; Phatak, *International dimensions of management*; Nichols, C. E., Rothstein, M. G., & Bourne, A. (2002) Predicting expatriate work attitudes: The impact of cognitive closure and adjustment competencies. *International Journal of Cross-Cultural Management*, 2, 297–320.

62. Bolino, M. C., & Feldman, D. C. (2000). The antecedents and consequences of underemployment among expatriates. *Journal of Organizational Behavior*, 21, 889–911.

63. Schneider, S. C., & Asakawa, K. (1995). American and Japanese expatriate adjustment: A psychoanalytic perspective. *Human Relations*, 48, 1109–1127; Ward, C., & Rana-Deuba, A. (2000). Home and host culture influences on sojourner adjustment. *International Journal of Intercultural Relations*, 24, 291–306.

64. Black, Gregersen, & Mendenhall, *Global assignments: Successfully expatriating and repatriating international managers*; Jordan, Have husband, will travel; Latta, G. W. (1999). Expatriate policy and practice: A ten-year comparison of trends. *Compensation and Benefits Review*, 31, 35–39; Lublin, No place like home; Selmer, J. (1999). Corporate expatriate career development. *Journal of International Management*, 5, 55–71; Solomon, C. M. (1996). Expats say: Help make us mobile. *Personnel Journal*, July, 43–52; Swaak, R. A. (1995). Expatriate management: The search for best practices. *Compensation and Benefits Review*, 27, 21–29; Swaak, R. A. (1995). Today's expatriate family: Dual careers and other obstacles. *Compensation and Benefits Review*, 26, 21–26.

65. Black, Gregersen, & Mendenhall, *Global assignments: Successfully expatriating and repatriating international managers*; Caligiuri, P. (2000). The big five personality characteristics as predictors of expatriate's desire to terminate the assignment and supervisor-rated performance. *Personnel Psychology*, 53, 67–88; Carpenter, Battling the overseas blues.

66. Carpenter, Battling the overseas blues; Phatak, *International dimensions of management*; Sanchez, J. I., Spector, P. E., & Cooper, C. L. (2000). Adapting to a boundaryless world: A developmental expatriate model. *The Academy of Management Executive*, 14, 96–106.

67. Black, Gregersen, & Mendenhall, *Global assignments: Successfully expatriating and repatriating international managers*; Deshpande, S. P., & Viswesvaran, C. (1992). Is cross-cultural training of managers effective: A meta analysis. *International Journal of Intercultural Relations*,

16, 295–310; Fitzgerald-Turner, B. (1997). Myths of expatriate life. *HR Magazine*, June, 1–7.

68. Black, J. S. (1992). Coming home: The relationship of expatriate expectations with repatriation adjustment and job performance. *Human Relations, 45*, 177–192; Black, Gregersen, & Mendenhall, *Global assignments: Successfully expatriating and repatriating international managers*; Harrison, J. K. (1994). Developing successful expatriate managers: A framework for the structural design and strategic alignment of cross-cultural training programs. *Human Resource Planning, 17*, 17–35.

69. Aryee, S., Chay, Y. W., & Chew, J. (1996). An investigation of the willingness of managerial employees to accept an expatriate assignment. *Journal of Organizational Behavior, 17*, 267–283; Black, Gregersen, & Mendenhall, *Global assignments: Successfully expatriating and repatriating international managers*; Parker, B., & McEvoy, G. M. (1993). Initial examination of a model of intercultural adjustment. *International Journal of Intercultural Relations, 17*, 355–379; Stroh, L. K., Dennis, L. E., & Cramer, T. C. (1994). Predictors of expatriate adjustment. *International Journal of Organizational Analysis, 2*, 176–192.

70. Solomon, Expats say: Help make us mobile.

71. Hagerty, B. (1993). Trainers help expatriate employees build bridges to different cultures. *The Wall Street Journal*, June 14, B1, B6.

72. Carpenter, Battling the overseas blues.

73. Adler, *International dimensions of organizational behavior*; Arthur, W., & Bennett, W. (1995). The international assignee: The relative importance of factors perceived to contribute to success. *Personnel Psychology, 48*, 99–114; Swaak, Today's expatriate family: Dual careers and other obstacles.

74. Adler, *International dimensions of organizational behavior*; Black, J. S., & Gregersen, H. B. (1991). The other half of the picture: Antecedents of spouse cross-cultural adjustment. *Journal of International Business Studies, 22*, 461–477.

75. Carpenter, Battling the overseas blues.

76. Tu, H., & Sullivan, S. E. (1994). Preparing yourself for an international assignment. *Business Horizons, 37*, January–February, 67–70; Zaslow, J. (2003). The fourth without fireworks: Americans' quiet patriotism abroad. *The Wall Street Journal*, July 3, D1.

77. Black, Coming home: The relationship of expatriate expectations with repatriation adjustment and job performance; Black, Gregersen, & Mendenhall, *Global assignments: Successfully expatriating and repatriating international managers*: Shilling, M. (1993). How to win at repatriation. *Personnel Journal*, September, 40–46.

78. Solomon, C. M. (1995). Repatriation: Up, down, or out? *Personnel Journal*, January, 28–37.

79. Wonocott, Mobility in China: Off to the city; Gross & Dyson, The iron rice bowl cracks; Hutzler & Leggett, For China's premier Zhu, a critical home stretch; Nyaw, Human resource management in the People's Republic of China.; Ramstad, E. (2003). Motorola sells China chip plant to small Shanghai manufacturer. *The Wall Street Journal*, October 27, B6; Shenkar & Nyaw, How to run a successful joint venture in China; Wonocott, China's secret weapon: Smart, cheap labor for high tech goods; Wozniak, L. (2003). Companies in China struggle to train, retain qualified managers. *The Wall Street Journal*, December 30, A8.

Chapter 13

1. Oddou, G., & Mendenhall, M. (1991). Expatriate performance appraisal: Problems and solutions. In M. Mendenhall & G. Oddou (Eds.), *International human resource management*, 364–374. Boston: PWS-Kent.

2. Oddou & Mendenhall, Expatriate performance appraisal: Problems and solutions.

3. Oddou & Mendenhall, Expatriate performance appraisal: Problems and solutions.

4. Cascio, W., & Bailey, E. (1995). International human resource management: The state of research and practice. In O. Shenkar, *Global perspectives of human resource management*, 15–36. Englewood Cliffs, NJ: Prentice-Hall.

5. Gregersen, H., Hite, J., Black, J. S. (1996). Expatriate performance appraisal in U.S. multinational firms. *Journal of International Business Studies, 27*, 711–738.

6. Dowling, P. J., & Schuler, R. S. (1990). *International dimensions of human resource management*. Boston: PWS-Kent.

7. Garland, J., & Farmer, R. N. (1986). *International dimensions of business policy and strategy*. Boston: PWS-Kent.

8. Dowling & Schuler, *International dimensions of human resource management*.

9. Dowling & Schuler, *International dimensions of human resource management*.

10. Dowling & Schuler, *International dimensions of human resource management*; Garland & Farmer, *International dimensions of business policy and strategy*.

11. Oddou & Mendenhall, Expatriate performance appraisal: Problems and solutions.

12. Oddou & Mendenhall, Expatriate performance appraisal: Problems and solutions.

13. Ali, A. (1988). A cross-national perspective of managerial work value systems. In R. N. Farmer & E. G. McGowen (Eds.), *Advances in international comparative management*. Greenwich, CT: JAI Press.

14. Arvey, R. D., Bhagat, R. S., & Salas, E. (1991). Cross-cultural and cross-national issues in personnel and human resources management: Where do we go from here? *Research in Personnel and Human Resources Management, 9*, 367–407; Vance, C. M., Paik, Y., Boje, B. M., & Stage, H. D. (1993). A study of the generalizability of performance appraisal design characteristics across four Southeast Asian countries: Assessing the extent of divergence effect. Paper presented to the International Management Division of the National Academy of Management.

15. Allen, L. A. (1988). Working better with Japanese managers. *Management Review, 77*, November, 55–56.

16. Early, P. C. (1986). Trust, perceived importance of praise and criticism and work performance: An examination of feedback in the United States and England. *Journal of Management, 12*, 457–473.

17. See also Morton, C. (1988). Bringing manager and managed together. *Industrial Society*, September, 26–27; see also Bolino, M. C., & Feldman, D. C. (2000). The antecedents and consequences of underemployment among expatriates. *Journal of Organizational Behavior, 21*, 889–911.

18. Trompenaars, F. (1994). *Riding the waves of culture: Understanding diversity in global business*. New York: Irwin.

19. Vance, Paik, Boje, & Stage, A study of the generalizability of performance appraisal design characteristics across four Southeast Asian countries.

20. Stull, J. S. (1988). Giving feedback to foreign-born employees. *Management Solutions*, *33*, July, 42–45.

21. Milkovich, G. T., & Newman, J. M. (1996). *Compensation*. Chicago: Irwin.

22. Kras, E. S. (1989). *Management in two cultures: Bridging the gap between US and Mexican managers*. Yarmouth, ME: Intercultural Press.

23. Milkovich & Newman, *Compensation*.

24. ———. (1994). Mexican labor's hidden costs. *Fortune*, October, 17, 32.

25. Bailey, E. K. (1995). International compensation. In O. Shenkar (Ed.), *Global perspectives of human resource management*. Englewood Cliffs, NJ: Prentice-Hall, 147–164.

26. ———. (2000). Chief executives' pay as a multiple of manufacturing employees' pay. *The Economist*, September 30, 110.

27. Parker-Pope, T. (1996). Executive pay: So far away. *The Wall Street Journal*, April, R12; Fryer, B. (2003). In a world of pay. *Harvard Business Review Case & Expert Commentary*, November, 31–40.

28. Mesdag, L. M. (1984). Are you underpaid? *Fortune*, March 19, 22–23.

29. Haigh, T. (1995). U.S. multinational compensation strategies for local nationals. *Compensation: Present practices and future concerns: A conference report*. New York: The Conference Board, Report no. 1129–95-CH, 15–18; Helms, M. (1991). International executive compensation practices. In Mendenhall and Oddou, *International human resource management*; Puffer, S. M., & Shekshnia, S. V. (1994). Compensating local employees in post-communist Russia: In search of talent or just looking for a bargain? *Compensation and Benefits Review*, September–October, 35–43.

30. Townsend, A. M., Scott, K. D., & Markham, S. E. (1990). An examination of country and culture-based differences in compensation practices. *Journal of International Business Studies*, *21*, 667–678.

31. Hewitt Associates (1991). *Total compensation management: Reward management strategies for the 1990's*. Cambridge, MA: Basil Blackwell.

32. Flynn, G. (1994). HR in Mexico: What you should know. *Personnel Journal*, August, 34–44.

33. Beatty, J. R., McCune, J. T., & Beatty, R. W. (1988). A policy-capturing approach to the study of United States and Japanese managers' compensation decisions. *Journal of Management*, *14*, 465–474.

34. Mroczkowski, T., & Hanaoka, M. (1989). Continuity and change in Japanese management. *California Management Review*, Winter, 39–52.

35. Gomez-Mejia, L. R., & Welbourne, T. (1991). Compensation strategies in a global context. *Human Resource Planning*, *14*, 29–41; ———. ORC Surveys of International Assignment Policies and Practices. In **www.orcinc.com/surveys/wws2003.html.**

36. See also Whenmouth, A. (1988). Is Japan's corporate culture changing? *Industry Week*, *237*(7), 33–35.

37. Gomez-Mejia & Welbourne, Compensation strategies in a global context; Hodgetts, R. M., & Luthans, F. (1993). U.S. multinationals' compensation strategies for local management: Cross-cultural implications. *Compensation and Benefits Review*, 42–48.

38. Taylor, A. (1996). Toyota's boss stands out in a crowd. *Fortune*, November 25, 116–122.

39. Fergus, M. (1990). Employees on the move. *HR Magazine*, *36*, No. 5, 44–46.

40. Mervosh, E. M. (1997). Managing expatriate compensation. *Industry Week*, July 21, 13–18; Gould, C. (1999). Expatriate compensation. *Workforce*, September, 40–46.

41. Black, J. S. (1991). Returning expatriates feel foreign in their native land. *Personnel*, *68*, 17.

42. Reynolds, C. (1994). *Compensation basics for North American expatriates: Developing an effective program for employees working abroad*. Scottsdale, AZ: The American Compensation Association.

43. Reynolds, *Compensation basics for North American expatriates*.

44. Oemig, D. R. A. (1999). When you say, "we'll keep you whole," do you mean it? *Compensation and Benefits Review*, *31*, 40–47.

45. Helms, International executive compensation practices; Infante, V. D. (2001). Three ways to design international pay: Headquarters, home country, host country. *Workforce*, January, 22–24.

46. ———. (1992). *Guide to major holidays around the globe*. Zurich: Union Bank of Switzerland.

47. U.S. Department of State. (1999). *Indexes of living costs abroad, quarters allowances, and hardship differentials*. Washington, DC: Government Printing Office; ———. (2002). Hardship rating. *The Economist*, October, 12, 98.

48. Reynolds, *Compensation basics for North American expatriates*.

49. ———. (1997). Market rents. *The Wall Street Journal*, January 24, B8.

50. Anderson, J. B. (1990). Compensating your overseas executives, Part 2: Europe in 1992. *Compensation and Benefits Review*, *22*, 25–35; Klein, R. B. (1992). Compensating your overseas executives, Part 3: Exporting U.S. stock option plans to expatriates. *Compensation and Benefits Review*, *23*, 27–38.

51. Anderson, Compensating your overseas executives, Part 2: Europe in 1992.

52. Reynolds, *Compensation basics for North American expatriates*.

53. ———. (2001). Cost of living. *The Economist*, January 20, 108; ———. (2001). Where expats spend the most. *Business Week*, June 25, 30.

54. ———. (2001). Big Mac currencies. *The Economist*, April 21, 74.

55. Vachris, M. A., & Thomas, J. (1999). International price comparisons based on purchasing power parity. *Monthly Labor Review*, October, 3–12.

56. Logger, E., Vinke, R., & Kluytmans, F. (1995). Compensation and appraisal in an international perspective. In A. Harzing & J. Van Ruysseveldt (Eds.), *International human resource management*, 144–155. London: Sage.

57. Reynolds, *Compensation basics for North American expatriates*.

58. Wilson, L. E. (2000). The balance sheet approach to expatriate compensation: Still with us after all these years. *Relocation Journal and Real Estate News*, *14*, 1–9.

59. Reynolds, *Compensation basics for North American expatriates*.

60. Dwyer, T. D. (1999). Trends in global compensation. *Compensation and Benefits Review*, *31*, 48–53; Milkovich, G. T., & Bloom, M. (1998). Rethinking international compensation. *Compensation and Benefits Review*, *30*, 15–23.

61. Reynolds, *Compensation basics for North American expatriates*.

62. Gould, C. (1999). Expat pay plans suffer cutbacks. *Workforce*, September, 40–46; Latta, G. W. (1999).

Expatriate policy and practice: A ten-year comparison of trends. *Compensation and Benefits Review*, *31*, 35–39.

63. McGowan, R. (2003). The days of the 'champagne lifestyle' expatriate assignments are numbered. *Mercer Human Resource Consulting*, January 29, 1–3.

64. Milkovich & Newman, *Compensation*.

65. Laabs, J. J. (1993). What it costs to house expatriates worldwide. *Personnel Journal*, *16*, 16; Laabs, J. J. (1993). What joint ventures in China are giving employees in pay and benefits. *Personnel Journal*, *16*, 16–20.

66. Phatak, A. V. (1995). *International dimensions of management*. Cincinnati, OH: South-Western.

67. Harvey, M. (1993). Designing a global compensation system: The logic and a model. *Columbia Journal of World Business*, Winter, 57–72.

68. Anderson, Compensating your overseas executives, Part 2: Europe in 1992; Young, D. (2000). Fair compensation for expatriates. *Harvard Business Review*, July–August, 117–126.

69. Harvey, M. (1993). Empirical evidence of recurring international compensation problems. *Journal of International Business Studies*, *24*, 785–799.

70. Shenkar, *Global perspectives of human resource management*.

Chapter 14

1. Neale, R., & Mindel, B. (1992). Rigging up multicultural teamworking. *Personnel Management*, January, 36–39.

2. Triandis, H. C. (1988). Collectivism v. individualism: A reconceptualism of a basic concept in cross-cultural social psychology. In G. K. Verma & C. Bagley (Eds.). *Cross-Cultural Studies of Personality, Attitudes, and Cognition*. New York: St. Martin's Press, 60–95.

3. Domino, G. (1992). Cooperation and competition in Chinese and American children. *Journal of Cross-Cultural Psychology*, *23*, 456–467.

4. Bond, M. H., & Hwang, K. (1986). The social psychology of the Chinese people. In M. H. Bond (Ed.), *The psychology of the Chinese people*, 213–266. Hong Kong: Oxford University Press.

5. Liden, R. C., Wayne, S. J., Jaworski, R. A., & Bennett, N. (2004). Social loafing: A field investigation. *Journal of Management*, *30*, 285–304.

6. Matsui, T., Kakuyama, T., & Ongltco, M. L. U. (1987). Effects of goals and feedback on performance in groups. *Journal of Applied Psychology*, *72*, 407–415.

7. Earley, P. C. (1989). Social loafing and collectivism. *Administrative Science Quarterly*, *34*, 565–581; Gabrenya, W. K., Latane, B., & Wang, Y. (1985). Social loafing on an optimizing task: Cross-cultural differences among Chinese and Americans. *Journal of Cross-Cultural Psychology*, *16*, 223–242.

8. Earley, P. C. (1993). East meets West meets Mideast: Further explorations of collectivistic and individualistic work groups. *Academy of Management Journal*, *36*, 319–348.

9. Triandis, Collectivism v. individualism: A reconceptualism of a basic concept in cross-cultural social psychology.

10. Espinoza, J. A., & Garza, R. T. (1985). Social group salience and inter-ethnic cooperation. *Journal of Experimental Social Psychology*, *23*, 380–392.

11. Earley, East meets West meets Mideast: Further explorations of collectivistic and individualistic work groups.

12. Merritt, A. C., & Helmreich, R. L. (1996). Human factors on the flight deck: The influence of national culture. *Journal of Cross-Cultural Psychology*, *27*, 5–24.

13. See also Earley, P. C. (1994). Self or group? Cultural effects of training on self-efficacy and performance. *Administrative Science Quarterly*, *39*, 89–117.

14. Earley, East meets West meets Mideast: Further explorations of collectivistic and individualistic work groups.

15. ———. (1992). Work team trivia. *The Competitive Edge*. March/April, 12; Dumaine, B. (1990). Who needs a boss? *Fortune*, May 7, 52–60.

16. Adler, N. J. (1991). *International dimensions of organizational behavior*. Boston, MA: PWS-Kent.

17. Adler, *International dimensions of organizational behavior*.

18. Browning, E. S. (1994). Computer chip project brings rivals together, but the cultures clash. *The Wall Street Journal*, May 3, A1, A8.

19. Earley, P. C., & Mosakowski, E. (2000). Creating hybrid team cultures: An empirical test of transnational team functioning. *Academy of Management Journal*, *43*, 26–49.

20. Jehn, K. A., Chadwick, C., & Thatcher, S. M. B. (1997). To agree or not to agree: The effects of value congruence, individual demographic dissimilarity, and conflict on workgroup outcomes. *International Journal of Conflict Management*, *8*, 287–305.

21. Houlder, V. (1996). How to get ideas to hatch. *Financial Times*, September 9, 10.

22. Some of these anecdotal observations have been supported with research findings. See, for example, Salk, J. E., & Brannen, M. Y. (2000). National culture, networks, and individual influence in a multinational management team. *Academy of Management Journal*, *43*, 191–202.

23. Guzzo, R. A., & Shea, G. P. (1992). Group performance and intergroup relations in organizations. In M. D. Dunnette & L. M. Hough (Eds.), *Handbook of industrial and organizational psychology* (2nd Ed.), vol. 3. Palo Alto, CA: Consulting Psychologists Press; Watson, W. E., Kumar, K., & Michaelson, L. K. (1993). Cultural diversity's impact on interaction process and performance: Comparing homogeneous and diverse task groups. *Academy of Management Journal*, *36*, 590–602.

24. Elron, E. (1997). Top management teams within multinational corporations: Effects of cultural heterogeneity. *Leadership Quarterly*, *8*, 393–412.

25. Earley & Mosakowski, Creating hybrid team cultures: An empirical test of transnational team functioning.

26. Harstone, M., & Augoustinos, M. (1995). The minimal group paradigm: Categorization into two versus three groups. *European Journal of Social Psychology*, *25*, 179–193.

27. Adler, *International dimensions of organizational behavior*.

28. Earley, P. C. (1999). Playing follow the leader: Status-determining traits in relation to collective efficacy across cultures. *Organizational Behavior and Human Decision Processes*, *80*, 192–212.

29. Tan, H. H., & Aryee, S. (2002). Antecedents and outcomes of union loyalty: A constructive replication and extension. *Journal of Applied Psychology*, *87*, 715–722.

30. Newman, B. (1993). Border dispute: Single-country unions of Europe try to cope with multinationals. *The Wall Street Journal*, November 30, A1 A22; Zachary, G. P. (1993). Like factory workers, professionals face loss of jobs to foreigners. *The Wall Street Journal*, March 17, A1, A9.

31. Fleming, C. (2004). Europe learns litigious ways. *The Wall Street Journal*, February 24, A16, A17.

32. Steinmetz, G. (1996). Americans, too, run afoul of rigorous German rules. *The Wall Street Journal*, February 2, A6.

33. ———. (1992). Employee dismissals can prove costly for companies in Europe. *HR Focus*, August, 18.

34. Bilefsky, D. (2003). The Dutch way of firing. *The Wall Street Journal*, July 8, A14.

35. Bourdette, N. E. (2004). As jobs head to Eastern Europe, unions in the West start to bend. *The Wall Street Journal*, March 11, A1, A6.

36. Briscoe, *International human resource management*.

37. Hollinshead, G., & Leaf, M. (1995). *Human resource management: An international and comparative perspective*. London: Pitman; Koretz, G. (1990). Why unions thrive abroad, but wither in the U.S. *Business Week*, September 10, 26.

38. Gunnigle, P., Brewster, C., & Morley, M. (1994). European industrial relations: Change and continuity. In C. Brewster & A. Hegewisch (Eds.), *Policy and Practice in European Human Resource Management: The Price-Waterhouse Cranfield Survey*, chapter 9, 139–153. London: Routledge.

39. Ferner, A., & Hyman, R. (1992). *Industrial relations in the new Europe*. Oxford: Blackwell.

40. Gunnigle, Brewster, & Morley, European industrial relations: Change and continuity.

41. ———. (2003). Working hours. *The Economist*, August 23, 80; ———. (2000). Germany: Rebirth of a salesman. *The Economist*, July 8, 22–24; Benjamin, D. (1993). Germany is troubled by how little work its workers are doing. *The Wall Street Journal*, May 6, A1, A7; Benjamin, D., & Horwitz, T. (1994). German view: You Americans work too hard—and for what? *The Wall Street Journal*, July 14, B5, B6; Koretz, G. (2001). Why Americans work so hard. *Business Week*, June 11, 34.

42. ———. (2004). German industrial relations: Slowly losing their chains. *The Economist*, February 21, 49; Wachter, H. (1997). German co-determination—Quo vadis? A study of the implementation of new management concepts in a German steel company. *Employee Relations*, 19, 27–37.

43. ———. (2004). How to pep up Germany's economy. *The Economist*, May 8, 65–67; Rhoads, C. (2003). In deep crisis, Germany starts to revamp vast welfare state. *The Wall Street Journal*, July 10, A1, A5; Rohwedder, C. (1999). Once the big muscle of German industry, unions see it all sag. *The Wall Street Journal*, November 29, A1; Sims, G. T., & Rhoads, C. (2003). New era for German labor movement? *The Wall Street Journal*, July 1, A9.

44. Hollinshead & Leaf, *Human resource management: An international and comparative perspective*.

45. Hollinshead, & Leaf, *Human resource management: An international and comparative perspective*.

46. Hollinshead & Leaf, *Human resource management: An international and comparative perspective*.

47. Brunstein, I. (1995). *Human resource management in Western Europe*. Berlin: Walter de Gruyter.

48. Brunstein, *Human resource management in Western Europe*; Matlack, C. (2003). France: Labor disarray is giving reform a chance. *Business Week*, June 16, 48.

49. Brewster, C., & Hegewisch, A. (1994). *Policy and Practice in European Human Resource Management: The Price-Waterhouse Cranfield Survey*. London: Routledge.

50. Reed, S. (1997). Will Stockholm give away the store? *Business Week*, February 10, 54.

51. Taylor, R. (1993). Union membership in Sweden still growing. *Financial Times*, December 21, 14.

52. Hees, M. (1995). Belgium. In I. Brunstein (Ed.), *Human resource management in Western Europe*. Berlin: Walter de Gruyter.

53. ———. (2003). Part-time workers. *The Economist*, November 23, 100; Templeman, J., Trinephi, M., & Toy, S. (1996). A continent swarming with temps. *Business Week*, April 8, 54.

54. ———. (2001). Spain cuts a Gordian labor knot. *The Economist*, March 10, 51.

55. Inohara, H. (1990). *Human resource development in Japanese companies*. Tokyo: Asian Productivity Organization.

56. Inohara, *Human resource development in Japanese companies*.

57. Browning, E. S. (1986). Japan's firms have a friend: The unions. *The Wall Street Journal*, April 28, B2, B8.

58. Nyaw, M. (1995). Human resource management in the People's Republic of China. In L. F. Moore & P. D. Jennings (Eds.), *Human Resource Management on the Pacific Rim*. Berlin: Walter de Gruyter & Co. (pp. 187–196).

59. Nyaw, Human resource management in the People's Republic of China.

60. Nyaw, Human resource management in the People's Republic of China; Wonacott, P. (2003). Poisoned at plant, Mr. Wu became a labor crusader. *The Wall Street Journal*, July 21, A1, A6.

61. Barnathan, J., & Forney, M. (1994). Damping labor's fires: Can Beijing calm workers and sustain growth? *Business Week*, August 1, 40–41; Kahn, J. (1994). China orders foreign firms to unionize. *The Wall Street Journal*, June 29, A14; Kuhn, A. (2003). China turns to back-pay issue. *The Wall Street Journal*, January 19, A11; Wonacott, Poisoned at plant, Mr. Wu became a labor crusader.

62. Poon, W. K. (1995). Human resource management in Hong Kong. In Moore & Jennings, *Human resource management on the Pacific Rim*.

63. ———. (2001). Getting organized, with Western help. *The Economist*, December 1, 57–58.

64. Koch, M., Nam, S. H., & Steers, R. M. (1995). Human resource management in South Korea. In Moore & Jennings, *Human resource management on the Pacific Rim*.

65. Brull, S. V., & Lee, C. K. (1997). Why Seoul is seething. *Business Week*, January 27, 44–48; ———. (1997). South Korea: Culture clash. *The Economist*, January 11, 35–36.

66. Solomon, J., & Choi, H. W. (2001). For Korea's Daewoo Motor, a hard sale. *The Wall Street Journal*, May 23, A21.

67. Briscoe, *International Human Resource Management*.

68. Smith, G. (2000). Mexican workers deserve better than this. *Business Week*, September 11, 127.

69. Chege, M. (1988). The state and labor: Industrial relations in independent Kenya. In P. Coughlin & G. Ikiara (Eds.), *Industrialization in Kenya: In search of a strategy*. Nairobi: Heinemann Kenya; Moll, P. G. (1993). Black South African unions: Relative wage effects in international perspective. *Industrial and Labor Relations Review*, 46, 245–261.

70. Moll, Black South African unions: Relative wage effects in international perspective.

71. Matthews, R. (1996). Another burden to carry. *Financial Times*, May 21, 15.

72. Newman, B. (1983). Border dispute: Single-country unions of Europe try to cope with multinationals. *The Wall Street Journal*, November 30, 1, 22.

73. Simpson, W. R. (1994). The ILO and tripartism: Some reflections. *Monthly Labor Review*, September, 40–45.

74. Hollinshead & Leaf, *Human resource management: An international and comparative perspective*.

75. Dowling, P. J., & Schuler, R. S. (1990). *International dimensions of human resource management*. Boston: PWS-Kent.

76. Parry, J., & O'Meara, G. (1990). The struggle for European unions. *International Management*, December, 70–75.

77. Martin, D. (1984). A Canadian split on unions. *The New York Times*, March 12, D12.

78. Forman, C. (1993). France is preparing to battle Britain over flight of jobs across the channel. *The Wall Street Journal*, February 3, A11.

79. Borrus, A. (2000). Workers of the world: Welcome *Business Week*, November 20, 129–133.

80. Burkins, G. (2000). Labor reaches out to global economy. *The Wall Street Journal*, April 11, A2.

81. Strauss, G. (1982). Worker participation in management: An international perspective. *Research in Organizational Behavior*, 4, 173–265.

82. But please see de Macedo-Soares, T. D. L., & Lucas, D. C. (1996). Key quality management practices of leading firms in Brazil: Findings of a pilot-study. *The TQM Magazine*, 8, 55–70.

83. McFarlin, D., Sweeney, P. D., & Cotton, J. L. (1992). Attitudes toward employee participation in decision-making: A comparison of European and American managers in a US multinational company. *Human Resource Management*, 31, 363–383.

84. McFarlin, Sweeney, & Cotton, Attitudes toward employee participation in decision-making.

85. Sparrow, P., & Hiltrop, J. M. (1994). *European human resource management in transition*. New York: Prentice-Hall.

86. ———. (2000). Labor disputes. *The Economist*, April 22, 96.

87. Sparrow & Hiltrop, *European human resource management in transition*.

88. ———. (2001). Labor disputes. *The Economist*, May 12, 108.

89. Sparrow & Hiltrop, *European human resource management in transition*.

90. Inohara, *Human resource development in Japanese companies*.

91. Poole, M. (1986). *Industrial relations: Origins and patterns of national diversity*. London: Routledge.

92. Neale & Mindel, Rigging up multicultural teamworking.

Name Index

Subject Index